IRELAND GUIDE

YOUR PASSPORT TO GREAT TRAVEL!

CRITICAL ACCLAIM FOR
OPEN ROAD TRAVEL GUIDES!

*Whether you're going abroad or planning a trip in the United States, take Open Road along on your journey. Our books have been praised by **Travel & Leisure, The Los Angeles Times, Newsday, Booklist, US News & World Report, Endless Vacation, American Bookseller, Coast to Coast**, and many other magazines and newspapers!*

Don't just see the world – experience it with Open Road!

ABOUT THE AUTHOR

Dan McQuillan is a professional writer specializing in travel and technical subjects. He is a direct descendant of Niall the First, who ruled Ireland from 380 to 405 AD. Dan makes his home in Denver, Colorado, with his wife and six children.

HIT THE OPEN ROAD -
WITH OPEN ROAD PUBLISHING!

Open Road Publishing now has guide books to exciting, fun destinations on four continents. As veteran travelers, our goal is to bring you the best travel guides available anywhere!

No small task, but here's what we offer:

• All Open Road travel guides are written by authors with a distinct, opinionated point of view – not some sterile committee or team of writers. Our authors are experts in the areas covered and are polished writers.

• Our guides are geared to people who want great vacations, great value, and great tips for both standard tourist sights *and* fun, unique alternatives.

• We're strong on the basics, but we also provide terrific choices for those looking to get off the beaten path and *experience* the country or city – not just *see* it or pass through it.

• We give you the best, but we also tell you about the worst and what to avoid. Nobody should waste their time and money on their hard-earned vacation because of bad or inadequate travel advice.

• Our guides assume nothing. We tell you everything you need to know to have the trip of a lifetime – presented in a fun, literate, no-nonsense style.

• And, above all, we welcome your input, ideas, and suggestions to help us put out the best travel guides possible.

IRELAND GUIDE

YOUR PASSPORT TO GREAT TRAVEL!

DAN McQUILLAN

OPEN ROAD PUBLISHING

This book is dedicated to Teague McQuillan, who courageously left his beloved Ulster in 1617 for the liberty America offered.

1st Edition

TABLE OF CONTENTS

CONTENTS

CONTENTS

CONTENTS

CONTENTS

CONTENTS

1. INTRODUCTION

I have traveled to many beautiful and exciting parts of the world, but I am always enchanted when I return to Ireland. And you'll be enchanted too. From the Cliffs of Moher to Dublin and Dunluce, from the Book of Kells to the Creevykeel Court Tomb, you'll experience some of the best and most beautiful sights this world has to offer.

On many of your previous travels you have probably sent postcards home to family and friends. Well, Ireland *is* a postcard. Grandeur and simplicity, mirth and meditation are all found in abundance on this beautiful green island.

And I'll help you experience it all. I have made every effort to ferret out each interesting nook and engaging cranny in Ireland.

But there's more to see than the scenery. Ireland is a place you must experience. Talk to the locals. Watch the buskers (street performers) ply their trade. Talk to the school children who want to have their pictures taken. Relax as your car or bicycle is engulfed by a sea of sheep or cattle headed nowhere in particular and in no hurry.

Ireland is a mystical, magical, mirthful land where leprechauns and shamrocks, miracles and massacres are woven together as tightly as the knit of an Aran sweater. I guarantee that you will have a rich and rewarding experience as you tour the Emerald Isle. An anonymous Irish poet wrote: "If you're lucky enough to be Irish...you're lucky enough." Even if your descendants do not come from the Emerald Isle (most unfortunate), you'll feel like an adopted member of the family during and after your visit.

So come along and prowl through the ruins of an ancient race. Drink their beer and listen to their tales. Learn of their past and appreciate their future. And maybe even envy their wee green corner of the world.

If this is your first trip to the Emerald Isle, it's a good bet it won't be your last. Ireland's many charms have a way of enticing you to return, again and again.

2. EXCITING IRELAND!
- OVERVIEW

If you've never been to Ireland, you are in for a treat. If you have been before, you're still in for a treat. Follow the pages of this book and you'll see some of the most popular Irish tourist attractions: the Blarney Stone and the Book of Kells, Waterford Crystal Factory, the Rock of Cashel. But you'll also see much more: I'll lead you through 5,000 year old passage graves in Newgrange, help you prowl the brooding ruins of Dunluce Castle, and direct you to the ancient remains of a ritual murder victim in the National Museum. In addition, you'll contemplate the fate of a million people as you visit the overgrown famine graveyard in Dungarvan, or, on the lighter side, share a banquet with the lord of a medieval castle.

Ireland is divided into four provinces, and so is this book. Since there is so much to see and do in Dublin, there's also a chapter devoted to Ireland's leading city. The last chapter addresses genealogy, since there is a seven-in-ten chance that you are Irish (70% of American and Canadian tourists who venture to the Emerald Isle have at least one Irish ancestor).

The following is a short synopsis of the high points of each of the destination chapters:

DUBLIN

Dublin is Ireland's capital city. It is also one of the Emerald Isle's oldest cities. And it is rich in wonderful hotels and inns, fine restaurants and fun pubs, and impressive sights. **Christchurch** and **St. Patrick's Cathedral** dominate Dublin's skyline, and are perhaps its most recognizable buildings. Find out which was known as the church of the people, and which was known as the church of the government, and why.

At St. Patrick's, you'll be awed by the immense beauty of the cathedral. Considered the National Cathedral of the Church of Ireland, St. Patrick's was founded in 1191. But its history goes back much farther.

Local historians will tell you this is perhaps the oldest Christian site in Dublin. It was on this spot that tradition holds that St. Patrick himself performed baptisms at his well. Physically, St. Patrick's is impressive. The largest church in Ireland, its west clock tower rises 141 feet above Patrick Street, and the spire atop the tower rises another 101 feet, making the tip of the spire nearly two hundred and fifty feet high!

The **Book of Kells** is one of the cultural sights you shouldn't miss in Dublin. Without a doubt, this is one of the most celebrated attractions in Ireland: four volumes worth of illustrations of the four Gospels painstakingly illustrated by 9th-century monks. The elaborate artwork that graces the pages of the Latin text are truly a sight to behold.

The **National Gallery of Ireland** is one of the gems in Dublin's tiara. Established by an Act of Parliament in 1854, it has grown to an impressive gallery of some of the finest art on display in western Europe. The great playwright George Bernard Shaw claimed he owed half his education to the National Gallery of Art, where he spent hours upon hours within its walls as a youth. There are over 2,400 paintings, 300 sculptures, and an incredible assortment of various other items. Feast on the works of impressive Irish artists as well as the fruit of such great artists as Degas, Rembrandt, Monet, and Van Dyck, to name a few.

A visit to Dublin isn't complete without a visit to the **National Museum of Ireland**. Sort of Ireland's Smithsonian Institution, this museum just celebrated its 100th birthday, and its second hundred years promise to be as great as its first hundred. A fabulous collection of antiquities specific to Ireland is highlighted by items in the National Treasury, including the Ardagh Chalice, Cross of Cong, and the Tara Brooch. Their collection of gold artifacts is held by many to be the finest collection in Europe. And if that's not enough to pique your interest, you can view the ancient remains of a ritual murder victim.

While Dublin is a delightful place to visit, it has had its share of dark days throughout history. **Dublin Castle** was the seat of government for the hated English conquerors, and **Kilmainham Jail** is the site of numerous executions and many more incarcerations. The **General Post Office**, fondly known as the GPO, is where patriots declared Ireland's independence from Britain. It was comparable to the shot heard round the world at Concord, Massachusetts. Eventually the revolution begun here resulted in Irish independence.

In recent years, there has been a bit of a food renaissance in Dublin. A number of Dublin restaurants have stepped to the fore in the preparation and presentation of quality cuisine. Follow my recommendations and your palate will be satisfied.

LEINSTER

Leinster province extends from County Louth north of Dublin to the southeastern end of the island in County Wexford and as far west as County Offlay in central Ireland. Historically, much of northern Leinster was under control of the English, conquerors and occupiers of Ireland. Today, Leinster offers a variety of great sights and attractions not far from Dublin.

The southern half of Leinster is rich in natural beauty. The **Wicklow Mountains**, south of Dublin, are tall and grand, and served in early times as hideouts for those not in favor with the English rulers. Immediately south of Dublin is **County Wicklow**, referred to as the Garden of Ireland. It offers a number of beautiful vistas and fascinating ancient ruins.

Foremost among the latter is **Glendalough**, site of a monastic settlement and hermitage dating back to the 6th century. At the west end of the valley, Glenealo stream cascades in a waterfall into the valley, which is encompassed by heavily forested mountains. Add to all this natural beauty some exquisite and ancient ruins, and this is a wonderful place to visit.

Not far from Glendalough is the absolutely fabulous **Powerscourt Gardens**. You've probably seen pictures of Powerscourt Gardens before – they are popular scenes used to depict the beauty of Ireland. The gardens were originally laid out beginning in 1745, and were revised to their present grand design in the mid-1800s. They cascade in a series of terraces down a slope from an ancient mansion house. The gardens are filled with greenery: sculpted shrubs, trees, and many varieties of flowering plants, and a number of statues, fountains, and walkways. From the top of the terraces, the views sweep across the pretty **Dargle Valley**, culminating in outstanding views of **Great Sugar Loaf Mountain** and **Kippure Mountain**. Nearby you can visit the **Powerscourt Waterfall**, the highest waterfall in Ireland, with water dropping more than 400 feet off the edge of Djouce Mountain. It is a favorite picnic area for tourists and locals alike.

County Wexford on the southeastern tip of Ireland offers a number of scenic white sand beaches and port towns that are interesting to poke around in. **Rosslare** is a favorite seaside vacation spot for Dubliners. A host of leisure activities are available, from golf to windsurfing, fishing and sunbathing. The central-western part of Leinster consists of the wide flat plain called the **Curragh**, and is the Kentucky of Ireland. It is here that a number of national horse races are held, as well as the location of a number of stud farms, including the **National Stud** in Tully.

An hour's drive north of Dublin is the **Boyne River Valley**. The valley played an important role in the history of Ireland. In ancient times, it was the gathering place of the kings of Ireland. It also served as the burial place for these same kings. Several well-preserved burial mounds dating back five millennia are found, most notably **Newgrange**, where you can see the cross-shaped ancient passage graves. Inside Newgrange, visitors are led down a passage lined with massive stones and into the central chamber. The Newgrange mound is a well-preserved grave dating back to nearly 3,000 BC. During the winter solstice (December 21), rays from the sun glide down the narrow passageway gradually lighting the burial chamber.

MUNSTER

Munster comprises six counties in the southwestern quarter of the island. Much of Munster is rural, and the scenic views in this province are a match for any in the rest of the country. Pretty seascapes, rugged offshore islands, and country roads wending through green fields are typical of the scenery here.

If you know of only one place in Ireland, it is probably the **Blarney Stone**. Many people are unaware that the Blarney Stone is part of **Blarney Castle**. The famous stone is located atop an ancient keep (castle stronghold) underneath its battlements. To kiss the stone – which legend says grants the kisser the gift of *blarney* (flattering eloquence) – you lay on your back and slide down and under the battlements. Locals are positioned to give you a hand. The verdant setting and the obligatory kiss of the Blarney Stone will be memorable parts of your visit to the Emerald Isle.

Waterford City is the location of **Waterford Crystal**, the world-renowned lead crystal manufacturer. Kings and queens, presidents and prime ministers have been presented gifts of this famous crystal in solemn ceremonies. Several years ago, the Super Bowl trophy was a large Waterford Crystal football on a pedestal (they have a replica of it in their showroom). The factory has a nice gallery, and their one hour tour takes you within a few feet of the artisans who blow and cut the glass – much as it has been done for several hundred years at this site. I guarantee you'll never look at a piece of hand-blown crystal again without a new appreciation.

One of the most impressive ruins in all of Ireland is the **Rock of Cashel**, found in **County Tipperary**. You'll want to save plenty of film for one of the most awe-inspiring sites in Ireland. The setting for this chapel/round tower/Cathedral is on a mound towering some 200 feet above the surrounding plains (the peak of the round tower is nearly 300 feet high). The ruins are amazingly well-preserved. Incredible views of the surrounding Tipperary plains await you.

On the western edge of Ireland, rising dramatically and abruptly from the foaming sea, are the **Cliffs of Moher**. These incredible cliffs feature sheer seven hundred foot drops to the crashing ocean. They make for an impressive photo opportunity regardless of the weather. When it's clear and bright, the cliffs are regal and majestic; when it's gloomy and rainy, they sulk silently, like giant brows gathered in a frown. And of course, little **Killarney**, nestled as it is in the heart of some of the prettiest scenery in the country, is a place you simply must see. The natural beauty of the area will leave you in awe as you wander through the woods, take a fun jaunting car ride through the grounds of **Muckross House** or over the **Gap of Dunloe**, or just walk the cool green paths to **Torc Waterfall**.

CONNACHT

Connacht is located in the western part of the country. Much of this province is wide open spaces with beautiful heather enhancements. It also has its share of pretty seaports in Galway and Westport counties. The **Connemara** district of **County Galway** is rugged and beautiful. Connemara is home of the **Twelve Bens**, twelve peaks that rise out of the solitude of Connemara – an area that many Irish will tell you is the soul of the real Ireland.

Off the western coast of Ireland, a trip to the **Aran Islands** is a trip into Ireland's past. Winding rock walls, ancient ruins, prehistoric forts, and megalithic tombs greet visitors with stony silence. Contrast that silence with the warmth of thatch-roofed cottages, amiable inhabitants, and the friendly pubs you'll find here.

Known as Ireland's Holy Mountain, **Croagh Patrick** sits regally on the south side of **Clew Bay** and holds an important position in Irish history and legend. This is where St. Patrick enticed all of the snakes in Ireland to gather. After they had all assembled, St. Patrick rang his bell, and the snakes cast themselves to their deaths over a cliff! It must be true, because there are no snakes in Ireland! Croagh Patrick is an impressive mountain, and the site of yearly pilgrimages by many Catholic faithful. Whether you hike to the top as part of a pilgrimage or whether you just want to see the views, you won't be disappointed for your efforts.

ULSTER

Ulster is a politically divided province. Consisting of nine counties, six of those counties make up **Northern Ireland**, which is a part of the United Kingdom, with the three remaining counties part of the Republic of Ireland. Despite this political segregation, scene for scene, vista for vista, Ulster may have the most spectacular scenery on the island. Unfortunately, due to the troubles of recent years, most American and Canadian visitors have chosen not to visit Ulster in general, and Northern Ireland in particular. Even during the most tumultuous times in Northern Ireland, however, visitors have encountered very few problems.

More recently, there has been a fragile peace between the Irish Republican Army and Great Britain, and it has really turned North

Americans on to Northern Ireland. Those who live in the North have warmly opened their arms to travelers, especially those from America and Canada.

What is there to see here? For starters, one of the most romantic ruins on the island is **Dunluce Castle**, on the northern coast of Northern Ireland. It is also one of the most photographed castles anywhere. Sitting romantically atop an outcropping that juts into the Atlantic, the sheer sides of the outcropping drop off directly into the sea. In ancient times, it made an impregnable defense, and today it makes for superb photos.

Giant's Causeway, just up the coast from Dunluce Castle, is one of the most amazing geologic sites on the Emerald Isle. The Causeway consists of more than 40,000 hexagonal basalt pillars of varying heights. The symmetry is astounding, and well worth a visit. If you are the adventurous type, then perhaps **Carrick-a-Rede** is the place for you – a rope bridge that stretches across an eighty-foot span from the mainland to an island. As you walk across it, the undulating bridge will convince you that someone behind you is jumping up and down on the bridge; a peek over your shoulder will tell you it is only the bridge's natural reaction to your passing. Hint: Hold on, and go slowly.

Along the eastern coast of Northern Ireland are the **Glens of Antrim**, and the Queen of the Glens, **Glenariff Forest Park**. You have a choice of numerous walking paths that allow you to stroll through lush green hills. Cascading waterfalls, beautiful wild flowers, and dense undergrowth add to the cool, quiet splendor of your walk. Not to be outdone by the sights of Northern Ireland, **County Donegal** on the northwest coast of Ireland is simply beautiful. Every turn of the road, every hill you top seems to reveal another beautiful lake or seascape. Donegal is one of the three counties in Ulster that is part of the Irish Republic.

GENEALOGY

I've included a chapter on genealogy in Ireland to help you find long lost relatives. There is a good chance that if you are traveling from the United States or Canada, you have Irish ancestry because 70% of North Americans who visit Ireland have Irish roots. So you're a Murphy? Then be sure and visit Counties Cork, Donegal and Mayo, since those are the ancestral counties of the Murphy clan. If you're a Ryan, then include Counties Limerick and Tipperary in your itinerary.

Are you hoping your family in the "ould country" is having a clan reunion? In Chapter 18, *Searching For Your Irish Roots*, I've included information on how to find out if, when, and where your family is having that reunion. Or, if you'd simply like to visit long-lost cousins, I've provided a suggestion or two on how to make that happen.

So, whether you are coming to Ireland to search out your roots, see splendid scenery, mosey through museums, gaze at galleries of art, or prowl ancient ruins, Ireland offers it all to you. And you can use this book to guide your journey throughout the country.

AROUND EVERY BEND ... ANOTHER MAGNIFICENT CASTLE!

3. SUGGESTED ITINERARIES

Here are a few suggested itineraries for varying lengths of stay in Ireland. I've outlined itineraries of three, four, seven, and fourteen days. Remember, these are just suggestions. If you are enjoying prowling around an old ruin longer than I suggest, by all means stay there. Remember: this is your vacation; go at your own speed. Conversely, if you find yourself a little ahead of schedule, stop at a **Tourist Information Centre** (TI) and ask for suggestions of things to see and do in the surrounding area. Or better yet, just follow your nose.

Whether you're in the city, the country, or somewhere in between, you should find something that will interest you, and it might even prove to be the highlight of your trip. Several of my most interesting pictures and best memories are of abandoned ruins on back roads I had taken on a whim.

Dublin is very different from the rest of Ireland. While it's a delightful city, many people's idea of Ireland runs more to romantic ruins, rolling fields of green, and stone walls wending their way through the verdant landscape. Nevertheless, Dublin is a wonderful city to visit. Museums, art galleries, and historical sights are plentiful.

If you visit Dublin, don't bother renting a car while you are there. Traffic is horrendous almost any time of day. Bicyclists, motorcyclists, and pedestrians will drive you batty, and it can be dangerous for you and those around you. If you do rent a car, it's probably easiest to park it several blocks from the city center and walk. In the past, I have been lucky and found parking around St. Stephen's Green. Most of the Dublin City sights are within easy walking distance from a central point like St. Stephen's Green.

There are a number of sights that are better as a part of a longer trip. The Skelligs, the Dingle Peninsula, the Ring of Kerry, and the Aran Islands are great places to visit, but they take the better part of a day to see. If your time is limited, I suggest you concentrate on the sights outlined below and save other areas for future visits.

Most sights close between 5:30 - 7:00 pm during the summer months, earlier other times of the year. One way to maximize your touring is to see all you can in an area during the day, and use the evening to drive to your next destination. During the summer, it stays light until well after 9:00 pm, and you can still see the beautiful countryside while you travel. This tactic makes B&B owners especially nervous, so be sure and call ahead to confirm your reservations and let them know you'll be late. Call in the afternoon if you can, but certainly no later than 6:00 pm.

In the following itineraries, I recommend staying in the last town you're touring because it makes for a more leisurely schedule.

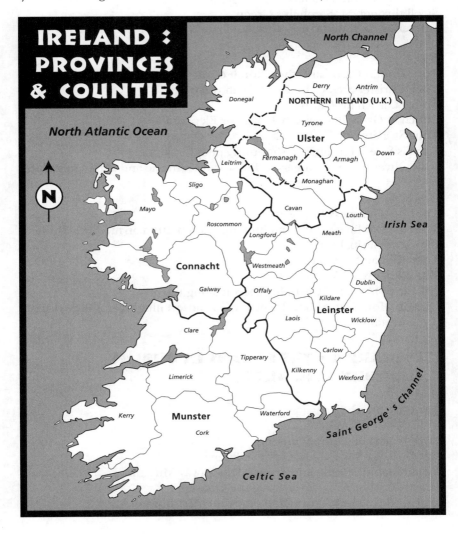

ITINERARY 1 - THREE DAYS IN DUBLIN
Day 1
Breakfast at Number 10
Trinity College: see multimedia show *The Dublin Experience* and Book of
    Kells
Visit the Bank of Ireland and the House of Lords
Grafton Street for window shopping and busker-watching
Lunch at Latchford's
Tour the National Museum
Tour the National Gallery
Stroll through St. Stephen's Green
Dinner at La Stampa or Patrick Guilbaud's (make reservations)

Day 2
Tour Dublin Castle and the Church of the Most Holy Trinity
Tour Christchurch Cathedral (watch the traffic!)
Tour St. Michans Church
Lunch at Gallagher's Boxty House or Elephant and Castle
Tour St. Patrick's Cathedral
Francis Street for antique shopping/people watching
Visit Oliver St. John Gogarty's Pub for Irish music and some pub grub

Day 3
Tour the Guinness Brewery
Tour the Dublinia exhibit (multimedia presentation on medieval Dublin)
Lunch at Garibaldi's
Tour Kilmainham Jail
Visit Phoenix Park
Take the DART to Howth for a stroll along the quay
Dine in Howth at Abbey Tavern; enjoy an evening of traditional Irish
    entertainment

ITINERARY 2 - THREE DAYS IN DUBLIN
& SURROUNDING AREAS
Day 1
Visit Monasterboice
Tour Mellifont Abbey
Tour Newgrange burial mound
Lunch at An Sos Cafe in Castlebellingham
Visit Malahide Castle and Fry Model Railway Museum
Howth Harbor for a stroll along the Quays
Dine at the Abbey Tavern and enjoy their Irish music show

Day 2
Visit Trinity College and the Book of Kells
Grafton Street
Tour the National Museum
Lunch
Tour St. Patrick's and Christchurch Cathedrals
Tour Kilmainham Jail
Phoenix Park
Drive to Rathnew to stay at Tinakilly Country House
Dinner at either Tinakilly Country House or Hunter's Hotel

Day 3
Visit Mt. Usher Gardens
Drive through the Vale of Avoca, stop and walk a bit
Visit Glendalough
Lunch
Visit Powerscourt Gardens and Waterfall
Tour Russborough House
Dine and spend the night at Mount Juliet

ITINERARY 3 - FOUR DAYS IN THE WEST

You can reach the west coast of Ireland from Dublin in about three or four hours driving, depending on your final destination. However, if you are going to spend your entire time in the west, then fly into Shannon and begin your tour from there.

Day 1
Drive to Killarney
Visit the shops in Killarney
Tour Muckross House and Kerry Life Experience
Have lunch at the snack bar at the Muckross House
Drive the Ring of Kerry up to Ladies' View
Drive part of the Dingle Peninsula, from Castlemaine to Dingle and back
Walk around Dingle Town
Rent a skiff to take you into the harbor to see Fungi, the Dingle Dolphin
     (or drive a little further out on the peninsula)
Spend the night in Killarney at Hotel Dunloe Castle

Day 2
Drive to Adare, tour the shops and the ruins of several abbeys
On to Limerick
Visit King John's Castle
Tour the Hunt Collection

Lunch in Limerick
Visit the Craggaunowen Project
Visit Bunratty Folk Park
Dine at Bunratty Castle Medieval Banquet

Day 3
Visit the Cliffs of Moher
Drive through the Burren; visit the Burren Display Center
Head for Galway City
Lunch at MacDonagh's Seafood Restaurant
See the sights in Galway, visit the shops
Spend the night at Cashel House Hotel or Ballynahinch Castle

Day 4
(Lots of driving today)
Head to Clifden, visit the shops
Tour Connemara National Park, including Kylemore Abbey
Lunch at Kylemore Abbey
On to Westport – visit the shops and sites to see in Westport
Head south toward Ballinrobe and Galway (inland route); swing by
   Ashford Castle to see the grounds in Cong
Spend the night in Galway (about 1 1/2 hours from Shannon Airport)

ITINERARY 4 - SEVEN DAYS IN IRELAND

Seven days is a pretty short time in which to see Ireland. This itinerary begins in County Wicklow just south of Dublin, circles the country, and ends in Dublin.

If the following itinerary seems a little rushed, you can divide the fourteen-day itinerary in half and just see half of the island. Days one through six and fourteen are a pretty good tour of the southern half of the island. Days seven through fourteen makes sense for the northern half of the island, and includes Northern Ireland. If you take the latter option, fly into Shannon and out of Dublin to maximize your time.

Depending on your rental car company, there may or may not be an extra charge to drop your car in Dublin if you rented it in Shannon.

Day 1
Head south for County Wicklow
Visit Mt. Usher Gardens
Drive through the Vale of Avoca, stop and walk a bit
Visit Glendalough
Lunch
Visit Powerscourt Gardens and Waterfall

Tour Russborough House
Dine and spend the night at Mount Juliet in Thomastown

Day 2
Visit Waterford City
Tour Waterford Crystal Factory
Head north for Cahir. Tour Cahir Castle
Lunch in Cashel
Visit the Rock of Cashel
Visit the Bru Boru Heritage Center
Head for Cork
Visit Blarney Castle and Blarney Stone
Spend the night around Blarney

Day 3
Head for Killarney
Visit the shops in Killarney
Tour Muckross House and Kerry Life Experience
Drive the Ring of Kerry up to Ladies' View, then back
Drive around the Dingle Peninsula (this will take about four hours)
Have lunch in and walk around Dingle Town
Rent a skiff to take you into the harbor to see Fungi, the Dingle Dolphin
Spend the night in or around Limerick

Day 4
Visit King John's Castle
Tour the Hunt Collection
Drive to Adare, tour the shops and the ruins of several abbeys
Lunch in Adare
Visit Bunratty Folk Park
Visit the Craggaunowen Project
Drive to the Cliffs of Moher
Spend the night at Gregan's Castle in Ballyvaughan

Day 5
Head for Galway
Tour the city, especially the shops
Drive to Clifden, visit the shops
Lunch in Destry's, or Quay House
Visit Kylemore Abbey
Drive to Westport
Tour Westport City, especially the shops
Spend the night at The Coral Reef outside Westport

Day 6
Drive cross-country to the Drogheda area (about three and a half hours)
Visit Monasterboice
Lunch at An Sos Cafe in Castlebellingham
Tour Mellifont Abbey
Tour Newgrange burial mound
Howth Harbor for a stroll along the Quays
Dine at the Abbey Tavern and enjoy their Irish music show
Spend the night at Ariel House in Dublin

Day 7
Visit Trinity College and the Book of Kells
Grafton Street
Tour Dublin Castle
Lunch at Garibaldi's
Tour the National Museum
Tour the National Art Gallery
Tour St. Patrick's and Christchurch Cathedrals
Spend the night in Skerries at The Reefs B&B (not far from the airport);
    enjoy sunset over the Irish Sea for your last evening in Ireland

ITINERARY 5 - FOURTEEN DAYS IN IRELAND

Fourteen days gives you plenty of time to tour Ireland. You won't see everything, but you'll see many of the major sights and have time for a few of the minor ones, too. This itinerary begins in County Wicklow, and encircles the island in a counter-clockwise manner. It ends in Dublin, so you can return your rental car, see Dublin without it, and save a few dollars. If you fly into Shannon, just start the tour in the middle.

Day 1
Head south for County Wicklow
Visit Mt. Usher Gardens
Drive through the Vale of Avoca, stop and walk a bit
Visit Glendalough
Lunch
Visit Powerscourt Gardens and Waterfall
Tour Russborough House
Dine and spend the night at Mount Juliet

Day 2
Head for County Wexford
Rosslare: visit their shops, walk along their beautiful beach
Tour Johnstown Castle and Gardens

Lunch
Visit Dunbrodey ruins in Ballyhack
Visit Waterford City
Tour Waterford Crystal Factory
Tour the Waterford Heritage Center
Spend the evening at Blenheim House

Day 3
Head for Ardmore
On the way, go through Dungarvan, visit the Famine Graveyard
Visit Ardmore. Walk around the town, visit the round tower, take the cliff-
    side walk
Head north for Cahir. Tour Cahir Castle
Lunch in Cashel
Visit the Rock of Cashel
Visit the Bru Boru Heritage Center
Head toward for Cork
Visit Blarney Castle and Blarney Stone

Day 4
Visit the sites that are of interest to you in Cork City (Shandon Steeple,
    Crawford Art Gallery, English Market)
Visit the Fota Wildlife Park
Lunch in Cobh
Visit Cobh (your ancestors may have bid farewell to Ireland from here)
Visit the Queenstown Project in Cobh
Head for Kinsale
Visit Charles Fort in Kinsale
Head for Bantry
Visit the Bantry 1796 French Armada Exhibition Center in Bantry
Enjoy Bantry Bay
Spend the night in Bantry

Day 5
Head for Killarney
Visit Muckross House and Kerry Life Experience
Walk up to Torc Waterfall
Lunch in Killarney at either Gaby's or Foley's Town House
Take a jaunting Car ride up the Gap of Dunloe
Drive a portion of the Ring of Kerry to Kenmare. (Stop to take pictures)
If there's time, visit the shops in Kenmare
Dine at Park Hotel Kenmare or La Cascade Restaurant at Sheen Falls
    Lodge

Stay in either the Park Hotel Kenmare, Sheen Falls Lodge, or Sallyport
  House

Day 6
Head for Waterville on the Iveragh Peninsula
In Waterville, catch a boat to the Skelligs
Lunch in Waterville
Finish driving the Ring of Kerry along the northern side of the Iveragh
  Peninsula
Spend the night in Killarney at Hotel Dunloe Castle

Day 7
Spend this entire day on the Dingle Peninsula
Visit Dingle, walk around the shops
Rent a skiff to take you into the harbor to see Fungi, the Dingle Dolphin
Gallarus Oratory
Slea Head
Visit the Blasket Center
Visit Dunquin Pottery
Take O'Connor Pass to Kilcummin, then into Tralee
Spend the night in Tralee

Day 8
Head north toward Limerick
Visit Adare, tour the shops and the ruins of several abbeys
On to Limerick
Visit King John's Castle
Visit the Hunt Collection
Lunch in Limerick
Visit the Craggaunowen Project
Visit Bunratty Folk Park
Dine at Bunratty Castle Medieval Banquet
Spend the night in a B&B near Bunratty Castle

Day 9
Head northwest to see the Cliffs of Moher
Visit the Burren and the Burren Display Center
Visit Ailwee Cave
Drive to Galway
Visit the shops of Galway
Find Lynch's Memorial Window
Look for Salmon off the Salmon Weir Bridge
Visit Spanish Arch

Visit the Galway City Museum
Spend the night in Galway

Day 10
Visit the Aran Islands today

Day 11
(Get out early – lots of driving today)
Head to Clifden, visit the shops
Tour Connemara National Park, including Kylemore Abbey
Lunch at Kylemore Abbey
On to Westport – visit the shops and sites to see in Westport
Spend the night at the Coral Reef B&B just outside Westport

Day 12
Get out early – head north to Donegal (long drive). Along the way, stop
    at Creevykeel Court Tomb, Drumcliffe and W. B. Yeats' grave
Visit the shops in Donegal Town.
Lunch in the Blueberry Tea Room.
Drive north and visit Glenveagh National Park
Skirt Derry (Londonderry)
Spend the night at Whitepark Country House in Ballintoy

Day 13
Visit Dunluce Castle, Giant's Causeway, and Carrick-a-Rede
Lunch in Ballycastle
Visit Bonamargy Friary. Find Julia McQuillian's gravestone
Take the Torr Head Drive out of Ballycastle to Cushendun
Take the inland route to Belfast
Visit sites in Belfast: Botanical Gardens, Ulster Museum, Crown Pub
Drive to Dundalk or Drogheda to spend the night

Day 14
Drive to Dublin
Visit Trinity College and the Book of Kells
Grafton Street
Lunch at Cafe En Seine
Tour the National Museum
Tour St. Patrick's and Christchurch Cathedrals
Tour Kilmainham Jail
Spend the night in Skerries at The Reefs B&B (not far from the airport);
    enjoy the sunset over the Irish Sea on your last evening in Ireland.

4. LAND & PEOPLE

THE LAND

The Emerald Isle is often said to be the size of Virginia or Kentucky (actually, it's a little smaller than both). In other words, it's not very large. The island is about three hundred miles long from its northern beaches to its southern coves, and one hundred and seventy miles from the Atlantic Ocean on the west to the Irish Sea on the east. No matter where you travel on this island paradise, you are never more than about seventy miles from the sea.

Ireland is divided into two political entities. The majority of the island (all but the northeastern portion) is called the Republic of Ireland. It is referred to as the Republic or alternately as "the South." There are approximately 3.5 million people living in the republic, which is about the size of Maine or Indiana.

Northern Ireland consists of six counties in the northeastern portion of the island and is a part of the United Kingdom. Northern Ireland, or "the North," is about the size of Connecticut, and is home to approximately 1.5 million people.

When I thought to ask the question, I was a little surprised to find that many who live in Northern Ireland consider themselves British, living in Ireland as opposed to being Irish living in Britain. There are, of course, those in the North and the South who feel Ireland is still occupied by invaders – the British – and who will not be happy until Northern Ireland is reunited politically with the Republic.

Geologists will tell you that Ireland has been an island for 8,500 years, having separated from the European continent during the thawing of the last Ice Age. The central portion of Ireland is a relatively level limestone plain. Rolling hills, rich foliage, and occasional peaks jutting up are typical of this area. The outer edge of the island is mountainous and blocks the interior from the sea. On the western shore of Ireland these mountains tend to drop off sharply to the sea, resulting in some dramatic seascapes. Indeed, some of the precipices are seven hundred feet high. Elsewhere on

IRELAND

North Channel

Londonderry

NORTHERN IRELAND (U.K.)

Donegal

Atlantic Ocean

Donegal Bay

Lough Neagh

Belfast

Sligo

Enniskillen

Ulster

Boyle

Irish Sea

Shannon

Boyne

Connacht

Galway

Dublin

Leinster

Wicklow

Ennis

Limerick

Kilkenny

Barrow

Suir

Wexford

Tralee

Munster

Waterford

Saint George's Channel

Killarney

Kenmare

Blackwater

Cork

Bantry

Celtic Sea

the island, the slope to the sea is more gradual, allowing for some wide sandy beaches fit for frolicking and romantic strolls along their sandy walkways. The beaches of Northern Ireland and of southwestern Ireland are especially inviting.

FACTS ON IRELAND

Highest mountain: Carrantuohill in County Kerry (3,414 feet)
Longest River: Shannon River (230 miles)
Total ocean shoreline: 3,497 miles
Largest city: Dublin, nearly 500,000 (within the city limits)
Largest lake: Lough Neagh (153 miles of shoreline)
Total population:
 – Republic: 3.52 million (over 40% lives within 60 miles of Dublin)
 – Northern Ireland: 1.59 million
Religious affiliation:
 – Republic: 93% Catholic, 4% Anglican, 3% other
 – Northern Ireland: 69% Protestant, 26% Catholic, 5% other
Unemployment:
 – Republic: 17.6%
 – Northern Ireland: 16.7%
Birth Rates:
 – Republic: 14.6 per 1,000
 – Northern Ireland: 15.9 per 1,000
Land use: 90% undeveloped or rural, 10% other
Total Area:
 – Republic: 32,595 square miles
 – Northern Ireland: 5,462 square miles
Form of Government:
 – Republic: constitutional democracy
 – Northern Ireland: monarchy (Great Britain)

The mountains of Ireland are spectacular. The **Mountains of Mourne** in the northwest are perhaps the best known, as they are mentioned in a number of poems and songs. "Sweeping down to the sea," as famed Irish poet and balladeer Percy French put it more than a hundred years ago, the Mournes are a great granite range that have rounded with age, and are rife with wildlife. South of Dublin and in County Wicklow are more granite hills known as the **Wicklow Mountains**. Inland, the granite is replaced by red sandstone and quartzite that form the **Galtee**, **Knockmealdown**, **Slieve Aughty**, and **Slieve Bloom mountains**.

In the southwest, especially in southwest Counties Cork and Kerry, the same red sandstone crumbles into a series of finger-like peninsulas reaching into the sea. This makes for some marvelous harbors and harbor towns, seascapes and landscapes.

Central County Kerry boasts the highest red sandstone peak in Ireland at **Carrauntuohill**. A steep and craggy peak, it lunges abruptly heavenward over 3,400 feet.

Up the western coastline to Galway, you come to the **Maamturk** and **Partry** ranges, quartzite mountains that provide wonderful jutting mounds. The most impressive and significant is **Croagh Patrick** near Westport, a peak surrounded by many legends and a place of pilgrimage for thousands each year. Farther north, you encounter the quartzite peaks of the **Nephin Mountains**, in County Mayo. Still farther north, you arrive at the **Bluestack Mountains**, the predominant feature of pretty County Donegal. Donegal is very mountainous by Irish standards, and the Bluestacks are the main range in Donegal. On the west coast of Donegal are the **Slieve League Mountains**, with their impressive drop to the sea.

Finishing a counter-clockwise loop of the island, you'll find the softly rounded mounds of the **Sperrin Mountains** in Counties Derry and Tyrone, and to the east of Northern Ireland you find the **Antrim Mountains**, whose wind-swept, rounded peaks drop off into the lovely glens of Antrim, home to an incredible number of wildflowers, and, some say, leprechauns.

Several Irish landscape characteristics seem like anomalies. First, the climate supports plant life that ranges from arctic tundra to sub-tropical plants, often growing side by side. Second, on the central-western edge of the island is the **Burren**, a vast area of gray limestone hills and plains. At first glance, it seems as though it should be called the *Barren* instead of the *Burren*. And yet, this lunar-looking area continues to draw naturalists from all over the world to study its amazing qualities. Thousands of tiny plants, including some rare species of orchids, grow in the seemingly inhospitable environment. Countless underground caves, turloughs (lakes that appear during the rainy seasons, then disappear as the weather gets drier), and fissures criss-cross the face of the Burren. The contrast of the Burren to the rest of Ireland is awesome.

It may seem to you that Ireland has a quilt-like quality: seams run across the width and breadth of the island. Those seams are in reality rock walls. In some parts of the country, that is obvious; in other parts, it looks like the fields are separated by massive, straight hedgerows. They are hedgerows, but those hedgerows cover ancient stone fences. How ancient? Well, some have been there for thousands of years, but most likely the walls you are seeing have been in place for no more than several hundred years.

Prior to the widespread appearance of landlords in the late 1600s, Ireland was relatively devoid of stone fences. Oh, there were plenty of stone forts from the Celtic period – over 30,000 of them are still found in the country. But these were small and were not the stone walls you see today. When landlords came in, they began fencing "their" property with stone walls, marking it off in five- and ten-acre parcels, to be sold to other Protestants. Over time, even the native Irish adopted the practice of building stone walls, and soon stone walls covered the country and became indelibly Irish.

TURF FIRES

*If you are driving along in the lovely Irish countryside and see individuals laboring in fields relatively devoid of vegetation, stop and witness a tradition that has gone on in Ireland for hundreds, if not thousands, of years. In many areas of Ireland, there are huge expanses of peat bogs – wet areas that contain the carbonized remains of peat moss. Some ingenius (or desperate) soul long ago discovered that if chunks of this wet earth were dried, they could be burnt in a fireplace. These **turf fires**, as they're called, provided cooking fires, warmth, and light for otherwise cold, drab cottages. Turf fires provide a low-flame, long-burning, aromatic fire.*

Back to the people you saw laboring in the bog. They are probably doing one of two things: either they are cutting the wet bog into brick-size pieces, and turning them over so they will dry out, or they are collecting turf bricks that have already been cut and dried. The government passed a law allowing anyone in the country to go to a bog, free of charge, and "harvest" turf to be used in their own personal turf fires. You'll often see a car pulled over to the side of the road near a bog, with its trunk open. Not too far away you'll see individuals – often entire families – picking up turf bricks to put in the car.

Once, turf fires were the primary heating fuel in Ireland. Today, the tradition has been largely abandoned in the big cities, but in the rural areas it is still very common. Many pubs, restaurants, and hotels in Ireland still burn turf fires to give their establishment that homey, Irish feel and smell. As you drive through small rural villages, if you'll roll down your window and sniff the air, I guarantee you'll catch a whiff of turf fires – they smell like burning grass. It works best in the mornings or evenings, but you'll be able to smell it during the day, too. It's one of my most memorable (olfactory) memories of Ireland, and it may prove to be one of yours, too.

The Irish discovered the stone walls were practical and useful. In addition to marking land ownership, they kept certain animals in, and certain animals out. They served as a place to meet and chat and everyone leaned on the sturdy walls. During the days of the Penal Laws, they served as protection for **hedge schools**, places where Catholics were educated since it was illegal for them to receive a formal education. And I suppose countless generations of children climbed on them, ran along them, hid behind them, and used them in any way their imaginations could come up with.

THE PEOPLE

There are many beautiful sights in Ireland: beaches, scenic sunsets, verdant valleys, and towering cliffs. But by far, the best part of Ireland is the people. They are among the most gracious and friendly people on the planet. From several people jumping up to give their seat to an elderly person or woman on a bus to the warm welcomes you receive in B&Bs to meeting your long lost cousins, you'll find Irish hospitality wherever you go.

Here are a few interesting tidbits about the Irish:
• Ireland has gone from a country where it was illegal for Catholics to receive a formal education to a 98% adult literacy rate today.
• It has produced more than its fair share of literary giants. From the early days of the Celts, poets and minstrels have been among the most honored and respected members of society. That reverence has spawned generations of internationally renowned poets, writers, and playwrights over the years: Jonathan Swift, George Bernard Shaw, W. B. Yeats, Oscar Wilde, Oliver Goldsmith, and James Joyce, including three Nobel Prizes for Literature.
• Christianity first came to Ireland in approximately the late 4th century. One of its earliest missionaries was St. Patrick, who is credited with establishing over sixty churches in Ireland. By the early 1500s, Ireland was predominantly Roman Catholic. Today, about 93% of the population in the Republic of Ireland is Roman Catholic, as are 26% of the people in Northern Ireland.

Irish Language

Irish is the official language of the Republic of Ireland, with English recognized as a second language under the Constitution. **Gaelic** and **Irish** are generally interchangeable terms, although today the language is almost always referred to as Irish. Gaelic is most often used to refer to the language of the ancient inhabitants of Ireland, the Celts.

During the past century, English has become the daily language of the majority of the Irish people. In a bid to combat this, the Gaelic League was formed in 1893. When the Irish state was formed in 1921, the government made the restoration and preservation of Irish one of its priorities. To this end, areas where Irish was still the daily language were designated as *Gaeltacht*, and special grants were made available. Large parts of counties Donegal, Galway, and Kerry, as well as parts of counties Mayo, Cork, Waterford, and Meath all qualified.

Regional accents abound. Around Dublin, the accents tend to have a strong English flavor. In County Cork in the southwest, accents have a more sing-songy quality. In the extreme west – Galway and Donegal in particular – accents are more what Americans would expect – quite frankly, the accent you hear on the "Irish Spring" soap commercials! In Northern Ireland, accents have a strong resemblance to a thick Scottish brogue, most likely due to the predominance of Scottish settlers over the centuries.

SEPARATED BY A COMMON LANGUAGE

When my wife and I visited long-lost cousins in Northern Ireland, we had a delightful time. As we were leaving, one of the cousins took my wife's hand, and shaking it vigorously, said, "We're so glad you came. You are so plain and homely." For a moment we were both stunned by this seemingly insulting comment. But the broad smile on her face and the enthusiastic nods of agreement from the other Irish cousins present made us realize that in American English she was saying: "We're so glad you came. You are so down-to-earth and comfortable to be with."

That experience reinforced for us the fact that while we share a similar language with the Irish, there are some distinct differences. Another difference is that there are still many vestiges of Gaelic in their vocabulary. Many towns and villages retain their ancient Irish names and children are given seemingly unpronounceable Irish names, for example: Aoife, Oísín, and Niamh to name a few.

Below are some of the more common Irish words you are certain to encounter during your visit. Many of them are anglicized versions of Irish words – for example, Bally is the anglicized Baile, which means town. Many small towns in Ireland carry the prefix Bally: Ballymena, Ballyconnell, Ballydonegan, Ballydoyle, etc.

ard	a high place
ath	ford
bally	town
ben	large hill or mountain
bord	office or board
burren	stone
cahir	stone fort
carrig	rock
cashel	stone fort
cavan	cave
ceile	dance
croagh	hill (especially a cone-shaped hill)
derry	oak

drum	low ridge or mound
dun	fort
êireann	Ireland
ennis	island
feile	festival or celebration
feis	feast or celebration
gal	river
grianan	palace
kil	church
knock	hill
lis	earthen fort
lough	lake
mac	son
mor	great
oughter	upper
quay	pier
rath	earthen ring fort
skerry	sea rocks
slieve	mountain
tully	small hill

Here are a few common English words that will be helpful to know in conversation, since the meanings are sometimes different in Ireland:

call	visit
hire	rent
homely	homey
on holiday	on vacation
pram	baby stroller
plain	down-to-earth
queue	line
ring	call on the phone
tariff	rate (as in the rate for a hotel room)

One last lesson: *Celtic* is pronounced differently than the way we pronounce the name of the NBA team from Boston. The Celtic you see in Ireland is pronounced Keltic, with a hard K, and it was spoken by Kelts. (Not Seltic spoken by Selts!)

OH, THOSE IRISH NAMES!

Sure, and I'm certain you are familiar with Irish names like Danny, Patrick, Darby, Mary, Molly, and maybe even Sean. But here are a few you might see that you may have problems pronouncing. Here's a little help:

Name	Pronounced
Aine	OWN-ya
Aishling	Ashling
Aoife	EE' fa
Caitriona	KA-trina
Ciaran	KEER-un
Colm	CALL-um
Donough	DUN-uh
Dymphna	DIM-pna (female)
Eamon	AY-mon
Eoin	Owen
Fiacha	Fee-AH-ka
Fionnala	Fi-nula
Kathleen	KAT-leen
Liam	LEE-um
Maeve	Mayve
Malachi	MAL-a-key
Moire	MOY-ra (Mary)
Niall	Neel or Nile
Niamh	Neev (female)
Oísin	O-SHEEN
Patrick	often Paddy (diminutive of Patrick)
Sean	Shawn
Seamus	SHAY-mus
Sinead	Shi-NAY-ud
Siobhan	SHI-vawn (female)

Irish Music

The written histories of Ireland are liberally sprinkled with references to music in the lives of the Irish people. Indeed, even today music is an important part of Irish celebrations, whether those celebrations are festivals, sporting events, parades, weddings, or even funerals.

The instruments? The **harp** was one of the most important musical instruments in ancient Ireland. Its place in Irish society was so revered that it has earned the honor of being the national emblem, and is stamped on all modern Irish coins. The harp was the main instrument of the Celtic minstrels, and references to harps and harpists can be found in eyewitiness accounts of Irish life as early as the 11th century.

Over the centuries, other instruments crept on the Irish stage with the harp. New settlers brought the instruments of their cultures, and many of those instruments were adopted by the Irish. The Scottish brought **bagpipes**, which evolved to the Irish *uillean*, also known as union pipes. Union pipes are similar to bagpipes in design and sound, but they differ fundamentally in the way they fill the bag with air. Instead of using your breath to fill the bag, a bellows-like device is used to fill it.

The **concertina**, a small accordian-like instrument, was introduced into Ireland by their English conquerors in the mid-1800s. Other important musical instruments include the fiddle, flute, tin whistle, and the *bodhran* (pronounced BOW-rawn), which is a small, goatskin-covered drum or tamborine that is played with a stick. It has a mesmerizing effect, as it sets the tempo for many an Irish song.

THREE FRIENDS!

5. A SHORT HISTORY

Ireland is one of the most tranquil places you will ever visit. Unfortunately, her peaceful repose belies her rocky history. Oppression and domination have played a major role in Ireland's history for over 1,000 years. From subtle politics to bloody uprisings, Ireland's past is checkered with intrigue, drama, and pathos that rivals today's fictional best-sellers.

And yet natives of this incredible island are resilient, and time and again have broken the chains of their oppressors through the centuries to become the free people you find today – although there are those who feel the tyrant's grasp is still on that part of the Emerald Isle known as Northern Ireland.

ANCIENT HISTORY

The earliest signs we have of mankind in Ireland are signs of his death. Ireland is littered with stone tombs from five millennia ago – some of them have been estimated to have been built as long ago as 3,000 BC. Who were these people, and where did they come from? Why did they go to the trouble to build immense passage graves? How did they lift fifty-ton stones onto pedestals to serve as tombs for their deceased? And why? Unfortunately, we can only speculate about what compelled these people to do all this.

The earliest Irish residents were probably **Mesolithic** hunters. It is widely believed that these ancient nomads arrived in the middle of the Stone Age, as people on the European continent expanded their fishing and hunting grounds to the western edge of the continent and on to what is today Ireland. They may have come afoot since some believe that Ireland was part of continental Europe at that time. Whether on foot or in skin coracles, they came, were seduced – by its beauty, abundance, or isolation – and stayed.

Little is known of these Mesolithic people. They left few traces of their passing. Ancient sites at the mouth of rivers and along the shores of lakes were taken over by succeeding generations, each making the settlement a little larger and a little better fortified against marauders.

The beginning of the New Stone Age was the first of many renaissances on the Emerald Isle, when **Neolithic** man appeared in Ireland. Perhaps the race multiplied beyond the rivers' abilities to support it, but it was during this time that these ancient groups moved into the interior of Ireland. Crude stone farm implements attest to their new occupation as tillers of the soil. As time went on, the crudeness of their tools softened to a unique sophistication. Stone axes were sharp and plentiful enough which made massive timbering projects possible on the island – as well as to provide protection if necessary. Remnants of their civilization indicate they mastered the arts of pottery and weaving.

It was these advanced Stone Age men that began the practice of building massive tombs for their dead. Thousands of these tombs can be found dotting the fields and hills of Ireland to this day. They include passage graves (so-called because of the presence of a central passage into the tomb), dolmens, stone circles along the same lines as Stonehenge, and a variety of other monuments, all apparently to honor their dead. Many of them also reflect a knowledge of astronomy, as they show some solar orientation. Some of the finest examples of these today include **Newgrange**, **Dowth**, **Knowth**, **Creevykeel**, and **Browne's Dolmen**.

The Bronze Age in Ireland lasted from about 2,000 BC to 500 BC, evidenced by a significant and eclectic collection of relics such as fine jewelry, weapons, and tools that have been unearthed in recent years. Many of the finer examples are on display in museums such as the **National Museum** in Dublin.

The Bronze Age gave way slowly to the Iron Age as wandering bands of iron-users made their way to this small island. These new settlers came to be known by today's historians as **Celts**, although it's doubtful that's what they called themselves.

The Celts had a long and event-filled history on this tiny island. Their religious leaders were called **Druids**, and their gods became the gods of the Irish people for many hundreds of years. The Druids worshipped a number of deities, and presided over the human sacrifices that were an important part of some of their ceremonies.

The language of the Celts is of Indo-Germanic origin, and soon became the predominant language of the island, eclipsing whatever form of communication had gone on before. **Gaelic**, still spoken in many parts of the country, evolved from the language spoken by the Celts.

By the time the seventh century BC rolled around, Ireland was known to the world beyond the Irish Sea as **Hibernia**. Maps of the period bear the name Hibernia for Ireland and Albion for Britain. They also show a number of towns – probably more like settlements than towns – around the country, primarily situated at the mouths of the rivers that emptied into the sea.

The next several hundred years saw the migration of various and sundry peoples to the Emerald Isle. Never coming in numbers large enough to alarm, much less subjugate the native Irish, these peoples were quickly absorbed into the culture, adding their own influences.

The Celtic culture was one regulated by a litany of laws and edicts. The law was passed on orally from jurist to jurist. Celtic law, which today is known as **Brehon Law**, covered everything from land and cattle ownership to the granting of kingships to divorce to control of "peeping Toms." During the English conquest, Queen Elizabeth is said to have found the laws "lewd, unreasonable, and barbarous."

THE BREHON LAWS

*These and similar laws were in place in Ireland for nearly 1,700 years, from the first century BC to the early seventeenth century. The quotes below are taken from **Irish Laws**, published by Appletree Press, Belfast, and are used with their gracious permission.*

Peeping Toms: *The fine for peering into your neighbor's house without permission is one cow.*

Debt: *If your neighbor does not repay the debt he owes you, you may prevent him from going about his daily business.*

Kindness: *If a pregnant woman craves a morsel of food and her husband withholds it through stinginess or neglect, he must pay a fine.*

Divorce: *February the first is the day on which a husband or wife may decide to walk away from a marriage.*

Doctor's responsibilities: *If the doctor heals your wound, but it breaks out anew because of his carelessness, he must return the fee you paid. He also must pay you damages as if he himself had wounded you.*

Hospitality: *Whoever comes to your door, you must feed him or care for him, with no questions asked.*

Health laws: *It is illegal to give someone food in which has been found a dead mouse or weasel.*

Intoxication: *The layman may drink six pints of ale with his dinner. But a monk may drink only three pints. This is so he will not be intoxicated when prayer-time comes.*

Liability: *If a chip of wood from the carpenter's ax hits a bystander, the carpenter is exempt from liability, unless he deliberately aimed the chip at the bystander.*

Neighbor's Dog: *If a dog commits a nuisance on a neighbor's land, the dog's ordure must be removed as far as its juice is found. The ground must be pressed and stamped upon by the heel, and fine clay put there to cover it. Compensation shall be paid in butter, dough or curds amounting to three times the size of the ordure.*

Celtic society was divided into various castes. At the top of the caste structure were the professional class of people consisting or jurists, poets, historians, Druids, smiths, artists, and musicians. Members of the professional caste were free to move among the people. The rest of the populace was relegated to the lower echelons of the caste system. Its grip was strong enough to last well into the era of Christianity.

During this period, it is highly unlikely that there were many formal towns, much less cities. The populace was scattered helter-skelter across the width and breadth of the country, tied to their level in the caste system and whichever noble to whom they owed their fealty.

During this period, upwards of one hundred and fifty kings ruled the 500,000 inhabitants of the Emerald Isle. Perhaps "king" is too strong a word; they were more appropriately chieftains, perhaps patriarchs, of their own extended families. Over time, this system gave way to four or five kingdoms, precursors to today's four provinces of Leinster, Munster, Connacht, and Ulster.

CHRISTIANITY & THE EMERALD ISLE

Celtic society embraced an institution that eventually caused the weakening and eventual loss of their power. The institution? Slavery. In approximately the late 4th century, a youngster was captured by slave traders in Britain and brought back to Ireland to serve as a sheep tender. That young man's name was Patrick – he later came to be known as **St. Patrick**. When he was finally able to throw off the chains of bondage, he escaped to the continent where he studied for the ministry. Later, he returned to the land of his captivity to begin his ministry.

St. Patrick was not the first Christian missionary in Ireland, but he was one of the earliest, and was perhaps the most indefatigable. Among other things, he is credited with establishing churches in over sixty locations in Ireland. His work to spread the Gospel in Ireland is mixed with so many legends that it seems nearly impossible to know what he did and what he didn't do. For example, did he or didn't he cleanse Ireland of snakes? Legend says he did. (By the way, there are no snakes in Ireland.) One thing is certain: during his ministry, Christianity grew by leaps and bounds. While it would be several hundred years before Christianity eclipsed the paganism practiced by the majority of the Celts, St. Patrick established a firm foundation for those who followed to build on.

In addition to bringing the *religion* of Christianity, St. Patrick, his predecessors, contemporaries, and successors brought the *education* of Christianity. While the rest of Europe sunk into the depths of the Dark Ages, Ireland actually enjoyed its own mini-renaissance, led by learned and scholarly priests. Lacking extensive towns during this period, monasteries became the centers to which the population migrated.

Over several hundred years, Christianity continued to gain acceptance from the inhabitants until close to the end of the 8th century when things changed drastically.

VIKING INVADERS

Some historians mark the date as 795, others as 800, and still others as late as 807, but the exact date of the first **Viking** invasion is immaterial. What does matter is that the Vikings made their appearance on the Irish scene with a large dose of brutality and destruction. Wooden monastic settlements all across the island made easy and flammable targets for these marauders from the north. The Vikings torched the settlements and plundered them of their precious treasures. Fortunately, some of the greatest treasures were left behind by the Vikings: books and manuscripts. Many ancient books perished in the fires started by the Vikings, but those that didn't perish were often ignored by the non-reading Vikings who saw no value in them. The richly illustrated books of Kells, Durrow, and Armagh (all on display at Trinity College) are examples of these unappreciated literary treasures that were left behind.

Like so many other visitors to the Emerald Isle, the Vikings liked what they found, and decided to stay. They are responsible for a number of settlements that became seaports around Ireland, including Dublin, Limerick, Wexford, and Waterford. During this period, the Irish were noted for their clannishness, and their unwillingness to unite against a common foe. For several hundred years, the Vikings took advantage of these divisions and used these and other towns as their base for plundering the rest of the country.

It was these Viking raiders that we have to thank for the distinctive round towers that dot the Irish countryside. Prior to the Viking invasion, the monastic settlements consisted primarily of wooden structures. The need for additional protection prompted the Irish to construct stone round towers to serve as repositories of manuscripts and documents, as well as other treasures. They also served as watch-towers and places of refuge. An interesting aspect of the round towers is that their doors are often off the ground – some as high as twelve feet above the ground. Portable ladders provided access to the towers; once all were safely inside, the ladders were then retrieved inside the towers, and invaders found the fortresses impregnable.

As mentioned earlier, the Vikings were able to plunder Ireland by taking advantage of the clannishness and lack of unity among the Irish. During most of the two hundred-plus years the Vikings maintained their foothold in Ireland, there was no single king to unite Irish forces against these northern pests. In the year 1002, a prince of the ruling family in Munster, **Brian Boru**, came to power as the undisputed High King of

Ireland. Brian Boru united the armies of the other Irish kings and drove the Vikings forever from the shores of the Emerald Isle. The final battle was the Battle of Clontarf, where the Vikings were finally defeated. Unfortunately, Brian Boru was killed during the fighting: some legends say it was while he was praying for victory. Regardless, his forces were victorious, and the Vikings were no longer a power nor menace in Ireland.

Three of the four Irish kings supported the ouster of the Vikings from Ireland. The fourth was less than supportive; in fact, he joined with the Vikings and fought against his countrymen. Nearly one hundred and fifty years later another Leinster king chose to oppose his royal peers. **Dermot MacMurrough** was viewed by some as a traitor. By others he was viewed as an opportunist. Whatever his motivation, we now know that his actions resulted in over seven hundred and fifty years of occupation and subjugation of the Irish by the British.

ENGLISH INVADERS

In 1152, Dermot MacMurrough was censured by the other Irish kings for conduct unbecoming a king. **Rory O'Connell**, High King of Ireland, announced the united decision of the kings: banishment from Ireland for MacMurrough.

The MacMurrough-O'Rourke Feud

In 1152, **Tiernan O'Rourke**, an Irish chieftain, and his wife Dervorguilla lived in relative happiness in their castle not far from what is today Innisfree. O'Rourke suddenly found himself under attack by Dermot MacMurrough, the king of Leinster, and his forces. MacMurrough had convinced the lovely Dervorguilla to flee with him and his armies. Actually, the story is a little muddled: some accounts say she was kidnapped, others say she ran off with MacMurrough. Whatever the case, O'Rourke marshaled his forces, formed an alliance with other Irish chieftains, and was able to retrieve his sweetheart.

Not one to take banishment sitting down, MacMurrough was granted an audience with **King Henry II** of England, during which he discussed the "injustice" he suffered in Ireland. Whether MacMurrough knew that King Henry had designs on Ireland is unclear. However, prior to the feud, Henry had applied and been granted a "bull of legitimation" from **Pope Adrian IV**, which allowed him to begin his conquest of Ireland. King Henry saw MacMurrough's plight as an opportunity to expand his kingdom and assure additional kingdoms for his sons.

King Henry agreed to support MacMurrough in his efforts to regain his crown in Ireland by allowing him to enlist the assistance of power-hungry barons in England and Wales. Many of them responded favorably, including the famous Earl of Pembroke, also known as **Strongbow**. Over the next generation and a half, Ireland was under siege from warlords based across the Irish Sea. To secure Strongbow's allegiance, MacMurrough promised his daughter to him. It must have worked: the wedding was consummated and the incursions into Ireland began.

Anglo-Norman success was initially along the eastern coast of Ireland, where their armored and well-coordinated attacks on settlements, towns, and villages were met with ineffectual resistance. In 1170, Strongbow and his soldiers defeated the Irish Forces. The establishment of the English colony was primarily located in a thirty-mile by twenty-mile strip of land referred to as **the Pale**. It was over 750 years before the British could be persuaded to leave.

CENTURIES OF BATTLES

The warfare that took place in Ireland during this period affected primarily the Irish rulers and their armies. The common class – the laborers who worked the fields and tended the sheep – were not directly involved, and their lives continued relatively unaffected, except that they often found themselves serving new landlords.

As time went on and the Irish continued to lose battles because of overwhelming odds, they finally decided it was necessary to unite their forces to fight the Anglo-Norman onslaught. They united under a series of kings – generals or warlords, really – and imported mercenaries from Scotland. These professional fighting men were called *galloglasses*, from the Irish word for "foreign soldiers." Their entry into the fray helped check further significant incursions into the Irish countryside, and kept the majority of the English influence and occupation within the Pale.

In the middle of the 14th century, the fighting took a respite while both sides struggled to survive the onslaught of another, deadlier invader – the Black Death. The plague took its toll among all castes and nationalities. Irish chieftains, galloglasses, and Anglo-Norman citizens were not exempt.

As time progressed, the Anglo-Norman invaders became more and more Irish and less and less English. They intermarried, adopted the dress and customs of native Irish, and even began to speak their language. In 1366, in an unsuccessful attempt to stem the tide that was pulling powerful new rulers in Ireland away from the crown, the **Statutes of Kilkenny** were drafted and approved. The statutes made intermarriage a treasonable offense, made it illegal for an Irishman to live within a walled town, and laid heavy penalties on those who spoke the Irish language or adopted their ways of dress or any of their customs. Alas, it was too late, as many of the very practices that were outlawed were already a normal way of life for the invaders.

Over time, the land settled into a relatively peaceful acceptance and toleration of the two peoples. Fighting became less common, and a sort of peace settled across the land. The Irish chieftains were allowed to roam the lands as they had been accustomed to doing, and the Anglo-Norman invaders were allowed to stay within their walled cities. Occasional skirmishes arose, mostly along the outlying edges of the Pale, but these were usually isolated affairs that lasted for short periods of time.

The schism between **Henry VIII** and the Roman Catholic Church further distanced native Irish from their occupiers. By now, Ireland was predominantly Catholic, and Henry's departure from the church would have dire consequences for the Irish in coming years. Gradually, the religion that was once embraced by the English was rejected, tolerated, and then disdained. It was this grand disdain for their religion that made the Irish more devout and the English more intolerant.

During the next generation, the Irish engaged in a series of rebellions and in turn experienced a series of crushing defeats at the hands of Elizabethan soldiers that were ever more prevalent throughout the country. This was the **Plantation Period**, during which soldiers were granted large tracts of land for their service to **Queen Elizabeth**. Elizabeth, in turn, felt she was protecting the "back door" to England. There were fears in London that if Catholicism continued in Ireland, Spain might use that site to launch attacks on the shores of England.

QUEEN ELIZABETH OUTLAWS IRISH MUSIC

Poets and musicians have always played an important role in Irish society. From the days of the Celts, these cynical minstrels were honored, respected, and even a little feared. For political leaders their favor was paramount because a poet could turn the people for or against a particular king or chieftain.

They were such a critical cog in the machinery of the Irish culture that they were allowed to go about their business of music-making and satire with little retribution for biting words and great honor for complimentary words and songs.

As you might imagine, the English conquerors did not fare well at the hands of the minstrels. Queen Elizabeth understood the power these men wielded in Ireland. She outlawed all traditional Irish music, and proclaimed, "Hang all the harpers where found, and burn the instruments."

In 1580, the Spanish sent an expedition of 600 men to Ireland; their stated purpose was to assist in the defense of the Catholic cause in Ireland. This hapless army surrendered to a better-armed English army, and was summarily executed. But their efforts were viewed as an example of the very activity Queen Elizabeth feared. Her response was to flood Ireland with soldiers in an attempt to "pacify" the rebellious Irish; unfortunately, this pacification took the form of brutal repression and slaughter.

The Spanish continued to assist the Irish in their fray with England. Ammunition, money, and soldiers were sent periodically. In late 1601, an army of 4,000 men was sent to assist the Irish cause. They arrived too late to assist the beleaguered Irish army, and they themselves were besieged and defeated by **Lord Mountjoy** on Christmas Day, 1601. The leading rulers of the Irish fled Ireland at this time, and their departure was referred to as the **Flight of the Earls**.

After the Flight of the Earls, Ireland entered a period when the enmity between the Catholic Church and the English government grew more deeply. The church fanned the discontent of the Irish people; they told them they were being ruled by a queen whose birth was illegitimate in the eyes of God, and whose religion was heresy, the result of Henry VIII's lust. They told the Irish that rebellion against the crown was lawful, and indeed it was their duty to throw off the yoke of bondage.

Meanwhile, the Flight of the Earls opened up Ireland for settlement. Ulster was the targeted area, and the Crown moved to settle the area with loyal Protestants from England, Scotland, and Wales. Partially due to the numbers who were sent there, and partially due to the remoteness of Ulster, the settlement took hold, and many of its inhabitants today trace their ancestry to those settlers.

Between 1610 and 1640, Irish Catholics watched as their land was usurped by settling Protestants. The enmity and distrust between the conquerors and conquered grew, but seldom erupted in violence. It was a time when the conqueror needed the conquered to work his fields, and the conquered could not survive without working the fields of the conqueror. Despite the relative peace, a vehemence was boiling beneath the surface, a boil in need of lancing, an explosion waiting to happen.

In an effort to introduce education and the reformed faith to Ireland, Queen Elizabeth founded **Trinity College** in Dublin in 1592. The college was located on the grounds of a priory (a monastery) suppressed by her father a generation earlier. But the Irish refused to attend; in fact, the Catholic Church specifically barred them from doing so. So, in a matter of several decades, we find a relatively educated Protestant populace and a relatively uneducated Catholic populace. The result was contempt for the Irish and resentment on the part of the Irish.

In 1641, the Irish Catholics in Ulster revolted. Led by **Phelim O'Neill**, Protestants were massacred by the thousands. Men, women and children were caught in the maelstrom. While the wrath of the Irish was probably no worse than anything the English inflicted on the Irish, the results were widely reported in London, and great indignation followed.

In 1649, **Oliver Cromwell** was dispatched to Ireland. His hatred for and intolerance of Catholicism was legendary even at that time. Within four years, Cromwell laid waste to almost every square inch of Ireland. You can scarcely drive through the countryside in Ireland without finding a castle, monastery, or town that was sacked by Cromwell and his armies.

As armies were defeated and lands claimed for the crown, they were immediately granted to loyal Protestants. Irish rebels forfeited their lands to those who could prove that they had not been involved in the rebellion. If they couldn't prove they did not participate, rebels (and suspected rebels) lost their lands outright. It is estimated that at the time of the 1641 Uprising, 60% of the land in Ireland belonged to Catholics; after Cromwell's efforts, less than 20% of the lands were held by the Irish, and that in the inhospitable and relatively barren lands of Connacht.

In 1685, a glimmer of hope lighted the lives of the oppressed Catholic populace. **James II** of Scotland, who was also called Catholic James because of his religious affiliation, ascended to the throne of England. His reign lasted only a short time: Catholics were apparently as hated on the throne of England as they were in Ireland. The "Glorious Revolution" of 1688 chased James II from the throne and he sought and won the support of Irish Catholics. In fact, James II was accepted as a savior of sorts by the Irish people.

Unfortunately, due to the interplay of religious and political complexities, Catholic James did not enjoy the favor of **Pope Alexander VIII**, the very pope for whom his support had resulted in his ouster from England. James had hoped to flee to Ireland and muster troops there, and with the help of the French, reclaim his throne. Unfortunately, **Louis XIV** was too busy fighting his own battles within his own country, as well as with the Dutch and the English, to provide anything more than token assistance to James.

When James arrived in Ireland, most of the country was under the control of the Irish army. One notable exception was Derry, where English troops were under siege. They held out for nearly four months, and were on the verge of surrender when reinforcements arrived by sea, and caused James' forces to abandon their designs.

Enter on the scene one **William of Orange**. William, a Protestant, landed in Ireland near Carrickfergus Castle on June 14, 1690. Two weeks later, on July 1, his troops engaged James' troops in a massive battle on the banks of the River Boyne. The **Battle of the Boyne**, as it came to be called, signaled the end of any opportunity for James to be restored to the throne. James fled to Waterford, boarded a ship and left for France, where he died in exile three years later.

Ireland was still full of Irish troops. One by one, these armies lost a series of skirmishes with William's better-armed and better-led forces. Finally, one year later, 10,000 Irish troops surrendered after the **Siege of Limerick**, and they were allowed to leave the country. The sailing of these rebels from the shores of Ireland to the Continent was spoken of by the bards as the "**flight of the wild geese**."

Undefended and leaderless, Ireland now faced some of its stiffest challenges – perhaps even greater than the trying times Oliver Cromwell brought. At the urging of Protestants in Ireland as well as those in England, William allowed Parliament to pass the infamous **Penal Laws**. These laws essentially disenfranchised the Catholics within the boundaries of their own country. They were not allowed to vote nor run for election to Parliament, they were excluded from military service and the legal profession, and they were not allowed to receive formal education. They could not possess arms, and they were not even allowed to own a horse worth more than five pounds. In short, they were rendered a nonentity in their own country. The practice of Catholicism was strictly controlled, and was only in the hands of a few licensed priests; ecclesiastical leaders at the level of bishop and above were banned from the country, and a death sentence was pronounced upon those who dared return. Catholic lands were forfeited to Protestants, and they were relegated to the status of tenant farmers.

The Penal Laws were a vicious retribution on what the British felt were a troublesome people. The laws were designed to keep the Irish down socially, economically, religiously, and politically. The laws were strictly enforced, and created a new caste system in Ireland. While there was some softening of its enforcement at times, Catholic emancipation was not completely won for another century and a half.

"Catholic emancipation" became the rallying cry for two generations of Irish patriots – or rebels, if viewed from the English side of the issue. It was during the early 18th century that **Jonathan Swift** (of *Gulliver's Travels* fame) penned the following sentiment that found its way across the ocean to bolster the cause of another English colony in rebellion: "All government without the consent of the governed is the very essence of slavery."

There were two primary classes in Ireland: the disenfranchised Catholics and the landed Protestants. Parliament and the Crown continued to meddle with the economy and lifestyle of the Irish, and found themselves alienating both the Irish natives and the "Old English," who by now had become quite Irish in most aspects except religion. Control of the lucrative Irish woolen trade, coining of Irish money by an individual investor in England, and other repressive actions on the part of the English led to the formation of an alliance between the rebellious Irish and the hitherto supportive Protestant landlords of Ireland.

The American Revolution provided some relief for the Catholics in Ireland. Fighting one major war on one front necessitated the attention of Parliament; they didn't want and could ill afford an active rebellion in another of their colonies. The American Revolution was strongly supported by Irish Catholics and the Protestants landlords. Indeed, the Irish in particular probably felt a certain kinship to these fellow colonists struggling for independence from the powerful crown. During this time, Ireland won important concessions from Parliament in the areas surrounding the Irish woolen market, relative legislative independence, and a lessening of some of the harsher aspects of the Penal Laws. But Catholics were still unable to vote, and they were still unable to stand for Parliament.

Near the end of the 18th century another movement called the **United Irishmen** gained prominence. Led by **Theobald Wolfe Tone**, the United Irishmen were encouraged by both the American and French Revolutions. They hoped to wrest control of Ireland from the English and to establish an independent Irish republic. To mollify the rebels, additional modifications were made to the Penal Laws, the most important of which extended voting privileges to Catholics, the first time in a century.

Despite this major surge forward toward full emancipation, the United Irishmen were not satisfied. Rebellion broke out in the Northeast and Southeast sections of the country, and English troops put them down with the ferocity of the former Cromwellian armies. French troops arrived too late to assist, and they, too, were defeated by the British army. Wolfe Tone was captured, and perished in prison.

During this period, individuals on both sides of the religious fence were working hard to effect a uniting of the kingdom. Catholics saw this move as a positive step that would assure them total emancipation; Protestants saw it as a means of greater stability and strength for the Irish economy. Their support and the efforts of men such as **Edmund Burke** and **William Pitt** finally led to the establishment of the **United Kingdom of Great Britain and Ireland** on New Year's Day, 1801.

Despite the Union, full emancipation still did not see the light of day. For the next 25 years a number of movements arose – and were crushed – without realizing their dream of emancipation. These movements again fomented for the establishment of a Republic of Ireland. Home Rule, or *Sinn Fein* (Irish for We Alone) became the rallying cry for this generation of Irish patriots.

The stage was now set for two of Ireland's most influential and revered men to step forward. **Daniel O'Connell** and **Charles Stewart**

Parnell are the men credited with achieving complete Catholic emancipation. Parnell was a Protestant member of Parliament who lobbied hard for Catholic franchise. O'Connell was a Catholic from County Clare who won a seat in Parliament in 1828, but was refused the opportunity to take that seat because of his religious beliefs. He was a tireless supporter of the cause, and considered one of the greatest orators of his day. His impassioned speeches, coupled with large mass meetings and an avid Catholic following, swayed Parliament, and in 1829 the final vestiges of the Penal Laws were repealed.

The political scene was relatively quiet for the next several decades, although there were a series of aborted efforts to establish Ireland as an independent republic. But Ireland was moving quickly toward an event that was to devastate, demoralize, and decimate one quarter of her population. Mother Nature accomplished what centuries of military campaigns, plans, and schemes of an antagonistic crown could not do. From 1845 to 1847, a scourge of epic proportion hit Ireland: the **Great Potato Famine**.

Ireland of the mid-1840s was primarily an agricultural nation. The vast majority of Ireland's eight million inhabitants relied on the hearty potato as the mainstay of their diet. The potato was a natural food to take the lead in the Irish diet: great quantities could be grown on relatively little land, and it seemed to flourish whether planted in rich, loamy soil or in less arable land. With so little of Ireland in Irish hands, this combination made potatoes the ideal crop. But it was also akin to putting all their eggs in one basket.

The potato crop of 1845 was meager; a blight hit the plants, and potatoes rotted in the ground before they could be harvested. Successive potato crop failures in 1845, 1846, and 1847 hit the nation, and the populace was devastated. It is estimated the between 1845 and 1848, one million Irish perished in the famine, and another million emigrated, mostly to America. One quarter of the population was gone from Ireland in a little over three years. Any talk of rebellion, independence, or an Irish Republic must have seemed like gossamer as the struggle to merely stay alive gripped the nation.

Much has been written on the famine over the years. Despite the enmity between the Irish and the English Crown, vast sums of money were spent by England to provide public works employment, soup kitchens, and a variety of other efforts aimed at reducing the hardships encountered by over two-thirds of the population. Some applaud their humanitarian efforts; others judge them as too little, too late.

THE IRISH COME TO AMERICA

As devastating as the famine was, it may have been the beginning of the end for the United Kingdom of England and Ireland. A million Irish left famine-devastated Ireland during the famine years, and hundreds of thousands followed in the decades thereafter. As financially humble as their new lives were in America, they were far better economically than they would have been in Ireland. They also continued their clannishness, living in the same Irish neighborhoods, voting for the same politicians. The Irish vote became a much sought-after commodity among politicians in Boston and New York in particular.

And these Irish did not forget their roots. Dreams of Irish independence once again rekindled in the hearts of Irishmen, but now some of those Irishmen lived in America and could support their dreams with more than a voice and a body: money began to pour into any movement that supported Irish independence. At the same time, politicians understood that a large percentage of their constituency favored Irish independence. Indeed, at that time English newspapers and members of Parliament commented on the difficulty in keeping the Irish down, since such a strong group was now out of their direct control.

MORE UPRISINGS

In an effort to help bring the famine to an end, the English government forced landlords to pay higher taxes in order to support relief projects underway. The landlords in turn put pressure on their Irish tenants to pay their rents. When they were unable to pay, landlords began evicting them in hopes of finding tenants who could – and would – pay the increased rents. These evictions became another hardship, and another reason to hate the English. Perhaps most important, it drove many who had previously been neutral on the idea of Irish independence to support it whole heartedly.

As soon as the famine was over, the business of independence began again with renewed vigor and grimmer tenacity. Groups committed to Irish independence sprung up seemingly overnight in America as well as in Ireland. Some of the groups sought independence through political means, others through more militaristic methods. The **Fenians**, the **Irish Republican Brotherhood**, **Fenian Brotherhood** (in America), and other groups vowed independence for Ireland.

One by one the military efforts of each of these groups was met and put down. Occasionally, their leaders were executed; more often they were imprisoned for their efforts. But the Fenians finally hit upon a tactic that moved the purpose of independence a giant step forward: it was called the **Land League**, and it was highly effective.

The strategy of the Land League was simple: choose landlords who had been particularly aggressive in their evictions, and apply all means of non-military pressure available in order to make them more reasonable. Two of their tactics proved exceptionally effective. The first was the practice of withholding services. Landlords saw acres and acres of crops either go unplanted or rot in the ground because of their inability to find willing laborers to do the work. The second tactic was the social ostracism of individuals who either rented the homes of those who had been evicted, or who continued to work the landlord's lands despite the Land League's sanctions.

One of the first landlords targeted with this strategy was one **Captain Boycott**. The sanctions against Captain Boycott were so effective in establishing negotiations that the hapless landlord forever lent his name to the practice of withholding labor and ostracizing workers who cross a picket line. Incidentally, the Land League and its members could not have implemented this strategy for any effective length of time without the monetary support of Irish-Americans.

Simultaneously, **Charles Stewart Parnell** had transitioned from a powerful ally to the chairman of the Irish parliamentary party. Mr. Stewart had a strong conviction for the Catholic cause in Ireland, despite his own Protestant beliefs. He was considered a leader of the Irish people by both the Irish and the English.

As a result of Parnell's influence, sweeping changes in Ireland came about. In 1881, the **Land Act** was passed. This historic act brought much-needed protection in the areas of rent control and provided protection against arbitrary eviction. This victory, coupled with a short imprisonment at Kilmainham Jail, secured Parnell's leadership among the Irish.

This immense following enabled Parnell's party to seat eighty-five members of Parliament – a group who held the balance of power in the House of Commons. Their efforts, coupled with those of several English legislators, nearly bought independence for Ireland through political means. A **Home Rule** bill was proposed and nearly passed. However, the political stage was set: English opinion was beginning to swing toward the Irish, and it seemed that with a little patience, Irish Home Rule was imminent.

Unfortunately, the Irish party suffered a major setback when Charles Parnell was named in divorce proceedings as the paramour of the wife of another member of Parliament. The Victorian mores of the day proved the undoing of Home Rule for a season. Parnell was deposed as the chairman of the party. Powerful support was lost from other members of Parliament, from within the Irish party itself, and from the Catholic church. The party was in disarray, and subsequent elections saw them lose the significant gains they had so recently made. Charles Stewart Parnell died a little over one year later at the age of forty-six, an Irish political enigma who had come so close to gaining independence for Ireland, but whose actions cost them – at least for awhile – the elusive prize.

INDEPENDENCE AT LAST

Despite this latest setback, Irish independence was not to be fore-stalled much longer. The flame of hope for independence burned too brightly to allow it to die out completely. Although Parnell's contemporaries abandoned him, the rising generation adored him. He became somewhat of a martyr for the cause among the youth, and gave them the strength to press forward in the cause he had embraced.

While Home Rule bill after Home Rule bill failed in Parliament, the first two decades of the twentieth century saw the rise of men who were learning the tactics that would win the fight.

Simultaneously, as it appeared evident that Ireland was heading for Home Rule eventually, strong resistance in Ulster arose. Protestants objected strongly to an independent Ireland on the grounds of religion. They fought the battle on two grounds: first to avert Irish independence, and second, if Irish independence were to be granted, that it should exempt Ulster. So strong was the Ulster resistance that they firmly declared they would wage civil war – and they prepared to do so – if Ireland was granted its independence.

This demand to leave Ulster out of Irish independence was repugnant to the majority of the Irish. The "partition" of Ireland, as the proposal was called, was favored by a minority of the country, yet a majority in the section of the country affected.

In November 1913, the **Irish Volunteers** were formed, a group of men bent on revolution. This small force of men – and a few women – eventually turned the tide and won independence for Ireland.

The Irish Volunteers chose Easter Sunday, 1916 to stage a country-wide uprising. The leadership was split on the issue, and orders canceling the rising were issued; those orders were repealed by yet another set of orders by other leaders. Confusion resulted, and only about 20% of the ten thousand members of the Irish Volunteers participated in the **Easter Rising**.

The leaders of the Irish Volunteers seized the General Post Office – the GPO – on O'Connell Street in Dublin. From its steps they proclaimed the free Republic of Ireland.

THE PROCLAMATION OF THE REPUBLIC OF IRELAND

Like the "Shot Heard Round the World," the following volley began the Irish War for Independence. Here are a few words from the Proclamation of the Republic, read Easter Sunday, 1916, from the steps of the GPO:

IRISHMEN AND IRISHWOMEN: In the name of God and of the dead generations from which she receives her old tradition of nationhood, Ireland, through us, summons her children to her flag and strikes for her freedom...

We declare the right of the people of Ireland to the ownership of Ireland and to unfettered control of Irish destinies, to be sovereign and indefeasible. The long usurpation of that right by a foreign people and government has not extinguished the right, nor can it ever be extinguished except by the destruction of the Irish people. In every generation, the Irish people have asserted their right to national freedom and sovereignty; six times during the last three hundred years they have asserted it in arms. Standing on that fundamental right and again asserting it in arms in the face of the world, we hereby proclaim the Irish Republic as a Sovereign Independent State, and we pledge our lives and the lives of our comrades-in-arms to the cause of freedom, of its welfare, and of its exaltation among the nations.

The uprising lasted a week. During that time, nearly five hundred people lost their lives in the fighting that ensued. Finally, out-manned and out-gunned, the rebels surrendered the GPO to the British. Fifteen men had signed the **Proclamation of the Republic**; after the smoke cleared, and the Easter Rising suppressed, all were executed at Kilmainham Gaol, and hundreds of participants were imprisoned. Their status in Ireland was immediately elevated to that of martyrs, and the cause of Ireland took a fierce and bloody step toward its goal: a free and independent nation.

As World War I ended, parliamentary elections were held in Ireland. Seventy-three seats went to members of the Sinn Fein party. Rather than journey to Westminster to claim their seats, these members of parliament instead established their own Republican Parliament and called it *Dail Eireann* (literally meaning Meeting of Ireland). On January 19, 1921, they ratified the Proclamation of the Republic that was read five years earlier on the steps of the GPO, and another bold step toward independence was taken. It is interesting to note that thirty-six of the original members of the Dail Eirann were not present for their first meeting; they were still imprisoned for their role in the Easter Rising.

In addition to ratifying the Proclamation, they declared that the Dail Eireann was the only legislative body that could pass laws relative to the Irish people, and called for the evacuation of the English military machine from the country. They elected a government, headed by President **Eamon de Valera**; they also set up their own judicial system.

The English government refused to bow to the wishes of the Dail Eireann and several years of guerrilla warfare ensued. Greatly outnumbered, the **Irish Republican Army** evolved from several former paramilitary organizations. Their goal was the disruption of the workings of the English government and military in Ireland through terrorist attacks. In response, the English retaliated swiftly and relied on "collective reprisals," openly admitting that some of those who were affected by the reprisals were not the perpetrators, but innocents that were in the wrong place at the wrong time.

This tactic was incredibly destructive to world public opinion. In England, America, Australia, and Canada, England was censured for their heavy-handedness. Ireland was increasingly becoming a political football where no matter what they did, England looked like the bad guy. And again, in this generation as in the last, funds from America kept the rebellion afloat and enabled the rebels to continue their cause.

The **1920 Government Act of Ireland** established separate parliaments for Northern and Southern Ireland. Elections that year returned Sinn Fein members for all seats except those representing the greater Dublin area. In the North, the seats were all won by Protestants favoring the Union. Once again, Sinn Fein members refused to take their seats in the Southern Ireland parliament, establishing the Second Dail Eireann instead.

It appeared there was to be no compromise: while southern Ireland was closer to independence than it had ever been, Ulster was as far away as it had ever been. Those in Ulster had vowed to fight any attempts at secession from England. They saw themselves more closely aligned with England than with Ireland, and they simply did not wish to be governed by the wishes of a Catholic majority in the South.

In June 1922, Eamon de Valera was invited to participate in peace talks. During the talks, Sinn Fein representatives and representatives from the crown agreed to terms that essentially created two political entities: the Irish Free State in the south, and six counties in Ulster called Northern Ireland. Seven decades of hindsight help us see that representatives for the crown were the better negotiators. Through a series of harangues, empty promises, and vague potentialities, the Irish representatives were encouraged to sign a treaty that recognized the South as the **Irish Free State**, and recognized the Dail Eireann as the governing body of that state.

However, in exchange, the Irish Free State was forced to swear allegiance to the crown and allow her ports to be under English control in times of war. Feeling perhaps that a bird in the hand was worth two in the bush, on December 6, 1921, the **Anglo-Irish Treaty** was signed, establishing southern Ireland as the Irish Free State.

These proceedings divided Sinn Fein into pro-treaty and anti-treaty factions. Those who opposed the treaty did so on the grounds that once Northern Ireland was separated, they felt no power could restore them to the Republic (very prophetic); the idea of allegiance to the crown was also repugnant to them. Those with these views were called **Republicans**. The pro-treaty party – called the **Free Staters** – felt that something was better than nothing, and that in the long run, Northern Ireland would come around and want to be a part of the Republic. De Valera, a Republican, was unable to win his seat in the Dail Eireann in the next election.. The ideological split caused a separation into two factions: the anti-treaty **Irish Republican Army** (IRA) and the **Free State Army**. Both moved into separate buildings in Dublin and continued their respective campaigns.

On June 22, 1922, an eleven-month civil war broke out between the two differing factions after **Sir Henry Wilson**, a military advisor to the Northern Ireland government, was assassinated by members of the IRA. During this time, many of the Republican leaders were either executed or imprisoned. Eamon de Valera spent over a year in prison as a result of his leadership role in the Republicans.

Over the next two and a half decades, bits and pieces of the treaty were rescinded. In 1949 the final ties of allegiance to the crown were severed and Ireland, after over seven hundred and fifty years of British occupation, was now a free republic in every way.

THE TROUBLES IN NORTHERN IRELAND

As outlined earlier, **the troubles** in Northern Ireland that exist today had their beginnings many generations ago. Today, hostilities still wax and wane, and as long as there are those who foment for one Republic, and those who fight against it, there will be clashes between the two forces.

Over the years, the differences between the two ideological positions have had a history of alternating between violence and peace. To categorize the violence as a struggle between Catholicism and Protestantism is inaccurate. It is true that in general those who want a united republic tend to be Catholic and those that want Northern Ireland to remain with Great Britain tend to be Protestant. But it is political opinion and who will get and hold political and economic power – not religious affiliation – that causes the continuing troubles in Northern Ireland. The opposing religious beliefs of the political camps merely serve to galvanize the parties and, to some extent, muddy the issue.

Bloody Sunday

As the press graphically reported in the late 1960s and 1970s, sometimes the clash of opinions erupted into violence and bloodshed. Sunday, January 30, 1972, was one of the darkest of many dark days in the recent history of Northern Ireland. Despite a ban on street demonstrations in Northern Ireland imposed by the British government, civil rights demonstrators planned and carried out a peaceful march on Derry. Their purpose was to protest the recent decision by the British government to jail suspected IRA terrorists without benefit of a trial.

An estimated 15,000 to 20,000 demonstrators marched into Derry carrying posters and chanting. As they entered the city, their intended route of march was interrupted as British army forces posted barricades across the roads. As the crowd began to turn away from the barricades, something went terribly wrong. Tear gas and rubber bullets were fired into the milling crowd of demonstrators. Within minutes, the tear gas and rubber bullets were replaced with real bullets, and panic swept through the demonstrators, many of them teenagers, as they fled from the withering fire of British army regulars.

The event was dubbed **Bloody Sunday**. When the gunsmoke cleared, thirteen demonstrators were dead and one would die several months later from gunshot wounds. Six of the dead were seventeen year olds. The next two decades saw a series of bombings and reprisals. There is no doubt that many innocent bystanders were injured and killed.

Northern Ireland Today

The last few years seem to have witnessed the dawn of a moderation of attitudes and extremist tactics. In the early 1990s, an armistice was agreed to between the Irish Republican Army and the British government. The armistice has received worldwide attention and approval. When the IRA became frustrated with the lack of progress in negotiations and resorted to several car bombings, international censure of their actions was quick in coming. At the time of this writing, that censure has kept extremist activities in check, and negotiations are continuing.

As a gesture of good faith, the British government removed all military check-points along the border between Northern Ireland and the Republic, and their presence is not so obvious in the historical flashpoints of Belfast, Derry, and Armagh. The longer the ceasefire is in place, the more peaceful Northern Ireland seems. As a result, tourism numbers in Northern Ireland are higher than they have ever been. The Irish are flocking to Northern Ireland as tourists, as are western European and North American tourists. While a return to violence cannot be ruled out, I have hope that differences will be ironed out peacefully in the future.

THE IRISH ECONOMY TODAY

Historically, Ireland's economy has been dependent on agriculture. In fact, even today 90% of the land in Ireland is undeveloped and considered agricultural. But the Irish government knew an agricultural economy would not meet the needs of their people. As early as 1950, the Irish government became active in subsidizing and otherwise supporting industry, and one of their biggest pushes today is in the area of jobs creation. Their efforts have slowly transformed Ireland's economy into one centered on industry, which today accounts for 37% of gross domestic product, over 75% of exports, and is responsible for the employment of 29% of the work force.

Employment in the agricultural sector, once by far the greatest area of employment for the Irish, stands at about 14%. By far, most people work in the service sector, where 57% of the Irish population is employed. But despite their efforts, unemployment in Ireland today still averages between 15% and 18%, and is a constant source of concern for the government and people of Ireland.

IMPORTANT PEOPLE IN IRISH HISTORY

You'll see their names on street signs, parks, bridges, and railway stations. You'll hear ballads sung about them or disgust in the voices that utter them. These are important men and women in Irish history:

__St. Patrick__ (389–461?) – St. Patrick is probably as revered in Ireland as George Washington or Abraham Lincoln is in America. But the feelings for St. Patrick go beyond revere – almost to the point of adulation. While not the first Christian missionary to Ireland, St. Patrick was perhaps the most tireless, and certainly the most well-known.

__St. Brigid__ (5th century) – Saint Brigid founded an abbey during the 5th century.

__Brian Boru__ (926–1014) – High King of Ireland whose armies defeated the Vikings in the Battle of Clontarf.

__Dermot MacMurrough__ (1110–1171) – As it turns out, MacMurrough assumes the role of Benedict Arnold in Irish history. It was his anger at his censure and exile by the other Irish kings that sent him to London to plead for support from King Henry II. The ensuing invasion of land barons and their armies resulted in over seven hundred and fifty years of English rule in Ireland.

__Richard le Clare__ (died 1176) – Richard le Clare is better known to historians as either the Earl of Pembroke, or simply as Strongbow.

__Oliver Cromwell__ (1599–1658) – The Darth Vader of Irish history. Probably the most powerful, ruthless, merciless, and efficient conqueror to invade Ireland. Many atrocities are attributed to him and his armies.

IMPORTANT PEOPLE CONTINUED

Cromwell roared through Ireland leaving death, devastation, subjugation, and broken lives in his path.

James II – Called Catholic James, he fought William of Orange for the English crown at the Battle of the Boyne in 1690. He lost, ending all hopes of relief from oppression for Catholics.

William of Orange – Husband of Mary Stuart, Protestant sister to James II. William defeated James, a Catholic king, for the crown of England. James' defeat signaled the end of a short period when Catholics in Ireland hoped for relief from Protestant occupation and conquest.

Jonathan Swift (1667–1745) – Swift was a writer and Dean of St. Patrick's Cathedral in Dublin. Perhaps best known for his satirical Gulliver's Travels. He was also a tireless writer against the tyranny of the English Crown.

Oliver Goldsmith (1728–1774) – Goldsmith was an author, born in County Longford.

Theobald Wolfe Tone (1763–1798) – Leader of the United Irishmen who were fighting for Irish independence.

Daniel O'Connell (1775–1847) – Daniel O'Connell was known as "the Liberator." It was he who was responsible for the repeal of the Penal Laws, resulting in emancipation for Catholics.

Charles Stewart Parnell (1846–1891) – Considered the leader of the Home Rule campaign for Ireland and the leader of the Irish people. At one time in his career, he was called the uncrowned king of Ireland. A Protestant, he was a tireless fighter for Irish independence. He was the leader of the Irish parliamentary party. His affair with Kitty O'Shea split the Irish party and he lost support from his own party, the Catholic Church, and the Irish people in general.

Oscar Wilde (1854–1900) – Playwright and author. His works included Lady Windemere's Fan and The Importance of Being Earnest.

George Bernard Shaw (1856–1950) – Famous playwright born in Dublin. Some of his works include Arms and the Man, John Bull's Other Island, and Pygmalion. Shaw won the Nobel Prize for Literature.

William Butler (W. B.) Yeats (1865–1939) – A world-renowned poet, Yeats won the Nobel Prize for Literature. Yeats also served as a senator in the Irish Free State.

James Joyce (1882–1941) – Novelist, poet, and playwright born in Dublin. His works include Ulysses, A Portrait of the Artist as a Young Man, and Dubliners.

6. PLANNING YOUR TRIP

WHEN TO GO - CLIMATE & WEATHER

Ireland enjoys a temperate climate year-round, thanks to the Gulf Stream. Most tourists find the weather pleasant and more than acceptable for vacationing from April through October. During April and May, the temperatures are generally in the mid-50s during the days. During the summer months, you can expect the temperatures to be in the 60s, with even an occasional day or two in the 70s. Fall temperatures generally emulate those of the springtime, with daytime temperatures ranging from the high 40s to mid-50s most of the time. For the most part, winters on the Emerald Isle are also mild, with average temperatures in the mid-30s to low 40s.

But beware! There is a reason Ireland is known as the Emerald Isle. There are more shades of green than you can count, and they remain that way due to the frequency of rain, which can be anytime, anywhere throughout the year. (The average annual rainfall in Ireland is 43 inches.) However, despite frequent rain showers, it seldom rains hard enough to dampen the enjoyment of the many sights there are to see. I've found that a sweater (purchased in Ireland, of course), a light-weight raincoat, and (perhaps) an umbrella will make your touring pleasant.

On a recent flight to Ireland, as we neared Shannon, the captain announced to the passengers that there was a light skiff of snow on the ground. I had an inkling this was uncommon when many of the *Irish* passengers moved to the windows to see their island in white. While it does snow occasionally during the winter, it is generally warm enough to rain instead.

July and August are the peak tourist months, and it is during these months that you may find yourself waiting in line to see some of the more popular sights such as the **Blarney Stone** and the **Book of Kells**. During April, May, September and October, the numbers of tourists are noticeably less, and during the winter months you're liable to be downright lonely for the company of fellow travelers. There will be a few sights that aren't open until May, but I note those for you throughout the book.

As you might expect, rates in hotels and B&Bs are seasonal, and you'll pay slightly more during the high season (from June through August) than you will the rest of the year. Some hotels have another rate from March to May and during September–October that is less than the high season, but higher than the rate they charge from November to February.

Ireland has plenty of "dull days" – the Irish term for overcast or cloudy days. But other than providing an opaque backdrop for most of your photographs, there's really no harm done by the dull days. But oh – when the sky is a shimmering blue it is a sight to behold! Washed clean by the rains and ocean breezes, its brilliance accentuates the majesty of brooding ruins, augments the tranquil effect of verdant glens, and coaxes the true turquoise tint from the sea.

During most months of the year, there is an omnipresent breeze. A light sweater or sweatshirt is usually enough to combat its effects. As you visit some of the coastal sights you'll experience more wind – so hold on to your hat!

The Emerald Isle has Daylight Savings Time – called Summer Time. It begins the last Sunday of March, and reverts to Standard Time the last Sunday in October. This is a complimentary bonus of extra daylight hours with which to continue your walks on the beach, or and extra hour or two to prowl around deserted ruins.

AVERAGE DAYTIME TEMPERATURES (FAHRENHEIT)			
January	43	July	60
February	41	August	61
March	44	September	56
April	45	October	49
May	53	November	44
June	59	December	41

GETTING TO IRELAND

You have several options for arranging your trip. If you are an experienced traveler, you may feel comfortable scouting for the best air fares around. Most of us, however, will benefit from the expertise of a qualified international travel agent.

Find an agent that specializes in international travel. Check with friends and relatives who have traveled abroad and get their recommendations. Interview several travel agencies until you find one with which you are comfortable. After you have decided on a travel agent, provide him or her with all the organizations you are affiliated with – AAA, AARP, your credit union, your company, etc. Sometimes these entities have negotiated special rates with the airlines, and your travel agent can find those rates for you. Also keep in mind that, depending on the season, airlines sometimes run discount fares that beat any affiliation-negotiated rates.

Every year, Aer Lingus and Delta come up with attractive travel packages that include airfare, car rental, and lodging. Depending on the time of year, travel packages may best meet your needs. Bear in mind, however, that packages are typically priced for travel from the cities on the East Coast from which Aer Lingus or Delta fly directly to Ireland. Getting to one of those cities may drive up your costs considerably.

Transatlantic flights enter Ireland in one of two airports: Dublin or Shannon. At the time of this writing, **Aer Lingus** and **Delta** are the only airlines that fly directly to Ireland from North America. Delta flies from Atlanta to Shannon, and from New York City (JFK) to Shannon or Dublin. Aer Lingus flies from New York City (JFK), Boston, and Chicago directly to Dublin and Shannon. Neither Delta nor Aer Lingus have direct flights from Canada.

Other major airlines occasionally announce new service to Ireland direct from the US, but as yet none of them have lasted. Other airlines fly to Ireland via London where you then transfer to one of their international partners: British Airways, British Midland, SAS, and a handful of others. One advantage of connecting in London is that you can get a flight to some of Ireland's minor airports: Cork, Galway, Kerry, Sligo, Knock, and Belfast. If your eventual destination involves one of these locations, you may want your travel agent to check on costs, times, etc.

ENTRY REQUIREMENTS

First and foremost, you must have a current passport to enter Ireland. If you have traveled internationally, you probably already have one; it's a good idea to check the expiration date well before you plan to travel. American passports are valid for five years for children and ten years for adults. Canadian passports are valid for five years. All US citizens traveling to Ireland must have a valid passport. For Canadian citizens, children under sixteen can be included on their parents' passports, but they must have their own passport if they are traveling alone.

If you are getting a new passport, you should apply six weeks before you plan to depart (four weeks in Canada). That should give you plenty of time to receive your passport. If you are inside the six week window, don't fear – you can still get a passport, but it will be more expensive, as you will have to pay for overnight mail charges. About five days is the quickest you can get a passport, but I wouldn't cut it that short! Applications are available at US or Canadian passport offices as well as at some post offices. Some Canadian travel agencies also have passport applications.

Ireland requires only a passport for entry into their country. No visa is necessary if you are a citizen of the United States, Canada, Australia, or New Zealand and if your stay is less than ninety days (one hundred and eighty days in Northern Ireland). If you plan an extended stay that lasts longer than that, you must demonstrate that you have adequate funds to stay and already possess a return airline ticket.

If you are getting a new passport, here is what will be required:
• a notarized copy of your birth certificate. A hospital copy won't work. Naturalization papers or an old passport are acceptable
• two identical passport photos taken within the last six months. I've found my local AAA agency to be the best place to get these.
• you'll need to bring a picture ID, such as a driver's license.
• if this is your first passport, you must apply in person.
• the cost is (currently) $65 if you are 18 or over, and $40 if you are younger than 18.
• if you are renewing a passport, and it was issued within the past twelve years, the cost is $55 (if you are over 18 and your last name is still the same.)

CUSTOMS REGULATIONS

American Citizens

Americans who have been out of the country for more than forty-eight hours may return to the US with up to $400 worth of goods without paying duty. In addition, you may return with up to two hundred cigarettes and one liter of alcohol (you must be at least twenty-one years old to bring liquor back). If you are traveling as a family, the exemptions apply to each person, but can be pooled as a group.

If the total value of your purchases is greater than $400, you will be expected to pay additional duty. Currently, you must pay 10% duty on the next $1,000 worth of items you are returning with. Beyond the $1,400 threshold (the $400 duty free and the next $1,000 worth of goods), you will be assessed a fee based on the category your purchases fall into. If you need to pay additional duty, cash, checks, travelers checks, and (in some places) credit cards are acceptable.

Canadian Citizens

Once a year, Canadian citizens are allowed to bring C$300 worth of foreign goods back home without paying duty. That applies if you have been out of the country for at least seven days. If you have been gone less than seven days, but more than forty-eight hours, you can bring back

C$100 duty-free each trip, and there is no limit to the number of times you can do this. Exemptions apply to all members of a family traveling with you, but the exemptions cannot be combined as a group.

You may also bring home, duty-free, 1.14 liters of wine or liquor or twenty-four 12 oz. bottles of beer or ale. If you are sixteen years of age or older, you may bring home, also duty-free, two hundred cigarettes, fifty cigars or cigarillos, and four hundred tobacco sticks or four hundred grams of manufactured tobacco.

Both American and Canadian citizens can mail gifts home duty-free if the gifts are valued at less than US$50 and C$60. You can only mail one package per day per addressee. Packages should be marked "Unsolicited gift." Packages should also be marked on the outside with the retail value. The value of these gifts is not part of your exemption, and they are duty-free.

During your return flight home, flight attendants will hand out Customs forms for you to complete. You are expected to declare the total value of all products you bring in with you.

HOTEL & INN TERMS

Most Bed and Breakfasts and hotels charge a slight premium for renting a double room to a single traveler, since their rates usually are **per person sharing**. For B&Bs, room rates are listed as per person sharing. The "norm" and expectation is that two people will share a room. If a B&B lists its rate as £16 per person sharing, the cost for the room is £32 for two people. If only one person rents the room, instead of charging the full £32 for the double room, a "single supplement" is charged, normally around £5. Therefore, if one person rents a double room, the cost is £21 (£16 + £5). If a B&B has a single room, they will generally list a single room charge (usually a few pounds less than a double room), with no single supplement added.

Given the above rates, if three people want to share a double room, the cost would be £48 (£16 per person sharing).

You'll also run across the term **en suite**, which I use in this guide as well. If you get a room en suite, this means you have a bathroom in your room or suite; otherwise, you'll have to use the bathroom out in the hall.

TRAVEL COSTS IN IRELAND

Obviously, the mode of transportation you choose for your travels and the lifestyle you lead while in Ireland will have great bearing on your travel costs. Having said that, here's some general information about travel costs in Ireland.

Generally speaking, costs in Ireland were about what you'd expect to pay for things in the United States, if you ignore the dollar/pound conversion rate. In other words, if I would expect to pay $4 for a sandwich, it generally costs around £4 (which is really about $6.40). Or if I'd expect to pay $69 for a room, it probably costs around £69 (which is really about $110). One notable exception is the cost of gasoline. For years, gasoline in Europe has been far more expensive than it is in the US. On my most recent trips, petrol was running about $3.60 per gallon.

Rates for Bed and Breakfasts (B&Bs) around the country generally range from about £14 to £22 per person sharing, guest houses run from £28 to £70 per person sharing, and hotels run from £40 to £100 per room, and luxury hotels run much higher. If you choose to stay in youth hostels, where the accommodations are usually clean but pretty basic, expect to pay from £5 to £9. Rooms in Dublin, Belfast, and Cork as well as the tourist centers of Killarney, Westport, and Galway will generally be at the higher end of the spectrum and rooms in rural areas at the lower end.

The rate for rental cars varies widely, so it pays to shop diligently. Generally speaking, the big international rental car companies are significantly more expensive than the smaller local companies, some-times as much as three times the smaller companies' rates. A weekly rental should run you in the neighborhood of $300, depending on the car size, time of the year, etc. Occasionally the big international companies run specials that are attractive, but they still tend to be too expensive.

Train and bus travel is viable in Ireland. Both are under the control of a state-run agency. Again, rates will depend on how long you wish to stay and travel in Ireland. For example, you can purchase a pass for train and bus travel for any eight days of travel within a fifteen day window. The cost is $136 for adults and $68 for children ages 5-15. This ticket is available for travel only within the republic; for a few pounds more, you can have the same travel privileges extended to Belfast and all of Northern Ireland.

Bicycling across Ireland has become fashionable in recent years. The mild climate and beautiful country lends itself to this mode of transpor-tation, even though the narrow roads do not. Bicycle shops are plentiful around the country, especially in areas such as Dublin, Killarney, Galway, Westport, Dingle, etc. Expect to pay around £7 per day, £30 per week, or £115 per month for a bicycle.

Shop owners usually require something of value for a deposit to be left behind, like your passport or a major credit card. Bicycling is an excellent way to augment motorized travel in Ireland, whether you've chosen car, bus, train, or hitchhiking. If you do rent a bicycle, please be careful. The roads are painfully narrow, with lots of curves. Bicycle riders are expected to ride with traffic, not against it.

WHAT TO PACK

I've packed for Ireland two ways: heavy and light. On my first trip, I packed for every conceivable weather condition and social occasion. On my next trip, I packed lightly, going for versatile clothing. I'm here to tell you the latter method is far superior. In each of my subsequent trips, I have been able to fit everything, including camera equipment, travel guides, maps, etc., into one carry-on suitcase (with wheels) and one over-the-shoulder satchel.

Here are the necessities: sweater, 3-4 shirts (usually long sleeve), a couple of pairs of casual-style pants, one skirt for women, comfortable shoes, several pair of underwear and socks. If you plan on eating in the finest restaurants in Ireland, of course you'll want to bring a suitable pair of slacks, a suit or sports jacket, and possibly a tie for men, and a nice dress, skirt and blouse, or pants suit and nylons and shoes for women. Children tend to go through their clothes faster, but I recommend you pack clothes comparable to what you pack for yourself, although they may need a few extra changes of clothes.

You should be prepared for rain. I prefer not to carry an umbrella, choosing instead to fend off the rain with a cap: it rarely rained hard enough to make me wish for an umbrella. I suggest taking one of those small retractable umbrellas, if a cap won't do the job for you. Since my first trip, I no longer take a raincoat either because I find that an Irish wool sweater does a fine job shedding the water and keeps me dry. You'll need to determine whether you think a raincoat is necessary.

You can get just about any toiletry you might need in Ireland: tooth paste, deodorant, shampoo, lotion, make-up and feminine care products. You'll have to decide how important your particular brand is to you, because it may not be sold in Ireland. If you require prescription drugs, I recommend you bring enough for your trip, but be sure you know exactly what you take, how often, and in what dose in case you lose your medication. Hair dryers are generally available in most hotels but in only a few B&Bs and guest houses. If you have to have a hair dryer, you should bring your own, but make sure you also bring a converter and plug adapter. Finally, there are places to have your clothes pressed; alternatively, you may want to purchase a small travel iron (with converter and adapter).

If you are traveling with kids, don't forget to bring books, crossword puzzles, magnetic games like chess, checkers, or backgammon, or a Gameboy (or whatever they like), to keep them entertained as you drive from town to town and in the evenings. Also, depending on their age, you should consider purchasing them their own disposable cameras so they can take pictures (it's their vacation too, after all), and they won't bug you to use your camera.

You will need good maps. If you are renting a car, the rental agency will give you one that is pretty general but not bad. You may want to pick up regional maps in the areas you are traveling to; they are usually available at the tourist offices. If you plan on being in Ireland for more than one week, ask the car rental agency for an extra map. I usually wear a map out in a week.

You may want to supplement this guide with another B&B or hotel guide. The Irish Town and Country Homes Association produces a yearly book on Bed and Breakfasts for the Republic called *Guest Accommodation – 1996* (£2.50), which is updated yearly. The Irish Hotels Federation publishes a book called *Be Our Guest* (£2). Both books list hundreds of Bord Failte-approved B&Bs, guest houses, and hotels throughout the country. Tourist offices will have them, and they are worth the money. Use this guide for personal insights into each accommodation; use these other two if you find you are out in the middle of nowhere and it's getting late, or if all the accommodations I have suggested are full.

IRISH REPRESENTATIVES ABROAD

Before you leave for Ireland, you may wish to contact some of the following organizations. They can be of great help in planning your vacation. Whether you are looking for brochures, travel information, advice, or just an Irish accent to listen to, they should be able to meet your needs.

United States
- **Irish Tourist Board**, *345 Park Avenue, New York, NY 10154. Tel. 212-371-9052, 800-223-6470.*
- **Irish Embassy**, *2234 Massachusetts Avenue NW, Washington DC 20008. Tel. 202-462-3939.*
- **Consulate General of Ireland**, *345 Park Avenue, New York, NY 10154. Tel. 212-319-2555.*
- **Consulate of Ireland**, *William McCarthy Building, 535 Boylston Street. Boston MA 02116. Tel. 617-267-9330.*
- **Consulate of Ireland**, *655 Montgomery Street, San Francisco, California 94111.*
- **Consulate of Ireland**, *Wrigley Building, 400 North Michigan Avenue. Chicago, Illinois 60611.*

Canada
- **Irish Tourist Board**, *160 Bloor Street East, Suite 1150, Toronto, Ontario M4W 1B9. Tel. 416-929-6783.*
- **Irish Embassy**, *170 Metcalfe Street, Ottawa, Ontario K2P 1P3. Tel. 613-233-6281.*

GETTING AROUND IRELAND

There are many ways to get around Ireland, and the mode depends entirely on your purpose, destinations, adventuresome spirit and desires. Bicycle, bus, rental car, hitchhiking, and train – or a combination of any of them – are the major options.

BY BICYCLE

If you choose to see the Emerald Isle on two wheels, congratulations. This is one of the most popular modes of transportation for tourists from May through October. Most cities of any size have bicycle rental shops with bicycles for hire on a daily, weekly, and monthly basis. Expect to pay about £7 per day, £30 per week, or £115 per month. Most bicycles for hire are the currently popular 18- or 21-speed mountain bikes.

Many of the bicycle shops close down during the off-season, so if you're going to Ireland from about November through March or April, you may want to call the Tourist Office in the city where you want to begin your cycling and get the names of companies that are open that time of year.

BY BUS

Bus Eireann is the state-run organization that runs the bus (and train) lines. They run all the long distance buses, as well as most of the local and sightseeing buses. If you choose to travel in Ireland by bus, you should purchase a **Provincial Bus Schedule** at any bus terminal, or at the many newsagents scattered across the country (typically in small grocery stores).

There are several types of passes available. The rates are current as of this writing:

• **Irish Explorer Rail/Bus** – Valid for any eight days of travel within a fifteen day window. The cost is £85 for adults and £42.50 for children ages 5-15. For travel in the Republic of Ireland only.

• **Emerald Card Rail/Bus** – Valid for any eight days of travel within a fifteen day window. Similar to the Irish Explorer Rail/Bus pass listed above, except this allows you to go to Belfast and elsewhere in Northern Ireland. The cost is £105 for adults and £52.50 for children ages 5–15. There is also a pass for travel on any fifteen days out of a thirty day window. The rates are £180 for adults, and £90 for children ages 5-15.

Children under age five travel free. If you'd feel more comfortable purchasing your passes before you leave, you can write to: **CIE Tours**, *108 Ridgedale Avenue, PO Box 2355, Morristown, New Jersey 07962.*

BY CAR

"Left is right and right is wrong" when it comes to driving in Ireland. That's right – the Irish drive on the left, as do the English.

Surprisingly, driving on the left is not difficult to get used to. However, if you rent a car with a manual transmission, you should have reasonable coordination since you'll be shifting with your left hand instead of your right. If you can't pat your head and rub your stomach at the same time, you may want to consider paying extra for an automatic transmission – but it will cost you from £8 to £15 extra per day, depending on the time of year, the agency, and the class of car you rent. That's a little pricey, and you have to make the decision, but it will be just one less thing to worry about. And one less thing to worry about is exactly what you'll need as you encounter your first "round-about."

If you live in the eastern United States, you are probably familiar with traffic circles – the US name for round-abouts. But if you are from west of the original thirteen colonies, they may be a mystery. Round-abouts are a traffic control system found at the intersection of two or more roads. Generally, no stop signs or traffic lights are employed – drivers merely enter the circle continuing on their journey until they reach the outlet that takes them in the direction they want to go (got that?). Initially a skeptic, I came to admire the smooth and efficient way they manage traffic.

ROUND-ABOUTS

Round-abouts can be intimidating the first few times you enter one. The following will help you navigate your way in and out:

• traffic in round-abouts moves clock-wise;

• traffic already in the round-about has the right-of-way and cars in the round-about and those behind you will expect you to stop if the road is not clear;

• round-abouts are generally well-signed going into and within them;

• round-abouts that handle lots of traffic are often augmented by traffic signals.

There are several types of roads in the Republic and in Northern Ireland. In Northern Ireland, roads are categorized as *A*- or *B*-roads. *A*-roads are the main roads, and *B*-roads are the local roads.

In the Republic, there are three primary types of roads: *M*-, *N*- and *R*-roads.

M-roads are about the same as interstate highways in the United States. The speed limit on these roads is 70 mph. There are not many of these roads in Ireland.

N-roads (national roads) are the same as two-lane highways in the United States. The speed limit on N-roads is 60 mph. Occasionally you'll see signs for a "dual carriageway." You'll come to love them. They are similar to divided highways and are a welcome sight after the narrow roads you primarily drive in Ireland.

R-roads (regional roads) make up the majority of the roads and are extremely narrow. They are well-maintained and the speed limit on these roads is also 60 mph, unless otherwise posted.

WATCH OUT FOR THOSE IRISH DRIVERS!

Many of the N-roads are two-lane highways with wide, flat, paved shoulders called hard margins. Even with oncoming traffic, cars behind you will pass you. You are expected to move over (to your left) and drive on the hard margin until they pass. Likewise, oncoming traffic will expect both the car they are passing and oncoming traffic – you – to move over, onto the hard margin. It's bizarre, but it works very well. Irish drivers faithfully use their turn signals before participating in this maneuver, and you should too.

Bear in Mind ...
• Drivers and front seat passengers are required to wear seat belts.
• It is unlawful for children under age twelve to ride in the front seat.
• Motorcyclists and their passengers are required to wear helmets.
• Ireland has very aggressive laws when it comes to driving under the influence of alcohol.
• A solid white line serves the same purpose in Ireland as the solid yellow line does here – it means no passing.
• Gasoline is more expensive in Ireland than in the US, but on a par with the rest of Europe. The last time I was there, the cost averaged about 60 pence per liter. That works out to about £2.25, or roughly $3.60 per gallon. The cost will vary, of course, depending on the exchange rate when you are traveling.
• Unless you are traveling on M-roads, remember travel times will be much slower than in the states due to narrow winding roads, frequent villages, tractors, sheep, cattle, etc. I found forty miles an hour is a pretty aggressive estimate for most roads.
• In general, locals tend to drive at much higher speeds than I am comfortable with. In those cases, I simply pull over and let them pass, then continue my driving and sightseeing at a leisurely pace.

Driving in Cities
Driving in the cities requires special attention. Bicyclists, motorcyclists, and pedestrians are more plentiful and far more aggressive than in most American cities. Motorcyclists in particular can be maddening: passing on your left or right, darting in and out of traffic, and making a general nuisance of themselves! Traffic lights are on the corners – not

hanging in the air over the intersections. I never did get accustomed to this, and had to consciously remind myself to watch closely. In the larger cities, (Dublin, Cork, Galway) it is virtually impossible, and dangerous, to sightsee while you are driving. Find a place to park, and walk around the cities, seeing all that you wish in relative safety.

I say relative safety, because as a pedestrian in Ireland you need to concern yourself with the different traffic patterns. Rather than looking left for traffic as you would in the US, you must look to the right! During World War II, Winston Churchill had an accident that underscores the importance of this. On a trip to New York City, he looked to the right for traffic – as he would in London – and stepped into the path of an oncoming taxi – coming from his left. Fortunately, he sustained only minor injuries. So remember: look to the right!

Road Signs

Both Ireland and Northern Ireland have great road signs. The US could take a lesson from these tourist-conscious countries.

Irish signposts have a unique design: a single pole with any number of vertical arrows with the name of towns and distances written on them. Each arrow is fastened to a pole with a circular clamp, much like those used on radiator hoses. It is a popular schoolboy prank to twist the signs around slightly, giving the unwary traveler a more...scenic...view of Ireland. If this happens, don't fret; enjoy the ride and the unplanned adventure – you'll find your way eventually!

SIGNPOSTS & ROAD NUMBERS

Once you get off the M- and N-roads, road numbers are pretty much just found on maps; there may be a sign with the road number on it out in the country at an intersection, but more than likely it won't be there (I'd guess 80% of the time it's not), and it's never posted on the road as you're driving along. The Irish are a little nonchalant about street addresses, and they're the same way about road numbers being marked anywhere on the roads themselves. The country is well-signposted with the names of towns, but not the road numbers.

Rental Cars

While airfares are usually fairly price-competitive, you will need to shop around for the best car rental rates. You can do this through your travel agent, or you can do it yourself. Rates on rental cars seem to change on a daily basis, and car rental agencies also have a series of discounts based on negotiated rates with affiliated companies and organizations. I recently checked the major rental car agencies – Hertz, Avis, National (which is Europcar in Ireland) – and found a surprisingly wide range of prices. For a two-week rental, I was quoted prices from $450 to over $1,400 for the same class of car! Perhaps that last rate was so high because the woman thought I wanted to *buy* the car!

When comparing rental car rates, be certain you are shopping "apples to apples," such as length of time, type of insurance, size of car, mileage charges, service charges and taxes. When I checked, I asked the companies to include Collision Damage Waiver (CDW), theft insurance, and Value Added Tax (VAT – it is a whopping 12.5%!). All the agencies I checked with included unlimited mileage in their rates, but ask just to make sure. Also, be sure you compare dollars to dollars, or pounds to pounds. Most agencies will quote their rates in dollars as well as pounds.

Regarding gasoline, some rental agencies give you a full tank of gas and require you to leave a £25 or £30 deposit. If you return the car with a full tank, they refund the deposit. Other agencies give you a full tank of gas and expect you to return it empty; they do not give you credit for any gas left in the tank, even if you filled it at the airport. Be sure and check which policy is in effect when you rent your car.

You'll need a valid US or Canadian driver's license and a major credit card to drive in Ireland.

Most car rental agencies in Ireland will only rent to drivers who are at least twenty-three years old and younger than seventy-five years old. Some rental agencies require you to be at least twenty-five.

Car Insurance: To Buy or Not To Buy

If you are accustomed to renting cars in the United States, you know your own car insurance usually covers you while you are driving a rental car in the US. *Such is not the case in Ireland.* Your domestic car insurance will not cover you while your are driving a rental car in Ireland. However, many credit card companies will cover your car rental insurance, so you can forgo the **Collision Damage Waiver** (CDW) charge. That amounts to about £8 or more per day.

Before you accept or forgo the CDW, check with your credit card company because you may be covered if you rent a car with your credit card. For example, my credit card company covers collisions, rollovers, vandalism, theft, tire blow-out or damage, and windshield damage. Also check what restrictions, deductibles, or requirements apply. My credit card company has the following restrictions: covers rental car for a maximum of 31 days; all drivers must be listed on the rental agreement; all claims must be submitted to the credit card company within 20 days; the entire car rental must be charged to the credit card

Most major credit card companies offer a similar service, but please don't assume yours does. Programs change, services expire, or new stipulations may be put in place. Before you go, check to be sure.

If you intend to take a rental car to the Republic to Northern Ireland (or vice versa), make certain the insurance you get covers you in both places. In the past, this was not always the case, although all the car rental agencies I checked with on my last trip covered both places.

IRISH DRIVING TERMS	
bonnet	*hood*
boot	*trunk*
caravan	*trailer (like a travel trailer)*
car park	*parking lot*
dip	*dim (as in: dim your lights)*
diversion	*detour*
dual carriageway	*divided highway*
Garda	*police*
give way	*yield*
lay by	*rest area*
margin	*shoulder*
M__, Motorway	*interstate highway*
N__, National road	*two-lane highway*
petrol	*gasoline*
way out	*exit*

As you might expect, there are several dozen car rental agencies in Ireland. The following are a few of the more notable agencies:

Car Rentals in Dublin
- **Argus Rent-a-Car**, *Argus House, 59 Terenure Road East. Tel. (01) 490-4444 Fax (01) 490-6328*
- **Atlas Car Rentals Ltd.**, *Desk 1, Arrivals Hall, Dublin Airport. Tel. (01) 844-4859 Fax (01) 844-0732*
- **Alamo-Treaty Rent-a-Car**, *800-522-9696*
- **Auto-Europe**, *800-223-5555*
- **Avis Rent-a-Car**, *800-331-1084*
- **Boland's Rent-a-Car**, *800-227-5577*
- **Budget Rent-a-Car**, *800-472-3325*
- **Casey's/Flannelly Car Rentals**, *212-935-0606*
- **Eurocar**, *800-6000*
- **Hamill's Rent-a-Car**, *800-346-5388*
- **Hertz Rent-a-Car**, *800-654-3001*
- **Holiday Autos**, *800-422-7737*
- **Kemwell Rent-a-Car**, *800-678-0678*
- **Long's Travel**, *96 Ridgedale Avenue, Cedar Knolls NJ 07927, 800-524-0555*

• **Tom Mannion Self Drive**, *800-666-4066*
• **Murrays Europcar Car Rental**, *Baggot Street Bridge, Dublin 4. Tel. (01) 668-1777, Fax (01) 660-2958; or toll-free 800-227-3876*
• **South County Car Rentals**, *Rochestown Avenue, Dun Laoghaire, County Dublin. Tel. (01) 280-6005 Fax (01) 285-7016; or toll-free 800-521-0643*
• **Windsor Car Rentals**, *South Circular Road, Rialto, Dublin 8. Tel. (01) 454-0800, Fax (01) 454-0122*

Car Rentals in Limerick
• **Cara Rent-a-Car Ltd.**, *Coonagh Cross, Ennis Road, Limerick. Tel. (061) 55811, Fax (061) 55369*
• **Dan Dooley/Kenning Rent-a-Car**, *Knocklong, County Limerick. Tel. (062) 53103, (062) 53392; or toll-free 800-331-9301*
• **Payless/Bunratty Car Rentals**, *Coonagh Cross, Ennis Road, Limerick. Tel (061) 52781, Fax (061) 52516; or toll-free 800-524-0555*
• **Thrifty Irish Car Rentals**, *Maxol Station, Ennis Road, Limerick. Tel. (061) 53049, Fax (061) 53433; or toll-free 800-367-2277*
• **Treaty Rent-a-Car**, *37 William Street, Limerick. Tel. (061) 24211 Fax (061) 412266*

BY HITCHHIKING

Hitchhiking is legal in Ireland, and in former years it was a wildly exciting and romantic way to see the country. More recently, however, several highly-publicized murders of hitchhikers has put a damper on it. However, having said that, you'll see far more people hitchhiking in Ireland than you do in the US. If you're going to hitchhike, use caution, go in pairs, and if you feel the least bit uncomfortable about a car or truck that stops to pick you up, wait for the next one.

BY TRAIN

The railways in Ireland literally criss-cross the country, and you'll be able to get within striking distance of just about any place in Ireland you'd like to go. From Sligo in the Northwest to Wexford in the southeast, from Dublin to Killarney, the trains will get you to where you want to go. Train service is a little sparse in the province of Connacht, however.

Bus Eireann is the state-run organization that runs the train (and bus) lines. If you choose to travel in Ireland by train, you should purchase a **Train Timetable** at any train terminal, or at the many newsagents scattered across the country (typically in small grocery stores).

There are several types of passes available. The rates are current as of this writing:

Irish Explorer Rail – Valid for any five days of travel within a fifteen day window – ideal if you want to stay a day or two and explore the surrounding areas before moving on to explore other cities or regions. The charge is £60 for adults and £30 for children ages 5–15. For travel in the Republic of Ireland only.

Irish Rover Rail – Valid for any five days of travel within a fifteen day window. Similar to the Irish Explorer Rail listed above, except this pass allows you to go to Northern Ireland. Rates are £70.00 for adults and £35 for youth ages 5-15.

Children under age five travel free. If you'd feel more comfortable purchasing your passes before you leave, you can write to: **CIE Tours**, *108 Ridgedale Avenue, PO Box 2355, Morristown, New Jersey 07962.*

RIDE IN A JAUNTING CAR!

A jaunting car is a small horse-drawn cart peculiar to Ireland. It generally holds the driver and from two to four passengers. If you saw the movie **The Quiet Man** *with John Wayne and Maureen O'Hara, they did their courting under the watchful eye of Barry Fitzgerald (as the driver) as they rode in his jaunting car.*

BORD FAILTE - THE IRISH TOURIST BOARD

The reception you receive as a tourist in Ireland will be warm and cheerful. The Irish take tourism in their country very seriously. Approximately one out of every thirty Irish citizens is employed in the tourism industry. Tourism in Ireland accounts for over 60% of all exports of services, and its growth rate is double that of the economy as a whole.

With that kind of impact on the Irish economy, you can be sure the **Irish Tourist Board** – *Bord Failte* (pronounced fall'-cha – which means "Welcome" in Irish) is anxious to see that you have a pleasant and enjoyable trip to their country. Several months prior to your trip, call or write to any of several Bord Failte locations, and they will provide you with an abundance of tourism material. You should request the specific type of information you are interested in: tourist attractions, Bed and Breakfasts, hotels, etc. Bord Failte also has an office in New York City *(Tel. 212-418-0800)*. Much of the material they send you is free. They'll also usually send you a price list for other materials you can purchase.

Bord Failte has a network of tourist offices throughout the width and breadth of Ireland. These local offices are a great source of information for points of interest in their respective areas. Following are the regional offices of Bord Failte:

- **Dublin City and County Regional Tourism Organization**, *1 Clarinda Park North, Dun Laoghaire. Tel. (01) 280-8571*
- **Northwest Regional Tourism Organization**, *Aras Reddan, Temple Street, Sligo. Tel. (051) 75823*

- **Southeast Tourism**, *41 The Quay Co., Waterford. Tel. (071) 61201*
- **Ireland West Regional Tourism Organization**, *Aras Failte, Eyre Square, Galway. Tel. (091) 63081*
- **Midland-East Tourism Organization**, *Dublin Road, Mulingar, Co. Westmeath*
- **Southwest Regional Tourism Organization**, *Tourist House, Grand Parade, Cork. Tel. (021) 273251*
- **Shannon Development**, *Shannon Town Centre, Co. Clare. Tel. (061) 361555*
- **Northern Ireland Tourism Board**, *St. Anne's Court, 59 North Street, Belfast, Northern Ireland BT1 1ND. Tel. (0232) 231221.*

IRISH ROAD SIGN

7. BASIC INFORMATION

BUSINESS HOURS

Businesses are generally open from 9:00 am to 5:00 pm, although most stores open at 9:30 am or 10:00 am. In some of the larger cities, stores will stay open later one night of the week. In Dublin, that day is Thursday.

ELECTRICITY

Electricity in Ireland is 220 volts (50 cycles) and an adapter is required. Most discount stores like Target, K-Mart, and Walmart, as well as Sears and J.C. Penny's carry inexpensive adapters that will do the job nicely. Remember, if you expect to use your hair dryer, curling iron, or electric razor, you'll need an adapter. Oh yes – and unless you're going to bring lots of very expensive (and heavy) batteries, you'll want that adapter to recharge the batteries for your camcorder (common oversight).

EMBASSIES & CONSULATES IN IRELAND

The **American Embassy** is located in Dublin at *42 Elgin Road, Dublin 4., Tel. (01) 668-8777*. They are open Monday through Friday from 8:30 am to 5:00 pm. If you have cause to visit there, look for what is probably the ugliest building in Dublin. Set in the splendor of a beautiful Georgian residential neighborhood, its unfortunate modernistic, gray concrete and glass architecture sticks out like a sore thumb. It really is an eyesore.

The **Canadian Embassy** is located at *65 St. Stephen's Green, Tel. (01) 478-1988*. They are open Monday through Wednesday from 8:30 am to 12:30 pm, and from 2:00 pm to 4:00 pm, and Thursday and Friday from 8:30 am to 12:30 pm.

The **American Consulate in Northern Ireland** is located at *14 Queen Street, Belfast, Tel. (01232) 328239*. They are open Monday through Friday from 9:00 am to 5:00 pm.

HEALTH & SAFETY

Before you leave for your holiday in Ireland, check with your health insurance company to see if you will be covered in the event of an emergency, illness, or injury during your travels in Ireland. If you are covered, find out the procedure they require you to follow before seeking treatment. As you may know, both Ireland and Northern Ireland have national health care systems, and unless you have insurance, you will only be treated in the event of an emergency. As of this writing, Medicare doesn't cover overseas medical expenses, but some of their supplemental plans do. Check before going.

Safety? If you use common sense in your travels you will be fine. Ireland is far from crime-free, although I suppose it is still one of the safest countries in which to travel.

I think the biggest concern I have in the area of safety is driving. Roads are narrow, speeds are fast, and there are a lot of Americans on the roads! Don't try to keep up with the locals until you have logged a few miles on these narrow roads. And on the exceptionally narrow roads of Counties Cork, Donegal, Connemara, and Donegal, give way to those who are driving faster than you, and enjoy the scenery.

LAUNDRY

If you are staying for more than a week, you probably will need to do your wash. That is easier said than done. But, if you are diligent, (and in a city) you should be able to find a place.

You have several options. Most major hotels have valet services. If you are staying in a B&B, many will allow you to use their washing facilities. The cost is usually minimal, roughly equivalent to what you'd expect to pay in a laundromat. But, don't assume the B&B will allow you to use its facilities. When you call to make a reservation or confirm your reservation, ask about the policy.

You can also ask your host to direct you to the laundromat, or you can use the local "yellow" pages or inquire at the local tourist office. They are called *washeterias* or *launderettes*, and are self-serve. A *laundry shop* is what we call a dry cleaners.

MONEY & BANKING

The currency is officially known as a **punt** (pronounced *poont*), but is generally referred to as pounds. As with all foreign currencies, the exchange rate fluctuates. The past several years the conversion rate has been in the neighborhood of US$1.50 to $1.65 and CD $2.05 to $2.25 for each Irish pound (£1). To find out what the conversion rate is, call any sizable bank, AAA, currency exchange office or check the *Foreign Ex-*

change box in the business section of your local newspaper. Since Irish money is not quite as common as other foreign currencies, your bank may need a few day's notice to obtain the currency.

If you forget or can't get to a bank or currency exchange office to exchange your money before you leave, don't worry. There are currency exchange kiosks in most city airports (Chicago, Boston, New York, and Atlanta), as well as at Shannon and Dublin airports. You'll have to pay a service charge.

In the Republic, businesses will accept either Irish or British pounds (UK£). However, in Northern Ireland, most shops won't accept the Irish pound – only British Sterling. During most of my trips to Ireland the exchange rate for British Sterling was a few pennies more than the Irish pound. The shops in the South charge a small fee – about 10p per pound - when you use British pounds.

Banks in Ireland are open, well, they're open bankers' hours. Traditionally, banks in the Republic are open Monday through Wednesday and Friday from 10:00 am to 12:30 pm, and from 1:30 pm to 3:00 pm. On Thursdays their *extended* hours are from 10:00 am to 12:30 pm and 1:30 pm to 5:00 pm. Banks in Northern Ireland are open from 9:30 am to 4:30 pm and closed from 12:30 pm to 1:30 pm. In the larger cities (Belfast and Derry), they don't close for lunch. The banks in the Shannon, Dublin, and Belfast airports, however, are open every day to service incoming international flights.

Post offices in the main cities in Ireland will also exchange money for you. Be aware, however, that most post offices will not accept $100 bills. Some larger hotels will also change money for you.

Automatic Teller Machines (ATMs) have started making their appearance in Ireland. Although they are nowhere near as ubiquitous as in America, they can usually be found on the outside wall of banks. **Cirrus** and **Plus** are the international networks most of these ATMs are part of. Most of the banks that provide ATMs charge a small transaction fee for withdrawals. Check with the bank that issued your ATM card to see if your current Personal Identification Number (PIN) will work overseas. Many of the ATMs overseas only accept four-digit PINs.

NEWSPAPERS

There are two main newspapers in Ireland: the *Irish Independent* and the *Irish Times*. If it's a hometown newspaper you're looking for, you may be in luck if you're from New York or consider the *Wall Street Journal* your hometown newspaper. Copies of the *Journal* and the *New York Times* can sometimes be found at Newsagents in the bigger cities, although they are usually a few days old.

POSTAL SERVICE

Letters sent from the Republic of Ireland to the United States and Canada cost 52 pence (written as "52p") and postcards cost 38p. If you have occasion to send them to Europe, letters cost 32p and postcards cost 28p. Stamps are available from the post office, or from most Newsagents. Postcards from the North to the United States cost 35p and letters cost 41p.

Most post offices in the country are open Monday through Saturday from 9:00 am to 6:00 pm. In the larger cities some of the post offices may have extended hours. For example, the General Post Office (GPO) in Dublin is open Monday - Saturday from 8:00 am to 8:00 pm.

If you're going to be in one place for a time, you can arrange to have your mail sent to a post office in your area. They will hold the mail for you free of charge for three months.

RADIO

You are almost always within distance of radio stations, the most common being several BBC stations out of England. There are two national radio stations in Ireland, **Radio 1** and **Radio 2**. Radio 1 is a conservative station that features talk shows. Gay Burne, who hosts the *Late, Late Show* on television also hosts a morning talk show on Radio 1. Radio 2 is geared much more toward the younger generation, and features rock music. There is also a national radio station called **Radio Gaeltachta**, which broadcasts in the Irish language.

In recent years, regional radio stations have emerged and become immensely popular. These small stations focus on regional news, covering regional athletic teams, local horseracing results, and obituaries for the area. In addition, livestock prices are also an important part of the broadcasts.

TAXES

Ireland has a **Value-Added Tax (VAT)** that is applied to all goods and services. This insidious tax now amounts to 12.5% in the Republic and 17.5% in Northern Ireland. All prices you are quoted and all prices you see posted in stores include VAT.

VAT also applies to food, but you do not get "cash back" on the VAT paid for food, nor for VAT paid on rental cars, hotel rooms, etc. You only get VAT refunds for purchased items such as an Aran sweater, Waterford crystal, or a Donegal tweed.

The good news is, if you are not from a country that is a member of the European Community (EC), you can get a refund on the VAT you pay. Whenever you make a purchase, ask the proprietor for a **CashBack** form.

Take the time to fill out all the forms you collect. Find the CashBack booth at the airport and present your forms to them. Be sure you give yourself time to do this at the airport.

If you made your purchases with a credit card, your VAT refund will either be mailed to you, or credited to your credit card. The refund company charges a small handling fee, but it's still worth your time to fill out the forms. They're pretty self-explanatory.

TELEVISION

Ireland has two television stations run by **Radio Teilifis Eireann**. The stations are called **RTE 1** and **Network 2**. Two of the most popular shows in Ireland are talk shows, similar to a serious Jay Leno (is there such a thing?). Friday nights at 9:30 pm (after the 9:00 pm news) you can watch the *Late, Late Show* hosted by Gay Burne. On Saturday evenings you can tune into another talk show called *Kenny Live*, hosted by Pat Kenny. Both shows are immensely popular, although the format is more restrained than you might be accustomed to in America. Typical guests might include a politician, CEO, rock star, or local athlete. The most popular Irish soap opera/drama is *Fair City*, a show about the (fictional) people of Dublin and their lives. *Fair City* airs Tuesday and Thursday evenings at 7:00 pm.

In addition to the two Irish television stations, cable or satellite will bring you numerous BBC stations from England. These stations carry English television shows, as well as American and Australian entertainment. *Coronation Street* (Monday, Wednesday, and Friday evenings at 7:30 pm) is a popular English soap opera about the people who live on a street in Manchester, England. American shows that are popular in Ireland include *Dr. Quinn, Medicine Woman*; *The Fresh Prince of Belair*; *Seinfeld*; and reruns of *Dallas*.

TIPPING

Tipping is acceptable and expected in Ireland. But be warned that if you give your customary 15% to 20% tip for outstanding service, you may in reality be giving over 35%. Many hotels and restaurants in the Republic automatically tack on a service charge of 10% to 15% to your room or meal. You might be interested to know that service charges are a hot issue in the hotel and tourism circles in Ireland. This should be settled one way or another within the next couple of years. Ever in tune with their customers, Bord Failte is well-aware that Americans in particular bristle at the idea of service charges on hotel rooms.

It's customary to tip cab drivers around 10% (they don't automatically add it to the fare), more if the driver acts as a tour guide, filling you in on interesting tidbits of trivia about the sites you're passing. Porters should be tipped £1 per bag.

TELEPHONE

Unless you are a hermit, in trouble with the law, or trying to lose yourself from the world, you will need to use Alexander Graham Bell's grand invention – the telephone. Be warned: you will not find the same consistent, user-friendly interface you are accustomed to in North America. Without a doubt you will experience uncooperative phones, occasional poor reception, and just plain frustration. It may take you two or three times dialing exactly the same numbers to get a call through, or you may need to deposit your coins two or three times before they'll register. But, with a little patience, you will be able to get your calls placed.

If you think you might need a phone soon, and you see one, use it! Public phones are not as prevalent as they are in the United States. The surest place to find them is in hotels, although this is not always the case in smaller hotels.

TELEPHONE CODES

International Direct Dialing 011
International Credit Card 01
Ireland 353
Northern Ireland 44
Dublin City 01

Calling Ireland

If you need to call Ireland or Northern Ireland prior to your trip, the country code for Northern Ireland is 44, and the country code for the Republic of Ireland is 353.

AT&T and MCI offer competitive direct dialing rates to and from the Emerald Isle. Check with them for their latest rates. They both routinely run special programs and rates.

Calling from Ireland

When calling home from the Republic of Ireland, dial *800-550-000* if you're using AT&T, or *800-551-001* if you are using MCI. If you are calling from Northern Ireland, dial *0500-890-011* if you're using AT&T, or *0800-890-222* if you're using MCI. You will be connected to an AT&T or MCI operator in the United States who will help you complete your calling card or collect call.

Another option that should be used only in an emergency, or if you wanted to enrich *Telephone Eireann,* is to use the international operator to place your calls. On my last trip, I priced a ten-minute call from Dublin to the United States using all three methods, and I think you'll find the differences surprising: **International Operator** *(111)*, $23.36 for the first five minutes, $3.90 each additional minute (total for 10 minutes: $42.86); **AT&T Credit Card** *(800-550-000)*, $4.29 for the first minute, $1.25 each additional minute (total for 10 minutes: $15.54); and **MCI Credit Card** *(800-551-001)*, $4.78 for the first minute, $1.25 each additional minute (total for 10 minutes: $16.03).

These rates were in effect at the time I called. They are surely different now, especially with the fierce competition between the long distance heavyweights. Be sure and check with the carriers to determine which is the best deal. About two-thirds of the rate for the first minute for both AT&T and MCI is an international surcharge that both are required to charge. When you call to ask for rates, one of the carriers quotes the entire amount, and the other leaves out the surcharge unless you ask them specifically, making it appear that their rates are significantly lower than their competitor's. Be sure and ask if there are any other charges or taxes.

Some hotels only allow you to place international calls through the operator (111) from their rooms. If that's the case in your hotel, you may want to use the pay phone in the lobby or on the street. While not as convenient, it's a lot more reasonable. Also, some hotels levy a surcharge for in-room international calls that can equal what the long distance carriers charge, effectively doubling the cost of your call. If this matters to you, check with the front desk before you make any calls from your room.

Calling within Ireland

Most of your calls within Ireland will be made from one of two types of public telephones: coin phones or phonecard phones.

Most **coin phones** are being updated and will accept only 20p and 50p coins – *Irish* in the Republic, and *British* in Northern Ireland! All calls are metered. A digital screen on the phone registers the amount of money you entered, and counts down to 0 as you talk. At 0, you receive three warning tones, and if you do not add additional coins within ten seconds, your call will be cut off. If you have credits remaining at the end of your call, you can push a button that allows you to make another call without adding additional coins. Unused, whole amounts will be returned to you.

Phonecard phones are becoming increasingly popular. Post Offices and some stores sell phonecards of varying denominations: £2, £3.50, £8, and £16. Like the coin phones, once the card is inserted, a digital readout on the phone displays remaining units. On local calls, one unit is roughly equal to three minutes; slightly less for long distance calls, depending on the distance involved.

Phonecards depict some typically Irish scene on the face of the card, with instructions for use on the back. I was anxious to see what scene of Ireland I would get the first time I purchased a phonecard. Imagine my surprise when Garth Brooks' smiling face greeted me from the front of my first phonecard!

Emergency Telephoning

In both the North and the Republic, remember **911 = 999**. If you have an emergency requiring police, an ambulance, or a fireman, dial 999.

USEFUL TELEPHONE NUMBERS

Emergency   999
Directory Assistance – National   1190
Directory Assistance – Great Britain   1197
Directory Assistance – International   114
Operator Assistance – National   10

Dublin Airport   (01) 844-4900
Shannon Airport   (061) 471-444
Aer Lingus   (01) 705-6705
Delta   (01) 844-4170

Irish Rail (passenger info)   (01) 836-6222
DART information   (01) 836-3333
Bus Eireann (Irish Bus)   (01) 836-1111
Dublin Bus   (01) 873-4222
Irish Ferries   (01) 661-0511

General Post Office   (01) 872-8888
Bord Failte (Tourist Board)   (01) 602-4000

TIME

Ireland is on Greenwich Mean Time, and for most of the year that means they are five hours ahead of New York and Montreal, and eight hours ahead of Los Angeles and Vancouver.

Ireland has Daylight Savings Time (called Summer Time), but it doesn't coincide exactly with the beginning and ending of Daylight Savings Time in North America. Summer Time begins one week earlier than Daylight Savings Time – the last Sunday of March. It reverts to Standard Time the last Sunday in October as it does here.

TROUBLE - AND HOW TO AVOID IT!

Crime is Ireland is far from non-existent, but it has tended to be of the non-violent type. Murders in Ireland send shock-waves through the country and they are always accompanied by front-page headlines and are the lead stories in newscasts. The **Gardi** (police) do not carry weapons, but are all "armed" with radios.

Dublin, like big cities all over the world, seems to be the most susceptible to crime. The majority of the crime there is petty theft and burglaries, although more violent crimes of rape and murder do occur. Throughout Dublin you'll see signs warning you of pick-pockets, who apparently work high-traffic areas like the DART stations, and Grafton and Henry Streets. Rental cars are also easy targets, especially if you leave purses, cameras, or other items of value in plain sight. Take the few extra seconds to put those things in your trunk.

The streets of downtown Dublin are pretty safe, but there are areas you will want to stay away from. The docks are notorious for crime, as are large areas of apartments – flats – to the west and northeast of the center of Dublin. If you stay in the areas outlined in this guide, you should have no problem. Notwithstanding the relatively low crime rate, don't be lulled into a false sense of security; there are malevolent people in every land who prey upon the innocent and unsuspecting. It would be a shame to spoil a delightful holiday by taking silly chances.

Of course, when traveling on your own you should take some precautions. Let someone back home know your tentative schedule and when you expect to be back, for example. Lone travelers tend to be more of a target than two or more people traveling together. Just be cautious, and use common sense.

Ireland has very aggressive laws when it comes to driving under the influence of alcohol.

If you do have trouble, remember that in Ireland **911 = 999**.

WEIGHTS & MEASURES

For the most part, Ireland uses the metric system. The main concern this has for you is that the petrol you purchase for your rental car will be measured in liters. If you're like me and have this fetish for knowing how many miles to the gallon your car is getting, there are 3.7854 liters in a gallon.

The few speed limits you will see in the country are posted in miles per hour, not kilometers per hour. Many of the road signs indicating distance to other towns have both miles and kilometers listed on them. If only one distance is given, well, there seems to be no standard for whether it is in miles or in kilometers. So ... assume miles, and if it's in kilometers, your trip will only take you about 5/8ths as long to get there!

8. SPORTS & RECREATION

There is a lot to do in Ireland, as a spectator and as a participant. For the purposes of this chapter, activities under sports involve professional athletes and your role as the spectator. Those activities under recreation involve your participation. That isn't to say that golf is not a sport; indeed it is.

PROFESSIONAL SPORTS

The Irish are sports fanatics. They love a good contest, and they are as avid as fans anywhere in the world. They are fiercely proud of their national teams, especially those that compete in international competition.

For example, when Ireland was competing in the World Cup in soccer, it was an all-consuming issue in the country.

Gaelic Football

Gaelic football is a rough and tumble (literally) game that is a cross between rugby and soccer. Having watched a few games, I'd say they reminded me of the Australian Football games I've seen on ESPN. Gaelic football aficionados claim the Aussies got it from the Irish; I suspect the Aussies have the reverse opinion. At any rate, each team consists of fifteen players who pass the ball to one another in an effort to move it down field and across an "end-zone." The ball is round and can be handed, passed, and kicked to move it. The sport is much faster than American or Canadian football.

Like hurling, Gaelic football is played in the spring and summer, with the All-Ireland finals held in Dublin in September. In recent years, the team from Kerry has been nearly unstoppable in Gaelic football.

Young Irish lads grow up dreaming of leading their county's team to the **All-Ireland title** (the equivalent of the Super Bowl), and becoming instant national heroes. Gaelic football was particularly good to one fellow named Jack Lynch. Lynch played for Cork (Gaelic football and hurling) and was the captain of teams that won six consecutive All-Ireland titles. His fans rewarded him by twice voting him Prime Minister!

Gaelic football can be watched throughout the season at **Croke Park** in Dublin (about fifteen to twenty minute's walk north of O'Connell Bridge), or you can catch a bus at O'Connell Bridge that will take you there. Games are played every other Sunday (the same stadium is used for Gaelic football and hurling). Tickets will cost £6 and £12.

For ticket information and schedules, contact the **Gaelic Athletic Association**, *Tel. (01) 836-3222.*

Horse Racing

Horse racing is followed as avidly as any other sport in the country. Results of races are broadcast hourly by many radio stations, and it is always part of the evening news sports section. At last count, races are held on two hundred and thirty-three days of the year, at twenty-seven different race tracks. (Remember – Ireland is about the size of Kentucky.)

Check the local newspapers or visit the local Bord Failte office for information on the location and times of the races closest to you. The **Jameson Irish Grand National** is run at **Punchestown Race Course** in County Kildare. Other popular race tracks are at Leopardstown (near Dublin), and in Galway, Fairyhouse in County Meath, Killarney, Tralee, and Listowel. Punchestown and Fairyhouse race tracks are the venue for the extremely popular steeplechase races.

Hurling

Hurling was a popular game in Ireland long before *Bill and Ted's Excellent Adventure* gave the term a different twist. Hurling is a high-speed game of ancient (probably Celtic) origin that is extremely popular with the Irish. Fifteen players per team use a short (approximately 3') stick – called a *caman* or *hurley* – that is curved on the end to bat, catch, and hurl a leather ball down-field and through their opponent's goal posts. It is incredibly fast-paced, and seems to combine elements of lacrosse, hockey, soccer, and rugby in its execution.

Along with Gaelic football, hurling is considered part of the "**National Games**," sponsored by the Irish Gaelic Athlete Association. Games are played throughout the summer, and the All-Ireland finals are held in Dublin in September. If you have the opportunity, stop and watch a game. I never could understand the scoring, but it was all very exciting.

Hurling can be watched throughout the season at **Croke Park** in Dublin (about fifteen to twenty minute's walk north of O'Connell Bridge), or you can catch a bus at O'Connell Bridge that will take you there. Games are played every other Sunday (the same stadium is used for Gaelic football and hurling). Tickets will cost £6 and £12.

For ticket information and schedules, contact the **Gaelic Athletic Association**, *Tel. (01) 836-3222.*

Rugby

Rugby is also a wildly exciting game in Ireland, and its followers are as avid here as they are anyplace else. If you've never seen rugby, it's sort of a non-stop football game where husky men try and ram an over-inflated football through the defense of their opponent. One interesting aspect of rugby in Ireland is that their international team consists of players from both the Republic and Northern Ireland – the only team sport on the Emerald Isle that ignores political differences and has one Irish team made up of players from both countries. Rugby is played at **Lansdowne Stadium** in Ballsbridge, right next to the DART station.

For ticket information and schedules, contact the **Gaelic Athletic Association**, *Tel. (01) 836-3222.*

Soccer

Ireland is considered a European nation, and as such, they play soccer. (I think this must be required to become a member of the European Economic Community!) But the Irish are not as obsessed as the rest of Europe with soccer – they save their obsession for Gaelic football and hurling.

Soccer is played primarily in and around Dublin (attesting to centuries of strong English presence there) and Belfast. Having said that, let Ireland's team compete in the World Cup, and soccer is followed avidly on the radio and television (yawn). Unlike Gaelic football and hurling, soccer has gone the way of many pro sports in America. Players play for whichever team pays the most, and many Irish players play on teams other than Ireland's team. In recent years, the English soccer team in Manchester has had significant Irish representation, and accordingly has a significant Irish following.

When Ireland's international soccer team plays in Dublin, they play at **Lansdowne Stadium** in Ballsbridge, right next to the DART station. Semi-professional soccer teams play at **Dalymount Park** in Phibsborough in north Dublin, at the corner of Phibsborough Road and Dalymount/ North Circular Roads. It's about two and a half miles northwest of the O'Connell Street Bridge.

RECREATION

The number one outdoor activity among visitors to Ireland is hill-walking, followed by golf and angling (fishing). But there are many other things to do as well - cycling, horseback riding and believe it or not, scuba diving.

While the Irish are great spectators, they are nowhere near as obsessed with fitness as Americans. In all my trips to Ireland I have seen two joggers – and they were probably both Americans. The one healthy activity that is regularly practiced is walking. But there is a difference. It's not like the power-walking you see in America, but rather strolls along country lanes, or young mothers pushing their babies in prams.

Angling

Ireland has a lot to offer in the way of fishing. Salmon, sea trout, brown trout, pike, and a variety of other fish are plentiful in Ireland's lakes and streams, not to mention those available off the coast.

You are required to have a license and the laws are a little confusing; you usually need at least one license or permit, and sometimes you need a license, a permit, and a "day ticket." It's best to ask at the local fishing shop for instructions. They'll be more than happy to help you out. A state license costs from £3 to £25, depending on how long you want it for, and whether it is for one particular angling district or multiple districts. The only fish requiring a state license are salmon and sea trout (you don't need a state license for brown trout). The other permits are available on an annual, weekly, or daily basis, and are relatively inexpensive.

The Irish angling industry uses two terms you may not be familiar with. They are **game fishing** and **coarse fishing**. Game angling refers to the pursuit of trout, salmon, and pike. Coarse angling refers to fishing for perch, tench, rudd, bream, etc. You need a state license for game fishing, but not for coarse fishing.

Don't worry about finding a good spot to fish. The proprietors of an angling shop in Dublin – **Patrick Cleere and Son** on Anglesea Street – told me that most Irish fishermen will be happy to take a fellow fishing "for the company."

In addition to getting a license, another good place to learn about the local hotspots is in the local angling shop. They are all over the country, especially in towns near lakes and streams.

Here are a few you can pop into:

- **Patrick Cleere and Son**, *Anglesea Street, Dublin, Tel. (01) 677-7406*
- **O'Neill's Fishing Tackle**, *6 Plunkett Street, Killarney, County Kerry, Tel. (064) 31970*
- **Jim Robinson's Angling Center**, *43 Lower Gerald Griffin Street, Limerick, County Clare, Tel. (061) 414900*
- **Nestor Brothers Sports Store**, *28 O'Connell Street Limerick, County Clare, Tel. (061) 414096*
- **Dermot Killeen**, *Main Street, Shannonbridge, County Offally, Tel. (0905) 74112*

• **Erne Marine**, *Bellanaleck, Enniskillen, County Fermanagh, Tel. (01365) 387077*
• **Lakeland Marina**, *Muckross, Kesh, County Fermanagh, Tel. (01365) 323481*

Here are good spots to try for the following fish:
• **Salmon** – River Shannon (Co. Limerick and Clare), River Clare (Co. Galway), River Fergus (Co. Clare), River Feale (Co. Kerry), River Moy (Co. Mayo), Mulcair River (Co. Limerick), River Maigue (Co. Limerick), and the Brosna River (Co. Offaly). Loughs Conn (Co. Mayo), Eske (Co. Donegal), Corrib (Co. Galway), Leane (Co. Kerry), and Melvin (Co. Leitrim). There are two primary seasons for salmon: from March to May and the end of May through September.
• **Sea trout** – River Feale (Co. Limerick), River Bandon (Co. Cork), Lough Eske (Co. Donegal), River Slaney (Co. Wexford), and Lough Glencar (Co. Leitrim and Sligo).
• **Brown trout** – the Shannon (Co. Galway), Blackwater (Munster), Clare (Co. Galway), Barrow (Co. Carlow/Kilkenny), Fergus (Co. Clare), Nore (Co. Laois), Laune (Co. Kerry) rivers and the following loughs: Derg (Co. Clare), Conn (Co. Mayo), Inchiquin (Co. Clare), Melvin (Co. Leitrim), Mask (Co. Mayo), and Leane (Co. Kerry).
• **Pike** – Lough Derg (Co. Clare), and the lakes of the River Fergus (Co. Clare).

Bird Watching

Ireland is noted for many fine locations for bird watching. Whether it's off **Bull Island** north of Dublin, or the **Skelligs**, or many of the loughs (lakes) in Northern Ireland, you'll have a great selection of sites to visit and birds to see.

In the southeast, the best place for bird-watching is off the coast at the village of **Kilmore Quay**. Just offshore are the **Saltee Islands**, and they have the distinction of being the largest bird sanctuary in Ireland. Ornithologists claim there are over three million birds representing forty-seven species located on and around the Saltee Islands. The most predominant birds are cormorants, guillemots, kittiwakes, petrels, puffins, and sea gulls. Boats in the harbor will take you out to the islands for a closer look.

Off the southwestern coast of Ireland lies little **Clear Island**, where another colony of birds has taken up residence. Though the numbers aren't quite as extensive as at the Saltee Islands, there are plenty to see. In addition to the species that can be spied at the Saltees, add the much rarer black-bowed albatross. As with the Saltees, boats can be hired in **Baltimore** (County Cork) to take you out for a closer look.

Further up the west coast of Ireland you come to the Skelligs, a small cluster of islands off the **Iveragh Peninsula**. In addition to the fine ruins of an ancient monastic site on the largest of the islands, there are two islands that have significant colonies of sea-birds. **Little Skellig** serves as the breeding ground for more than 20,000 pairs of gannets, and **Puffin Island** hosts thousands of petrel, shearwaters, and puffins. Boats can be hired in Waterville to take you out to the Skelligs.

On to **Northern Ireland** for your bird-watching pleasure. Ireland is the first stop for many autumn-migrating birds, and Northern Ireland is their first chance to rest their weary wings after many miles. Northern Ireland is one of the few places left where ornithologists can see species such as chough and corncrake.

At the northwest point of Northern Ireland is **Lough Foyle**, a large lake that draws a great number of species to its mud-flats and saltwater marshes. Species that can be seen here include curlew, bar-tailed godwits, Greenland white-fronted geese, and whooper swans. In addition, there are large numbers of buzzards, gyrfalcon, finches, kestrel, larks, merlins, peregrine falcons, petrel, and sparrowhawks.

Lough Neagh is the largest freshwater lake in the British Isles. It is a wonderful place to see many different species of birds, including golden-eye, crested grebe, pochard, scaup, whooper and Bewick's swans.

In County Down, Belfast, Carlingford, and Strangford Loughs are havens for a number species of birds, including dark- and pale-bellied brant geese, cormorants, curlews, dunlin, gadwall, godwits, golden plover, greenshank, knot, lapwings, oystercatchers, red-breasted mergansers, redshank, sandwich terns, shelduck, and whooper swans.

Cycling

Cycling in Ireland is probably the all-around best way to see Ireland (if the roads just weren't so darned narrow!). As with walking, you have several options. First, you can rent the bike at a bicycle shop, and roll out of there, and you're on your way. Or, you can engage a company that provides excursions for bikers. You'll see these companies all over Ireland. For a reasonable fee, they'll rent you a bicycle and helmet, shuttle your personal belongings to the location where you'll be spending the night, and they'll even pack lunch for you if you wish. They also provide maps and details about the routes you'll be taking.

These companies usually provide package deals that include meals, bike rental, maps, itinerary, luggage transport, roadside maintenance, and accommodations (usually at B&Bs) for a set price. The prices vary according to your requirements, but figure on paying around £300 for a week and £575 for two weeks. When you figure what a week's bicycle rental (about £30) and one week's B&B accommodations (about £140) would run you, that's not really too bad a deal. Most of the companies listed here will also arrange to pick you up at the airport and return you there at the end of your journey as part of the package.

CYCLING TOUR OPERATORS	
Celtic Cycling Ltd.	*Tel. (0503) 75282*
Cycle Ireland	*Tel. (064) 32536*
Irish Cycle Hire	*Tel. (041) 41067*
Irish Cycling Safaris	*Tel. (01) 260-0749*
Shannon Cycle Center	*Tel. (061) 361280*

Golf

It's hard to get an accurate count of how many golf courses there are in Ireland. Sources that should be "in the know" vary in their information; I've seen numbers quoted from two hundred to over three hundred. As a golfer, I prefer to think of the number as over three hundred. That means there is one golf course about every one hundred square miles in Ireland, so theoretically, you should never have to travel more than ten miles to find a golf course.

As you might suspect, the golf courses in Ireland are verdant, lush, and about everything you've ever dreamed of for a game of golf. Some courses have fairways that have cliff hazards along the edge of the fairway – don't slice, or you'll watch your golf ball sail over the edge to the ocean two hundred feet below (great distance, but...). Others have the pins set on the far side of tall drumlins (mounds) that have a stick at the top to tell you where to hit your nine iron.

Green fees vary, of course, but you can expect to pay between £15 and £30 for 18 holes. Green fees are slightly more on the weekends. Most courses have clubs available for rent (the term in Ireland is "club hire"), as well as golf carts and caddies, but you should ask to be sure when you make your tee-time.

Many of Ireland's golf courses are actually part of a golf club. But unlike America, these courses welcome players who do not belong to their club. The only restriction is that weekends are generally reserved for club members (as are some other days at some courses).

While it's not practical to list all three hundred golf courses in Ireland, here's a sampling of some of the better courses, with a bit of information about each. Green fees are given in weekday/weekend format.

Courses in The Republic of Ireland

Adare Manor Golf Club, *Adare, Co. Limerick, Tel. (061) 396566*, £30 (resident)/£35 (nonresident). Visitors welcome weekdays. Par 72, 7,138 yards.

Ballybunion, *Ballybunion, Co. Kerry, Tel. (068) 27146*, £25/£35. Visitors welcome weekdays. Par 72, 6,216 yards.

Connemara Golf Club, *Clifden, Co. Galway, Tel. (095) 23502*, £18/£18. Visitors welcome every day except Sunday. Par 72, 7,174 yards.

County Tipperary Golf Club, *Dundrum, Co. Tipperary, Tel. (062) 71116*, £15/£20. Visitors welcome any time. Par 72.

Deer Park Golf Course, *Howth, Co. Dublin, Tel. (01) 832-2624*, £11/£12. Visitors welcome any time. Par 72.

Donegal Golf Club, *Murvagh, Co. Donegal, Tel. (073) 34054*, £15/£18. Visitors welcome any time. Par 73, 7,153 yards.

Dooks Golf Club, *Glenbeigh, Co. Kerry, Tel. (066) 68205*, £15/£16. Visitors welcome on weekdays. Par 70, 6,010 yards.

Dromoland Castle, *Newmarket-on-Fergus, Co. Clare, Tel. (061) 368144*, £20/£25. Visitors welcome weekdays. Par 71.

Portmarnock, *Portmarnock, Co. Dublin, Tel. (01) 846-2968*, £40/£50. Visitors welcome Monday, Tuesday, and Friday. Par 72, 7,051 yards.

Royal Dublin Golf Club, *Bull Island, Co. Dublin, Tel. (01) 833-6346*, £35/£45 Visitors welcome Monday and Tuesday, Thursday and Friday. Par 73, 6,763 yards.

Shannon Golf Club, *Shannon, Co. Clare, Tel. (061) 471849*, £20/£25. Visitors welcome anytime. Par 73.

Courses in Northern Ireland

Ballycastle Golf Club, *Ballycastle, Co. Antrim, Tel. (012657) 62536*, UK£13/UK£18. Visitors welcome any time. Par 68, 5,692 yards.

Malone Golf Club, *Dumnurry, Belfast, Co. Antrim, Tel. (01232) 612758*, UK£25/UK£30. Visitors welcome Monday, Thursday, and Friday. Par 71, 6,642 yards.

Portstewart Golf Club, *Portstewart, Co. Derry, Tel. (01265) 832015*, UK£22/UK£27. Visitors welcome Monday, Tuesday, and Friday. Par 72, 6,784 yards.

Royal Portrush Golf Course, *Portrush, Co. Derry, Tel. (01265) 822311*, Dunluce course: UK£37.50/UK£45, Valley Course: UK£15/UK£20. Visitors welcome weekdays except Wednesday and Friday afternoons. Dunluce course: Par 72, 6,772 yards; Valley course: Par 72, 6,273 yards.

Horseback Riding

You knew horseback riding would be available in Ireland, didn't you? There are a number of equestrian centers in Ireland, centered primarily in Leinster, which is the heart of Ireland's horse country. There are other places outside of Leinster that offer horseback riding too, but the majority of the places are here. Whether you are interested in riding trails, jumping, or even hunting, you can find it in Leinster. Contact the Tourist

Office in the area where you are going to be to get more information on riding.

Cashel House Hotel on Cashel Bay and **Hotel Castle Dunloe** in Killarney have riding stables for their guests and the hotels are reviewed in the *Where to Stay* sections of the Connacht and Munster chapters, respectively.

Scuba Diving

It might surprise you to learn that scuba diving is available in Ireland. It's not widespread, but it is gaining in popularity. Some of the towns where scuba diving is offered are Bantry, Dalkey, Donegal, Kilkee, Killybeg, Kinsale, Tralee, Waterford, and Westport. Check with the local angling shop or Tourist Office in the city you're going to be in for more information.

Surfing

There are a several beaches along the west coast of Ireland that are gaining reputations as decent surfing beaches. In fact, just outside **Waterville** (near Rossnowlagh) in County Donegal, the **Irish Surfing National Championships** are held every year.

Walking

Ireland has become a haven for walkers and hikers the world over; in fact, according to statistics kept by Bord Failte (Irish Tourist Board), hill-walking is the number one activity tourists participate in when they come to Ireland. The terrain and climate lend themselves to walking. The terrain is seldom arduous, and more often than not your walking will consist of treks up pleasant rolling hills or across flat plains. For those of a more adventurous nature, there are also a number of strenuous walking trails that conquer the peaks of numerous Irish mountain ranges. The weather is almost always pleasant, and seldom too cold. With summer hiking temperatures rarely above the low- to mid-60s, it's ideal weather for walking. Rain, of course, is a threat at any time, but is seldom of the heavy down-pour variety.

Trails criss-cross the country. Some are very popular and well marked; others are more obscure, and not sign-posted well, if at all. Some of the more popular walking trails are the **Wicklow Way**, the **Ulster Way**, and the **Dingle Way**. The Wicklow Way was the very first sign-posted walking trail in Ireland, and it was established in 1982. Since that time, nineteen additional trails have been established and sign-posted. These twenty paths are called **Waymarked Ways**, and have been developed and are maintained under the auspices of Bord Failte and the Irish Forestry Board.

These Waymarked Ways have been developed to provide walkers with a good day's walk, not a marathon. In general, the longest leg of a walk is fourteen to eighteen miles, although some of the very rural walks are a little further. Generally speaking, B&Bs, hotels, and youth hostels are conveniently located along the Waymarked Ways, and cater to walkers. Many of them provide drying facilities (for your damp clothes), pack storage, and even sack lunch preparation if you wish.

There is no charge for walking these paths, of course, unless you employ a guide to take you to show the way, comment on the topography, flora, and fauna, etc. But these trails were generally designed for freelance walkers.

If you think this sounds like an ideal activity, there are several books that will be helpful to you. The first is published by Bord Failte, and is called *Walking Ireland – The Waymarked Ways*. It gives you an overview of each walking way and is available at most Tourist Offices. Another book that is available in bookstores in Ireland is called *Irish Long Distance Walks – A Guide to the Waymarked Trails* by Michael Fewer. It covers ten of the trails in detail. One other book by Paddy Dillon is *The Trail Walker Guide*, and it covers six of the trails. Between the two books, twelve of the twenty trails are covered (four of Paddy Dillon's trails are also covered in Michael Fewer's book).

Maps of the Waymarked Ways can be obtained in most bookstores in Ireland, as well as from **An Oige**, the Youth Hostel organization in Ireland, and may be obtained by writing or calling them. Contact An Oige at: *61 Mountjoy Street, Dublin 7, Tel. (01) 830-4555.*

Remember, the Waymarked Ways are walking trails. You are requested not to ride mountain bikes or horses on the trails. Also, since many of the trails traverse pastures where sheep and cattle graze, dogs are not welcome on the trails.

If you want to be a little more adventurous, or if you would feel more comfortable having a guide along to show you the way and teach you a little of the history of the area, there is an entire industry that has grown up around this activity. Most of these organizations offer a wide variety of tours, beginning with city tours for as little as £4 up to and including two-week excursions that include room and board along the way for £200 or more per person. Virtually all these groups have set excursions, but are quite willing and adept at tailoring a program to fit your interest and pocket-book.

WALKING TOUR OPERATORS

Ballyhoura Country Holidays	*Tel. (063) 91300*
Ballyknocken House	*Tel. (0404) 44614*
Burren Walking Holidays	*Tel. (065) 74411*
Connemara Walking Center	*Tel. (095) 21379*
Croagh Patrick Walking Holidays	*Tel. (095) 26090*
Crutchs Hillville House Hotel	*Tel. (066) 38118*
Hidden Ireland Tours	*Tel. (066) 51868*
Irish Walking Way Holidays	*Tel. (055) 27479*
Mourne Country (N.I.)	*Tel. (013967) 24059*
Nature Reserves of Fermanagh	*Tel. (01356) 21588*
Southwest Walks Ireland	*Tel. (061) 419477*
Western Trekking	*Tel. (091) 25806*

9. SHOPPING

Ireland is a wonderful place to purchase all those things that remind you of Ireland: sweaters, Irish linen, Irish whiskey, wools and tweeds, and crystal, to name a few. There are a number of traditional "shopping towns" in Ireland, including Clifden, Donegal, Galway, Killarney, and Westport. However, I was pleasantly surprised to find that merchandise prices varied little across the width and breadth of the country. The cost of items seemed driven more by the variations in their design than by the area of the country where they were purchased. Remember, it is a small country, smaller than the majority of the states in the United States.

The following table will give you an idea of what you can expect to pay for a variety of items:
- Sweaters   £25 – £100
- Tweed jackets   £80 – £150
- Tweed skirts   £40 – £60
- Irish linen tablecloths
        54" X 90"   £ 55
        72"X108"   £100
- Irish lace handkerchief £55
- Crystal wine goblet   £17 – £35
- Claddagh Ring (gold)   £39 and up
- Claddagh Ring (silver) £7 and up

Both the Dublin and Shannon airports have large "Duty-Free" shops. Not only are they duty-free, but they are also free of the dreaded VAT. And their prices are actually pretty good. I recently saw a television special that compared Duty-Free shops in airports all over the world. While some of them are horrendous rip-offs, the Dublin and Shannon shops were named as two of the best. The only problem I have with these shops is that the selection may not be as broad as you would like it to be. This seems to be especially true when it comes to sweaters, linen, and tweeds. They do a pretty good job of stocking a good selection of other items, such as Waterford and Tipperary Crystal.

Shopping hours in Dublin are slowly beginning to expand, but the rest of the country still doggedly clings to the hours they have had for at least a generation. Typically, stores are open from 9:00 am to 5:30 pm Monday through Saturday, and closed on Sunday. Some Dublin stores (primarily on Grafton Street and several new downtown malls) are open late on Thursday evenings (6:30 pm or 7:00 pm), and some are even beginning to stay open on Sunday. But this latest venture is the exception rather than the rule. When you're in the rural parts of Ireland, expect Sunday to be a pretty slow day for shopping.

Newsagents in the towns tend to open a little earlier than most stores – around 7:00 am, as do bakeries. Newsagents have sort of a country store

CLOTHING SIZES IN IRELAND

Clothing sizes in Ireland do not strictly follow the American, Canadian, or European sizing formats. Below is a chart comparing Irish sizes to sizes in the United States, Canada, and Europe. Your best bet, however, is to try on any article before buying it.

Men's suits

Irish/US/Can. 36	38	40	42	44	46
European 46	48	50	52	54	56

Shirts

Irish/US/Can. 14	15	16	17	18
European 36	38	41	43	46

Women's dresses

Irish	32	34	36	38	40	42	44
US	8	10	12	14	16	18	20
Canadian	10	12	14	16	18	20	22
European	38	40	42	44	46	48	50

Men's shoes

Irish	6	7	8	9	10	11
US/Can.	$6 \frac{1}{2}$	$7 \frac{1}{2}$	$8 \frac{1}{2}$	$9 \frac{1}{2}$	$10 \frac{1}{2}$	$11 \frac{1}{2}$
European	40	41	42	43	44	45

Women's shoes

Irish	2	3	4	5	6	7
US	$3 \frac{1}{2}$	$4 \frac{1}{2}$	$5 \frac{1}{2}$	$6 \frac{1}{2}$	$7 \frac{1}{2}$	$8 \frac{1}{2}$
Canadian	4	5	6	7	8	9
European	$34 \frac{1}{2}$	$35 \frac{1}{2}$	$36 \frac{1}{2}$	$37 \frac{1}{2}$	$38 \frac{1}{2}$	$39 \frac{1}{2}$

feel, even in the city. They are typically small, with cribs full of fresh produce, and a little bit of everything.

CRYSTAL

The name Waterford is synonymous with lead crystal in Ireland, although there are several other glass manufacturers that make lead crystal on the Emerald Isle. Waterford Crystal products have become world-renowned, and with good reason. These hand-crafted items, from Superbowl trophies to chandeliers, from goblets to vases, are exquisite in every detail. (A tour of their factory gives you an idea how incredible the human effort is.)

Waterford and Tipperary (a nearby competitor) crystal both consist of 33% lead oxide. The resulting works of art are heavy, to say the least. The products from other competitors around the country generally only have 22% lead content. Both Waterford and Tipperary crystal are blown and hand-etched. The results are exquisite. Waterford Crystal is proudly sold throughout the country.

The prices vary little from store to store, and buying in the town of Waterford is no guarantee of lower price. The lowest prices I have found are in the Duty-Free shops in the Dublin and Shannon Airports, and these prices don't include the dreaded VAT. They carry a pretty good selection of goblets, wine and water glasses, vases, and the like.

If you buy lead crystal because of the prestige of the name, Waterford Crystal is for you. But it you buy because of the sheer beauty and craftsmanship, Tipperary Crystal might be your choice. In recent years, many have recognized the quality craftsmanship of Tipperary, as well as the price tag that is substantially lower than for Waterford. I recently purchased eight Tipperary Crystal water glasses for about two-thirds the cost of similar glasses from Waterford.

ARAN SWEATERS

Aran sweaters have become extremely popular with tourists the last several years. As a consequence, the prices for these woolen works of art have risen significantly.

These heavy sweaters were originally knitted for the men and boys who earned their way in life by fishing in the inhospitable Atlantic waters off the west coast of Ireland. The sweaters served a dual purpose: they were heavy and dense and so afforded maximum protection from the omnipresent wind and rain. A slightly grimmer and equally practical purpose was to identify the bodies of drowned fishermen. These original sweaters featured a combination of stitches unique to each fishing village; drowned sailors could then be returned to their village of origin by those who found them.

Many Aran sweaters today are machine-made of lighter wools than that used for hand-made sweaters. The hand-made sweaters are heavier and a little more expensive than those made by knitting machines. If you want a hand-knit masterpiece, check the tag, ask the store owner, or simply feel the difference in weight. If it's the pattern, stitch, and functionality you seek, the machine-made sweaters will be a little less expensive. **Hehirs Woolens** *(Clifden, Tel. 095 21282, Market Street)*, **Padraic O'Maille's** *(Galway, Tel. 091 562696, 35 Eyre Square)*, and **Standun's Irish Heritage Store** *(Spiddal, Tel. 091 553108)* have good selections of Aran sweaters.

IRISH LACE

Hand-made Irish lace is a great gift and an elegant adornment to any table. The art of tatting lace is liable to be a lost one in the coming generations: fewer and fewer women have the patience or time to continue the time-intensive practice of tatting Irish lace. Today, the majority of Irish lace comes from convents, where the art is kept alive through the fingers of these religious tatters. Occasionally, the Duty-Free shops in the Dublin and Shannon airports have some Irish lace, but when they do, their selection is limited.

One place with a good selection is the **Good Shepherd Convent**, *Clare Street in Limerick*. The cost of an Irish lace handkerchief will run about £55.

CLADDAGH RINGS

Claddagh rings are incredibly popular with the Irish as well as tourists. In fact, as I boarded the plane to return home on my last trip, I noticed that about half of the women were wearing either a Claddagh ring or a Claddagh necklace. These symbolic rings that are oh-so-Irish feature a heart with a crown on it. On either side of the heart are hands holding onto the heart. The heart represents love, the crown represents loyalty, and the hands represent friendship. With its symbolism, you can appreciate how popular the ring is as an engagement or wedding ring.

But beware –there is a right and a wrong way to wear a Claddagh ring! If your heart is taken (by a sweetheart, fiancee, or spouse), then the bottom of the heart should be worn facing toward your wrist. If, however, your heart is available, you wear the ring with the bottom of the heart facing out – toward the end of your finger. That lets prospective suitors know your availability, or lack thereof!

Claddagh rings are available in every jewelry store in Ireland, as well as in most souvenir and craft shops. They are available in gold as well as silver. One of the most extensive selections in the country is at **Faller's Jewelers** *(Galway, Tel. 091 561226, Williamsgate Street)*, but you'll have no trouble finding them anywhere in the country.

TWEEDS

Ireland's northwest coast is known for its Irish tweeds, in particular Donegal tweeds from the county of the same name. These woven woolens are made into coats, capes, scarves, and skirts. If you're in Donegal, most clothing shops will carry Donegal tweeds, including **Magee's** *(Donegal Town, Tel. 073 22660, The Diamond)*.

You can also pick up some fine tweeds from the **Avoca Handweavers** *(Avoca, Tel. 0402 35105)* south of Dublin in County Wicklow.

10. TAKING THE KIDS

If you are thinking about sharing your vacation with your children, Ireland is definitely the place to do it. Ireland is a young country; over 45% of the country is under age 25 and large families are typical.

Most tourist attractions have discounted fares for children, as do most Bed and Breakfasts and many of the hotels in the country. The discount for attractions and activities is generally about 50% off the adult fare, and many attractions offer family fares, typically discounted rates covering the admission charge for two adults and four children.

There are a number of activities around the country targeted specifically for families with children. As the father of six children, I know well how quickly children tire of a steady diet of museums, cathedrals, and art galleries. If you can find diversions to break up the day for your children, you (and your children) will have a pleasant visit to Ireland.

Don't forget to bring books, crossword puzzles, magnetic games like chess, checkers or backgammon, or a Gameboy (or whatever they like), to keep them entertained as you drive from town to town and in the evenings. Also, depending on their age, you should consider purchasing them their own throw-away cameras so they can take pictures (it's their vacation too, after all), and they won't bug you to use your camera.

SUGGESTED KID'S ITINERARY FOR DUBLIN

To have a successful family vacation in Ireland, you should intersperse "kid-activities" between those things you want to see. For example, here's a sample itinerary for a day in Dublin with children:

I recommend spending the morning at the **National Museum of Ireland** while the kids are still fresh.

When you leave the museum, let the kids lead you through **Grafton Street**. Let *them* decide how long to look at which buskers (street entertainers), which stores to stop at, which side lanes to explore, etc. They'll get a kick out of it and feel that the vacation is theirs as well. Give them a time limit, perhaps an hour, or you may end up there all day!

From Grafton Street, head to **Trinity College** for a look at **the Book of Kells,** and maybe even watch the audiovisual presentation called **The Dublin Experience** if they're not too fidgety. That might be pushing it, but it will give everyone a chance to sit down and rest and hopefully learn something.

From Trinity College, head back up Grafton Street, stop along the way (at **Bewley's,** maybe?) and pick up a little something to eat. Get it "take away", and head for **St. Stephen's Green** at the top of Grafton Street for a picnic. Be sure and buy some rolls or bread because there will be plenty of ducks to feed when you get there.

After lunch, while you're still in St. Stephen's Green, have your kids close their eyes (unless you carry a blindfold with you), and take them on a tour of the Braille gardens. These gardens have signs written in Braille for the blind, and the flora in the garden is resilient enough to be handled by those who "see" with their hands. It is a fun and educational activity for your children (you, too!).

If you are fortunate, there will be an afternoon concert serenading you from the Victorian bandstand in St. Stephen's Green. You can just listen as you go about your planned activities, or if your kids like music you can sit and listen for awhile.

After lunch, with rested children, head for **Kilmainham Gaol** (Jail). This is a tough call, not all kids will be interested in Kilmainham Gaol, it really depends on the age of your children.

Following your journey into Kilmainham, head over to **Phoenix Park.** There's a host of activities here, and what you should do again depends on the ages and interests of your children. There's a zoo (the number one tourist attraction in Ireland every year), polo fields (they may really enjoy watching the horses), cricket fields, rose gardens, and of course, the obligatory ducks to feed.

Ride the **DART** out to **Howth** and **Abbey Tavern** for an evening of Irish entertainment. Unless your children are very, very young, they'll enjoy the action and merriment. If you arrive early for dinner and the show, walk along the quay, or over to see the fishing boats up close.

OTHER FUN ACTIVITIES

There are a number of other things to do in addition to those mentioned in the suggested itinerary. Ireland is made for outdoor activities, and since the weather rarely runs to extremes, outdoor activities are especially enjoyable in Ireland.

Take a ride in a jaunting car around the grounds of Muckross House, or ride a steam train through the countryside in Tralee. Delve into one of Ireland's numerous caves and see stalagmites and stalactites, have a fisherman row you out into Dingle Harbor in search for Fungi, the Dingle Dolphin, or take a ferry out to Aran Islands or the Skelligs.

These are just a few of the many activities that await you and your children. Put yourself in their shoes and look for activities that will enrich as well as entertain your children. But above all, have a good time with them in Ireland.

Farms & Zoos

There are perhaps forty or fifty farms throughout Ireland that allow children to handle, pet, and hold farm animals. **Newbridge House** north of Dublin is an example of one of those farms. Most children love animals, and enjoy seeing them up close and personal. Some farmers will let the kids bottle-feed a baby lamb or milk a cow.

There are a number of good zoos around Ireland, including **Phoenix Park** and the zoo at **Westport House**, as well as the fascinating **Fota Wildlife Park** in Cork.

Folk Villages

Dotting the Irish countryside are Irish Folk Villages that recreate the past for you and your children. Watch your daughter's eyes as she learns the art of candle-making, pottering, or weaving; see how your son responds to the arduous work of a blacksmith (or vice-versa). Help them learn perspective as they realize families of eight or ten people shared entire houses no larger than the room they complain about having to share with their little brother or sister.

Some of the better examples of these folk villages include the one at the **Ulster Folk and Transport Museum** in Bangor (near Belfast), the **Bunratty Castle and Folk Park** in County Limerick, the **Kerry Country Life Experience** in Killarney, County Kerry (next to Muckross House), and the **Folk Village** at Glencolmkille in County Donegal.

Ruins that offer an opportunity for young imaginations to run wild include **Dunbrodey Abbey** (County Wexford), **Bonamargy Friary** (County Antrim), **Mellifont Abbey** (County Meath), and about 10,000 unnamed ruins across the countryside.

Hiking

Hiking is one of the most popular tourist activities in Ireland. And kids love to hike (run, skip, jump). Whether you are a family that's into serious hiking and want to hike fifteen miles a day, or whether you just need a mile or two of trail to work off some energy, Ireland has it all. There are thousands of miles of walking trails throughout Ireland and you'll easily find the trail to suit your family.

Lakes & Rivers

Ireland is blessed with a considerable number of lakes and rivers. There are nearly 9,000 miles worth of rivers, and over 4,000 loughs (lakes) in this small country. The lakes are all beautiful, and perfect places for shoreline picnics, inexpensive boat rides out to islands lush with greenery and guarded by ancient ruins, and fishing (angling equipment can be rented).

As you can imagine, there is a great selection of lakes and rivers to choose from for your children to explore. Start with the **Grand Canal** that runs along the south side of Dublin near the Ballsbridge area. Nice walking paths are available for enjoying the canal. The **Shannon River** is a pretty river that wends its way through a large portion of the country, and offers lots of opportunities for exploration. You might also try the **River Suir** at Carrick on Suir – it's very picturesque.

When it comes to lakes, one of my favorite is island-studded **Lough Corrib** in County Galway. **Lough Derg** also has some islands to explore, including some impressive ruins. **Lough Dan** and **Lough Tay** in the Wicklow Mountains are pretty. **Glencar Lough** in County Leitrim is pretty and features a few a waterfalls to explore at the north end of the lake. And, of course, any of the lakes around Killarney are beautiful and worth taking the time to explore.

Ocean & Sea

There is no place in Ireland that is more than seventy miles from the ocean, and there are many shores that children in particular would enjoy. Whether they want to swim, skip along the shore, build sand castles, or just throw rocks in the water, the ocean is always near-by. But the Irish do swim in the Atlantic and Irish Seas. Their swimming season usually doesn't begin until around mid- to late-June, and extends into September. The water never gets really warm, but (apparently) warm enough for hardy swimmers.

The beaches to watch for are those that have been designated as **Blue Flag** beaches. These beaches have been judged safe for swimming, and they will have a tall flag pole with a blue flag flying. Many of them also have lifeguards on duty throughout the day. Some popular blue flag beaches around the country are in **Rosslare** (County Wexford), **Brittas Bay** and **Jack's Hole** (County Wicklow), **Waterville** (County Kerry), **Rossknowlagh** and **Downings** (County Donegal).

If you are in Ireland when the water is too cold to swim, don't automatically discount the beaches. If your kids are like mine, they will still enjoy the sand between their toes, the jetsam and flotsam that washes up on the shores, and the thrill of being at the ocean.

Ruins

There are ruins all over Ireland, castles, abbeys, friarys, houses, stables, and burial grounds. If your kids need to burn off some energy, look for a deserted ruin, (you'll only have to look a short time), and let the kids explore them and give flight to their fantasies. Let them pretend they are defending or attacking a castle, or let them imagine what it would have been like to be a monk looking desperately for a place to hide the literary treasures of your monastery from an approaching army.

11. FOOD & DRINK

FOOD

In recent years, prepared food in Ireland has undergone somewhat of a renaissance. In the past, food critics the world over described the food in Irish restaurants as unimaginative, bland, and relatively unexciting. (Supporters of Irish food call it "simple.") The Irish food industry took the criticism to heart. Chefs trained in Europe were brought in, and the food took on a decidedly European flavor. In Dublin, "French-Irish" or "Irish with Continental influences" are rapidly becoming popular specialties, and there is now a wide selection of ethnic restaurants. If you are a gourmand, on the other hand, Ireland's highest rated restaurant, and there's only one, is a two-star restaurant (by Michelin).

Throughout the rest of Ireland, the food can still be described as unimaginative (simple), since the culinary changes sweeping Dublin have not spread to the rest of the country. There are exceptions, of course, as marvelous chefs have been hired to whip up delicacies that rival meals any of the Dublin restaurants produce. The province of Munster, for example, has a number of top-flight restaurants.

As an island nation, Ireland is particularly proud of their seafood. Salmon, scallops, prawns, lobster, sea trout, mussels, and oysters are generally plentiful especially in Ireland's seaport towns such as Galway, Kinsale, Westport, Dublin, Wexford, and Waterford.

What can you expect from a traditional Irish meal? Well, potatoes are a good start. Potatoes have been a mainstay in the Irish diet for many years. Potato scones are a specialty in the northern part of the island.

SOME IRISH DINING PHRASES

creamed potatoes	mashed potatoes
gammon	thickly cut grilled ham
jacket potatoes	baked potatoes
take away	take-out (as in: take-out food)

Spread with butter or honey, these are mouth-wateringly delicious. Potato cakes are also eaten, primarily for breakfast with bacon and eggs, as are baked and boiled potatoes. Irish stew contains healthy portions of potatoes. And of course, a plain baked potato (called a jacket potato) with butter is always available and filling.

An Irish specialty that should not be missed is Irish soda bread. This flavorful brown bread is made from stone-ground wheat flour. Its crust is, well, crusty, and covers a soft and succulent dough on the inside. It is used to accompany just about any meal, but more particularly it is served with seafood platters of salmon, mussels, or scallops.

A RECIPE FOR IRISH STEW

Ireland's national dish is **Irish Stew**. *There are probably as many recipes for Irish Stew as there are Irish cooks. Here's one for you to try:*
- *5 pounds of lamb shoulder chops*
- *20 baby red-skinned potatoes*
- *6 large carrots, peeled and sliced*
- *3 medium onions*
- *2 medium leeks*
- *1/3 cup chopped fresh parsley*
- *1 1/2 tablespoons chopped fresh thyme*
- *2 cups water.*

Trim the fat and bones from the lamb shoulder chops, and cut the remaining meat into 1" to 2" square chunks. Put the fat in a large pot and cook on medium high temperature until about 3 tablespoons of drippings are present (5 to 7 minutes). Remove large pieces of fat from the pot.

Salt and pepper the chunks of lamb, add them to the pot and sauté until brown (you'll probably have to do this a little at a time until all the lamb is browned). Remove lamb, add the bones to the pot with the drippings and cook for about 5 minutes. Remove the bones.

Add the carrots, onions (peeled and quartered), leeks (slice only the white and pale green parts into 1/2" pieces), parsley, and thyme into the pot and stir regularly so nothing burns.

Return the meat and the bones to the pot, along with 2 cups of water. Bring to a boil, then reduce to medium-low heat. Cover pot tightly, simmer and stir occasionally until the lamb is tender and the vegetables are soft (about an hour and a half).

Remove approximately one cup of the vegetables, puree, and return to the stew. Season to taste with salt and pepper. Serves six.

The stew can be made one day ahead of time.

Most restaurants, and especially those in the country, boast that they use only the freshest ingredients. It is not an idle boast. Many of the country restaurants use herbs and vegetables from their own kitchen gardens, and they are assuredly some of the freshest and most flavorful you'll ever have. And the freshest ingredients are not limited to herbs and vegetables. You can also be served eggs from free-range hens, seafood from the ocean your table overlooks, or venison from the local farmer's fields.

In recent years, Irish farmhouse cheeses have become quite popular. Once you taste them you'll understand why. These hand-made delicacies are considered among the finest in the world. As often as not, you'll be asked to choose from a selection the restaurant presents on a cheese trolley, similar to the dessert trolleys you might be more familiar with. Several favorites to keep your eye out for include *Knockalara* (made with sheep's milk), *Cahills, Round tower*, and smoked *Gubbeen*. There are others, certainly – over forty kinds at last count.

IRELAND'S BEST RESTAURANTS

My criteria for the best restaurants in Ireland include quality, presentation, selection, service and ambiance.

DOYLE'S SEAFOOD BAR, *4 John Street, Dingle, County Kerry, Province of Munster. Tel. (066) 51174. Set dinner menu for £13.50. Diners Club, MasterCard, and Visa accepted. 10% service charge.*

Doyle's gets my vote for the best seafood restaurant in Ireland. The setting isn't bad either, out on Dingle Peninsula. John and Stella Doyle have been cooking seafood for the local populace and tourists since the 1970s, and they do a pretty good job of it. Doyle's combines a homey atmosphere with fresh and exceptionally well prepared seafood to the delight of all their guests. One of their specialty dishes is millefeuille of warm oysters with Guinness sauce, a dish that has received international attention. Other dishes include baked lemon sole, mussels in herb and garlic sauce, and fried scallops.

KEE'S RESTAURANT, *Stranolar, Ballybofey, County Donegal, Province of Ulster. Tel. (074) 31018. £10.95 to £17. All major credit cards accepted.*

The Kee family has a right to be proud of their restaurant that serves both their guests (this is a part of their hotel) and the general public. In fact, I think so highly of this restaurant that I made a special effort to find it again. Several years ago during a trip to Ireland, my wife and I stumbled across this restaurant. We were delighted with what we found: *wonderful* service (even by Irish standards), a sumptuous meal, and exquisite presentation, almost too pretty to eat! But, we forgot where it was. I remembered that it was in County Donegal somewhere. So, on my last trip to Ireland, I retraced as nearly as I could remember the route through the county that my wife and I had taken, and just as I was ready to give up, I stumbled across it again.

I had to eat there again, and it was as delicious as the first time I visited. Chef Frederic Souty is the master behind the fare, and he doesn't disappoint. The menu is well represented by beef, lamb, seafood, and other wonderful concoctions. Try the roast rack of Donegal spring lamb or the grilled fillet steak with wild mushroom essence. Add one of the finest wine lists in the country, and you have a combination that's difficult to beat.

The restaurant's dark wood enhances the quiet, private atmosphere of the room. The framed tapestries around the walls are the work of past owners of the hotel and restaurant.

NUMBER 10, *10 Fitzwilliam Street Lower, Dublin. Tel. (01) 676-1367. £13.95 to £24.95. All major credit cards accepted.*

If exquisite dining is what you are looking for in Dublin, look no further. Number 10, the restaurant that also serves Longfield's Hotel, is arguably one of the finest dining establishments in Dublin. As you descend white and black tile steps below street level, you emerge into a small but engaging restaurant. The open fire, accentuated by the crystal and linen on the tables immediately lets you that you've come to the right place. But that is only the beginning. The service, the food, and the ambiance all combine to provide an elegant and graceful dining experience.

Their internationally trained chef, Tommy Donovan, whips up meals fit for a king. His presentation is as tasteful and exquisite as is the food itself. Michael Blake, the manager, assures that the staff is attentive and that top-notch service is a reality. Michael describes their fare as light French cuisine with Irish influences. The chef from Ireland's only two-star restaurant occasionally frequents Number 10 on his days off. Need I say more? Number 10 seats only thirty-five or so, and it fills up quickly. Reservations are strongly recommended, and you'll probably not get in without them on the weekends.

ARBUTUS LODGE RESTAURANT, *Montenotte, Cork City, Province of Munster. Tel. (021) 501237. Set dinner menus for £22.95 and £27.75. All major credit cards accepted.*

The restaurant for Arbutus Lodge is considered one of the ten finest in Ireland by most food critics. Traditional Irish food prepared with care and presented with an artistic flair all topped by outstanding service are hallmarks of the restaurant. From seafood to steak, lobster to lamb, all the meals are cooked with fresh ingredients, many of them from Arbutus Lodge's own kitchen garden.

Hungry for seafood? Try their pan-fried mussels with a walnut and garlic dip, or perhaps you prefer Irish beef. If that's the case, try their spiced beef with chutney or fillet of steak. If it's wild game you like, there's always the roast venison with raspberry coulis, or the chartreuse of pigeon and rabbit with fresh chanterelle sauce. As a bonus that you don't get in many upscale restaurants in Ireland, the portions are large.

LONGUEVILLE HOUSE PRESIDENTS' RESTAURANT, *Mallow, County Cork, Province of Munster. Tel. (022) 47156. Set dinner menu for £28. All major credit cards accepted.*

This elegant country restaurant is something special. On the walls surrounding the dining area are the somber portraits of former Irish Presidents overseeing the service and food in the dining room.

They needn't be concerned: the food is exquisite, the service impeccable, and the experience memorable. The freshness, ingenuity, and interesting combinations of delicious edibles all combine to make your dining an event rather than just another meal.

Part of the success of the restaurant is Chef William O'Callaghan's insistence on the freshest of ingredients; indeed, many of the vegetables, fruit, herbs, lamb, and salmon are from within a few hundred yards of the house. The others come from nearby farms or waters.

Mr. O'Callaghan tempts his guests with a variety of exceptional offerings, including an ever-popular *Surprise Taste Menu*, which is a seven course treat. Other tempting specialties include such favorites as roast of Longueville lamb with a gratin of turnips, pan-fried medallions of monkfish, or Kilbrack pork. Desserts will leave you dreaming of the ones you didn't order – you may decide to come back just for a new dessert! Longueville House is renowned for their pyramid of chocolate with an enchanting orange sauce.

ASSOLAS COUNTRY HOUSE RESTAURANT, *Kanturk, County Cork, Province of Munster. Tel. (029) 50015. Set dinner menu for £28. All major credit cards accepted. No service charge.*

The restaurant at Assolas Country House is as elegant and delightful as you'd expect it to be. The fruits, the vegetables, and the herbs impart such magnificent subtleties of taste to the food and all are grown in Assolas Country House's kitchen garden. The menu changes daily, but the quality is always the same. Typical offerings include fillet of brill oven-baked in a basil butter sauce, Kenmare mussels, sautéed oysters with shallots and cream in brioche, or confit of duck. If wild game is your preference, several options are usually available, including venison, pheasant and quail.

CASHEL HOUSE RESTAURANT, *Cashel, County Galway, Province of Connacht. Tel. (095) 31001. Set dinner menu for £29. All major credit cards accepted. 12.5% service charge.*

Cashel House the restaurant is as impressive as Cashel House the accommodation. For starters, the dining room overlooks the pretty grounds. Heads of state have eaten here. The menu is simple, yet offers plenty of options, such as sautéed monkfish with a shrimp sauce, roast rack of spring lamb, filo chicken in a tarragon sauce, and even guinea fowl with grapes and Madeira. Vegetarian dishes are also available.

EARL OF THOMOND ROOM, *Newmarket-on-Fergus, County Clare, Province of Munster. Tel. (061) 368144. Set lunch menu for £18, set dinner menu for £35 and £45. All major credit cards accepted. 15% service charge.*

I was totally captivated by the restaurant in Dromoland Castle. High ceilings, rich dark wood, gorgeous crystal chandeliers, crisp starched linen tablecloths, gleaming china, and an Irish harpist, singer or fiddler all contribute to an elegant and opulent dining experience. As you dine, the watchful eyes of the former Lords and Ladies of the castle gaze down at you from larger-than-life-size portraits spread around the room.

The menu is beyond exquisite, and the food exceeds all expectations. Typical offerings include picatta of milk-fed veal, in classic "Nicoise" style, pan-fried fillet of John Dory set upon a nage of leeks and mushrooms, and terrine of Dromoland estate venison with fig chutney. All are tastefully presented, and the service is impeccable and personalized, but not overbearing.

RESTAURANT PATRICK GUILBAUD, *46 James Place, Dublin. Tel. (01) 676-4192. £10 to £46. All major credit cards accepted.*

If you want to eat in *the* restaurant in Ireland, this would be the place. On a recent trip, I noticed that the newspapers were trumpeting Ireland's latest achievement: Restaurant Patrick Guilbaud had just been awarded a second Michelin star, the first restaurant in Ireland ever to gain this distinction.

Restaurant Patrick Guilbaud is not soft candlelight and quiet conversations. Rather, it is a bright, lively place where people come to enjoy exquisite food and animated conversation with friends and family. Live plants hang overhead. White walls accentuate the paintings that are judiciously hung throughout the restaurant. The paintings are by Irish artists who lived and painted in France. Mr. Guilbaud is proud to have acquired these paintings and returned them to their native Ireland.

As you would expect, the food is marvelous. From the roast quail to the poached Connemara lobster, it is as tasteful to the eye as it is to the palate. Set menus are available for £18.50 for lunch and £30 for dinner. There is even a *Menu Surprise* for £46 for those wishing a dining adventure!

You are likely to meet Mr. Guilbaud, as he is active in serving, greeting and conversing with his customers. Be sure to congratulate him on his second Michelin star.

DRINK

People all over the world associate **pubs** with Ireland – and rightfully so. There are an unbelievable number of pubs in Ireland. By some estimates, there are over 10,000 pubs in Ireland - one for every five hundred inhabitants. Indeed, if you come to a spot in the road with two buildings, one of them is sure to be a pub! Dublin alone is reported to have nearly 1,000 pubs, giving rise to the nickname *Publin*.

Liquor is big business in Ireland. There is a wide range of ales, beers, and lagers, although Ireland is probably best known for the bitter dark stout **Guinness** exports all around the world. Whether you've tried Guinness before or not, you must try it in Dublin. All Irish agree that it tastes better when sipped within the Dublin city limits. Beer experts (to be found in pubs all over Ireland) claim there are a number of factors that add to the flavor of Guinness. These include esoterica such as a constant temperature from the brewery to the cellar to the tap, frequency of flow, and just the right pressure from the tap. Throw in a healthy dose of pub atmosphere, and you've got all the makings of a velvety smooth drink.

Ireland also produces a variety of other liquors, including gin, vodka, and whiskey. They are proud to be the nation that brought the world whiskey. Whiskey was introduced into Ireland in the sixth century by none other than monks. In fact, the word whiskey comes from the anglicized Irish words *uisce beatha* (pronounced ISK-kee-BAH-hah), which means the "water of life." By the time Anglo-Norman invaders hit the shores of Ireland, whiskey was well-established in the Irish culture. Unable to pronounce *uisce beatha*, the English soldiers shortened it to *uisce*, which they eventually anglicized to whiskey.

John Jameson established the **Jameson Distillery** in Dublin in 1780, and over the centuries his successors have perfected the recipe and process to give us the most recognizable of Irish whiskies. Irish whiskey is made from malted and unmalted barley and other native grains such as wheat, oats, and a little rye. The whiskey is matured in wooden casks from three to twelve years. Connoisseurs of whiskey will immediately notice the difference between Irish whiskey and Scotch whisky (other than the fact that one uses an "e" in its spelling, and the other does not). The difference is attributed to the malt: Irish whiskey is dried in a closed kiln, as opposed to dried over open peat fires as Scotch is. The latter method imparts a distinct smoky flavor to Scotch whisky that is absent in Irish whiskey. Irish whiskey is also distilled three times, while Scotch is distilled only twice.

Jameson is perhaps the best-known Irish whiskey, but the local favorite is **Power's Gold Label**. Running a close third is the whiskey distilled in the **Bushmills Distillery** in Northern Ireland. You should try all three to determine which is your personal favorite. But don't bother trying it before you come to Ireland. Irish whiskey, like Guinness, is reputed to be best when taken within the shadow of its distillery.

As quaint and fun as pubs are, they are also of great concern for Ireland. Alcoholism is higher here than in just about any other European nation. That statistic, coupled with an unemployment rate consistently over 15%, poses a staggering challenge for the country. Put another way by one who hosted me at a pub, "Aye, lad," said he, " 'tis a real difficulty for us here."

As you wind down your Irish holiday, and you lift your glass to toast Ireland, think of this famous Irish toast:

May the road rise to meet you
May the wind be always at your back
May the sun shine warm upon your face
And the rain fall soft upon your fields
And until we meet again
May God hold you in the hollow of His hand.

HOW TO MAKE AN IRISH WHISKEY PUNCH!

Irish Whiskey Punch is a favorite holiday treat, or a favorite treat for any other occasion you can think of! They say it's good for what ails you.
- *1 3/4 cups Irish (of course!) whiskey*
- *1/4 cup golden brown sugar*
- *1 large (or 2 small) lemons sliced into six wedges*
- *24 whole cloves*
- *3 cups hot water*

Put the whiskey and brown sugar into a pitcher and mix thoroughly (until the sugar is dissolved). Place in six cups. Put four cloves into each lemon slice, and place in each cup. Pour 1/2 cup of hot water into each, stir; drink; enjoy.

12. IRELAND'S BEST HOTELS & INNS

While most of the accommodations I've stayed in over the many years I've been going to Ireland were quite good, there are a few that still linger in my memory. These were the ones I couldn't wait to tell my family and friends about when I got home.

Some of these hotels and B&Bs you'll remember for their history and beauty; others for their genuine warmth and the people you meet there. For each selection – other than those for Dublin, which simply list the Dublin street address – I've included the province as part of the address, so you'll have an easier time finding it in this book (each province is a separate chapter) and in your travels around Ireland.

THE ARCHES COUNTRY HOUSE, *Lough Eske, Barnesmore, County Donegal, Province of Ulster. Tel. (073) 22029. 5 rooms. Rates for singles: £21, doubles: £16 per person sharing. Rates include breakfast. No credit cards accepted. No service charge.*

Hands down, the Arches Country House is my favorite Irish B&B and Mrs. Noreen McGinty is the primary reason for that. She is a gracious and enjoyable hostess. Her immaculate B&B rests on a hill with stunning views of Lough Eske.

Three arches grace the front porch and entryway to this relatively new Bed and Breakfast. The rooms are all well-lit and decorated in a bright and cheery manner. The rooms at the front of the house have large windows that provide spectacular views of Lough Eske in the distance. The rooms at the back of the house are equally as nice, and their views are of the lovely Bluestack Mountains.

A nice sitting room is available for visiting with other guests or just relaxing after the rigors of your touring. All in all, The Arches — the rooms, the views, the great breakfast, and the warm hospitality — is a special place to stay.

ARIEL HOUSE, *50 - 52 Lansdowne Road, Dublin 4. Tel. (01) 668-5512, fax (01) 668-5845. 30 rooms. Rates for doubles: £25 to £68, superior doubles: £90, suites: £150. Rates include breakfast. MasterCard and Visa accepted. No service charge.*

Without a doubt, one of the warmest welcomes and most pleasant stays you can have in Ireland is at the Ariel House. Three Victorian (not Georgian) townhouses, built in the 1850s, have been converted into the award winning "Best Small Hotel in Ireland" for 1995. Michael O'Brien, who has been the proprietor of Ariel House since 1960, is your gracious host. Referred to by some as "The grandfather of the Bed and Breakfast industry in Ireland," Mr. O'Brien is a pleasure to visit with.The front sitting room is equally as wonderful, furnished with comfortable leather chairs surrounded by antiques all situated before a lovely fireplace.

Twenty of the thirty rooms are furnished almost exclusively with furniture from the Victorian era. (Ask Mr. O'Brien why Victorian furniture is so much better suited to B&Bs than Georgian furniture.) The rooms range from lovely to elegant. Ask to see the junior and senior honeymoon suites, also called the presidential suites depending on the occasion. They are nothing short of spectacular. The large four-poster bed, the seven foot tall armoire, and the crystal chandelier complement one another nicely and combine for a marvelous effect. All the rooms have upgraded bathrooms, televisions, ironing boards and hair dryers.

There are an additional ten rooms added onto the back of Ariel House that are strictly functional. Their style and feel are more like small hotel rooms, and are a let-down after seeing the rest of the house. But they are less expensive than the other rooms, and are a nice clean place to stay.

ARIEL HOUSE, PRESIDENTIAL/HONEYMOON SUITE

Your stay at Ariel House will be enchanting, and as you rise to partake of breakfast before you begin your day, that enchantment will continue. Breakfast itself is wonderful – eggs, Irish bacon, brown bread, and coffee or tea all prepared exactly to your liking. But the ambiance of the conservatory overlooking the gardens and lush backyard add a touch that's nothing short of marvelous.

While Ariel House is several miles from downtown Dublin, it is one hundred yards from the Lansdowne DART station, about a three minute ride to downtown.

THE RUSSELL COURT HOTEL, *Harcourt Street, Dublin 2. Tel. (01) 478-4066, fax (01) 478-1576. 48 rooms. Rates for singles: £60, doubles: £82, suites: £82. Rates include continental breakfast. One restaurant, a pub and several lounges. All major credit cards accepted. 12.5% service charge.*

What a find! The Russell Court Hotel is one of the best-kept secrets in Dublin. The Hotel does not advertise because they have a loyal clientele – mostly business people – that keeps them full all year long.

From the moment you walk into this hotel – three converted Georgian townhouses – you'll feel comfortable and at home. No two rooms are alike, except for the fact that they are all large, with high ceilings, and are beautifully decorated. Rich wood molding, solid wood doors, and attention to detail makes this a beautiful hotel. Combine all that with its close proximity to Grafton Street and St. Stephen's Green, and this is the perfect place to stay.

On-site is Dicey Reilly's Pub, with a beer garden that's very popular in the spring and summer, and four nights a week of live music, from traditional Irish to jazz to contemporary.

If you want to stay here, you'd better make your reservations several months in advance.

BALLYNAHINCH CASTLE HOTEL, *Recess, County Connemara, Province of Connacht. Tel. (095) 31006, fax (095) 31085. 28 rooms. Rates for singles: £55 to £69, doubles: £80 to £104, suites: £94 to £120. Rates include breakfast. Restaurant, gardens, croquet, riding, shooting, walking trails. All major credit cards accepted. 10% service charge.*

Simply put, Ballynahinch Castle is a lovely hotel, with a real red fox that often greets tourists at the front door. Ancestral home of the Martin Clan of Connemara, Ballynahinch Castle has been converted into a four-star hotel. The rooms – all individually decorated – are spacious and offer beautiful views of either the mountains or the lake. The service is impeccable.

During the 1930s, the eccentric (and wealthy) Maharajah Ranjitsinji purchased Ballynahinch Castle as a winter get-away to relax and entertain his friends. Pictures of the Maharajah grace some of the walls and help put a name with the face.

In recent years, Ballynahinch Castle Hotel has earned the reputation as a shooting center, where sporting folk come from all over the world to participate in five annual woodcock bird hunts sponsored by the hotel.

In addition to the exceptional service and the warmth of Ballynahinch Castle, the restaurant is also impressive. Looking out over the Owenmore River as it quietly fills Ballynahinch Lake, the flood-lit shores add a peaceful touch to your dining experience. The food is delicious, the service efficient, and the atmosphere tranquil.

Ballynahinch Castle Hotel is rightfully proud of their designation as Ireland's Hotel of the Year in 1994.

CASHEL HOUSE HOTEL, *Cashel, County Connemara, Province of Connacht. Tel. (095) 31001, (095) 31077, US toll free 800-223-6510. 32 rooms. Rates for singles: £49 to £66, doubles: £49 to £66 per person sharing. Rates include breakfast. Restaurant, gardens, riding, walking trails. All major credit cards accepted. 12.5% service charge.*

This is a very impressive hotel. The owners, Dermot and Kay McEvilly, have been in the hotel business since 1968 and are responsible for Cashel House emanating the feel and personality of a B&B, but the facilities and amenities of a hotel. Built in the 19th century, Cashel House has been magnificently renovated. Antiques, old (*old!*) oil paintings, and plush hand-made Connemara rugs grace the floors throughout the hotel.

Each room is lavish and unique from one another. Each is tastefully wallpapered and carpeted, and flowers from the extensive gardens are found daily in your room – just the right touch to make you feel all that much more welcome.

And if that's not enough, their restaurant is considered one of the best in Ireland. Located at the front and side of the house, the dining room has large windows that look out onto the grounds of Cashel House. Dermot McEvilly and his crew of cooks are excellent chefs; their specialty is seafood.

Riding stables on-site are constantly in use by the guests, and in keeping with their thoughtful manner, the owners provide boots and riding helmets for their guests to ensure safe and enjoyable rides. And their luxurious gardens make for a quiet beginning or a romantic end to your day. Pound for pound, pence for pence, this is probably the best lodging for the money in western Ireland!

TINAKILLY COUNTRY HOUSE, *Rathnew, County Wicklow, Province of Leinster. Tel. (0404) 69274, fax (0404) 67806. 29 rooms. Rates for singles: £85 to £93, doubles: £55 to £63 per person sharing, suites: £70 to £100 per person sharing. One restaurant, putting green, croquet. All major credit cards accepted. No service charge.*

Tinakilly feels more like being at home – well, a very expensive home, than staying in a hotel. Antiques abound, from the sitting room with its blazing fire to the spacious rooms, most with lovely views of the Irish Sea. They also have a marvelous restaurant. This old Victorian mansion was built in the 1870s as a token of appreciation for Captain Robert Halpin, who commanded the *Great Eastern*, which laid the first telegraph cable that linked Europe and America.

PARK HOTEL KENMARE, *Kenmare, County Kerry, Province of Munster. Tel. (064) 41200, fax (064) 41402. 50 rooms. Rates for singles: £115 to £135, doubles: £96 to £138 per person sharing, suites: £165 to £199 per person sharing. One restaurant, croquet, tennis. All major credit cards accepted. No service charge.*

I must admit, I was probably more curious to meet the owner of the Park Hotel in Kenmare than I was to actually stay at his hotel. It seemed that nearly every hotelier to whom I mentioned my upcoming stay at the Park Hotel asked me to say "Hello" to Francis Brennan for them. Several of them, general managers at some of Ireland's most prestigious hotels, had learned their craft at Francis' hand. I wasn't disappointed, either in Mr. Brennan, his staff, or in the hotel.

The hotel was built in 1897 to serve as the hotel for the railroad that dead-ended there. Since that time, it has been renovated and expanded, and the results are marvelous. From the turned-down beds to the bathrobes and slippers, to the clean windshield in the morning "...to get a clear view of our Emerald Isle," you'll be delighted you stayed. The rooms are nice-sized, and the ones in the back are the nicest, offering views of Kenmare Bay and most of the eleven acres of gardens. The halls are filled with antiques and portraits.

On-site is an award-winning restaurant that overlooks Kenmare Bay. The menu offers a good selection, but on my last visit I finally settled on the grilled fillet of beef studded with truffles and a fricasee of wild mushrooms. It was, without a doubt, one of the most delicious meals I had while I was in Ireland. The beef was tender and practically dissolved in my mouth, and the flavor was as exceptional as I have ever experienced.

Note: the Park Hotel Kenmare is only open from mid-April through mid-November. After their season is over, Mr. Brennan takes his entire staff on an all-expense paid international vacation as a reward for their fine service. Believe me, they deserve it.

SHELBOURNE HOTEL, *27 St. Stephen's Green, Dublin 2. Tel. (01) 676-6471, fax (01) 661-6006. 164 rooms. Rates for singles: £120 to £135, doubles: £140 to £160, and suites: £265 to £680. One restaurant and two bars. All major credit cards accepted. 15% service charge.*

The Shelbourne Hotel receives my vote for the nicest of the nice in Dublin. From the rich dark wood to the lovely antique Waterford crystal chandelier in the Lord Mayor's lounge, to the flawless service, you'll be delighted with every aspect of your stay at the Shelbourne.

The Shelbourne isn't as flamboyant as some of the other brass and crystal hotels you'll find in Dublin. Instead, it is all grace and grandeur, refinement and splendor. No impressive lobby awaits your arrival, but a rather understated journey from the front door to the reception desk. But that's all that is understated. The rooms and the furnishings, the fine equestrian art, and the ambiance are as rich and lovely as you'll find in Dublin.

The Shelbourne, like so many other hotels in Dublin, is three Georgian townhouses that were converted in 1824. The rooms are large and spacious, and no two are alike in their layout, size, or decor. All the rooms are lavishly furnished and very comfortable. Ask for a room overlooking St. Stephen's Green – the views are among the best in Dublin.

For a treat, ask to see the Presidential Suite – more fondly referred to as the Princess Grace Room in honor of that grand lady's stay here several years prior to her death. It is a large, attractive, multi-roomed suite overlooking St. Stephen's Green. Near one of the windows is a picture of Princess Grace, and it adds a touch of, well...*grace*...to the room! If the room is not occupied, the front desk staff assures me it is possible to have a short tour.

History buffs will be interested to know that the Irish Constitution was drafted in the Shelbourne in 1922. The Shelbourne boasts many heads of state, actors, and actresses, and many of the world's *glitterati* as their honored guests. And you will feel equally honored during your stay here.

DROMOLAND CASTLE, *Newmarket-on-Fergus, County Clare, Province of Munster. Tel. (061) 368144, fax (061) 363355, U.S. toll free 800-346-7007. 73 rooms. Rates for standard rooms: £116 to £202, deluxe rooms: £180 to £245, state rooms and suites: £245 to £414; children under age 12 stay free with parents. One restaurant, indoor swimming pool, spa, sauna, fitness center, beauty salon, tennis, snooker, golf, riding, fishing, shooting, bicycles. All major credit cards accepted. No service charge.*

"A fantasy come true," "A piece of heaven," "Exceeded every expectation I had" – these were the last three entries in the guest book on the morning after I stayed at Dromoland Castle, and they represent my feelings pretty well. Dromoland Castle is the sister castle to Ashford Castle, and you can certainly see the family resemblance. But if Ashford is the elegant, classic beauty, Dromoland is the sister with the personality. Dromoland exudes grace and charm.

Dromoland Castle was once the estate of the powerful O'Brien Clan, blood descendants of Brian Boru, High King of Ireland. Chock full of antiques and portraits of the previous inhabitants, it retains its regal feeling without being stuffy. Adding to the fairytale feeling, Dromoland Castle is set amid 370 acres of wood, parks, and golf fairways and greens.

DROMOLAND CASTLE HOTEL

The rooms are spacious and tastefully decorated. The rooms in front have lovely views of a small lake and the golf course. All rooms come with nightly turn-down service, warm robes, and chocolates on your pillow.

On-site is an outstanding restaurant – the Earl of Thomond Room – that provides one of the most delectable dining experiences in the country. I'm not sure whether it was the exceptional food, or the Irish harpist and singer softly serenading the diners, or the beautiful views out the dining room windows, or the feeling that I was dining where kings and queens would feel comfortable, but meals at Dromoland Castle are superb in all respects. For a full review of the restaurant, see Chapter 11, *Food & Drink*.

ASHFORD CASTLE, *Cong, County Mayo, Province of Connacht. Tel. (092) 46003, fax (092) 46260, U.S. toll free 800-346-7007. 83 rooms. Rates for standard rooms: £116 to £202, deluxe rooms: £180 to £245, state rooms: £180 to £292, suites: £245 to £414. Restaurant, gardens, tennis, grounds, fishing, walking trails, golf. All major credit cards accepted. No service charge.*

What an exquisite hotel this is. Ashford Castle is far better experienced than described (although I'll try). Just to give you a point of reference, Ashford Castle has been highlighted several times on television, and was one of the hotels President Ronald Reagan stayed in during his visit to Ireland.

Resting regally amid 350 acres of luscious park land, this 13th-century Norman castle is a sight to behold. Inside, the scores of high quality antiques and old portraits combined with rich paneled walls and plush carpets give you the feeling you've stumbled into the private chambers of an ancient ruler. The public rooms are elegant, filled with rich leather chairs, dark paneling, and views of the verdant grounds. The bedrooms are all different, and are probably the largest you'll find in Ireland for each class of room. All have antiques aplenty, plush carpets, and marvelous bathrooms. Thick robes, slippers, mineral water, and a bowl of fruit greet you upon arrival.

If you are romanced by the hotel, you will be positively seduced by the dining expeience here. The Connaught Room is a small, intimate restaurant overlooking the grounds of the estate. Rich, dark paneling, an exquisite Waterford crystal chandelier and an open fireplace are the perfect touches to put you in the mood for a wonderful dinner. The specialty is French cuisine. Typical offerings include Cleggan lobster tail in a ginger fish consomme with tomato and leeks, or whole duckling (carved at your table.

But wait – you've only learned about one of the restaurants in Ashford Castle. In addition to the Connaught Room, there is the equally lovely George V room, with an open fire, gorgeous chandeliers, and beautiful panelling – light oak, giving the room less of a regal feel and more of a traditional Irish feel, which is the perfect complement to the traditional Irish cuisine featured here. Whether you prefer fish or beef, either is prepared to perfection and served with elegant efficiency.

Ashford Castle is the *créme de la créme* of hotels in Ireland. However, as exquisite and elegant as Ashford Castle is, it also has a reputation for a certain amount of stuffiness. The service is supremely efficient but lacking in the customary Irish warmth and friendliness. Having said this, Ashford Castle will definitely provide a memorable experience.

ASHFORD CASTLE HOTEL

13. DUBLIN

INTRODUCTION

With slightly over one million people in the greater Dublin area, Dublin is the largest city on the Emerald Isle. Its original Irish name, *Baile Atha Cliath*, means "Town of the Hurdle Ford." However, British conquerers renamed it Dublin after a nearby important trading area called Dubh-Linn (Black Pool in English). Located on the eastern coast of Ireland, Dublin has been an important seaport for nearly a millennium. The **River Liffey** is the major waterway in Dublin, and it bisects the city from east to west.

Dublin is the ideal place to both begin and end your journey to the Emerald Isle. Cultural, architectural, and historical sights and sounds are present on nearly every corner and around every bend in Dublin. Museums, art galleries, historic sites, marvelous shopping, and quiet sunsets all vie for your time and attention.

Dublin's history begins with the Viking settlement of *Dylfin*, founded in 841. Sailing up into the mouth of the River Liffey, these intrepid Norsemen founded a small community that would one day become the most important seaport in Ireland. The native Irish were not pleased with their presence, and the next one hundred and fifty years saw a series of battles between the Irish and these northern interlopers. But it wasn't until 988 (some historians say 989) that the town was permanently wrested from foreign hands. Despite its initial founding in 841, Dubliners consider 988 as the founding date for their hometown.

In 1170, English and Norman mercenaries under the Earl of Pembroke, also known as Strongbow, came to the aid of the King of Leinster in a dispute with other Irish kings. These invaders overwhelmed the walled town's defenses and established a firm stronghold in Dublin. It was the beginning of over seven hundred and fifty years of English domination over Dublin and Ireland. Shortly after the invasion, Dublin swelled with the arrival of immigrants from England. This was the beginning of a number of waves of English settlement. Even today the accents of native Dubliners have a strong British flavor.

This began a period of renaissance, maturing, and building for this small seaport town. Some of Dublin's existing attractions came into being during this period. Small churches were rebuilt on a grand scale during this time: **Christchurch Cathedral** (1173), **St. Audoen's Church of Ireland** (1190), and **St. Patrick's Cathedral** (1190 and 1220). In addition, **Dublin Castle** was built in 1204, although the structure in place today has been rebuilt numerous times. The **Record Tower** is the only remaining part of the original castle.

As the center of English rule and power in Ireland, Dublin found itself ostracized from the rest of Ireland. Over the ensuing years, Anglo-Norman control over Ireland was exercised from within the walled city of Dublin and their influence and domination became firmly implanted along the eastern coastline, centered in Dublin. This area came to be known as **The Pale**.

DUBLIN'S MUST-SEE SIGHTS

BOOK OF KELLS – *Housed at Trinity College. Ancient monks hand-illustrated the four gospels over eleven hundred years ago.*

CHESTER BEATTY LIBRARY AND GALLERY OF ORIENTAL ART – *This is a pretty impressive museum. Currently in Ballsbridge, it is slated to move to Dublin Castle.*

CHRISTCHURCH CATHEDRAL – *The two finest cathedrals in Ireland are located in Dublin. St. Patrick's is one, Christchurch is the other.*

GENERAL POST OFFICE (GPO) – *There aren't many cities where I'd suggest going to see the main post office. But the GPO has played such an important part in Irish history, it's a must.*

GRAFTON STREET – *This pedestrian shopping street provides ample opportunity for shopping and people-watching.*

GUINNESS BREWERY – *Visit the brewery that made Dublin famous. The tour no longer takes you back into the brewery itself, but provides a video tour.*

HUGH LANE MUNICIPAL GALLERY OF MODERN ART – *Another fine art gallery in Dublin. This one focuses on contemporary art.*

NATIONAL GALLERY OF IRELAND – *The National Gallery is the best art gallery in Ireland, and is well worth a visit.*

NATIONAL MUSEUM – *If you see only one museum in Ireland, let this be the one.*

PHOENIX PARK – *Phoenix Park has a lot to offer if you are interested in lots of greenery, cricket games or polo matches, ducks and ponds, a fabulous zoo, or people-watching.*

ST. PATRICK'S CATHEDRAL – *So indelibly associated with the history of Ireland you have to visit.*

Dublin served as the launching point for various and sundry military campaigns against the native Irish during the 16th through 19th centuries. It enjoyed a resurgence of prominence during the mid-17th century as a result of the successes of Oliver Cromwell.

During the 19th century, massive efforts to revitalize and restore Dublin were undertaken. As a lasting tribute to the Georgian period in Dublin's history, streets were laid out and widened and beautiful townhouses were erected.

ARRIVALS & DEPARTURES

Dublin can be reached in a variety of ways: by air, trains, and car. It can also be reached by ferry if you are coming from France, England, or Wales.

BY AIR FROM THE UNITED STATES

Dublin International Airport, *Tel. (01) 705-2222*, is about six miles north of Dublin's city center. It is the principal airport for flights from Europe, England, Scotland, and the United States. The airport code is DUB.

Nearly two dozen flights a day arrive from London's Heathrow and Gatwick airports. In addition, daily flights arrive from Edinburgh and Glasgow as well as from a number of England's regional airports, including Birmingham, Bristol, Liverpool, Luton, Manchester, and Newcastle.

Airlines flying to Dublin from London and England's regional airports include Aer Lingus, British Airways, British Midland Airways, and Ryanair. Flights from Ireland's regional airports (Cork, Galway, Knock, Sligo, and Waterford) also land at Dublin Airport.

Transatlantic flights to Ireland from the US land in Dublin (some flights land in Shannon first, then continue on to Dublin). **Aer Lingus** and **Delta** are the only two carriers at this time that fly directly to Ireland from the United States. Canadian passengers flying to Dublin or Shannon must connect in Chicago, Boston, New York, or London.

Dublin Airport is a small, but modern airport. The fact that it has only one terminal also makes it easy to navigate. Signs are plentiful, and if you're the least bit confused or lost, there are plenty of helpful airport employees willing to lend a hand.

Don't be alarmed if you see military personnel leisurely patrolling the halls with Uzi machine guns slung over their shoulders. This is a common sight in most European airports, and Europeans pay as little heed to their presence as Americans pay to pistol-toting police officers in America.

From the airport to Dublin's city center you can choose a taxi, bus, express bus, or rental car.

BY AIR FROM ENGLAND

Since many international carriers do not fly directly into Ireland but connect in London, many tourists visiting Ireland first spend a few days in England. If that's the case with you, it's relatively easy to get to Ireland from England, and you have several choices.

As mentioned above, a number of airlines fly into Dublin (and other Irish airports), and if your airfare doesn't already include a trip to Ireland, the fares are quite competitive. Depending on the time of year, and your days of travel (weekdays are more expensive than weekends), you can expect to pay an additional £85 to £140 for round-trip airfare from London.

Getting to Town By Taxi

The taxi stand is just outside the doors of the Arrivals hall. If you hire a taxi, the twenty-five minute ride from the airport will cost you around £15 including tip, and is certainly the quickest way to get into town.

Getting to Town By Bus

You have two choices for a bus ride into the city: express or regular bus.

The **express bus** gets you into town nearly as quickly as does a taxi, but at a considerably lower cost. The thirty-five minute ride costs £2.50. It can take about fifteen minutes longer during rush hour. The express bus takes you into the heart of Dublin, stopping at **Busaras Station** *(Tel. 01 836-6111, Store Street)* in the O'Connell Street District north of the River Liffey. The service runs daily every half hour from 7:30 am to 11:00 pm. To catch the express bus, turn left coming out of the Arrivals hall, and walk about one hundred feet to bus stop #1.

To catch the **regular bus** into the city, go about fifty feet further than the express bus stop to bus stop #2. This bus stops all along the way into downtown Dublin, but it only costs £1.10. Of course, it takes a bit longer – about forty-five minutes without heavy traffic. This bus takes you to any number of places in downtown Dublin, but not to Busaras, the main bus station.

Renting a Car at the Airport

If you are renting a car when you arrive, your path through Customs will deliver you into a large hall where Avis, EuroDollar, Hertz, and Murray's EuropCar are located. If you are using one of the other, lesser known car rental agencies, they are tucked around the corner at the far end of the hall (the opposite end from where you enter after Customs). If you don't find them right away, ask for directions from any of the uniformed airport employees.

BY BUS

If you are arriving in Dublin on a bus from elsewhere in Ireland, you will arrive at **Busaras Station** on Store Street. You'll be about four blocks west of O'Connell Street, and two blocks north of the River Liffey. The neighborhood is marginal – not too bad, but I wouldn't advise walking too far west or northwest of there. The closer you get to O'Connell Street, the better the neighborhood gets.

BY FERRY FROM ENGLAND

If you want to continue to use the rental car you rented in England, drive to Holyhead or Fishguard in Wales. From there, ferries depart for Ireland on a regular basis. The **B&I Line** *(Tel. 0171 491-8682 in England)* runs ferries from Holyhead to Dublin, and **Stena Sealink** *(toll free in the US and Canada: 800-677-8585 or 01233 647047 in England)* runs ferries from Holyhead to Dun Laoghaire.

Ferries may sound romantic and fun, and that may be. But they are no bargain compared to airfares. Expect to pay about £200 one way, or £350 round-trip for your car, yourself, and three passengers. You'll pay less if it is just you, or just you and a companion, but it is still roughly equivalent to airfare. Ferries run three to five times daily, depending on the time of year. The trip across the Irish Sea takes about an hour and forty-five minutes.

BY TRAIN

Ireland has a well-regulated and much-used rail system, with stations in many towns and cities across the country. If you are coming to Dublin by train from elsewhere in Ireland, you will either arrive at Heuston Station or Connolly Station.

If you are coming from (or going to) Belfast, Rosslare, or Sligo Town, you will use **Connolly Station** *(Tel. 01 836-6222, Amiens Street)*. From there it is a ten-minute walk to Dublin's city center, or a short and inexpensive (£3) taxi ride.

If you are coming from (or going to) anywhere else in Ireland, your train will be at **Heuston Station** *(Tel. 01 836-6222, King's Bridge)*, about a twenty-minute walk to Dublin's city center, a £5 cab ride, or a ten minute, 60p bus ride to O'Connell Bridge. Buses depart frequently from Heuston Station headed for O'Connell Bridge.

Like the neighborhood around Busaras Station, the closer you get to O'Connell Bridge, the better the neighborhoods become. Nothing too scary around Heuston or Connolly Stations, but the areas are marginal.

ORIENTATION

Dublin is a relatively easy town to get around in, once you get used to the way the streets change names every other block or so (really!). While that sounds strange, it is really incredibly efficient for finding places. For example, rather than having to know where the 2500 block of Elm Street is, all you need to know is what names a given thoroughfare has over a distance. For example, the street on the north side of St. Stephen's Green is called, interestingly, St. Stephen's Green North. If you walk east on that street for six blocks, the name changes to Merrion Street, Baggot Street Lower, Baggot Street Upper, and then Pembroke Street. At first I found it frustrating, but I soon figured out how easy it is to follow. Probably 60% of the restaurant and hotel owners I spoke with didn't even know the addresses of their own businesses, they just knew the street name!

Most of the major streets in Dublin are wide and easy to negotiate. Many of the streets are one-way. When the streets are not one-way, remember to drive on the left, not the right. They have come up with a unique way to protect people who come from countries where they drive on the right hand side of the road. As you step off the curb at cross-walks, written on the road in big bold letters are the words **LOOK TO THE RIGHT -> ** or **< - LOOK TO THE LEFT**, depending on which side of the street you're on and whether you are on a one-way or two-way street.

Traffic in Dublin is a good reason to leave your rental car parked or wait until you are ready leave Dublin before you rent one. Drivers in Dublin are maniacal. Add to their craziness aggressive motorcyclists and daring pedestrians, and you'll be tempted to turn in your AAA card and international drivers license if you try to drive in Dublin!

The principal sights in Dublin are located in a four by three mile rectangle covering the heart of Dublin city. From the Dublin Area Rapid Transit (DART) rails on the east to Phoenix Park on the west, and from Parnell Square on the north to the Ballsbridge area on the south, you'll have lots to see and do, as well as plenty of places to stay and eat.

Streets & Districts

O'Connell Street is north of the River Liffey and was once one of the finest residential areas in the city. Off O'Connell street is the still-popular Henry Street shopping district. It is also the location of the theater district, and numerous fine museums are found in this area.

The **Temple Bar** district is an area just south of the River Liffey. It is one of the oldest parts of the city, and in recent years it has seen a revitalization and is becoming the cultural center of the city. Jazz festivals, public art exhibits and some of the best bistros in the city are located here.

Grafton Street is the newest hub for shopping in Dublin. In recent years it has unseated the former shopping hub, **Henry Street**, as a favorite for tourists. Grafton Street and many of its intersecting streets are closed to cars and is a shoppers' and people-watchers' paradise. Buskers – street entertainers – ply their talents all along the way. Surrounding Grafton Street are many restaurants, cafes, and bistros, as well as a number of the nicest hotels in Dublin.

Ballsbridge is southeast of Dublin proper, but is singled-out because of its fine hotels, guest houses, and restaurants. Georgian and Victorian architecture dominates the area, and is a wonderful district to stroll through and admire this well-kept residential neighborhood.

The Irish Tourist Board

There is a **Bord Failte** office in the Dublin airport that can assist you when you arrive in Dublin. If you have left the airport, the main Bord Failte office in Dublin is located at the corner of Lower Baggot Street and Wilson Terrace, *Tel. (01) 676-5871,* just inside the Grand Canal.

There are two other locations: on Upper O'Connell Street, *Tel. (01) 674-7733,* and in the heart of Dublin on Suffolk Street, *Tel. (01) 605-7777.*

GETTING AROUND TOWN

Dublin is a very easy city to get around. Most of the interesting sights are within a relatively compact area, and well within walking distance. Of course, there are alternatives to walking: taxis, buses, bicycles, and the DART. With a good map of the city, one that includes bus and DART lines, you should have no problem getting around. Maps can be had at most Newsagents, the Irish Tourist Board and possibly your hotel concierge.

There are several **taxi stands** throughout the city: the airport, the Busaras station, Connolly, Pearse, and Heuston train stations, on O'Connell Street, College Green (in front of the Bank of Ireland), and St. Stephen's Green North. You can also call a cab company and have a taxi pick you up, although there is usually an additional charge (£2 to £4) to have them do so. In the past you couldn't hail a taxi, but that is changing. I have witnessed numerous unsuccessful attempts to hail empty, on-duty taxis when I was last in Dublin.

Buses crisscross the city on a regular basis, and are relatively inexpensive. Fares are charged based on distance to your destination, from 50p to £1.10. They run regularly from 6:30 am (9:30 am on Sundays) until 11:30 pm each night. You can catch the bus at any number of stops in the city. Most routes begin at or near O'Connell Bridge and bus starters at O'Connell bridge will be more than happy to point you to the correct bus stop (bus-starters are bus company employees at the O'Connell Street station to make sure individuals – especially tourists – get on the right bus). If you are planning to use the bus, it's best to get a map since

O'Connell Bridge may not be convenient. If you are on the outskirts of the city, just look for the bus destination signs that say *An Lar*, Irish for "the center."

Bicycling is another way to see Dublin. There are several dozen bicycle rental shops in the city. Rates average about £7 per day and £30 per week. In fact, there is a bike rental shop, called Rent-a-Bike, right around the corner from the Busaras station, at the corner of Lower Gardener Street and French Lane. If you do rent a bicycle to see Dublin, please use caution. The main thoroughfares in the city are often congested with traffic, especially at rush hour. However, once you get out of the heart of the city, bicycling is quite pleasant.

The **Dublin Area Rapid Transit** (**DART**) is an electrified train that reaches from Dublin's city center to outlying communities as far north as Howth and as far south as Bray. It runs every fifteen minutes (every five minutes during rush hours) from 6:30 am until 11:30 pm. If you are heading north on the DART, you need to be on the west platform, and if you are headed south, you should be on the east platform. These green trains are models of efficiency that zip their passengers to their destinations swiftly and relatively quietly. DART has a well-deserved reputation for timeliness, and you can practically set your watch by it. Fares are reasonable and distance-dependent. You can purchase an all-day DART pass for £3.20 if you plan to ride it for more than just a few trips. There is no smoking on DART and the fine for doing so is £400!

At some stations you may feel a moment's disorientation due to the use of a common word in an uncommon manner. Watch for signs directing you to the "subway". This is not an underground train with which you may be familiar, but rather a "subterranean walkway" that takes you under the tracks to the exit. If you are really confused, just follow the crowds, or ask someone.

WHERE TO STAY

In Dublin, you have the full spectrum of lodging from which to choose: austere youth hostels to luxurious five-star hotels, and everything in between. I've tried to give you plenty of selections in each price category.

The prices for hotels are typically room prices – that is, you are quoted the rate for a room, no matter how many people stay in it (sometimes they have additional person costs – be sure and ask). However, guest houses, Bed and Breakfasts (B&Bs), and hostels usually quote their prices as "per person sharing" with various numbers of people sharing a room. When you make your reservations, be sure and clarify whether the price is for the room or per person and how many people to a room.

Most hotels in Ireland tack on a service charge to the cost of their rooms. These charges range from 10% to 15%. The proceeds from these charges are divided among the hotel staff – from the maids to the front desk personnel. I have made an effort to identify all the hotels that add a service charge, but it's still a good idea to check if there is a charge and how much it is when you make your reservations.

Most of the hotels have in-room dialing, bathrooms (referred to as ensuite), televisions, hair dryers, coffee and tea facilities, and trousers presses.

DUBLIN'S TOP HOTELS

The following hotels are listed from least to most expensive. You can get more information on each selection in reviews that follow. I've left the numbers at the front of each selection for easy reference in the reviews and on the hotel map.

6. OLIVER ST. JOHN GOGARTY'S YOUTH HOSTEL, *18-21 Anglesea Street, Dublin 2. Tel. (01) 671-1822, fax (01) 671-7637. 27 rooms, 130 beds. Rates for twins: £14 to £18, three beds: £12 to £15, 10 to £18, four beds: £11 to £14, dormitory: £10 to 14. One of the nicest and most comfortable hostels in Ireland.*

22. ARIEL HOUSE, *50 - 52 Lansdowne Road, Dublin 4. Tel. (01) 668-5512, fax (01) 668-5845. 30 rooms. Rates for doubles: £25 to £68, super doubles: £90, suites: £150. Probably the best guest house in Ireland, with a proprietor in the same category!*

14. THE RUSSELL COURT HOTEL, *Harcourt Street, Dublin 2. Tel. (01) 478-4066, fax (01) 478-1576. 48 rooms. Rates for singles: £60, doubles: £82, suites: £82. A gem of a hotel. Mid-range in price, top-flight in ambiance. One of the best-kept secrets in Dublin (but not any more!).*

28. BURLINGTON HOTEL, *Upper Leesom Street, Ballsbridge, Dublin 4. Tel. (01) 660-5222, fax (01) 660-5064, toll-free 800-448-8355. 451 rooms. Rates for singles: £115, doubles: £135, suites: £330. If the Shelbourne exemplifies "old money" grace, the Burlington symbolizes "new money". Plenty of marble, brass and dark wood await you here.*

17. SHELBOURNE HOTEL, *27 St. Stephen's Green, Dublin 2. Tel. (01) 676-6471, fax (01) 661-6006. 164 rooms. Rates for singles: £120 to £135, doubles: £140 to £160, and suites: £265 to £680. The best "old money" elegance in Dublin. The best of the upper-class hotels.*

Youth hostels are typically spartan places to lay your head, get a shower, eat some basic food, and that's about it. Accommodations range from singles to dormitory-style (ten to eighteen beds). Costs are low, ranging from £5 to £10 for the dormitories to the equivalent of B&B rates for a single room (£20+). These days, you'll see "youth" from ages eighteen to seventy (literally), so don't let the label "youth hostel" stop you from considering it if you are looking for inexpensive lodging. Most hostels provide a small cafe or self-catering kitchen (for cooking your own food). Some charge extra for sheets and towels, and some include them in the price. Most take credit cards, some do not. Most do not include breakfast in their prices. All in all, hostels are an excellent way to lower your costs while in Ireland.

In Ireland, there is no set way to list telephone numbers. They used to be listed as a five- or six-digit string of numbers. However, several years ago it became necessary to add a seventh digit to Dublin phone numbers, and the Dubliners haven't decided how best to deal with that. Until they decide on a format, I have Americanized all the telephone numbers for Dublin – any published telephone number in Dublin with less than seven number is out of date. If you're going to call Ireland from the United States to make hotel reservations, you must dial the country code (353 for Ireland; 44 for Northern Ireland), and the city code, then the telephone number. *Sort of.* In the case of Dublin telephone numbers, the city code is 01, but you drop the 0 when dialing. Therefore, if you were calling the Berkeley Court Hotel from the United States, you should dial 011-353-1-497-8275. (011 is the international long distance direct dialing code. 01 is the international code for credit card calls.)

The rates I have listed are "rack" rates. Chances are if you work for a major corporation, or belong to an organization like AAA, you can get a reduced rate, especially in the major hotels.

"All major credit cards accepted" means Access, American Express, EuroCard, MasterCard, and Visa. If any one of these is not accepted, I have specifically listed those that are accepted.

Finally, you'll see that I've numbered the hotels in this section to correspond with the hotel map on page 137.

NORTH DUBLIN

At Or Near The Airport

1. FORTE CREST HOTEL, *Dublin Airport, Dublin 9, Tel. (01) 844-4211, fax (01) 842-5874. 188 rooms. Rates for singles: £79 to £89, doubles: £85 to £95. One restaurant and one bistro. All major credit cards accepted. 15% service charge.*

The only hotel located at the airport, the Forte Crest serves business travelers well. The rooms are about average size, but nicely furnished and very comfortable. They offer a business center with secretarial services and conference facilities that can accommodate up to 150 people. There is a shuttle bus that runs from the hotel to the airport on demand.

2. THE DOYLE SKYLON HOTEL, *Drumcondra Road, Dublin 9, Tel. (01) 837-9121, fax (01) 837-2778, US toll free 800-448-8355. 90 rooms. Rates for singles: £83, doubles: £103. One restaurant and one bar. All major credit cards accepted. 15% service charge.*

This is probably the most basic of the Doyle Hotel Group properties. On the main road into Dublin from the airport, the Doyle Skylon is a rather uninspiring building from the outside, and mostly functional on the inside. The main floor was recently remodeled, and the results are very nice, especially in the new bar and Rendezvous Restaurant. The rooms are a nice size, but they lack some of the plushness of other Doyle properties.

The Doyle Skylon is a convenient place for conducting business if that is what brings you to Dublin.

O'Connell Street District

3. ISAACS YOUTH HOSTEL, *2 French Lane, Dublin 1, Tel. (01) 836-3877. 200 beds. Rates for singles: £17, six bed dorms: £7.75, 12 bed dorms: £6.25. No credit cards accepted – cash only! No service charge.*

One of the most spartan of the spartan, Isaacs Youth Hostel is nonetheless clean and inexpensive. The rooms are generally just large enough to house the number of beds they are made for. There are large lockers in each of the dorm rooms. They are not large enough to hold a standard suitcase, but certainly large enough to store any objects you may be uncomfortable leaving out, such as cameras. Common bathrooms and showers serve each of the dorm room floors and men and women do not stay on the same floors.

There is no restaurant or cafe, but there is a self-catering kitchen on the premises.

The Isaacs Youth Hostel is located just around the corner from the Busaras bus station. Ask around for the hostel – the employees all know where it is. I wasn't overly impressed with the neighborhood; it was marginal at best.

4. THE ROYAL DUBLIN HOTEL, *O'Connell Street, Dublin 1, Tel. (01) 873-3666, fax (01) 873-3120. 117 rooms. Rates for singles: £70 to £93, doubles: £84 to £114, and suites: £140 to £170. One restaurant. All major credit cards accepted. No service charge.*

Don't be fooled by the name. The Royal Dublin isn't very royal. Perhaps a better name would be The *Functional* Dublin. This older hotel is located right on O'Connell Street, but lacks the elegance and finery of some of the other hotels in the area. It is certainly not a dump, but the rooms are small and uninspiring, and were in bad need of fresh paint and new carpeting. But it is functional, and if you really want to stay on O'Connell Street, it's a decent choice.

LONGFIELD'S HOTEL

ARIEL HOUSE

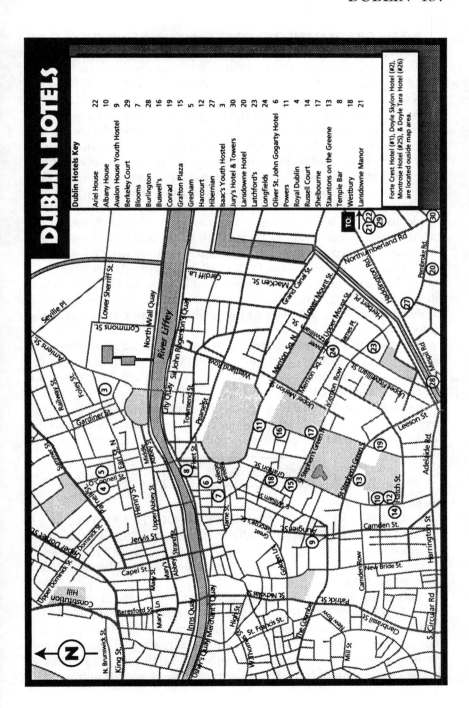

DUBLIN HOTELS

Dublin Hotels Key

Ariel House	22
Albany House	10
Avalon House Youth Hostel	9
Berkeley Court	29
Blooms	7
Burlington	28
Buswell's	16
Conrad	19
Grafton Plaza	15
Gresham	5
Harcourt	12
Hibernian	27
Isaac's Youth Hostel	3
Jury's Hotel & Towers	30
Lansdowne Hotel	20
Latchford's	23
Longfields	24
Oliver St. John Gogarty Hotel	6
Powers	11
Royal Dublin	4
Russell Court	14
Shelbourne	17
Stauntons on the Greene	13
Temple Bar	8
Westbury	18
Lansdowne Manor	21

Forte Crest Hotel (#1), Doyle Skylon Hotel (#2), Montrose Hotel (#25), & Doyle Tara Hotel (#26) are located ouside map area.

5. THE GRESHAM HOTEL, *23 Upper O'Connell Street, Dublin 1, Tel. (01) 874-6881, fax (01) 878-7175. 206 rooms. Rates for singles: £ 125 to £140, doubles: £150 to £180, suites: £200, £250, £400, £500. One restaurant and two pubs. Free parking for guests. All major credit cards accepted. 12.5% service charge.*

Built in 1817, the Gresham Hotel was probably something to behold back then. Now, the marble in the lobby is a little older and the chandelier doesn't gleam quite as brightly. But it is still a fine hotel, and speaks more of elegance, grace, and refinement than the many new hotels with their brass and Italian marble. Old it may be, but run-down it is not. Freshly painted walls in cream and light yellow give it a bright and cheery feeling.

The Gresham has served as the host for many important and famous people in the world, including Ronald Reagan, Dwight Eisenhower, Richard Burton and Elizabeth Taylor, Bob Hope, and other luminaries. The rooms are nice and large, and are tastefully furnished. Those at the front of the hotel overlook busy O'Connell Street with all its comings and goings. These rooms are a little noisier (though not too bad). If you like quieter surroundings, ask for a room away from the front. They also have a range of nice suites, although a little smaller than you'd expect from a four-star hotel.

For those who are traveling on business, there is a 24-hour business center equipped with secretarial assistance, PCs with standard software, and a laser printer. Their on-site travel agency is also helpful in the event you need to adjust flight arrangements.

Close to a number of museums, the theater district, and shopping on Henry Street, The Gresham is also an easy five to ten minute walk to Trinity College and Grafton Street.

SOUTH DUBLIN

Temple Bar District

6. OLIVER ST. JOHN GOGARTY'S YOUTH HOSTEL, *18-21 Anglesea Street, Dublin 2, Tel. (01) 671-1822, fax (01) 671-7637. 27 rooms, 130 beds. Rates for twins: £14 to £18, three beds: £12 to £15, £10 to £18, four beds: £11 to £14, dormitory: £10 to 14. One cafe. American Express, MasterCard, and Visa accepted. No service charge.*

This is the newest and one of the nicest youth hostels in Ireland. Opened in October 1995, it is in very good condition, with new plumbing, comfortable (albeit bunk) beds, and clean linens. The small cafe provides a continental breakfast for £1.10 or a full breakfast for £2.95. There is a television room if you need to rest your tired feet after a long day trekking around Dublin. Often, youth hostels are not in the best parts of town, but this is not the case with Gogarty's. If you are looking for budget accommodations in Dublin, this is the place to stay. As it gets better known, you may find it difficult to just drop in and get a room. I was there recently in the winter, and they were already taking reservations for the summer months. So make your reservations in advance.

7. THE BLOOMS HOTEL, *6 Anglesea Street, Dublin 2, Tel. (01) 671-5622, fax (01) 671-5997. 86 rooms. Rates for singles: £55 to £65, doubles: £65 to £75. One restaurant, one cafe and one pub/nightclub. All major credit cards accepted. 12.5% service charge.*

The Blooms Hotel is located in the heart of the Temple Bar District, and is a relatively inexpensive hotel in the heart of Dublin. They are refurbishing many of the rooms – new paint, upgraded bathrooms, new furniture, etc. Typical of Irish hotels, the rooms are on the small side, although they are comfortable. Several of the rooms have balconies, which are nice in the spring and summer, although the views are mostly of the tops of Dublin buildings.

Their nightclub plays live music seven nights a week, and the music can be dimly heard throughout most of the hotel. If you are accustomed to turning in early, or are bothered by a little noise, you may want to look elsewhere.

8. TEMPLE BAR HOTEL, *Fleet Street, Dublin 2, Tel. (01) 677-3333, fax (01) 677-3088. 108 rooms. Rates for singles: £90, doubles: £120, suites: £150. Rates include breakfast. One restaurant and one disco bar. All major credit cards accepted. No service charge.*

Don't let the unconvincing exterior dissuade you from staying at the Temple Bar Hotel (although the rates might). The hotel itself is very nice and comfortable. The rooms are good sized and comfortably if not lavishly decorated. The bathrooms are upgraded and modern. The Terrace restaurant serves Temple Bar Hotel patrons as well as the public. It's a pleasant, light and airy restaurant.

This hotel does a lot of travel package business, so they are relatively full most of the year. A little pricey for my taste, especially compared to some of the other hotels in the area.

Grafton Street District

9. AVALON HOUSE YOUTH HOSTEL, *55 Aungier Street, Dublin 2, Tel. (01) 475-0001, fax (01) 475-0303. 185 beds. Rates for singles: £14 to £17, twins: £11 to £14, four beds: £9 to £12, dormitory: £7.50 to £10.50 (rates include light continental breakfast). One cafe. American Express, MasterCard, and Visa accepted. Cafe on site. No service charge.*

The Avalon House Youth Hostel is probably the busiest and offers the most amenities of any of the hostels in Dublin. There is a small cafe in the Avalon House, as well as a Bureau de Change, self-catering kitchen facilities, laundry service, TV room, luggage storage, and secure bicycle storage. Linens are provided in the rate. The cafe had a wonderful bohemian feel and always seems to be busy.

All twin and single rooms are ensuite (have bathrooms), but the larger rooms and the dormitory rooms share community bathrooms. None of the rooms are huge, but you'll marvel at the way they utilize every available square foot. Men and women share the same shower facilities, each shower having its own locking stall.

The only real drawback to the Avalon House is that the neighborhood didn't "feel" as good as most of the others in this guide. I am a little uneasy walking some of the dark side streets around the Avalon House at night.

10. ALBANY HOUSE BED AND BREAKFAST, *84 Harcourt Street, Dublin 2, Tel. (01) 475-1092. 13 rooms. Rates for singles: £50, doubles: £35 per person sharing. All major credit cards accepted. No restaurant. No service charge.*

This lovely old Georgian mansion is inviting from the moment you step into the lobby, which is dominated by a large fireplace. The rooms, typical for these Georgian mansions, are large and spacious, and the furnishings are lovely. The Albany House is located just up the street from the southwest corner of St. Stephen's Green on Harcourt Street.

11. THE POWERS HOTEL, *42-47 Kildare Street, Dublin 2, Tel. (01) 679-4388, fax (01) 679-4914. 32 rooms. Rates for singles: £45, doubles: £65. Rates include breakfast. One restaurant. All major credit cards accepted. No service charge.*

Just before going to press, the Powers Hotel was under extensive renovation, so it's a little difficult to fairly judge it. It is an older hotel – a converted Georgian home, and it appeared to be feeling its age. But it is clean and is convenient to Grafton Street, Trinity College, and St. Stephen's Green. There is no elevator, so if you're not into climbing stairs, this will present a problem.

12. THE HARCOURT HOTEL, *60 Harcourt Street, Dublin 2, Tel. (01) 478-3677, fax (01) 475-2013. 53 rooms. Rates for singles: £40 to £50, doubles: £60 to £80, and suites: £100 to £120. Rates include breakfast. One pub and nightclub. All major credit cards accepted. No service charge.*

The Harcourt Hotel is located just up the street from St. Stephen's Green and Grafton Street. Like so many of the hotels and guesthouses in Dublin, the Harcourt Hotel is a conversion of three old Georgian townhouses. Prior to its conversion into a hotel, George Bernard Shaw rented a room in one of the townhomes from 1874 to 1876. His portrait hangs in the lobby, and his stern visage stares down at guests. Unfortunately, the rooms and furnishings in the hotel are unremarkable, and the hotel has a bit of a tired feeling.

The rooms feel small and cramped, even though most have high ceilings that usually offset the smallness of the room. About half the rooms have their own bath and shower, and there are shared bathrooms for the rest.

The pub and nightclub on the premises provide live music seven nights a week, from traditional Irish to jazz to New Age.

13. STAUNTONS ON THE GREEN, *83 St. Stephens Green South, Dublin 2, Tel. (01) 478-2300, fax (01) 478-2263. 38 rooms. Rates for singles: £48 to £55, doubles: £66 to £85, suites: £105 to £130. Rates include breakfast. No service charge.*

On the south side of St. Stephen's Green, Stauntons is a series of converted Georgian townhouses. The rooms are large and no two are the same. The rooms at the front of the house overlook St. Stephen's Green and those at the back of the hotel overlook pretty gardens. If you are overly-sensitive to traffic noise, forego the views of the Green and opt for the views of the garden. The rooms are all comfortable and functional, although quite basic.

14. THE RUSSELL COURT HOTEL, *Harcourt Street, Dublin 2, Tel. (01) 478-4066, fax (01) 478-1576. 48 rooms. Rates for singles: £60, doubles: £82, suites: £82. Rates include continental breakfast. One restaurant, a pub and several lounges. All major credit cards accepted. 12.5% service charge.*

What a find! The Russell Court Hotel is one of the best-kept secrets in Dublin. They do not advertise because they have a loyal clientele – mostly business people – that keeps them full all year long.

From the moment you walk into this hotel – three converted Georgian townhouses – you'll feel comfortable and at home. No two rooms are alike, except for the fact that they are all large, with high ceilings and beautifully decorated. Rich wood molding, solid wood doors, and attention to detail in every respect makes this a beautiful hotel. Combine all that with its close proximity to Grafton Street and St. Stephen's Green, and you've got a great place to stay.

On site is Dicey Reilly's Pub, with a beer garden that's very popular in the spring and summer, and four nights a week of live music, from traditional Irish to jazz to contemporary.

If you want to stay here, you'd better make your reservations several months in advance, because they are a favorite and it may be difficult to get a room if you don't.

15. GRAFTON PLAZA HOTEL, *2 Johnson's place, Dublin 2, Tel. (01) 475-0888, fax (01) 475-0908. 75 rooms. Rates for singles: £75, doubles: £95, suites: £115. Restaurant and pub/nightclub. All major credit cards accepted. No service charge.*

The Grafton Plaza is located just around the corner from Grafton Street and all the activities that abound there. The rooms at the Grafton Plaza are not big, but light, cheery and nicely furnished. They reminded me of a standard Marriott room in the US, just a little smaller.

The Grafton Plaza sports an interesting pub and disco. The pub is quite large with a large square serving island. Plenty of room for talking, drinking, and enjoying the atmosphere.

16. BUSWELL'S HOTEL, *25 Molesworth Street, Dublin 2, Tel. (01) 676-4013, fax (01) 676-2090. 60 rooms. Rates for singles: £78, doubles: £130. Rates include breakfast. One restaurant and bar. All major credit cards accepted. No service charge.*

This nice older hotel is just a few steps from the Leinster House and the National Museum. The hotel has recently undergone extensive renovation, and the results are marvelous. As you walk into the lobby, you'll be impressed with the deep blue carpet that complements the rich dark wood reception desk. The rooms are decent size, although there are a few that are a bit small.

The restaurant is the Emily Room, and it is known locally as a restaurant of quiet elegance. The silver and crystal and linen table cloths make for a nice dining experience.

Perhaps a little on the expensive side for what you get, Buswell's is still a nice place to stay. It is close to Grafton Street but far enough away that it has a less harried feel.

17. SHELBOURNE HOTEL, *27 St. Stephen's Green, Dublin 2, Tel. (01) 676-6471, fax (01) 661-6006. 164 rooms. Rates for singles: £120 to £135, doubles: £140 to £160, and suites: £265 to £680. One restaurant and two bars. All major credit cards accepted. 15% service charge.*

The Shelbourne Hotel receives my vote for the nicest of the nice in Dublin. From the rich dark wood to the lovely antique Waterford crystal chandelier in the Lord Mayor's lounge, to the flawless service, you'll be delighted with every aspect of your stay at the Shelbourne.

The Shelbourne isn't as flamboyant as some of the other brass and crystal hotels you'll find in Dublin. Instead, it is all grace and grandeur, refinement and splendor. No impressive lobby awaits your arrival, but a rather understated journey from the front door to the reception desk. But that's all that is understated. The rooms and the furnishings, the fine equestrian art, and the ambiance are as rich and lovely as you'll find in Dublin.

The Shelbourne, like so many other hotels in Dublin, is three Georgian townhouses, converted in 1824. The rooms are large and spacious, and no two are alike in their layout, size, or decor. All the rooms are lavishly furnished, and they are all very comfortable. Ask for a room overlooking St. Stephen's Green – the views are among the best in Dublin.

For a treat, ask to see the Presidential Suite – more fondly referred to as the Princess Grace Room in honor of that grand lady's stay here several years prior to her death. It is a large, attractive, multi-roomed suite overlooking St. Stephen's Green. Near one of the windows is a picture of

Princess Grace, and it adds a touch of, well...*grace*...to the room! If the room is not occupied, the front desk staff assures me it is possible to have a short tour.

History buffs will be interested to know that the Irish Constitution was drafted in the Shelbourne in 1922. The Shelbourne boasts many heads of state, actors and actresses, and many of the world's *glitterati* as their honored guests. And you will feel equally honored during your stay here.

18. WESTBURY HOTEL, *Grafton Street, Dublin 2, Tel. (01) 679-1122, fax (01) 679-7078, US toll free 800-423-6953. 156 rooms. Rates for singles: £155, doubles: £175, suites: £275 to £565. Two restaurants and one bar. All major credit cards accepted. 15% service charge.*

Your first view of the Westbury Hotel will help you understand why this is one of the brightest gems in the Doyle Hotel Group tiara. The contemporary lobby, decorated in cream and red marble with brass and crystal aplenty, lets you know your high expectations will likely be met. Comfortable sofas and chairs are placed throughout the lobby where guests can visit quietly, take afternoon tea, or simply enjoy the serene splendor of the hotel. The grand piano tinkling in the background adds to the quiet ambiance that is the Westbury Hotel.

The rooms are smallish by American standards, although they are nicely decorated. The modern furniture is almost plush. The junior and senior suites were much nicer. Cherry wood desks and tables add to the rich and extravagant setting.

The Russell Room is their elegant and graceful restaurant, and downstairs is the Sandbank Seafood Bar with its rich wood and brass furnishings. A small fitness center with rowing machine, stair stepper, and treadmill are available to help you work off some of those calories you are sure to consume during your stay.

Another plus for the Westbury Hotel is its location: just a half block off Grafton Street (even though their address is given as Grafton Street), it is in the hub of activity in Dublin. Free parking for guests is included.

19. CONRAD HOTEL, *Earlsfort Terrace, Dublin 2, Tel. (01) 676-5555, fax (01) 676-5424, US toll free 800-Hilton. 191 rooms. Rates for singles: £165, doubles: £190, suites: £365 to £720. Two restaurants and one pub. All credit cards accepted. 15% service charge.*

If it feels as though you have walked into a Hilton when you enter the lobby of the Conrad, it is because the Conrad is a part of the Hilton Hotels group. From its glimmering marble and brass lobby to its ultra-luxurious Presidential Suite, everything is top quality.

The rooms are ample size, and very nicely decorated with quality furnishings and soft salmon-colored decor. The Conrad is also one of the few hotels in Ireland that is air conditioned. Most of the rooms have relatively boring views, but the rooms in the front of the hotel overlook the National Concert Hall across the street. When there is a concert (most nights), the Concert Hall is lit up and makes for a stunning view out your bedroom window. The suites are spacious and lavish, and are among the nicest in all of Ireland. Most of their guests are business travelers.

The Alexandra Restaurant offers elegant dining. There is also a more informal cafe-style dining facility, the Plurabelle, which offers a more relaxed and less expensive meal.

Ballsbridge District

20. LANSDOWNE HOTEL, *27 Pembroke Road, Dublin 4, Tel. (01) 668-2522, fax (01) 668-2309, US toll free 800-527-3460. 30 rooms. Rates for singles: £30 to £50, doubles: £50 to £90. One restaurant and one pub. MasterCard and Visa accepted. No Seville charge.*

This converted Georgian townhouse is in a very quiet residential neighborhood in Georgian Dublin. Set back off the street a little further than most of the hotels in this area, you will be assured of a quiet and pleasant stay. The rooms are large and plainly decorated. The furnishings are functional and comfortable, although not particularly memorable.

The Green Blazer Bar is the pub located in the basement of the hotel, and it is a pleasant place to quaff your thirst and meet some of the locals, who always seem willing to talk to you.

21. LANSDOWNE MANOR GUEST HOUSE, *46 - 48 Lansdowne Road, Dublin 4, Tel. (01) 668-8848, fax (01) 668-8873. 22 rooms. Rates for singles: £40 to £50, doubles: £60 to £90, suites: £70 to £120. Rates include breakfast. All major credit cards accepted. No service charge.*

This four-star guest house is a lovely converted Victorian house. The rooms, typical of converted townhomes, are large and the light paint makes each room feel expansive. They are tastefully decorated. Lansdowne Manor is located in a very nice, low-crime Ballsbridge area. Many of the overflow guests from the five star Berkely Court Hotel are referred to Lansdowne Manor.

22. ARIEL HOUSE, *50 - 52 Lansdowne Road, Dublin 4, Tel. (01) 668-5512, fax (01) 668-5845. 30 rooms. Rates for doubles: £25 to £68, superior doubles: £90, suites: £150. Rates include breakfast. MasterCard and Visa accepted. No service charge.*

Without a doubt, one of the warmest welcomes and most pleasant stays you can have in Ireland is at the Ariel House. Three Victorian (not Georgian) townhouses, built in the 1850s, have been converted into the award-winning "Best Small Hotel in Ireland" for 1995. Michael O'Brien, who has been the proprietor of Ariel House since 1960, is your gracious host. Referred to by some as the grandfather of the Bed and Breakfast industry in Ireland, Mr. O'Brien is a pleasure to visit with.

The front sitting room is furnished with comfortable leather chairs surrounded by antiques all situated before a lovely fireplace. Twenty of the thirty rooms are furnished almost exclusively with furniture from the Victorian era. (Ask Mr. O'Brien why Victorian furniture is so much better suited as B&B furniture than Georgian furniture.) The rooms range from lovely to elegant. Ask to see the junior and senior honeymoon suites, also called the presidential suites depending on the occasion. They are nothing short of spectacular. The large four-poster bed, the seven foot tall armoire, and the crystal chandelier complement one another nicely and combine for a marvelous effect.

There are an additional ten rooms added onto the back of Ariel House that are strictly functional. Their style and feel are more like small hotel rooms, and are a let-down after seeing the rest of the house. But they are less expensive than the other rooms, and are a nice clean place to stay. All rooms in the hotel have upgraded bathrooms, televisions, ironing boards and hair dryers.

While Ariel House is several miles from downtown Dublin, it is one hundred yards from the Lansdowne DART station, only about a three minute ride to downtown.

23. LATCHFORDS OF BAGGOT STREET, *99 - 100 Lower Baggot Street, Tel. (01) 676-0784, fax (01) 662-2764. 22 rooms. Rates for studios: £45 to £69, superior studios: £60 to £85, one bedroom: £55 to £79, two bedroom: £60 to £99. One restaurant. All major credit cards accepted. No service charge.*

Latchfords offers self-catering for those who want to cut corners by cooking their own food while on vacation. Each room is furnished with an efficiency refrigerator, microwave oven (some have hot plates), and a sink. The rooms in this converted Georgian townhouse are large and high-ceilinged and brightly decorated. There is a separate entrance to the facility which guests are given a key to, so that they can come and go as they please without the need of a night manager.

If you tire of eating your own cooking, next door is Latchfords, one of the most affordable restaurants in the area.

24. LONGFIELD'S HOTEL, *10 Fitzwilliam Street Lower, Tel. (01) 676-1367, fax (01) 676-1542. 28 rooms. Rates for singles: £83, doubles: £99, superior doubles: £115. One restaurant. All major credit cards accepted. No service charge.*

Longfield's Hotel has all the ingredients that make for a nice stay: lovely comfortable rooms, and personable, outgoing staff. This is one of the nicest hotels in Dublin.

Located just a few blocks east of St. Stephen's Green, Longfield's is a converted Georgian townhouse. The rooms are nice size – not huge – with tall ceilings and light colors. All the rooms are ensuite, although some have a shower with no bathtub, so if that matters to you, be sure and specify that you want a tub. The rooms that overlook Fitzwilliam Street are a little noisy due to traffic, so you may want to request a room at the back of the hotel. There is an elevator, by the way.

Number 10 Restaurant is located in the basement of Longfield's, and it is one of the best restaurants in Dublin. And their lunch menu is every bit as exquisite as their dinner menu at half the price.

25. MONTROSE HOTEL, *Stillorgan Road, Dublin 4, Tel. (01) 269-3311, fax (01) 269-1164, US toll free 800-448-8355. 179 rooms. Rates for singles: £83, doubles: £103. One restaurant and one pub. All major credit cards accepted. 15% service charge.*

The Montrose Hotel on the southern outskirts of Dublin is another outstanding hotel belonging to the Doyle Hotel Group. It recently received an extensive (and expensive) facelift – inside as well as outside. The results are a success.

The bedrooms fared well in the renovation. Fresh paint, new wall paper, furnishings, and carpet make these rooms pleasant and luxurious. Mahogany furniture and marbled bathrooms give the Montrose a plush feeling. The suites are equally as spacious and luxurious, and you'll be impressed not only with their size, but with the lavishness of the furnishings. Belfield Bar is a good pub located on the premises, with an open fireplace welcoming weary travelers as well as locals. The restaurant – the Belfield Room – provides elegant dining in a bright atmosphere.

Unlike most of the hotels in this guide, the Montrose is a little removed from the action. It is about a fifteen minute cab ride from the city center, and is a bit too far to walk. Still, it is a lovely hotel, and if your plans include trips to the south of Ireland, this is a good jumping-off point.

26. DOYLE TARA HOTEL, *Merrion Road, Dublin 4, Tel. (01) 269-4666, fax (01) 269-1027, US toll free 800-448-8355. 114 rooms. Rates for singles: £83, doubles: £103. One restaurant and one pub. All major credit cards accepted. 15% service charge.*

Perhaps the most prominent feature in the Doyle Hotel Group's Tara Hotel is its view of Dublin Bay. Located only a quarter mile from the bay, the views are outstanding. As with all of the Doyle properties, the lobby is elegant and well-appointed. The feeling carries throughout the facility, from the Joycean Bar and its finely carved dark wood and period furnishings to the contemporary airiness of the Conservatory Restaurant. Despite its loveliness, the Doyle Tara is a little more relaxed than its glitzy sister hotels. The rooms are all large and comfortable, with bright floral patterns on many of the bedspreads and window coverings that complement the cherry wood furnishings. Ask for a room on the Dublin Bay side of the hotel for the views.

The hotel is about four miles from St. Stephen's Green, so it's a bit far to walk. It is about a half mile from the Booterstown DART station, or a short cab ride from the city center.

27. THE HIBERNIAN HOTEL, *Eastmoreland Place, Dublin 4, Tel. (01) 668-7666, fax (01) 660-2566. 40 rooms. Rates for singles: £90 to £95, doubles: £120 to £135, suites: £160. Rates include breakfast. One restaurant. All major credit cards accepted. No service charge.*

Built originally as a nurses' home, this pretty red brick building has been recently converted into a very comfortable hotel. Just off Baggot Street between Ballsbridge and St. Stephen's Green, this hotel offers you both warmth and comfort. The rooms are not huge, but certainly more than ample for the nice cherry wood furnishings in each room. Most of the bathrooms need updating, but they are clean. There is a nice library and lounge for relaxing at the end of a day's sightseeing. The Patrick Kavanaugh Room is their restaurant and features a nice selection.

While the price is a little steep, it is a nice hotel and you'll be impressed with the personal service and warmth of the staff.

28. BURLINGTON HOTEL, *Upper Leesom Street, Ballsbridge, Dublin 4, Tel. (01) 660-5222, fax (01) 660-5064, US toll free 800-448-8355. 451 rooms. Rates for singles: £115, doubles: £135, suites: £330. Two restaurants, one lounge and one pub. All major credit cards accepted. 15% service charge.*

The Doyle Hotel Group certainly seems to know what it is doing when it comes to providing luxurious hotels, and the Burlington Hotel is no exception. Crystal chandeliers, marble and brass, dark wood and plush carpet all welcome you with surprising warmth and gaiety as you enter the lobby of the hotel. The only thing that compares is the warm reception you'll receive from the hotel staff. They seem genuinely glad to see you.

The rooms are large and bright, and the furnishings are top quality. The bathrooms are similarly luxurious. Together they combine to make your stay a pleasant one. The suites are expansive and lavish and filled with lovely comfortable furnishings.

The Burlington Hotel boasts two fine restaurants on their premises: the Sussex and the Diplomat. Both offer elegant surroundings and delicious meals. But my favorite place here is Buck Mulligan's Pub. For nearly twenty years, the Burlington Hotel has hosted a traditional Irish dinner and cabaret that provides a fun and rollicking evening, £33 for the dinner and show, £23 for the show only. The cabaret runs from early May through October.

29. BERKELEY COURT HOTEL, *Lansdowne Road, Ballsbridge, Dublin 4, Tel. (01) 660-1711, fax: (01) 497-8275, US toll free 800-423-6953. 200 rooms. Rates for singles: £155, doubles: £175, suites: £240 to £550; Penthouse Suite: £1,600. Two restaurants and a lounge. All major credit cards accepted. 15% service charge.*

If you want plush, elegant, and the extraordinary, the Berkeley Court Hotel is the place to stay. Another hotel in Dublin belonging to the Doyle Hotel Group, this five-star hotel is about as far as you'll get from the stereotypical one-room cottage warmed by a turf fire. Beautiful furnishings abound. If you have business with the American Embassy, this is a convenient hotel, as the embassy is within a five to ten minute walk.

From the moment you enter the magnificent lobby with its deep blue and gold carpet you'll be transported into a world of luxury that only a handful of hotels in Ireland can offer. There is rich dark paneling in the Royal Court Bar and a serene elegance in the Berkeley Room restaurant. The bedrooms are large and equally as inviting and luxurious as the public rooms. Decorated in soft pastels, the rooms are light and airy, with comfortable, classic furniture.

The Berkeley Court is located in the quiet residential area of Ballsbridge on Lansdowne Street. Its grounds were once the site of the Botanical Gardens of University College Dublin, and much of that beauty has been retained for guests to enjoy.

30. JURY'S HOTEL AND TOWERS, *Pembroke and Lansdowne Roads, Ballsbridge, Dublin 4, Tel. (01) 660-5000, fax (01) 660-5540. 300 rooms. Rates at Jury's Hotel for singles: £123, doubles: £142, suites: £300. Rates at The Towers for singles: £172, doubles: £191, and suites: £350 to £450. Two restaurants, a coffee bar, and a pub. Indoor and outdoor swimming pools, spa, sauna, beauty salon, and masseuse. All major credit cards accepted. 12.5% service charge.*

Jury's Hotel and Towers is in reality two separate hotels – Jury's Hotel and a connected exclusive wing called The Towers. Guests at The Towers share the common facilities of Jury's Hotel: pool, sauna, whirlpool, as well as two restaurants, a coffee bar, and the Dubliner Bar. But separate entrances and electronic locks into The Towers lets you know it's exclusive.

You'll be impressed when you walk into the lobby – modern, plush, and very busy. Unfortunately for the Jury's Hotel, that's the most impressive part of your visit there. The rooms are a little cramped, and the furnishings are underwhelming but functional – far less than you'd expect from a luxury hotel. One of the favorable aspects of the Jury's complex is their internationally famous Irish Cabaret. It runs from early May through October, and makes for a wonderfully enjoyable evening.

The rooms at The Towers, on the other hand, are much larger and more elegantly and tastefully decorated, more befitting the price of the rooms. Their suites are particularly inviting – spacious, elegant, and comfortable. My favorite feature is the television built into a ledge at eye-level with the bathtub! Room rates include a continental breakfast for guests at The Towers. The Towers is air conditioned; Jury's is not.

There are two restaurants associated with the hotel. The Kish restaurant specializes in seafood, and the Embassy Garden Restaurant features international cuisine. Both restaurants are frequented by locals as well as hotel guests.

Jury's Hotel and Towers is located near the American Embassy and a short walk from the business district along Baggot Street. If you're looking for an exclusive lodging experience, The Towers is a good choice. Pay the extra few pounds for a room there rather than in the main part of the hotel.

NORTH OF DUBLIN

31. THE REEFS BED AND BREAKFAST, *Balbriggan Coast Road, Skerries, Co. Dublin. Tel. (01) 849-1574. 4 rooms. Rates for singles: £19.50 to £21.50, doubles: £14.50 to £16.50 per person sharing. Rates include breakfast. No service charge. Open from April 1 through October 31.*

About half an hour north of Dublin lies the small harbor town of Skerries, and less than a mile up the road from Skerries is The Reefs Bed and Breakfast, run by Mrs. Violet Clinton. Views of the sea as well as the Mourne Mountains add spice to this pleasant B&B. Sitting right on the seashore, with views of both the Irish Sea and the Mourne Mountains, this relatively new place is a pleasant place to stay. There is no DART station nearby, so you probably need a car to stay here.

32. THE VILLA BED AND BREAKFAST, *150 Howth Rod, Clontarf, Dublin 3, Tel. (01) 832-2377. 5 bedrooms. Rates for singles: £28, Doubles: £20 per person sharing, Single. Rates include breakfast. No service charge.*

The Villa, run by Mrs. Nuala Beston, is a pleasant older Victorian home set on nice grounds. Inside, the home is comfortable, although a little cramped. But the rooms are nice size, very clean, and comfortable.

33. SHASTON BED AND BREAKFAST, *20 Mount Prospect Avenue, Clontarf, Dublin 3, Tel. (01) 833-6336. 3 rooms. Rates for singles: £28, doubles: £20 per person sharing. Breakfast included in rates. No service charge. Open March 1 through October.*

Mrs. Ann O'Dolan runs a nice B&B. This beautiful home is tastefully and richly decorated, and is a pleasant place to stay. Since it is in Clontarf, you're within easy reach of the airport as well as the city center.

34. AISHLING HOUSE BED AND BREAKFAST, *20 St. Laurence Road, Clontarf, Dublin 3, Tel. (01) 833-9097, fax (01) 833-840. 9 rooms. Rates for singles: £28, doubles: £20 per person sharing. Rates include breakfast.*

Aishling House is run by Joe and Mary Mooney. A lovely Victorian residence, you'll not be disappointed in either the furnishings or the welcome you'll receive here. Aishling House has an impressive collection of antiques, as well as a lovely Waterford crystal chandelier. In addition, the dining room features crystal and crisp, starched Irish linen to complement your breakfast. And what a breakfast it is! Mrs. Mooney does a wonderful job of whipping up a tasty Irish breakfast of eggs, bacon, brown bread, and coffee.

35. DEER PARK HOTEL, *Howth, Co. Dublin, Tel. (01) 832-2624, fax (01) 839-2405. 49 rooms. Rates for singles: £25, doubles: £35 to £41. Rates include breakfast. One restaurant. All major credit cards accepted. No service charge.*

The setting for the Deer Park Hotel is probably as green and serene as any in Ireland. The hotel is surrounded by five golf courses and a thirty acre rhododendron patch, with a view of the Irish Sea that prompted H.G. Wells to describe it as "the finest view west of Naples."

With all that beauty, the hotel itself pales in comparison. With fresh paint and wallpaper, as well as an interior decorator's touch, the hotel could be spectacular. Instead, it feels much like a 1960s era hotel. The rooms are large, and the furnishings adequate.

If you don't drive from Dublin, the best way to get to the hotel is to call a cab. The hotel is about a mile from the DART station, but the last half mile or so is uphill, and would be a bear if you were carrying luggage. However, if you have little or no luggage, and the weather is nice, it is a beautiful twenty minute walk from the DART station. Turn right as you leave the Howth DART Station, and the entrance to Deer Park Hotel is about one half mile down the road on your left. From there, you have a another half-mile walk (slightly uphill) to reach the hotel. They have no shuttle bus.

36. HOWTH LODGE HOTEL, *Howth, Co. Dublin, Tel. (01) 832-1010, fax (01) 832-2268. 46 rooms. Rates for singles: £50 to £75, doubles: £68 to £95. Rates include breakfast. One restaurant, one bistro and one pub. All major credit cards accepted. No service charge.*

Nestled comfortably beside the sea, Howth Lodge Hotel offers beautiful scenery and fresh sea breezes. Family owned and operated by the Hanratty family, you'll feel more like a guest in their home than a patron at their hotel. Many of the rooms have views of the sea and the impressive "Ireland's Eye" – a quartzite island that sits just offshore. Once the site of a 7th-century monastery, the island is now a bird sanctuary.

Back to Howth Lodge — the views *are* distracting! The rooms themselves are large and bright and cheery. They are furnished comfortably and tastefully. The hotel recently added a nice leisure center with a swimming pool, gym and weight room, jacuzzi, steam room/sauna, and a beauty salon. They even have a tanning room (for a small fee). Their restaurant is a popular place for Dubliners. Specialties are seafood, caught fresh each day by local fishermen, and steak, for which they are deservedly proud.

If you take the DART to Howth, your two options to get to the hotel are to catch a taxi or walk. The walk is very pleasant, only about ten minutes from the Howth DART station, which is about a twenty minute ride from downtown. Turn right as you leave the DART station, and Howth Lodge is about one half mile down the road on your right.

SOUTH OF DUBLIN

37. HARKIN HOUSE BED AND BREAKFAST, *7 Claremont Villas, Glenageary, Dun Laoghaire, County Dublin, Tel. (01) 280-5346. 5 rooms. Rates for singles: £21 to £23, doubles: £16 to £18 per person sharing. Breakfast included in the rate. No service charge.*

If you like well-kept Victorian homes, try this Bed and Breakfast run by Mrs. Ann Harkin. This spacious home is in a quiet upscale residential area. The rooms are nice sized, and the greeting warm and cheery.

38. ANNESGROVE BED AND BREAKFAST, *28 Rosmeen Gardens, Dun Laoghaire, Co. Dublin, Tel. (01) 280-9801. 4 rooms. Rates for singles: £21 to £23.50, doubles: £16 to £18.50 per person sharing. Breakfast included in the rate. No service charge.*

Mrs. Anne d'Alton runs the lovely Annesgrove, located in a quiet neighborhood. Annesgrove is relatively close to the Sandycove DART Station.

39. CHESTNUT LODGE, *2 Vesey Place, Monkstown, Tel. (01) 280-7860, (01) 280-1466. 5 rooms. Rates for singles: £30 to £38, doubles: £23 to £28 per person sharing. Rates include breakfast. MasterCard and Visa accepted. No service charge.*

Mrs. Nancy Malone's welcome to her mid-19th-century Georgian is as warm as the croissants she prepares for breakfast. The rooms are large and spacious, and the ones at the front of the house have views of chestnut trees and an occasional glimpse of the sea beyond.

40. COURT HOTEL, *Killiney, Co. Dublin, Tel. (01) 285-1622, fax (01) 285-2085. 86 rooms. Rates for singles: £45 to £65, doubles: £82 to £89. Breakfast included in the rates. One restaurant and grill. All major credit cards accepted. 12.5% service charge.*

Killiney Bay provides magnificent views for guests at the Court Hotel. About ten miles south of Dublin, the hotel can be reached either by car or DART. The Killiney DART Station is about one hundred yards from the hotel. In fact, the hotel employees are fond of saying they have their own DART station!

The hotel was formerly a seven-room mansion built about 180 years ago. It has since been renovated and expanded. The rooms are smallish, and many of the back rooms have a rather close-up view of the hillside the hotel is built up against. The front rooms, especially those on the third floor, have beautiful views of Killiney Bay. For the most part, the rooms are not especially memorable, but they are clean and adequate.

41. ROYAL MARINE HOTEL, *Marine Road, Dun Laoghaire, Tel. (01) 280-1911, fax (01) 280-1089. 104 rooms. Rates for singles: £45, doubles: £45 to £100. Restaurant, pub. All major credit cards accepted. 10% service charge.*

Located in Dun Laoghaire overlooking Dublin Bay, the Royal Marine Hotel was probably a pretty nice hotel when built in the 1960s. Today, the original rooms are in need of some good attention: upgraded furnishings, wall coverings, and bathroom facilities. The newer addition is much nicer, and the rooms have more comfortable furnishings and more acceptable decor.

42. FITZPATRICK CASTLE HOTEL, *Killiney Hill Road, Killiney, Co. Dublin. Tel. (01) 284-0700, fax (01) 285-0207. 90 rooms. Rates for singles: £79 to £94, doubles: £96 to £124, suites: £180. Two restaurants, a pub and a nightclub. All major credit cards accepted. 15% service charge.*

The Fitzpatrick Hotel is located about ten miles south of Dublin. Their literature says they are near the DART station, but don't make the mistake of walking there from the Killiney DART Station. It may only be a mile or two (depending on the DART station you get off at), but it is all uphill. They do have a shuttle bus, but they seem to be unable to find anyone to drive it on a consistent basis! Your best bet is to drive there yourself if you have a car.

Originally a castle built in 1741, in recent times it has been renovated by the Fitzpatrick family into a hotel. Before I arrived I had seen several pictures of the hotel, and it looked enchanting. In person, the exterior is old and dumpy, but indoors you'll see that it is enchanting, beginning with the suit of armor near the front desk. The rooms in the hotel are somewhat small, but the tall ceilings give the rooms a larger feel. The furnishings are comfortable and functional, but that's about it. Ask for a room in the front of the hotel. They all have small patios from which you can sit and enjoy the spectacular views of Dublin Bay. They have seven suites, and they are quite nice. Two of them are end rooms, and they have large windows overlooking the bay. Each suite has a jacuzzi.

In addition to the two restaurants (the Truffles Restaurant is popular with Dubliners), the hotel offers other amenities, including a pool, sauna, small gym, aerobics classes, and a beauty salon.

WHERE TO EAT

The Irish are a lively people, insisting on good friends, good pubs, and good food – not necessarily in that order! Fortunately they are all easy to come by in Ireland, and in Dublin in particular. From small bistros to hotel dining rooms to top-notch restaurants, Dublin offers you a wide selection. Over the past few years, Dublin has seen the introduction of a number of fine restaurants, the renovation of a number of older restaurants, and the rapid growth of good ethnic restaurants. French, Italian, Indian, Spanish,

Greek, and Chinese restaurants, as well as just about any other ethnic restaurant you can think of, are now quite plentiful.

Since the majority of the sights in Dublin are south of the River Liffey and Trinity College, most of the restaurants I review are also south of the River Liffey, in the Temple Bar, Grafton Street, and Ballsbridge areas. I've also included several in the suburbs. The Temple Bar and Ballsbridge areas are about a five to ten minute walk from Grafton Street.

For each restaurant, I've included samples of what's on the menu and their price. Remember, however, that prices are subject to change, and restaurants tend to change their menus daily or seasonally. Unless specifically noted, all the prices listed here are for dinner (salad, entree, dessert, and coffee). Often the lunch menus are merely scaled-down versions of the dinner menus, at about half to two-thirds the cost of dinner.

I have also provided their hours of business. In most cases, the closing times listed are the last time they will accept orders, although for many it also depends on business. If business is really slow due to weather or some other reason, they might close a little early; if business is brisk at closing time, they might stay open longer. Most if not all of these restaurants are closed on Christmas and Easter.

"All major credit cards accepted" means Access, American Express, EuroCard, MasterCard, and Visa. If any one of these is not accepted, I have specifically listed those that are. As in the hotel section, I have Americanized the telephone numbers.

Dublin, and most of Ireland, is very casual, and restaurants are no exception. Every restaurant I've been to in Dublin except one (Number 27 the Green) says casual dress is fine, although a number of the more upscale restaurants request no blue jeans or grubbies. In practice, however, most of the clientele in the nicer restaurants wear suit and tie and dresses.

Dublin restaurants automatically tack a 10% to 15% gratuity onto your bill. If you feel the service was exceptional beyond that level, feel free to leave an additional tip. The legal drinking age is eighteen, although many restaurants (especially) and some pubs enforce a house minimum of twenty-one years.

As in the hotel section above, the restaurants are numbered to correspond with the restaurant map on page 157.

DUBLIN'S TOP RESTAURANTS

The following restaurants are listed from least to most expensive. You can get more information on each selection in the reviews that follow.

23. LA STAMPA, *35 Dawson Street. Tel. (01) 677-8611. £8.95 to £17.95. All major credit cards accepted. Despite bad art, the restaurant is considered one of the best in Ireland.*

24. THE IMPERIAL CHINESE RESTAURANT, *13 Wicklow Street. Tel. (01) 677-2580. £9 to £18. All major credit cards accepted. The Imperial Chinese Restaurant is probably the best Chinese restaurant in Dublin, if not the best in Ireland.*

34. NUMBER 10, *10 Fitzwilliam Street Lower. Tel. (01) 676-1367. £13.95 to £24.95. All major credit cards accepted. All things considered (price, service, presentation, flavor, etc.), this is my favorite restaurant in Dublin.*

41. ABBEY TAVERN RESTAURANT, *Abbey Street. Tel. (01) 839-0307. £19 to £24.95, American Express, MasterCard, and Visa accepted. You have to go here just to experience the traditional Irish Cabaret.*

37. LE COQ HARDI, *35 Pembroke Roke Road. Tel. (01) 668-9070. £21.95 to £35. All major credit cards accepted. Quiet dining in an old Georgian mansion, Le Coq Hardi features French cuisine that is marvelous.*

28. THE COMMONS RESTAURANT, *85 - 86 St. Stephen's Green South. Tel. (01) 475-2597. £32 to £42. All major credit cards accepted. Downstairs on the south side of St. Stephen's Green, The Commons Restaurant features candlelight and crystal decor.*

38. RESTAURANT PATRICK GUILBAUD, *46 James Place. Tel. (01) 676-4192. £10 to £46. All major credit cards accepted. Ireland's only Michelin-rated two star restaurant. Wonderful food, fun atmosphere.*

SOUTH DUBLIN

Temple Bar District

The Temple Bar District is south of the River Liffey, and just a few minute's walk west of Trinity College. Cafes dominate here, and as a rule are less expensive than the cafes and restaurants closer to Grafton Street.

1. THE ALAMO, *22 Temple Bar, Tel. (01) 677-6546. £3.95 to £7. Open 10:00 am to midnight Monday through Thursday, and 10:00 am to 12:30 am on Fridays and Saturdays. MasterCard and Visa accepted.*

For a little bit of Tex-Mex, Irish-style, try this little cafe. You'll smile at the "longhorn" skull and horns over the heating stove – it's really a water buffalo skull and horns! The food is typical Mexican fare, such as tacos and chimichangas and is just okay. It just seems strange to me to have Mexican food in Ireland (your call, though)! Very casual dress.

2. CAFE LEOPOLD, *6 Anglesea Street, Tel. (01) 671-5622. £4 to £10. Open every day 10:30 am to 11:30 pm. All major credit cards accepted.*

Located in Bloom's Hotel, this little cafe has a limited menu, but pretty decent food. It has a modern feel and a pleasant chatty atmosphere. Reservations are not required and the dress is casual. Examples of their fare include chicken Kiev and minute steak.

3. PIZZERIA ITALIA, *23 Temple Bar, Tel. (01) 677-8528. £4 to £10. Open every day 12:30 pm to 11:00 pm. No credit cards accepted.*

This is one of the best places in Dublin (and therefore, probably in all of Ireland) to get a pizza. They offer a surprisingly large selection of items in addition to pizza. There's not much in the way of atmosphere; this is just a small eatery with stools and counters around the windows and one long rectangular table with eight chairs. Examples of their selections are Napoli pizza, fettuccine Italia, and spaghetti carbonera. Very casual dress.

4. ELEPHANT & CASTLE, *18/19 Temple Bar, Tel. (01) 679-3121. £4.75 to £10.95. Open from 12:30 pm to 11:30 pm. No reservations taken. All major credit cards accepted.*

Kind of an "art deco in wood" style, this place is pleasant, coffee-shop noisy, and very busy. During the spring and summer seasons you will probably have a bit of a wait during lunch and dinner. The music selection piped in is typically light jazz, and the black and white pictures on the walls are an eclectic assortment, ranging from scenes from the old west to early Dublin. Casual dress.

5. BAD ASS CAFE, *2 Crown Alley, Tel. (01) 671-2596. £5 to £10. Open daily from 9:00 am until 11:00 pm during the winter, and until midnight during the tourist season. All major credit cards accepted.*

To be honest, the reason this is in the book is because it is a pretty popular place to go; why, I don't know. But it does have an almost cult following. It is in an old warehouse, where little has been done to decorate it. The food, like the decor, is underwhelming. They have a variety of dishes, pizza, chicken, steak, and burgers. Perhaps its biggest claim to fame is that Sinead O'Connor worked here prior to making it big. Perhaps that, their "Eeyore-like" logo, or the name contributes to its success. At any rate, it's always pretty full during the tourist season. Casual dress.

6. GALLAGHER'S BOXTY HOUSE, *20-21 Temple Bar, Tel. (01) 677-2762. £5.45 to 12.95. Gallagher's is open from 11:00 am to 11:30 pm Monday though Thursday, and until midnight on Fridays and Saturdays. No reservations. MasterCard and Visa accepted.*

A "boxty" is a potato, but Gallagher's Boxty House offers more than just potatoes. From the sweet smell of the turf fire in the fireplace (a turf

GALLAGHER'S BOXTY HOUSE

WALL ART AT THE AULD DUBLINER PUB

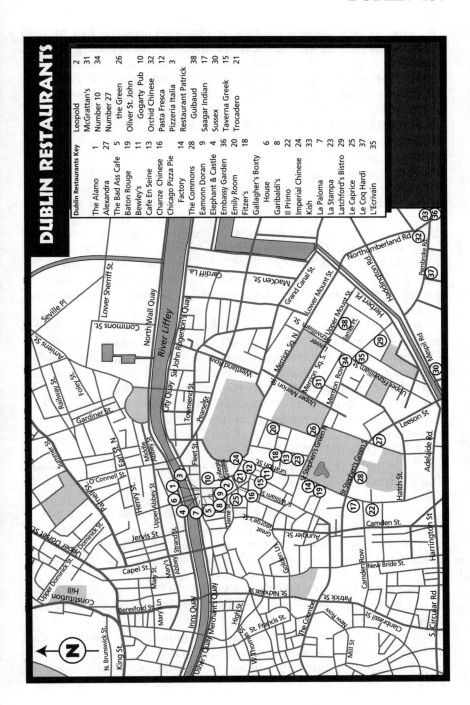

DUBLIN RESTAURANTS

Dublin Restaurants Key		
The Alamo	1	
Alexandra	27	
The Bad Ass Cafe	5	
Baton Rouge	19	
Bewley's	11	
Cafe En Seine	13	
Chanze Chinese	16	
Chicago Pizza Pie Factory	14	
The Commons	28	
Eamonn Doran	9	
Elephant & Castle	4	
Embassy Garden	36	
Emily Room	20	
Fitzer's	18	
Gallagher's Boxty House	6	
Garibaldi's	8	
Il Primo	22	
Imperial Chinese	24	
Kish	33	
La Paloma	7	
La Stampa	23	
Latchford's Bistro	29	
Le Caprice	25	
Le Coq Hardi	37	
L'Ecrivain	35	
Leopold	2	
McGrattan's	31	
Number 10	34	
Number 27		
the Green	26	
Oliver St. John Gogarty Pub	10	
Orchid Chinese	32	
Pasta Fresca	12	
Pizzeria Italia	3	
Restaurant Patrick Guibaud	38	
Saagar Indian	17	
Sussex	30	
Taverna Greek	15	
Trocadero	21	

fire is dried peat moss set ablaze, traditionally used as fuel in the countryside) to the antique pine tables to their Irish Stew, you'll get a very traditional Irish meal and atmosphere here. Menu selections include corned beef and cabbage, poached salmon steak, and Irish stew. They also have a set menu for £9.95, which includes an appetizer, entree, tea or coffee, and dessert.

7. LA PALOMA, *17B Asdylls Road, Tel. (01) 677-7392. Lunch from £3 to £5, dinner £8.95 to 10.95, Open from noon until midnight every evening. MasterCard and Visa accepted.*

This pleasant restaurant is around the corner from Elephant & Castle, and is easy to miss if you're not careful. Dining at this lovely Spanish restaurant is a great way to get away from the bustle, eat tapas and listen to Spanish music. Specialties include Milanesa de Ternera, pollo al chilindron, and their tapas platter, £8.95 each. The dress is casual, and on weekends during the tourist season you'll need reservations.

8. GARIBALDI'S RESTAURANT, *15 - 16 Crown Alley, Tel. (01) 671-7288. £5.50 to £12.95. Open from noon until 11:00 pm during the week, and until midnight on the weekends. They do not take reservations. American Express, MasterCard, and Visa accepted.*

Just a few doors up from The Bad Ass Cafe, this two-story bistro features contemporary, light jazz, and blues music playing unobtrusively in the background. Modern and impressionistic artwork graces the walls. Ask for a table on the second floor. They pride themselves on their use of fresh Irish ingredients, and they have their own butcher to ensure the best cuts of fresh meat. Their specialties are seafood and various meat dishes, including fresh salmon, T-bone steak, and a variety of burgers. Casual dress.

9. EAMONN DORAN, *3A Crown Alley, Tel. (01) 679-9773. £6.50 to £14.95. Open from 11:30 am to 11:00 pm Monday through Saturday. Reservations are recommended during the tourist season, especially on weekends. All major credit cards accepted.*

This restaurant is sort of a cross between a pub, a cafe, and a restaurant. There are lots of interesting pictures on the wall to keep you entertained as you wait for your meal. Some of their specialties are Gaeltacht chicken, Irish salmon dijonaise, and New York sirloin steak (with Irish beef, of course). Casual dress.

10. OLIVER ST. JOHN GOGARTY, *58 - 59 Fleet Street, Tel. (01) 288-4707. £7.95 to £14.95. Open every day from 12:30 pm until late. All major credit cards accepted.*

"Pub grub" is getting increasingly more popular in Ireland, and the traditional Irish food served at Oliver St. John Gogarty's pub is among the best. The crowded, noisy atmosphere doesn't detract from the decent food.

Most nights they have traditional Irish music in a small bar upstairs, and there is often Irish music on the first floor also. Dress is very casual.

Grafton Street District

11. BEWLEY'S, *78 - 79 Grafton Street, Tel. (01) 677-6761. £4.95 to £8.95. Open Monday through Friday from 9:00 am to 7:00 pm (until 9:00 pm on Thursdays) and 11:30 am to 6:30 pm on Saturdays. They do not take reservations, but tables turn over quickly. American Express, MasterCard and Visa are accepted.*

Bewley's is sort of a cross between McDonald's and a bistro. There is a very busy cafeteria on the first floor, and a slightly less busy mezzanine section as well as the James Joyce Room. All serve relatively inexpensive and decent fare. Located on Grafton Street, it's a convenient place to stop for a bite to eat while you're shopping. It's worth going to either the mezzanine or the James Joyce Room to look out on the Grafton Street crowd below. Be sure and ask for a table near the window. The fare is simple, consisting mainly of sandwiches. They have a few other dishes such as Chicken Creole and Irish oak smoked salmon. Dress is very casual (it's mostly shoppers).

12. PASTA FRESCA, *2 - 4 Chatham Street (near the Westbury Hotel off Grafton Street), Tel. (01) 475-2597. £3.75 to 9.95. Open Monday through Saturday from 7:30 am to 11:30 pm, and from noon until 8:00 pm on Sundays. MasterCard and Visa accepted.*

The atmosphere in this Italian restaurant is light and cheerful. Their pasta has delighted patrons for over a decade now. Their main claim to fame is that they make their own pasta fresh daily and there always seems to be people in here, especially at lunch time. Examples of items on the menu include fettuccine pasta fresca and bistecca al Pepe. Dress is casual.

13. CAFE EN SEINE, *40 Dawson Street, Tel. (01) 667-4369. £3.95 to £10.95. Open Monday through Friday from 10:30 am until 11:00 pm, and on Sundays from noon until 11:30 pm. All major credit cards accepted.*

This is a trendy cafe on Dawson Street, one block east of Grafton Street. This art-deco, quasi-Parisienne restaurant attracts all kinds – from the bohemian to the business person, from the avant-garde to the traditionalist. Contemporary jazz music greets you as you step into this long restaurant. They specialize in sandwiches and soups. It's worth a stop if only to stroll through and do a little people watching. Offerings include sandwich au poulet, le grand plateau, and filet mignon.

14. THE CHICAGO PIZZA PIE FACTORY, *2 St. Stephen's Green, Tel. (01) 478-1233. £4.95 to £10.95. Open noon to 11:00 pm Monday through Saturday, and 12:30 pm to 10:30 pm Sundays. All major credit cards accepted.*

This is a sports bar, not your local Pizza Hut. It is definitely not a family restaurant, except for Sundays, when the restaurant promotes "family day." Patrons are encouraged to bring their children in, and are entertained in a variety of ways – from jugglers to face painters to balloon animal sculptors.

The Chicago Pizza Pie Factory is a large, well-lit restaurant and bar with a fun and lively atmosphere. Thursday through Saturday evenings there's a disco, with many of the chairs and tables in their large dining area cleared out for dancing. The rest of the week they have a juke box in the early evening and a disk jockey for later on. The food isn't gourmet, but it is filling. They have pizza (of course), and an assortment of burgers. Dress is casual.

15. TAVERNA GREEK RESTAURANT, *33 Wicklow Street. £6.95 to £12.95. Open Monday through Saturday from noon until midnight, and Sundays from 3:00 pm until 11:30 pm. Reservations are recommended during the tourist season. Diners Club, MasterCard, Visa accepted.*

Absolutely *the* best Greek restaurant in Ireland! Well, actually, according to the owner, it is the *only* Greek restaurant in Ireland. (I did find one other fine Greek restaurant in County Wicklow.) At any rate, this nice little restaurant about a half block off Grafton Street is a great place to visit. It has two rooms, both set with about a dozen small tables, all with red-checkered tablecloths. The Greek music adds to the pleasant atmosphere. If you're lucky, and usually toward the end of the evening, patrons may literally be dancing in the aisles – just enjoying one another's company, the food, and the moment. It's always packed on the weekends and during the tourist season. Try the souvlakia, the lamb kleftiko or if you have the time and appetite, the house special: mezes – three courses of a variety of Greek dishes. The dress is casual.

16. CHANZE, *7 St. Andrews Place, Tel. (01) 679-9866. £6 to £12.95. Open 11:00 am until midnight Monday through Saturday, and 5:00 pm until midnight on Sundays. Reservations are recommended on weekends during the tourist season. All major credit cards.*

This is a nice, quiet Chinese restaurant not far from Grafton Street. While not as upscale as The Imperial Chinese Restaurant (just around the corner), it is roughly half the price. The food is quite good. Try their pork Szechuan, the Cantonese roast duck, or the filet of beef. Casual but nice dress.

17. SAAGAR INDIAN RESTAURANT, *16 Harcourt Street, Tel. (01) 475-5060. £7 to £12.95. Open 7:00 pm until 11:00 pm Monday through Saturday. Reservations are suggested. All major credit cards accepted.*

As I entered Saagar's one evening, I met a journalist friend of mine coming out of the restaurant. He is a food critic for one of the London newspapers, so I figured he'd be a good person to ask about the food. He responded enthusiastically, "This is by far the best Indian food I have had in years, and certainly the best in Ireland." I took that as a pretty sound endorsement (especially because he was exceptionally caustic about other restaurants in the area – none of them in this book).

The owner, Meera Kumar, is proud of his restaurant and likes to point out they are the only Indian restaurant in Ireland that is owned and run by people from India. The chefs, Yen Bhadhur Rawat and Vivek Sahni, are internationally trained and world famous. Examples of dishes they serve include lamb curry, murgh sufed korma, and kachche gosht ki biryani. Dress is casual.

18. FITZER'S CAFE, *51 Dawson Street, Tel. (01) 677-1155. £9.95 to £12.95. Open Monday through Saturday from 10:00 am until midnight. All major credit cards accepted.*

This is a nice, inexpensive eatery located on Dawson Street, which runs parallel to Grafton Street. The atmosphere is relaxed and easy, and it is very casual. The lunch menu items include chicken breast and ricotta cheese (£7.50) and prawns and fried potatoes (£7.95). The dinner menu offers such treats as Duck liver and sweet potatoes (£9.95) and roast duck stuffed with pistachio nuts (£12.95). The cafe has...interesting...artwork on the walls. Dress is casual.

19. BATON ROUGE, *119 St. Stephen's Green West, Tel. (01) 475-1181. £9.95 to £12.95. Open Monday through Saturday from noon to 3:00 pm, and daily from 6:00 pm until 12:30 am. Reservations are recommended year-round on Thursday through Saturday evening, and every night during the tourist season. All major credit cards accepted.*

This trendy New Orleans-style cafe is just south of the end of Grafton Street, across from St. Stephen's Green. You'll find a spacious cafe that specializes in blackened fish dishes. The fish, of course, are of the freshest variety, caught daily in Dublin Bay. They have a live band that plays New Orleans jazz and Dixieland several nights a week. Downstairs they have an enjoyable sing-along piano bar. Very popular with the young folks, it also attracts many business people and tourists. They have a pretty varied menu, including such items as veal la Louisiana, Creole seafood au gratin and blackened fish – the type varies daily. Dress is casual but nice.

20. THE EMILY ROOM, *23 Molesworth, Tel. (01) 676-4013. £7.95 to £14.95. Open daily from 7:30 am to 10:30 am for breakfast, 12:30 pm to 2:30 pm for lunch, and 6:00 pm to 9:30 pm for dinner. Reservations are recommended on the weekends during the tourist season. All major credit cards accepted.*

This is the restaurant for Buswell's Hotel. You'll find a quieter crowd here, several blocks away from both Grafton Street and Trinity College, which may be just what you are looking for after a bustling, long day. Examples of their menu items include filet steak chasseur, chicken Kiev, and lamb cutlets. Casual but nice dress.

21. TROCADERO RESTAURANT, *3 St. Andrews Street, Tel. (01) 677-5545. £8 to £15. Open Monday through Saturday from 6:00 pm until 12:15 am,* *and 6:00 pm to 11:00 pm on Sundays. Reservations are recommended throughout the year on the weekends. All major credit cards accepted.*

This restaurant, between Grafton and Trinity Streets, is popular with the theater crowd – those in front of the stage as well as on it. Examples of their fare include chicken fromage, escalope of pork, and tagliatelle al pesto. They also do a good job with their steaks – priced around £12.95. Casual but nice dress.

22. IL PRIMO, *16 Montague Street, Tel. (01) 478-3373. £9 to £14.95. Open Monday through Friday from noon to 2:30 pm and 6:00 pm to 11:00 pm. Reservations recommended during the tourist season and on the weekends. All major credit cards accepted.*

It's a little difficult to find, but Il Primo Restaurant is worth the hunt. At the south end of Grafton Street, continue walking south on St. Stephen's Green West. At the corner, bear just slightly to your right on Harcourt Street. About a block down on your right will be an alley marked Montague Street. Turn right, and it's one of the first buildings on your left.

The outside is relatively unremarkable, as is the view when you enter from the street into their bar area. You ascend a steep, narrow staircase to reach the dining room, which is only slightly less narrow than the staircase. The dining room is probably no more than ten feet wide and about thirty feet long, and seats about thirty. The paintings on the wall are by local artists and are for sale if you are so inclined. That's the bad news.

The good news is that as plain as the surroundings are, the food is absolutely exquisite. It has been referred to as new-wave Italian, but the owner, William Frisby, says they serve Italian with special Irish variations, such as lasagna with chicken and mushrooms in a red wine sauce, ravioli il Primo, canneloni il Primo, and insalata d'Anitra. Casual but nice dress.

23. LA STAMPA, *35 Dawson Street, Tel. (01) 677-8611. £8.95 to £17.95. Open 12:30 pm to 2:15 pm for lunch, and daily from 6:30 pm to 11:00 pm. Reservations are suggested on the weekends. All major credit cards accepted.*

This upscale award-winning restaurant features a variety of European dishes. As you move from the entrance into the dining room, you'll pass a number of bizarre paintings by Irish-born avant-garde artist Graham Kmuttel. They are filled with scowling people, distrustfully looking at one another (many have their hands in their coats as though they are preparing to draw a gun). Once you forget the art, the service as well as the food is great. The dining area has high ceilings, and is long and narrow with floor-to-ceiling mirrors. Examples of their varied offerings include char-grilled fillet of beef, buttered linguini with baby spinach, and confit lamb. The clientele is varied, and you'll see dress from chinos to tuxedos. (Maybe the management will replace the pictures before you dine here!)

24. THE IMPERIAL CHINESE RESTAURANT, *13 Wicklow Street, Tel. (01) 677-2580. £9 to £18. Open daily from 12:30 pm until midnight. Reservations are strongly recommended every day during the tourist season, and on weekends throughout the year. All major credit cards accepted.*

Beautiful indigo carpets accentuate the light rose-colored walls at The Imperial Chinese. As you enter the dining area, you'll pass a small fish pond and rock fountain. All this gives the restaurant a quiet, serene ambiance. One of the next things you notice is the number of Chinese patrons dining here – always a good sign in a Chinese restaurant. The Imperial Chinese Restaurant has become a popular dining spot for the Dublin Chinese community, and with good reason.

Although a little pricey, the food is excellent. They have several set menus, one of which is £16 per person (minimum of two), and another that is £18 per person (minimum of three). A la carte specialties include Peking duck, king prawns, and fried squid. While the dress is casual but nice, most of the diners dress in suits and ties and dresses.

25. LE CAPRICE, *12A St. Andrew Place, Tel. (01) 679-4050. £5.95 to £19.95. Open from 6:00 pm until 12:30 am daily. Reservations are strongly recommended on weekends and during the tourist season. All major credit cards accepted.*

This is a nice, tidy little Italian restaurant a block and a half off Grafton Street. Dinner music by first-class pianists adds to the pleasant and lively atmosphere and is a special touch. Specialties of the house include fresh fish caught locally, as well as escalope of veal champignon, lasagna Caprice, and sole of grilled meuniere. Nice casual dress requested.

26. NUMBER 27 THE GREEN, *27 St. Stephen's Green, Tel. (01) 676-6471. £12.95 to £23. Open daily from 7:30 am to 10:30 am for breakfast, 12:30 pm to 2:30 pm for lunch, and 6:00 pm to 10:30 pm for dinner (Sundays until 10:00 pm). Reservations are strongly recommended on the weekends during the tourist season. All major credit cards accepted.*

This is the main restaurant for the Shelbourne Hotel. The same impeccable service, pleasant ambiance, and beautiful surroundings that characterize the hotel extend to the restaurant. They have received numerous awards for their breakfast, and their dinners are excellent as well. They have a set dinner menu for £23, as well as á la carte items such as fillet of cod, grilled filet of beef, and hickory fillet of salmon, all for £14.50 each; there's an extensive wine list. Jacket and tie are expected, and they will provide you one if you are without.

27. THE ALEXANDRA, *Earlsfort Terrace, Tel. (01) 676-5555. £15.95 to £33. Open Monday through Friday from 12:30 pm to 2:30 pm for lunch, and from 6:30 pm until 10:30 pm for dinner. Saturdays they are open only for dinner from 6:30 pm until 10:30 pm. Reservations are required. All major credit cards accepted.*

Located in the Conrad Hotel, the Alexandra Restaurant is elegant and courtly. The room is richly accented with dark wood, lovely paintings, and shimmering chandeliers. This marvelous, intimate restaurant serves a delicious variety of taste treats, including blackened sole, mignon of beef, and Chateaubriand. Jacket and tie are requested.

28. THE COMMONS RESTAURANT, *85 - 86 St. Stephen's Green South, Tel. (01) 475-2597. £32 to £42. Reservations are required for dinner, and recommended for lunch. All major credit cards accepted.*

The Commons is one of the nicest restaurants in Dublin. Located on the south side of St. Stephen's Green in about the middle of the block, it is easy to miss because it is below street-level, and is not particularly well marked. Unlike many of the restaurants in Dublin, tables are not too close together and allow you to converse quietly, enjoy your candlelit meal, and relax in the romantic glow created by the fire in the large fireplace. During the spring and summer they use their lovely garden patio for drinks and socializing. The walls are covered with artwork commissioned by the owners of the restaurant. Irish artists were asked to paint their impressions of the writer James Joyce, and their works grace the walls.

Their menu is primarily French with an Irish influence, and they have several set menus ranging in price from £32 to £42. Dress is jacket and tie.

Ballsbridge District

29. LATCHFORDS BISTRO, *99 - 100 Lower Baggot Street, Tel. (01) 676-0784. £10.95 to £14.95. Open Monday through Friday for lunch from 12:30 pm to 3:00 pm, and Monday through Saturday from 6:00 pm to 11:00 pm for dinner. Reservations are recommended. All major credit cards accepted.*

This family-run bistro has a warm, comfortable atmosphere topped only by the excellent cuisine. It is very popular with the locals, and it hasn't been discovered by tourists yet. They specialize in a sort of contemporary French/Italian menu ranging from roast pheasant in a lentil and orange sauce (outstanding) to noisettes of lamb to fillet of salmon, or you can choose their set dinner menu for £18.95. They also have a pretty impressive wine list. The presentation of the dishes is nearly as impressive as the flavor. Save room for dessert – the sticky toffee gateau on a raspberry coulis is to die for! The lunch menu is comparable for about half the price. Dress is casual but nice, although most dress in suits.

30. SUSSEX RESTAURANT, *Upper Leeson Street, Tel. (01) 660-5222. £7 to £18. Open 7:00 am to 10:00 am for breakfast, 12:30 pm to 2:30 pm for lunch, and 6:30 pm to 10:30 pm for dinner. Reservations are recommended most weekends, and every evening throughout the tourist season. All major credit cards accepted.*

The Sussex Restaurant is the formal restaurant associated with the Burlington Hotel. It is one of the few restaurants listed here that request at least a jacket, if not a tie. The atmosphere is pleasant and open. They have a set menu from £16.50, and á la carte items including medallions of beef au poivre and fillet of lemon sole.

31. MCGRATTAN'S RESTAURANT, *76 Fitzwilliam Lane, Tel. (01) 661-8808. £10.95 to £18.50. Open daily from 12:30 pm to 2:30 pm (noon to 5:00 pm on Sundays), and from 6:00 pm until midnight for dinner. Reservations are recommended on the weekends and during the tourist season. All major credit cards accepted.*

The ambiance here is candlelight and crystal, with a large fireplace and live piano music (Thursday through Sunday evenings). The food is excellent, from appetizer to dessert.Their clam chowder is probably the best I have ever had. While seafood is the specialty, they have a varied menu, from a set menu (£18.50) to á la carte items such as grilled swordfish, salmon, and chicken Kiev. The food was outstanding, and there is lots of it. Save room for dessert, which is delicious, especially the Bailey's mouse with fresh fruit coulis – it's light and superb! Dress is casual, but patrons tend to dress in jacket and tie and dresses.

32. THE ORCHID RESTAURANT, *127 Pembroke Road, Tel. (01) 660-0629. £8 to £20. Open Monday through Saturday for lunch from noon to 2:15 pm, and for dinner from 6:00 pm until midnight. Due to its close proximity to the Jury's Hotel and Towers, reservations are necessary on the weekends, especially so during the tourist season. All major credit cards accepted.*

As I stood outside this restaurant debating whether or not to eat here, a local Dubliner stopped and volunteered that it was a marvelous Chinese restaurant. With that unsolicited recommendation, I ventured in, and was not disappointed. The Orchid offers a set menu (£18 to £20) as well as á la carte selections. On the á la carte menu, you can select from such savory dishes as Cantonese roast duck, Szechuan spicy chicken, and sweet and sour pork. Dress is casual but nice.

33. KISH RESTAURANT, *Pembroke Road, Tel. (01) 660-5000. £12.50 to £20.95. Open Monday through Saturday from 6:30 pm until 10:45 pm. Reservations are recommended, especially on the weekend. All major credit cards accepted.*

Associated with the Jury's Hotel, this seafood restaurant provides a nice selection of fresh fish. Scallops and prawn flambe, mussels á la mainiere, and sole walesha are samples of their offerings. Dress is casual but nice. Because of the popularity of the Jury's Hotel and Towers, the Kish Restaurant is usually very busy.

34. NUMBER 10, *10 Fitzwilliam Street Lower, Tel. (01) 676-1367. £13.95 to £24.95. Open seven days a week for breakfast from 7:30 am until 10:00 am, and for dinner from 7:00 pm until 11:00 pm (9:00 pm on Sundays); open for lunch Monday through Saturday from noon to 3:00 pm. Reservations are* *strongly recommended, and you'll probably not get in without them on the weekends. All major credit cards accepted.*

If exquisite dining is what you are looking for in Dublin, look no further. Number 10, the restaurant that also serves Longfield's Hotel, is arguably one of the finest dining establishments in Dublin. As you descend white and black tile steps below street level, you emerge into a small but engaging restaurant. The open fire, accentuated by the crystal and linen on the tables, immediately signals you that you've come to the right place. The service, the food, and the ambiance all combine to provide an elegant and graceful dining experience.

Their internationally trained chef, Tommy Donovan, provides meals fit for a king. His presentation is tasteful and exquisite. Michael Blake, the manager, assures that the staff is attentive and that top-notch service is a reality. The fare is light French cuisine with Irish influences. From confit of French duck to an outstanding ravioli stuffed with fresh crab, you'll enjoy this savory adventure. They offer a set dinner menu for £24.95 that includes appetizer, salad, soup, granite (like a sorbet, only with no sugar), entree and dessert. They offer an equally excellent award-winning breakfast menu for £8.50, and their lunch menu is as delectable as their dinner menu for about half the price.

The chef from Ireland's only two-star restaurant occasionally frequents Number 10 on his days off. Need I say more? The restaurant seats only thirty-five or so, and it fills up quickly. Dress is casual but nice, although diners are usually dressed in jacket and tie and dresses.

35. L'ECRIVAIN, *109 Lower Baggot Street, Tel. (01) 661-1919. £21.95 to £27.95. Open Monday through Friday for lunch from 12:30 pm to 2:30 pm, Monday through Saturday for dinner from 7:00 pm to 11:00 pm (open at 6:30 pm on Saturdays). Reservations are a must. All major credit cards accepted.*

L'Ecrivain means "the writer" in French, and the walls of this restaurant are decorated with paintings that pay homage to a number of Irish writers – present as well as past. A traditional French restaurant, L'Ecrivain offers a set dinner menu for £27.50 with a surprisingly wide selection, including crisp confit of duck and rack of lamb. They also have an excellent four-course set lunch menu. Their extensive wine list is considered one of the best in Dublin, with nearly one hundred and fifty selections. For dinner, a jacket is required and a tie is suggested.

36. EMBASSY GARDEN, *Pembroke Road, Tel. (01) 660-5000. £12.95 to £30. Open daily from 7:00 am to 10:00 am for breakfast, 12:15 pm to 2:00 pm for lunch, and 6:00 pm to 9:45 pm for dinner. Reservations are recommended on the weekends. All major credit cards accepted.*

Located in Jury's Hotel, just walk across the footbridge and over the stream into the relaxed, fine dining room. Ask for a table by the windows overlooking the hotel's garden and pool. This restaurant specializes in

French food, including chateaubriand, osso buco (veal), and a variety of beef, lamb, and veal dishes. Dress is casual but nice.

37. LE COQ HARDI, *35 Pembroke Road, Tel. (01) 668-9070. £21.95 to £35. Open Monday through Friday from 12:30 pm until 3:30 pm for lunch, and Monday through Saturday from 7:00 pm until 11:00 pm for dinner. Reservations are required for dinner. All major credit cards accepted.*

Located in a converted Georgian home, Le Coq Hardi is perhaps the best place in Ireland for French cuisine. The restaurant is expensively and elegantly decorated with rosewood and brass, and linen, fine china, and crystal make for elegant table settings.

Try the house special: coq hardi, baked chicken breast stuffed with potatoes, mushrooms and a variety of seasonings wrapped in bacon, and flamed at your table. If that doesn't strike your fancy, there's lobster, prawns, and turbot, rack of lamb, Gaelic steak, and roast goose to choose from. You can't go wrong with any choice here. Only the freshest ingredients are used, and the fish is as fresh as any you'll find on the Emerald Isle. Their wine list is extensive, with some of the finest French wines available. Dress is definitely jacket and tie – you'll feel uncomfortable and out of place in anything else.

38. RESTAURANT PATRICK GUILBAUD, *46 James Place, Tel. (01) 676-4192. £10 to £46. Open Tuesday through Saturday for lunch from 12:30 pm to 2:00 pm, and for dinner from 7:30 pm until 10:15 pm. Reservations are a must all year. All major credit cards accepted.*

If you want to eat in *the* restaurant in Ireland, this would be the place. On a recent trip, I noticed that the newspapers were trumpeting Ireland's latest achievement: Restaurant Patrick Guilbaud had just been awarded a second Michelin star, the first restaurant in Ireland ever to gain this distinction.

Restaurant Patrick Guilbaud is not soft candlelight and quiet conversations. Rather, it is a bright, lively place where people come to enjoy exquisite food and animated conversation with friends and family. Live plants hang overhead. White walls accentuate the paintings that are judiciously hung throughout the restaurant. The paintings are by Irish artists who lived and painted in France. Mr. Guilbaud is proud to have acquired these paintings and returned them to their native Ireland.

The food is marvelous. From the roast quail to the poached Connemara lobster, it is as tasteful to the eye as it is to the palate. Set menus are available for £18.50 for lunch and £30 for dinner. There is even a *Menu Surprise* for £46 for those wishing a dining adventure! The dress is casual, but nice. Most people are dressed in coat and tie and dresses.

You are likely to meet Mr. Guilbaud, as he is active in serving, greeting and conversing with his customers. Be sure to congratulate him on his second Michelin star.

Restaurant Patrick Guilbaud is a little difficult to find. From St. Stephen's Green, head east on St. Stephen's Green North a little over two blocks. The street is now named Lower Baggot Street. Keep walking and just after you pass Fitzwilliam Street, watch for James Street. Turn left onto James Street, go about fifty yards, turn right into an unmarked alley (James Place), and it's about seventy-five yards up on your left.

NORTH OF DUBLIN

There are many delightful and affordable restaurants north of Dublin. Many are on the DART system. Howth, Clontarf, Swords, and other small towns are all popular due to their close proximity to Dublin.

39. ADRIAN'S RESTAURANT, *3 Abbey Street, Howth, Tel. (01) 839-1696. £8 to £18.50. Open Monday through Thursday from 12:30 until 11:00 pm, Friday and Saturday from 12:30 pm until 3:30 pm, and from 6:00 pm until 11:30 pm. They are open on Sundays from 1:00 pm until 10:00 pm. All major credit cards accepted.*

This small award-winning restaurant is very reasonable. Fish caught daily by local fishermen are presented in a very appealing manner. Dress is casual.

40. HOWTH LODGE RESTAURANT, *Howth Harbor, Tel. (01) 832-1010. £11.95 to £18.50. Open Monday through Saturday from 7:00 pm until 9:30 pm. Reservations are suggested for the weekends. All major credit cards accepted.*

You'll love the views of Howth Harbor when you dine at Howth Lodge Restaurant. Local fisherman supply the entrees each day. In addition to their excellent seafood, Howth Lodge Restaurant is known for its excellent Irish beef. Their fare includes medallions of Monkfish, sea trout, and layered salmon. The atmosphere is casual and comfortable.

Turn right as you leave the Howth DART station, and walk about a half mile down the road, the restaurant is on your right.

41. ABBEY TAVERN RESTAURANT, *Abbey Street, Howth, Tel. (01) 839-0307. £19 to £24.95. Open from 7:00 pm until 11:00 pm Monday through Saturday. Reservations are a must during the tourist season. American Express, MasterCard, and Visa accepted.*

This is one of the most popular tourist and dining attractions in the Dublin area. The unmistakable smell of peat burning in the fireplace (turf fire) and the original 16th-century stone walls and gas lights give you a sense of having stepped back in time. Along with their fantastic traditional Irish music program, the folks at the Abbey Tavern serve remarkably good food, especially seafood. Try the sole of Abbey, a decadently-prepared specialty. Dress is casual but neat, although many of the diners will have jackets.

As you leave the Howth DART station, turn left and head toward the quay. Several blocks down on your right is Abbey Street, and Abbey Tavern is up the hill about 100 yards on the right.

42. KING SITRIC, *East Pier, Howth Tel. (01) 832-5235. £17.50 to £30. Open Monday through Friday for lunch from 12:30 pm to 3:00 pm, and from 6:30 pm to 11:00 pm for dinner. Reservations are strongly suggested on the weekends and during the tourist season. All major credit cards accepted.*

The harbor master who formerly lived here never had as good a meal as you'll find at the King Sitric Restaurant. Located at the tip of Howth Harbor, the only thing separating you from the sea is the road and a retaining wall. Striking views of the sea complement the wonderful meals prepared here. This comfortable, yet elegant restaurant was named for the famous Norse King Sitric Silkenbeard. Surrounded by antiques, you'll enjoy just sitting back and taking it all in. As you would expect, seafood is the specialty, and it is excellent. From baked haddock to fillet of lemon sole, if you are a seafood lover you won't be disappointed. Dress is casual but nice, although most diners will be in jacket and tie.

The King Sitric is about a seven minute walk from the Howth DART Station. As soon as you walk out of the station, turn left and walk up the street. The restaurant is at the end of the street just as you get to the quay.

SOUTH OF DUBLIN

These restaurants are well south of Dublin, and will require you to drive or take the DART.

43. DE SELBY'S, *17 Patrick Street, Dun Laoghaire, Tel. (01) 284-1761. £9 to £12.95. Open daily from 5:30 pm to 11:00 pm for dinner, and from noon until 10:00 pm on Sunday. All major credit cards accepted.*

Near the shopping district and both the Dun Laoghaire and Sandycove DART Stations, De Selby's is a nice family-run seafood restaurant with an acceptable selection available for beef-eaters and vegetarians. The wine list seems to go for quality rather than quantity. Try the prawn stir-fry – it's great.

44. LIBRARY GRILL, *Killiney Bay, Killiney, Tel. (01) 285-1622. £4 to £7. Open from noon to 11:30 pm. Reservations are not taken. All major credit cards accepted.*

This nice little grill is located in the Court Hotel overlooking Killiney Bay. It has a pleasant atmosphere and adequate food. Menu items include burgers, fillet of plaice, and Chicken Marcus. Dress is casual.

45. JOHNNIE FOX'S PUB, *Glencullen, Tel. (01) 295-5647. £7.95 to £17.95. Open Monday through Saturday from 10:30 am to 11:30 pm, and Sunday from noon to 2:00 pm and from 4:00 pm to 11:00 pm. All major credit cards accepted.*

Located in the mountains south of Dublin, Johnnie Fox's was recently awarded the "Bar Food of the Year" award by a major industry watcher. The atmosphere smacks of pure schtick – sawdust-strewn stone floors, old photographs on the walls along with a ton of knick-knacks everywhere, and traditional Irish music. But it's fun, and the food is a real treat. In keeping with the setting, the menu is traditional Irish, but not boringly so. The selection is surprisingly wide, and ranges from wild oak-smoked salmon with prawns and salad, to hot crab claws in butter, to roast rack of spring lamb, and of course you can always get an excellent steak.

46. ISLAND RESTAURANT, *Killiney Bay, Killiney, Tel. (01) 285-1622. Set menu £19.95. Open from noon to 2:30 pm for lunch, and 6:30 pm to 11:00 pm for dinner. Reservations during the tourist season and on the weekends. All major credit cards accepted.*

This is a very popular restaurant for Dubliners to come to for lunch and dinner. It is the main restaurant for the Court Hotel, and is right across the street from Killiney DART Station – a mere twenty minute ride from downtown Dublin. The restaurant looks out on Killiney Bay, and the views are frankly spectacular. The entry is the original to the old mansion and it is gorgeous. Much of the original dark woodwork has been preserved. The best part of this restaurant is the view. Jackets are recommended.

47. TRUFFLES, *Killiney Hill Road, Killiney, Tel. (01) 284-0700. £15 to £23. Open daily from 7:00 am to 10:00 am for breakfast, noon to 2:30 pm for lunch, and 6:30 pm to 10:30 pm for dinner. All major credit cards accepted.*

This nice restaurant is located in the Fitzpatrick Castle Hotel, about eight miles south of Dublin City. You'll have a nice, quiet dining experience here. The food is acceptable although not remarkable. The best part of the dining experience may well be the views of Dublin Bay you can enjoy during a walk before or after dinner, especially at night. If you decide to try this restaurant, you'll probably need a car. The Killiney DART Station is about a mile to a mile and a half from the hotel, but it's mostly uphill. They do have a shuttle, but they seem to have a hard time finding the driver just when you need a ride. Dress is casual but nice.

48. THE TREE OF IDLENESS, *on the waterfront, Bray, County Wicklow, Tel. (01) 286-3498. £15 to £21. Open Sunday through Friday from 7:30 pm until 11:00 pm (10:00 pm on Sunday). Closed Monday. All major credit cards accepted.*

This wonderful little Greek-Cypriot restaurant on the waterfront in Bray is a winner. The original Tree of Idleness was in Bellapais, Cyprus. Located in an old Victorian house, owner Susan Courtellas has managed a winning combination: fine Greek food (the result of chef Ismail Basran's expertise), a marvelous wine list, stunning dessert selection, and a pleasant atmosphere. Your selection is wide and varied and ranges from spinach ravioli stuffed with crab mousse to filet of Irish beef to pheasant with grapes and chestnuts. The Roast lamb and feta cheese is also wonderful.

SEEING THE SIGHTS

Dublin is the most populous city in Ireland, and has many interesting and historical sights. There's plenty to do, from pub crawls to shopping malls, from castles to dungeons.

While you're in Dublin, I highly recommend that you *do not* rent a car. It would be counter-productive. The things to see in Dublin are for the most part within walking distance, and those things that are not are a short bus or DART ride away. If you rent a car, you'll spend all your time looking for a parking place, and then end up walking further than if you had walked from a centrally located hotel!

DART STATIONS

From Howth on the extreme north to Bray on the extreme south, here is a list of the DART Stations in the Dublin area. With the exception of one six minute span (between Connolly and Killester), all the stops are about two minutes apart.

The stops are: Howth , Sutton, Bayside, Howth Junction, Kilbarrack, Raheny, Harmonstown, Killester, Connolly, Tara Street, Pearse, Lansdowne Road, Sandymount, Sidney Parade, Booterstown, Blackrock, Seapoint, Monkstown, Dun Laoghaire, Sandycove, Glenageary, Dalkey, Killiney, Shankill, and Bray.

North Dublin

O'Connell Street only runs for two blocks north of the River Liffey, but it is one of the most important streets in Dublin. It is not nearly as long as you'd expect it to be, given its seeming importance in Dublin: only a little over two blocks long. But it seems to have a mesmerizing affect on all those who visit. Home of one of the finest hotels in Dublin (the Gresham), one of the most important buildings in Dublin (the General Post Office – the GPO), and the namesake of one of Ireland's most revered individuals (Daniel O'Connell), O'Connell Street was once a grand thoroughfare where the ladies and gentlemen of Dublin's High Society liked to be seen.

It's not quite as impressive today as it may have been in those bygone days. Many of the lovely old Victorian homes and buildings are gone and have given way to more modern structures. Still, the wide central island is punctuated with large green trees and statues of Irish greats: Daniel O'Connell (former Dublin mayor and winner of Catholic emancipation), William Smith O'Brien (leader of one of Ireland's many rebellions against

British authority), Sir John Gay (newspaper editor), James Larkin (a historic union leader), Father Theobald Mathew (a revered priest known as "the apostle of temperance, and honored for his tireless efforts during a cholera epidemic in 1832), and Charles Stewart Parnell (key figure in the Home Rule campaign).

Included with all these impressive statues along O'Connell Street is the **Anna Livia Millennium Fountain** (in the center island across from the GPO). Unveiled as part of the festivities during Dublin's one thousand year celebration (1988), Anna Livia represents the River Liffey. I stood in front of the fountain for half an hour and questioned Dubliners about the fountain. None of them knew anything about Anna Livia, but they all knew the site by the more common appellation *The Floozie in the Jacuzzi*. Ah, the Irish sense of humor!

Like the Grand Canal in the south, the **Royal Canal** begins at Dublin Bay and bounds the north side of Dublin, then runs into the countryside until it joins the Shannon river in the middle of the country. Forty-seven locks along its route compensate for the rise in elevation as the Canal runs into the countryside. Construction on the canal began in 1792, and was completed in 1817.

The Royal Canal was used to bring turf for fires and heating into Dublin. It was also used extensively by the Guinness Brewery. Grain was brought into Dublin on barges for use in the brewery, then kegs of Guinness were transported to the interior of the country. When the kegs were empty, they made the trip back to Dublin to be refilled. The canal was used for that purpose up until the canal closed in 1960. Now anglers and pleasure boaters are its most frequent users.

General Post Office (**GPO**), *O'Connell Street, open Monday through Saturday 8:00 am until 8:00 pm, Sundays from 10:30 am to 6:30 pm. Tel. (01) 872-8888.* This is probably the most talked-about building in Dublin. It is the main post office, and as such everyone is familiar with it. But its mark on history goes much beyond postal service: it was the flash point of the 1916 Easter Rising. It was from the seized GPO that Irish rebel leaders proclaimed their message of a new republic. The ensuing battle destroyed most of the area around O'Connell Street. Some of the GPO's massive stone columns are still chipped from flying bullets. As a result of the fighting, the GPO was virtually gutted by fire and British artillery. Its renovation was completed in 1929 and faithfully restored the GPO to its former grandeur. The words of the proclamation read by the rebel leaders on that fateful Easter morning is inscribed in green marble. All those who signed the proclamation also signed their death warrants. All were taken to Kilmainham Prison and executed.

Inside the GPO is a magnificent statue of **Cuchulainn** – the legendary Irish warrior who has been idolized by generations of Irish children.

Mortally-wounded, Cuchulain is said to have fought single-handedly against overwhelming numbers. As he felt his strength failing, he lashed himself to a stone in order to face his assailants standing – even in death. His last moments are depicted by the statue. It is an appropriate tribute to those few warriors who took on the British Empire almost single-handedly and wrested Ireland from her grasp. The three stone statues atop the portico represent **Mercury, Hibernia** and **Fidelity**.

The intersection in front of the GPO – Henry and North Earl Streets and O'Connell Street – was formerly the location of one of the city's most recognizable landmarks – the **Nelson Pillar**. A one hundred and thirty-five foot pillar, complete with spiral staircase leading to the viewing platform at the top, was a tribute to British Admiral Nelson. On a March night in 1966, a tremendous blast reduced the pillar to rubble, an act of Irish loyalists who resented Admiral Nelson's lofty position in the city center. The demolition took place just prior to the 50th anniversary of the 1916 Easter Rising.

Henry Street bisects O'Connell Street one block north of the River Liffey. Like Grafton Street on the south of the river, Henry Street is a pedestrian shopping area. It has been largely replaced as *the* shopping street in Dublin by Grafton Street, but it is still crowded with shoppers most hours of the day and evening. The stores are a little older and the architecture a little more tired, but the atmosphere is similar to Grafton Street.

About a half block off O'Connell Street on the right is a large tile mosaic on the walkway that announces the entrance to **Moore Street,** which for generations has been the fruit, vegetable, and flower market of Dublin. You can hear the (mostly) women vendors shouting to call your attention to their produce. In days gone by, many of the shops lining Moore Street were butcher shops, but they have been slowly replaced by discount stores and other shops. It's a fun place to go, and it's especially colorful and cheery on a sunny day.

The **Rotunda Maternity Hospital**, *Parnell Street, Tel. (01) 873-0700*. Originally known as the Lying-in Hospital, this was the brainchild of **Dr. Bartholomew Mosse**, a Dublin midwife (twenty years before the American revolution). His vision and mission in life was to provide a "modern" hospital for pregnant women and childbirth. As a fundraising project, Mosse and a group of investors purchased a set of adjoining gardens (now the site of the Garden of Remembrance), where a series of benefit concerts were held to raise money to fund the work Mosse was doing on the hospital.

Through much tribulation, Mosse saw the completion of the hospital in 1757, and immediately began work on a chapel. The chapel is at the top of the central staircase of the hospital, and its ornate ceiling – a tribute to

DUBLIN CASTLE

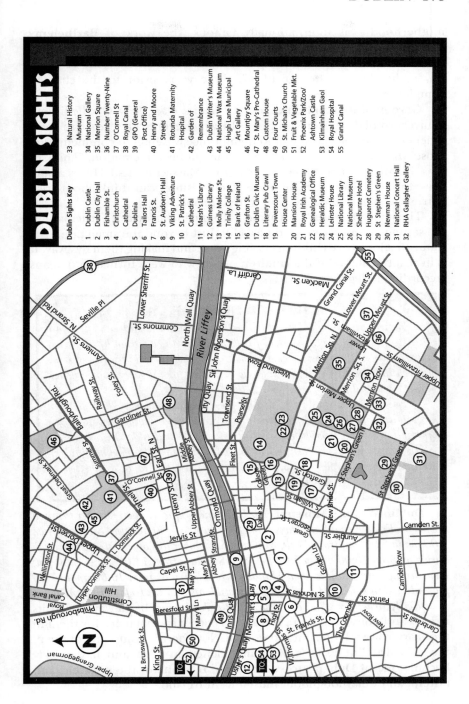

DUBLIN SIGHTS

Dublin Sights Key

1 Dublin Castle
2 Dublin City Hall
3 Fishamble St.
4 Christchurch Cathedral
5 Dublinia
6 Tailors Hall
7 Francis St.
8 St. Audoen's Hall
9 Viking Adventure
10 St. Patrick's Cathedral
11 Marsh's Library
12 Guiness Library
13 Molly Malone St.
14 Trinity College
15 Bank of Ireland
16 Grafton St.
17 Dublin Civic Museum
18 Literary Pub Crawl
19 Powerscourt Town House Center
20 Mansion House
21 Royal Irish Academy
22 Genealogical Office
23 Heraldic Museum
24 Leinster House
25 National Library
26 National Museum
27 Shelburne Hotel
28 Huguenot Cemetery
29 St Stephen's Green
30 Newman House
31 National Concert Hall
32 RHA Gallagher Gallery

33 Natural History Museum
34 National Gallery
35 Merrion Square
36 Number Twenty-Nine
37 O'Connell St
38 Royal Canal
39 GPO (General Post Office)
40 Henry and Moore Streets
41 Rotunda Maternity Hospital
42 Garden of Remembrance
43 Dublin Writer's Museum
44 National Wax Museum
45 Hugh Lane Municipal Art Gallery
46 Mountjoy Square
47 St. Mary's Pro-Cathedral
48 Custom House
49 Four Courts
50 St. Michan's Church
51 Fruit & Vegetable Mkt.
52 Phoenix Park/Zoo/ Ashtown Castle
53 Kilmainham Gaol
54 Royal Hospital
55 Grand Canal

motherhood – is internationally famous, the work of **Barthelemy Cramillion**. The mahogany pews, paneling and fluted columns are all some of the finest craftsmanship in Ireland. Unfortunately, Mosse never saw it: he died at the age of 47, three years prior to the chapel's completion.

Garden of Remembrance, *Parnell Square. Open daily.* On the fiftieth anniversary of the Easter Rising of 1916, which eventually lead to Ireland's independence, the Garden of Remembrance was built to commemorate those who gave their lives that Ireland might be a free nation. (Think of it as the Minuteman statue in Lexington, Massachusetts.) This is a very peaceful and contemplative place where visitors can think about Irish patriots who gave their lives for a free Ireland.

The square features an ornamental pond in the form of a crucifix, and the setting is very serene and peaceful. Just beyond the small pond is a statue that looks like children chasing geese and making them fly away. It is in reality a statue of the children of Lir, who were turned into swans (according to legend).

THE CHILDREN OF LIR

Lir was an ancient Celtic chieftain who lived nine hundred years before Christianity came to the shores of Ireland. After the death of his wife, Lir married an enchantress named Aoife. Aoife was insanely jealous of Lir's four children by his first wife, and used her magic to change the poor children into swans (talk about a wicked step-mother).

Even though they were swans, the children retained their human capabilities, and used their voices to sing songs that brought great joy to the inhabitants of the surrounding countryside. The spell ended nine hundred years later when Christianity was introduced into Ireland. The children resumed their former personalities, and were said to be converted to Christianity by St. Mochaomhog.

Dublin Writer's Museum, *18/19 Parnell Square, open October through March on Fridays and Saturdays from 10:00 am to 5:00 pm, and Sundays from 1:00 pm to 5:00 pm; from April, May and September it is open Tuesday through Saturday from 10:00 am to 5:00 pm, and Sundays from 11:00 am to 6:00 pm; June through August it is open Monday through Friday from 10:00 am to 7:00 pm. Admission is £2.60 for adults, £2 for students and £1.10 for children. There is a family ticket for £7. Tel. (01) 872-2077.* Ireland has always loved its writers and poets, and there has always been a special place for them in the heart of every Irish man and woman. Now there is a museum for them, too. The Dublin Writer's Museum opened in 1991 and has quickly become one of Dublin's top attractions. It is one of the most elegant, tasteful and well thought-out museums in Ireland.

This exquisitely restored Georgian home houses the Gorham Library on the first floor. Be sure to take a look at its beautiful ceiling. Permanent exhibits in the museum feature famed Irish authors such as **Samuel Beckett, Brendan Behan, George Bernard Shaw, Jonathan Swift,** and **Oscar Wilde**. Paintings, photographs, letters, and memorabilia are all part of the various exhibits.

Adjacent to the museum is the Irish Writer's Centre, a gathering place for current writers to meet, talk, and host readings. If the exhibits sparks an interest in the works of these writers, there is a bookstore that sells most of the works of the authors represented in the museum. If it's food you're thinking of, they also have a cafe on site.

National Wax Museum, *Granby Row, open Monday through Saturday from 10:00 am to 5:30 pm, and Sunday from noon to 5:30 pm. Admission is £3 for adults, senior citizens and students £2.50, children £2. Tel. (01) 872-6340.* It's okay for a wax museum, but to be honest, I find most wax museums, well, sort of lifeless. You can see Madonna's paraffin persona here, along with a host of Irish personalities.

Hugh Lane Municipal Gallery of Modern Art, *Parnell Square, open Tuesday through Friday, 9:00 am to 6:00 pm, Saturday from 9:30 am to 5:00 pm, Sunday from 11:00 am to 5:00 pm. Admission is free. Tel. (01) 874-1903.* Built in the mid-18th century, this former townhouse of Lord Charlemont has been restored and now houses a fine collection of modern art. Works by Picasso, Monet, Renoir, Degas, and Manet are all part of the collection of artworks owned at one time by Hugh Lane. Upon Mr. Lane's death on the *Lusitania* off the southwest coast of Ireland in 1915 (which some claim was the work of the English to bring America into the first world war, but that's another story), his collection of art was to go to the Dublin Corporation.

But several years prior to his death, Mr. Lane was angered when the Dublin Corporation decided not to build a special gallery to house his collection, so he stipulated that thirty-nine of his paintings were to go to London instead. However, after his death, a contested (unwitnessed) codicil was discovered reversing his decision and bequeathing the paintings to the Dublin Corporation, his original preference. The collection was tied up in legal proceedings for nearly fifty years until London and Dublin decided on a compromise: the paintings would rotate every five years between the two cities. Included with Lane's collection are a number of other fine works by 19th and 20th-century artists, as well as a room devoted to stained glass artisan Harry Clarke.

Mountjoy Square, *Upper Gardiner Street.* A couple of blocks north and east of O'Connell Street is Mountjoy Square, a large greenbelt area the size of a city block. Once in the midst of one of the ritziest neighborhoods in Dublin, the area now borders on a section of the city that's been a bit neglected. Mountjoy Square is named after **Luke Gardiner**, the third Viscount Mountjoy, hence the name.

St. Mary's Pro-Cathedral, *Marlborough Street, open daily 8:00 am to 6:00 pm. Admission is free. Tel. (01) 874-5441.* If you've been to the Temple of Theseus in Athens, you might think that St. Mary's Pro-Cathedral was trying to imitate it, with its portico supported by six columns and you'd be right. Completed in 1825, the interior is done in Grecian-Doric architectural style, and is very nice.

This church (it was never endowed with cathedral status) has been the location of the funerals for key government officials for years. It is considered the main Catholic church in Ireland. The crypt is open irregular times, but is interesting. Ask if it is open when you arrive, or call ahead for times.

The Custom House, *Custom House Quay, not open to the public (unfortunately).* If you spend any time whatsoever in Dublin, you are certain to wonder what the large, obviously governmental-type building is that faces the River Liffey two blocks east of O'Connell Street. It is the Custom House, and it is a very impressive sight, especially at night when it is brightly lit.

The Custom House is a building that evokes strong feelings of pride in Dubliners – it really is a beautiful, stately building. But that wasn't always the case. When construction began in 1781, opponents hired ruffians on more than one occasion to attack the builders. Notwithstanding these efforts and numerous death threats to the builder, James Gandon, work on the building continued. However, Mr. Gandon felt the threats were sincere enough that he began wearing his sword to the job site!

A suspicious fire broke out in a portion of the unfinished building in 1789, but the damage was repaired and the Custom House opened on schedule in 1791. But, unlike characters in fairy tales, the Custom House did not live happily ever after. Another fire struck in 1833, and then a fire of monumental proportions devastated the structure in 1921. Local fire crews were unsuccessful in putting out the fire, and it burned out of control for five days. The fire was so hot that it melted brass door fittings and cracked stonework.

Once again restoration and repair work put the building back in commission. In the early 1970's, it was determined that additional cracks in the stonework, probably caused by the fire in 1921, would need to be fixed. An aggressive restoration program was completed in the early 1990s. The Custom House has once again been restored to its prior grandeur. And you benefit from the work.

Four Courts, *Inns Quay, open Monday through Friday 10:00 am to 4:00 pm. Admission is free. Tel. (01) 872-5555.* The Four Courts is a landmark building. Its dome, sitting regally above the River Liffey is a familiar site, and very impressive at night. Housing the Irish Law Courts, the Four Courts has been on the Dublin scene since its completion in 1802.

During the Irish Civil War in 1922, the Four Courts was nearly destroyed by fire and artillery shelling and the Public Records Office next to it was destroyed, along with generations of irreplaceable legal, land, and genealogical records, a most regrettable loss. Fortunately the building was not razed, and years of renovation have restored it to its previous glory.

The front portico is supported by six massive columns, and Moses, the Law Giver, stands tall at the center of the top of the portico and is flanked by the statues of Justice and Mercy. Behind and above the portico is an immense circular dome.

If you have the time, be sure and visit the upper rotunda of the dome. It provides some nice views of Dublin.

St. Michan's Church, *Church Street, open March through October Monday through Friday from 10:00 am to 12:45 pm, and from 2:00 pm to 4:45 pm, and Saturdays from 10:00 am until 1:00 pm, and November through February Monday through Friday 12:30 pm to 3:30 pm, and Saturday 10:00 am to 1:00 pm. Admission to the vaults is £1.20 for adults, and £1 for children and senior citizens. Tel. (01) 872-4154.* Originally built in 1095 as a Viking parish church (the only one north of the River Liffey for over 500 years), St. Michan's was rebuilt to its current state in 1686, and has had several facelifts since then. The woodwork throughout the chapel is beautiful.

Legend has it that **Handel** played St. Michan's magnificent 18th-century organ while composing *The Messiah*. (It's the Irish equivalent of "George Washington slept here.")

One of the oddities at St. Michan's is the "stool of repentance," where misbehaving parishioners did public penance. Perhaps the most unusual aspect of St. Michan's is the partially mummified remains of three 17th-century people. The limestone in the ground of the vaults removed moisture from the air, preserving the bodies remarkably well. If the mummified cat and mouse at Christchurch made you queasy, you might want to pass!

Dublin Corporation Fruit and Vegetable Market, *Mary's Lane.* Another of Dublin's Fruit and Vegetable Markets, this one was established a little over a hundred years ago in 1892. To get there, walk down Henry Street from O'Connell Street. Continue west as Henry Street turns into Mary Street, and eventually it will turn into Mary's Lane. On your left, watch for the Dublin City Arms over the archway of the main entrance. The red and yellow brick building hosts another cacophony of fruit and vegetable vendors hawking their produce. Personally, I liked Moore Street better, but this is close. Both offer a taste of the Irish way of life.

South Dublin – Temple Bar District
The **River Liffey** is the lifeblood, the main artery of Dublin. Dublin itself is here because of the inland access the river provided for its earliest and most intrepid settlers – the Vikings. With its beginnings in the Wicklow mountains to the south, the river meanders its way through the Irish countryside. Poems have been written about The River, songs have been sung to it, and it is fondly regarded by the populace of Dublin, like a favorite uncle. Dark and musty, it is not a particularly pretty river, but it is still special to Dubliners.

Two of the most beautiful evening sites in Dublin are along the banks of the River Liffey. The Custom House and the Four Courts offer gorgeous lighted views at night.

The River cuts through the center of Dublin, and most addresses are geographically described as either north or south of the River Liffey. Once it enters Dublin, an even dozen bridges span its girth. The most familiar and popular are the **O'Connell Bridge** and the **Ha'penny Bridge**. The former has been in place for about two hundred years. Originally called Carlisle Bridge, its name was changed to honor **Daniel O'Connell**, who fought long and hard for Catholic emancipation – the right of Catholics to be elected to parliament and to participate in the governance of Ireland. The bridge is nearly as wide as it is long and the large statue in the center island of O'Connell Street, as you pass from the south to the north side of Dublin, is a monument to Mr. O'Connell. Ha'penny (pronounced hay'-penny) Bridge, the only strictly pedestrian bridge in Dublin, derives its name from the toll charged to use the bridge in earlier days. Originally called Wellington Bridge, it's officially called the Liffey Bridge. However, most continue to call it the Ha'penny.

Dublin Castle, *Castle Street, open Monday through Friday 10:00 am to 12:15 pm and 2:00 pm to 5:00 pm, Saturdays and Sundays 2:00 pm until 5:00 pm. Admission is £1.75 for adults and £1 for children. Tel. (01) 677-7580.* Dublin Castle is symbolic of English rule over Ireland for six hundred years, from the early 13th century until the independence of Ireland in 1922. As such, it is not exactly well liked by Dubliners.

However, it *is* a great place to visit. There is a guided tour around the grounds and through the State Apartments, which formerly served as the residences for the English Viceroys. These elaborate rooms are adorned with rich Donegal carpets and Waterford crystal chandeliers, and are truly luxurious. Today the State Apartments are used primarily for ceremonial affairs from time to time. The remainder of the castle has been converted into government offices.

Several of the rooms are exceptionally exquisite. You'll marvel at most of the rooms, but the ones that elicit the most "Oohs" and Ahs" are the Apollo Room (sometimes called the Music Room), the Round

Drawing Room, and the Wedgewood Room. The highlight of the Castle is St. Patrick's Hall. This large room (82 feet by 40 feet) is graced with a hand painted ceiling and beautiful gilded pillars. It is the venue for Irish presidential inaugurations and various state functions.

The oldest section of Dublin Castle is the Record Tower, a part of the original structure dating from 1220. Over the years the Record Tower was also called at one time or another the Black Tower, Gunner's Tower, and Wardrobe Tower. Unfortunately, the public is not allowed in Record Tower.

On the grounds of Dublin Castle is the **Royal Chapel**, also known as the **Church of the Holy Trinity**. This charming little (by cathedral standards) church has beautiful oak panels and lovely stained-glass windows. The exterior is embellished with the carved heads of all the kings and queens of England. The Royal Chapel was completed in 1814 based on the designs of Francis Johnston. It served the Anglican Church for over one hundred and twenty-five years. However, beginning in 1943, the Catholic Church began using it for their services, and continue to do so today.

Arrangements have recently been made to move the outstanding collection of Oriental art and antiquities now residing in the **Chester Beatty Library and Gallery of Oriental Art** in Ballsbridge to Dublin Castle in 1997. (Chester Beatty was an American millionaire who moved to Dublin in 1953. He had an extensive book collection, which he donated to Ireland in his will). The collection contains over 22,000 items, including rare books and manuscripts, miniature paintings, ancient copies of the Koran, clay tablets from Babylon, and some of the earliest known Biblical papyri in existence.

Dublin City Hall, *Castle Street/Cork Hill, open Monday through Friday 9:00 am to 5:00 pm. Admission is free. Tel. (01) 679-6111.* City Hall is the home of the Dublin Corporation, the Dublin City government. The building was completed in 1769. The entry hall contains fluted columns that tend to cause your eyes to lift upward, where you'll see an impressive domed ceiling. Further on in the Muniment Room you'll find the Dublin City sword and mace. There are no public tours, but you can walk about in the public areas.

Fishamble Street is the location of historic Dublin. Look for a narrow street next to the relatively modern (great controversy in Dublin over that!) Civic Offices; this is Fishamble Street. The area between Christchurch Cathedral and Wood Quay is where the original Viking settlement of Dylfin was founded in 841. It was originally a fish market, bustling with activity. Excavations in this area during the 1970's unearthed a treasure-load of Viking artifacts, many of which are now housed in the National Museum.

An ironworks now stands on the site of a Music Hall that once stood on the corner of Fishamble Street. Next door, a house with a plaque marks the site of the first public performance of **Handel's** *The Messiah* on April 13, 1742. The event drew over seven hundred of Dublin's well-heeled aristocracy. The space was limited, and as large crowds were expected, ladies were asked to refrain from wearing hoop skirts and men were asked to leave their swords home!

Christchurch Cathedral, *Christchurch Place, open Monday through Saturday 10:00 am until 5:00 pm and Sundays between church services. Call for an appointment between November and April. Admission is free, although a small donation is appreciated. Tel. (01) 677-8099.* Christchurch Cathedral was built in 1038 for the Norse King Sitric Silkenbeard. Originally a wooden structure, major renovation was undertaken between 1173 and 1220, and the wooden structure was replaced with stonework. In 1831, the cathedral received one final major facelift, and was redone in the Gothic style you see today.

This magnificent cathedral includes a self-guided tour through the ancient crypt below the cathedral. It's a little dusty, so if you suffer from asthma you may want to forego this part of the cathedral. Two of the more surprising sights in the crypt are the mummified bodies of a cat and rat that apparently participated in a deadly game of "cat and mouse" in days gone by. The rat raced into an organ pipe with the cat hot on his tail. The cat became lodged in the pipe, and both diner and dinner perished.

The tomb of **Strongbow**, the first Norman conqueror of Ireland, is located in the cathedral. Not to burst your enthusiastic bubble at seeing the image of the eight centuries-old great Norman conqueror of Ireland, but Strongbow's actual tomb was destroyed four hundred years ago when part of the roof caved in. The tomb was replaced with the effigy of a long-forgotten knight. However, the heart (yes, the real heart) of St. Lawrence O'Toole is preserved in a metal casket at the east end of the cathedral. He was the Archbishop of Dublin at the time of Strongbow's invasion.

The most noticeable aspects of the interior of Christchurch Cathedral are the elaborate stonework and elegant stained glass that grace the walls of the cathedral. Like St. Patrick's, Christchurch Cathedral belongs to the Church of Ireland.

Dublin Medieval Heritage Centre, *Christchurch Place, open daily from 10:00 am until 5:00 pm from April through September, and Monday through Saturday 11:00 am to 4:00 pm, Sundays and holidays from 10:00 am to 4:30 pm. Admission is £3.95 for adults, and £2.90 for students and senior citizens. There is a family pass available (2 adults and 2 children) for £10 (children under 5 are free). Tel. (01) 679-4611.* Located in Synod Hall across from Christchurch Cathedral, the Dublin Medieval Heritage Centre (more commonly called Dublinia), allows visitors to step back into four hundred years of Dublin history. This is one of the best history learning centers in Dublin. You'll receive an audio headset that will guide you through the exhibit, beginning with the invasion of Strongbow in 1170, after which you'll be whisked through the sights and sounds of medieval Dublin up until the mid-1500's. Life-size models and rebuilt city scenes will help transport you back to days gone by. The tour is enlightening, educational, and entertaining – truly an enjoyable way to learn about Ireland's medieval times.

Tailors Hall, *Back Lane of Christchurch Place, open Monday through Friday from 9:00 am to 5:00 pm. Admission is free. Tel. 454-4794.* Tailors Hall is the last of what was once many guild halls in Dublin. Dating from 1706, this building has served as the guild hall of a number of trades, including saddlers, tanners, surgeons, and hosiers. Currently, it is the home of *An Taisce*, the Irish National Trust, whose charter is to preserve and restore the many ancient buildings in Ireland. Be sure to check out the carved musician's balcony.

Francis Street has become the de-facto antique section of Dublin. Although you'll find antique shops elsewhere in Dublin, nowhere is there the concentration as thick as you'll find here on Francis Street, just a block west of St. Patrick's Cathedral. Visitors will be enticed by many of the small shops, some of whose owners are as precious and delightful as the antiques they peddle.

Church of Ireland St. Audoen's, *High Street, open daily from 10:00 am until 4:30 pm. Admission is £1.50. Tel. (01) 679-1855.* St. Audoen's Church is the only existing medieval church in Dublin. It was originally called St. Ouen's, but has been altered through the years to its present name – St. Audoen's. The church is in a lovely park-like setting, surrounded by portions of the old city wall, and includes the only surviving gate to the city, **St. Audoen's Arch**. St. Audoen's boasts a set of bells that were made in 1423, and they are thought to be among Ireland's oldest. An extra treat is a good audiovisual presentation called *The Flame on the Hill*, which covers the history of Ireland before the arrival of the Vikings.

If you walk down the steps from the grounds of St. Audoen's to the Arch, you'll be on Cork street, originally the location of most of Dublin's coffin-makers!

Don't mistake this St. Audoen's for the nearby Catholic St. Audoen's. This one is a mere seven hundred or so years newer than the Catholic church of the same name.

The Dublin Viking Adventure, *Essex Quay, Open daily 10:00 am until 5:00 pm.* The Dublin Viking Adventure does its best to transport its visitors back to the days when Vikings ruled this part of Ireland. You are escorted about the recreated Viking city, including houses and shops and other typical sights, – even the sounds and smells. If you can, stay into the evening and enjoy a Viking dinner banquet.

The adventure all takes place within the walls of the converted Saints Michael and John Church. This former Catholic church has also served as a playhouse, so the Viking actors are right at home there.

St. Patrick's Cathedral, *Patrick Street, open Monday through Friday 9:00 am to 6:00 pm, Saturdays 9:00 am to 5:00 pm, and Sundays 10:00 am to 4:30 pm (it closes at 4:00 pm on weekends between November and March). Admission is £1.20 for adults and 50p for children and senior citizens. Tel. (01) 475-4817.* If you see only two cathedrals in Dublin, this should be one of them. Aside from the peaceful grounds, the immense beauty of the cathedral is truly a sight to behold.

Considered the National Cathedral of the Church of Ireland, St. Patrick's was founded in 1191. But its history goes back much farther. Local historians will tell you that this is perhaps the oldest Christian site in Dublin. It was on this spot that tradition says St. Patrick himself performed baptisms. Originally built outside the Dublin city walls, the location earned St. Patrick's the reputation of being the "church of the people," while Christchurch, which was built within the city walls, was considered by some to be the "church of the government."

Physically, St. Patrick's is impressive. The largest church in Ireland, its west clock tower rises 141 feet above Patrick Street, and the spire atop the tower rises another 101 feet, making the tip of the spire nearly two hundred and fifty feet above your head! As you walk into St. Patrick's, if it feels like the front of the cathedral is about a football field's length away, you're exactly right: the interior of the cathedral is three hundred feet long. As you might expect, St. Patrick's also boasts a number of stunning stained glass windows.

It's hard to believe that Oliver Cromwell showed his contempt for the cathedral by demanding that his horses be stabled inside the cathedral. This was a practice he replicated throughout the country at other churches, cathedrals, and town halls.

Jonathan Swift, the author of *Gulliver's Travels*, was Dean of St. Patrick's for over thirty years, from 1713 to 1745. His pulpit is still on display in the cathedral, along with sundry items belonging to him. At the west end of the nave you'll find Jonathan's bust, along with his pointed epitaph which he wrote: "Here he lies, where bitter indignation can no longer lacerate his heart. Go traveler and imitate if you can one who was, to the best of his powers, a defender of Liberty."

The organ, one of the more modern additions to the Cathedral, was installed in 1902, and is considered the most robust and powerful in all of Ireland.

The year Columbus set sail for America, two of Ireland's most powerful men, the Earl of Kildare and the Earl of Ormond, had been warring. The Earl of Ormond sought sanctuary in the Chapter House, and a standoff ensued. Tired of the war, the Earl of Kildare approached the Chapter House and chopped a hole in the door. As an act of reconciliation, he thrust his arm through the hole and grasped the hand of his enemy, ending the war. The door – called the "Door of Reconciliation" – is on display in the northeast section of the cathedral.

Marsh's Library, *St. Patrick's Close, Patrick Street, open Monday, Wednesday through Friday from 10:00 am to 5:00 pm, and Saturdays from 10:30 am until 12:45 pm. A £1 donation is requested. Tel. (01) 454-3511.* If you are a book lover, this is a place you'll want to visit. The first public library in Ireland, Marsh's Library was established in 1701 by Narcissus Marsh, the Archbishop of Dublin. The brick exterior of the library is unpretentious, and doesn't prepare you for what you'll find inside.

The decor is magnificent, and dark oak bookcases and wire cages house over 25,000 books and some 300 rare manuscripts. Most of the books are from the 16th through 18th centuries. Famed writers like Jonathan Swift and James Joyce used the library in their day. The Stillfleet Collection alone has over 10,000 books that date back to 1705. Books can no longer be checked out at Marsh's, but you can view some of the volumes in one of the wire cages.

Marsh's Library is located behind St. Patrick's Cathedral.

Guinness Brewery, *Crane Street, open Monday through Friday 10:00 am until 5:00 pm. Admission is £2 for adults, £1.50 for students, and 50p for senior citizens and children. (01) 453-8364 (information line), Tel. (01) 453-6700 (for reservations for large groups, or to talk to the Hop Store).* A trip to Ireland would not be complete unless you try their world famous Guinness beer. And there is no better place than the sprawling, sixty acre Guinness Brewery where Dubliners swear the beer tastes better! For the uninitiated, Guinness is a dark, heavy, bitter beer with a creamy head served at room temperature. For many, it is an acquired taste, but all beer lovers should try it at least once.

The brewery was founded on the banks of the River Liffey in 1759 by Arthur Guinness, and his descendants have carried on his work. The brewery produces an amazing four million pints of Guinness beer *per day*. Tours of the brewery itself are no longer conducted, but a fine audiovisual presentation on the history of the brewery is available in the Hop Store. At the close of the presentation, a complimentary sample of Guinness is available to those who wish to sample the dark brew.

The four-story Hop Store has been attractively converted into a museum, and the top floor serves as a venue for art shows.

South Dublin – Grafton Street District

Molly Malone statue, *Suffolk and Grafton Streets*. O'Connell Street may have *The Floozie in the Jacuzzi*, but Grafton Street has the bronze statue of

Molly Malone, *The Dish with the Fish!* Molly Malone, standing at the corner of Suffolk and Grafton Streets, is a featured character in an old Irish folk song. The song is taught to school children, sung in pubs, and bellowed at rugby, soccer, hurling, and Gaelic football games. The bodice on Molly's dress is so scandalously low (even for a statue!) that she has another name: *The Tart with the Cart.*

Trinity College, *College Street, open daily from 8:00 am to 10:00 pm. Admission is free.* Stately Trinity College is always alive with activity, both inside and outside its grounds. Personally, one of the things I like best about Trinity College is its *presence.* During your stay in Dublin, you will see it in paintings and drawings that are hundreds of years old – it was such an important site in the 16th through 19th centuries. It still is, for that matter.

Trinity College was built during the reign of **Queen Elizabeth I** in 1592 on the grounds of confiscated Catholic property, the Augustinian Priory of All Hallows. Most of the buildings now date from the early 1700s to the mid-1800s. Its buildings and grounds cover some forty acres in the heart of the city center.

Currently, Trinity College has about 8,000 full-time students. It was the first European university to allow women to earn degrees. However, for most of Trinity College's history, Catholics were barred from entering, not by the college, but rather by the Catholic Church. In the 1960s, this ban was lifted and Trinity College has become the renowned university it is today.

The front gate (known curiously as *The Front Gate!*) is flanked by two statues of the famous orator **Edmund Burke** and the poet **Oliver Goldsmith**, alumni of Trinity College. As you move beyond its huge wooden doors, check out the many announcement boards to see what's going on. Often, lunch-time concerts are scheduled, and everyone is welcome to attend.

Book of Kells, *Trinity College Colonnades, open Monday through Saturday 9:30 am to 4:30 pm, Sunday noon to 4:30 pm (last tour begins at 4:30 pm). Admission is £2 for adults, £1.50 for senior citizens, £1 for children, and there is a family ticket available for £5 (two adults and four children). Tel. (01) 677-2941.* Without a doubt, the most important holding at Trinity College is the Book of Kells, the ornately illustrated four Gospels written by the monks of the Kells monastery in County Meath. Written (drawn?) in the 9th century, the Book of Kells is four volumes of elaborate ornamental drawings of the four the Gospels. The title pages of each Gospel are particularly elaborate. There are also gorgeous pictures depicting many scenes from Christ's life, including his temptation and arrest.

The Book of Kells is kept in a glass case in a room with muted lighting. Two Gospels are shown at a time, and the pages are turned each day. The pages are calfskin made from 185 calves! As you look at the incredible craftsmanship and stunning artwork of the books, it's hard to imagine that these lovely works were once hidden under a roll of sod to protect them from the ravages of invaders!

As you enter the room, there are also cases along the walls (which you walk past while in line), that contain other ancient books, including the **Book of Durrow**, which was written in 675, and is the earliest surviving decorated book of the Gospels. The **Book of Armagh** is another you'll see, and it was written in 807.

To see the Book of Kells, you'll probably have to stand in line, but the line moves quickly thanks to college employees who gently encourage you to look and move along your way, a fact you appreciate more when the line moves than you do when you are finally the one who gets to look at the beautiful pages.

After you view of the Book of Kells, you are treated to a fascinating stroll through the lavish **Long Room of the Old Library** on your way out. This impressive room is over 200 feet long and forty feet wide. For nearly 200 years, Trinity College has been receiving a copy of every book published in Ireland and England, and many of them are on display here in the Old Library. You'll also be in the midst of another of the library's prized possessions: tall oak bookcases filled with over 200,000 old volumes of books. You walk between busts of Plato, Cicero, Newton, Demosthenes, and many other scholars.

The Dublin Experience, *Trinity College Davis Theater, Arts Building, open daily between 10:00 am and 5:00 pm from late May through the end of September. The shows run every hour on the hour. Admission is £2.75 for adults (£5 for the combined Book of Kells and the Dublin Experience), £2.25 for students and senior citizens (£4 combined ticket), £1.50 children. Tel. (01) 702-1688.* Trinity College has developed an excellent multimedia presentation on the first 1,000 years of Dublin history, although it covers much of the same ground other similar presentations in the city do. If you've seen any of them, pass on this one.

Bank of Ireland, *College Green, open Monday through Friday from 10:00 am to 12:30 pm and 1:30 pm to 4:00 pm. Admission is free. Tel. (01) 671-1671.* Across from Trinity College at the corner of College and Dame Streets is the semi-circular Bank of Ireland. When the edifice was completed in 1729, it housed both houses of Parliament – the House of Commons and the House of Lords, and was the first building ever built for the express purpose of housing Parliament.

In the House of Lords hangs two very old and very impressive tapestries: one portrays William of Orange's defeat of King James II at the Battle of the Boyne in 1690, and the other depicts the fifteen-week Siege of Derry in 1689. These were significant turning points in Ireland's history. Both tapestries have hung here since 1735 – over two hundred and fifty years! Encased in glass at one end of the room is the ornate speaker's mace.

In 1800, the Irish Parliament did something no other Parliament had done or has since done – they voted themselves out of existence, handing over all governance to the good graces of London. The building was then sold to the Bank of Ireland, who has been its only tenant since then. When the Bank of Ireland purchased the building, they converted the House of Commons into a spacious lobby, but left the House of Lords intact.

You can browse around the House of Lords (it's not very big), and nearby attendants will answer questions and tell you a little of the history of the room and building.

DUBLIN LITERARY PUB CRAWL

Meets at The Duke Pub, Duke Street. Easter through October 31: Monday - Saturday 3:00 pm, Sundays at noon, nightly 7:30 pm. November through Easter: Sundays at noon, Thursday through Saturday 7:30 pm. Admission is £6. Tel. (01) 454-0228. As you walk south on Grafton Street from Trinity College, look for their temporary sign along the left side of the walk directing you onto Duke Street. The admission charge doesn't cover the cost of any drinks you consume as you move from pub to pub.

*Officially called the **Jameson Dublin Literary Pub Crawl**, this trip around the Dublin is well worth your time. Local actors (eight of them) take turns entertaining, informing, shocking, and delighting their guests with tales of Ireland's most noteworthy writers: **Behan, Joyce, Yeats, Wilde, Goldsmith, Shaw**, and others. Each session is conducted by a two-some (mine were Derrick and Donough).*

These very accomplished actors take your group on a tour of several pubs frequented by famous writers – usually four or five, as well as onto the grounds of Trinity College. Along the way they regale you with stories and anecdotes from the lives of these writers. You'll find out which journalist referred to himself as a "bicycle built for two" (and why) and learn which writer characterized himself as "A good drinker who had trouble with writing." Blended in is some of the history of Irish struggles against the English, but it's done without a lot of serious political rhetoric.

A rollicking good time, full of literary one-liners, a little irreverence, lots of laughs, a little bawdy at times, and plenty of good clean (mostly) fun!

Across from Trinity College is **Grafton Street**, a long pedestrian open air mall. Grafton Street is a fascinating blend of antique, jewelry, and upscale shops, with a generous mix of *buskers*, street entertainers, ranging from musicians to magicians, jugglers to Marionette masters, and a host of other talented individuals. Street peddlers also hawk their wares, ranging from silk ties and silver rings to cassettes and macramé.

Dublin Civic Museum, *South William Street, open Tuesday through Saturday 10:00 am to 6:00 pm, Sundays 11:00 am to 2:00 pm. Free admission. Tel. (01) 679-4260.* This small museum is a winner for history buffs. The museum's primary focus is the history of Dublin, its people, and its environs. The eclectic collection includes Stone Age implements to Viking tokens to the sculpted head of Admiral Horatio Nelson. Admiral Nelson's image once had a slightly more dignified location atop Nelson's Pillar beside the General Post Office. However, in 1966, on the fiftieth anniversary of the Easter Rising, Admiral Nelson lost his head, and pillar, to a bomb. Seems as though Irish loyalists resented the good Admiral's image presiding over the goings-on at the GPO!

Powerscourt Townhouse Centre, *Clarendon Street.* As you are walking south on Grafton Street, turn right onto narrow Johnston's Court and you'll find Powerscourt Townhouse – a converted Georgian townhouse chock full of a score of shops and cafes. It's one of the most charming "malls" you'll ever visit.

Mansion House, *Dawson Street.* The official residence for the Lord Mayor of Dublin, the Mansion House was built in 1710 for **John Dawson**. Five years later he sold it to the Dublin Corporation to serve as the Mayor's residence, which it has served as since that time. Several important events in modern Irish history happened within the four walls of the Mansion House: the first Irish Parliament met here in 1919; the Declaration of Independence from England in 1919 was adopted, and the truce that ended the fighting between England and Ireland in 1921 was signed here.

Unfortunately, the house is not generally open to the public, although it is often the site for various exhibits such as antique shows and book fairs.

The Royal Irish Academy, *19 Dawson Street, open Monday through Friday 10:30 am to 5:00 pm. Admission is free. Tel. (01) 676-2570.* The Royal Irish Academy was founded in 1752 and has been located here since 1852. The leading scholarly society in Dublin, the Royal Irish Academy takes great pride in its collection of ancient manuscripts. One of its most valuable is the Psalter of **Saint Columcille**, a partial copy of the Vulgate version of Psalms. Another is the Book of the Dun Cow, a 12th-century manuscript penned at Clonmacnoise. Each week the Academy presents an exhibition of an ancient manuscript.

Genealogical Office, *2 Kildare Street, open Monday through Friday from 9:30 am to 5:30 pm. Admission is free.* So your mother was an O'Kelly and your grandfather a Murphy, and you'd like to do a little genealogical research into the family tree? The Genealogical Office is a good place to begin. The employees here are helpful in assisting you identify those long-lost cousins.

Researching your genealogy in Ireland is like doing it anywhere in the world: the more information you have the better. Pump Mom and Dad, your grandparents and anyone else in your family for as much information as you can: dates of birth (even approximate year), county, town, parish, maiden names, parent's names, etc. See the *Genealogy* chapter in this book for more information.

Heraldic Museum, *2 Kildare Street, open Monday through Friday from 10:30 am to 12:30 pm and 2:00 pm to 4:30 pm. Admission is free. Tel. (01) 661-4877.* Located with the Genealogical Office, the Heraldic Museum has a fine display of coats of arms that extend back many centuries. Go in and see if you can find yours!

Leinster House, *Kildare Street, open when Parliament is not in session. Admission is free. Tel. (01) 678-9911.* Built over two hundred and fifty years ago (1725) for the Duke of Leinster, Leinster House serves as the meeting place for the Irish House of Representatives (*Dail Eireann*) and the Senate (*Seanad Eireann*).

Visitors are only admitted to the visitor's gallery upon invitation of a member of Parliament. Check with the Dublin Tourism Centre, *Tel. (01) 605-7777,* to see if they can arrange a visit (they often can). The Irish sometimes view their elected officials with humor. As an example, Leinster House has sometimes been referred to as "The National Home for the Terminally Bewildered."

The National Library of Ireland, *Kildare Street, open Monday 10:00 am until 9:00 pm, Tuesdays and Wednesdays 2:00 pm until 9:00 pm, Thursday and Friday 10:00 am until 5:00 pm, and Saturdays 10:00 am until 1:00 pm. Admission is free.* The National Library of Ireland is so much more than a library. First of all, it is a visual treasure. Architecturally stunning, the highlights of the library are the large rotunda and the domed reading room. In addition, exhibits are frequently available on Irish art and history.

National Museum of Ireland, *Kildare Street, open Tuesday through Saturday 10:00 am to 5:00 pm and Sunday from 2:00 pm to 5:00 pm. Admission is free (except for special exhibits). Tel. (01) 661-8811.* The National Museum of Ireland recently celebrated its 100th anniversary (1890 – 1990) and is looking forward to another outstanding 100+ years. Located next to the Leinster House, the National Museum of Ireland was originally the combination of several historical collections. It has a number of fascinating displays which take you through the history of Ireland from the Bronze Age (2200 BC to 700 BC) to the present.

The Treasury Exhibition (the only part of the museum requiring a modest admission fee) includes the lovely Tara Brooch (8th-century), the Ardagh Chalice (8th-century), and the silver and bronzed Cross of Cong (12th-century), and much more. One of the highlights of the museum is a replica of the New Grange passage grave in County Meath. The actual cross-shaped tomb – about an hour north of Dublin – is nearly 5,000 years old and is wonderfully preserved. If you can't make the drive, be sure and see the replica at the museum. *Ar Thóir na Saoirse*, which means "The Road to Independence," is a permanent exhibit that deals with the major personalities and events that took place from 1916 to 1922 in the struggle for Ireland's independence.

Shelbourne Hotel, *27 St. Stephen's Green North, Tel. (01) 676-6471*. The Shelbourne Hotel bears mentioning here. Across the street from the north side of St. Stephen's Green, The Shelbourne is where the drafting of the Irish Constitution took place in 1922. The staff does not mind you coming in and looking around a bit. Better yet, stop in for a spot of tea or coffee in the superb Lord Mayor's lounge.

Huguenot Cemetery, *St. Stephen's Green North*. Next to the Shelbourne is Hotel is the Huguenot Cemetery, final resting place of French Huguenots who left persecution in their native lands for Ireland. Alas, you cannot walk through the grounds, but you can view them from the wrought-iron gates.

St. Stephen's Green, *at the south end of Grafton Street*, is a very peaceful, serene city park. In the 17th century this twenty-two acre area was an open common, but in the early 1800s it became a private garden for residents whose property circled it. An annual one guinea (about $1.75) maintenance fee was charged for upkeep and access to the gardens. In 1877, Sir Arthur Guinness (of brewery fame) was instrumental in passing an act of Parliament that opened the park to the public. Because of his magnanimous gesture, Dubliners allowed him to personally pay for many of the improvements to the park, including the lake, fountains, trees and many of the gardens.

There are a number of memorials in the park that are worthy of your attention. The Romanesque arch over the main entrance at the northwest corner of the park is called the Fusiliers Arch, and it is a memorial to the Dublin Fusiliers who fought and died during the Boer War. There is a memorial dedicated to the memory of **W. B. Yeats**. Don't miss the fountain and statue of the Three Fates, a statue given to the Irish by a grateful German government for the relief they provided to the needy at the close of World War II. Other individuals memorialized in St. Stephen's Green include **James Joyce**, **Wolfe Tone**, and those who perished in the potato famine.

There is a children's playground, lots of ducks for the children (and you) to feed, a Victorian bandstand (where free lunch time concerts are given throughout the summer), and a unique garden designed especially for the blind. The plants are labeled in Braille, and they are also resilient enough to be handled.

Newman House, *85/86 St. Stephen's Green South, open June through September Tuesday through Friday from 10:00 am until 4:30 pm, Saturdays 1:00 pm until 3:30 pm and Sundays from 11:00 am until 1:00 pm. Admission is £1 for adults, and 75p for children and senior citizens.* Across the street from the south side of St. Stephen's Green is Newman House. Newman House is named after **Cardinal John Henry Newman**, who founded the first Catholic University in Dublin at Number 86, St. Stephen's Green South. **James Joyce** was one of the more illustrious individuals to call the Catholic University his alma mater (he attended from 1899 to 1902). In fact, one of the rooms has been renovated to look as classroom would have looked at the turn of the century. The period furniture nicely accents the masterful plaster work in both houses. The small admission fee includes a guided tour of both buildings, as well as a short video presentation on the history of the building.

Don't forget to take a peek at **Iveagh Gardens** that run behind Newman House and **Iveagh House**. The entrance to the gardens is around the corner, left at Harcourt Street, then left on Clonmel Street to the garden gate.

National Concert Hall, *Earlsfort Terrace, prices range from £5 to £15. Tel. (01) 671-1533.* At the southeast corner of St. Stephen's Green and across the street from the Conrad Hotel is the National Concert Hall. Formerly the location of the University College of Dublin, the Concert Hall is the site of many events throughout the year. It is especially pretty on performance nights, when it is lit with spotlights.

Royal Hibernian Academy (RHA) Gallagher Gallery, *Ely Place, open Monday through Wednesday and Friday through Saturday from 11:00 am to 5:00 pm; Thursday from 11:00 am to 9:00 pm, Sundays from 2:00 pm until 5:00 pm. Admission is free.* This small Gallery houses an eclectic collection of Irish and continental art. With several other more notable art museums close by, this one tends to get passed over by most visitors. I enjoyed it.

Natural History Museum, *Merrion Street, open Tuesday through Saturday from 10:00 am to 5:00 pm, Sunday from 2:00 pm until 5:00 pm. Admission is free. Tel. (01) 661-8811.* The Natural History Museum, founded in 1857, is part of the National Museum of Ireland. George Bernard Shaw reportedly said that he owed much of his education to the gallery and showed his gratitude by leaving one third of his estate to the museum.

The collection includes an outstanding exhibit of Irish fauna, including an especially impressive skeleton of a giant Irish deer, a distant cousin of the elk, African and Asian animals, and two large whale skeletons suspended from the ceiling. (The whales are former Irish residents *of sorts* – they washed up on Irish shores!) The museum is also internationally renowned for its extensive entomological collection.

If you are vacationing with children, I'm sure they'd enjoy this museum.

National Gallery of Ireland, *Merrion Square West, open Monday through Saturday 10:00 am to 5:30 pm, (Thursday until 8:30 pm), Sunday from 2:00 pm until 5:00 pm. Admission is free. Tel. (01) 661-5133.* Established by an Act of Parliament almost one hundred and fifty years ago (1854), the National Gallery of Ireland spent ten years collecting paintings, sculptures, and other pieces of art before opening in January 1864. The grand opening of the museum boasted over one hundred paintings and numerous statues. Today there are over 2,400 paintings, 300 sculptures and an incredible assortment of various other pieces to catch your eye.

If you are hoping to see works of art by Irish painters, you won't be disappointed. I suppose every major Irish artist – and many not-so-major artists – are represented here. In addition, there is a fine European collection, including works by such notables as Rembrandt, Degas, El Greco, Goya, Monet, Reynolds, Rubens, Titian, Van Dyck, and others. One of the museums most extraordinary aspects is a four story circular staircase lined with paintings of three centuries worth of notable personalities in Irish history, a kind of wall of fame.

Guided tours are offered on Saturday afternoons at 3:00 pm and Sundays at 2:30 pm, 3:15 pm, and 4:00 pm. If you find yourself here around lunch time, there is an award-winning self-serve restaurant.

Laid out in the center of one of the most impressive displays of Georgian architecture in the city, **Merrion Square** is a place to get away from the omnipresent Dublin traffic. Merrion Square is about a half-block south and east of the Trinity College grounds. The park dates from 1762, and is a lovely assemblage of gardens, shrubs, and trees. Over the years, a number of Ireland's most important and esteemed citizens called the fine Georgian townhouses around Merrion Square home, including **Oscar Wilde's** parents *(Number 1)*, **Daniel O'Connell** *(Number 58)*, **W. B. Yeats** *(Numbers 52 and 82)* and the **Duke of Wellington** *(Number 24 Upper Merrion Street)*. Many of the homes have plaques identifying their famous inhabitants.

Number Twenty-Nine Fitzwilliam Street, *open Tuesday through Saturday from 10:00 am to 5:00 pm, Sunday from 2:00 pm to 5:00 pm. Admission is free. Tel. (01) 702-6165.* The National Museum of Ireland and the Electricity Supply Board have combined their talents and funds to restore Number Twenty-Nine as it likely was in the late 18th century – the home of a middle-class family. Great attention to detail has been given to everything from the woodwork to the furnishings, walls and ceilings. Take special note of the floor and window coverings, as well as the numerous paintings. Number Twenty-Nine is a little more subdued than a similar exhibit at the **Newman House**, but both are nice (and this one is free).

South Dublin – Ballsbridge District

The **Grand Canal** runs from Dublin Bay in a semi-circular route around the south side of Dublin and then it wends its way out into the Irish countryside all the way to the river Shannon in the center of the country. The Gand Canal was used to transport passengers as well as fragile cargo such as pottery and glass products (manufacturers preferred the smooth canal to the bumpy roads). Farmers also used the canal to bring produce to market.

Construction on the canal began in 1756 and was completed in 1804, and was formerly in constant use for commercial ventures, as small barges and canal boats navigated its waters through a series of locks. Today, the paths along the canal see the most use as Dubliners and others stroll along the banks.

The Chester Beatty Library and Gallery of Oriental Art, *20 Shrewsbury Road, Ballsbridge, open Tuesday through Friday from 10:00 am to 5:00 pm and Saturday from 2:00 pm to 5:00 pm. Admission is free. Tel. (01) 269-2386.* In 1956, Sir Alfred Chester Beatty bequeathed his private collection of Oriental art to Ireland. This outstanding collection of Oriental art and antiquities contains over 22,000 items, including rare books and manuscripts, miniature paintings, over 270 ancient copies of the Koran, clay tablets from Babylon, and some of the earliest known Biblical papyri in existence. In fact, their extensive Biblical collection includes Armenian, Coptic, Ethiopian and Syriac texts. The collection is scheduled to move to its new home, Dublin Castle, in 1997.

Sandymount Strand is the closest beach to Dublin. The beach is about three miles long, and when the tide goes out, it extends about a mile out. A favorite beach of **James Joyce**, Sandymount Strand has a prominent role in Joyce's work *Ulysses*. This is a popular place to collect shellfish. The walk out to Poolbeg lighthouse is a pleasant one, and a favorite of locals and tourists alike. This isn't a particularly good beach for swimming, though, as the surf has a tendency to come in very rapidly. Walk along its shores, or search for shellfish, but be alert for the rapidly rising tides.

You can reach Sandymount Strand by taking the DART to Sandymount Station. Head east on Sandymount Avenue to Gilford, then you can turn left or right: either way will get you to Sandymount Strand. It's about a three hundred yard walk.

Waterways Visitors Centre, *Ringsend Basin, open June to September every day from 9:30 am to 6:30 pm, March through May and October, every day from 10:00 am to 5:00 pm (closed from 1:00 pm to 2:00 pm for lunch). Call for appointment November through February. Admission is £1.50 for adults and 60p for children.* This unique modern building sits on stilts in the Grand Canal Basin near the Pearse Street Bridge. It houses an interesting exhibit on the history and importance of the various waterways in Ireland, including a working model of a canal lock. There is also a section on the marine life – animal and plant – found throughout the canals.

West Dublin

Phoenix Park originally opened to the public over two hundred and fifty years ago, is the largest city park in Europe at over 1,700 acres, and it is a delightful place to visit. If you enjoy parks and have the time, you could easily spend a half day here; a full day if you also go to the zoo, watch a polo match or a cricket game. With green fields punctuated by pools and ponds, the park serves as a relaxing contrast to the hustle and bustle of the city. Phoenix Park is about two miles from the Dublin's city center.

As you enter the park from its main gate on the southeast side, you're greeted by the 195 foot monument honoring **Arthur Wellesley**, the first Duke of Wellington. You may ask yourself why this British general who defeated Napoleon at Waterloo rates a monument in Dublin? After all, a similar monument to the British **Admiral Nelson** – another victor over Napoleon – was so ill-received by Dubliners that it was blown to pieces by some unknown hand. The answer is Wellington was a native Dubliner. Despite his choice of armies, his victory at Waterloo earned him fame and hero status in Ireland.

Across the road from Wellington's monument is the **People's Garden**, a lovely set of banked gardens surrounding a small lake.

Just ahead on your right is the **Phoenix Zoo**, which was founded in 1831. It has a wide variety of animals, and an area for the children to get "up close and personal" with a number of less exotic creatures like rabbits, chickens, and goats.

The **polo grounds** are just beyond the zoo, and practices or matches are fun to watch, whether you understand all the rules or not (I don't). The horses are magnificent, and to see them wheeling and charging is really a treat. The riders aren't bad either.

Just past the polo grounds is the home of the president of Ireland, called **Aras an Uactarain**. In 1882, the British Chief Secretary to Ireland and his assistant were murdered outside the house by five extremists, members of a rebel band called "The Invincibles." One of the killers turned state's witness, and his four partners were executed at Kilmainham jail. Shortly afterwards, the pardoned killer tried to flee the country for Cape Town, but was assassinated by another member of the Invincibles. The murderer of the murderer/informant was later convicted and executed.

On the far south side of the park is the former site of the **Dublin Dueling Grounds**, where the gentility of Dublin came to shoot at each other. Today the area hosts far more civilized hostility and competition in the form of hurling, cricket, and football. Matches/games are typically played around 3:00 pm on Saturdays and Sundays from mid-May through September.

The beautiful park is not named after the mythological bird that rises from the ashes, but rather from the Irish words *fionn uisce* (clear water), which sounds like Phoenix in English. On nice days, old men and women in their Sunday best sit on many of the park benches, just enjoying the nice weather and watching the people go by. Families cavort on the grass, visit the zoo, and feed the omnipresent ducks. Lovers walk arm and arm oblivious to the beauty around them.

Dublin Zoo, *Phoenix Park, open daily (closed Christmas) from 9:30 am until 6:00 pm. Admission is £5.50 for adults and £2.75 for senior citizens and children under 16, 3 and younger are free. Family tickets available for £13 (two adults and two children), or £15.50 (two adults and four children). Tel. (01) 677-1425.* The zoo's main claim to fame is that lions breed here almost as well as they do in the wild. They are one of the few zoos in the world that can make that claim. And they do it in a big way – over seven hundred lions have been bred here since they began the program in 1851. The famous MGM lion claims the Dublin Zoo as his birthplace.

Ashtown Castle, *Phoenix Park, open daily 10:00 am until 5:00 pm (closed from 1:00 pm until 2:00 pm) March through May, 9:30 am to 6:30 pm June through September, and in October from 2:00 pm until 5:00 pm. Admission is £1.50 for adults and 60p for children under 16. Senior citizens are £1. Family tickets are available for £4. Tel. (01) 677-0095.* This unassuming medieval fortress was built in the 17th century. The small visitors center hosts presentations on the history of Phoenix Park and on the various plants and animals you'll find there. I was frankly underwhelmed, but you might find it interesting.

Kilmainham Gaol Historical Museum, *Inchicore Road, open daily from 11:00 am until 6:00 pm (May through September), and Monday through Friday from 1:00 pm until 4:00 pm and Sundays 1:00 pm until 6:00 pm (October through April). The last tour begins one hour before closing. Admission is £2 adults, £1.50 senior citizens, £1 for children. A family pass is also available for £5. Tel. (01) 453-5984.* Step into the darker side of Ireland's past. This restored prison gives its guests a peek into the terrible conditions endured by Irish patriots awaiting execution or a one-way ticket to Australia. From its first political prisoners in 1796 until its last in 1924, Kilmainham Gaol meant nothing but misery for Irish patriots. Among the most infamous acts committed here was the execution of those who penned their names to the Proclamation of the Republic in 1916.

After the last prisoner was released in 1924 (it happened to be the former president of the rebel Irish Republic, Eamon de Valera) the prison fell into disrepair, and it was through the efforts of a few who didn't wish for this chapter to be forgotten that the jail was restored. You'll chill as you view the Hanging Room and cringe at the prison yard where executions took place.

A short audiovisual presentation is included in the tour, and gives you the highlights of the Irish struggle for independence.

Royal Hospital Kilmainham/Irish Museum of Modern Art, *Kilmainham Lane, open Monday through Saturday 10:00 am to 5:30 pm, Sundays from noon until 5:30 pm. Admission is free. Tel. (01) 671-8666.* This splendid building was formerly the Royal Hospital Kilmainham (RHK). It was built in 1684 after the manner of *Les Invalides* in Paris, and its original purpose was to house ill and infirm soldiers, a tribute to their service to Britain. After the establishment of the Irish Free State in 1922, the building was closed and fell into severe disrepair. A fifteen year, $30,000,000 renovation project has paid handsome dividends – the building is once again a grand structure.

Now the RHK is home to the Irish Museum of Modern Art (IMMA): four galleries surrounding a large and lovely courtyard. An eclectic array of 20th-century art is exhibited throughout the museum, and there always seems to be a one man show, or theme exhibit going on. The Banqueting Hall is now the site of frequent concerts and special activities. Perhaps the prettiest room is the chapel, which has rich wood paneling and a Baroque ceiling.

This grand structure is worth a visit even if you have no interest in modern art.

OUTSIDE THE CITY LIMITS - NORTH OF DUBLIN

National Botanic Gardens

Glasnevin Road, Glasnevin, open during the summer months Monday through Saturday from 9:00 am until 6:00 pm, Sundays from 11:00 am to 6:00 pm; open during the winter months Monday through Saturday from 10:00 am to 4:30 pm, and Sundays from 11:00 am to 4:30 pm. Admission is free. Tel. (01) 837-7596 or (01) 837-4388. This is a real treat and worth the short drive (or bus – numbers 13, 19, or 34, or cab ride). Visitors have enjoyed these gardens for over two hundred years.

The gardens boast over 20,000 plant species spread over 45 acres, but the oversized arboretum threatens to steal the show. Completed in 1869, it recently went through an extensive restoration. The greenhouses – over 400 feet of them – house an astounding variety of exotic plants and trees, such as orchids, banana trees, and palm trees. The Tolka River runs through the gardens. Cross over the pretty wooden bridge into the gorgeous rose gardens for a special treat.

Clontarf

Two and a half miles north of Dublin along the seaside is the residential community of Clontarf. Running east of Clontarf is the **North Bull Wall**, a man-made wall built to prevent silt from building up in Dublin Harbor. Not only did it succeed in doing that, but it also added a new geographical sight to Ireland, North Bull Island. Due to the gradual build-up of silt, North Bull Island is over three miles long and still growing. Other unforseen benefits are new plant and animal life along the sand dunes and salt marshes. Tens of thousands of migrating birds, such as ducks and geese, can now be seen here during the winter months.

Howth

Lying about nine miles north of Dublin city center, Howth (pro-nounced Hoath) is a small, picturesque seaside fishing village. In recent years, Howth has spruced up its appearance, and the town is really quite nice to visit. A short twenty-minute DART ride from Dublin, Howth offers several excellent restaurants, splendid views, and stunning sunsets. They have a nice quay that extends out into the harbor that is popular with Dubliners, locals, and tourists.

Howth Cliff Walk begins at the end of the main street in Howth, near King Sitric Restaurant. This one and a half mile cliff walk takes you along the edge of the cliff to the apex, where you'll find the Bailey Lighthouse, built in 1814 as a beacon for generations of incoming sailors.

Transport Museum, *Howth, open July to September daily 10:00 am to 6:00 pm, October through June Saturday and Sunday from noon until 5:00 pm. Admission is £1 for adults and 50p for children. Tel. (01) 848-0831.* Near the Howth DART station is the Transport Museum. A variety of transport vehicles are on display from the horse and buggy days to the present time. Horse-drawn vehicles, old tractors, military vehicles, and double-decker buses are on display. The star of the show is the old Number 9 – the Hill of Howth tram. The tram ran to the top of Howth Hill and back for nearly sixty years before its retirement in 1960. In recent years volunteers have been working to restore it to its former condition.

Howth Castle Gardens, *Howth, open daily year-round from 8:00 am to sundown. Admission is free.* Behind Deer Park Hotel, the Howth Castle Gardens offer a distinct treat: over thirty acres of rhododendron gardens. They are best seen from April through June, when there are in full bloom. There are over 2,000 varieties of rhododendrons, including many rare species. Also located in the gardens is a large Neolithic dolmen.

Marino Casino, *Malahide Road, Malahide, open mid-June through mid-September from 10:00 am to 6:30 pm. Admission is £1. Tel. (01) 833-1618.* About two and a half or three miles north of the Dublin city center is Marino Casino. Don't worry about bringing lots of money to gamble with, because the term "Casino" in this case does not refer to a gambling hall at all. It takes its name from the Italian *cassino*, which means "small house." In other words, it merely identifies this smaller house that is associated with a larger house. In this case, Marino Casino was once associated with the much larger Charlemont Mansion, the residence of **James Caulfield**, the first Earl of Charlemont, which was destroyed in 1921.

Fortunately, the Casino, whose neo-classical architecture gives it a sense of classical prowess and grace, still stands proudly. Restored in 1984, the sixteen room Casino has been refurbished with appropriate ornamentation, period furnishings, and antiques.

Look closely at the exterior of this fine building that dates from 1780. The urns at the top double as chimneys and the ultra-impressive columns are actually hollow, serving as drainage pipes for frequent rains!

Malahide Castle, *Malahide, open January through December Monday through Friday from 10:00 am to 5:00 pm, November through March on Saturdays and Sundays from 2:00 pm to 5:00 pm, April through October on Saturdays and Sundays from 11:30 am to 6:00 pm. Admission for adults is £2.75, students (12 to 18 years) and senior citizens £2.15, and children (3 to 11 years) £1.40. There is a family ticket (two adults and four children) for £7.50. Combination tickets (with the Fry Railway Museum) are available for adults £4.35, students and seniors £3.35, children £2.25, and a family ticket for £10.95. Tel. (01) 846-2184.* This ancient fortress was built in 1174, and was lived in by members of the Talbot family until 1973, when the last Lord Talbot died. A jewel set in a crown of over two hundred and fifty luscious acres of land, Malahide Castle is remarkably well-preserved. Unlike many of the fortresses and castles in Ireland, it did not go through years of neglect and destruction.

The Banqueting Hall, Oak Room, and Drawing Room are just a few of the rooms you'll see as you tour the castle. Each is furnished in exquisite period furniture, such as a side table decorated with a beautiful, detailed inlay of oak leaves. Many of the antiques here were originally used in the castle. On July 1, 1690, fourteen members of the Talbot family breakfasted together at the long table that still exists in the Banqueting Hall. It was to be their last meal together; by nightfall, all had been killed in the Battle of the Boyne. Included on the grounds is a botanical garden containing over 5,000 varieties of plants, all labeled and the Fry Model Railway Museum. There is also a gift shop and restaurant on the castle premises if you get hungry or are looking for souvenirs.

The Fry Model Railway Museum, *Malahide Castle, open April through September Monday through Thursday from 10:00 am to 6:00 pm, and Saturday from 11:00 am to 6:00 pm, Sunday from 2:00 pm to 6:00 pm. June through August also open Fridays from 10:00 am to 6:00 pm, and October through March Saturday and Sunday from 2:00 pm to 5:00 pm. Admission for adults is £2.35,* *students (12 to 18 years) and senior citizens £1.75, and children (to 11 years) £1.30. There is a family ticket available for £6.75 (two adults and four children). Combination tickets (with Malahide Castle) are available for adults £4.35, students and seniors £3.35, children £2.25, and a family ticket for £10.95. Tel. (01) 846-3779.* Located in the gardens of Malahide Castle, the railway museum is the result of the life-long work of a passionate railroad fan, Cyril Fry. Fry, a railroad engineer, spent years painstaking working to build the trains and a miniature Dublin, complete with models of Cork and Heuston stations, O'Connell and Ha'penny bridges, cars, boats, barges (on the River Liffey, of course!) and elevated tracks. The "city" and railway is laid out on a 72 feet by 32 feet display.

Mr. Fry began his work on the railway in the 1920s, and continued adding, reworking and retouching his masterpiece over the ensuing decades.

Newbridge House, *Donabate, open April through October, Monday through Friday from 10:00 am to 5:00 pm and Sunday 2:00 pm to 6:00 pm, and November through March Sundays from 2:00 pm until 5:00 pm. Admission is £2.50 for adults and £1.25 for children. Tel. (01) 843-6534.* This Georgian home set on 350 acres of land has been restored for your enjoyment. The main house was built in 1740, and an addition was added fifteen years later. Not all of the house is open to the public, but there is a lovely Drawing Room, several reception rooms, and the original 18th-century kitchen and laundry, both purporting to have the actual original utensils used in both rooms, that you can see. Each room has been painstakingly restored with many original furnishings to represent what it might have looked like in the 1700s. Paintings, furniture, and a variety of knick-knacks will make you feel as though you've walked into the parlor of the Archbishop of Dublin, for whom the house was built.

Tara's Palace, a miniature dollhouse, has over two dozen decorated rooms. There is also an antique doll collection that has over 150 dolls.

Outside in the courtyard you'll find the dairy, blacksmith's and carpenter's shops. There is even a mini-farm, where children can pet rabbits, sheep, goats, and other sundry farm animals.

Not as grand as some of the other Georgian homes that are open to the public in Dublin, the Newbridge House offers a little more, such as the doll collection and the mini-farm.

OUTSIDE THE CITY LIMITS - SOUTH OF DUBLIN

Dun Laoghaire

Dun Laoghaire, pronounced *Dunleary* (really!), is a favorite escape for Dublin city dwellers as well as tourists. In Irish the name means Leary's Fort. A short DART ride south of Dublin (about 7 miles), this pleasant, predominantly residential town is also where you can catch the ferry to Holyhead (and visa versa), three and a half to four hours away.

People come to relax, take in the salt air and walk out on the two fine piers that extend about a mile and a half into the Irish Sea. Sundays are the most popular days in Dun Laoghaire. Today, the town still proudly exhibits its Victorian homes along with many excellent pubs and restaurants.

For nearly one hundred years, from 1821 to 1920, Dun Laoghaire was called Kingstown in honor of a brief visit from England's King George IV. But the citizens decided to reclaim the original Irish name during the Civil War with England.

To get here, take the subway to the Dun Laoghaire DART Station.

The National Maritime Museum, *Haigh Terrace, Dun Laoghaire, open May through September Tuesday through Sunday 2:30 pm to 5:30 pm. Admission is £1. Tel. (01) 280-0969.* The National Maritime Museum is housed in Mariner's Church, and is home to an eclectic collection of nautical novelties, including a captured French longboat and the Bailey Optic, which until 1972 illuminated the night for many seafarers from the old 1814 Bailey lighthouse at Howth Head.

People's Park, *Dun Laoghaire.* On the road from Dun Laoghaire to Sandycove, this small public park is a pleasant retreat with pretty views, lovely landscaping, and a playground for active children.

James Joyce Tower, *Dun Laoghaire, open April through October Monday to Saturday from 10:00 am to 5:00 pm (closed from 1:00 pm to 2:00 pm for lunch) and Sunday from 2:00 pm to 6:00 pm. The rest of the year you need to call for an appointment. Admission fee is £2 for adults, students (12 to 18) and seniors are £1.60, and £1.10 for children (3 to 11 years). There is a family ticket for £5.80 (2 adults and 4 children). Tel. (01) 280-9265 or (01) 872-2077.* Strange as this may seem, we can thank Napoleon for this exhibit. From 1804 through 1815, the Martello Towers were built on strategic promontories on the south and east coasts of Ireland to give early warning of Napoleonic forces. Strongly fortified in the event of attack, these impressive structures are made of forty feet high, eight feet thick granite, and offer a commanding view of the sea for miles around. In modern times, many of the Towers were converted into living quarters.

James Joyce lived in one such tower for a short time around the turn of the century as a guest of his friend **Oliver St. John Gogarty** (who had rented it from the Army for the princely sum of 67 pence a month). He was so impressed with the tower that it figures prominently in the opening pages of his famous book *Ulysses.* He was also impressed with his friend; Gogarty was to Buck Mulligan what Tom Blankenship was to Mark Twain's Huckleberry Finn. (For those of you who may not have read *Ulysses*, the main character is Buck Mulligan.)

A collection of Joycean objects are on view in the James Joyce Tower: his waistcoat, cigar case, a tie, numerous first editions of his book, a piano and guitar once belonging to him, and his death mask, taken in 1941.

Forty Foot Bathing Pool, *Dun Laoghaire*. Near the James Joyce Tower is Sandycove Beach, a beach traditionally frequented by nude male swimmers. In recent years, however, women have made inroads into this male haven, but generally speaking, men are still the predominant bathers here.

NIGHTLIFE & ENTERTAINMENT

There is a lot of fun nightlife in Dublin, centered around pubs and nightclubs. Within each category of nightlife, the selections are listed in alphabetical order.

Traditional Irish Music

ABBEY TAVERN, *Howth, Tel. (01) 839-0307.*

As mentioned in the *Where to Eat* section, Abbey Tavern could be one of the best places in Ireland for an evening of traditional Irish music.

THE AULD DUBLINER, *Anglesea Street, Tel. (01) 677-0527.*

The Auld Dubliner Pub is a typical Irish pub, offering lively traditional Irish music several nights a week, and almost every night during the tourist season. Call to find out when, and who is performing, or better yet, just wander in during your strolls around the Temple Bar District.

BRAZEN HEAD, *Bridge Street, Tel. (01) 679-5186.*

One of the most famous venues for traditional Irish music in Dublin., the Brazen Head is reputed (and disputed) to be Dublin's oldest pub. It has served many a pint continually since 1688. When you walk in, it feels like a pub ought to feel. Particularly enjoyable are the Sunday evening sing-alongs for which they have become famous.

BURLINGTON HOTEL, *Upper Leesom Street, Ballsbridge, Tel. (01) 660-5222.*

From early May through October, the Burlington runs one of the most enjoyable traditional Irish cabarets around. Lots of music and laughs.

THE CELLARS, *Merrion Square, Tel. (01) 661-6799.*

Located in the Mont Clare Hotel, The Cellars provides an enjoyable evening of traditional music. Not as rustic as others around town, they still put on a good show filled with music, singing, storytelling, and lots of laughs.

CISS MADDEN'S, *Donnybrook Road, Tel. (01) 283-0208.*

New but trying hard to have that ancient feel, Ciss Madden's offers traditional Irish evenings. Call to find out which evenings they are performing, as the schedule is not set.

DOHENY & NESBITT, *5 Lower Baggot Street, Tel. (01) 676-2945.*

This pub hasn't changed much through the years, but it's a favorite of locals and tourists alike.

FITZWILLIAMS, *Temple Bar.*

Trendier than most of the pubs listed here, they offer traditional Irish music several times a week.

JOHNNIE FOX'S PUB, *Glencullen, Co. Dublin, Tel. (01) 295-5647.*

About eight to ten miles (depending on if you get lost, and for how long) from downtown Dublin, Johnnie Fox's caters specifically to tourists. Advertised as "The highest pub in Ireland" (I'm not so sure – others claim the same title), Fox's offers enjoyable evenings of traditional Irish song and dance. Its rustic interior, antiques, pretty colleens, and lively atmosphere are a lot of fun. Call for directions before you go.

JURY'S HOTEL, *Pembroke and Lansdowne Roads, Ballsbridge, Tel. (01) 660-5000.*

Jury's has been offering a traditional Irish cabaret for years, and they are pretty good at it.

MOTHER REDCAP'S TAVERN, *Christchurch Back Lane, Tel. (01) 453-8306.*

The decorators have done a nice job here in their efforts to recreate the feel and atmosphere of a 17th-century pub. Traditional Irish evenings are held; call to find out which evenings.

O'DONOGHUE'S, *15 Merrion Row, Tel. (01) 676-2807.*

Lively is the adjective usually applied to O'Donoghue's. And the traditional music is among the best in Dublin. It is frequented by a young crowd as well as tourists. One young Dubliner told me that the place is "mad and lunatic" (her actual words). I believe she meant it as a compliment of the highest order.

OLIVER ST. JOHN GOGARTY'S, *59 Fleet Street, Tel. (01) 671-1872.*

Nothing spectacularly different about this pub, it's typical of many of the pubs in Ireland. The atmosphere is pleasant, and they offer traditional Irish music several evenings a week.

SLATTERY'S, *129 Capel Street, Tel. (01) 872-7971.*

Nothing particularly noteworthy about Slattery's other than the excellent traditional music show held most evenings. Locals I spoke with about Slattery's told me you can find quite a collection of characters here most evenings.

THE STAG'S HEAD, *1 Dame Court, Tel. (01) 679-3701.*

At this location since before the American Revolution, the Stag's Head is an authentic, smoke-filled pub. Owing to its south central location, there is a good cross-section of people here: local Dubliners, students, and tourists.

Trendy, Modern Pubs

While traditional Irish pubs are what many tourists look for when they go to Ireland, that's not all that is there. Here are a few pubs known more for their trendiness.

BAD BOB'S BACKSTAGE BAR, *35 East Essex Street, Tel. (01) 677-5482.*

Bad Bob's is the place to go if you have a yearning for a steel guitar and a little country western music, Irish-style.

THE BARGE, *42 Charlemont Street, Tel. (01) 475-1869.*

This is a nice pub, decorated like (interestingly enough) an old Barge. It is really more interesting than perhaps that sounds, and you should check it out.

BREAK FOR THE BORDER, *2 Johnson's Place, Tel. (01) 475-0888.*

This nice, large pub and nightclub is associated with the Grafton Plaza Hotel. The pub features a DJ until 10:30 pm, at which time the pub closes and patrons are invited (for £8) to continue their merriment in the downstairs nightclub, where a live band is featured.

BRUXELLE'S, Harry Street, *Tel. (01) 677-5362.*

If you want to practice your German, here's a good place to do so. For whatever reason, in recent years this seems to have become a haunt of German tourists (probably in some German guidebook!). A little pricey.

BUSKER'S, *Fleet Street , Tel. (01) 677-3333.*

This lively pub is pretty much for the younger set who like loud music. It's a nice place if you like loud music.

THE CHANCERY INN, *Charles Street West, Tel. (01) 677-0420.*

This small pub is pleasant enough, although there's nothing exceptional about it.

CLUB M, *Blooms Hotel, Anglesea Street, Tel. (01) 671-5622.*

In the Temple Bar section of town, Club M is a popular nightclub for tourists because of its close proximity to a number of hotels, the live music, and their laser light show.

THE HARCOURT HOTEL, *60 Harcourt Street, Tel. (01) 478-3677.*

The pub of the Harcourt Hotel features live music seven nights a week. It ranges from jazz (one of the best places in town), to New Age to traditional Irish. Call ahead to see what's playing.

THE PINK ELEPHANT, *South Frederick Street, Tel. (01) 677-5876.*

A favorite hangout of Trinity students, The Pink Elephant is a popular spot that brings rising European rock groups into their establishment.

Nightclubs

There aren't nearly as many nightclubs as there are pubs in Dublin. But there are a few here and there (some are both pubs and clubs, so I've included them here too). All have cover charges ranging from £5 to £8.

BAD BOB'S, *35 East Essex Street, Tel. (01) 677-5482.*
In the Temple Bar District you'll find Bad Bob's, a nightclub specializing in country music. I was surprised to find a lot of interest in country music in Ireland. In fact, you might say there's a bit of a cult following there. And Bad Bob's is where they'll probably be on any given evening.
BREAK FOR THE BORDER, *2 Johnson's Place, Tel. (01) 475-0888.*
Another of the country-western venues in Dublin.
GARDA CLUB, *Harrington Street*
This nightclub is more of a discotheque, catering to the mid-20s crowd. The music is mostly contemporary Top 40 stuff.
THE KITCHEN, *Temple Bar, Tel. (01) 677-6178.*
The Kitchen is a nightclub in the Clarence Hotel, and both are owned by the rock group U2. You'll find the young and the restless, and the wild and wonderful crowds here.
POD, *Harcourt Street, (01) 478-0166.*
The POD (which stands for Place of Dance), is the place to be for the upwardly mobile and socially conscious in Dublin. The artistic professionals (models, artists, advertising, etc.) find their way here.
THE ROCK GARDEN, *Crown Alley, Tel. (01) 679-9114.*
Another of the nightclubs in the Temple Bar District, The Rock Garden caters almost exclusively to the younger college crowd.

Theaters
The Irish are generally a demonstrative people, outgoing, and gregarious by nature. They also seem to enjoy seeing their fellow countrymen and women display their talents on stage. The principal theaters in Dublin are the Gate, Abbey, Peacock, Gaiety, and Olympia. Buy a local paper at any Newsagent (located throughout the city, in bus depots, and train stations) to see what's playing. Most shows are reasonably priced, generally ranging between £5 to £15.
ABBEY THEATER, *Lower Abbey Street, Tel. (01) 478-7222.*
The Abbey theater has been the venue for many important dramatic plays in Ireland's history. It opened in 1904, and some of its most important patrons and benefactors included **W. B. Yeats** and one **Lady Gregory**, a member of the Dublin gentry who spent enormous amounts of time and money furthering the arts in Dublin. In addition, Lady Gregory wrote and directed dozens of plays that appeared at the Abbey. Playwright **J. M. Synge** benefited from their interest in the arts and also presented a number of plays at the Abbey.
The original theater burned in 1951 in a fire many felt was arson, and it took fifteen years for it to be rebuilt (1966).
GAIETY THEATER, *South King Street, Tel. (01) 677-1717.*
The Gaiety Theater provides family-oriented entertainment.

GATE THEATER, *Cavendish Row, Tel. (01) 874-4045*.
The Gate Theater has a rich history, with the likes of Orson Welles and James Mason, who have graced their stage. Today it features contemporary efforts of young native dramatists.
OLYMPIA THEATER, *Dame Street, Tel. (01) 677-8962*.
Along with the Gaiety Theater, the Olympia provides the Dublin arts scene with a host of family-oriented entertainment.
PEACOCK THEATER, *Lower Abbey Street, Tel. (01) 478-7222*.
The Peacock Theater, in the same building as the Abbey Theater, might best be classed as an experimental theater. One man shows, novelty presentations, and plays in Gaelic are typical.

DAY TRIPS & EXCURSIONS

Virtually all of Ireland is reachable within a day from Dublin. However, there are a couple of interesting excursions that lie just outside of Dublin that are worthwhile day trips. You can find more detail on these excursions in Chapter 15, *Leinster*.

North of Dublin

About an hour's drive north of Dublin on the N2 is the Boyne River Valley, one of the most historically important areas in Ireland. Just west of Drogheda is **Newgrange**, a passage grave archaeologists believe to be 5,000 years old. The grave itself is an impressive architectural feat, and contains fascinating stone carvings that have baffled archaeologists: are they some ancient form of writing, an ancient message, or merely stone "doodling?"

From Newgrange, head northeast on the N2 to the ruins of 11th-century Mellifont Abbey. In former days, **Mellifont Abbey** must have been an enormous and impressive set of buildings. You can still see the outlines of the community, along with several well-preserved ruins.

Watch for signs directing you to the back roads to **Monasterboice**. In this part of the country, many of the winding country lanes are not on any map, and sometimes there are signs, and sometimes there aren't. If you get frustrated, head east to Drogheda, and then north out of Drogheda on the N1. Take the first Dunleer exit north of Drogheda, then follow the signs to Monasterboice. It is not particularly well-signed off the N1, but you can see Monasterboice's round tower off the N1 – if you miss the exit, just work your way over to it.

Monasterboice was a monastery founded by **St. Buithe** in the 5th century. Two of the high crosses found at Monasterboice are among the best examples of high crosses in the world. One of them, the seventeen foot Cross of Muiredach, is remarkably well-preserved and is about 1,000 years old. An inscription at the base of the cross says, "A prayer for

Muiredach by whom this cross was made." The crosses have images of biblical stories from the Old and New Testaments engraved on them.

On your return to Dublin, work your way over to the coast and hug the coastline on your way south. Take your time, get out and feel the sea breezes as you walk along the shore or on the quay around Skerries. There are no sandy beaches here, but the rock and shale beaches provide a pretty setting as you look out over the Irish Sea. Sunsets over Skerries are a sight to behold. Some of the finest ocean sunsets I've ever seen are from this small port town.

As you near Dublin, watch for signposts directing you to Donabate. In Donabate you'll find **Newbridge House**, a restored Georgian Mansion. Parts of the home are open, including the restored kitchen which boasts a number of the original implements. There is also an impressive dollhouse and an antique doll collection that has over one hundred and fifty dolls. In the courtyard there is a mini-farm, where children can pet rabbits, sheep, and goats.

From Donabate, watch for signs to Malahide and **Malahide Castle**. Built in 1174, Malahide Castle is remarkably well-built fortress that has seen continuous use the past eight-hundred years. Many of the furnishings in the house are antiques, reflecting the elegant lifestyle the lords of Malahide Castle were accustomed to.

One of the most poignant episodes in its history is connected with the Battle of the Boyne. On July 1, 1690, fourteen members of the Talbot family breakfasted together at the long table that's still in the Banqueting Hall. It was to be their last meal together: all were killed by nightfall.

An added bonus to Malahide Castle are the lovely gardens with over 5,000 varieties of plants. While at Malahide Castle, be sure and visit the Fry Model Railway Museum. The museum features the painstaking miniaturization of Dublin City with trains and tracks running all around and through it.

Depending on the time, you may want to return to Skerries to see the sunset, or go on to Howth where you can walk along the quay and enjoy a meal and traditional Irish music and entertainment at Abbey Tavern.

South of Dublin

South of Dublin are several sites that are definitely worth a day trip.

Leaving Dublin on the N11, head south for Rathnew. Just before you reach Rathnew, you'll come to Ashford and **Mount Usher Gardens**. These gardens are the pride of County Wicklow.

From Ashford, continue south on the N11 to Arklow, then head northwest on R747, then R752 north out of Avoca. (Just follow the signposts for the Vale of Avoca.) **The Vale of Avoca** is a luxurious, verdant valley that was immortalized by Thomas Moore in his poem "The Meeting of the Waters." It really is pretty here, and you should take the time to get out and walk along any of the trails that wend through the valley.

At the end of the Vale of Avoca is Rathdrum. Take R755 north to Laragh, and watch for signs pointing you to **Glendalough**. Glendalough is the site of an impressive set of ruins that was once one of the world's most renowned monastic settlements. Established by **St. Kevin** in the 6th century, many of the buildings, high crosses, and the round tower are still in excellent condition. It's easy to see why St. Kevin found solitude in Glendalough. Even with numerous tourists, it still imparts a serene and tranquil feeling.

From Glendalough, head north to the town of Enniskerry. Watch for signs directing you to **Powerscourt Gardens and Waterfall**. The beautiful terraced gardens are filled with sculpted shrubs, trees, and many varieties of flowering plants, as well as a number of statues, fountains, and walkways. From the top of the terraces, the views sweep across the pretty Dargle Valley, culminating in outstanding views of Great Sugar Loaf Mountain and Kippure Mountain. You've probably seen pictures of Powerscourt Gardens without realizing it: they are popular and are in many brochures of Ireland. As impressive as the gardens is Powerscourt Waterfall. It is three miles south of the gardens. The highest waterfall in Ireland, the water free-falls over 400 feet off the edge of Djouce Mountain. It is a favorite picnic area for tourists and locals alike.

From Enniskerry, head for tiny Glencree and the **German War Cemetery**. This pretty little cemetery was established to inter the bodies of German soldiers who crash-landed on Ireland after bombing runs in England. It was a thoughtful act by a kind people.

From Glencree, backtrack a bit and head west for Blessington. Just south of Blessington is **Russborough House**, an impressive 18th-century Palladian mansion set in the beautiful Wicklow Mountains. The park-like grounds are gorgeous, and set the stage for the exquisite interior of the House. There is also a nice art collection here, which features the work of a number of well-known artists such as Goya, Reynolds, Rubens, and Velasquez.

As you wrap up this day trip, you may want to work your way back over to Rathnew and dine at either the Tinakilly Country House or Hunter's Hotel. Both are recognized as two of the finest restaurants in Ireland, and it would be a shame to be so close and let the opportunity pass you by.

PRACTICAL INFORMATION

American Express

The American Express office in Dublin, *116 Grafton Street, Dublin 2, Tel. (02) 677-2874,* can be your best friend if you lose traveler's checks, need money exchanged, or need some travel agency assistance.

Automobile Association - AA

The **Automobile Association**, *23 Rockhill Street, Blackrock, Dublin. Tel. (01) 283-3555*, can help out if you run into problems getting your car to start, or if you need to be towed.

Banks

Banks in Dublin are generally open Monday through Wednesday and Friday from 10:00 am to 3:00 pm. On Thursdays, they are open from 10:00 am to 5:00 pm. Most banks in Dublin have an ATM machine either outside their main doorways or just inside the bank. The ATMs are part of the Cirrus and Plus international networks. Be sure to check with your bank to see if your personal identification number (PIN) will work on international ATMs. Most international ATMs only accept four-digit PINs.

The bank at Dublin International Airport is open daily from 6:00 am to 8:00 pm to service international flights.

Buses, Planes, & Trains

- **Bus Eireann**, *Tel. (01) 836-6111*
- **Aer Lingus**, *Tel. (01) 844-4777*
- **Delta Airlines**, *Tel. (01) 844-4170*
- **DART information**, *Tel. (01) 836-6222*
- **Irish Rail**, *Tel. (01) 836-6222*

Embassies & Consulates

- **US Embassy**, *42 Elgin Road, Dublin 4, Tel. (01) 668-8777*
- **Canadian Embassy**, *65 St. Stephen's Green, Dublin 2, Tel. (01) 478-1988.*

Emergencies

Remember this: dialing 999 in Ireland = dialing 911 in the States. Use it in the event of any emergency where you need assistance from the police, fire department, or the medical community.

Exchanging Money

You can exchange money at banks, most post offices, larger hotels, and at change booths in Dublin International Airport.

Lost Credit Cards & Traveler's Checks

- **American Express Card**, *Tel. 288-3311*
- **American Express Traveler's Checks**, *Tel. 800-626-0000*
- **Diners Club**, *Tel. 800-709-944*
- **Visa/MasterCard**, *Tel. 269-7700*

Pharmacies

In Ireland, pharmacies are called "Chemists," and can be located through any of the Tourist Offices, or in the "Yellow Pages."

Post Offices

The **General Post Office** is located on O'Connell Street and is open Monday through Saturday from 8:00 am to 8:00 pm. Smaller branch offices are scattered around the city, and their hours are shorter, usually Monday through Saturday from 9:00 am to 6:00 pm.

Restrooms

Public restrooms are not prevalent in Ireland; your best bet is usually a hotel or a pub. (Most hotels have at least one pub, and the restrooms are usually located near the pub.)

Taxi Companies

• **A1 Taxis**, *Tel. 285-9333*
• **Blue Cabs**, *Tel. 676-1111*
• **Capital Cabs**, *Tel. 490-8888*
• **Central Cabs**, *Tel. 836-5555*
• **City Group**, *Tel. 872-7272*
• **Metro Cabs**, *Tel. 668-3333*

Tourist Information

There are a number of tourist offices in Dublin. The **main tourist office** is located at *Suffolk Street, Dublin 2, Tel. (01) 605-7777*. Another is located at *Baggot Street Bridge, Dublin 2, Tel. (01) 676-5871*. There is also a tourist office in the Arrivals hall at Dublin International Airport.

14. LEINSTER

Leinster is the province that lies along Ireland's southeastern seaboard. Its principal city is Dublin, but the majority of the province is much less populated than Ireland's capital city.

On the whole, the ancient kings of Leinster were perhaps the most acrimonious of all the monarchs of Ireland. History bears record that the people of Leinster sided with the foreign enemies of their fellow Irishmen nearly as often as they joined hands to clear their land of the foreign invaders.

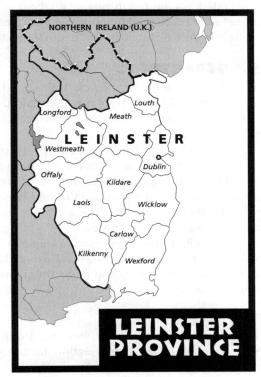

In fact, it was the dispute of Dermot MacMurrough with the other Irish kings that first brought English forces into Ireland. Initially fighting on the side of the king of Leinster, these Anglo-Norman invaders took a liking to the Emerald Isle and decided to stay – for seven hundred and fifty years!

Leinster consists of twelve counties, five of which lie along the Irish and Celtic Seas on Ireland's east and southeast. The remaining counties are landlocked, with the exception of County Kilkenny, which has access to the sea via the River Barrow and Waterford Harbor. The inland counties west and south of Dublin consist of the wide flat plain called the **Curragh**, and is the Kentucky of Ireland. It is here that a number of national horse races are held, as well as the location of a number of stud farms, including the famous **National Stud** in Tully.

In the northern portion of Leinster, in the **Boyne River Valley** are 5,000 year old passage graves and burial mounds. These were the burial places of the ancient kings of Ireland. Here, too, is the fabled **Hill of Tara**, the seat of power for those kings. It was also in the Boyne River Valley in 1690 that Irish Catholic hopes for tolerance and equality from the English were dashed when Protestant William of Orange defeated Catholic King James II and succeeded him on the throne of England.

Many sights in Leinster are readily accessible from Dublin, making it an easy place to explore even if Dublin is your main destination in Ireland.

ARRIVALS & DEPARTURES

Leinster is easily accessible via planes, trains, and automobiles. Dublin Airport on the outskirts of Dublin is the main point of arrival where foreign travelers enter not only the province of Leinster but Ireland as well.

From Dublin, roads venturing throughout the province are plentiful, as are railways and bus lines. Railways shoot north and south along the coast to the farthest extremities of Leinster, and they also reach west and southwest into her heart. The northwest portion of Leinster – Counties Longford, Meath, and Westmeath – are unreachable by train; you'll have to drive or take a bus to see those counties.

Dublin is the main city in the north part of Leinster, and the main cities in the southern portion of Leinster are **Wexford** and **Kilkenny**. Both have regular bus and train service to and from Dublin as well as other towns throughout the country.

BY AIR

If you're flying into and out of Leinster, you'll use **Dublin Airport**. See Chapter 13, *Dublin*, Arrivals & Departures section, for complete information on air travel into and out of Dublin.

BY BUS

Bus service runs between Dublin's **Busaras Station**, *Store Street, Tel. (01) 836-6111*, and Wexford's **O'Hanrahan Station**, *Redmond Square, Tel. (053) 22522*, five times a day. The two hour ride will cost you £9 for a round-trip ticket, and £8 for a one-way ticket. O'Hanrahan Station is about a third of a mile from the town center, and the neighborhood is fine to walk through.

Bus service runs from Busaras Station in Dublin to Kilkenny's **McDonagh Station**, *Tel. (056) 22024*, five times a day. McDonagh Station is just off the center of town on Castlecomer Road, an easy walk to the sights and shopping Kilkenny has to offer. The area around McDonagh Station is a nice neighborhood. The bus ride from Dublin costs £7 for a one-way ticket, and £8 for a round-trip ticket.

BY CAR

To get to the southern portion of Leinster, take the N11 if you want a semi-coastal route; the N7, N9, and N81 roads strike out through south-central Leinster. Heading north, take the M1/N1 or the N2. The N3 and N4 will take you to the northwest and central portions of Leinster.

LEINSTER'S PREMIER SIGHTS

GLENDALOUGH – This ancient monastic site is remarkably peaceful and beautiful.

JERPOINT ABBEY – These impressive ruins contain intriguing stonework.

MELLIFONT ABBEY – Mellifont Abbey was once the most important religious center in Ireland. Not far from Monasterboice, you can see from the extent of the ruins what an impressive sight this must have been.

MONASTERBOICE – The ruins of this ancient monastery include a round tower and a number of well-preserved high crosses.

MOUNT USHER GARDENS – On an island that is considered a garden spot itself, in a county that is called "The Garden of Ireland," Mt. Usher Gardens are some of the prettiest anywhere.

NATIONAL STUD – The Irish love their horses, and the National Stud is, as the name suggests, the national stud farm, where Irish race horses are bred. There is also an interesting museum here.

NEWGRANGE – Lots of questions still remain about this passage grave that is 5,000 years old. The site is well-preserved and well-worth the visit.

POWERSCOURT GARDENS AND WATERFALL – This impressive estate is well worth the time to stop and visit. The grounds are incredible, and the waterfall is pretty impressive, too.

BY TRAIN

Train service runs from Dublin's **Heuston Station**, *Tel. (01) 836-6222*, to Wexford's **O'Hanrahan Station**, *Redmond Square, Tel. (053) 22522*, three times a day, and will cost you L12 for a round-trip ticket, L11 for a one-way ticket. The trip takes about three hours.

Train service runs from Dublin's Heuston Station to Kilkenny's **McDonagh Station**, *Castlecomer Road, Tel. (056) 22024*, four times a day. The one and a half hour trip costs £12 for a round-trip ticket and £11 for a one-way ticket.

WHERE TO STAY

Without a doubt, the majority of hotels in Leinster are located in Dublin and its environs. Still, there are a good number of hotels, manor houses, guest houses, and B&Bs spread throughout the province. Lodgings below are listed by county.

GREAT LEINSTER ACCOMMODATIONS

HUNTER'S HOTEL, *Rathnew, Tel. (0404) 40106, fax (0404) 40338. 16 rooms. Rates for singles: £47.50, doubles: £90. Don't let the outside fool you. This is a great place!*

MOYGLARE MANOR, *Maynooth, Tel. (01) 628-6351, (01) 628-5405. 17 rooms. Rates for singles: £75, doubles: £60 per person sharing. Impressive mansion, bountiful antiques, a warm welcome, and fabulous service.*

TINAKILLY COUNTRY HOUSE, *Rathnew, Tel. (0404) 69274, fax (0404) 67806. 29 rooms. Rates for singles: £85 to £93, doubles: £55 to £63 per person sharing, suites: £70 to £100 per person sharing. This marvelous old mansion has been lovingly restored and offers large, comfortable rooms, antiques, and views of the Irish Sea.*

RATHSALLAGH HOUSE, *Dunlavin, Tel. (045) 403112, fax (045) 40334. 17 rooms. Rates for singles: £70, doubles: £55 to £85 per person sharing. Eighteenth-century converted horse stables have never been so comfortable!*

MOUNT JULIET, *Thomastown, Tel. (056) 24455, fax (056) 24522. 54 rooms. Rates for singles: £130 to £140, doubles: £175 to £195, suites: £395. One of the premier country houses in Ireland, Mount Juliet is set in 1,500 acres of park land. The rooms are nearly as spacious, and the views are incredible.*

KILDARE HOTEL, *Straffan, Tel. (01) 627-333, fax (01) 627-3312. 45 rooms. Rates for singles: £170, doubles: £245 to £265, suites: £320 to £850. Kildare Hotel is an exquisite five-star hotel that will make you feel like you are a member of the privileged class.*

County Kilkenny

LAUNARD HOUSE B&B, *Kells Road, Kilkenny, Tel. (056) 51889. 4 rooms. Rates for singles: £21, doubles: £16 per person sharing. Rates include breakfast. Visa accepted.*

This pleasant B&B in Kilkenny is modern and provides a pleasant place to stay as well as wonderful hosts, John and Sandra Cahill. The rooms are average size and comfortably furnished.

SONORA B&B, *Drakelands, Kilkenny, Tel. (056) 22877. 5 rooms. Rates for singles: £23 to £25, doubles: £18 to £20 per person sharing. Rates include breakfast. No credit cards accepted. No service charge.*

Mrs. Hayes runs a lovely B&B with beautiful gardens round about. There are five rooms, three of which are ensuite; all are light and pleasant and decorated with antiques. The conservatory offers serene views of the gardens.

BOW HALL, *Castletownshend, Tel. (028) 36114. 3 rooms. Rates for singles: £28 to £30, doubles: £28 to £30 per person sharing. Rates include breakfast. No credit cards accepted. No service charge.*

If you want a warm Irish welcome by authentic Irish hosts, don't look for it here. Actually, you will get a warm Irish welcome, but it will be from the American owners, Dick and Barbara Vickery! Nationality notwithstanding, they run a top-notch guest house. There are only three rooms, but they are comfortable and pleasant.

BLANCHVILLE HOUSE, *Dunbell, Maddoxtown, Tel. (056) 27197. 6 rooms. Rates for singles: £25 to £35, doubles: £25 to £35 per person sharing. Rates include breakfast. MasterCard and Visa accepted. No service charge.*

Just a few miles north of Kilkenny Town quietly sits an elegant 19th-century Georgian home. The home has been refurbished magnificently, and the resulting effect is one of quiet grandeur. The country setting of the house lends itself to a tranquil stay. The bedrooms are pleasant and airy, and those on the front of the house overlook the grounds.

LACKEN HOUSE, *Kilkenny, Tel. (056) 61085, fax (056) 62435. 8 rooms. Rates for singles: £35, doubles: £30 to £36 per person sharing. One restaurant. All major credit cards accepted. Rates include breakfast. No service charge.*

While the Lacken House is perhaps more famous for its excellent restaurant (see the *Where to Eat* section), their guest house is no slouch either. The rooms are fair-sized and comfortably furnished.

NEWPARK HOTEL, *Kilkenny, Tel. (056) 22122, fax (056) 61111. 84 rooms. Rates for singles: £48, doubles: £41 to £52 per person sharing. Two restaurants, indoor swimming pool, sauna, jacuzzi, fitness center. All major credit cards accepted. No service charge.*

This older hotel (built in the 1960's) is still a comfortable place to stay, and offers a number of additional amenities, such as pool, sauna, and fitness center. Several years ago twenty-four rooms were added, and these rooms are of course nicer than the older rooms. They are average size, and furnished comfortably, if not memorably.

MOUNT JULIET, *Thomastown, Tel. (056) 24455, fax (056) 24522. 54 rooms. Rates for singles: £130 to £140, doubles: £175 to £195, suites: £395. One restaurant, indoor swimming pool, spa, sauna, fitness center, beauty salon, tennis, snooker, golf, shooting, bicycles. All major credit cards accepted. 12.5% service charge.*

This is the way the other half lives. Situated amidst 1,500 acres on a gorgeous estate, Mount Juliet is truly one of the gems of County Kilkenny. The rooms are large, well-appointed, and come with a box of chocolates, a bowl of fruit, plush bathrobes, and full turn-down service in the evenings. There isn't a bad view in the place – the rooms either overlook the River Nore or the grounds of the estate; it's hard to say which would be considered the "premium" view. A little more pricey than other accommodations in the area, this is a nice place and will leave you with pleasant memories of friendly service and exquisite surroundings. Their award-winning restaurant is elegant; see *Where to Eat.*

County Kildare

KILDARE HOTEL, *Straffan, Tel. (01) 627-333, fax (01) 627-3312. 45 rooms. Rates for singles: £170, doubles: £245 to £265, suites: £320 to £850. Restaurant, tennis, croquet, golf, indoor swimming pool, fitness center, squash, sauna, shooting, horse-back riding, beauty salon. All major credit cards accepted. 12.5% service charge.*

The Kildare Hotel and Country Club is a relatively new (1991) five-star hotel located just seventeen miles from downtown Dublin in the peaceful town of Straffan. The cost, of course, is commensurate with the surroundings.

From outside, the structure suggests opulence. The grounds – including a mile-long stretch of the River Liffey and five lakes – are nothing short of spectacular, as are the gardens. Leaflets at the front desk provide you with details of walks you can take through the grounds. Inside, you'll not be disappointed – the interior is as exquisite as the exterior. Lavish furnishings are complemented by antiques, including a fine collection of artwork. The bedrooms? Large and tastefully (and expensively) outfitted. Luxurious bathrobes, slippers, hand-made chocolates, bowls of fruit and mineral water are nice touches in the rooms.

For those of you who have a passing interest in golf, the Kildare Country Club was the venue for the European Open for 1995 and 1996, and is slated to serve as the site again in 1997. It presides over the Arnold Palmer-designed course.

MOYGLARE MANOR, *Maynooth, Tel. (01) 628-6351, (01) 628-5405. 17 rooms. Rates for singles: £75, doubles: £60 per person sharing. Restaurant, tennis, garden. All major credit cards accepted. 12.5% service charge.*

As you enter the grounds of Moyglare Manor, you'll feel lost in the midst of verdant beauty. Splendid gardens and sprawling lawns and park land serve as the backdrop for this imposing Georgian mansion.

However, the only thing imposing about Moyglare Manor is the manor house itself. Once you darken the doorway, you'll feel welcomed and warmed immediately. Your stay will be punctuated with friendly service and serenity – most of the rooms do not have television to ensure the tranquillity of the experience. The Lady of the house is Norah Devlin, and even in antique-crazy Ireland she is known for her eye for antiques – many of which are displayed throughout the width and breath of Moyglare Manor. The rooms are large and comfortable. Most have four-poster beds and tasteful decor. To preserve the peaceful nature at Moyglare Manor, you are respectfully requested not to bring children under age twelve.

County Louth

BOYNE VALLEY HOTEL, *Castlebellingham, Tel. (041) 37737, fax (041) 39188. 37 rooms. Rates for singles: £33 to £40, doubles: £33 to £40 per person sharing. Rates include breakfast. Restaurant. All major credit cards accepted.*

The Boyne Valley Hotel is a lovely country house, set amid sixteen acres of park land. Its gardens are serene, and make for a nice evening walk. The rooms are nice sized, and pleasantly furnished.

County Westmeath

HODSON BAY HOTEL, *Athlone, County Westmeath, Tel. (0902) 92444, fax (0902) 92688. 100 rooms. Rates for singles: £55 to £70, doubles: £70 to £110, suites £165. One restaurant, pub, indoor swimming pool, fitness center, sauna. All major credit cards accepted. 10% service charge.*

The Hodson Bay Hotel is a pleasant hotel on the shores of Lough Ree. Most of the rooms are fair size, although those in their recent addition are a little nicer. The rooms at the front of the hotel offer nice views of Lough Ree.

County Wexford

LEMONGROVE HOUSE, *Enniscorthy, Tel. (054) 36115. 5 rooms. Rates for singles: £21, doubles: £16 per person sharing. Rates include breakfast. Credit cards not accepted. No service charge.*

This lovely, large, newer B&B offers a pleasant place to stay and a warm Irish welcome from Colm and Ann McGibney.

HILLSIDE HOUSE B&B, *Gorey, Tel. (055) 21726. 6 rooms. Rates for singles: £23, doubles: £18 per person sharing. Rates include breakfast. Visa accepted. No service charge.*

This quiet B&B is a nice center for exploring Counties Wexford and Wicklow. This country home has a rural setting that enhances the nice-sized rooms.

CLONARD HOUSE, *Great Wexford, Wexford, Tel. (053) 43141. 9 rooms. Rates for singles: £18, doubles: £18 per person sharing. Rates include breakfast. All major credit cards accepted. No service charge.*

So you've always wanted to be a dairy farmer? Well, the Clonard House is located on a dairy farm overlooking Wexford Harbor. John and Kathleen Hayes run a pleasant and enjoyable guest house. The rooms are average size, but nicely furnished.

WHITE'S HOTEL, *George Street, Wexford, Tel. (053) 22311, fax (053) 45000. 82 rooms. Rates for singles: £28 to £33, doubles: £28 to £41 per person sharing; children under 3 stay free, and children ages 3 to 12 stay for half price. Rates include breakfast. One restaurant and pub, gym, spa, sauna. All major credit cards accepted. No service charge.*

This older hotel has been well-cared for, and has had numerous renovations in its public areas. The rooms tend to have an older feel, although all are clean.

NEWBAY COUNTRY HOUSE, *Newbay, near Wexford, Tel. (053) 42779, fax (053) 46318. 6 rooms. Rates for singles: £40, doubles: £35 per person sharing. Rates include breakfast. Diners, MasterCard, and Visa accepted. No service charge.*

Located just a few miles outside Wexford in Newbay, the Newbay Country House offers a nice place from which to explore the Wexford peninsula. While the outside of the house is not particularly memorable, the interior will be more to your liking. A number of antiques combine with a warm welcome to make Newbay House a pleasant place to stay.

The bedrooms are all spacious and nicely furnished. Four-poster beds are a treat, but don't expect to flop on the bed and catch CNN – there are no televisions in the rooms, helping to foster that rustic country feeling that pervades the rest of the house.

KELLY'S RESORT HOTEL, *Rosslare, Tel. (053) 32114, fax (053) 32222. 99 rooms. Rates for singles: £40; doubles: £77 to £104. Two bars, one restaurant, tennis, swimming pools, squash, snooker, croquet, miniature golf, bicycling, children's playroom. All major credit cards accepted.*

Rosslare is a noted resort town, and Kelly's Resort Hotel does all they can to cater to those who come here looking for a resort vacation. Four generations of the Kelly family have put together a sound sleeping and resort package for their guests. The rooms in this hotel are wonderful, bordering on elegant. All are tastefully furnished and spacious. Ask for a room overlooking the bay, or perhaps you'd like the rooms that open out into the hotel's gardens.

GREAT SOUTHERN HOTEL, *Rosslare Harbor, Tel. (053) 33233, fax (053) 33543, 100 rooms. Rates for singles: £50; doubles: £80 to £102. Swimming pool, fitness room, sauna, snooker, hairdresser. All major credit cards accepted.*

The recently refurbished Great Southern Hotel overlooks Rosslare Harbor and is a pleasant and enjoyable place to stay. The rooms are of a nice size and comfortably furnished. Their remodeled lounge and reception area are light and airy, and give you a feeling of casual hospitality. But the service is anything but casual. You'll enjoy your stay here immensely.

County Wicklow

HUNTER'S HOTEL, *Rathnew, Tel. (0404) 40106, fax (0404) 40338. 16 rooms. Rates for singles: £47.50, doubles: £90. One restaurant and pub. All major credit cards accepted. No service charge.*

You'll be surprised by this hotel, especially if you have the tendency to judge a book by its cover. Unbecoming on the outside, it nonetheless offers old-world charm and...creakiness on the inside. Run by the Gelletlie family since 1820, you feel as though you're being hosted by long-lost relatives.

Old – perhaps better classified as well-seasoned – but clean and warm, Hunter's Hotel oozes personality. The rooms are all nice-sized, and offer a collection of antiques. Their restaurant is considered one of the best south of Dublin (see *Where to Eat* section.)

THE OLD RECTORY, *Wicklow Town, Tel. (0404) 67048, fax (0404) 69181. 5 rooms. Rates for singles: £65, doubles: £45 per person sharing. Rates include breakfast. One restaurant. All major credit cards accepted. No service charge.*

This old Georgian home has been warmly renovated with a floral decor throughout. The rooms are large and decorated in soft pastels, giving it a restful feel. A fine restaurant is also on the premises.

RATHSALLAGH HOUSE, *Dunlavin, Tel. (045) 403112, fax (045) 403343. 17 rooms. Rates for singles: £70, doubles: £55 to £85 per person sharing. Rates include breakfast. Restaurant, garden, croquet, indoor swimming pool, sauna, tennis, golf, snooker. All major credit cards accepted. No service charge.*

In 1798, a lovely Queen Anne house burned down, leaving only the stables. Pity the house, but rejoice that the stables were spared, because they have been converted into a romantic hide-away that may well be one of your most pleasant memories of your stay in Ireland.

There are two types of rooms here – large and spacious, and smaller but warmer. The choice is yours, but either should serve your needs well.

Rathsallagh House is set in over 500 acres of emerald greenery, and the feeling is one of getting away from it all. You can golf on the 18-hole golf course, curl up with a book in the drawing room in front of the fire, or walk around the lovely grounds. And all this about forty-five minutes from downtown Dublin.

TINAKILLY COUNTRY HOUSE, *Rathnew, Tel. (0404) 69274, fax (0404) 67806. 29 rooms. Rates for singles: £85 to £93, doubles: £55 to £63 per person sharing, suites: £70 to £100 per person sharing. One restaurant, putting green, croquet. All major credit cards accepted. No service charge.*

What a lovely hotel. It feels more like being at home (well – maybe at a very expensive home!) than like being at a hotel. Antiques abound, from the sitting room with its blazing fire to the splendid pieces in the rooms. This old Victorian mansion was built in the 1870s as a token of appreciation for Captain Robert Halpin, who commanded the *Great Eastern* as it laid the first telegraph cable that linked Europe and America. He must have been very pleased with the gift.

The rooms are wonderful – spacious, antique-laden, and most with lovely views of the Irish Sea. They also sport a marvelous restaurant (see *Where to Eat* section).

WHERE TO EAT

Leinster has its share of excellent restaurants, but throughout the province you'll find a number of good, hearty establishments offering good fare at good prices.

LEINSTER'S BEST RESTAURANTS

HUNTER'S HOTEL, Newrath Bridge, Rathnew, Tel. (0404) 40106. Set lunch is £14.00 and set dinner is £18.50. All major credit cards accepted. The award-winning restaurant is quietly elegant.

CROOKEDWOOD HOUSE, Crookedwood, Mullingar, Co. Westmeath, Tel. (044) 72165. £12.95 to £19.95. All major credit cards accepted. The Crookedwood House is best known for its exceptional beef dishes. Featured in a recent special edition of Bon Appetit magazine.

LACKEN HOUSE, Dublin Road, Tel. (056) 61085. Set dinner menu £23. All major credit cards accepted. The meals at this country house are legendary.

TINAKILLY COUNTRY HOUSE RESTAURANT, Rathnew, Tel. (0404) 69274. £15.95 to £30. All major credit cards accepted. The restaurant at Tinakilly Country House is recognized as one of the best in the country.

*MOUNT JULIET HOTEL RESTAURANT (called **Lady Helen McCalmont Dining Room**), Tel. (056) 24455, Thomastown, set dinner menu for £33. All major credit cards accepted. The Franco-Irish fare at the Lady Helen McCalmont Dining Room is award-winning and exceptional.*

County Kilkenny

AN CAISEAN UI CUAIN, *2 High Street, Kilkenny Town, Tel. (056) 65406. £5.95 to £9.95. Open daily 12:30 pm to 3:00 pm, and 5:30 pm to 8:30 pm. No credit cards accepted.*

This bar has succeeded in mixing traditional and trendy Irish atmosphere and is very popular with the younger crowd in particular. The food is branded "pub grub," and is tasteful and substantial. Officially, Monday evenings feature traditional Irish music, but with the artsy crowd, live music can break out spontaneously at any time.

KILKENNY KITCHEN, *Kilkenny Design Centre, Castle Yard, Kilkenny Town. £4.95 to £12.95. Open 9:00 am to 5:00 pm daily. All major credit cards accepted.*

This sizable restaurant (it seats 165 people) serves a pretty varied menu for you to choose from. No real specialties other than their breads and pastries, the Kilkenny Kitchen is a nice place to stop for a bite to eat. Fish, poultry, and a variety of cheeses are offered.

SHEM'S, *61 John Street, Kilkenny, Tel. (056) 21543. £15.95 to £30. Open daily noon to 9:30 pm (only snacks are available on Sundays). All major credit cards accepted.*

Shem's is a delightful country pub with a pleasant ambiance and excellent food. Julie Lawlor presides over the kitchen and serves up soups, salads, sandwiches, and a few pasta dishes.

LANGTON'S, *69 John Street, Kilkenny Town, Tel. (056) 65133. £4.95 to £17.95. Open all day for bar food. All major credit cards accepted.*

Langton's has earned a reputation as sort of a smorgasbord of bars, where you'll find a collection of bars in varying decors and atmospheres. But the reason they are listed here is because of the quality of their pub grub. Salads, chicken, seafood, and beef grace their menu.

LACKEN HOUSE, *Dublin Road, Tel. (056) 61085. Set dinner menu £23. Open Tuesday through Saturday from 7:00 am to 9:00 pm. All major credit cards accepted.*

The restaurant housed in this old Victorian home offers a solid Irish menu, a mix of traditional Irish dishes and progressive dishes. Salmon, trout, and a bevy of seafood dishes including crab gateau and lobster complement a varied meat menu that features Irish beef and lamb as well as several wild meats. Fresh produce from the farms of local farmers guarantees a freshness to all the menu items.

MOUNT JULIET HOTEL RESTAURANT *(also called **Lady Helen McCalmont Dining Room**), Tel. (056) 24455, Thomastown. Set dinner menu for £33. Open daily for dinner from 7:00 pm to 10:00 pm. All major credit cards accepted.*

The dining room at Mount Juliet Hotel is everything you'd expect it to be: elegant, bordering on opulent. Wedgewood china, starched Irish linen, and gleaming silverware punctuate your dining experience. The meal? Equally as exquisite. French with an Irish flair (or is it Irish with a French flair?), the presentation of your fare is as spectacular as it is tasteful. The menu changes, but you might expect the likes of baked escalope of salmon, roast breast of Barbary duck with fruit sauce, or roast rack of spring lamb. Jacket and tie are requested.

County Louth

AN SOS CAFE, *Castlebellingham, Tel. (042) 72149. £3 to £7. Open during the summer months Monday through Saturday from 8:00 am to 6:00 pm, and Sunday from 11:00 am to 4:00 pm. Winter hours vary, but are generally Monday through Friday 9:00 am to 4:00 pm, Saturday 9:30 am to 2:30 pm, and closed Sundays. MasterCard and Visa accepted.*

Flight attendants have a reputation for knowing where to eat, and an Aer Lingus flight attendant tipped me off to this outstanding little cafe that is easily missed if you're not looking for it. As you are zooming along the N1 between Drogheda and Dundalk, slow down as you go through the hamlet of Castebellingham and watch for the thatched cottage known as *An Sos* Cafe. This charming cafe run by Julie McMahon specializes in breakfast and a warm welcome. You'll probably sit among locals, and the mornings in particular are quite busy. The menu is surprisingly varied, from a full traditional Irish breakfast for only £3, to smoked salmon, to Julie's special-recipe lasagna (including garlic, spinach, and ricotta cheese).

County Westmeath

CROOKEDWOOD HOUSE, *Crookedwood, Mullingar, Tel. (044) 72165. £12.95 to £19.95. Open Monday through Saturday 6:30 pm to 10:00 pm for dinner, and for lunch on Sunday from 12:30 pm to 2:30 pm. All major credit cards accepted.*

Welcome to one of the top beef restaurants in Ireland! While there are a number of other items on the varied menu (roast pigeon, salmon and trout, roast duck, etc.), the Crookedwood House is best known for its exceptional meat dishes. Featured in a special edition of *Bon Appetit* magazine, owner/chef Noel Kenney is a master at his art. Try any of his beef plates, like his sirloin steak with colcannon and a mead/tarragon sauce that's exceptional. Wild meat specialties include medallions of venison with port and cranberries.

County Wexford

GALLEY CRUISING RESTAURANT, *New Ross, open Easter through October. Lunch is £11, afternoon tea is £5, and dinner is £20. Tel. (051) 21723.*

If you find yourself in New Ross around meal time, you might enjoy a lunch cruise on the River Barrow. Fish caught locally is the specialty.

County Wicklow

Perhaps because of its close proximity to Dublin, County Wicklow seems to have its fair share of excellent, award-winning restaurants. Several are associated with a manor house or guest house. The short drive from Dublin (roughly forty-five minutes), the relaxed atmosphere, and pretty countryside all make the restaurants of County Wicklow a popular venue for Dubliners and tourists alike.

HUNTER'S HOTEL, *Newrath Bridge, Rathnew, Tel. (0404) 40106. Set lunch is £14 and set dinner is £18.50. Open daily for lunch from 1:00 pm to 3:00 pm and for dinner from 7:30 pm to 9:00 pm. All major credit cards accepted.*

Don't let the exterior of Hunter's Lodge put you off, as you'll miss a dining treat if you do. Mrs. Gilletlie is justifiably proud of the traditional meals prepared here for her hotel guests as well as those who journey here specifically for a meal. The menus vary day to day, but you'll always find quality, such as oak-smoked trout fillet, and Irish lamb and beef, all complemented with vegetables fresh from Hunter's Hotel's gardens.

ROUNDWOOD INN, *Roundwood, Tel. (01) 281-8107. £7.95 to £21.95. Open for lunch daily from 1:00 pm to 2:15 pm, and for dinner from 7:30 pm to 9:30 pm. If the restaurant is closed, the bar serves from a scaled-down menu from noon until 10:00 pm. All major credit cards accepted.*

This German-style restaurant in the Wicklow Mountains is a real find. The German owners, Jargen and Aine Schwalm, have combined the best of German and Irish cuisine to come up with a distinctive and tasteful menu. There are numerous German dishes (wiener schnitzel, blueberry pancakes, veal) alongside traditional Irish dishes on the menu. Seafood, beef, and wild meat dishes are plentiful.

The Roundwood House is a cross between a pub and restaurant, and the ambiance is casual, from jacketed business people to hill-climbers in shorts and walking boots.

TINAKILLY COUNTRY HOUSE RESTAURANT, *Rathnew, Tel. (0404) 69274. £15.95 to £30. Open daily from 12:30 pm to 2:00 pm for lunch and from 7:30 pm until 9:00 pm for dinner. All major credit cards accepted.*

Set in the corner of the exquisite Victorian mansion once belonging to Captain Robert Halpin, Commander of the *Great Eastern*, and leader of the expedition to lay the first cross-Atlantic telegraph cable to America, the restaurant at Tinakilly House is a touch of elegance complemented by serenity and dining excellence.

The menu is wide-ranging, and main courses are augmented by fresh produce that is grown on the estate. They have gained some renown of late for their treatment of lamb. Other menu items include seafood (of course), Irish beef, and several vegetarian dishes. Aside from any of the lamb dishes, you might consider their excellent beef tenderloin with spring vegetables and champignon. Other specialties include baked tartlet of mushrooms, baked escalope of salmon, and roast breast of Barbary duck with fruit sauce. Their table d'hote menus are £18.50 for lunch and £30 for dinner.

OLD RECTORY, *Wicklow Town, Tel. (0404) 67048. £18.95 to £27. Open daily 8:00 pm to 9:30 pm for dinner. All major credit cards accepted. 10% service charge.*

The small Old Rectory restaurant is run by Linda Saunders, and blends the best of French and Irish cuisine to present an appetizing addition to your Irish holiday. The menu is not particularly extensive, and varies on a regular basis. Depending on when you are there, you may be treated to such specialties as fillet of black sole, roast quail with wild mushrooms, or sea trout and smoked salmon.

SEEING THE SIGHTS
County Carlow
Carlow Town. The county seat of County Carlow, this busy burg of about 12,000 sits quietly beside the River Barrow. Carlow has more industry than many of its neighboring towns, mostly centered on processing agricultural products such as sugar beets, wheat, and malt. Its Irish name is *Ceatharlach*, which means "Fourfold Lake."

Serving during much of Ireland's recent history as one of the southern borders of the English Pale, the area has a history rife with violence, as Irish chieftains often sought to throw off the chains of their oppressors. They fought and bled much in County Carlow. During the uprising of 1798, 640 patriots perished here. Their efforts are remembered by a Celtic high cross erected on the site of their graves on Church Street.

Today, things are a little quieter in Carlow. Located about fifty miles south of Dublin on the N9, it offers salmon and trout fishing (called angling here), golfing, and river cruising along the Barrow. Sights in and around Carlow that are of interest include the Cathedral of the Assumption, Carlow Castle, Carlow County Museum, and Browne's Dolmen.

Cathedral of the Assumption, *Tullow Street, Carlow, open daily from 10:00 am until 8:00 pm. Tel. (0503) 31227.* Built in the shape of a cross, the late 19th-century Gothic Cathedral of the Assumption is known for its lovely stained-glass windows. In addition, its lantern tower soars an impressive 151 feet above the street. You'll also be impressed with a fine marble monument to the builder of the cathedral, Bishop James Doyle (1786-1834). Bishop Doyle was a tireless agitator for Catholic emancipation at a time when it was exceptionally hazardous to do so. He was a prolific political writer, and his pen was continually busy for the Catholic cause.

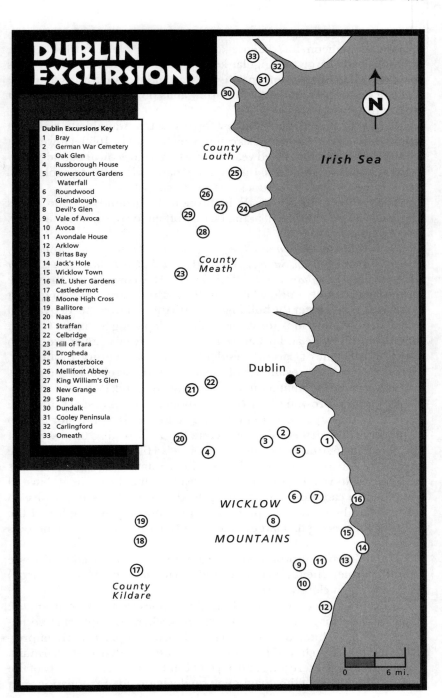

DUBLIN EXCURSIONS

Dublin Excursions Key

1 Bray
2 German War Cemetery
3 Oak Glen
4 Russborough House
5 Powerscourt Gardens
    Waterfall
6 Roundwood
7 Glendalough
8 Devil's Glen
9 Vale of Avoca
10 Avoca
11 Avondale House
12 Arklow
13 Britas Bay
14 Jack's Hole
15 Wicklow Town
16 Mt. Usher Gardens
17 Castledermot
18 Moone High Cross
19 Ballitore
20 Naas
21 Straffan
22 Celbridge
23 Hill of Tara
24 Drogheda
25 Monasterboice
26 Mellifont Abbey
27 King William's Glen
28 New Grange
29 Slane
30 Dundalk
31 Cooley Peninsula
32 Carlingford
33 Omeath

County Louth

Irish Sea

County Meath

Dublin

WICKLOW

MOUNTAINS

County Kildare

0   6 mi.

Carlow Castle, *Castle Hill Street, Carlow*. Built in the 13th century to provide a modicum of defense against local raiders, Carlow Castle originally had a large rectangular keep with a round tower at each of its corners. Today, all that remains are one wall and the two towers that abut it. It still stands poised to defend Carlow at its point near the bridge that crosses the River Barrow.

Carlow Castle is one of the few fortresses that was able to repel the advances of Oliver Cromwell's armies, which it did in 1650. However, it fell to idiocy several hundred years later when its new owner accidentally destroyed most of the castle through the inauspicious use of explosives. (He was trying to alter the thickness of the walls.)

Today, access to the Castle is through the grounds of Corcoran's Mineral Water Factory. Ask at the factory office for permission to enter. (Weekdays only.)

County Museum, *Centaur Street, Carlow, open Tuesday through Saturday from 9:30 am to 5:30 pm, Sunday from 2:30 pm to 5:30 pm. Admission is £1 for adults and 50p for children. Tel. (0503) 31759.* The Town Hall is the venue for the small County Carlow Museum. The exhibits are interesting if not extensive. As you enter the building beneath the two-story portico upheld by massive columns, look for several exhibits depicting life in old Carlow. A blacksmith's forge and primitive kitchen will give you an appreciation for the life of some of Carlow's residents in the 19th century. In addition, there are several fine examples of carpentry and barrel-making tools, as well as a number of military items from the 18th and 19th centuries.

Dolmen on Browne's Hill, *Carlow*. About two miles east of Carlow on the R725 is the largest *dolmen* in Ireland (a dolmen is a prehistoric tomb or monument which consists of a large flat rock resting on a series of upright smaller stones). Located in Browne's Hill demesne (estate), the large rock on top was once elevated by a number of smaller stones underneath. Its weight (102 tons!), the weather, and the elements have all combined to cause one end to drop to the ground. It's impressive to contemplate how on earth prehistoric man possibly accomplished the feat of maneuvering that large stone into place with the few ancient tools he had.

The dolmen is approached in a circuitous two hundred yard route around a farmer's field, and is protected by a few cows in a nearby (fenced) field who watch closely as you pass.

Killeshin Church, *Carlow*. About three miles west of Carlow on the R430 are the ruins of Killeshin Church, an excellent example of Hiberno-Romanesque architecture. The arched doorway is particularly impressive. Killeshin Church is a 6th-century monastery founded by St. Diarmuid. There are several interesting and ancient tombstones in the vicinity of the church. This is one of those ruins you can let your kids' imaginations run wild in; see which is the oldest date they can identify. Chances are there won't be a lot of other tourists around, and you can explore to your heart's content here with few distractions.

Black Castle, *Leighlinbridge*. Seven miles south of Carlow on the N9 are the ruins of Black Castle. Sitting near the River Barrow, the castle dates from the Anglo-Norman conquest of Ireland in the late 12th century. Its peaceful demeanor belies the fact that it was a place of great violence in days gone by. As one of the first strongholds of the Anglo-Norman invaders, it was the scene of many sieges and attacks, and the surrounding grounds have been moistened with great quantities of blood over the centuries. Not much of the castle remains today other than a decrepit tower.

St. Laserian's Cathedral, *Old Leighlin*. A couple of miles west of Leighlinbridge on a minor road (watch for the signposts) is the hamlet of Old Leighlin, the site and ruins of St. Laserian's Cathedral. St. Laserian founded a monastic settlement on this site in the 7th century. In the 12th century a church was built to commemorate St. Laserian's work, and was expanded in the 16th century. This was the cathedral for the diocese of Leighlin, and it became one of the most important monastic sites in Ireland during the 14th century. There are several well-preserved relics here: an ancient Cross of St. Laserian and an eight hundred year old baptismal font. There are also several ancient tombs inside the cathedral.

Muine Bheag. Also called **Bagenalstown**, this attractive little hamlet is just a few miles southeast of Leighlinbridge on the R750. It serves as a popular fishing center. Nearby Muine Bheag are the ancient ruins of Ballymoon Castle. Ballymoon Castle is a mere shadow of its former self, with only its extensive eight foot thick, twenty foot walls remaining.

County Kildare

Castletown House, *Celbridge, open April through October Monday through Friday from 10:00 am until 6:00 pm, Saturday 11:00 am to 6:00 pm, and Sunday from 2:00 pm until 6:00 pm. From November through March open Sundays from 2:00 pm until 6:00 pm. Admission is £2.50 for adults and £1 for children. Tel. (01) 628-8252.* Castletown House is another of Ireland's impressive Palladian-style mansions. Built in 1722 as the home of William Conolly, Speaker of the Irish House of Commons, the two wings are connected to the main house by colonnaded galleries.

The interior hallway features the handiwork of those talented Italian brothers Francini – they were considered to be among the best plaster workers on the continent and very much in demand in Ireland. The interior is exquisitely decorated with period furnishings, and makes for an awe-inspiring visit. The Long Gallery is especially impressive with its soft blue paint, Venetian chandeliers, and period furnishings.

Maynooth Castle, *Maynooth, open from June through September daily from 3:00 pm until 6:00 pm. Other times by appointment. Admission is free.* Just off the N4 (watch for the signposts) lies the small village of Maynooth, and with it Maynooth Castle. Its ruins greet the Catholic seminarians who attend nearby St. Patrick's College. The keep is still in relatively good condition, as is the gate tower, although most of the rest of the castle was destroyed during the Cromwellian period.

Straffan Butterfly Farm, *Straffan, open May through August daily from 10:00 am until 6:00 pm. Admission is £1. Tel. (01) 627-1109.* Located in the tiny town of Straffan, just a ten minute ride from Maynooth on the R408, the Straffan Butterfly Farm is a unique and interesting diversion from the ruins and cathedrals that abound in Ireland. The greenhouse features exotic and tropical plants, and a host of butterflies and moths.

Straffan Steam Museum, *Straffan, open Easter through September Tuesday through Sunday from 11:00 am until 6:00 pm. Admission is £3 for adults and £2 for children and seniors. Tel. (01) 627-3155.* This museum is devoted to the history of steam power in Ireland. Over twenty steam locomotives are on display, in addition to steam engines (called Stationary Industrial Engines) that were used for more sedentary work, such as churning butter and threshing wheat. Some of the steam engines are activated on days called "live steam" days; call ahead to find out when the "live steam" days are going to be. You can end your visit with a stop in the adjacent Steaming Kettle Tea House and Gift shop.

Robertstown. Sitting next to the Royal Canal, the tiny hamlet of Robertstown is a nice place to pause, walk along the canal, and maybe take a canal cruise. The Canal Hotel found here was built in 1801, and is now a popular venue for candlelight dinners and canal cruises in horse-drawn canal boats. The dinner and cruise cost £24.95.

Punchestown Racecourse, *Punchestown.* Punchestown Racecourse lies amid the verdant undulating foothills of the Wicklow Mountains. About three miles southeast of Naas, the racecourse is a popular place among horse racing fans, and perhaps is most famous for its steeplechase event that takes place every April.

Jigginstown House, *Naas.* Just south of Naas on the N7 is Jigginstown House, one of the most intriguing residential structures in this part of the country. The mansion is only partially finished – it was begun in 1633 as a residence by the Earl of Strafford. But it was never finished due to the premature death of the Earl in 1641 (he was executed). The front of the red brick mansion is over a football field's length – almost 375 feet long.

Hill of Allen, *near Newbridge.* Take a few minutes and drive to the Hill of Allen, about five miles northwest of Newbridge. The hill rises 676 feet above the famous Curragh Plain. As one of the lone hills in the area, it offers pretty panoramas. As you might imagine, due to its wide views it was formerly the location of the residences of several royal palaces during medieval times. The hill was also reputed to be the home of the legendary Fionn MacCumhaill, warrior leader of the vaunted Fianna during the 3rd century.

St. Brigid's Cathedral, *Kildare, open daily from 10:00 am to 6:00 pm. Admission is free.* St. Brigid's Cathedral is built on the original site chosen by St. Brigid in the 5th century. The cathedral was built in the early 13th century, and boasts several fine medieval tombs. The interior offers serenity and some lovely stained-glass windows. In the churchyard a round tower rises over 100 feet, and offers fine views of the surrounding area for those who make the effort to climb to the top.

Japanese Gardens, *Tully (near Kildare), open Easter through October Monday through Saturday from 10:00 am until 5:00 pm, and Sunday from 2:00 pm until 6:00 pm. Admission £1.50. Tel. (045) 21617.* A little over a mile south of Kildare is the village of Tully, with its famous Japanese Gardens. Early in this century, Lord Wavertree commissioned famous Japanese landscape designer Tassa Eida to design and lay out these gardens. The results of his work are exquisite. The design symbolizes man's passage through mortality and into eternity. This is really worth a visit.

National Stud and Iron Horse Museum, *Tully (near Kildare), open Easter through October Monday thorough Saturday from 10:00 am until 5:00 pm, and Sunday from 2:00 pm until 6:00 pm. Admission £1.50. Tel. (045) 21617.* In case you didn't know it, Ireland loves horses, and that love is probably centered in Tully at the National Stud. This is where breeding stallions are kept and where horse groomers and trainers work their magic on the mares of Ireland.

Located with the National Stud is the Iron Horse Museum, a museum that traces equestrian history from the Bronze Age to the present. If you're really into horses and horse racing, you'll know the name of Arkle, probably the most famous (and winningest) Irish racehorse. His skeleton is on display at the museum. Visitors to the National Stud have fairly free access to the fine horses that are stabled here.

Quaker Museum, *Ballitore, open May through September on Sunday from 2:00 pm to 6:00 pm. Tel. (045) 31109. Admission is £1.* South of Naas on the N9 is the tiny town of Ballitore. Its main attraction is the small Quaker Museum housed in an old schoolhouse. The community was founded by Quakers in the 18th century.

Moone High Cross, *Moone (near Ballitore).* Just south of Ballitore is the small hamlet of Moone with its famous high cross. Over seventeen feet tall, the cross has a number of carvings depicting biblical scenes. My favorite is of Shadrach, Meshach and Abednego facing the fiery furnace. Can you identify any of the others?

Castledermot. About seven miles northwest of Carlow is the market town of Castledermot. There is a well-preserved round tower that's over one thousand years old, as well as several high crosses which are also well-preserved.

County Kilkenny

Kilkenny Town. Kilkenny Town's Irish name is *Cill Cainneach,* which means "Canice's Church;" the town and county both owe their name to the 6th-century St. Canice. Kilkenny Town, straddling the River Nore, is home to just over 8,500 people. It is an ancient and royal town. In former days, it was the capital of the Kingdom of Ossory. During the Anglo-Norman invasion, it was presided over by William le Mareschal, the son-in-law of the Irish arch-enemy **Strongbow**.

As pretty and peaceful as Kilkenny is today, it is associated with infamy. In an effort to segregate the Anglo-Norman conquerors from the "Irish rabble," the 1366 Statutes of Kilkenny was passed here. The statutes laid out strict punishment for Anglo-Normans who deliberately embraced Irish culture. For example, marriage by an Anglo-Norman to an Irish citizen was punishable by death; Irishmen were forbidden to live within walled cities; Anglo-Normans were banned from wearing Irish clothing, naming their children with Irish names, and from learning Gaelic. This segregation and separation widened the two hundred year-old rift – physical as well as political – between the native Irish and the invaders from across the Irish Sea.

Kilkenny Castle, *The Parade, Kilkenny, open April and May daily 10:30 am to 5:00 pm, June through September daily 10:00 am until 7:00 pm, October through March Tuesday through Saturday from 10:30 am to 12:45 pm and 2:00 pm to 5:00 pm, Sunday from 11:00 am to 12:45 pm and 2:00 pm to 5:00 pm. Admission is £1 for adults, and 40p for children. Tel. (056) 21450.* In the 12th century, The Earl of Pembroke – Strongbow – built a wooden fortress on a high bank above the River Nore. It was a commanding position. In the 13th century the wooden structure was replaced with an even stronger stone fortress. Over the centuries, the castle has been added to, and it is now a mixture of Gothic and classical architectural styles. In 1391, the powerful Butler family purchased the castle in anticipation of King Richard II's visit to Ireland. They seemed to like the house and the neighborhood – Kilkenny Castle was the family residence until 1935. The Butlers were known as the Earls and Dukes of Ormonde.

Begin your tour of Kilkenny Castle on the richly landscaped grounds. They are immaculate with hardly a blade of grass or mum out of place. The castle sits along the bank of the River Nore, and is surrounded by acres of manicured lawns, fountains, and flowers. When you've had your fill of the grounds, venture into the house. Delightful hosts and hostesses will greet you and see that you have a pleasant visit. The tour includes visits to a number of the castle's rooms, including the drawing and dining rooms, the library, and some of the bedrooms, which are imposing: ample numbers of antiques, tremendous tapestries, and plenty of paintings. But by far the most impressive room in the castle is the impressive Long Gallery, a cavernous room one hundred and fifty feet long. Its walls are decked out with the portraits of the Butler family – five hundred years' worth!

Kyteler's Inn, *St. Kieran's Street.* After you visit Kilkenny Castle, stop at Kyteler's Inn on St. Kieran's Street. This old limestone coaching inn is the oldest house in Kilkenny, but the real story here belongs to the former owner of the house, Dame Alice Kyteler. Dame Kyteler was born in 1280, and the attractive lass earned a lucrative living as a "banker" in the small town. By the time she was forty-four years old, she had outlived four husbands. Unfortunately, Bishop de Ledrede accused her of witchcraft, and a plentiful stock of herbs, ointments, and other oddities in her home were enough to convict her and her maid of the charge. Dame Kyteler fled the scene, never to be heard of again; Petronella, her maid, wasn't so quick, and she was burned at the stake. Check out the inn. In addition to its fascinating history, it serves a pretty good meal, too.

Shee's Alms House, *Rose Inn Street, open May through September Monday to Saturday from 9:00 am to 6:00 pm, Sunday from 10:00 am to 5:00 pm, and October through April Tuesday through Saturday from 9:00 am to 5:15 pm. Admission to CityScope is £1 for adults and 50p for children. Tel. (056) 51500.* Next to St. Mary's Hall on Rose Inn Street is the old stone front of Shee's Alms House, a house of charity founded in 1582 by Sir Richard Shee as a hospital for the indigent of Kilkenny. It served in that role until 1895. Today, instead of dispensing medicine and compassion, it serves up tourist information – it contains the local office of the Tourist Information Office. They offer a short show called CityScope which gives the history of 17th-century Kilkenny. If you need a rest, the CityScope presentation isn't too bad; otherwise, pass on it and see the town first-hand.

Rothe House, *Parliament Street, Kilkenny, open April through September daily from 10:00 am until 12:30 pm, and from 3:00 pm to 5:00 pm, October through March Saturday and Sunday from 3:00 pm until 5:00 pm, or call for an appointment. Admission is £1.50 for adults, £1 for students and senior citizens, and 60p for children. Tel. (056) 22893.* Rothe House is the home of an English merchant built in 1594 around a double courtyard. Currently it serves as the headquarters of the Kilkenny Archaeological Society. It contains a small museum and a 19th-century collection of costumes.

Black Abbey, *Abbey Street, Kilkenny.* On Abbey Street in Kilkenny is the 13th-century Black Abbey, named after the color of the Dominican Friar's robes. In recent years, the Black Abbey was restored and is now in use as a Dominican friary (called Black Friar's Church). All that remains of the original abbey is the nave, south transept, and the tower.

St. Canice's Cathedral, *corner of Dean and Parliament Streets, Kilkenny, open Easter through September Monday through Saturday 9:00 am until 6:00 pm, Sunday from 2:00 pm until 6:00 pm, and October through Easter Monday through Saturday from 10:00 am to 1:00 pm, and 2:00 pm to 4:00 pm, and Sunday from 2:00 pm until 4:00 pm. Admission is free.* St. Canice's Cathedral is an impressive gray granite structure. Modeled after many of the English churches of the period (13th century), St. Canice's stands firm and straight despite the efforts of a number of plunderers, including Cromwell's forces.

St. Canice's Library, *Dean Street, Kilkenny, open daily from 9:00 am until 1:00 pm, and from 2:00 pm until 6:00 pm. Admission is free.* Next to St. Canice's cathedral is St. Canice's Library, the repository of over 3,000 16th and 17th-century manuscripts.

St. Cainneach (anglicized as Canice – pronounced Kenny) founded a monastery on this site in the 6th century, and this cathedral was built in the early 1200s. It is the second largest medieval cathedral in Ireland, next to St. Patrick's Cathedral in Dublin.

The Gothic interior is majestic and the view from the back of the chapel to the stained glass windows is memorable. A number of tombs are contained in the cathedral. Many are interesting to study. One of them, that of Viscount Mountgarrett, is in full armor. Be sure and check out the carved black marble of St. Ciaran's chair in the north transept.

Standing next to the cathedral is a 101 foot tall round tower, the only vestige of the original monastic settlement. If you've the desire, 167 steps lead you to the top and a nice view of Kilkenny Town.

THE BLACK DEATH IN IRELAND

Ireland has had its share of tragedies through the centuries. But one of them was not unique to Ireland: the Black Death, a terrible scourge that spread like wildfire through Europe and Asia in the mid-1300s. Modern medicine believes the culprit was most likely the Bubonic Plague.

As Ireland was not immune, neither was tiny Kilkenny, nor its Dominican friary, the Black Abbey. Eight priests succumbed to the deadly disease as it spread through Ireland. One of the inhabitants of the Black Abbey, Friar Clyn, recorded that no household in Kilkenny had lost fewer than two individuals. His last words read, "I leave parchment to carry out the work if perchance any man survives..." The next entry was the record of Friar Clyn's death, written by another scribe.

Dunmore Cave, *near Kilkenny, open mid-March through June Tuesday through Saturday from 10:00 am to 5:00 pm, Sunday from 2:00 pm to 5:00 pm. Mid-June through September it is open daily from 10:00 am until 7:00 pm, and October through mid-March it is open weekends from 10:00 am until 5:00 pm. Admission is £1 for adults and 40p for children. Tel. (056) 67726.* About seven miles north of Kilkenny is Dunmore cave, a series of natural limestone caves. There are three primary chambers and one mighty 20 foot tall stalagmite (remember – stalagmites attach to the floor) called Market Cross.

Dunmore Cave was once considered the gateway to hell, as most caves were in ancient Irish times. Perhaps the most interesting aspect of Dunmore Cave is the stories of tragedies that occurred here, including stories of Viking massacres. If you've never been in a cave, this might be a good time to go. Like most other caves, this one is damp and clammy. The history of the cave makes it a little more interesting, however.

Jerpoint Abbey, *near Thomastown, open April to mid-June and mid-September to mid-October Tuesday through Sunday 10:00 am to 1:00 pm and 2:00 pm to 5:00 pm, mid-June to mid-September daily from 9:30 am to 6:30 pm. From November through March, see the caretaker who lives on-site for access to the grounds. Admission is £1.50 for adults and 60p for children. Tel. (056) 21755.* Jerpoint Cisterian Abbey is two miles south of Thomastown on the N9. It is considered one of the best monastic ruins in Ireland. Spend a few minutes walking among the ample ruins, imagining what the life of a monk in the late 12th century would have been like at this monastery. The abbey was built in 1158 for the Benedictine order by Donagh MacGillapatrick, but later passed to the Cisterians in 1180. It functioned under the Cisterians until 1540, when it was abandoned as a result of King Henry VIII's suppression order.

After the abbey was abandoned, the lands were given to the Ormond family. The ruin is large – it is nearly the exact length and width of a football field. There are a series of interesting sculptures in the cloister, thought to be the work of the renowned sculptor Rory O'Tunney. Judging from the flowing robes on many of them, they may represent some of the monks who served at Jerpoint Abbey during that time. (O'Tunney is thought to have sculpted them in the first half of the 16th century.) There are several interesting tombs in the church, including one of Bishop Felix O'Dulaney. Bishop O'Dulaney's effigy is interesting: it depicts a snake biting the crosier (a hooked staff, like a shepherd's crooked stick) held by the good bishop.

The small visitors center provides a history of the monastery. The monastery is a wonderful subject for photographers – amateur as well as professional. It is impressive, and is well worth the small admission fee.

Duiske Abbey, *Graiguenamanagh*. If you can pronounce (correctly) the name of this small town – Graiguenamanagh – you are doing better with your Irish than me. It is a pretty, unspoiled little village located on the R703. Its main attraction is the pretty Duiske Abbey, which is currently in use as a Catholic parish church. It's worth a peek inside – while the Gothic arches are the most impressive, the church is quietly reverent.

The abbey was built in 1204, and the monks quickly endeared themselves to their fellow countrymen by being exceptionally generous and compassionate to the poor and ill. They earned a reputation for kindness in that part of the country. As was often the case in ancient Ireland, a community sprung up near the abbey. The name was a tribute to the goodly monks: *Graigneunmanagh* is the Irish name for "Village of the Monks." The abbey was abandoned in 1540 when Henry VIII ordered the closure of all monasteries in Ireland, and the abbey fell into disrepair. In the early 1980s, the townsfolk began repairing the abbey.

County Laois

Emo Court and Gardens, *near Portarlington, Gardens open daily from 10:30 am to 5:30 pm, house open April through mid-October Monday 2:00 pm to 6:00 pm or by appointment. Admission to the gardens is £2 for adults and £1 for senior citizens and children. Admission to the house is £2.50. (0502) 26110.* About five miles outside of Portarlington is Emo Court and Gardens. James Gandon, who designed the Custom House and The Four Courts in Dublin, also designed the house. You'll note he seems to have been unable to do anything on a small scale. The house is exquisite, and is truly a sight. It has an impressive domed rotunda, and the lighting currently in use accentuates its grandeur.

The grounds are quiet and serene, and include numerous statues, shrubs, and walkways. This is a nice quiet diversion.

Irish Veteran Car Museum, *Ivyleigh, open Monday through Saturday from 10:00 am until 5:00 pm. Admission for adults is £2.50 and £1 for children.* This pleasant detour is on the outskirts of Portlaoise. The museum is devoted to antique cars; most of them are pre-World War I.

County Longford

Carriglass Manor, *near Longford, open mid-June through September Thursday through Monday from 1:00 pm to 5:00 pm, and Sunday from 2:00 pm to 6:00 pm. Admission is £3 for adults and £2 for children. Tel. (043) 45165.* Carriglass Manor is about three miles outside Longford on the R194 road. Built in 1837, this dreamy Tudor house boasts fine plaster-work and 19th-century furnishings.

The Motte of Granard, *Granard*. On the southwest outskirts of the small village of Granard silently sits the Motte of Granard. A *motte* is a stockade atop a flat mound. In ancient times a motte generally had a tower in the center of the stockade. Some believe the motte here is the largest of its kind in Ireland. A statue of St. Patrick was erected on the site in 1932 to celebrate the 1,500th anniversary of St. Patrick's arrival in the Emerald Isle.

County Louth

Drogheda. Drogheda is one of the busiest towns in Ireland. Its Irish name is *Droichead Atha,* which means "The Bridge of the Ford." At one time, Drogheda was one of the most important cities in Ireland. Today it is a bustling industrial town of some 30,000 or so. Its main industry is cement, which it provides to the entire country.

Spanning the River Boyne, Drogheda was formerly two towns – one on each side of the river. But the towns grew together, and it made sense to some medieval city fathers to combine the name of the towns and call them one. It's interesting to realize that Drogheda physically resides in two counties: Louth and Meath, since the River Boyne separates the two counties at this point.

Drogheda's history extends back to its founding as a permanent site by Vikings in the early 10th century. Prior to that, a small community lived here where the River Boyne empties into the Irish Sea. Considering the presence of Newgrange, Knowth, and Dowth just up the Boyne Valley from Drogheda, it is likely that this area was host to some of Ireland's earliest inhabitants. The passage graves at these three sites, for example, date to 3,000 BC.

Several hundred years after the Vikings inhabited the site and established Drogheda as one of the most important trading centers on the island, the town – as with many others across the country – was taken by the Anglo-Norman **Hugh de Lacy**. Over the next several hundred years Drogheda's importance and its position on the borders of "the Pale" justified the heavily fortified city wall. Ten gates allowed access into the city, but only one remains for visitors to see today: **St. Lawrence's Gate**, *on St. Lawrence Street,* is freely accessible. Impressive towers and a vaulted arch overlook the low passageway.

In 1649, Drogheda was unable to withstand the onslaught of **Oliver Cromwell's** armies, and between 2,500 and 3,000 captured soldiers were executed. According to Cromwell, the executions were "...a righteous judgment of God upon those barbarous wretches...."

At the opposite end of St. Lawrence Street from St. Lawrence's Gate is the domed 18th-century *Tholsel,* or city hall. The building is no longer used as city hall and now houses a bank. Nearby, at the corner of St. Peter's and William Street, is the proud **St. Peter's Church**, a 19th-century Gothic structure. The church was built in memory of a Catholic martyr, Oliver

Plunkett. At one time he was the Archbishop of Armagh. He was one of many to be martyred in London in 1681 (he was canonized by the church in 1975). Not only was the church erected in his honor, but he is remembered today in a singular manner: his head is preserved in a shrine in the church. Macabre, at best.

Other sites worth seeing in Drogheda are the ruins of the 13th-century **St. Mary d'Urso Augustinian Abbey**. All that remains is the tower, which rises slightly over 100 feet above Abbey Lane. On the south side of town is a hill called **Millmount Mound**. It is said that the mound was built over the final resting place of the son of Milesius around the 11th century BC. Its 14th-century fort was taken by Cromwellian forces.

Today it houses the **Millmount Museum**, *Millmount Mound, Drogheda, open May to October Tuesday through Sunday from 3:00 pm until 6:00 pm, and November though April Wednesday, Saturday and Sunday from 3:00 pm until 6:00 pm. Admission is £1 for adults and 50p for children. Tel. (041) 36391. (The craft shops are open all year from 9:30 am until 6:00 pm Monday through Saturday.)* On Millmount Mound are a set of old English barracks, part of which have been converted into a museum featuring eight centuries of Droghedan history. Also included in the barracks are crafts shops and a picture gallery. The museum spends far more space on the domestic history of Drogheda than on its military history. A number of exhibits highlight Drogheda's progression from a settlement whose principle occupations were fishing and farming to the industrial center it is today.

Monasterboice, *near Drogheda*. Located on the R132 just off the N1 about six miles north of Drogheda, watch for the first Dunleer exit north of Drogheda, then follow the signs to Monasterboice. It is not particularly well-signed off the N1, but you can see it off the N1. This is one of the premier exhibits of finely preserved high crosses in Ireland is the monastic settlement of Monasterboice. It takes its name from the Irish *Mainstir Buithe*, which means "St. Buithe's Abbey."

St. Buithe founded a monastery on this site during the 5th century. In 1097, the round tower suffered a devastating fire, destroying the monastic library that was kept there for safe keeping. The monastery was abandoned in the 12th century. The site consists of the ruins of two churches, a round tower, and three high crosses.

Two of the high crosses are among the best examples of high crosses in the world. One of them, the **Cross of Muiredach**, is remarkably well-preserved. An inscription at the base of the cross says, "A prayer for Muiredach by whom this cross was made." The crosses have images of biblical stories from the old and new testaments engraved on them.

The 10th-century Cross of Muiredach stands almost seventeen feet tall, and has scenes depicting Adam and Eve, Cain and Abel, Christ as the Judge, and Michael weighing souls. It also contains a depiction of the crucifixion. **Tall Cross** (twenty-one feet high) depicts the sacrifice of Isaac by Abraham, the Vigil at the Tomb, Judas' kiss of betrayal, and the crucifixion. One other cross, the **North Cross**, only partially survived the years.

The round tower stands nearly 110 feet tall, even without its peaked cap, which was lost many centuries ago. There is also a six foot tall granite sundial enclosed with a railing that is interesting to see. In 1979, Monasterboice hosted a visit from Pope John Paul.

Mellifont Abbey, *near Tullyallen, open from May through mid-June daily from 10:00 am to 5:00 pm, and mid-June through October 1 daily from 9:30 am until 6:30 pm. Admission is free. A guided tour is available at £1.50 for adults, £1 for seniors, and 60p for children. A family ticket is available for £4.*

Located about three miles northwest of Drogheda just off the R168 is Mellifont Abbey, which was founded in 1142 by St. Malachy O'Morgair, and was the first Cisterian monastery in Ireland. A chapter house is the meeting place for a chapter (group) of monks.

Only bits and pieces of the original buildings are still available to see, but the remains are enough to tell you it was an extensive site in its day. In fact, its Irish name *An Mhainistir Mhor,* means "The Big Monastery." Portions of the cloister still exist, along with parts of a chapter house built in the 12th century.

King William's Glen, *near Drogheda.* About seven miles west of Drogheda off the N51 is King William's Glen. This is the area that part of King William's army secreted themselves just prior to the Battle of the Boyne. The site of their battle on July 1, 1690 is marked nearby. This was a pivotal battle, and marked the beginning of many difficult and arduous years for the Irish in general and Irish Catholics in particular.

Ledwidge Cottage and Museum, *Slane, open year around Monday through Wednesday from 10:00 am to 1:00 pm and 2:00 pm to 6:00 pm, Saturday from 10:00 am to 1:00 pm and from 2:00 pm to 7:00 pm, and Sunday from 2:00 pm to 6:00 pm. Admission is £1. Tel. (041) 24285.* On the east side of Slane is a small stone cottage that once belonged to celebrated Irish poet Francis Ledwidge. He was an up-and-coming lyric poet who was killed during World War I. The home has been restored and stocked with period furnishings as a tribute to his short life.

Slane Castle, *Slane.* About a mile outside Slane is the 19th-century Gothic Slane Castle. On the grounds of the castle is the 16th-century church called the Hermitage of St. Erc, the first bishop of Slane. In addition to the buildings, you can take peaceful strolls through the tree-filled estate.

Slane Hill, *near Slane.* A mile north of Slane is Slane Hill, one of the most famous hillocks in Ireland. It is revered as the place where **St. Patrick** lit a paschal fire in 433 AD, signifying the arrival in Ireland of Christianity and proclaiming the beginning of his ministry. The lighting of the Paschal fire defied a royal prohibition against such acts.

Atop the hill are the remains of a 16th-century Franciscan friary, which were built on the ruins of the church St. Patrick built on that same spot.

Ratheddy. The village of Ratheddy, a mile outside of Knockbridge, is home to *Clochafermor*, which means Cuchulainn's Stone. Cuchulainn is a legendary hero, a member of the Red Branch Knights. The legend says that as Cuchulainn was fearlessly facing a daunting number of foes, he bravely fought on and on. Mortally wounded, he is said to have thrown his sword into a nearby lake and then lashed himself to a stone so that he could face his enemies standing. His foes wouldn't approach his body, the legend says, until a bird landed on the shoulder of the lifeless warrior.

At any rate, the stone stands in Ratheddy. Interestingly, a nearby bog bears the Irish name *Lochan an Chlaiomh*, which means "The Lakelet of the Sword."

Dundalk. The harbor town of Dundalk is about fifty miles north of Dublin. Driving there takes about an hour and fifteen minutes from Dublin. Bus and train service runs there also. Trains leave Dublin's Connolly Station and take about an hour to an hour and a half; buses take two hours.

Dundalk's Irish name, *Dun Dealgan* means Delga's Fort. The town has been here at the mouth of Dundalk Harbor since the 7th century, and has a history of attacks, sacks, and burnings. Dundalk is not far from the small town where death came to the legendary hero Cuchulainn of the Red Branch Knights. A statue commemorating his fearless stand and brave death graces the lobby of the General Post Office in Dublin.

The town was walled in about 1185 by Bertram de Verdon. For nearly 300 years, Dundalk was considered a frontier town at the northern end of the English-controlled Pale. Because of this, it was frequently visited by native chieftains with murder and mayhem on their minds.

Today, it is a bustling town of about 25,000. One of the more interesting sights in Dundalk is **St. Patrick's Church** (1847) with its stone-carved high altar and pulpit. Its Newry-granite exterior is an imitation of King's College Chapel in Cambridge, England. On Clanbrassil Street is one of Dundalk's oldest surviving structures, **St. Nicholas' Church**, originally built in 1207. It was added to in the 1400s and renovated in 1707. In the adjoining graveyard, its most celebrated resident is Agnes Galt, the sister of Scottish poet Robert Burns, who is also commemorated by a pillar on the right side of the entrance to the church. On Castle Street stand the ruins of "The Castle," which really wasn't (and isn't) a castle at all. Rather, it is actually the bell-tower of a ruined 13th-century Franciscan friary.

Perhaps the most interesting sight in Dundalk isn't man-made. On the outskirts of the city are extensive salt flats and marshes, home to about a trillion different species of birds.

Tourism in Dundalk suffers from the plethora of more rustic ruins, scenic settings, and dazzling displays elsewhere in the country. Unless your family came from Dundalk, or lives here now, you may want to travel on to other locales.

Cooley Peninsula Drive, *north of Dundalk*. Northeast of Dundalk on the N1, watch for the R173 and signposts to the Carlingford and the Coast Road. This six-mile drive around the peninsula is pretty, and affords nice views of the Irish Sea.

Proleek Dolmen, *Ballymascanlon*. In the little town of Ballymascanlon, behind the hotel of the same name, is the Proleek Dolmen, which has been here for roughly 5,000 years. A *dolmen* is a simple megalithic tomb that has three or more stones that serve as pillars or pedestals for a large stone (called a capstone) that is placed on top of them. Sometimes these capstones weigh up to one hundred tons. The capstone for the Proleek Dolmen *only* weighs about fifty tons!

The medieval town of **Carlingford** sits on the north side of the Cooley Peninsula, nestled at the foot of Slieve Foye (1,935 feet) on the south shore of Carlingford Lough. There are a number of interesting medieval ruins in the town, although only one of them is available to the public. **King John's Castle** is a picturesque ruin still guarding the mouth of the harbor, as King John directed in the 13th century. It sits on the south end of town between the N1 and Carlingford Lough. Take a few minutes to explore the ruin, or take the half-mile or so walk on the quay that goes out into the lough. Other interesting ruins include the 15th-century **Mint House** and **Taafe's Castle**, an immense square keep off Newry Street and a contemporary of the Mint House.

Omeath. At the head of Carlingford Lough is the tiny town of Omeath. Ask the locals for directions to Long Woman's Grave, and you'll find yourself presented with a lovely view of Carlingford Lough and the opposite shoreline. Along the quays, catch a jaunting car (like a horse and buggy) up to the Calvary and Stations of the Cross at the Charity Fathers' Monastery.

St. Mochta's House, *Louth*. About four miles southwest of Dundalk on the R171 (after you go through Rathneddy) lies the hamlet of Louth. This pretty little hilltop town is traditionally given as the site of the first church built by St. Patrick in the 5th century. Nothing remains of that ancient house of worship. What remains is the 10th-century oratory named after the first bishop of Louth, now called St. Mochta's House. An excellent example of the Irish stone house, its tall stone roof is splendid.

County Meath

Navan. The small city of Navan, population 3,500, is about a forty-five minute drive from Dublin on the N3, or about twenty minutes from Drogheda on the N51. Navan serves as an important furniture manufacturing location for the country. Its Irish name is *An Uaimh*, which means "The Cave." It has ancient beginnings, but like so many other towns in this part of Ireland it saw its greatest growth and stature when Hugh de Lacy walled and fortified the city, as he did Drogheda, and secured it as one of the frontier towns of the English Pale.

The main street in Navan is Trimgate Street, and on it you'll come across **St. Mary's Church**, a 19th-century Catholic church. It's most striking feature is the 18th-century carving of the Crucifixion, one of the finest ever done by Irish wood carver and sculptor Edward Smyth.

Hill of Tara, *near Navan*. Eight miles south of Navan just off the N3 (watch for the signpost) is the Hill of Tara, one of the most significant hills in Ireland. It is the ancient site of the coronation of the Celtic kings of Ireland. Every three years a great *feis* (pronounced fesh) or large assembly was held to pass laws, regulate trade, settle disputes, and forge alliances. It was revered through the centuries as a place of awe. With the lighting of **St. Patrick's** paschal fire not far away on Slane Hill, the power and influence of the Hill of Tara began to wane.

Atop the hill is a statue of St. Patrick, and a small pillar called the *Lia Fail*, the stone believed to have been used as an ancient coronation stone. The pagan Celtic kings would roll over in their graves to have the statue of this zealous Christian missionary erected on the hill of their ancient coronations. Little else is on the hill except grass-covered mounds and the occasional grazing sheep – the new kings of Tara.

Hill of Tara Interpretive Center, *near Navan, open in May and September daily from 10:00 am until 5:00 pm, and June through August daily from 9:30 am until 6:30 pm. Admission is free. Tel. (041) 24824.* Located in a converted Church of Ireland building, a small interpretive center gives you the background of the Hill of Tara. The center features a short audiovisual presentation that helps you understand the historical significance of the Hill of Tara.

Trim. South of Navan on the R161 is the small market town of Trim. Sitting pretty on the banks of the River Boyne, Trim's Irish name means "Town of the Elder-Tree Ford" (*Baile Atha Truim*). Religious and secular history swirled around this quiet little town through the centuries. Like so many towns in Ireland, it was stormed and taken by Oliver Cromwell's armies, and like so many others, most of its inhabitants were put to the sword. Places to see in and around Trim include Trim Castle, Yellow Steeple, and St. Patrick's Church.

Trim Castle, *Trim, admission is free.* Overlooking the River Boyne looms Trim Castle, a massive Anglo-Norman fortress said to be the largest in Ireland. The ruins of the castle cover more than two acres. Built by Hugh de Lacy, he seemed to be preparing for Armageddon – the huge fortress consists of a massive square keep with turrets soaring 70 feet, and towers in the middle of each wall. The walls themselves are a mere eleven feet thick! The fortress originally featured a drawbridge, which has long since disappeared. It spanned a moat which was filled from the River Boyne. The outer wall is over a quarter of a mile long, and originally its walks joined the town's walls. This was one impressive fortress in its day; the ruins are impressive today.

Yellow Steeple, *Trim.* The Yellow Steeple is what remains of a 13th-century Augustinian abbey (although the steeple is much newer – it was built in 1368!). Most of the tower was destroyed to prevent Cromwell's troops from taking it, and now only the 125 foot wall remains, a silent witness of the ugliness that dogged this pretty little town through the centuries.

Newgrange, *open Mid-June through mid September daily from 10:00 am until 7:00 pm, April through mid-June and mid-September to mid-October Monday through Saturday from 10:00 am until 5:00 pm and Sunday from 2:00 pm until 5:00 pm, and from mid-October through March 31 it is open Tuesday through Saturday from 10:00 am until 5:00 pm with an hour lunch from 1:00 pm to 2:00 pm, and Sunday from 2:00 pm until 5:00 pm. Admission is £2 for adults and £1 for children.* Between the N2 and N1 north of Dublin is the Boyne River Valley in County Meath, where a number of important archaeological discoveries have been made in recent years. Newgrange, Dowth, and Knowth, within close proximity to one another, are the sites of three ancient burial mounds.

Of the three, Newgrange's cross-shaped passage grave is the most impressive. Inside Newgrange, visitors will be led down a passage lined with massive stones and into the central burial chamber.

The Newgrange mound is a well-preserved grave dating back to nearly 3,000 BC. During the winter solstice (December 21), rays from the sun glide down the narrow passageway gradually lighting the burial chamber. For those unable to be at Newgrange during the winter solstice, modern technology recreates the effect. On December 21, the rising sun strikes an aperture in the roof of the passage grave. The sunlight is directed down into the passage grave, and as the sun rises its rays slowly move down the passage until they arrive in the main burial chamber, illuminating it. The rest of the year the effect is simulated by shining a light down the passage and into the burial chamber, as though it was really December 21, simulating the path the sun's rays take.

The burial mounds at Dowth and Knowth are also impressive, though neither has the dramatic winter solstice effect Newgrange offers. Dowth, in fact, has two chambers to its passage-tomb, and Knowth offers two main tombs surrounded by eighteen others. Both Dowth and Knowth are in the process of excavation, and sometimes parts of them are open to visitors. When they are, the hours are the same as those listed above for Newgrange.

All three sites offer splendid examples of ancient artistic/ritualistic craftsmanship, as the tombs are all graced with wonderful stone carvings. These are really impressive reminders of ancient man's devotion to his god or gods. These were the burial sites of the ancient kings of Ireland, and are well worth a visit.

Newtown. Less than a mile east of Trim, nestled along the banks of the River Boyne, are the ruins of what was at one time the largest cathedral in Ireland. Built in 1210 by Simon de Rochfort, all that remain of this magnificent building are the choir, crossing, and a portion of the nave. What a beautiful sight this must have been!

Kells. Near the intersection of the N3 and the N52 northwest of Dublin lies the monastic settlement of Kells. Its Irish name *Ceanannus Mor*, meaning "Great Residence." Built around the 6th century by **St. Columcille**, Kells survived repeated raids over several hundred years from their ill-mannered Viking neighbors. Their greatest claim to fame, however, is the 9th-century production of the richly illustrated *Book of Kells*, now on display in Dublin at Trinity College. But there is a modern reproduction of the Book on display at St. Columba's Church in Kells.

St. Columba's also features a graveyard with five ancient high crosses. As with other high crosses, these are elaborately carved with scenes from the scriptures. See if you can identify any of the stories depicted (hint: look for Cain and Abel, Christ's Judgment, Daniel in the Lion's Den, Abraham's sacrifice of Isaac in the wilderness, and the miracle of the loaves and fishes). Four of the crosses are still in relatively good shape, but only a portion of the fifth survives. Sadly, in more troubled times, the fifth cross was used as a gallows during the 1798 uprising.

High Crosses first began to appear in Ireland in the 8th century. Theological experts have theorized that they served another purpose beyond merely representing the crucifixion. They speculate that the Biblical figures on the crosses may have helped the priests teach their non-reading parishioners stories from the scriptures. This theory may be true; or it may simply be that someone wanted to express his adulation and remembrance on a grand scale, and the idea caught on.

Nearby is **St. Columba's House**, an impressive example of the craft of building an entirely stone building, including the steeply pitched stone roof. St. Columba's House is similar in design to those found at Glendalough (St. Kevin's House) and at Cashel (Cormac's Chapel). The building itself measures 24 feet by 21 feet, is 40 feet tall at the ridge, and has walls that are more than four feet thick.

Near the church is a wonderfully erect round tower, dating from before the 12th century. The tower is nearly 100 feet tall, and there are five windows at the top, each providing a view of the various entrances to the ancient city. The tower no longer has its conical cap but is still an impressive sight.

County Offaly

Birr Castle Demesne, *Birr, open April through October daily from 9:00 am to 6:00 pm, November and December daily from 9:00 am to 1:00 pm and 2:00 pm to 5:00 pm. Admission for adults is £3 and £1.50 for children.* In the small, quiet town of Birr, you'll find the Birr Castle, a romantic castle built in Gothic style in the early 1600s. Unfortunately, the castle isn't open to the public (it's still lived in by the earls of Rosse), but the grounds are, and they are well worth the time it takes to see them.

The castle is set in a gorgeous 100 acre park-like setting. Spring is a particularly good time to visit, as the cherry trees, magnolias, and a host of other trees and flowers are in full bloom. Of particular interest are the 30-plus foot tall hedges.

Clonmacnoise, *Co. Offaly, open mid-June through September daily from 9:00 am to 7:00 pm, and October to May daily from 10:00 am until 6:00 pm (or dusk during the winter months). Admission is £1.50 for adults, £1 for senior citizens, and 60p for children. Tel. (0905) 74195.* On a ridge above the Shannon River lies the 6th-century monastic site of Clonmacnoise. Its Irish name means "Meadow of the son of Nos" (*Cluain Mic Nois*). Founded by St. Ciaran in 548, the goodly saint never realized how important the monastery would become – he died the year he founded it. It was once considered the most important religious center in Ireland.

Over the years, monks laboring within its walls produced several valuable manuscripts that are still in existence: *The Book of the Dun Cow* (currently on display at the Royal Irish Academy in Dublin) and the *Annals of Tighernach*. Alas, like so many other monastic sites around Ireland, Clonmacnoise suffered repeated attacks, plunderings, and burnings during its turbulent history. It seems every invading group conducted attacks against the community, from the Vikings to the Normans to the English under Oliver Cromwell.

The walled monastery is littered with ruins and crosses. Central to the ruins is the cathedral, which due to un-neighborly visits consists of various building and rebuilding(!) efforts, ranging from the 10th to the 15th centuries. Little is left except the walls. In addition to the cathedral, there are the ruins of eight churches and two round towers within or adjacent to the walls of the site.

One of the ruins is that of the 9th-century oratory called Temple Kieran. Tradition says that St. Ciaran's tomb is contained therein.

Scattered over the site are gravestones of varying ages. In addition, there are three high crosses, the most famous of which being the Cross of the Scriptures. It is said to mark the gravesite of **King Flann Sinna**, who died in 914. Like its counterparts in several other parts of Ireland (Glendalough and Monasterboice, to name two), this cross is richly carved with various scenes from the scriptures. Watch for the betrayal, arrest, and crucifixion of Christ, and the Judgment, all popular scenes for these crosses. In addition, this cross depicts King Dermot helping St. Ciaran laying the cornerstone of the church.

The Royal Irish Academy in Dublin, in addition to having *The Book of the Dun Cow*, also has in its possession the Crosier of Clonmacnoise, and it is considered to be one of the finest, best-preserved ancient Irish crosiers in existence. (A crosier is a staff with a crook in it, generally carried by or before a bishop or abbot. It is symbolic of his pastoral role as shepherd of the flock of God.)

Clonmacnoise is definitely worth a few hours.

Charleville Castle, *Tullamore, open April and May Saturdays and Sundays from 2:00 pm to 6:00 pm, and from June through September Wednesday through Sunday from 11:00 am until 5:00 pm.* This grand mansion is set in a pretty park-like setting amid trees and gardens. Built while the War of 1812 was raging in America, this house is a splendid example of the way the wealthy Irish of the day lived.

County Westmeath

Tullynally Castle and Gardens, *near Castlepollard, open May through October daily from 10:00 am to 5:00 pm. Admission is £3 for adults and £1.50 for senior citizens and children. Admission to the gardens only is £1 for adults and 50p for children. Tel. (044) 61159.* Tullynally Castle and Gardens are located about a mile from the outskirts of Castlepollard on the R394. The house has served as the main residence for the Earls of Longford from the 1600s until the present, and is an impressive example of a Gothic manor house, with its many turrets and towers. Inside, you'll find an impressive two-story hall with a number of paintings, lovely china, and antique furniture. Outside, the peaceful grounds and gardens are available for a stroll.

Fore Abbey, *Fore.* From Castlepollard, take the R195 to Fore. Follow the signposts that point you to Fore Abbey. These ancient ruins date from the 10th century.

Belvedere House Gardens, *near Mullingar, open May through September daily from noon to 6:00 pm. Admission is £1 for adults and 50p for children. Tel. (044) 40861.* Five miles south of Mullingar on the N52 is Belvedere

House Gardens. Pretty terraced gardens set with the backdrop of Lough Ennel greet you.

County Wexford

New Ross. The village of New Ross, population 5,000, is due west of Wexford Town. Its Irish name is *Ros Mhic Treoin*, which means "The Wood of the Son of Tream." The town is built against and on a steep hill which leads down to the River Barrow. An ancient town dating to the early 6th century (a monastery was founded here by St. Abban), its real importance emerged as an inland port during the 13th century. It was one of many towns in this part of the country that fell to the advancing Cromwellian armies.

Sinister intrigue swirled around New Ross during the 1798 uprising. Rebel forces fighting for Bagenal Harvey were attempting to negotiate peace with the British commander, **Lord Mountjoy**, who was garrisoned with his forces in New Ross. The rebels sent a peace envoy into the garrison; he was summarily shot. Realizing the magnitude of the error, Lord Mountjoy sought a meeting to placate the rebels. He was shot and killed in reprisal for the envoy's death, which in turn ignited fierce fighting for the town. The British forces finally gave way and vacated. But while the exhausted rebel forces were enjoying their hard-fought victory, fresh British reinforcements arrived and inflicted heavy casualties on the rebels before forcing them from the town.

New Ross is immensely quieter these days. Take a few minutes to stretch your legs here. If you do, you'll find a town with a medieval feel, with narrow winding streets, many of which are closed to vehicular traffic. If you're up for a river cruise dining experience, check out the Galley Cruising Restaurant (see *Where to Eat* above).

Ballylane Farm, *near New Ross, open May through September daily from 10:00 am to 6:00 pm. Admission is £2.50 for adults and £1 for children. A family ticket is available for £7 (2 adults and 4 children). Tel. (051) 25666.* Two hundred acres of interesting sights, sounds, and smells await your visit to Ballylane Farm. This working farm presents a variety of things for you to see and experience, including activities on tillage, pheasant and deer raising, sheep and forestry. The hour tour is educational and interesting.

John F. Kennedy Memorial Forest Park, *near Dunganstown, open daily from 10:00 am to dusk. Admission is £2 for adults and £1 for children. Tel. (051) 388171.* Located at Dunganstown is the small cottage that was the birthplace of John F. Kennedy's great-grandfather. Perhaps you have seen this cottage in old films of President Kennedy's visit here in the 1960s. Nearby is the 400 acre memorial park, wherein the Irish people pay homage to President Kennedy's life and works. The cost of the park was footed by Americans of Irish descent.

Enniscorthy Castle & County Wexford Museum, *Enniscorthy, open mid-June through August, Monday through Saturday from 10:00 am to 6:00 pm, and Sunday from 2:00 pm to 5:00 pm. Admission is £2 for adults, £1.50 for students, and 50p for children. Tel. (054) 34699.* This massive square keep is wonderfully preserved. Originally built in 1199 by one of the early Anglo-Norman invaders, the castle was rebuilt in 1586. It withstood the guns of Cromwell in 1649, and has served as a prison, residence (of the English poet Edmund Spenser), and now serves as the county museum. The museum has a number of interesting exhibits, including two that focus on the uprisings that occurred in 1798 and 1916. Don't miss the country "still" that was used for brewing Ireland's own brand of white lightning. It's called *poteen* (pronounced potcheen), and the Irish say a good batch will knock you for a loop.

Tacumshane, *near Kilmore Quay.* Follow the signposts from Wexford to the beautiful village of Kilmore Quay, where you'll find thatched-roof cottages and pleasant villagers. Ask the locals to direct you to Tacumshane, site of one of the few thatched windmills remaining in Ireland. The windmill was built in 1846, and part of its workings are the original wooden mechanisms. It makes for great photos!

Wexford Town. The town of Wexford sits along the Slaney River as it enters Wexford Harbor. The town is ancient, showing up on 2nd-century maps drawn by Ptolemy. Its Irish name, *Loch Garman*, means "Garman's Lake." However, like Wicklow, it takes its current name from an anglicized Viking word. The Viking name of the town was *Waesfjord*, which means "the harbor of the mud flats."

One of the first towns taken by the Anglo-Norman invaders during the 12th century, Wexford always seemed to be up for a fight. In 1649, Oliver Cromwell took the city and slaughtered its inhabitants. For a short period during the 1798 uprising, the town was held briefly by Irish rebels, who met ignominious defeat at Vinegar Hill.

Today, Wexford is a fascinating place to visit. When in Wexford, just follow your nose, and it's sure to take you someplace interesting. There are so many things to see and do, you need to let your interests guide you. From the Maritime Museum to the Irish National Heritage Park, to gorgeous sandy beaches on the Irish and Celtic Seas, you can't go wrong. The Wexford Peninsula seems to be made for tourists of all ages and interests.

Wexford Waterfowl Preserve. There is a reason why the Vikings called this town *Waesfjord*, "the harbor of the mud flats." As the River Slaney empties into Wexford Harbor, its silt build-up was noticeable even a thousand years ago. Perhaps it wasn't as bad then, but bad enough to call it by that name. Today, the north bank of the River Slaney provides a broad waterfowl preserve on those same silt mud flats. Walking across the bridge that spans the River Slaney at the west end of town takes you to the preserve. Over half of the year, Greenland white-fronted geese make this their home.

Statue of Commodore John Barry, *Crescent Quay, Wexford.* If you are a veteran of the United States Navy, you may want to make your way to the large bronze statue of John Barry, considered the "Father of the American Navy." Born in Ballysampson in 1745, he immigrated to America and became one of her most brilliant naval officers during the War for Independence.

Vinegar Hill, *Wexford, guided tours of the site are available from mid-May through September for £3. Tel. (054) 36800.* East of town you come to Vinegar Hill, the site of a pivotal battle between the British and the Irish during the 1798 uprising. Over 20,000 Irish rebels made a valiant stand against the British army. Their only weapons were spears, and they took a frightful pounding from the constant artillery barrage leveled at them by the British.

Following the battle, the rebel leader Bagenal Harvey fled to a cave on an island off the south Wexford coastline, where he was later captured.

Church of the Immaculate Conception/Church of Assumption, *Rowe and Bride Streets.* These two churches are called "the Twin Churches," because these 19th-century Gothic churches are identical on the exterior, from the base of their corner stones laid on the same date to the tips of their lofty, 230 foot spires.

Selskar Abbey, *Wexford.* Tradition has it that Selskar Abbey is located on the oldest site of Christian worship in County Wexford. Built on the former site of a Viking temple to Odin, the ruins of Selskar lie just to the south of Westgate Tower Heritage Center.

Westgate Tower, *corner of Westgate and Slaney Streets, open May to December Monday to Saturday from 9:30 am to 1:00 pm, and from 2:00 pm to 5:30 pm. In July and August it is also open on Sunday from 2:00 pm to 6:00 pm. From January to April call for appointment. Admission is £1.50 for adults and £1 for children. Tel. (053) 20733.* This gate tower, a red sandstone remnant of the old city wall, has been meticulously restored. It is the only one of five original gate towers that remains today. It serves now as the home of the Westgate Heritage Center, where you can see a short audio-visual presentation of the history of Wexford.

Franciscan Church, *School Street.* Built on the site of a former Franciscan abbey, the abbey features marvelous plaster work on its ceiling. A glass case enshrines the remains of St. Adjutor, a young man who is considered an early Christian martyr. The son of a pagan father and Christian mother, the lad was raised as a Christian by his mother, unbeknownst to his father. When the news reached his father, he was so incensed that he slew his son with an ax.

Wexford Bull Ring, *Quay Street*. Many of us look disapprovingly on sports that require cruelty to animals. Such was the sport of bull-baiting, for which the Wexford Bull Ring was used. Bull-baiting was a popular sporting event for the Anglo-Norman rulers. Worse still, this ring was used by Cromwell's soldiers to execute over 300 townspeople who had gathered there to pray for safety when the city was attacked by British forces.

Irish National Heritage Park, *Ferrycarrig, open March to November from 10:00 am to 7:00 pm (last admittance at 5:00 pm). Admission is £3 for adults and £2 for senior citizens and children. Tel. (053) 41733.* This fun and educational park traces Ireland's heritage from the Stone Age through the conquest of the Anglo-Normans. Thirty acres are filled with a myriad of life-size structures – dwellings, forts, a monastery, Norman castle, etc., to give you an idea of how the ancient Irish lived, worked, and were buried. Actors in period dress answer questions and share their skills at weaving, pole lathing, and pottery through frequent demonstrations.

This is a lot of fun and very interesting. In about an hour and a half you'll get a good overview of about 4,000 years of Irish history.

Johnstown Castle Gardens, *Johnstown, open April, May and September through November Monday trough Friday from 9:00 am to 1:30 pm and 2:30 pm to 5:00 pm, Saturday and Sunday from 2:00 pm to 5:00 pm; June to August Monday through Friday from 9:00 am to 5:00 pm, Saturday and Sunday from 2:00 pm to 5:00 pm. Admission is £1.75 for adults and £1 for children. Tel. (053) 42888.* Johnstown Castle is an impressive 13th-century Anglo-Norman castle. It is located about three miles south of Wexford. The castle has been converted into an agricultural museum, and it has a fine collection of farm implements used through the years in Ireland. Aside from the agricultural exhibits, the castle is not open to the public, although the extensive gardens are.

Rosslare Beach, *Rosslare*. Rosslare and its pretty beach are about ten miles from downtown Wexford Town. Take the N25 south out of Wexford, and then take either the R736 or the R740.

This is one of the prettiest beaches along the eastern coast of Ireland (some would argue that it's the prettiest in the country). Long stretches of sandy beaches (about five miles' worth) and safe swimming areas make this a popular place for tourists as well as the Irish. Rosslare is a booming metropolis of 700 people; from May through October visitors outnumber locals by a significant number.

Kilmore Quay. The word for Kilmore Quay is picturesque. It is a pretty little village with thatched roofs and white-washed cottages. Sitting on a small peninsula on the Celtic Sea, the sea views are fabulous.

Ring of Hook Drive. The Ring of Hook Drive is undoubtedly as peaceful a seaside drive as you are likely to take, with serene seascapes all along the way. From Wellington Bridge, take the R733 toward Fethard-on-the-Sea. While on your way, take the time to meander along the many coves and exquisite beaches along the way. It's a great place to take plenty of pictures.

Duncannon. The Ring of Hook ends at Duncannon, just across the harbor from Waterford. Duncannon's Irish name (*Dun Conan*) means "The Fort of Conan."

For many years Duncannon was a site of military importance, particularly as protection against marauding ships of (take your choice) Vikings, Anglo-Normans, Irish rebels, the Spanish Armada, Napoleon's navy, etc. No matter who currently controlled this site, they kept the three acre fort fortified and ready to greet any foes. The ruins are still visible on a rocky promontory.

Ballyhack. Little Ballyhack sits at the mouth of Waterford Harbor on the R733. It has been an incredibly popular locale for artists and photographers from all over the world. This stereotypical fishing village offers plenty to paint, sketch, or photograph: fishing boats, old **Ballyhack Castle**, and the assorted local residents, full of character. Ballyhack Castle was originally part of the preceptory (a religious house) of the Knights Templar; today its ivy-covered and weathered rock walls keep watch over the harbor. A short car ferry ride that will set you back £5 across the harbor will take you to another picturesque Irish fishing village in County Waterford: **Passage East**, which competes with Ballyhack for its share of photographers and artists. It's nice competition – everybody wins.

Dunbrody Abbey and Castle, *near Campile, visitor center open April through September Monday through Friday from 10:00 am to 6:00 pm, Saturday and Sunday 10:00 am to 8:00 pm. Admission is free (but there is a £1 charge for the car park). Tel. (051) 88603.* Three miles north of Ballyhack on the R733 are the brooding ruins of Dunbrody Abbey and Dunbrody Castle. The Abbey was built in the late 12th century, and the castle (right next to the Abbey) is of similar vintage. A small visitors center next to the ruins encompasses a museum, tea room and gift shop.

County Wicklow

County Wicklow is the county immediately south of Dublin County, and is a popular place for both vacationing Dubliners fleeing the big city and foreign tourists. In a country that has an abundance of luscious flora, the fact that County Wicklow is referred to as the **Garden of Ireland** gives you some indication of the beauty of this part of the Emerald Isle.

The Wicklow Mountains run from the north end of the county to the south, tapering gently into the Irish Sea on the east and dropping smoothly down to the River Barrow plain. These mountains are a series of hills and dales, conical peaks and wooded glens. So secluded and relatively inaccessible are parts of these mountains that they served for hundreds of years as resorts of escape for feisty Irish chieftains and their followers who thumbed their noses at the representatives of the British crown. Even today there are only two passes through these mountains that allow them to be traversed from east to west.

These heavily wooded hills, some of which rise over 3,000 feet from the Irish sea, conceal some of the prettiest spots in Ireland. Powerscourt Gardens and Waterfall, Loughs Dan and Tay, Glendalough, and Devil's Glen are just a few of the spectacular places to be visited throughout County Wicklow.

County Wicklow is accessible via automobile, as well as a number of bus and train routes that run from Dublin on a regular basis. The trains leave from Connolly and Pearse stations, and buses leave from Busaran as well as from the Dublin Quay, depending on your destination.

Bray. The farthest point on the DART service line – about 25 minutes from downtown Dublin – is the pretty Victorian town of Bray, situated along the southern sweep of Killiney Bay. Its beaches are of the sand and shingle variety, good for walking and feeling the sea breeze on your face. Worth seeing in Bray are the Heritage Center in the Old Courthouse, the Bray Esplanade with its aquarium, and Bray Head. It's also a popular get-away point for Dubliners.

Bray Esplanade, *Bray*. A mile and a half-long esplanade that skirts the beach is extremely popular for strolling, feeling the sea breezes, and watching people, especially on nice summer evenings when the walkways can be fairly populated. There's also a new **National Aquarium** with over seven hundred different species of aquatic life on display that has proven quite popular.

Bray Head, *near Bray*. South of the Bray Esplanade is a walking path that takes you to Bray Head, a promontory that rises 800 feet above the shores of the Irish Sea. Needless to say, views from here are beautiful on a clear day. The hike up and back takes a couple of hours.

Bray Cliff Walk, *Bray*. Skirting the base of Bray Head is a pleasant trail called the Cliff Walk. It heads south from Bray Head to Greystones, four miles away. The walk is a pleasant one, requiring less effort than climbing Bray Head, but it also provides serene seascape views.

Kilruddery House and Gardens, *Bray, open May, June, and September daily from 1:00 pm until 5:00 pm. It is possible to make an appointment in April, July, and August by calling ahead. Admission is £1 for adults and 50p for children. Tel. (01) 286-7128.* On the Bray-Greystones Road is Kilruddery House and Gardens, a pretty gray granite Elizabethan mansion that sits amid verdant trees and colorful gardens. The home was built in 1820. Kilruddery House is one of two County Wicklow sites for the annual **Festival of Music in Great Irish Houses** (the other location is Russborough

House). Irish musicians come to Kilruddery House during the first or second week of June each year (it varies according to the musicians' schedules) and perform their musical magic. Violinists, cellists, or chamber orchestras are usually the featured performers. For schedule and ticket information on the concerts – both at Kilruddery and Russborough Houses, as well as around the country – write to: *Mr. Crawford Tipping, 31 Beechwood Lawn, Dun Laoghaire, County Dublin, Ireland.*

German War Cemetery, *Glencree.* West of Enniskerry is a secluded garden spot that represents a little sanity and humanity during a time of insanity and hatred. In the little town of Glencree is a well-kept graveyard for German airmen who crash-landed in Ireland as a result of damage incurred in their bombing runs and air battles over England.

Oak Glen, *near Glencree.* On the road between Glencree and Enniskerry, closer to Glencree on the south side of the road, is Oak Glen, an experimental tree farm where thousands of native oaks have been planted in an effort to re-vegetate the valley with the original flora that was here before being stripped for various building projects over the centuries. You can only access the lands by foot, but it's a pretty, serene stroll, not overrun by tourists.

Poulaphouca Reservoir, *near Blessington.* This is the reservoir that supplies much of Dublin's drinking water. It was formed by flooding the King and Liffey Rivers. Now the reservoir is an important place of play for those who like water-sports such as boating, water-skiing, wind surfing, and the like.

Blessington. Established as a town in 1682 by Michael Boyle after a grant from King Charles II in 1669, Blessington is a small, quiet market town.

Russborough House, *between Hollywood and Blessington, open from June to August daily from 10:30 am until 5:30 pm, April through May and September through October on Sundays from 10:30 am to 5:30 pm. Admission is £2.50 for adults, £1.50 for children (50p for children under 12). Tel. (045) 652329.* Wow! It only seems fitting that this Palladian mansion should be found near a town called Hollywood. It's actually closer to Blessington (two miles south), but its visage conjures up movie stars and the rich life. Built between 1740 and 1750, this impressive granite manor sits in the Wicklow Mountains, viewing them across an expanse of grass and a small lake. Its two wings on either side are connected to the main building by semicircular colonnaded galleries.

Now owned by Sir Alfred Beit, the house features the current owener's inspiring art collection, consisting of a number of paintings by well-known artists (**Goya, Reynolds, Rubens,** and **Velasquez,** among others), as well as a variety of bronze sculptures. The collection was once much more extensive, but a series of criminal activities prompted the donation of a number of the more valuable works to the National Gallery of Ireland in Dublin. The house itself is an art treasure also; particularly the plaster work which was crafted by the **Francini** brothers, artisans of great fame in their day.

If you like the wooded grounds that surround the house, they are available for strolls.

Powerscourt Gardens and Waterfall, *Enniskerry, the gardens are open March through October daily from 9:30 am until 5:30 pm. Admission is £3 for adults, £2.50 for students, and £2 for children under 12 (under 5 free). The waterfall is open all year from 10:30 am until 7:00 pm (in the winter from 10:30 am until dusk). Admission to the waterfall area is £1 for adults and 50p for children. Tel. (01) 286-7676.* If heaven is half as pretty as Powerscourt Gardens, I'll die a happy man! You've probably seen pictures of Powerscourt Gardens before – they are popular scenes used to depict the beauty of Ireland.

Powerscourt House was completed in 1740 for Sir Richard Wingfield, the first viscount of Powerscourt. The house is in the classical Roman Palladian style, and was designed by Richard Castle, who designed the Russborough House while overseeing the construction of Powerscourt House. Unfortunately, an accidental fire gutted the lovely home in 1974; plans are underway to restore it to its previous splendor. But the gardens were unscathed, and offer a good reason to come to Enniskerry.

The gardens were originally laid out beginning in 1745, and were revised to their present grand design in the mid-1800s. They cascade in a series of terraces down a slope from the house. The gardens are filled with verdant greenery: sculpted shrubs, trees, and many varieties of flowering plants, set among statues, fountains, and walkways. From the top of the terraces, the views sweep across the pretty Dargle Valley, culminating in outstanding views of Great Sugar Loaf Mountain and Kippure Mountain. In addition to the views, Powerscourt offers a tearoom, garden center and small shop.

Three miles south of the gardens is the Powerscourt **waterfall**. The highest waterfall in Ireland, the water free-falls more than 400 feet off the edge of Djouce Mountain. It serves as a favorite picnic area for tourists and locals alike.

Roundwood. Tiny Roundwood has the distinguished honor of being the highest village in Ireland at about 900 feet above sea level. It's a small, relatively quiet town, but they have a lively market each Sunday afternoon where home-made wares such as jellies, jams, and baked goods are peddled. Perhaps the best product they have at the market, however, is the bustling congeniality of the event.

Not far (less than five miles) to the west of Roundwood lie two beautiful lakes, **Lough Dan** and **Lough Tay**. You can drive to Lough Dan and catch any of a number of walking trails that ascend the surrounding mountains and afford lovely views of the area. Watch for signposts in Roundwood directing you to Lough Dan. If you prefer walking to Lough Dan, you can catch the Wicklow Way about halfway between Roundwood and Sally Gap on the R759. It's a short walk to Lough Dan through the valley that lies between Lough Dan and Lough Tay. (You can see Lough Tay, but you cannot visit: it's on private land.)

Devil's Glen, *north of Ashford.* Just north of Ashford, you'll come to spectacular Devil's Glen (watch for the road signs). This area is stunningly beautiful, and has a number of walking paths well-laid out that provide some magnificent views. Devil's Glen is a deep gorge whose sides are graced with trees and shrubbery. The River Vartry tumbles nearly 100 feet into a pool called the Devil's Punchbowl.

Glendalough, *Co. Wicklow. Visitors Center open March through May and September through October daily from 9:30 am to 6:00 pm, and June through August daily from 9:30 am until 7:00 pm. November through February it is open Tuesday through Sunday from 10:00 am until 4:30 pm. Admission is £2 for adults, £1.50 for seniors, and £1. Tel. (0404) 45325.* "The glen of the two lakes" – *Glen Da Locha* – is perhaps one of the most serene places in the world. In the 6th century, St. Kevin sought refuge from the world, and founded a hermitage here. It is easy to see why. At the west end of the valley, Glenealo stream cascades in a waterfall into the valley. Two lakes grace the valley with their elegance and beauty – they are called simply Upper Lake and Lower Lake. The valley is encompassed by heavily forested mountains. Add to the natural beauty some exquisite and ancient ruins, and this is a wonderful place to visit. But don't rush your visit here – take your time and see all there is to see. A webwork of walking paths laces the woods all around Glendalough, and if you're interested in that aspect of touring, they offer wonderfully serene views.

The best place to begin your tour of Glendalough is at the visitors center. Here they have a fine audio-visual presentation on Glendalough and its history.

In the 6th century when St. Kevin originally sought his solitude here, it is said he slept on a shelf above the Upper Lake. Tradition indicates that the place of Kevin's repose is a small hole in the rock of a cliff about thirty feet above the lake. It is called **St. Kevin's Bed**. After Kevin's death, the monastic settlement that he founded burgeoned. The settlement saw both its share of peace and serenity, as well as war and carnage. Repeated attacks by the Vikings in the ninth and tenth centuries took their toll, but it wasn't until English attacks in 1398 that the settlement was finally abandoned.

At the south end of Upper Lake is **Teampaill na Skellig** (Church of the Rock), a small (25 feet by 14 feet) granite church. This small church dates from the 6th century, as do the ruins of the **Reefert Church**, another small stone church of the same era. Tradition holds that Reefert Church is the burial place of local chieftains. Near Reefert Church are the ruins of a small beehive-shaped hut called **St. Kevin's Cell** that also served as home for the lonely St. Kevin. The south end of the lake is only accessible by a locally hired boat.

Moving from the Upper Lake to the Lower Lake, you encounter some of the finest religious ruins in Ireland.

To begin with, the gateway, next to the Royal Hotel (pretty setting for a hotel, but it's a shame to have it in the midst of these old ruins), is the only surviving structure of its kind in Ireland. Inside the gateway is the graveyard with many intricately-carved crosses.

Towering above the trees, the well-preserved one hundred foot tall **Round Tower** stands as a mute witness of past oppressors and as a sentry against future invaders. Built in the 10th century, the only entrance is a doorway a mere twenty-five feet above the ground!

The **Cathedral** located at Glendalough is in relatively good shape, given its age (11th century) and the history of conquest this valley has had. The nave, chancel, and small sacristy are still intact.

St. Kevin's Kitchen is nearby, and this small church has a high-pitched stone roof. It is thought this structure was also built in the 11th century. And don't miss **St. Kevin's Cross**, (it would be hard to), an eleven foot granite cross thirteen hundred years old.

Other ruins of interest in Glendalough include **St. Saviers's Church** (12th century), **Church of our Lady** (the oldest ruin in the lower valley), and the **Priest's House**, site of burials for priests. On the east end of Upper Lake you'll find an old fort (**Caher**) dating from the late Bronze or early Iron age. Look for the five crosses between the Reefert Church and Lower Lake. These crosses once marked the boundary of the monastic settlement.

Vale of Avoca, *near Woodenbridge and Avoca*. From Glendalough, head south to Rathdrum, and watch for the signposts to Avoca. The trip takes you through the famous Vale of Avoca, a lush green valley immortalized by **Thomas Moore**. It was in this wooded valley, about a mile and a half north of Avoca at the point where the Avonbeg and Avonmore rivers mingle their waters and change their name to the Avoca River, that he penned the poem *The Meeting of the Waters*. Splendid nature trails wend through the heavy woods and provide a nice diversion. If you're fortunate to be here in early spring, the verdant green of the valley is punctuated with the snow-white cherry blossoms of wild cherry trees.

The stretch of road between Woodenbridge and Rathdrum is all considered the Vale of Avoca.

Avoca. On the R752 between Woodenbridge and Rathdrum lies the quiet little berg of Avoca. This pretty village sits amid wooded hills and the remains of an active copper industry that thrived until the early 1980s, when the industry closed down.

Avoca Handweavers, *Avoca, Tel. (0402) 35105. Open Monday through Friday from 9:30 am to 5:30 pm, and Saturday and Sunday from 10:00 am to 6:00 pm.* Next to the natural beauty of the area, the main attraction in Avoca is Avoca Handweavers, reportedly the oldest handweaving mill in Ireland. Take a few minutes and stop by the mill. They'll tell you that some of their weavers are second- and third-generation weavers. Their hand weaving looms produce a colorful assortment of woven garments. Visitors can purchase items that catch their eye in a small shop, as well as snag a cup of coffee and a snack before continuing your trip. You can purchase a variety of items, from coats and scarves to bedspreads and caps.

Avondale Forest Park/Avondale House, *open March through October daily from 11:00 am to 5:30 pm, November through February daily from 11:00 am to 5:00 pm. Admission is £2 for adults and £1 for children and senior citizens. Tel. (0404) 46111.* Avondale Forest Park is the setting for Avondale House, once birthplace and residence of **Charles Stewart Parnell** (1846-1891), one of the most famous and influential players in Ireland's drive for independence. Charles was a gifted and eloquent Parliamentary speaker and untiring advocate for the cause of home rule for Ireland. Unfortunately, his much-publicized affair with Kitty O'Shea *(Mrs.* Kitty O'Shea) scandalized the country and split his political allies. He died a year after the revelation, some say of a broken heart.

Parnell's home has been meticulously restored and is a pleasure to visit. Built in 1779, the original owner, Samuel Hayes, spent years planting a variety of trees around his estate, and the results are evident all around you when you visit. Parnell's great-grandfather, John Parnell purchased the property in 1795.

Arklow. A village of a little under 10,000 souls, Arklow sits on the Irish Sea just a few miles south of Wicklow. Not as pretty as many of the towns you'll see in Ireland, it is nonetheless a nice place to visit for its walking paths along the Avoca River. Arklow is an important fishing and marine port in Ireland.

Arklow Pottery Factory, *the Quays, Arklow, open weekdays from 9:30 am to 1:00 pm, and 2:00 pm to 4:45 pm. Open weekends from 10:00 am to 4:45 pm. Tel. (0402) 32401.* The Arklow Pottery Factory is on the quays, and they offer tours for those who have an interest in pottery.

Maritime Museum, *in the public library, Arklow, open June through September weekdays from 10:00 am until 5:00 pm. Admission is £1 for adults and*

50p for children and senior citizens. Tel. (0402) 32868. Small though it may be, the Arklow Maritime Museum has a number of fine exhibits and objects relating to the area's nautical history.

Wicklow Way. The Wicklow Way is a well-marked walking path that wends its way through some of the most beautiful scenery in Ireland. Beginning up in County Dublin at Marley Park in Rathfarnham, it runs a little over eighty miles to its endpoint in County Carlow at Clonegal. Along the way, beautiful vistas are part and parcel of the trip.

Don't have the time to take an eighty-mile hike? That's okay, because you can hop on and off the Wicklow Way in a number of places. Watch for the signposts. Some of the more popular places to join the trail for a short time are Glendalough, Lough Dan, Glenmalure, Aghavannagh, Knockree and Crone.

Several maps of the Wicklow Way are available at most Tourist Information offices; in Wicklow Town, they're located at: *Rialto Center, Fitzwilliam Square, Wicklow Town, Tel. (0404) 69117.* You can get maps that cover segments of the trail or the entire trail.

Brittas Bay, *south of Wicklow Head.* This scenic sweep of sandy beach is a favorite among Dubliners and many of the Irish on holiday. Long (more than three miles) and pretty, it's a picturesque place to walk along the beach.

Jack's Hole, *south of Wicklow Head.* Six miles south of Wicklow Town is the spacious silky sands of Jack's Hole, a secluded seaside beach.

Wicklow Town. The county seat, Wicklow Town, lies about thirty miles south of Dublin on the coast of the Irish Sea. County Wicklow is often called the Garden of Ireland, but Wicklow Town is a little less than a bed of roses. Congested and confusing, it is not particularly user-friendly to get around. However, it does have a pretty setting, overlooking a beautiful curved bay of the Irish Sea. Wicklow Town can be reached by automobile by driving south from Dublin on the N11.

In the fifth century, a contemporary of St. Patrick's built a monastic settlement on the site and called it *Cill Mhantain* (St. Mantan's Church). However, in the 8th century, the Vikings saw the value of the area as a protected harbor, and moved in, calling the new settlement *Wykinglo*, which means Viking meadow. Over the years, the name was anglicized somewhat to the present day Wicklow.

The town itself has a lovely main street lined with trees. At one edge of town are the ruins of a **Franciscan friary**, built in the 1200s. The ruins are not generally open to the public, but can be visited by arrangement with the priest who lives in a nearby home *(Tel. 0404 67196).*

On the north side of town is **Broad Lough**, a saltwater lake which receives the River Vantry before it empties into the Irish Sea. Walkways around the lake are popular for morning and evening strolls.

Black Castle, *Wicklow Town*. Black Castle, an Anglo-Norman stronghold built in 1176 by Maurice Fitzgerald, one of **Strongbow's** cronies, sits atop a rocky cliff just south of Wicklow harbor. Commanding views of much of the Wicklow coastline made this castle a valuable strategic position. Because of that, it was the site of many attacks from warring Irish chieftains through the years. The extensive ruins are accessible to the public.

Mount Usher Gardens, *Ashford, open daily from May 17 through October 31 from 10:30 am until 6:00 pm (Sundays from 11:00 am until 6:00 pm). Admission is £3 for adults and £2 for children. Tel. (0404) 40205.* A little over four miles northwest of Wicklow Town is the small town of Ashford, and its main claim to fame: Mount Usher Gardens. In the 1860s, **Edward Walpole** planted a half acre garden here, and it has expanded to the twenty acres you can see today. Located along the banks of the River Vartry, the verdant area is covered with a medley of trees, shrubs, flowers, and plants.

As you enter Mount Usher Gardens, you'll pass by a series of craft shops and a small restaurant. You are free to wander through the paths that wend their way through the gardens and over the river.

PRACTICAL INFORMATION

Banks

Banks in Leinster are open Monday through Friday from 10:00 am to 12:30 pm, and from 1:30 pm to 3:00 pm. In the larger cities, the banks are usually open a little longer one day a week (the day varies throughout the province) until 5:00 pm.

Some of the larger banks in Leinster have an ATM machine either outside their main doorways, or just inside the bank. The ATMs are part of the Cirrus and Plus international networks. Note: check with your bank to see if your personal identification number (PIN) will work on international ATMs. Most international ATMs only accept four-digit PINs.

Buses & Trains

For both buses and trains, you'll want to use the following stations:
- **Kilkenny**: *McDonagh Station, Castlecomer Road, Tel. (056) 22024*
- **Wexford**: *O'Hanrahan Station, Redmond Square, Tel. (053) 22522*

Emergencies

Remember this: dialing 999 in Ireland = dialing 911 in the States. Use it in the event of any emergency where you need assistance from the police, fire department, or the medical community.

Exchanging Money
You can exchange money at banks, most post offices, and at larger hotels.

Lost Credit Cards
• **American Express Card**, *Tel. (01) 288-3311*
• **American Express Traveler's Checks**, *Tel. 800-626-0000*
• **Diners Club**, *Tel. 800-709-944*
• **Visa/MasterCard**, *Tel. (01) 269-7700*

Restrooms
Public restrooms are not prevalent in Ireland; your best bet is usually a hotel or a pub. (Hint: most hotels have at least one pub, and the restrooms are usually located near the pub.)

Tourist Offices
Tourist offices are located throughout Leinster. Some of them are as follows:
• **Bray**: *Florence Road, County Wicklow, Tel. (01) 286-7128*
• **Kilkenny**: *Rose Inn Street, Tel. (056) 51500*
• **Wexford**: *Crescent Quay, County Wexford, Tel. (053) 23111*

15. MUNSTER

Munster is the province that comprises the southwestern quarter of Ireland. It consists of six counties, and all but Tipperary are on the ocean – though County Limerick just barely, by virtue of the River Shannon estuary. Munster has the most developed tourist industry in the country. Part of the reason is that until just a few years ago, all international flights into Ireland from North America were required to land first at Shannon Airport. This provided great strength to the tourist industry in and around the airport, including the entire province of Munster.

The major cities in Munster are Cork, Limerick, Killarney, Tipperary and Waterford. Five of Ireland's top ten tourist attractions are found in Munster. Over a third of a million people visit **Bunratty Castle and Folk Park** every year, and nearly a quarter of a million people visit **Blarney Castle** to kiss the magical **Blarney Stone**. The **Fota Wildlife Park** outside Cork City, **Muckross House and Gardens** in Killarney, and the **Rock of Cashel** each draw nearly 200,000 people a year.

Killarney is probably the most frequently visited town in Ireland by American and Canadian tourists, and the town has been well-tuned to tourism for many years now. In addition to being blessed with great natural beauty, Killarney has honed its image as "the real Ireland" by providing jaunting car (horse and buggy) transportation to and through many of the sights in the city. To some, it's a tad overdone, but for me, I am always enthralled with Killarney each time I visit.

Munster is where many important events in Irish history have taken place, most of them tragic. For example, the little town of Cobh (pronounced like Cove) on the southern shore near Cork City has seen her fair share of tragedy. It was from Cobh harbor that hundreds of thousands of Irish immigrants fled Ireland from 1845 to 1848, the **Great Potato Famine** snapping at their heels. Again it was Cobh harbor that served as the last port-of-call for the **Titanic** on her first – and last – fateful cruise in April 1912. Almost exactly three years later in May 1915, nearly 1,200 souls perished in the sinking of the **Lusitania** just twelve short miles down the coast from Cobh.

Oliver Cromwell destroyed many castles, cathedrals, monasteries, and towns throughout the width and breadth of Munster during his ruthless military campaign that began in 1649. In 1690, **Catholic James** (James II), King of England, fled Ireland forever from Waterford harbor, and died three years later while in exile in France. He had been the only hope of an oppressed populace for the easing of their oppression. The new king, **William of Orange**, was a Protestant, and things got worse for the Catholics in Ireland. In fact, during his reign the infamous "Penal Laws" were passed, essentially rendering the Irish people non-entities in their own country. Gone was the ability to vote or be voted for, gone the ability to gain an education, serve in the military, and own arms. The laws were not to be repealed for over one hundred and twenty-five years, when a Munster lad named **Daniel O'Connell** fought valiantly for their repeal.

Munster spawned a number of uprisings throughout the years by patriots seeking to release the shackles so firmly clasped by the English. The **1798 Uprising** had its beginning – and ending – in Munster.

There's a beauty about Munster that is somehow different from the rest of Ireland. Whether it's the impressive Rock of Cashel, or the spectacular Skellig Islands, or pretty Dingle Peninsula, or the beautiful little town of Adare, I can't tell. Or maybe it's the excessively narrow roads that seem to run helter-skelter throughout western County Cork. You'll have to venture here and decide for yourself what it is that makes Munster's beauty just a little different from the rest of Ireland.

ARRIVALS & DEPARTURES

Next to Leinster, Munster is the the most readily accessible province in Ireland. For many years, Shannon Airport was the only airport where flights from North America could land. There are regional airports in Cork, Killarney, and Waterford that make air access convenient, as well as pretty thorough coverage of the province by bus and train lines.

If you are planning to spend a significant portion of your Irish holiday in Munster, or on the west coast of Ireland, you may want to consider flying into Shannon instead of Dublin. It will save you a few hours' driving time if you do so. Or you can fly into Shannon, then work your way over to the east coast, and fly home from Dublin. Most rental car agencies in Ireland will allow you to rent at Shannon and return the car to Dublin (or vice versa) with no "drop charge." (Be sure and check on this before renting to see if the company you choose allows this.)

BY AIR INTO SHANNON

As mentioned above, **Shannon Airport** (airport code SNN) is formerly the only airport in Ireland that accepted transatlantic flights; it now shares that privilege with Dublin International Airport. If you fly into Shannon, you'll find an older but well-maintained airport. If you need to exchange money here, the bank at Shannon Airport is open daily from 6:30 am to 5:30 pm.

Shannon Airport is about twenty miles from Limerick. To leave Shannon, you can rent a car, take a bus, or hail a taxi.

As soon as you clear Customs, you'll see over a dozen rental car agencies awaiting you with open arms. If it's bus service you prefer, the bus stop is right outside the Arrivals hall, and for £4, it will take you into Limerick. Buses leave every half hour throughout the day, beginning at ten minutes ater the hour (e.g. 7:10 am, 7:40 am, 8:10 am, etc.). Evening bus service isn't quite as frequent, with buses leaving for Limerick at 6:00 pm. 7:00 pm, 9:00 pm, and midnight. If you want a taxi, the taxi stand is right outside the Arrivals hall, and the ride into Limerick will cost about £16.

BY AIR INTO CORK

The **Cork Airport**, *Tel. (021) 313131*, is located ten miles south of Cork City. A number of airlines fly into Cork Airport, including Aer Lngus, Air Southwest, British Airways, British Midlands, and Ryanair. Flights arrive directly in Cork from England and other European cities.

As soon as you enter the Arrivals hall, on your left you'll see a number of car rental agencies. Buses are also available at the airport to take you to Cork City. They are just outside the Arrivals hall, and the twenty-minute ride to the city will cost you about £2.50. Cab stands are also right outside the Arrivals hall, and a cab ride into Cork wil run about £6.

BY AIR INTO KERRY

The **Kerry Airport**, *Tel. (066) 64644*, is about eight miles outside Killarney in the small town of Farranfore. Flights from some of England's regional airports land in Kerry Airport. There are a few rental car agencies available at the airport, but no bus service into Killarney. You'll either have to rent a car or take a £14 cab ride into town.

BY AIR INTO WATERFORD

The **Waterford Airport**, *Tel. (051) 75589*, is about six miles out of Waterford in Killowen. Flights from England and Glasgow via Dublin land in Waterford. You can rent cars at the airport only if you have pre-booked them (Avis, Hertz, EuroCar). Otherwise, there are no rental cars available at the airport. There is also no bus service into town, although you can catch a taxi outside the main doors. The short ride into town will cost about £8.

BY BUS

All bus service to Munster from Dublin leaves from **Busaras Station**, *Store Street, Tel. (01) 836-6111*. There are frequent routes into Munster, and the rates are inexpensive. In most cases, the round-trip fare is the same as the one-way fare, and if it's different, it's be only a pound or two. The frequency listed for trips between Dublin and these locations are for travel Monday through Saturday. Sundays typically offer fewer daily trips. Call Busaras Station at the number listed above for exact schedule information.

Many of the small towns in Munster are served by the bus lines, but the main destinations are Cork, Killarney, Limerick, and Waterford. If you are interested in going to other towns in Munster, call the train information line in Dublin at Busaras Station, *Tel. (01) 836-6111*.

For **Cork City**, the bus depot is **Parnell Station**, *Parnell Street, Tel. 021 508188*. It is located downtown in a decent neighborhood. There are four buses a day that run between Cork and Dublin, and the fare is £16 for the four and a half hour ride.

For **Killarney**, the bus depot is **Killarney Station**, *Tel. (064) 34777*, where the three daily buses from Dublin arrive. The six hour trip from (or to) Dublin will cost you £18. The bus station is located on Cork Road (N22) across from the Killarney Great Southern Hotel. The neighborhood is fine – quite nice, in fact.

For **Limerick**, the bus depot is **Colbert Station**, *Parnell Street, Tel. (061) 313333*, where seven buses daily arrive from Dublin. The three and a half hour trip costs £13. The neighborhood is marginal, and although it's not a far walk into the center of town, you may want to take an inexpensive (£2 or £3) cab ride if you arrive at night.

For **Waterford**, the bus depot is **Plunkett Station**, *Plunkett Street, Tel. (051) 73401.* Seven buses arrive daily from Dublin, and the cost for the three hour ride is £8. The station sits across the River Suir from town, and is just a couple hundred yards' walk.

BY CAR

If you are driving, there are a number of ways to get to Munster from Dublin. The main road out of Dublin toward Munster is the N7, and depending on your eventual destination, you may branch off of it at some point. The N7 will take you directly into Limerick. From there, the N21/N22 takes you to Killarney, the N20 to Cork, and the N24 to Tipperary. The quickest way to Waterford is via the N7 to the N9. These are the straight-shot routes, but you may wish to wend your way along to get to your destination, seeing the sights as you go.

BY FERRY

Ferry service reaches Munster from the European continent as well as from Britain. Ferries from Swansea, Le Havre, and Roscoff dock at Cork. Check with **Swansea Cork Ferries**, *Tel. 01792 456116 in England*, for schedules and rates.

BY TRAIN

All train service to Munster from Dublin leaves from **Heuston Station**, *King's Bridge, Tel. (01) 836-6222.* There are frequent routes into Munster, and the rates are reasonable. In most cases, the round-trip fare is the same as the one-way fare, and if it's different, it's only by a pound or two. The frequency listed for trips between Dublin and these locations are for travel Monday through Saturday. Sundays typically offer fewer daily trips. Call Heuston Station at the number above for exact schedule information.

For **Cork City**, the main train depot is **Kent Station**, *located at the edge of the center of town on Lower Glanmire Road, Tel. (021) 506766.* There are twelve trains a day that run between Cork and Dublin, and the fare is £32 for the three and a half hour ride. Kent Station is in a fairly decent neighborhood, and it would take you about ten or fifteen minutes to walk into the center of town. Taxis are also available outside the station, and will take you downtown for around £5.

For **Killarney**, the main train depot is **Killarney Station**, *located behind the Killarney Great Southern Hotel just off Cork Road (N22), Tel. (064) 31067.* Six trains a day make the four-hour trip between Dublin and Killarney, and the fare is £34. The neighborhood is fine, and within easy walking distance of downtown.

For **Limerick**, the main train depot is **Colbert Station**, *Parnell Street, Tel. (061) 315555*, where eight trains a day arrive after the two and half hour ride from Dublin. The trip will cost you £27. The neighborhood is marginal, and although it's not a far walk into the center of town, you may want to take an inexpensive (£2 or £3) cab ride if you arrive at night.

For **Waterford**, the main train depot is **Plunkett Station**, *Plunkett Street, Tel.(051) 73401*, where four trains a day arrive from Dublin after a three-hour trip. The cost for the ride is £13. Located across Bridge Street from downtown, the walk into town is only a couple hundred yards.

MUNSTER'S BEST SIGHTS

ADARE – *Adare is arguably the prettiest town in Ireland.*

BLARNEY CASTLE/BLARNEY STONE – *Everyone who comes to Ireland needs to see the Blarney Stone, which is part of Blarney Castle.*

BUNRATTY CASTLE AND FOLK PARK – *Sure it's touristy, but what a lot of fun! The castle hosts a medieval banquet; the folk park portrays life in ancient Ireland.*

CLIFFS OF MOHER – *The Cliffs of Moher are perhaps the most spectacular scenery in Ireland. Don't miss this incredible sight.*

DINGLE PENINSULA – *The Dingle Peninsula provides incredible seascapes.*

FAMINE GRAVEYARD – *Outside Dungarvan, this over-grown famine graveyard is a solemn reminder of one of the darker chapters in Irish history: the Great Potato Famine.*

GAP OF DUNLOE – *Outside Killarney, the Gap of Dunloe is a wonderful opportunity to take a jaunting car ride through a beautiful work of nature.*

MUCKROSS HOUSE – *Muckross House is nice, but the impressive sights here are the grounds themselves. Walk through them, or take a jaunting car ride through the estate for a more extensive view.*

ROCK OF CASHEL – *This is an impressive sight looking over the Golden Vale of Tipperary.*

THE SKELLIGS – *Lying off the southwestern coast of Ireland are the Skelligs, rocky islands that jut dramatically out of the sea. One houses a colony of birds, and the other is home to a set of ruins from ancient monks that will make you wonder why on earth they came here, and what they did once they arrived. The Skelligs are well worth the boat trip out to see.*

WATERFORD CRYSTAL FACTORY – *Home of the famous Waterford crystal, the factory includes an hour-long tour that will change the way you look at crystal for the rest of your life.*

WHERE TO STAY

Accommodations in Munster include quite a few excellent hotels and inns. Lodgings are listed by county, as they are throughout this book.

MUNSTER'S BEST HOTELS

SALLYPORT HOUSE B&B, Kenmare, Tel. (064) 42066. 5 rooms. Rates for singles: £40, doubles: £30 per person sharing. Warm hospitality and wonderful rooms.

THE MOORINGS, Scilly, Kinsale, Tel. (021) 772376, fax (021) 772675. 8 rooms. Rates for singles: £45, doubles: £35 to £55 per person sharing. This pleasant guesthouse right on the harbor is a nice place to base your exploration of Kinsale.

GREGAN'S CASTLE HOTEL, Ballyvaughan, Tel. (065) 77005, fax (065) 77111. 22 rooms. Rates for singles: £56 to £76, doubles: £60 to £95, suites £80 to £110. Gregan's is at the edge of the Burren in County Clare, and many of the rooms have beautiful views of this remarkable 100 square mile rock formation.

HOTEL DUNLOE CASTLE, Killarney, Tel. (064) 44111, fax (064) 44583, US toll free 800-221-1074. 120 rooms. Rates for singles: £65 to £84, doubles: £98 to £132, suites: £200. Romantic ruins of the old castle are on the grounds amid beautiful gardens.

HOTEL ARD NA SIDHE, Caragh Lake, Killorglin, Tel. (066) 69105, fax (066) 69282, US toll free 800-221-1074. 20 rooms. Rates for singles: £68, doubles: £102 to £132. This is a very comfortable hotel away from the hustle and bustle of Killarney.

WATERFORD CASTLE, The Island, Ballinakill, Waterford, Tel. (051) 78203, fax (051) 79316. 19 rooms. Rates for singles: £110 to £150, doubles: £150 to £200, suites: £275. Sitting on its own island, Waterford Castle is a nice place to stay if you're in County Waterford.

DROMOLAND CASTLE, Newmarket-on-Fergus, (061) 368144, (061) 363355 (fax), US toll free 800-346-7007, 73 rooms. Rates for standard rooms: £116 to £202, deluxe rooms: £180 to £245, state rooms and suites: £245 to £414. This beautiful old castle has been lovingly restored.

ADARE MANOR, Adare, Tel. (061) 396566, fax (061) 396124, US toll free 800-462-3273. 64 rooms. Rates for singles: £110 to £209, doubles: £148 to £209. Adare Manor is one of the most beautiful hotels in the country.

SHEEN FALLS LODGE, Kenmare, Tel. (064) 41600, fax (064) 41386. 40 rooms. Rates for singles: £135 to £185, doubles: £160 to £240, suites: £300 to £400. The setting for Sheen Falls Lodge is one of the prettiest in the country.

Cork City

BRANDON HOUSE B&B, *South Douglas Road, Hillgrove Lawn, Tel. (021) 893859. 5 rooms. Rates for singles: £21, rates for doubles: £14 to £16 per person sharing. No credit cards accepted. No service charge.*

Mrs. Barbara Ahern offers warm accommodations and a pleasant Irish welcome to her five-room B&B, four of which are en suite. Her modern home on a cul-de-sac is a nice place to spend an evening or two. Brandon House's central location puts you within easy reach of all that Cork City has to offer. If you want to kick back and enjoy some Irish television shows, you can do so from your own room, as all rooms have TV. There are special rates for guests with children. Mrs. Ahern respectfully requests that guests not smoke.

BEECHWOOD HOUSE B&B, *Curra, Riverstick, (near Cork City), Tel. (021) 771456. 4 rooms. Rates for singles: £21, rates for doubles: £16 per person sharing. No credit cards accepted. No service charge.*

This pretty B&B on the main Cork to Kinsale road is a pleasant find. Mrs. Brid O'Connor serves as a gracious hostess. Off the street enough to avoid street noises, and situated amid wooded areas, the rooms are average size but quite comfortable. Beechwood House features televisions in each of the bedrooms. For those of you with special needs, Beechwood House is wheelchair accessible.

FORTE TRAVELODGE, *Cork City, Tel. (021) 310722, fax (021) 310707. 40 rooms. Rates for room: £33.50. All major credit cards accepted.*

Nothing spectacular, but the rooms at the Forte Travelodge are fastidiously clean and comfortable at a rate more closely akin to a B&B than a hotel. The rooms are ample for two, and would serve a family of four or five nicely. In addition to a television and telephone, each room features tea and coffee-making facilities. The two-story Forte Travelodge is located at the Kinsale roundabout several miles from the city center, on your way to the airport. The hotel is wheelchair accessible.

ISAAC'S HOSTEL, *48 MacCurtain Street, Cork City, Tel. (021) 500011, fax (021) 506355. 220 beds. Rates for dormitory: £5.50, double room: £27, family room (sleeps 5): £44. MasterCard and Visa accepted.*

This is one of the nicest hostels in Ireland. Modern and upbeat, its vibrant atmosphere is infectious. The hostel is divided into dormitories of up to sixteen beds, with a few single, double, and family (sleeps 5) bedrooms. The facilities are clean, bright (some have called them *sassy*), and comfortable. There is a self-catering kitchen and a vibrant brasserie-style restaurant, as well as a small cafeteria that serves the guests. Linens and towels are provided. This is a pretty popular place, and extremely busy from mid-May through August. Call ahead for reservations, probably as much as a month or two in advance for the weekends. Nice place – you'll like it for budget accommodations.

SILVER GRANGE HOUSE, *Tivoli, Tel. (021) 821621, fax (021) 821800. 4 rooms. Rates for singles: £50, doubles: £30 per person sharing. Rates include breakfast. Restaurant, gardens. All major credit cards accepted.*

This stately Georgian manor house sits pretty in the midst of five acres of gardens. The decor is elegant, the rooms are spacious and inviting, and the welcome is warm and sincere. The Silver Grange House is better known for their restaurant – just another benefit of staying here – but you'll find the accommodations much more than acceptable.

MOORE'S HOTEL, *Morrison's Island, Cork City, Tel. (021) 271291, fax (021) 272485. 35 rooms. Rates for singles: £50, doubles: £25 to £35 per person sharing. Rates include breakfast. Restaurant. All major credit cards accepted. No service charge.*

In Cork City's business center, Moore's Hotel offers you decent and relatively inexpensive lodging. The hotel overlooks the River Lee, and the rooms at the front offer the best views. They are a little noisy, but not too bad. The rooms are average in size and comfortably furnished. As a family-run hotel, Moore's appreciates what it's like to travel with children. Special rates for children and specially priced meals in their restaurant are examples of their commitment to make your trip with the kids the most pleasant possible. In addition, they offer special rates for seniors (excluding July and August).

JURY'S CORK INN, *Anderson's Quay, Cork, (021) 276444, (021) 276144 (fax), 133 rooms. Rates for singles: £27.50, doubles: £55. All major credit cards accepted. No service charge.*

Jury's Inn's are a new idea in Irish accommodations: these inns offer rooms that sleep three adults (or two adults and two children) for one room rate. This relatively new five-story Jury's Inn is located in the center of the city. The rooms are simple, but very pleasantly furnished. In addition to television and telephone, each room offers tea and coffee making facilities. The bathrooms are a little small, but they are well-lit and adequate. They also offer a number of rooms that are handicap accessible.

ROCHESTOWN PARK HOTEL, *Rochestown Road, Douglas, Cork City, Tel. (021) 892233, fax (021) 892178. 63 rooms. Rates for singles: £57, doubles: £85. Rates include breakfast. Restaurant, indoor swimming pool, fitness center, sauna, spa, solarium, gardens. All major credit cards accepted. 12.5% service charge.*

This converted and expanded Georgian home is a nice hotel to stay in while you are in the Cork area. It was originally a home that once housed young men studying for the priesthood, as well as one of the residences of the Lord Mayors of Cork.

The main house is where you'll find the public rooms: reception, sitting rooms, and dining rooms. The bedrooms are in extensions to the main house. The rooms are nice size and include writing desks – they are designed to meet the needs of the business traveler as well as tourists. Additional amenities such as a bowl of fruit, mineral water, and robes give you an extra welcome. The hotel also boasts a fairly extensive fitness center, pool, sauna, steam room and solarium. And if you just want to walk, there are seven acres worth of gardens that surround the hotel.

MORRISON'S ISLAND HOTEL, *Morrison's Quay, Cork City, Tel. (021) 275858, fax (021) 275833. 40 rooms. Rates for singles: £80, doubles: £40 to £63 per person sharing. Restaurant. All major credit cards accepted. No service charge.*

Morrison's Island Hotel is the business person's dream. Located in the main business section of Cork City, the hotel focuses on providing roomy, comfortable suites for business travelers, or for travelers who like a little extra room. As you walk into the small, marbled lobby, you can feel the richness of the experience you'll have during your stay here.

Each room is a suite, and each has an adjoining room that can be used for meetings, quiet work sessions, or just relaxing. All but four of the rooms have kitchenettes, and several are two-bedroom suites. If you have the need for such, baby-sitting services are available through the hotel.

County Clare

BUNRATTY VILLA, *Bunratty, Tel. (061) 369241. 5 rooms. Rates for single: £21, doubles: £16 per person sharing. Rate includes breakfast. No credit cards accepted.*

A short walk from this B&B puts you at Bunratty Castle. This modern B&B offers pleasant and comfortable lodging just ten minutes from Shannon Airport. Mrs. Rohan is a gracious and genial hostess, and she requests that her guests not smoke.

LAKESIDE HOUSE, *Deerpark, Tel. (061) 369160. 4 rooms. Rates for single: £22, doubles: 16 per person sharing. Rate includes breakfast. No credit cards accepted.*

As the name implies, this modern Georgian home is in a beautiful setting at the edge of a lake, amid large, mature trees. The rooms are bright and cheery, and offer a pleasant place to hang your hat after visiting Bunratty Castle, just five minutes away.

BUNRATTY WOODS HOUSE B&B, *Bunratty, Tel. (061) 369402. 16 rooms. Rates for single: £22, doubles: £16.50 per person sharing. Rate includes breakfast. No credit cards accepted.*

Located near Bunratty Castle, this recently expanded B&B is a delight, as is its hostess, Mrs. Sheila O'Meara. The rooms are of average size, but clean and comfortable.

BUNRATTY LODGE, *Bunratty, Tel. (061) 369402. 4 rooms. Rates for single: £25, doubles: £17.50 per person sharing. Rate includes breakfast. No credit cards accepted.*

This impressive B&B is the winner of a number of awards in the B&B industry, and is recognized as one of the best around. Near Bunratty Castle, this modern home has nice sized, comfortable rooms. And Mrs. Mary Browne is a gracious hostess who will enhance your stay.

BUNRATTY CASTLE HOTEL, *Bunratty, Tel. (061) 364116, fax (064) 364891. 61 rooms. Rates for singles: £30, doubles: £22 per person sharing. Restaurant. All major credit cards accepted. No service charge.*

This old Georgian mansion house across the street from Bunratty Castle has been expanded and converted into a hotel. The lobby and pub are in the main house, and most of the rooms are in newer extensions to the house. Unfortunately, the extensions made no effort to continue the feel or quality of the original Georgian mansion, but the rooms are comfortable and clean, albeit a little small. A recent addition added fifty new rooms, and they are the nicest. Several evenings a week, live entertainment is offered in the pub.

GREGAN'S CASTLE HOTEL, *Ballyvaughan, Tel. (065) 77005, fax (065) 77111. 22 rooms. Rates for singles: £56 to £76, doubles: £60 to £95, suites £80 to £110. Rates include breakfast. Restaurant. Visa and MasterCard accepted. 15% service charge. Closed from November 1 to early April.*

If you're driving to Gregan's Castle Hotel, especially after a long day, you'll swear you'll never get there. It just seems to be out in the middle of nowhere. But once you get there – whether for dinner at their award-winning restaurant or for a night's lodging – you'll be glad you made the trip.

The welcoming turf fire represents the warmth you'll feel from the staff, the decor, and the views that await you here. Situated in a valley at the foot of a road with multiple hairpin curves called Corkscrew Hill, Gregan's Castle – which isn't really a castle at all – has remarkable views of Galway Bay and of the Burren, a limestone rock garden that extends for one hundred square miles throughout County Clare.

The rooms are individually decorated to top standards and many have lovely views. However, if you are looking forward to relaxing in front of the TV in your room, you'll be disappointed – to preserve the tranquil atmosphere, the rooms do not have televisions. The hotel is isolated, but offers a wide variety of outdoor activities. You can walk through their lovely gardens, take a stroll or more aggressive trek through the burren, or stroll along the shores of Galway Bay. If you've brought your children with you, you'll like the discounts they give, and you may want to take advantage of the baby-sitting service they will arrange for you.

DROMOLAND CASTLE, *Newmarket-on-Fergus, Tel. (061) 368144, fax (061) 363355, US toll free 800-346-7007. 73 rooms. Rates for standard rooms: £116 to £202, deluxe rooms: £180 to £245, state rooms and suites: £245 to £414; children under age 12 stay free with parents. One restaurant, indoor swimming* *pool, spa, sauna, fitness center, beauty salon, tennis, snooker, golf, riding, fishing, shooting, bicycles. All major credit cards accepted. No service charge.*

"A fantasy come true," "A piece of heaven," "Exceeded every expectation I had" – these were the last three entries in the guest book on the morning after my last stay at Dromoland Castle, and I couldn't agree more. Dromoland Castle is the sister castle to Ashford Castle, and you can certainly see the family resemblance. But if Ashford is the elegant, classic beauty, Dromoland is the sister with the personality. Beautiful in her own right, Dromoland also exudes a quiet grace and charm.

Dromoland Castle was once the estate of the powerful O'Brien Clan, blood descendants of Brian Boru, High King of Ireland. Chock full of antiques and portraits of the previous inhabitants of Dromoland Castle, it retains its regal feeling without being stuffy. Adding to the fairytale feeling, Dromoland Castle is set amid 370 acres of woods, parks, and golf fairways and greens.

The rooms are spacious and tastefully decorated; those in the front have lovely views of a small lake and the golf course. Nightly turn-down service, warm robes, and chocolates on your pillow are just some of the amenities here.

On-site is an outstanding restaurant – the Earl of Thomond Room – that provides one of the most delectable dining experiences in the country. (See the *Where to Eat* section.)

All-in-all, this is a dream place to stay if you can afford the rather steep price tag. The owners accurately say: "Dromoland Castle – perfectly combining old world charm with the facilities the new world demands."

IMPERIAL HOTEL, *South Mall, Cork, Tel. (021) 274040. 98 rooms. Rates for singles: £65, doubles: £85 per person sharing, suites: £170. Restaurant. All major credit cards accepted. 10% service charge.*

If you want to be in the middle of the Cork action, this is the place. Located in the center of the Cork city financial district, the Imperial Hotel is just minutes from many sights in town.

The hotel is not all that impressive though, with its eclectic architectural styles: it seems like they were unsure whether to retain their 19th-century roots or modernize from top to bottom. So they did a little of both. Some of the rooms are graced with antiques, as are a number of locations in the hotel, but most of the rooms are quite modern – to the point of white furnishings and chrome and glass coffee tables.

On the main floor they offer a 1930's style cocktail bar complete with a pianist; they also offer a pub that is frequented by a number of locals as well as tourists. If you are traveling with children, you will benefit from discounts for the young ones on the room rate as well as in the restaurant, where lower-priced children's meals are available. If you want to go out on the town, the hotel will also arrange babysitting for you.

There is a bit of a parking problem – parking at the hotel is limited, although there is covered parking a short distance from the hotel.

JURY'S HOTEL, *Western Road, Cork, Tel. (021) 276622, fax (021) 274477. 185 rooms. Rates for singles: £75, doubles: £85 per person sharing, suites: £135 per person sharing. Restaurant, gardens, outdoor swimming pool, sauna, spa, squash court. All major credit cards accepted. 12.5% service charge.*

Many of the rooms face onto a green courtyard, with well-kept lawns and gardens. The rooms, while somewhat small, are brightly decorated in a floral design. They are enhanced with a complimentary bowl of fruit and bottles of mineral water, and the nightly turn-down service is a nice touch.

Jury's Hotel offers a wide variety of leisure activities to help you relax during your stay. You can take advantage of the indoor/outdoor swimming pool, sauna, fitness center, and even a squash court. There's even a playground for youngsters to work their wiggles out. Discounted room rates for the children as well as children's meals in the restaurant help hold down costs if you're here with kids.

County Cork

KILLARNEY HOUSE, *Station Road, Blarney, Tel. (021) 381153. 4 rooms. Rates for singles: £22, rates for doubles: £17 per person sharing. No credit cards accepted. No service charge.*

Here's a nice B&B to stay in if you want to begin or end your day in Blarney seeing the famous castle and stone. Built specifically as a B&B, there's an acre of ground with pretty gardens that invite a visit. The rooms are average size but nicely furnished. Baby-sitting service is available should you need it.

BALLYMAKEIGH HOUSE, *Killeagh, Tel. (024) 95184, fax (024) 95370. 5 rooms. Rates for singles: £25, doubles: £20 per person sharing. Restaurant. No credit cards accepted. No service charge.*

Margaret Browne is the hostess, a working dairy farm is the setting, and the combination seems to work magic for those who stay at Ballymakeigh House. Many who stay here once vow it won't be the last time.

Sitting on a lush green hillside and presiding grandly over the luxurious farmland all around, Ballymakeigh House presents a regal appearance. Inside, you'll find a delightful mixture of hospitality, fresh flowers, and starched linen to complement your stay. If you've brought the kids, you'll really like the discount for children and you can take advantage of their baby-sitting service.

The older house has been renovated to provide a nice set of en suite bedrooms that are individually decorated and comfortably furnished. But the warm Irish welcome seems to be what brings 'em back. This truly is a special place that you shouldn't miss if it fits your schedule.

LOTAMORE HOUSE, *Tivoli, near Cork City, Tel. (021) 822344, fax (021) 822219. 20 rooms. Rates for singles: £27, doubles: £25 per person sharing. Rates include breakfast. American Express, MasterCard and Visa accepted. No service charge.*

Overlooking the River Lee just a few minutes outside Cork City is pretty Lotamore House. The first impression you have of this restored Georgian mansion is of the lovely verdant setting and the splendid gardens that accent the house. The rooms are large and spacious, and each is individually decorated to retain the warmth and character of the home.

BALLYVOLANE HOUSE, *Castlelyons, Tel. (025) 36349, fax (025) 36781. 6 rooms. Rates for singles: £42 to £52, doubles: £35 to £45 per person sharing. Restaurant. All major credit cards accepted. No service charge.*

The renovated Ballyvolane House is located in the countryside southeast of Fermoy between Rathcormac and Castlelyons. Built in 1728, the home has seen a number of renovations and refurbishments throughout the years. The results are splendid indeed, and you're fortunate that the Greens share its beauty through their guest house.

Ballyvolane House is situated in an emerald setting of woods and farmland. As you enter the house, you'll be impressed with the entryway: pillared and presided over by a baby grand piano. The sitting rooms are large rooms decorated with rich, dark wood and portraits of ancestors sternly watching Ballyvolane's guests. Your next impressions will be the collection of antiques that are liberally sprinkled throughout the house, including the bedrooms. The bedrooms themselves are a variety of sizes, but are all most comfortable and pleasant. If you're calling ahead to make reservations, ask for one of the rooms with the old claw-footed bathtubs – they're like taking a bath in a small swimming pool!

Ballyvolane House offers wheelchair access; children are welcome and pets allowed.

AHERNES SEAFOOD RESTAURANT AND ACCOMMODATION, *163 North Main Street, Youghal, Tel. (024) 92424, fax (024) 93633. 10 rooms. Rates for singles: £40, doubles: £35 to £50 per person sharing. All major credit cards accepted.*

It's difficult to say which aspect of Ahernes is most popular: its award-winning restaurant or its award-winning accommodations. For a review of the restaurant, see *Where to Eat* below. Ahernes has almost a cult following among tourists and the Irish alike. Much of their business is repeat, and new groupies join the ranks every season, having been directed there by the effusive comments of friends and strangers.

The Fitzgibbon family is probably responsible for this following – Kate carries on the tradition of three generations of Fitzgibbon hospitality. And they are small enough – just ten rooms – to provide attention at an individual level. Open turf fires welcome those who come to Ahernes. The seafood in the restaurant is exquisite, and the rooms are spacious and sumptuous. None of the rooms have memorable views, but the rooms and service are marvelous enough to compensate. This is perhaps the best lodging for the price in County Cork.

THE MOORINGS, *Scilly, Kinsale, Tel. (021) 772376, fax (021) 772675. 8 rooms. Rates for singles: £45, doubles: £35 to £55 per person sharing. Restaurant, tennis, croquet. MasterCard and Visa accepted.*

This marvelous guesthouse overlooks the marina in Kinsale Harbor. The rooms are large and light, and most of them have balconies that overlook the harbor. Talk about relaxation! If you're staying in Kinsale, this guest house would get my vote. But call ahead. With only eight rooms and gorgeous views, it fills up quickly from late May through August.

Parking in Kinsale can sometimes be very tough and expensive, especially in the summer months. That makes the private carpark for The Moorings all that much more attractive.

THE OLD BANK HOUSE, *11 Pearse Street, Kinsale, Tel. (021) 774075, fax (021) 774296. 9 rooms. Rates for singles: £45, doubles: £35 to £60 per person sharing. American Express, MasterCard, Visa.*

The Old Bank House takes its name from its previous use: it was formerly a branch office for the Munster and Leinster Bank. Much of the quiet dignity old banks have is retained in the guest house that now features a plethora of antiques and quality furnishings. The feeling you get is one of refined, old-world elegance.

Since this is an old Georgian home, the rooms are large and spacious. But you may not realize that they, too, are liberally endowed with antiques that provide just the right feel to the rooms. To provide a pleasant and enjoyable stay for all, the owners graciously request that their guests not smoke in the public areas of the guesthouse. Children above the age of seven years old are welcome.

ASSOLAS COUNTRY HOUSE, *Kanturk, Tel. (029) 50015, fax (029) 50795. 9 rooms. Rates for singles: £40 to £55, doubles: £50 to £77 per person sharing. Restaurant, tennis, croquet. All major credit cards accepted. No service charge.*

Just a few minutes outside of Kanturk sits pretty ivy-covered Assolas House, the courtly country home of the Bourke family. Inside the creeper-clad walls you'll find an impressive collection of antiques and an open fire in the fireplace.

The rooms are large, clean and well-maintained, and several have outstanding views of the grounds. Three of the rooms you will have to choose from are located out in the courtyard in a restored stone cottage. They are nonetheless nice, and you'll be exceptionally comfortable whether you stay in the rooms in the house or in the the stone cottage.

THE BLUE HAVEN HOTEL, *3 Pearse Street, Kinsale, Tel. (021) 772209, fax (021) 774268. 18 rooms. Rates for singles: £45, doubles: £35 to £60 per person sharing. Restaurant. All major credit cards accepted. 10% service charge.*

The Blue Haven Hotel in downtown Kinsale was recently named Ireland's small hotel of the year by a hotel industry organization. Part of the reason is doubtless the building itself; equally important, however, is the warm country welcome that is part and parcel of the package. Recently refurbished and expanded, the Blue Haven is a slice of peace and tranquillity. From the moment you enter the simple but nice reception area, to the open fire in the pub to the cane-furnished conservatory, you'll find a relaxed and cordial air here.

The rooms are unfortunately on the small size, but simply and comfortably furnished. The recent refurbishment work has gone a long way to making the rooms more comfortable, especially the rooms at the front of the hotel overlooking the street. The Blue Haven is centrally located, but in the past that centrality meant bothersome street noise in the rooms. The rooms have been recently renovated and include double-glazed windows, which cut down on the street noise immensely.

If you'd like to stay the Blue Haven during the summer months, be sure and call ahead for reservations as soon as you know your schedule. The hotel is very popular, and tends to fill up quickly.

LONGUEVILLE HOUSE, *Mallow, Tel. (022) 47156, US toll-free number 800-223-6510, fax (022) 47459. 21 rooms. Rates for singles: £51 to £77, doubles: £51 to £77 per person sharing. Garden, fishing. All major credit cards accepted. No service charge.*

Talk about an impressive Georgian house! Longueville House was built in 1720 by the ancestors of the current owners, Michael and Jane O'Callaghan. In the 1960's, they converted their large home into a country hotel, and it's obvious they know and love the business they've chosen. Their service is legendary, and those who stay here swear they'll be back. You will too!

As you enter the spacious foyer, you'll notice the lavish ornamentation of the house. Gilded portraits of past O'Callaghans greet you with somber expressions, but they'll be the only duskiness you'll experience at Longueville House. The house is rife with antiques and elegant furnishings, well-endowed with quality craftsmanship, from its ornate plaster work to the rich and beautiful woodwork.

To say the bedrooms are spacious would be an understatement; your bedroom at Longueville House may very well be the largest you experience during your stay in Ireland. The furnishings in the bedrooms are all top-of-the line, and most of the bathrooms are marble and offer first-rate facilities. The bedrooms at the front of the house are especially nice: they overlook the Blackwater River Valley, including the ruins of the 16th-century O'Callaghan castle.

ARBUTUS LODGE, *Montenotte Cork, Tel. (021) 501237, fax (021) 502893. 20 rooms. Rates for singles: £37 to £50, doubles: £85 to £115, suites: £135 to £200. Rates include breakfast. Gardens, tennis. All major credit cards accepted. No service charge.*

Formerly the home of the Lord Mayor of Cork, Arbutus Lodge sits grandly above Cork city with commanding views of the sprawling city and the River Lee. Exquisitely furnished with antiques throughout, the hotel also boasts a fine collection of Irish art – new as well as old.

The bedrooms are those befitting the family of the Lord Mayor – large and well-furnished. The four most impressive rooms are in a mansion across from the hotel, and are more like mini-apartments. This is a nice place, one of the nicest you'll find in and around Cork city.

BALLYMALOE HOUSE, *Shanagarry, Midleton, Tel. (021) 652531, fax (021) 652021. 32 rooms. Rates for singles: £55 to £65, doubles: £55 to £65 per person sharing. Restaurant, garden, croquet, outdoor swimming pool, tennis, golf. All major credit cards accepted. 10% service charge.*

About forty-five minutes east of Cork city sits the pretty, creeper-clad Ballymaloe House. Once a castle, then a farm, and now a hotel, Ballymaloe House seems to have retained the best of all three. It has the grandeur of the castle, the warmth of a family farm, and the efficiency of a well-run hotel. The Allen family are busy proprietors. In addition to the hotel, they have a highly regarded restaurant on-site, they run the Ballymaloe Cookery School, have a craft and kitchen shop, and run a restaurant in Cork city. Yet they still manage to greet each of their guests with a warmth typical of what you will come to expect in Ireland.

The bedrooms are an eclectic collection ranging from traditional to modern; all are comfortably furnished, and many open out onto lawns and gardens. Perhaps the most intriguing room is one which is housed in the 16th-century gatehouse. It offers kind of a rustic experience: twin beds, with the bathroom up a steep wooden staircase.

You can relax in the country splendor here, or you can spend some time participating in horseback riding, tennis, a playground for the children, and a swimming pool. In addition, you're only about two miles from the ocean. If you've brought the children along, you'll also appreciate the children's discount available for both the hotel and the restaurant. Several of the rooms have wheelchair access.

County Kerry

SALLYPORT HOUSE B&B, *Kenmare, Tel. (064) 42066. 5 rooms. Rates for singles: £40, doubles: £30 per person sharing. Rates include breakfast. No credit cards accepted. No service charge.*

At the edge of Kenmare you'll find this delightful country house. I originally became aware of Sallyport House when I encountered a variety of tourists who raved about the house, the hospitality, and the setting. I found their enthusiastic recommendations right on the money, from the warm turf fire in the lobby to the dining room overlooking lovely gardens.

The rooms are pleasantly decorated with antiques and reproductions. Depending on your preference (and how far ahead you call!), the bedrooms at Sallyport House offer you views of Kenmare Bay or green orchards and mountains.

CASTLEROSSE HOTEL, *Killorglin Road, Killarney, Tel. (064) 31144, fax (064) 31031, US toll free 800-528-1234. 110 rooms. Rates for singles: £40 to £50, doubles: £32 to £52 per person sharing, suites: £165 to £199 per person sharing. Rates include breakfast. One restaurant, indoor pool, sauna, fitness center. All major credit cards accepted. No service charge.*

Castlerosse Hotel sits at the edge of Killarney. This low-rise hotel is a member of the Best Western Hotel group. The hotel is looking a little old, with a need for updated lighting, carpets, and new paint. The rooms are simple and functional, but not very large. Many of the rooms offer fine views of the mountains.

The biggest draw for the hotel (besides its location in Killarney) is their extensive leisure center. They offer an indoor swimming pool, sauna, and fitness center. They offer children's discounts.

HOTEL DUNLOE CASTLE, *Killarney, Tel. (064) 44111, fax (064) 44583, US toll free 800-221-1074. 120 rooms. Rates for singles: £65 to £84, doubles: £98 to £132, suites: £200. One restaurant, gardens, riding, fishing, swimming pool, sauna, fitness center and tennis court. All major credit cards accepted. No service charge.*

As you turn into the gate of Hotel Dunloe Castle, it's almost like pulling through the gates of a Kentucky horse farm: white rail fences and beautiful horses grazing contentedly in fields of green. The rooms are comfortable with modern pine furnishings, and many have outstanding views of the Gap of Dunloe, those grazing horses, or exquisite award-winning gardens in the back of the hotel. The gardens surround the ancient ruins of the 13th-century Dunloe Castle, from which the hotel draws its name. A quiet walk through the gardens also brings you to a point where you overlook the softly flowing Leane River.

Hotel Dunloe Castle considers itself a country inn serving families. They succeed in their efforts with a variety of activities that cater to families. Those pretty horses grazing serenely as you enter the grounds are available for horseback riding. In addition, there is a playground and playroom available for the kids to romp in while you check out the indoor swimming pool, sauna, fitness center and tennis court (the kids are welcome here, too). The hotel offers room discounts and special meals for children in their restaurant. If your children are younger, the hotel can arrange baby-sitting for you. Pets are also welcome at the hotel.

HOTEL EUROPE, *Killarney, Tel. (064) 31900, fax (064) 34340, US toll free 800-221-1074. 200 rooms. Rates for singles: £74 to £96, doubles: £98 to £132, suites: £114 to £400. Two restaurants, indoor swimming pool, gym, sauna, spa, beauty salon, snooker, riding, fishing. All major credit cards accepted. No service charge.*

The Hotel Europe is a lovely five-star hotel sitting on the shores of Lough Leane. It's a popular site for incentive travel – corporations looking for a place to really treat their top-performing people. The rooms are comfortable, and those in the back of the hotel offer the prettiest views of the lake and the mountains, although they cost an extra £35.

A host of activities and amenities await you when you stay at Hotel Europe. They include a boutique, beauty salon, fishing, boating, cycling, indoor swimming pool, fitness center, and a sauna. In addition, Hotel Europe is within minutes of six championship golf courses.

KILLARNEY PARK HOTEL, *Kenmare Place, Killarney, Tel. (064) 35555, fax (064) 35266. 66 rooms. Rates for singles: £80 to £100, doubles: £55 to £85 per person sharing, suites: £70 to £100 per person sharing. One restaurant, bar, indoor swimming pool, fitness center. All major credit cards accepted. 10% service charge.*

The Killarney Park Hotel is centrally located in Killarney and promises a warm reception and pleasant stay. From the turf fire burning in the entrance hall to the front desk reception to the warm dark furnishings, you'll feel welcome and comfortable. The hotel has been recognized by a number of organizations for their delightful service and top-notch accommodations.

In addition to being close to all that Killarney has to offer, the Killarney Park Hotel also has their own set of activities to keep you occupied. They include an indoor swimming pool, fitness center, sauna, peaceful gardens to stroll in, and daily entertainment in their lounge.

The rooms are nice and large, some of them bordering on spacious. While not particularly memorable, they are comfortable, clean, and quiet and offer a lot of room, especially nice if you are traveling with children. If you have your children with you, you'll be able to take advantage of the special children's rates for the rooms and in their restaurant. In addition, baby-sitting service is available.

KILLARNEY RYAN HOTEL, *Cork Road, Killarney, Tel. (064) 31555, fax (064) 32438. 168 rooms. Rates for singles: £50, doubles: £35 to £69 per person sharing. One restaurant, two bars, indoor swimming pool, spa, sauna, tennis. All major credit cards accepted. 10% service charge.*

About a mile from the Killarney city center is the Killarney Ryan Hotel. This pleasant low-rise hotel offers a wide variety of activities.

Whether you are a serious health fiend or prefer to putter around at miniature golf, you should find something to interest you. Their fitness center includes an indoor swimming pool, jacuzzi, sauna, and a sports hall, with facilities for basketball, volleyball, soccer, and ping-pong. A miniature golf course (goofy golf) and tennis courts round out their athletic offerings.

And yes – they also offer bedrooms. The rooms are nothing special, but are pleasant and comfortable, clean and close to town. They also include a discount for children.

KILLARNEY GREAT SOUTHERN HOTEL, *Tel. (064) 31262, fax (064) 35300, US toll free 800-448-8355. Rates for singles: £67 to £77, doubles: £50 to £57 per person sharing. Restaurant, garden, indoor swimming pool, sauna, fitness center, spa, beauty salon, boutique. All major credit cards accepted. 12.5% service charge.*

As you walk into this hotel, the lobby speaks of old elegance: a turf fire burning in the fireplace, dark oak floors, crystal chandeliers, plush rugs, and marble pillars. Formerly a railway hotel, it was built in 1854 and has been busy ever since.

The hotel is set in the midst of thirty-six acres of gardens; the gardens wend their way around the hotel, and offer nice views from some of the public rooms as well as some of the bedrooms. The rooms are of average size, well-maintained, and nicely furnished. The creeper-clad hotel boasts a fine set of fitness facilities that include an indoor swimming pool, sauna, jacuzzi, steam room, fitness center, and tennis court. If you have your children along with you, you can take advantage of their discount for children.

HOTEL ARD NA SIDHE, *Caragh Lake, Killorglin, Tel. (66) 69105, fax (066) 69282, US toll free 800-221-1074. 20 rooms. Rates for singles: £68, doubles: £102 to £132. One restaurant. All major credit cards accepted. No service charge.*

The house was built in 1880 by an English woman who called it the "House of the Fairies." It is approximately seventeen miles from Killarney – watch for the signposts on the Killarney-Killorglin Road.

With lots of antique furnishings and an inviting open fireplace, the Hotel Ard na Sidhe feels like you've come home to a regal baronial manor at the end of the day. Beautiful gardens surround the hotel – gardens that have twice won first place in national garden competitions. The rooms are spacious and tastefully furnished with a bevy of antiques. They feel as though you have stumbled on the bedchambers of royalty.

Hotel Ard na Sidhe is owned by the same group that owns Hotel Europe and Hotel Dunloe Castle. You can take advantage of the leisure activities offered by those two larger hotels, including their swimming pools, horseback riding, etc.

PARK HOTEL KENMARE, *Kenmare, Tel. (064) 41200, fax (064) 41402. 50 rooms. Rates for singles: £115 to £135, doubles: £96 to £138 per person sharing, suites: £165 to £199 per person sharing. One restaurant, croquet, tennis. All major credit cards accepted. No service charge. Only open from mid-April through the mid-November.*

I must admit, I was probably more curious to meet the owner of the Park Hotel in Kenmare than I was to actually stay at his hotel. It seemed that nearly every hotelier to whom I mentioned my upcoming stay at the Park Hotel indicated a desire for me to say "Hello," to Francis Brennan. Several of them, general managers at some of Ireland's most prestigious hotels, had learned their craft at Francis' hand.

I wasn't disappointed, either in Mr. Brennan or in the hotel. Mr. Brennan is a wonderful host, and those who serve with him are equally enthusiastic.

Built in 1897 to serve as the hotel for the railroad that dead-ended there, it has since been renovated and expanded, and the results are marvelous. The rooms are a nice size; those in the back are the best, offering views of Kenmare Bay and most of the eleven acres of gardens. The halls are graced with a multitude of antiques and portraits. Some of them are interesting pieces, including a 19th-century wheelchair and an ancient wine press. Amenities include turn-down service, bathrobes, and slippers.

On-site is an award-winning restaurant overlooking Kenmare Bay and providing a delicious repast to augment your experience (see *Where to Eat* section). The simple elegance of the dining room is a fitting complement to the rest of the hotel. Crisp Irish linen and gleaming silverware accent the fine meals prepared by Chef Bruno Schmidt. The ambiance, food, and views all add up to a satisfying and impressive dining experience.

SHEEN FALLS LODGE, *Kenmare, Tel. (064) 41600, fax (064) 41386. 40 rooms. Rates for singles: £135 to £185, doubles: £160 to £240, suites: £300 to £400. One restaurant, croquet, tennis, gym, sauna, spa, beauty salon, riding, shooting, fishing, golf. All major credit cards accepted. No service charge.*

In the 17th century, William Petty commissioned the building of a luxurious manor house along the banks of Kenmare Bay. Three hundred years later, you can experience the same level of luxury William became accustomed to by staying at Sheen Falls Hotel, which is built around William's original home. The result is a hotel rich in tradition if not actual history. Sitting amid 300 acres of park-like surroundings, the Sheen Falls Lodge is a popular resort spot for the Irish as well as tourists.

The hotel has been expensively and richly decorated, from leather couches to mahogany paneling, from marble to crystal to roaring fireplaces. The rooms are of exceptional size, and each has views of Kenmare

Bay or the Sheen Falls on the Sheen River. The rooms come with a bowl of fruit, bathrobes, slippers, personal safe, and nightly turn-down service.

If you can pull yourself away from the beautiful bedrooms and public rooms, you'll have other treats awaiting you. If you like woodland walks or horseback rides along sprawling parks, or if you prefer tennis or trap shooting, you can do any or all of these on the grounds of Sheen Falls Hotel. I highly recommend Sheen Falls Lodge.

County Limerick

LIMERICK INN, *Ennis Road, Limerick, Tel. (061) 326666, fax (061) 326281. 153 rooms. Rates for singles: £52, doubles: £68. Rates include breakfast. Restaurant, pub, indoor swimming pool, sauna, spa, tennis, fitness center, snooker. All major credit cards accepted. No service charge.*

At the edge of Limerick City on Ennis Road sits the inconspicuous low-rise Limerick Inn. The hotel offers its guests a wide range of fitness activities including an indoor swimming pool, fitness center, sauna, solarium, snooker room, and tennis courts. The rooms are fairly large and are furnished with comfortable beds and pleasant furnishings. Trouser presses, an iron and ironing board in each room are nice touches (I always feel wrinkled when I travel!).

WOODLANDS HOUSE HOTEL, *Adare, Tel. (061) 396118, fax (061) 396073. 57 rooms. Rates for singles: £37 to £50, doubles: £27 to £40 per person sharing. Rates include breakfast. Restaurant. All major credit cards accepted. No service charge.*

Located in the tidy town of Adare, the Woodlands House Hotel is run by the Fitzgerald family. This mid-size one-story hotel has been serving visitors to Adare since 1983. In addition to being an excellent place from which to explore Adare and the Limerick area, the hotel is a popular site for weddings, banquets, and other functions.

Originally a four-bedroom farmhouse, the hotel has been expanded several times over the past decade. Some of the rooms are getting a little outdated, while others are fresh and lively. But all are well-maintained, clean, and comfortable. There are also price reductions for children and senior citizens.

TWO MILE INN HOTEL, *Ennis Road, Limerick, Tel. (061) 326255, fax (061) 453783. 123 rooms. Rates for singles: £49 to £63, doubles: £59 to £85. Rates include breakfast. Restaurant. All major credit cards accepted. No service charge.*

This new hotel, located about three miles from the center of Limerick City, offers a bit of a different look from most Irish hotels. One-story units containing bedrooms surround greenbelt areas, giving you the feeling more akin to a country inn than a big city hotel. The rooms are well-proportioned and comfortable. During the summers, the greenbelt is furnished with tables and chairs. The hotel is especially popular with families who are traveling with children, as discounts are offered on room rates and in their restaurant. Babysitting service is available if needed.

DUNRAVEN ARMS HOTEL, *Adare, Tel. (061) 396633, fax (061) 396541. 66 rooms. Rates for singles: £57 to £72, doubles: £84 to £104; children under age 4 stay free with their parents. Restaurant, tennis, riding center. All major credit cards accepted. 12.5% service charge.*

One of the most popular places to stay in Adare is the Dunraven Arms Hotel. The public areas of the hotel are lovely, with their traditional warmth and comfortable furnishings. The hotel was established in 1792, and has won a number of industry awards for both its restaurant and hotel over the past several years. One of the reasons is the excellent service provided by everyone associated with the hotel.

The rooms are splendid, furnished with antiques and comfortable beds and upgraded bathrooms. The rooms provide views of the thatched roofs of Adare's cottages, and some look out onto the meticulous gardens of the hotel. Your room will be complemented with fresh-cut flowers, a bowl of fruit, and mineral water from local springs. The nightly turn-down service is a nice touch, with a wee bit of chocolate candy left on your pillow. There are no tea- or coffee-making facilities in your room, but there's room service available around the clock.

A brand new leisure facility (late 1996) offers a variety of activities for guests.

LIMERICK RYAN HOTEL, *Ennis Road, Limerick, Tel. (061) 453922, fax (061) 326333. 181 rooms. Rates for singles: £70, doubles: £90. Two restaurants, pub, indoor swimming pool, sauna, spa, tennis, fitness center, snooker. All major credit cards accepted. 10% service charge.*

Another of Limerick's older hotels, this one has a wing that dates to the 1780s. The rooms in this hotel are of average size, but they are quite nicely furnished. The hotel is within a mile of Limerick's city center, and a convenient place to stay while you are exploring the area. The hotel welcomes families with children, and offers discounts on room rates and children's meals in their restaurant. They offer one room that affords wheelchair access.

JURY'S HOTEL, *Ennis Road, Limerick, Tel. (061) 327777, fax (061) 326400, US toll free 800-843-3311. 95 rooms. Rates for singles: £82, doubles: £102. Two restaurants, pub, indoor swimming pool, sauna, spa, tennis, fitness center, snooker. All major credit cards accepted. 10% service charge.*

Just as you enter Limerick on Ennis Road you'll come upon Jury's Hotel. This four-star hotel is set on its own five-acre plot next to the River Shannon, and offers pleasant and tranquil surroundings within a stone's throw of the city. There are two restaurants and a popular pub called Limericks Bar included at the hotel.

There is a mixture of old and new rooms available. Both are about average in size, although they are all comfortably if not elegantly furnished. Nice additions to the rooms include trouser presses and tea- and coffee-making facilities.

A fitness center rounds out the package that Jury's Hotel offers its guests. It features an indoor swimming pool, sauna, exercise room, and jacuzzi. Tennis courts are also available. If you've brought youngsters along with you, Jury's offers discounts on room rates as well as special meals in their restaurants. Baby-sitting service is also available.

ADARE MANOR, *Adare, Tel. (061) 396566, fax (061) 396124, US toll free 800-462-3273. 64 rooms. Rates for singles: £110 to £209, doubles: £148 to £209; children under age 12 stay free with their parents. Rates include breakfast. Restaurant, garden, gym, sauna, snooker, games room, riding, fishing, shooting. All major credit cards accepted. No service charge.*

If you want to see what it was like to live like 18th-century royalty, spend a night or two in Adare Manor. Located in the spotless town of Adare (and I do mean spotless: thatched cottages without a thatch out of place, white-washed walls, and so on), aside the meandering River Maigue, Adare Manor is the former home to the Earls of Dunraven. The hotel features exquisite furnishings, including crystal chandeliers, many antiques, stained-glass, and rich mahogany furniture. Stroll into the gallery, patterned after a room in the Versailles Palace outside of Paris. Sit in the drawing room and look out over magnificent gardens.

The enthusiasm you feel after your initial impressions will carry right on through to the bedrooms. Spacious, individually decorated rooms include hand-crafted fireplaces and elegant furnishings. Large, high-quality bathrooms complement the views you'll have out your bedroom windows.

A number of activities are available to Adare Manor's guests, including golf on their Robert Trent Jones-designed golf course, an indoor swimming pool, sauna, fitness center, and a game room. Children are welcome, and kids under twelve years of age stay free in their parents' room. Facilities for pets are also available.

Even with all these amenities, perhaps the most pleasant aspect of the hotel is the pampering you'll get from the staff. It really is a pleasant and memorable place to stay.

CASTLETROY PARK HOTEL, *Dublin Road, Limerick, Tel. (061) 335566, fax (061) 331117. 107 rooms. Rates for singles: £93, doubles: £113, suites: £160 to £250. Two restaurants, pub, indoor swimming pool, sauna, spa, beauty salon, tennis, fitness center, snooker. All major credit cards accepted. No service charge.*

This hotel is located on the outskirts of Limerick on the main Limerick-Dublin road in an attractive red-brick building. The rooms at the

Castletroy Park Hotel are large and comfortable. Their focus on business travelers means niceties for tourists as well: plenty of extra space in the rooms, writing desks, two phones, trouser presses, and extra lighting. The hotel offers a slightly upgraded series of rooms called Executive Rooms as well as a number of suites – Junior and Presidential – all of which include nightly turn-down service.

A leisure center available to guests includes an indoor swimming pool, fitness center, sauna, and solarium. There is also a beauty salon on the premises, and there are two rooms available with wheelchair access.

County Tipperary

BALLYCORMAC HOUSE, *Aglish, (near Borrisokane), Tel. (067) 21129, fax (067) 21200. 5 rooms. Rates for singles: £25, doubles: £20 per person sharing. Restaurant. All major credit cards accepted. No service charge.*

In recent years, Ballycormac House has gained some renown as a mini-fishing and hunting lodge. The proprietors, Herb and Christine Quigley, arrange *ghillies* (guides) for guests who would like to fish, ride, or shoot in the nearby countryside.

Their guest house has five rooms, including one small suite with its own private open fire and a lovely four-poster bed. The other rooms vary in size, several are small and the others are adequate, but all are clean and cheerily decorated. The restaurant here is also considered one of the best in this part of the country.

It's a little difficult to find since Aglish isn't on all maps. A phone call for directions will help immensely. It is north of Borrisokane, which is due north of Nenagh on the N52.

County Waterford

KNOCKBOY HOUSE, *Dunmore Road, Waterford, Tel. (051) 73484. 6 rooms. Rates for singles: £19 to £21, doubles: £14 to £16 per person sharing. Rates include breakfast. Credit cards not accepted. No service charge.*

This is a lovely Georgian residence overlooking the River Suir. There are three en suite rooms, and three standard rooms. Mrs. Jacinta Jackman-Kavanagh is your hostess, and she'll make you feel welcome indeed.

THE PINES, *Knockboy, Dunmore Road, Waterford, Tel. (051) 74452. 5 rooms. Rates for singles: £19 to £21, doubles: £14 to £16 per person sharing. Rates include breakfast. Credit cards not accepted. No service charge.*

This is a beautiful ivy-covered cottage in a rural setting. The rooms are tastefully decorated and very comfortable. There are four rooms en suite, and one without a bathroom.

BLENHEIM HOUSE, *Blenheim Heights, Waterford, Tel. (051) 74115. 6 rooms. Rates for singles: £18 to £21, doubles: £16 per person sharing. Rates include breakfast. Credit cards not accepted. No service charge.*

Just outside town, this beautifully restored Georgian residence is older than the United States. Built in 1763, it has been furnished with lovely antiques throughout. The rooms are comfortable, tastefully decorated, and well-furnished. Blenheim house is set at the end of a country lane on its own pretty park-like setting with plenty of grass, gardens, and large trees. Across from the house is a fenced area where you are liable to see a herd of deer peacefully feeding.

FOXMOUNT FARM, *Passage East Road, Waterford, Tel. (051) 74308, fax (051) 54906. 6 rooms. Rates for singles: £20, doubles: £20 per person sharing. Rates include breakfast. Credit cards not accepted. No service charge.*

Foxmount Farm is a farm first, and a B&B second. Not that you'd notice from the reception your hostess, Mrs. Margaret Kent, will give you. While the farm is a going concern that demands the attention of the Kent family, the B&B prospers just fine under Mrs. Kent's watchful eye.

The regal 18th-century home is a delightful place to stay. Set amid two hundred and thirty verdant acres, the house sits atop a small swell, assuring its guests marvelous views of lawns, gardens, and meadows. Children will particularly like the attention they can give to several farm animals on-site. The house features numerous antiques and comfortable public rooms, including a drawing room that offers a snug and warm atmosphere. The rooms vary in size, but all offer lovely views and comfort.

GRANVILLE HOTEL, *1 Meagher Quay, Waterford, Tel. (051) 55111, fax (051) 70307. 74 rooms. Rates for singles: £54, doubles: £44 per person sharing, suite: £100 per room; children under age 12 stay in parents' room free. Rates include breakfast. All major credit cards accepted. No service charge.*

The Granville Hotel is in the center of Waterford on the quay. An old Georgian Hotel from days gone by, it has been lovingly refurbished and meticulously maintained by owners Liam and Ann Cusack and their crack staff. There is a wide variety of rooms available, but some are a little on the small side. The rooms in the front of the hotel offer views of the river, although they suffer a bit from street noise. Children under twelve years of age stay free in their parents' room.

WATERFORD CASTLE, *The Island, Ballinakill, Waterford, Tel. (051) 78203, fax (051) 79316. 19 rooms. Rates for singles: £110 to £150, doubles: £150 to £200, suites: £275. Gardens, indoor swimming pool, tennis, bicycles, golf. All major credit cards accepted. No service charge.*

Just outside Waterford heading towards Dunmore you'll come across Waterford Castle, an 18th-century castle converted to a five-star luxury hotel. Proudly sitting on its own 310 acre island, Waterford Castle is set amid woods and an 18 hole golf course. The hotel is approached via car ferry that takes you across the water to the hotel. Upon landing, you'll get a close-up look at the impressive carved arch and heavy oak doors that serve as the entrance to the hotel.

Inside, the great hall boasts a huge fireplace, the Fitzgerald coat-of-arms woven into the carpet, and dark paneled walls. There's a liberal sprinkling of antiques throughout the hotel, in the public areas as well as in the rooms, which are lavish and spacious, nicely decorated, and comfortably furnished. Virtually all the rooms have attractive views of the water and grounds surrounding the hotel.

WHERE TO EAT

Munster has a number of excellent restaurants, perhaps the largest quantity outside Dublin. Selections below are arranged by county.

MUNSTER'S BEST RESTAURANTS

DOYLE'S SEAFOOD BAR, 4 John Street, Dingle, County Kerry, Tel. (066) 51174. Set dinner menu for £13.50. Diners Club, MasterCard, and Visa accepted. 10% service charge. Doyle's gets my vote for the best seafood restaurant in Ireland.

FLEMINGS, Silver Grange House, Tivoli. Set lunch menu for £13.50, and set dinner menu for £21. All major credit cards accepted. One of the nicest French restaurants in the country, still relatively unknown.

BLUE HAVEN HOTEL RESTAURANT, 3 Pearse Street, Kinsale, Tel. (021) 772209. £12.95 to £21.95. All major credit cards accepted. 10% service charge. Excellent seafood.

ARBUTUS LODGE RESTAURANT, Montenotte, Cork City, Tel. (021) 501237. Set dinner menus for £22.95 and £27.75. All major credit cards accepted. Award-winning fare.

GABY'S SEAFOOD RESTAURANT, 27 High Street, Killarney, Tel. (064) 32519. £10.95 to £24.95. All major credit cards accepted. Considered by many to be the best seafood restaurant in Killarney.

ASSOLAS COUNTRY HOUSE RESTAURANT, Kanturk, Tel. (029) 50015. Set dinner menu for £28.00. All major credit cards accepted. No service charge. Elegant and delightful.

LONGUEVILLE HOUSE PRESIDENTS' RESTAURANT, Mallow, Tel. (022) 47156. Set dinner menu for £28. All major credit cards accepted. Great country restaurant.

LA CASCADE RESTAURANT, Kenmare, Tel. (064) 41600. Set lunch menu for £17.50, set dinner menus for £29.50 and £37.50. A la carte menu also available. All major credit cards accepted. Quiet dining enhanced by lovely views of the falls (flood-lit at night).

EARL OF THOMOND ROOM, Newmarket-on-Fergus, Tel. (061) 368144. Set lunch menu for £18, set dinner menu for £35 and £45. All major credit cards accepted. 15% service charge. The restaurant for Dromoland Castle is exquisite in every detail.

Cork City

FARMGATE CAFE, *Old English Market, Princes Street, Cork City, Tel. (021) 278134. £2.95 to £9.95. Open Monday through Saturday from 8:30 am to 5:30 pm. MasterCard and Visa accepted. No service charge.*

While you're seeing Cork, stop by the Farmgate Cafe above the Old English Market for a bite to eat. This smallish cafe offers a pretty good selection of snacks, breakfast, lunch, and high tea menu items. Breakfast is served until 11:00 am. The freshest ingredients – many of them procured from the Old English Market – are used to enhance the quality and flavor of the simple traditional Irish dishes available. Dress is casual.

REIDY'S WINE VAULTS, *Western Road, Lancaster Quay, Cork City, Tel. (021) 275751. £3.95 to £14.95. Open daily from 10:30 am to 11:30 pm (Sundays from 12:30 pm to 2:00 pm, and 4:00 pm to 11:00 pm). All major credit cards accepted.*

Inside Reidy's is an eclectic collection of styles, from country antiques to modern black and white tiles. The impressive and immense mahogany bar presides over the pub's proceedings. Use Reidy's for a nip, or for a quick bite of their bar food, which is pretty basic but quite good. Home-made soups and sandwiches join steaks, fresh seafood, and chicken on the menu.

BULLY'S, *40 Paul Street, Cork City, Tel. (021) 27355. £7.95 to £10.95. Open Monday through Saturday from noon to 11:30 pm, and Sunday from 1:00 pm to 11:00 pm. No credit cards accepted. No service charge.*

Bully's is sort of a cross between a pizzeria and an Italian fast-food restaurant. The food is good, featuring solid Italian specialties, including pizza, calzone, and a number of home-made pasta and seafood dishes. A few vegetarian dishes are also available.

THE GINGERBREAD HOUSE, *Paul Street, Cork City, Tel. (021) 276411. £2.95 to £14.95. Open Monday through Saturday from 8:15 am to 10:30 pm; they serve dinner from 6:00 pm to 10:30 pm. No credit cards accepted. No service charge.*

For a quick bite while out shopping or sight-seeing, you may want to give Barnaby Blacker's Gingerbread house a try. Open basically all day long, the Gingerbread House has gained some reputation for its excellent pastries and breads (try their home-made carrot cake or French chocolate). They have also developed a decent though limited dinner menu.

ISAAC'S RESTAURANT, *48 MacCurtain Street, Cork City, (021) 503805, £7.95 to £17.95. Open Monday through Saturday for lunch from 12:30 pm to 2:30 pm, and daily for dinner from 6:30 pm to 10:30 pm. All major credit cards accepted.*

This brasserie-style restaurant, part of the hotel/hostel by the same name, is light and bright, and belies the building's beginnings as an 18th-century warehouse. The menu is trendy, and seems to follow no particular cuisine. The offerings range from such mundane fare as minute steak with onions to more exotic offerings like lamb curry with *poppadums* to grilled prawns in garlic butter.

CRAWFORD GALLERY CAFE, *Emmet Place, Cork City, Tel. (021) 274415. £3.95 to £19.95. Open from 9:00 am to 5:00 pm Monday through Saturday. No credit cards accepted.*

The Crawford Gallery is located on the first floor of the Crawford Municipal Art Gallery. It makes a convenient spot to stop for everything from a snack to a full meal before, after, or during your visit to the art gallery. Dress is casual.

BLUE HAVEN HOTEL RESTAURANT, *3 Pearse Street, Kinsale, Tel. (021) 772209. £12.95 to £21.95. Open from 12:30 pm to 3:00 pm for lunch, and from 7:00 pm to 10:30 pm. All major credit cards accepted. 10% service charge.*

The restaurant at the Blue Haven Hotel has earned quite the reputation as an excellent seafood restaurant, which speaks volumes when that restaurant is located in a port town. The atmosphere is elegant – crisply starched Irish linen, china, crystal, and appropriate lighting enhance the flavor and presentation of the meals. The pianist helps continue the tranquil feeling you encounter throughout the hotel. That feeling isn't diminished as you look out the conservatory windows to the flood-lit gardens and fountain.

One of the excellent specialties of the house is Blue Haven thermidor, fish, and miscellaneous seafood cooked in cheese sauce. Other offerings include sole with lemon and parsley butter, or more traditional offerings such as oysters, poached salmon, or sea trout. Even though the specialty is seafood, the chefs do a fine job on other dishes as well, including lamb and beef. Finish off your meal with a selection of fine Irish farmhouse cheeses.

MICHAEL'S BISTRO, *4 Mardyke Street, Cork City, Tel. (021) 276887. £12.95 to £24.95. Open Monday through Saturday for lunch from noon to 3:00 pm, and for dinner from 6:00 pm to 10:30 pm. (They are closed on Monday from mid-October through the end of May.) MasterCard and Visa accepted.*

Just around the corner from Cliffords Restaurant, and owned by the same couple, Michael's offers more of an intimate atmosphere than the more formal Cliffords. The menu here is traditional Irish, with some poetic liberties taken. The fare ranges from such offerings as seafood sausage on a bed of leeks to traditional Irish stew. The dessert and cheese selections are surprisingly good.

JIM EDWARDS PUB AND RESTAURANT, *Market Quay, Kinsale, Tel. (021) 772541. £15 to £24.95. Open for dinner from 6:30 pm to 9:30 pm. All major credit cards accepted. 10% service charge.*

Jim Edwards Pub and Restaurant has successfully bridged the gap between the two enterprises of pub and restaurant. They are noted for excellent seafood as well as fine steaks. The decor is simple, although I found it a little dark, with dark wood tables and greens and reds being the predominant colors. Try the fillet of Irish beef, or any of the local seafood specialties.

IVORY TOWER RESTAURANT, *35 Princes Street, Cork City. £12.95 to £25. Open for lunch daily from noon to 4:00 pm and 6:30 pm to 11:00 pm for dinner. MasterCard and Visa accepted.*

The easy-going and relaxed atmosphere at the Ivory Tower Restaurant is one of the things that makes this a popular dining spot for residents of Cork as well as tourists. The menu is sort of "Irish eclectic," and seems to offer a wide range of fare. Entrees range from scallops and prawns to eel and sushi. Vegetarian dishes are plentiful, and they are well-known for their home-made bread and Irish farmhouse cheeses. Dress is casual.

THE OYSTER TAVERN, *Market Lane, Cork City, Tel. (021) 272716. £14.95 to £24.95. Open Monday through Saturday from 12:30 pm to 2:30 pm and 6:30 pm to 10:30 pm. All major credit cards accepted.*

The Oyster Tavern is a landmark restaurant in Cork City, having served numerous generations of Irish for the past two hundred years. As you walk in, you have the unmistakable feeling of walking into the old Victorian period – dark woodwork, red upholstery, a friendly staff, and decent food. The food itself is not extraordinary, but it's good and filling, and the surroundings are a nice complement. Casual dress is fine.

JACQUES, *9 Phoenix Street, Cork City, Tel. (021) 277387. £14.95 to £24.95. Open Monday through Saturday from 11:30 pm to 3:00 pm and 6:00 pm to 10:30 pm. All major credit cards accepted.*

This brightly colored cafe is a pleasant place to grab a bite to eat. The Barry's run a nice eating establishment, and have gained a good reputation for their breads and Irish cheeses. Sample menu items might include such treats as warm salad of lamb's kidneys, escalope of fresh salmon on a ginger and spinach bed, and a variety of vegetarian dishes.

CLIFFORDS, *40 Paul Street, Cork City, Tel. (021) 275333. Set lunch menu for £11.50, and set dinner menu for £27. Open for dinner Tuesday through Saturday from 7:00 pm to 10:30 pm, and they're open for lunch Tuesday through Friday from 12:30 pm to 2:30 pm. All major credit cards accepted.*

Located on the west side of the city, this elegant modern restaurant in a converted Georgian townhouse is really a treat. The furnishings are simple and the walls are bedecked with contemporary Irish art. The tables are set with crisp Irish linen and a simple floral center-piece.

The food is traditional Irish with a decidedly continental flair. Typical menu items (most of which change monthly) include fresh brace of quail in a honey and cider vinegar sauce, pan-fried brill with mussels, noisettes of spring lamb with confit of baby onion, and black sole and prawns in a pepper and lime sauce.

ARBUTUS LODGE RESTAURANT, *Montenotte, Cork City, Tel. (021) 501237. Set dinner menus for £22.95 and £27.75. Open Monday through Saturday from 1:00 pm to 2:00 pm, and from 7:00 pm to 9:30 pm. All major credit cards accepted.*

The restaurant for Arbutus Lodge is considered one of the ten finest in Ireland by most food critics. Traditional Irish food prepared with care and presented with an artistic flair all topped by outstanding service are hallmarks of the restaurant. From seafood to steak, lobster to lamb, all the meals are cooked with fresh ingredients, many of them from Arbutus Lodge's own kitchen garden.

Hungry for seafood? Try their pan-fried mussels with a walnut and garlic dip, or perhaps you'd prefer Irish beef. If that's the case, try their spiced beef with chutney or fillet of steak. If it's wild game you'd like, there's always the roast venison with raspberry coulis, or the chartreuse of pigeon and rabbit with fresh chanterelle sauce. As a bonus that you don't get in many upscale restaurants in Ireland, the portions are large enough to satisfy you.

County Clare

AN FEAR GORTA – THE TEA ROOMS, *Ballyvaughan, Tel. (065) 77023. £4.95 to £9.95. Open Monday through Saturday from 11:00 am to 5:30 pm, June through the end of September. No credit cards accepted. No service charge.*

This tea room offers an eclectic collection of furniture and snack items for weary travelers. Scones, pastries, Irish cheeses, soups, salads, and a few light seafood lunches are available.

FLEMINGS, *Silver Grange House, Tivoli, , set lunch menu for £13.50, and set dinner menu for £21. Open daily from 12:30 pm to 2:30 pm for lunch, and from 6:30 pm to 10:30 pm for dinner. All major credit cards accepted.*

This is one of the nicest French restaurants in the country, and as yet it is still relatively unknown. Michael Fleming, owner and chef of Flemings, cooks up sumptuous offerings, from traditional French to his own delicious concoctions. You might be tempted by baby clams poached in a champagne sauce, pan-fried frog's legs with shallots on an apple and potato gallette, or bran-coated marinated mussels with an orange cream sauce. If your high school French fails to help you decipher the menu (which is written in French), don't despair – English translations are provided. The wine list aims for quality rather than quantity, and I doubt you'll be disappointed. A jacket is requested.

GREGAN'S CASTLE RESTAURANT, *Ballyvaughan, Tel. (065) 77005. Set dinner menu for £28. Open daily from 7:00 pm to 8:30 pm. Like the hotel, the restaurant is closed from mid-October through Easter. All major credit cards accepted. 15% service charge.*

Gregan's Castle restaurant is a dining delight (once you get past the unappetizing mustard-colored walls!). Gregan's touts the fact that they use only the freshest local ingredients for their meals, from local seafood, lamb, and beef to fresh herbs and vegetables. In addition, locally made farmhouse cheeses are available to tempt you.

EARL OF THOMOND ROOM, *Newmarket-on-Fergus, Tel. (061) 368144. Set lunch menu for £18, set dinner menu for £35 and £45. Open for lunch from 12:30 pm to 2:00 pm, and for dinner from 7:30 pm to 9:30 pm. All major credit cards accepted. 15% service charge.*

I was totally captivated by this restaurant associated with Dromoland Castle. High ceilings, rich dark wood, gorgeous crystal chandeliers, crisp starched linen tablecloths, gleaming china, and Irish harpists, singers, or fiddlers all contribute to the elegance and even opulence of the dining experience in the Earl of Thomond Room. As you dine, the watchful eyes of the former Lords and Ladies of the castle gaze down at you from larger-than-life portraits spread around the room. Doubtless their expectations are as high as yours, as their stern expressions show.

The menu is beyond exquisite, and the food exceeds all expectations. Typical offerings include picatta of milk-fed veal in classic "Nicoise" style, pan-fried fillet of John Dory set upon a nage of leeks and mushrooms, or perhaps even terrine of Dromoland estate venison with fig chutney. All are tastefully presented, and the service is impeccable and personalized without being overbearing. Jacket and tie are required to dine here.

County Cork

AHERNE'S SEAFOOD RESTAURANT, *163 North Main Street, Youghal, Tel. (024) 92424. £4.95 to £14.95. All major credit cards accepted.*

Aherne's came to my attention after several tourists I spoke with strongly recommended that I not miss it. Their praise was exuberant. When I showed up at Aherne's, I could see why they were ebullient. As a port city, you'd expect one of the top restaurants in the area to specialize in seafood, and they don't disappoint you. The selection is extensive and varied, and just the sound of the dishes spurs your appetite: prawns in garlic butter or hot creamed oysters, Youghal Bay Lobster, smoked salmon and pasta, grilled black sole, or plaice stuffed with oysters in a red wine sauce are just a few of the choices in this wonderful restaurant.

All in all, you won't go wrong with Aherne's if you like seafood. If not, there are also a few token dishes for meat-eaters.

RESTAURANT IN BLUE, *Crookhaven Road, Schull, Tel. (028) 28305. Set dinner menu for £22.50. Open Monday through Saturday from 7:15 pm to 9:45 pm. (During the off-season they are only open Thursday through Saturday evenings.) All major credit cards accepted. No service charge.*

The tiny town of Schull is home to the smallish Restaurant in Blue. This delightful cottage-style restaurant is furnished with antiques and provides a perfect setting for dinner. The menu is decidedly Irish, with numerous seafood selections, pork and lamb, and good Irish beef. Local cheeses are also available. Dress is nice casual.

LOVETT'S, *Churchyard Lane, Douglas, Tel. (021) 94909. Set lunch menu for £14.50, and set dinner menu for £24. Open Monday through Saturday for dinner from 7:00 pm to 9:45 pm, or for lunch Monday through Friday from 12:30 pm until 2:00 pm. All major credit cards accepted.*

Lovett's has a loyal following from the residents of Cork, and many tourists as well. And with good reason: it's difficult to know whether its popularity flows from Dermod Lovett's warm Irish welcome or the fine food prepared by his wife Margaret. Probably both contribute to their success. The menu is extensive, and features excellent seafood, beef, and vegetarian choices. Typical offerings might include grilled black sole with lemon butter, roast rack of spring Cork lamb, or poached salmon. All the ingredients are fresh, most coming from the local countryside.

LONGUEVILLE HOUSE PRESIDENTS' RESTAURANT, *Mallow, Tel. (022) 47156. Set dinner menu for £28. Open daily for dinner from 7:00 pm to 9:00 pm. Reservations are needed from June through August. If you'd like to stop by for lunch, Sunday is the only day they serve it, and they are open for lunch from noon until 1:45 pm. All major credit cards accepted.*

Try to eat at this elegant country restaurant. On the walls surrounding the dining area are the somber portraits of former Irish Presidents overseeing the service and food in the dining room. They needn't be concerned: the food is exquisite, the service impeccable, and the experience memorable. The freshness, ingenuity, and interesting combinations of delicious edibles all combine to make your dining an event rather than just another meal.

Part of the success of the restaurant is Chef William O'Callaghan's insistence on the freshest ingredients; indeed, many of the vegetables, fruits, herbs, lamb, and salmon come from within a few hundred yards of the house. The others come from nearby farms and waters.

Mr. O'Callaghan tempts his guests with a wide variety of exceptional offerings, including an ever-popular Surprise Taste Menu, which is a seven course treat. Other tempting specialties include such favorites as roast of Longueville lamb with a gratin of turnips, pan-fried medallions of monkfish, or Kilbrack pork. Desserts will leave you dreaming of those you couldn't order – you may decide to come back another day just for a new dessert! Longueville House is renowned for their pyramid of chocolate with an enchanting orange sauce.

All in all, you may not wish to pass this restaurant by. Jacket and tie are requested.

ASSOLAS COUNTRY HOUSE RESTAURANT, *Kanturk, Tel. (029) 50015. Set dinner menu for £28. Open daily from 7:00 pm to 8:30 pm. All major credit cards accepted. No service charge.*

The restaurant at Assolas Country House is elegant and delightful. The fruits and vegetables you eat, and the herbs that impart such magnificent subtleties of taste to the food, are all grown within the kitchen garden for Assolas Country House. The menu changes daily, but the quality is always the same. Typical offerings may include fillet of brill oven-baked in a basil butter sauce, Kenmare mussels, sautéed oysters with shallots and cream in brioche, and confit of duck. If wild game is your preference, several options are available, including venison, and at times pheasant or quail. Dress is nice casual.

BALLYMALOE HOUSE RESTAURANT, *Shanagarry, Tel. (021) 652531. Set dinner menu for £30. Open daily for lunch from 12:30 pm to 2:00 pm, and for dinner from 7:00 pm to 9:30 pm. All major credit cards accepted.*

The restaurant for Ballymaloe House is open to the public, and that's fortunate for all of us. Chef Rory O'Connell works wonders with the traditional Irish food prepared with a continental flair. The menu isn't extensive, but the food is marvelous, relying on only the freshest local produce and meats – much of which comes from Ballymaloe farm itself. Typical fare includes Shanagarry pork with apple sauce and broccoli, grilled sirloin with béarnaise sauce and fried onions, and a rich variety of farmhouse cheeses from throughout County Cork. Following the main course, the dessert trolley will tempt the most prodigious dieter. The set lunch menu is £16.50 and dinner is £30. Dress is nice casual.

County Kerry
DOYLE'S SEAFOOD BAR, *4 John Street, Dingle, County Kerry, Tel. (066) 51174. Set dinner menu for £13.50. Diners Club, MasterCard, and Visa accepted. 10% service charge.*

Doyle's gets my vote for the best seafood restaurant in Ireland. The setting isn't bad either, out on the Dingle Peninsula. John and Stella Doyle have been cooking seafood for the local populace and tourists since the 1970s. Doyle's combines a homey atmosphere with fresh and exceptionally prepared seafood. One of their specialty dishes is millefeuille of warm oysters with Guinness sauce, a dish that has brought them international attention. Other dishes include baked lemon sole, mussels in herb and garlic sauce, and fried scallops. All in all, if you are a seafood *aficionado*, this is an excellent restaurant for you.

FOLEY'S TOWN HOUSE, *23 High Street, Killarney, Tel. (064) 31217. £10.50 to £25. Open daily from 5:00 pm to 11:00 pm. Bar food is available from 12:30 pm to 3:00 pm. American Express, MasterCard, and Visa accepted. No service charge.*

Foley's has been an institution in the Killarney area for nearly fifty years. By comparison, even though the present owners are new in the business – they've *only* been at it since 1967 – they bring a great deal of knowledge and expertise to the table. While the specialty is seafood, there is also a good selection of beef and lamb dishes. Typical offerings include crab claws in garlic butter, lobster bisque, smoked salmon, fillet of steak, herb-stuffed fillet of pork with creamy apricot sauce, or roast duckling. Add to these dishes an appetizing dessert cart and a surprisingly good wine list, and you have a winner. Dress is casual.

GABY'S SEAFOOD RESTAURANT, *27 High Street, Killarney, Tel. (064) 32519. £10.95 to £24.95. Open for lunch Tuesday through Saturday from 12:30 pm to 2:30 pm, and for dinner Monday through Saturday from 6:00 pm until 10:00 pm. All major credit cards accepted.*

Gaby's is considered by many to be the best seafood restaurant in Killarney, although nearby Foley's gives it a run for its money. Geert and Marie Maes have over twenty years experience in the seafood restaurant business, and it shows. Fresh local produce enhances the offerings of the day. The seafood portion of the menu changes daily, depending on the success of the local fishermen. Possible offerings include salmon salad, Kerry seafood platter, and Lobster Gaby in cognac, wine, and cream sauce. They have an extensive wine list. Gaby's has garnered many local and national awards over the years.

LA CASCADE RESTAURANT, *Kenmare, Tel. (064) 41600. Set lunch menu for £17.50, set dinner menus for £29.50 and £37.50. A la carte menu also available. Open Monday through Friday from 11:00 am to 1:00 pm, Sunday from 1:00 pm to 2:00 pm, and daily for dinner from 7:30 pm to 9:30 pm. All major credit cards accepted.*

The restaurant for Sheen Falls Lodge is wonderful. Quiet dining is enhanced by lovely views of the falls (flood-lit at night). The style is contemporary Irish with a heavy continental influence. You can enjoy a good selection of vegetarian dishes, but the real specialties are salmon, fillet of Irish beef, and some excellent wild dishes, including venison and quail. The restaurant has earned a well-deserved reputation for its fine wine list. Their farmhouse cheeses from the area are also quite good.

PARK HOTEL RESTAURANT, *Kenmare, Tel. (064) 41200. Set dinner menus for £31.80 and £45. Open from 7:00 pm to 8:45 pm. Reservations are a must from June through August. All major credit cards accepted.*

For an adventure in fine dining, try the restaurant at Park Hotel Kenmare. The dining room is pleasantly situated at the back of the hotel, offering views of the hotel's gardens and grounds, extending to Kenmare Bay in the short distance. The atmosphere is a combination between relaxed and elegant. The tables are set with crisp Irish linen, china, and gleaming silver.

But the real treat is the menu. Chef Bruno Schmidt has crafted a series of masterpieces: subtle influences of herbs and sauces complement the natural freshness and presentation of each course. Sample menu items include roast salad of quail with Parma ham, grilled fillet of beef studded with truffles fricassee of wild mushrooms. The dessert menu offers a number of tempting delicacies. The wine list is extensive, and offers a wide range of wines from France, California, Australia and Italy.

Jacket and tie are required for dining. The restaurant, like the hotel, is only open from mid-April through mid-November.

County Limerick
COPPER ROOM, *Ennis Road, Limerick City, Tel. (061) 327777. £9.95 to £16.95. Open from 6:30 pm until 10:00 pm. All major credit cards accepted. 10% service charge.*

The main restaurant for the Jury's Hotel in Limerick, the Copper Room is a pleasant, bright eatery. Bright colors are a nice contrast to the rich dark wood used on the walls. The food is not particularly memorable, but it's good enough for a quick meal and reasonably priced. Dress is casual but nice.

SEEING THE SIGHTS
Cork City
Next to Dublin, **Cork** is one of the most widely recognized Irish city names around the world. Compared to Dublin, it's a little more cramped, confusing to get around in, and, well, a big city. But this third-largest Irish city is rich in history and pride.

Originally granted its city charter over eight hundred years ago (1185), Cork's importance in Ireland's history has waxed and waned. Cork's Irish name, *Corcaigh*, means "marshy place." Perhaps it once was, but the marshlands were drained to make way for the city. It was originally built along the banks of the River Lee, but over the years it has grown upwards onto the hills on the north and south sides of the river. Its deep harbors served to ensure Cork's importance as a port city.

Cork City lies between and along the banks of the **River Lee**. As the River Lee flows into the valley where Cork sits, it splits into two channels. Centuries ago, the marshy area between the north and south channels were filled in, and the city grew between those channels. But the River Lee was unable to contain the booming city, and long ago the city spread north and south beyond the confines of the River and up the hills that flowed down to the river.

Today, Cork is a busy metropolis with lots of traffic, pedestrians, and one-way streets. The best way to see Cork is to find a carpark and explore the city's sights by foot. Most of the sights are in an area a little over a mile

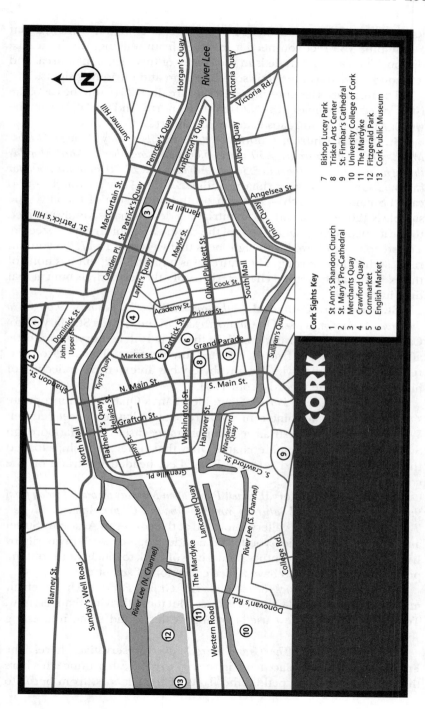

CORK

Cork Sights Key

1 St Ann's Shandon Church
2 St. Mary's Pro-Cathedral
3 Merchants Quay
4 Crawford Quay
5 Cornmarket
6 English Market
7 Bishop Lucey Park
8 Triskel Arts Center
9 St. Finnbar's Cathedral
10 University College of Cork
11 The Mardyke
12 Fitzgerald Park
13 Cork Public Museum

long and a half mile wide. Buses frequently criss-cross this section, and if at any time you feel you need a breather from walking, they're a nice option. The **Grand Parade** is in the center of this rectangular area, and is a good place to center your search for fun and intriquing sights.

The main arteries entering Cork City are the N25 (from the east), the N8 (from the northeast), the N20 (from the north) and the N22 (from the west). All these main roads lead into the heart of Cork City.

St. Anne's Church, *Church Street, Cork, open May through October Monday through Saturday 9:30 am to 5:00 pm, November to April Monday through Saturday 10:00 am to 3:30 pm. Admission is £1.50 for adults, 60p for children.* One of Cork's primary landmarks, St. Anne's Church – also called Shandon Church – sits high on the north side of the city. The steeple is 120 feet tall, and has an intriguing design that is fondly referred to as the "pepperpot." Nice views of the city are available from the steeple. The steeple is endowed with eight bells that were cast in 1750 – you can request that they be rung. The church was built in 1722, but has none of the exquisite architectural characteristics of other cathedrals built at that time in Ireland.

St. Mary's Pro-Cathedral, *Cathedral Walk, Cork, open daily 9:00 am to 6:00 pm. Admission is free.* On the north side of the city sits St. Mary's Pro-Cathedral. The cathedral was built in the early 19th century, and shortly afterward suffered a fire that gutted the interior. The interior was renovated in Gothic style. The presbytery has an extensive collection of birth and marriage records from 1784.

Merchant's Quay, *Patrick Street.* Merchant's Quay is an appropriate site for the large shopping center that resides on Patrick Street between Winthrop Street (a pedestrianized shopping street itself), and Marlborough Street. It was here along Merchants Quay that yesteryear's ships loaded their cargo and slipped into the River Lee, headed for trade on the continent.

Crawford Art Gallery, *Emmett Place, open Monday through Friday from 9:00 am to 5:00 pm, and Saturday from 9:00 am to 1:00 pm. Admission is free. Tel. (021) 273377.* The gallery is located at the corner of Academy Street and Emmet Place. Inside you'll find a wide range of work primarily by Irish artists, from 18th-century renderings of Cork to much more contemporary works. They also have a nice collection of sculptures.

Cornmarket, *Patrick Street and The Grand Parade.* The open-air market known as "Coal-Quay" was once a lot more thriving than it is now. Today, you'll find a few used-clothing dealers amid some interesting shops.

English Market, *The Grand Parade.* No preservatives here! The English Market is the place to go in the city to get fresh produce. It's here that the local farmers peddle the fruits of their labors, from herbs to vegetables to chicken, beef, tripe, drisheen, etc. It's a busy place that has changed very little over the centuries.

Bishop Lucey Park, *The Grand Parade*. Bishop Lucey Park is an oasis of green in the city. Among other things, the small park features the statuesque work of local Cork artisans.

Triskel Arts Center, *Tobin Street, open Monday through Friday from 11:00 am to 6:00 pm, and Saturday from 11:00 am to 5:00 pm. Admission is free. Tel. (021) 272022.* This small arts center is tucked away down an alley (watch for the signpost), and presents small but interesting exhibitions of modern art and crafts. Spend a few minutes here (that's all it will take) admiring the works of various artists, mostly local.

St. Finbarr Cathedral, *Bishop Street, open daily from 9:00 am to 6:00 pm. Admission is free.* Three steeples mark the Gothic St. Finbarr's Cathedral, sitting quietly in the southwest portion of the city. St. Finbarr established a monastery on this site over 1,300 years ago, and the Church of Ireland cathedral now bears his name. This cathedral was built in the 19th century.

University College Cork, *open Monday through Friday from 9:00 am to 5:00 pm. Tel. (021) 276871.* The University College of Cork sits along the River Lee in scholastic reverence. Most of the University's buildings were built in the 19th century, and sport the Tudor-Gothic style of architecture.

Walking tours of the college grounds and some of its buildings are available from mid-June through the end of August. During other times of the year, you are free to wander the campus and see the sights for yourself, or you can arrange for a tour by calling the university's main number. Rates for the tours are £2.50 for adults, 75p for children, or £6 for a family ticket.

The tour will take you into the main quadrangle building, where you'll see a number of historical exhibits. The tour also incorporates the **Republican Grave Plot**, a cemetery for those rebels who gave their lives through the years struggling for Ireland's independence.

The Mardyke. In the eastern part of the city center lies the green-belt area known simply as The Mardyke. It is a favorite place for riverside strolls, frisbee tossing, and people-watching. On the weekends, you may be fortunate enough to catch a game of cricket being played.

Fitzgerald's Park. Just to the east of The Mardyke and sprawling along the River Lee is spacious Fitzgerald Park. This is a popular spot for mothers walking their babies in prams (strollers), young men and women walking hand-in-hand or talking quietly on the grass, and kids running and jumping around.

Cork Public Museum, *open Monday through Friday from 11:00 am to 5:00 pm, and Sunday 3:00 pm to 5:00 pm. Tel. (021) 270679.* The Cork Public Museum is housed in an old Georgian Mansion in Fitzgerald Park. It isn't particularly large, but it contains a nice amount of information and exhibits that chronicle Cork's history.

As you tour the museum, you'll view exhibits that tout Cork's role in their centuries-long struggle for Irish independence. You'll learn of Cork's mayor, Terence MacSwiney, who felt so deeply about the cause that he died after a hunger strike of seventy-five days in 1920. Another exhibit features Michael Collins, the hard-as-nails Director of Intelligence for the IRA during the years that eventually led to Ireland's freedom. Among other things, Collins is credited with eliminating informers in the IRA and placing his own informers in Dublin Castle, the seat of English power in Ireland.

Elsewhere in County Cork

Blarney Castle & Blarney Stone, *Blarney. Open in May on Monday through Saturday from 9:00 am to 6:30 pm, June through August Monday through Saturday from 9:00 am to 7:00 pm, September Monday through Saturday from 9:00 am to 6:30 pm, and October through April Monday through Saturday from 9:00 am until sundown. They are also open year round on Sunday from 9:30 am to 5:30 pm. Admission is £3 for adults, £2 for senior citizens and £1 for children (children under 8 are free). Tel. (021) 385252.* Five miles north of Cork City is the town of Blarney and its famous stone. Before my first visit to Ireland, I had no idea the Blarney *Stone* was part of Blarney *Castle*. The famous stone is located atop the ancient keep underneath its battlements.

To kiss the stone – which legend says grants the kisser the gift of *blarney*, or flattery – you lay on your back and slide down and under the battlements. Locals are positioned to give you a hand. (They would appreciate a tip. After all – they do keep you from falling on your head!) One hundred and twenty-ish steps up a spiral staircase will precede your kiss. The castle and surrounding grounds are delightful. Be prepared to wait in line during the peak tourist season (June to September). But the grounds are pretty, so relax, enjoy yourself, and meet the people around you.

Cormac McCarthy, Lord of Blarney Castle, was a renowned negotiator and flatterer. On one occasion, an exasperated Queen Elizabeth I declared of McCarthy's honeyed words and crafty negotiations: "This is nothing but Blarney – what he says, he never means!"

Almost lost in the excitement of kissing the Blarney Stone is Blarney Castle itself. A massive square keep, it stands now as a mere shell of the impressive structure it must have been in its younger days. Its history, like so many other castles in Ireland, is pock-marked with sieges, attacks, and burnings. Cromwell visited here, as did William of Orange after the Battle of the Boyne.

There is a large home and breathtaking gardens adjacent to Blarney Castle that you can tour for an additional £2.50. These, however, are only open from mid-June through September.

Blarney Town itself is one of the few places in Ireland that look and feel like a tourist trap. Thankfully, this only holds for the town itself; the castle and stone are set in a lovely demesne (estate) that keeps them solitary and apart from the rest of the town.

Blackrock Castle, *Blackrock, near Cork City*. At the edge of town in the small village of Blackrock stands Blackrock Castle. Sitting on a small jetty that juts into the River Lee just as it widens into Lough Mahon, this 16th century castle was spruced up in the 19th century and now serves the area as a pub and restaurant.

Fota Demesne and Wildlife Park, *near Cork City, open from mid-March through the end of October Monday through Saturday from 10:00 am to 6:00 pm, and Sunday from 11:00 am to 6:00 pm. Admission is £3.30 for adults, £3 for students, and £2 for senior citizens and children. The car park costs £1, but includes entrance to the arboretum and gardens. Tel. (021) 812678.* Kind of a mini-San Diego Zoo, the Fota Wildlife Park is a seventy acre open-air zoo, where many of the tamer animals roam free. You can see emus and ostriches, zebras, giraffes, monkeys, flamingos and kangaroos. The more dangerous animals, such as the cheetahs, do not have free run of the zoo, for obvious reasons.

In addition to the wildlife park, there is a lovely arboretum, which boasts a wide variety of trees, including a significant number that have been imported from all over the world. There is also a fine collection of Irish landscape paintings.

Barryscourt Castle, *Carrigtwohill, near Cobh, open daily from 11:00 am to 6:00 pm. Admission is free. Tel. (021) 883864.* Watch for the signposts directing you to Barryscourt Castle, a 13th-century castle. It's an interesting old structure.

Cobh Town. Cobh (pronounced "cove") is unalterably associated with three grand marine catastrophes in Irish history. This small town (current population around 6,200), lived in the memories of a generation of Irish immigrants, for it was from tiny Cobh that hundreds of thousands of starving Irish left farms, families, and certain death during the Great Potato Famine in 1845 through 1847. Most of them were headed for America and a fresh start.

A scant sixty years later another maritime tragedy involved Cobh as the *Lusitania* was sunk in 1915 (ostensibly) by German U-boats not far from Cobh's harbor. Every available boat, dory, dingy and skiff was pressed into service in an effort to retrieve survivors of the attack. Hundreds of the victims of the disaster are buried in the Old Church Cemetery in Cobh, and a memorial to them stands on the quay.

And finally, one last disaster of titanic proportions had roots in Ireland as well as Cobh. The oceanliner *Titanic* was built in the shipyards of Belfast, and Cobh was its last port-of-call before sailing to its watery fate. So if you're the least bit superstitious, you may not want to take the ferry to Cobh!

Roche's Point, *near Cobh*. Five miles away from Cobh, looking out to the Celtic Sea, is Rochestown Point, a picturesque white-washed lighthouse sitting alongside several houses.

The Queenstown Project, *Cobh railway station, open February through November daily from 10:00 am to 6:00 pm. Admission is £3 for adults, £2.50 for senior citizens and children. Tel. (021) 813591.* This new heritage center in an old building (the old railway station) contains a maritime museum that primarily chronicles the experience Irish immigrants had as they bid the Emerald Isle farewell over the past several hundred years. Two well-done exhibits focus on the sea disasters associated with the *Lusitania* and the *Titanic*, both of which touched the town and lives of the residents of Cobh. The name Queenstown was the name Cobh carried from 1849 until 1922, in commemoration of a visit by **Queen Victoria** in 1849. The name Cobh was reclaimed after independence, meaning "The Haven" in Irish.

Kinsale. The Irish name for Kinsale is *Ceann Saile*, which means "Tide Head," and alerts you that Kinsale is a seaport town. The town is a tidy affair of narrow winding streets, Georgian homes, quays, sea breezes, and intriguing ruins. For hundreds of years Kinsale was an important seaport, until the size and draft of ships overcame the ability to use the harbor in the 18th century. At that point, Kinsale was relegated to serving the fishing industry.

One Kinsalean who made good was William Penn, founder of the state of Pennsylvania. William's father served as the governor of Kinsale, and William was a clerk of the Admiralty Court prior to seeking his fortune in the new world.

In recent years, Kinsale has rebounded by offering tourists a clean picturesque harbor town, noted for deep-sea fishing trips and fine seafood restaurants. (see the *Where to Eat* section for County Cork). If you're game, the Kinsale office of *Bord Failte* offers a booklet (£1) that will direct you into some of the more interesting nooks and crannies in town.

Kinsale Museum, *The Old Courthouse, Market Place, open Monday through Saturday from 11:00 am to 5:00 pm, and Sunday from 3:00 pm to 5:00 pm. Admission is (£1). Tel. (021) 772144.* The smallish Kinsale Museum has a number of interesting exhibits highlighting the history of Kinsale. Learn of the time the Irish and Spanish joined forces to fight the English who were garrisoned at Kinsale (the English won). There is also an interesting display about the Lusitania, which was sunk nearby.

Desmond Castle, *Cork Street, Tel. (021) 774855. Open mid-April to mid-June on Tuesday from 10:00 am to 1:00 pm and Sunday from 2:00 pm to 5:00 pm; mid-June to mid-September daily from 9:00 am to 6:00 pm, and mid-September to early October Monday through Saturday from 9:00 am to 5:00 pm, and Sunday from 10:00 am to 5:00 pm. Admission is £1 for adults, 40p for children, and there is a family ticket for £3.* The three-story square keep on Cork Street is Desmond Castle, or as it's also known, the French Prison. Built in 1500 to serve as the residence of the Earl of Desmond, Desmond Castle has served a variety of uses over the centuries.

When the Spanish descended upon Kinsale in 1601, the castle was found to be an excellent location to house soldiers; it was used as a place to house American prisoners of war during the American Revolution; and it was used as a prison for French seamen during 1754 when it caught fire, killing fifty-four prisoners. During the Great Potato Famine, it was used as a workhouse (like a soup kitchen) to provide relief for the starving population of Kinsale.

Today, you can see a number of exhibits dealing with Kinsale's history and the uses Desmond House saw during its first three centuries.

Charles Fort, *near Summer Cove, open mid-June through mid-September daily from 10:00 am to 6:30 pm, mid-April through mid-June on Tuesday through Saturday from 10:00 am to 5:00 pm, and Sunday from 2:00 pm to 5:00 pm, and mid-September through mid-April Monday through Friday from 8:00 am to 4:30 pm. Admission is £2 for adults and £1 for senior citizens and children. Tel. (021) 772684.* From Kinsale, get back on the Kinsale-Cork road and watch for the signposts directing you to Charles Fort. This hilltop fort is nearly four hundred years old, and covers nearly twelve acres. Guided tours are offered during the summer months.

Old Head, *near Kinsale.* An ancient castle once belonging to the de Courcy family sits atop Old Head outside of Kinsale. The views from here are splendid, and the site is quietly romantic. Farther out on the end of Old Head is a lighthouse.

Ballinspittle. Ballinspittle's main claim to fame is a grotto containing a statue of the Virgin Mary – nothing extraordinary, especially in this heavily Catholic country. But in 1985, a local lass claimed to have seen the statue rocking back and forth. She ran home and told her family and others, who returned and witnessed the same thing. The incident was reported in the county newspaper, *The Cork Examiner,* and the grotto was suddenly deluged with pilgrims. Thousands reported seeing the statue move as a result of the pilgrimage. Unfortunately, vandals destroyed the statue, and its replacement has been as still as a statue since that time. But many still journey here to see it.

Timoleague. Timoleague is on the R600 west of Kinsale. The Irish name for Timoleague means the "House of Molaga," and is named after

St. Molaga, who founded a monastery here. The ruins located there are of a 14th-century Franciscan friary.

Timoleague Castle Gardens, *Timoleague, open Easter weekend, then from mid-May through September daily from noon until 6:00 pm. Admission is £2 for adults and £1 for senior citizens and children. Tel. (023) 46116.* While Timoleague Castle is no longer around, visitors can still enjoy the gardens that originally graced its grounds.

Courtmacsherry. Courtmacsherry sits at the edge of Courtmacsherry Bay on the R601 southwest of Kinsale. This pretty little town with the big name offers several nice beaches, boat rides out into the bay, and fishing. If you are continuing southwest in County Cork, cling to the sea and follow the R601 through Butlerstown and on into Clonakilty and you'll be treated to some lovely views.

Clonakilty. Clonakilty is at the confluence of the R588, R601, and the R600 as it comes from Timoleague. The Irish name for this town of 2,400 is *Clanna Chaoilte*, which means "O'Keelty's Clan." Clonakilty caters, as most Irish towns do, to tourists. The image they present is squeaky-clean, and the small market town has a pleasant and energetic feel to it. While it's not as popular as Killarney, it has been discovered by tourists the last few years, and the slightly slower pace (and lighter traffic!) is nice.

Near Clonakilty are several enjoyable beaches if you'd like to get out of the car and walk in the sea breeze. Watch for the signpost directing you south of Clonakilty to **Inchadoney**, where you'll find a pretty sandy beach.

Castletownshend. Castletownshend lies southeast of Skibbereen on the R596. If you're coming from Clonakilty, take the R600 to Rosscarbery, then the R597 until it dead-ends into the R596, then turn left for Castletownshend – but it's really easier just to watch for the signpost directing you there.

Castletownshend is renowned as the home of Edith Somerville and Martin Ross, two writers who collaborated on the popular *Tales of an Irish Resident Magistrate*. If that doesn't interest you, then perhaps the town's main street that plunges precipitously toward the sea will. If you're a naval history buff, you might be interested to know that the Castletownshend harbor was the site of a ferocious sea battle between a host of Spanish and English ships in 1602.

Baltimore. Baltimore lies south of Skibbereen on a small peninsula (watch for signposts south of Skibbereenon on the R596). The sleepy image that Baltimore portrays belies a turbulent past. Witness the ruins of O'Driscoll Castle on a rocky outcropping above the harbor, or reflect on the 1631 sack of the village by Algerian pirates. Residents were slaughtered, and several hundred villagers were shipped to north Africa to serve as slaves. Today the village is a lot quieter, offering visitors such tranquil activities as sailing, fishing, and strolling.

Sherkin Island. Just off-shore from Baltimore is Sherkin Island. Quiet beaches are one of the attractions to this sparsely populated island; there are also the ruins of an ancient Franciscan abbey and an old castle. Ferries run several times a day from Baltimore.

Cape Clear Island. Cape Clear Island has the distinction of being the southernmost point in Ireland. It's also a *Gaeltacht* (Irish speaking area). The ferry ride from Baltimore takes an hour, and offers some splendid scenery on the ride out. The main activity on the island (besides chasing your hat) is the extensive colonies of birds that draw flocks of bird-watchers here. In addition to the omnipresent gulls, cormorants, and puffins, there are a number of rare species of feathered attractions. The facilities on the island are spartan in the event you choose to stay.

Skibbereen. Skibbereen is located on the N71 between Rosscarbery and Bantry. While the name sounds so classically Irish, the town of Skibbereen doesn't have a lot else to draw (or keep) tourists inside its town limits, aside from a few shops.

While Skibereen may not be a big draw for tourists today, it did produce a number of brave souls who fought valiantly for Ireland's independence during the Elizabethan and Cromwellian periods. Two of the most notable were also two of the least likely: Bishop Owen MacEgan, who lost his life against Elizabethan soldiers during a battle in 1602, and Bishop Boetius MacEgan, who was hanged in 1650 after an unsuccessful encounter with Cromwell's troops.

Bantry. This small town on the N71 sitting near the head of Bantry Bay is worth a visit, if for no other reason than to see the pretty bay. In the middle of the bay is **Whiddy Island**, and from views above Bantry it is easy to see old fortifications still in existence on the island.

Bantry's Irish name is Beanntraighe, which means "Descendants of Beann." The primary industry in Bantry for generations upon generations has been fishing. In the center of town on the main square is a statue of St. Brendan the Navigator. Many prayers have been directed to this saint for the return of loved ones who were on the waters in search of fish. (Legend says that St. Brendan found America a mere seven hundred years before Columbus.)

Bantry House, *Bantry Road, Bantry, open daily 9:00 am to 6:00 pm (later during the summer). Admission is £3 for adults, £1.75 for students and senior citizens, and free for children under 14. (027) 50047.* On the southern outskirts of Bantry proudly sits Bantry House, a beautiful mansion sitting amid beautiful gardens looking out to sea. The gardens offer a variety of plant life on their terraced levels. The best views are from the highest terrace. The house itself was built in the early 18th century, and offers lovely period furnishings, statuary, and most impressive are some ancient tapestries. They also have an eclectic European art collection.

The Bantry 1796 French Armada Exhibition Center, *Bantry House, open 10:00 am until 6:00 pm daily. Admission is £2.50 for adults, £1.50 for senior citizens and students, and free for children under 14. There is a family ticket available for £5. Joint ticket for the Armada Exhibition and Bantry House at £4.50 for adults and £3 for students. Tel. (027) 51796.*

In the courtyard of Bantry House is an exhibit that memorializes the attempted French rescue of Ireland from the British. In 1796, **Wolfe Tone** had been successful in persuading the French to send an invasion force of over 15,000 men to assist in rousting British troops from the Emerald Isle. Nearly fifty warships left Brest, France, for Bantry Bay. Unfortunately for the Irish, fierce storms arose and sunk almost one-fourth of the ships and the men on them. One of the unfortunate ships was the frigate *Surveillante*, which was no longer seaworthy as a result of the storms. It was scuttled off Whiddy Island. One of the highlights of the exhibit is the cross-sectional scale model of the frigate.

During this period, Wolfe Tone kept a very detailed journal, and it has delighted historians: it sheds light on the sequence of events that took place in the grand scheme gone awry due to the uncertainties of the sea. Excerpts from his journal are on display.

Glengariff. Head north out of Bantry on the N71 and you'll find the town of Glengariff, a pretty little village (population around 250) situated amid a pretty forest glen. Its Irish name is *Gleann Garbh*, which means "Rugged Glen." A harbor town, Glengariff lies at the head of a long valley that is the River Glengariff's final fling before emptying into Bantry Bay. As you might expect, Glengariff was once a fishing village; nowadays they have found that catching tourists is far more profitable! Pretty much the entire village caters to tourists in one way or another. Shops, restaurants, and hotels are plentiful here.

The warm Gulf Stream makes Glengariff a bit of an oddity here in Ireland – the warm winds foster a very pleasant climate, and the local flora responds well. You can see a number of normally semi-tropical plants here: fuchsia, arbutus, yews, hollies, magnolias, rhododendrons, camellias, and others. There are a number of serene wooded walks available. Ask at the post office for directions to the Poulgorm, Cromwell's Bridge, Lady Bantry's Look-out, and Eagle's nest. If you would like to swim, or just walk along the beach, ask for Biddy's Cove. All of these areas are within a few minutes' walk from the post office.

Garinish Island, *Glengariff, boat rides cost around £5 (negotiable, depending on the demand, weather, and the boatman's general mood).* While you're in Glengariff, see if you can talk a local boatman into taking you out to Garinish Island (I guarantee you'll be able to). The island sits at the mouth of Glengariff Harbor, and is worth a visit to see the formal gardens and other plant life there.

The Beara Peninsula. Glengariff is located on the Beara Peninsula, and the peninsula gets fewer visitors than some of its more famous neighbors. But it is a pretty drive, as most of the peninsula is quite mountainous. If you are into rugged beauty, take the R572 out of Glengariff and follow your nose.

County Clare

The Shannon River. Next to the River Liffey, the Shannon River is perhaps the most recognizable Irish River. The river wends and winds its way through the Emerald Isle for over 170 miles, making it the longest river in Ireland. It's a picturesque river, narrowing to rapids in places, and widening out to beautiful, island-dotted lakes in other places.

Bunratty Castle, *on the N18, open daily from 9:30 am to 5:30 pm. Admission is £4.75 for adults and £2.30 for children. Prices for the banquet are £30.50 for adults, £22.85 for children 10 to 12, £15.25 for children ages 6 - 9, and children under five are free. Tel. (061) 360788. If you are confident enough in your schedule before you leave the United States, you can call 800-243-8687 to make reservations.* Bunratty Castle and Bunratty Folk Park is about 10 miles west of Limerick on the Shannon airport road. Bunratty Castle is a magnificently restored 15th-century castle. Originally the home of the Earls of O'Brien, it was considered one of the most outstanding structures of its day. As you enter the castle, look for the "murder holes" – portals in the roof where various boiling concoctions were dumped on the heads of unsuspecting invaders.

However, if you can fit it into your schedule, your most lasting memories of Bunratty Castle will be of the reception and medieval banquet you'll receive inside. Period costumes, traditional Irish songs, harp music, and lots of fun are in store for you. You'll be greeted in the main reception hall by the Lord of the castle, and all guests are served honey mead – a fruity wine – or a non-alcoholic fruit drink if you prefer. Then off to the banquet hall where you'll be serenaded by lovely Irish colleens while you dine – sans silverware except for a knife – on a meal similar to what the original Lord of the castle would have eaten.

The banquet is held twice nightly throughout the year, at 5:30 pm and 8:45 pm. From May through October you should make your reservations at least the day before you arrive. On weekdays you may have luck getting a reservation for that evening, but weekends are usually heavily attended, so be sure to call the day before for reservations. The late banquet usually fills up first.

Across the street from Bunratty Castle is a wonderful traditional Irish Shop called Bunratty Cottage. This tax-free shop is fun to browse through whether you buy anything or not.

Bunratty Folk Park, *on the N18, open September through May from 9:30 am to 5:30 pm, and June to August from 9:30 am to 7:00 pm (last tours allowed to begin one hour prior to closing time). Admission is £4.75 for adults and £2.30 for children. There is a family ticket available for £11.50 (2 adults and 4 children). Tel. (061) 361511.* Adjacent to Bunratty Castle is the Bunratty Folk Park. The Folk Park is a wonderful recreation of 19th-century Ireland complete with artisans replicating the various vocations of that time period: candle makers, blacksmiths, millers, basket weavers, etc. It's a lot of fun and very informative.

Knappogue Castle, *near Quin, open daily from 9:30 am to 4:30 pm. Admission is £2.55 for adults and £1.55 for children. Prices for the banquet are £30.50 for adults, £22.85 for children 10 to 12, £15.25 for children ages 6 - 9, and children under five are free. Tel. (061) 368103. If you are confident enough in your schedule before you leave on vacation, you can call 800-243-8687 to make reservations.* Knappogue Castle is three miles southeast of Quin on the R469. It's a 15th-century tower house of the warrior-clan MacNamara. It's kind of a romantic setting, out in the middle of the country. A similar program to Bunratty Castle's medieval banquet is held here.

Craggaunowen Project, *Quin, open mid-April through September daily from 10:00 am to 6:00 pm (last admission 5:00 pm). Admission is £3.80 for adults and £2.50 for children.* At Quin, you'll discover the ruins of an old Franciscan friary sitting quietly beside a brook. From Quin, follow the signposts to Craggaunowen Castle. The castle was recently part of a historical project whose goal was to restore the old tower house and furnish it with period furnishings, tools, and assorted knickknacks. They have succeeded in their goal, and there are a number of things to see and catch your eye. You'll also find a replica of the small boat of **St. Brendan the Navigator**, who legend claims discovered America some seven hundred years *before* Columbus! (Columbus must have had a better PR agent!)

The small *crannog* – a fortified island dwelling – is particularly interesting. It's reached by a narrow bridge. In medieval times, people protected themselves from unfriendly visitors by building their homes on islands in lakes. This is a reproduction of one such structure.

Quin Abbey, *Quin.* Just southeast of Ennis are the ruins of Quin Abbey, built in the early 15th century. Originally the benefactor of the MacNamara family, many of the tombs of that family are well-preserved within the ruins of the abbey. The view from the top of the preserved tower is impressive, and worth the effort to climb the spiral staircase to its apex.

Cliffs of Moher, *Visitors Center is open April through October daily from 10:00 am until 6:00 pm. Admission is free, although the carpark costs £1.* The dramatic Cliffs of Moher, which run along the coast for about five miles, have awed visitors and locals alike for centuries with their 650 foot drops to the sea. The Irish name for the cliffs is *Aillte an Mhothair*, "Cliffs of Ruin."

Buskers (street entertainers) work the crowds in the car park on an ad hoc basis primarily from June through August or September. Your first stop should be at the visitors' center at the edge of the parking lot. Here you'll learn a little of the history of the area, and they will give you information on the best cliff-side walks available. Take time for them – they will provide some of your favorite memories of the Emerald Isle.

In the past, visitors to the cliffs could walk right out to the edge of the Cliffs and peer over the dizzying edge. Large stones along the path now block your ability to do that, and signs ask visitors not to venture too close to the edge. But if you'll walk past O'Brien's Tower, the stone walking path takes you out for additional beautiful views. If the weather cooperates, you can see the Aran Islands.

O'Brien's Tower, *Cliffs of Moher*. Built originally as a teahouse (really!) in 1835, this tower offers some of the most impressive views in Ireland. If you've seen Irish tourist brochures with a picture of a lonely tower sitting atop monstrous cliffs, this is O'Brien's Tower. During the summers, the tower serves as a small visitor center and gift shop.

Spanish Point, *Ennis*. At Ennis, watch for signposts to Milltown Malbay (R474). At the town, follow signposts to Spanish Point, where you can contemplate the hapless case of a number of Spanish sailors – a small contingent of the ill-fated Spanish Armada. In 1588 these sailors were fortunate enough to survive both their battle with the English and the wreck of their ship off this point, only to be captured and executed by the inhospitable Turlough O'Brien!

Ailwee Cave, *near Ballyvaughan, open March through early November daily from 10:00 am to 6:00 pm, July and August daily 10:00 am to 7:00 pm (last tours begin half hour before closing). Admission for adults is £3.50 and £2 for children. Tel. (065) 77036.* Stop here if you're into caves – otherwise skip it. Ailwee Cave has over 3,400 feet of passages that run underneath the lunar-like terrain of the Burren. Guided tours are well lit – both with lights and Irish mirth.

The Burren. South of Galway Bay lies the forbidding wasteland called The Burren (from the Irish *Boirinn*, which means "Great Rock"). The Burren is an area of vast limestone slabs with fissures running all through them. The dull gray of the stones is an abrupt change of scenery from all the green you've encountered elsewhere in the Emerald Isle.

The Burren is a hangout of botanists – amateur and professional – the world over. For some reason this inhospitable section of Ireland hosts a wide variety of plant life, including plants that normally grow only in Arctic regions, alongside other plants more comfortable in the Mediterranean! Take some time to wander around on foot in the Burren. It is really quite fascinating.

Burren Display Center, *Kilfenora, open July and August daily from 9:30 am to 6:00 pm, March through June and September through October daily from 10:00 am to 5:00 pm. Admission is £2 for adults and £1 for children. Tel. (065) 88030.* If the Burren proves puzzling to you, the Burren Display Center is a good place to stop. A short audio-visual presentation and numerous exhibits explain the geology and flora of the Burren.

Corcomroe Abbey, *Ballyvaughan.* Just northeast of Ballyvaughan just off the N67 you'll find the quiet ruins of Corcomroe Abbey. This Cisterian abbey was built in the late 12th century (1180). The ruins are in pretty good shape, and are pleasant to wander through.

Dysert O'Dea Castle Archaeology Center, *Corofin, open May through September daily from 10:00 am to 6:00 pm. Admission is £2 for adults and £1 for children. Tel. (065) 37722.* A place to visit for archaeology buffs, the Dysert O'Dea Castle Archaeology Center is located on the R476 at the outskirts of the town of Corofin. Interesting exhibits on the Burren are well done.

County Kerry

Killarney. For all the tourists Killarney receives, it is not a large town by any means. There are several main arteries that will carry you to Killarney. If you're coming from Bantry, the N71 enters Killarney from the south. From the north, you'll take the N22, unless you're coming from Limerick, in which case you'll take the N21/N23/N22. If you're coming from Cork, the N22 is your road, and if you're coming from Mallow, you'll want to be on the N72.

Once you arrive in Killarney, you'll find a busy little town full of cars and pedestrians, bicycles and jaunting cars. The main town consists of a handful of streets, in addition to the three arteries (N22, N71, and N72) that enter town. Main Street is, well, the main street in Killarney, and runs north through town, turning into High Street and Rock Street by the time you get to the north end of town. There are two main east-west streets: Plunkett/College/Fair Hill/Park Road runs east off of Main Street, and New Road/St. Anne's Road runs east to west almost the width of town as it crosses High Street/Rock Street. The town's streets are filled with churches, shops, pubs (of course!) and restaurants, including a few very good ones (see the *Where To Eat* section).

Killarney is one of the hottest tourist destinations in Ireland, especially among American visitors. Before you see any of the many sights in and around Killarney, take the time to explore the town first. Because of its popularity with the Irish as well as tourists, expect a lot of traffic during the season. Regardless, it is a delightful town to merely wander the streets

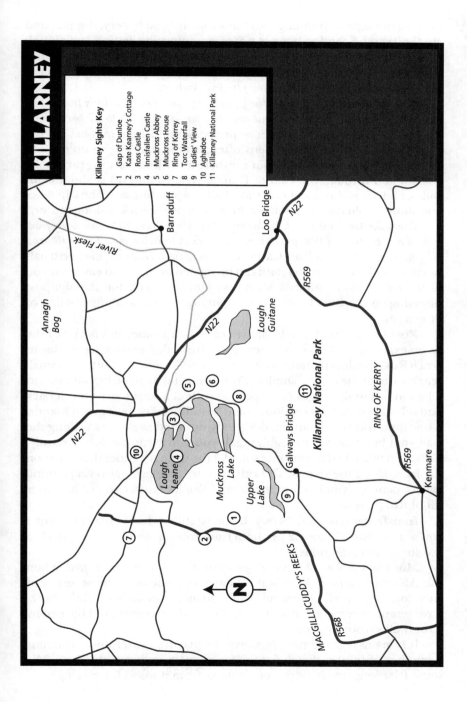

KILLARNEY

Killarney Sights Key

1 Gap of Dunloe
2 Kate Kearney's Cottage
3 Ross Castle
4 Innisfallen Castle
5 Muckross Abbey
6 Muckross House
7 Ring of Kerrey
8 Torc Waterfall
9 Ladies' View
10 Aghadoe
11 Killarney National Park

and see the sights – popping into this shop and that bakery, this pub and that knit shop. Spend an hour or two of your morning getting acquainted. (Leave your car at your B&B, or park in the nearest car park you can.) While driving in and around Killarney, watch for pedestrians, bicycles, and jaunting cars, as they seem to be everywhere.

Gap of Dunloe, *near Killarney, jaunting cars available daily from April through September. Rates vary, but expect to pay around £5 to £7 per person.* Pretty, pretty, pretty! And never so pretty as after a light rain has left the Gap a little misty, which happens often around here. Drive up to **Kate Kearney's Cottage** and park your car there and hire a jaunting car to take you up and through the Gap of Dunloe. The round-trip is about eight miles, and takes about an hour and a half in a jaunting car. The trip takes you along an old road that skirts a number of pristine lakes along the way.

Ross Castle, *Ross Road, Killarney, open May through October daily from 9:00 am to 6:30 pm, (5:00 pm during October). Admission is £2 for adults and £1 seniors and children.* Ross Castle, on Ross Road, is about one and a half miles from the town center, and can be walked or driven to easily. As you head out of town towards Muckross House, watch for the signpost directing you to Ross Castle. Turn right and continue along the line of lime trees.

Ross Castle sits along the shores of Lough Leane, and is one of the finest examples of 14th-century castles in Ireland. The most scenic way to reach Ross Castle is to make your way to Lord Brandon's Cottage (a small tea shop) near the Gap of Dunloe. From there, take a stroll (about two and a half miles) to the edges of Upper Lake. Rent a boat there and sit back and relax as you are taken along some beautiful lakes, past green islands, along limestone caves, and under a long-deserted eagle aerie. Along the way, your boatman will probably regale you with a trumpet solo. Actually, he'll use a bugle to demonstrate some of the strange echoes that occur on the lakes along the shores. The ride back to your car is also via jaunting car (remember, you left it at the Gap of Dunloe?) after you've had your fill of Ross Castle.

Innisfallen Island, *Killarney.* If you're still up for a boat ride, rent a rowboat at Ross Castle (£2 per hour) and row out to Inisfallen Island to see some romantic ruins.

Muckross Abbey, *Killarney, open year round. Admission is free.* When this Abbey was built in 1448, it must have been one of the most serene of such locations in all of Ireland. Unfortunately, the abbey didn't always have serene times: it was raided in 1589 by British troops, and burned by Cromwell's troops in 1652.

It remains a grand ruin, however. Its massive center tower contains a number of tombs. Watch for the large yew tree, probably planted by some friar long ago in hopes of gleaning from it wood for carving.

Muckross House, *N71, Killarney, from June 1 through October 1 open daily from 10:00 am to 7:00 pm, October through March 16 open Sunday from 2:00 pm to 6:00 pm, March 17 through May 1 open Saturday and Sunday from 2:00 pm to 6:00 pm, May 2 through June 1 daily from 2:00 pm to 6:00 pm. Admission to Muckross House or Kerry Life Experience for adults is £3.30, £2 for seniors, and £1.50 for students and children. A combined ticket is £4.50 for adults, £3 for seniors, and £2.50 for students and children. Tel. (064) 31440.* On the outskirts of town on the main road is Muckross House and the newly-completed **Kerry Country Life Experience**. The two are side-by-side, and give a view of the way both rich and poor lived in the mid-1800's. Muckross House was built in 1843 by a former Member of Parliament, Henry Arthur Herbert, and has been beautifully restored. The exquisite sculptured grounds are equally elegant.

While here, invest the time and money in a ride around the grounds via a "jaunting car" – a two-wheeled horse-drawn cart driven by a guide around the grounds of Muckross House, the ruins of Muckross Abbey, two lakes and a gorgeous waterfall. Two to four people can fit in the jaunting car, and the cost is around £20 (negotiable with the driver).

Across the parking lot is the Kerry Country Life Experience, a representation of the lifestyles of the rural Kerry folk before the advent of electricity.

The Ring of Kerry

The Ring of Kerry is one of the most celebrated drives in Ireland. It is a 110-mile scenic drive from Killarney around the Iveragh Peninsula. Traveling 110 miles should take about two hours, right? *Wrong!* It will take you three to three and a half hours easily. It is filled with beautiful views, striking panoramas, rustic ruins, and lots of pretty countryside. The views from Killarney to Kenmare are truly beautiful – if you have a clear day you will see some magnificent scenery as you look back down the valley toward Muckross House and the area's many lakes. Plan to take a lot of pictures.

It's immaterial whether you drive the Ring of Kerry in a clockwise or counter-clockwise direction. The scenery is the same both ways, although the traffic tends to be a little lighter if you go counter-clockwise. Unfortunately, the large tour buses go both directions! To go clockwise on the Ring of Kerry, head out of town toward Muckross House, and follow the signs for the Ring of Kerry; to go counter-clockwise, take the R562 toward Killorglin, then follow the signposts for the Ring of Kerry.

I've highlighted the most interesting and pretty stops for you along the Ring of Kerry below (the stops begin with the Torc Waterfall and end at Killorglin):

Torc Waterfall, *Ring of Kerry*. Along the Ring of Kerry on the N71, watch for the signs indicating the car park for the Torc Waterfall. Eight to ten minutes from your car you arrive at a pretty waterfall. The water that comes crashing over the 60 foot cliff comes there innocently enough from a small lake called the Devil's Punchbowl. Admire the waterfall, then take the path that ascends higher up **Mangerton Mountain**. The higher you go, the more lovely and panoramic the scenery becomes.

Ladies' View. Continuing on the N71 toward Kenmare, you come to Ladies' View, an area of wonderful views back down Killarney Valley.

Aghadoe. Further along the Ring of Kerry you'll come to the little town of Aghadoe. Look back toward Killarney for some splendid views.

Killarney National Park. The lake district around Killarney is beautiful, and much of it lies within the 25,000 acre Killarney National Park. Set in the midst of verdant mountains and shimmering lakes, there are lots of walking paths through the park that lend themselves to getting away from it all.

Sneem. The Irish name for Sneem is *An tSnaidhm*, which means "the Knot." This pretty little town on the Ring of Kerry route is reminiscent (to me, anyway) of a basket of Easter eggs, what with its pastel-colored houses. Sneem has terrific natural assets: the location on an estuary of the Ardsheelaun River, with a bevy of mountain peaks as a pretty backdrop.

Castlecove and Westcove. If you're still following the Ring of Kerry, you'll soon come to Castlecove and Westcove. These quiet little villages sit near a nice, sandy beach that is generally not very crowded. Take a few minutes to take your shoes off and sample the sand and sea.

Staigue Fort, *Castlecove. Admission is in the form of a small "trespass fee" charged by a local farmer for crossing his property to get to the fort.* Look for the signposts off the N70 near Castlecove directing you to Staigue Fort, an impressive (and largely intact) fort dating from the Iron Age. Archaeologists estimate its age at roughly 2,500 years old. The fort is a massive circular structure whose walls are thirteen feet thick at the base and nearly seven feet thick at the top. The undulating walls are of varying height owing to erosion, gravity, and theft, but they are about seventeen feet at their highest points and eleven feet at their lowest. All around the inside are steps that lead to the top of each wall. There's one small entrance into the fort on the south side, and the fort is ditched around the outside (i.e., there's a shallow ditch that runs around the base of the walls).

Derrynane House, *Caherdaniel, open June through September daily from 10:00 am to 7:00 pm, and October through May Tuesday through Saturday from 10:00 am to 1:00 pm and 2:00 pm to 5:00 pm, Sunday from 2:00 pm to 5:00 pm. Admission is free. Tel. (066) 75113.* Derrynane House was the former house of **Daniel O'Connell**, the man called the "Liberator" by his Irish compatriots for his unceasing efforts to obtain emancipation for Catholics. The house has been perfectly restored with period furnishings, including some of O'Connell's own furniture and appurtenances. The house sits amid gardens and greenery – three hundred and twenty acres worth – that run down to the crashing Atlantic. The whole area is known as **Derrynane National Park**.

Waterville. Continuing on the Ring of Kerry (N70), you'll come to the pretty town of Waterville, which sits quietly along the shores of Ballinskelligs Bay between the ocean and picturesque Lough Currane. Famed as a phenomenal fishing site, Waterville also boasts a fine sandy beach.

Valentia Island. Valentia Island off the coast boasts the distinction of the westernmost terminal of the first intercontinental telegraph cable. The island is reached at its southeast end via a bridge from the little town of Portmagee (on the R565). Valentia Island offers its visitors pretty seascapes, magnificent cliffs, and a bouquet of subtropical flowers throughout the island.

The Skellig Islands

The Skelligs. *The boat trip to the islands is £15 to £20*. Jutting abruptly out of the foaming Atlantic are a small group of islands – rocks, really – called variously The Skelligs, Skellig Islands, and Skellig Rocks. Nine miles off the coast, these small islands are fascinating to view from afar, and hold surprises when visited.

If you wish to see the islands up close and personal, tour boats leave from Ballinskelligs, Cahirciveen, Derrynane Pier, Valentia Island, and Waterville. One of the local boat operators is Dermot Walsh, and you can reserve a trip out to the islands by calling him, *Tel. (066) 76115*. He'll take you out to Skellig Michael and let you roam around there for about three hours before heading back. Another local boatsman is Des Lavelle, *Tel. (066) 76124*. If you just want to ride around the Skelligs, but not disembark on any of them, contact the **Skellig Experience Heritage Center**, *Tel. (064) 31633*. One boat a day goes out at 2:30 pm. It's a good idea to call ahead and make reservations for this boat trip.

Note: the trips to the Skelligs are only available when the weather is good. Stormy seas and rough rocks don't make a good combination.

Unbelievably, **Skellig Michael**, the largest of the islands, has the ruins of a 9th-century monastic settlement perched on its craggy ridges. If St. Finan was looking for solitude and an inhospitable location, he found it on Skellig Michael. Even during the best of weather, the wind can blow ferociously here. More than 650 stone steps hewn out of the mountain lead to the settlement. When you arrive, you'll marvel at the ruins – six old beehive huts, stone walls, two oratories, two churches and various and sundry remains. It is thought that those who came here were practicing "green martyrdom," which called for the diligent seeker of Christ to voluntarily seek exile in remote (and often inhospitable) places. The Skelligs would certainly fall into that category!

The settlement was abandoned in the 13th century, but for years the faithful continued to make pilgrimages to its site, climbing to the top of the island and kissing a rock inscribed with a cross. There is a lighthouse that silently and solemnly stands vigil on the island. Manned from 1820 to 1987, it must have had its own set of hearty inhabitants.

The boat trip also includes a trip past **Little Skelligs**, a smaller set of sea rocks. They are noted for their vast colonies – over 20,000 by some counts – of various species of birds. The most prevalent birds you'll see are gannets. As you near the island, the cacophony of sound that arises from the screeching birds is incredible, if not unnerving.

Take the time and visit these islands – I guarantee they'll be some of your most vivid memories.

The Skellig Experience, *Valencia Island, open April to June and September from 9:30 am to 5:00 pm, July and August from 9:30 am to 7:00 pm. Admission is £3 for adults and £1.50 for children. A combined ticket is available that includes the trip to the islands. It is £20 for adults and £10 for children. Tel. (066) 76306 3.* Just across the bridge to Valentia Island is The Skellig Experience, an exhibit concerned primarily with the Skellig Islands. Interesting information is presented on the monastic settlement on Skellig Michael, the lighthouse and its keepers, the variety of local seabirds who have chosen to roost in this part of the Emerald Isle, and the underwater creatures that inhabit this part of the great Atlantic.

If you don't feel like your sea-legs will handle a boat trip out to the Skelligs, you will probably enjoy the fifteen-minute audio-visual presentation on the monastic ruins on Skellig Michael.

Back to the Ring of Kerry

Cahirciveen. Cahirciveen on the N70 is the westernmost point of the Ring of Kerry. The Irish name for Cahirciveen is *Cathair Saidhbhin*, which means "Sabina's Stone Fort." The town has a neat, clean, and tidy feel to it, and there are a number of interesting shops.

The trip from Cahirciveen to Glenbeigh (or vice versa, depending on the direction you are traveling the Ring of Kerry) is one of the most scenic portions of the Ring. Views across Dingle Bay to the peaks of the Dingle Peninsula are wonderful.

Glenbeigh. *Gleann Beithe*, as it is called in Irish, means "The Glen of the Birches." Lots of hikers head for Glenbeigh, as the surrounding mountains offer some wonderful hikes with stunning views of Dingle Bay and Peninsula.

You might also want to stop and gaze upon the infamous "Wynne's Folly," a mansion that was built at the direction of Lord Headley Wynne in 1867. The mansion was built to simulate a castle, but was poorly constructed and not particularly livable – the roof and walls leaked when it rained, which was often. Thankfully, the mansion was destroyed during the destruction that accompanied the troubles in 1922. Lord Wynne did choose a great site for his folly, however; the views are superb.

Kerry Bog Village Museum, *Glenbeigh, open March through November daily from 8:30 am to 7:00 pm. Admission is £2 for adults, £1.50 for senior citizens, and £1 for children. Tel. (066) 69184.* If you haven't taken the time to stop and visit any of the many open-air museums that feature old cottages with period furnishings, this is a pretty good one. It's not extensive, but well done.

Killorglin. Killorglin is the northernmost point on the Ring of Kerry (N70) and is either the end of a long 110-mile drive, or near the beginning, depending on which direction you've chosen to travel the Ring of Kerry. In Irish, *Cill Orglan* means "Orgla's Church," and if ever you want to visit, you should do so during the second week of August. Why the second week of August? **Puck Fair**, that's why. This three-day jubilee is looked forward to by the townsfolk and other locals for most of the year.

Locals differ on the origin of the fair; some (the more intellectual types) will tell you it is the remnant of a long-forgotten pagan harvest festival. Others will tell you that it commemorates the time sheep saved the town from Oliver Cromwell's armies. The legend says that the terrified sheep fled before Cromwell's approaching army, flooding the main street of Killorglin with wool and alarmed bleating. The alerted villagers were aroused and able to defend their village against the approaching army. (Maybe the scores of other towns sacked by Cromwell should have stationed watch sheep?)

The fair features cattle-, horse-, sheep-trading, free concerts, and lots of drinking. The livestock trading is less now than in years past, but the drinking is greater. A wild goat is bedecked with ribbons and presides over the festivities.

The Dingle Peninsula

This is a beautiful part of Ireland! The Dingle Peninsula extends into the Atlantic Ocean, and has the honor of being the most westerly point of Europe. Glaciers in eons gone by have sculpted a masterpiece on this parcel of real estate. Towering mountains give way to silky valleys and gleaming lakes. The coastline alternates between sandy beaches and treacherous cliffs that sweep down to the foamy Atlantic.

The Dingle Peninsula is officially a *Gaeltacht* – a district where Irish is the predominant language. But don't worry, English is also spoken and you'll get along just fine. All the signposts are in Irish first with English underneath (well, *most* of the time the English name is given).

The drive around the peninsula is a mere one hundred miles. But don't think you can drive it in two hours. The roads, especially along the coastlines, are exceptionally narrow. And with numerous interesting villages to stop in, countless landscapes and seascapes to photograph, and a lot of beauty to take in, you'll want to set aside plenty of time. A full day will allow you the time to see this stunning area.

There aren't many choices for accessing the Dingle Peninsula. The most common is either the N86 from Tralee or the R561 from Castlemaine. Another way, much less traveled, is from the north side of the peninsula, taking the N86 out of Tralee to the R560 and going through Castlegregory. Just past Castlegregory, at Kilcummin, watch for signposts directing you to Connor Pass to cut across the interior of the Dingle Peninsula. You'll come out at the little town of Dingle.

Dingle. Your first stop during your tour of the Dingle Peninsula is little Dingle itself – signposted in Irish as *An Daingean* (O'Cush's Fortress). Dingle is located on the southern coast of the Dingle Peninsula on the N86.

If you listen casually, you will hear Irish spoken as the primary language. If you're fortunate, you can tune your car radio to an Irish-speaking station. You'll be amazed – it doesn't sound much like English. Get out and explore this old port town. There are a few interesting shops.

While in Dingle, take a boat ride out into Dingle Bay and see if Fungi, the Dingle Dolphin, is still around playfully jesting with tourists and fishing boats. Fungi has become a local legend, popular with locals as well as visitors. A ride out into the harbor in search of Fungi with a local fisherman runs about £5 for adults and £2 for children. Most of the fishermen guarantee a "Fungi sighting" or your money back.

Stretch your legs by walking around town (it's not large – the population is about 1,200). Be sure and visit the **Cearolann Craft Village**, where you can purchase silver, leather, knitted goods, and many other Irish crafts.

Ventry and Slea Head. As you head further out on the Dingle Peninsula, you'll come to Ventry, whose fine sandy beaches are the main attraction. Slea Head is the westernmost edge of Europe. Staggering views of the Atlantic Ocean, with the Blasket Islands in the foreground, await those who stop to gaze, gape, and click their shutters.

Dunquin. The small seaport village of Dunquin lies at the northwestern end of Slea Head. During the summer months, you can take a boat ride out to the Blasket Islands. Dunquin Pottery is also located in Dunquin (where else?). Their pottery would make a nice gift for those back home. When in town, stop by the **Blasket Centre**, *open Easter through September daily from 10:00 am to 6:00 pm. Admission is £2 for adults and £1 for children. Tel. (066)56371.* The Blasket Center (you can't miss it – it's the only modern building around) has a short presentation on the life and times of those who lived on the Blasket Islands.

Blasket Islands. Off the Dingle Peninsula lie the Blasket Islands, and the most obvious one is the largest of those islands, called **The Great Blasket**. These islands were inhabited until 1953 by a particularly hearty folk. Apparently they had a lot of time to think up stories and tell them to the few people they met, as they were renowned as story-tellers.

Clogher Strand. This is the spot to get a close-up look at the power of the Atlantic as it pounds the Irish shore. Crashing waves and foaming surf make for great photos.

Gallarus Oratory, *Dingle Peninsula*. Between Ballyferriter and Ballydavid, watch for signposts directing you to Gallarus Oratory, and there you'll find an incredibly preserved church – one of the earliest in Irish history. The mortar-free masonry has been watertight for over 1,000 years. It's impressive, but I can't get over the fact that it reminds me of an upside down rowboat. The inside of the church is about 10 feet by 15 feet.

Kilmakedar Church, *Kilmakedar, Dingle Peninsula*. Just a couple miles beyond the Gallarus Oratory is Kilmakedar Church, a superb example of a Hiberno-Roman church. In addition, there are a number of examples of Ogham stones and an alphabet stone.

Connor Pass. Connor Pass is a thrilling and beautiful mountainous drive. Be sure and stop at the carpark at the apex of the pass and check out the views. Whether you're looking toward Tralee or back toward Dingle, the views are incredible.

Limerick City

Like so many towns along the Irish coastline, Limerick was once a Viking stronghold. And like so many other such towns its history is speckled with violence and death. Originally used as a base for plunder across the countryside, the city became accustomed to warfare and siege.

Originally founded in the 9th century, Limerick was repeatedly attacked throughout its early years by its Irish neighbors. But it wasn't until **Brian Boru** and his forces made a concerted effort in the 10th century that the town was claimed from the Vikings and these unfriendly neighbors made to leave. In the latter end of the 12th century, Strongbow's men claimed the city for themselves, but were unable to hold it long before it was retaken by the powerful **O'Brien** clan.

The city was visited in 1210 by King John, and he ordered a castle built on the banks of the Shannon. The castle, which bears his name was obediently built, and is one of the most recognizable landmarks in Limerick today.

The next four hundred years saw many battles waged and many lives lost. After the Irish forces lost to **William of Orange** at the Battle of the Boyne, they pulled back to Limerick to lick their wounds. But William pursued them and laid siege to the city. William's forces made three unsuccessful attempts to conquer the city before abandoning their siege. A year later, the Irish armies negotiated a truce with another of William's armies, and signed the Treaty of Limerick after a two month siege. The Irish troops were allowed to leave the city peaceably. The treaty, which included a clause granting religious freedom to Catholics, was never ratified by the Protestant congress. Over 11,000 of those soldiers left the shores of Ireland to fight for **King Louis** of France rather than join the Protestant forces of King William.

Today, Limerick is the third largest city in Ireland, with a population just under 60,000. They are proud of their heritage, and to answer the question that's been burning in your mind: yes, Limerick did lend its name to the humorous poetic ditties that we all learned in junior high school – although some spoilsports disagree.

See *Arrivals & Departures* at the beginning of this chapter for information on getting to Limerick.

St. Mary's Cathedral, *corner of Nicholas Street and St. Augustine Place, Limerick, open Monday through Saturday from 9:00 am until 1:00 pm and from 2:00 pm to 5:00 pm. Admission is free. Tel. (061) 416238.* In 1168, **Donal Mor O'Brien** gave his palace to the church to be used as they saw fit. They saw fit to convert it into a cathedral. At the western entrance you'll find pillars and a Romanesque entrance. Inside are a number of sights that may catch your eye. Of particular note are the choir stalls with their misericords and their carvings in black oak. They are so incongruous that they have become an attraction in and of themselves. Other interesting sights include stone effigies of the fourth Earl of Thomand and his wife, and an immense stone coffin lid thought to be from the coffin of the cathedral's benefactor, Donal Mor O'Brien.

King John's Castle, *corner of Castle Street and The Parade, Limerick, open daily from mid-April through October from 9:30 am to 5:30 pm, and year-round on Saturday and Sunday from noon to 5:00 pm. Admission is £3.30 for adults and £1.70 for children. A family ticket is available for £8.50 (2 adults 4 children). Tel. (061) 411201.* As you enter Limerick from the southwest, one of the most prominent sights you'll see is the 13th century King John's Castle on the Shannon River. Head for it, and enjoy the short but informative slide show about the history of Limerick. Following that is a short tour of the castle. There's not much to go into, mostly just the outside walls remain. Several years ago, while attempting to do some restoration work on one of the walls, workers unearthed a pre-Norman village the castle had been built on top of! Currently archaeologists are working on the find, and tourists are welcome to get some up-close views of the work in progress.

Limerick Regional Archives, *Michael Street, Limerick, open Monday through Friday from 9:30 am to 5:00 pm. Admission is free. Tel. (061) 410777.*

On Michael Street you'll find the old Granary, a relatively new building by Limerick standards (1774). The Granary now houses the Limerick Regional Archives, and for a fee will research your Irish ancestors.

Hunt Collection, *University of Limerick, Plassey (on the outskirts of Limerick), open from May to September daily from 9:30 am to 5:30 pm. Admission is £3 for adults and £1.50 for children. Tel. (061) 333644.* While in Limerick, head over to the University of Limerick and the adjacent Hunt Museum. It offers a unique collection of Irish art and craftsmanship extending from the Neolithic period to contemporary times. Its most impressive exhibit is that of Celtic and medieval treasures, probably the most extensive outside of the National Museum in Dublin. Exhibits include European and Irish religious art, ancient (and exquisite) gold jewelry and Christian brooches, as well as every-day medieval items such as pottery, crucifixes, forks, and spoons.

Elsewhere in County Limerick

Ashkeaton. The small town of Ashkeaton lies west of Limerick on the N69. The town was a former stronghold of the Fitzgeralds of Desmond. A small rocky island in the River Deel is almost completely submerged by the ruins of a 15th-century castle. Nearby on the banks of the River Deel are the nicely preserved ruins of a 15th-century Franciscan friary. Feel free to wander through this ruin.

Adare. When you reach Adare, slow down. Stop. Adare is without a doubt one of the prettiest towns in Ireland. Somehow, it just looks and feels like an Irish town ought to. Clean. Tidy. Neat. Friendly. Quaint. Picturesque. Ruins of ancient origin. Thatch-roofed cottages. Its Irish name *Ath Dara*, means "The Ford of the Oak Tree."

Across from the Dunraven Arms Hotel are the large ornamental gates that lead to Adare Manor. Built in 1832, this lovely and imposing structure is now a luxury hotel (see *Where to Stay*). Drive through the gates and take in the beauty of the grounds. Adare Manor is open to the public, so spend a few minutes here. The town is small enough that you can easily explore it on foot. There are a number of ruins to visit, including several 13th to 15th-century friaries, and portions of an old Desmond Castle. The River Maigue alongside the Adare Manor moves languidly past one of the ruins at the edge of town. You can see it from the bridge.

Lough Gur, *near Holycross*. About twelve miles south of Limerick just off the R512 (look for the signposts) is Lough Gur, and on Lough Gur is an interesting prehistoric site. Up until the 19th century, this prehistoric settlement was unknown. But when the lough was drained, they discovered the Neolithic ruins of a community that archaeologists estimate is nearly 4,000 years old. Extensive burial grounds, passage graves, stone forts, and a number of other worthwhile sites are here.

De Valera Museum and Bruree Heritage Centre, *Bruree, Tuesday through Friday 10:00 am to 5:00 pm, Saturday and Sunday from 2:00 pm until 5:00 pm. Admission for adults is £2, and £1 for children. Tel. (063) 91300.* This recently refurbished museum covers the life and times of one of Ireland's most influential politicians. De Valera served as the first president of the rebel Irish Republic. It is interesting to learn about the modern history of Ireland through the various exhibits here. You'll enjoy an audio-visual presentation that gives you a history of the area as well as a history of Eamon de Valera himself. There are a number of graphic panels and exhibits that feature Mr. de Valera, including some of his clothing, medals, and other personal effects.

County Tipperary

Kilcooley Abbey, *near Urlingford.* Due east of Kilkenny, and south of Urlingford on the R689, lay the intriguing ruins of Kilcooley Abbey, a sister abbey to Jerpoint Abbey near Thomastown. The original portion of the abbey was built in 1200 by command of King Donagh O'Brien. In ensuing years, new buildings were added to the abbey.

Today, the abbey is a treasure-trove of sculptural prizes. At the north end is an ancient font with intricate carvings; the wall of the south transept has an abundance of well-preserved reliefs. Above the Gothic doorway is a fine carving of the crucifixion.

Lough Derg, *Counties Clare and Tipperary.* Lough Derg forms a portion of the boundary between Counties Clare and Tipperary. This pretty lake is formed by a widening of the River Shannon over a stretch of several miles. There are several routes around the lake that are noted for their beauty. The R494 on the east and R352 on the west are particularly nice.

Mitchellstown Caves, *near Clogheen, open daily from 10:00 am to 6:00 pm. Admission is £2 for adults and 50p for children. Tel. (052) 67246.* If you're into stalactites and stalagmites, Mitchelstown Cave is worth a stop. Just north of Clogheen, the half-mile tour has some intriguing shapes and sights. For centuries, the caves were used as a hideout for those not wishing to be found by the authorities, including the Earl of Desmond in the 1500s.

Cahir Castle, *open April through June and late September daily from 10:00 am to 6:00 pm, from June to mid-September daily from 9:00 am to 7:30 pm and from November to March daily from 10:00 am to 1:00 pm, and from 2:00 pm to 4:00 pm. Closed the month of October. Admission is £1 for adults and 40p for children. Tel. (052) 41011.* Continue north on the R668, and you'll come to Cahir (pronounced "care") Castle, one of the most recognized castles in the world since it has been used as a setting for several medieval movies. Built in 1142, the castle sits on a rocky outcropping of the River Suir.

Glen of Aherlow, *near Aherlow*. Between Cahir and Tipperary, watch for the signpost to the hamlet of Aherlow and the Glen of Aherlow (on the R663). Enjoy the drive through the beautiful Glen of Aherlow, or better yet take the time to walk through some of the many wooded walking paths.

As you revel in the beauty of the Glen, you would not suspect that it was the site of many important battles in ancient days. It also served as a refuge for many an Irishman hiding out from enemies. One of the more notable was Geoffrey Keating. Dr. Keating was an early 17th-century preacher who went a bit too far in his remonstrations, earning the severe ire of one of the powerful families of Tipperary. Fearing for his life, he fled to the seclusion of the Glen of Aherlow, where he spent several years quietly writing a history of Ireland.

Tipperary Town. Tipperary Town is at the junction of the N24 from Limerick on the northwest and Cahir on the southeast, and on the N74 from Cashel. Tipperary's Irish name is *Tiobrad Arann*, which means "The Well of Ara." Tipperary sits amid the lovely Golden Vale of Tipperary, a rich agricultural plain. In the 12th century, King John built a castle here and began the settlement of this area. Today, Tipperary is known for two things: dairy farming and racehorses.

Rock of Cashel, *Cashel, open mid-March to June daily from 9:30 am to 5:30 pm, June to September daily from 9:00 am to 7:30 pm, and October to mid-March daily from 9:30 am to 4:30 pm. Admission is £2.50 for adults £1.75 for seniors, and £1 for children. Family ticket available for £6. Tel. (062) 61437.* Save plenty of film for one of the most awe-inspiring sites in Ireland. The setting for this chapel/round tower/cathedral is on a mound towering some 200 feet above the surrounding plains (the peak of the round tower is nearly 300 feet high). The ruins are amazingly well-preserved, and the visitors' center at the foot of the Rock of Cashel is informative. Incredible views of the surrounding Tipperary plains await visitors to the site.

Local legend has it that one day the devil was flying over Ireland. As he approached the Slieve Bloom Mountains, rather than fly over them, he opted to bite a chunk out of them. (Locals will be happy to point out the missing section in the nearby mountains. It's called Devil's Bit.) Displeased with the taste, he spat the earth out here north of Cashel Town.

The Rock of Cashel (also called St. Patrick's Rock) long held a position of prominence in the history of Ireland. It was used for the coronation of Munster kings from 370 until 1100. The great Brian Boru was crowned here. In 1101, the site was given to the Church by An O'Brien, and it was dedicated "to God, St. Patrick, and St. Ailbhe." A little over two decades later, Bishop Cormac MacCarthy began construction on **Cormac's Chapel**. It can still be seen, and is a fine example of the Romanesque architecture used.

THE BAPTISM OF KING AENGUS

The Rock of Cashel has hosted many important events, religious as well as secular. One of the most important was St. Patrick's baptism of King Aengus. The story is told that in 450 AD as St. Patrick was preparing to baptize the good king, he tripped and planted his staff rather forcibly into the earth to maintain his balance. After the ceremony, it was discovered that the staff had instead pierced the king's foot, and the grass underneath was moistened by the king's blood. The king hadn't cried out or brought attention to St. Patrick's error, as he thought the pain and suffering were part of the ceremony!

St. Patrick's Cathedral is particularly impressive also. Now roofless, it is nonetheless easy to see the grandeur this structure once represented. At the corners of the nave and transepts, spiral staircases run up, up, and up (127 steps) in small round towers up to roof-walks. Connected to the cathedral is the well-preserved **round tower**, which is 92 feet tall. Its door is 12 feet above the ground. The round tower was built in the early 12th century. During the main tourist season (mid-June through September 1), the Rock of Cashel is besieged with tourists, but it is still well worth your time to stop and spend some time here.

Cashel Folk Village, *Main Street, Cashel, open daily 9:30 am to 8:00 pm. Admission is £1.50 for adults and 60p for children. Tel. (062) 61947.* The Cashel Folk Village in town provides replicas of 19th-century houses, storefronts, and shops. It is a little small in comparison to others around the country. If you've been to any of the others, skip this one.

GPA Bolton Library, *John Street, Cashel, open March through October Monday through Saturday 9:30 am to 5:30 pm, Sunday 2:30 pm to 5:30 pm. Admission is £1.50 for adults and 60p for children. Tel. (062) 61944.* The GPA Bolton library in Cashel houses an extensive (12,000+) collection of old books and manuscripts, with a few of them dating back to the early days of the printing press. This makes for a fascinating diversion.

Bru Boru Heritage Center, *Cashel, open June through October daily 9:30 am to 11:00 pm, November through May daily from 9:30 am to 5:30 pm. Admission to the Heritage Center is free, and the admission to the cultural evenings is £5 for adults and £2 for children. Tel. (062) 61122.* In the shadow of the Rock of Cashel, (or at least at the bottom of the hill) lies the Bru Boru Heritage Center, a center dedicated to the study of Irish culture, dancing, music and folklore. Exhibits change frequently, so if you've been before, stop in again. There is also a craft shop and genealogy center on-site, as well as a small restaurant. In the evenings from May through September, folk singing, story telling and traditional Irish dancing are demonstrated.

Famine Museum, *St. Mary's Lane, Thurles, Co. Tipperary, open Sundays 1:30 pm to 5:00 pm, weekdays by appointment. Admission for adults is £2 and for children is £1. Tel. (0504) 2133.* In 1994, the minutes of the Thurles/ Rahelaty Food Committee were uncovered. This important discovery shed light on the way rural congregations attempted to deal with the deadly famine that gripped Ireland in the mid-1840s.

During the 1840s, Archbishop Henry Cotton was the Rector of St. Mary's Church in Thurles. He was so moved by the suffering of his parishioners that he served as the chairman of the local famine food committee. The museum contains a number of interesting documents dealing with the famine period. This isn't a large museum, but rather the efforts of the current parishioners to honor the memory of a million of their countrymen and women who perished in the famine. As such, it's a poignant and heartfelt remembrance.

Carrick-on-Suir. The pretty village of Carrick-on-Suir straddles the Tipperary and Waterford County line. Located on the N24 between Clonmel and Waterford, or, coming from Kilkenny, the N76 terminates here. Sitting along the River Suir, it's Irish name means "Rock of the Suir" (*Carraig na Suire*). Carrick-on-Suir grew up during the Elizabethan period as English nobles came to Ireland and established themselves. Legend has it that Carrick-on-Suir is the birthplace of Anne Boleyn, although there are several other towns claiming the honor. Anne was the second wife of Henry VIII, and her daughter (Elizabeth I) ascended the throne of England when Henry was unable to produce a male heir.

Ormonde Castle, *Carrick-on-Suir, open mid-June through September daily from 9:30 am to 6:30 pm. Admission is £1 for adults and 40p for children. Tel. (051) 40787.* The most interesting attraction in Carrick-on-Suir is the beautiful Tudor mansion formerly owned by the Dukes of Ormonde. Built in 1584, it still stands regally overlooking the River Suir.

County Waterford

Waterford City. Owing to the famous crystal factory of the same name located in this city, you probably have already heard of Waterford. Sprawling along the southern bank of the River Suir, Waterford has been, and continues to be, an important Irish seaport. Reaching the Celtic Sea via Waterford Harbor, it maintains an active trade association with major European ports. The River Suir at this point is quite deep, as it must be to allow ships to come to port here.

The Irish name for Waterford is *Port Lairge*, which means "Lairge's Port." How did they get Waterford from this? Because Waterford is anglicized from the Viking word *Vadrefjord*. The town grew from a small gathering of farmers and fishermen in the 9th century into an important port town when the Vikings ran off the native settlers and established yet another stronghold here. They held this advantage for several centuries until Strongbow took the city from them. It quickly became an important city, at times rivaling Dublin.

Shortly after ousting the Danes, Strongbow married the daughter of the Irish chieftain he had come to Ireland to support – Dermot MacMurrough. The wedding was performed in Waterford. Perhaps because of that early union, Waterford generally sided with the British crown over the next five centuries, much to the distaste of her neighbors.

But Catholicism proved to be stronger than political bonds, and Waterford refused to acknowledge the King's supremacy over the Pope in matters of religion. They hoped to walk the tenuous line of supporting the Roman church and the London government. But the king didn't appreciate that, and Oliver Cromwell was dispatched to help them understand where their loyalties – their whole loyalties – needed to be placed. Initial efforts at taking the city failed, but in 1650 Cromwell's troops were successful.

Today, with a population in excess of 40,000, Waterford is one of Ireland's largest cities.

Waterford Heritage Centre, *Greyfriar's Street, Waterford, open April, May and October Monday through Friday 10:00 am to 1:00 pm and 2:00 pm to 6:00 pm, Saturday from 10:00 am to 1:00 pm; June through September Monday through Friday from 10:00 am to 8:00 pm, Saturday from 10:00 am to 1:00 pm and from 2:00 pm to 5:00 pm. Admission is £1. Tel. (051) 71227.* The Waterford Heritage Center is one of the finest and most elaborate museums in the country. Over 75,000 artifacts from Waterford's earliest beginnings are owned by the museum, and many of them are on display here. Many of the exhibits focus on the Viking and Anglo-Norman periods, and are quite interesting.

Reginald's Tower, *The Quay, Waterford, open April, May and October Monday through Friday 10:00 am to 1:00 pm and 2:00 pm to 6:00 pm, Saturday from 10:00 am to 1:00 pm; June through September Monday through Friday from 10:00 am to 8:00 pm, Saturday from 10:00 am to 1:00 pm and from 2:00 pm to 5:00 pm. Admission is £1. Tel. (051) 73501.* On the water's edge is Reginald's Tower, a squat, solid structure built by the Vikings in 1003. The walls are ten feet thick, and eighty feet tall. It served as the home to a number of Anglo-Norman kings, and is thought to have been the site where Strongbow married Dermot MacMurrough's daughter. It currently houses Waterford's Civic Museum, and has an eclectic assortment of items from the city's history.

City Hall, *Waterford, open Monday through Friday from 9:00 am to 1:00 pm and from 2:00 pm to 5:00 pm. Admission is free. Tel. (051) 73501.* The home for Waterford's City Hall is a splendid Georgian building built in the late 18th century. Inside are a number of treasures worth seeing. The first is an immense antique Waterford crystal chandelier that's nearly two hundred years old. There is also some American Civil War memorabilia including an old American flag as well as the uniform, battle flag, and sword that was carried into the Battle of Fredericksburg by **Thomas Francis Meagher**, a home-town boy who served as a brigadier general in the American Civil War. His birthplace is next door to City Hall in a house converted into the Granville Hotel.

Blackfriar's Abbey, *O'Connell Street, Waterford,*. Look for a 13th-century tower at the corner of Bridge and O'Connell Streets. It is all that remains of a Dominican abbey, also referred to as Blackfriars, that ran afoul of Oliver Cromwell's troops in the 17th century.

Victorian Clock Tower, *Merchant's Quay, Waterford*. On Merchant's Quay stands an impressive Victorian Clock Tower. Completed just as the American Civil War was coming to a close (1864), the clock tower still stands tall and serene.

City Walls, *Waterford*. Waterford says it has more ancient city walls than any other Irish city, with the exception of Derry in Northern Ireland. Some of the walls were built by the Vikings (9th century), and others are the handiwork of the Normans (13th century). The best places to see the walls are near Mayor's Walk, Castle Street, and near the railway station.

Christ Church Cathedral, *Peter Street, Waterford*. Christ Church Cathedral was built in 1779 and boasts a roomy interior and several fine medieval tombs.

French Church, *Greyfriars Street, Waterford*. During the 13th century the Franciscans built an abbey on this site. The ruins are extensive, and feature a pretty east window. The ruins take their name from the Huguenots, who were given the church for their worship in 1695. They worshipped there until early in the 19th century.

Waterford Crystal Factory, *Cork Road, Waterford, open weekdays from 9:00 am to 5:00 pm. The first tour begins around 9:30 am. Admission is £2 for adults and £1 p for children. Tel. (051) 73311.* The Waterford Glass Factory is the main draw to Waterford and southeastern Ireland. It's easy to find, and well worth the visit. You'll never look at a piece of lead crystal the same again! The factory has a nice gallery, and their one hour tour takes you within a few feet of the artisans who blow the glass – much as it has been done for several hundred years at this site. You cannot take photographs or videos while on the tour. (If you visit the Tyrone Crystal Factory later on your trip, they allow photographs and videos.)

Dunmore East. Ten miles southwest of Waterford is the beautiful fishing village of Dunmore East. The pier that extends into the Waterford Harbor was built in 1830 at a cost of over £100,000 – quite a bit of money for those days. Quiet and clean, Dunmore is worth a stroll if you have a few extra minutes on your itinerary.

Tramore. The seaside village of Tramore is southeast of Waterford on the R682. At Tramore is **Celtworld** – a high-tech presentation on Ireland during the days of the Celts and the Druids (admission is £3.75 for adults and £2.75 for children). It provides an interesting look at the early inhabitants of the Emerald Isle. The glitz, however, is out of character with most of the rest of the sights you will see in Ireland. Tramore also offers several peaceful and beautiful seaside walks.

Famine Graveyard, *near Dungarvan*. Several miles on the Cork side of Dungarvan just off the N25, watch closely for a small signpost entitled **Famine Graveyard**. The Potato Famine, which lasted from 1845 to 1847, is estimated to have been responsible for more than a million deaths and provided the primary motivation for more than a million immigrants to leave the Emerald Isle for America, Australia, and other countries. The graveyard is located about one hundred yards off the road, and is marked only by an old rock cross. Access is through a weed-choked drive (walk it, please). The last time I was there, the English signpost was down, and only the Irish sign remained to mark the way. It reads *"Reilig A' TSLE' An Gorta 1847"*.

It is not known how many victims of the famine are buried in unmarked graves here, but the shrine is a silent reminder of a terrible period in Irish history. There are countless gravesites such as this throughout the width and breadth of Ireland.

Ardmore. Ardmore is just a few miles south of the N25 between Dungarvan and Youghal on the R673. In a country that typifies tidy, the little town of Ardmore proudly boasts the title of "Ireland's Tidiest Town." – they actually won a contest to receive the honor. Its Irish name *Ard Mor* means "Great Hill." At the edge of town is a beautiful cliff walk that skirts the sea and offers magnificent views of the Celtic Sea.

Ardmore Tower, *Ardmore*. Atop a hill overlooking Ardmore is one of the finest examples of a round tower in Ireland. Nearly one hundred feet tall, the tower was used as protection by monks from various and sundry raiders over the course of the years in this tumultuous part of Ireland. As is typical with many round towers, the "front" door is fifteen feet off the ground – enabling the monks to get inside, then pull their ladder up with them to keep the invaders at arm's length.

Youghal. A short distance from Ardmore, on the N25 about half-way between Dungarvan and Cork, you'll encounter Youghal (pronounced *yawl*), a lovely seaside resort with a fascinating ruin – Molana Abbey. Overgrown and mysterious, the ruins invite a personal inspection. If you are a fan of old movies, you may have seen Youghal without realizing it. In the movie *Moby Dick*, Youghal was the setting for Captain Ahab's home town. Its narrow streets and memorable clock tower apparently provided just the setting the director was looking for.

Cathedral of St. Declan, *Ardmore.* The Cathedral of St. Declan was originally built in the 12th century, although it has been added to at least three different times since then. In the west gable are carved deep relief figures depicting various biblical scenes. (Look for *The Wisdom of Solomon*, among others.)

St. Declan's Oratory, *Ardmore.* Near Ardmore Tower sits a diminutive stone church called St. Declan's Oratory. Tradition has it that St. Declan's remains were buried there. It is a little sad to consider that while they were once there, they no longer are. The tomb is empty, its contents having been emptied over the years by the devout seeking St. Declan's intercession in their behalf.

Lismore. Lismore is east of Dungarvan on the N72, and north of Youghal via the R671. This tiny village has a big Irish name: *Lios Mor Mochuda*, which means "Mochuda's Great Enclosure." As with so many other ancient Irish towns, Lismore's beginnings were as a monastic settlement. In the 7th century this quiet spot on the Blackwater River was chosen by St. Carthach as the site for his monastery. And as with so many monastic settlements, its history was marred by plunder and burnings. It was burnt no fewer than four times in the 11th and 12th centuries.

Lismore Castle, *Lismore, gardens open May through September Monday through Friday and Sunday from 1:45 pm to 4:45 pm (closed Saturday). Admission is £2 for adults and £1 for children. Tel. (058) 54424.* Built in the 12th century by King John, Lismore Castle stands vigil over the Blackwater River from atop its perch on a cliff above the river. The castle changed hands through the centuries. One of its most noted residents was Robert Boyle. He was born and lived in the castle, and his later work in chemistry resulted in "Boyle's Law."

Unfortunately, the castle is not open to the public, but the gardens are. There are several walking paths through them, and the variety of flowers is astounding.

Knockmealdown Mountains/The Vee. If you travel between Lismore and Clogheen on the R668, you'll go through the pass in the Knockmealdown Mountains called "The Vee." The sweeping panoramic views of the "Golden Vale of Tipperary" are fabulous. If you are fortunate enough to take the drive when the heather is in bloom (late summer), you'll have a colorful addition to your views.

Between The Vee and Clogheen, watch for a rock cairn (it looks like a large beehive) on the side of the mountain; it is the final resting place of Colonel Samuel Grubb, who insisted on being interred upright in order to keep an eye on his lands! (Now *that's* a stubborn Irishman!) On clear days you can see the Rock of Cashel twenty miles to the north. Even on days that aren't so clear, you'll have stirring views of storms moving across the Golden Vale.

PRACTICAL INFORMATION

Banks

Banks in Munster are open Monday through Friday from 10:00 am to 12:30 pm, and from 1:30 pm to 3:00 pm. In the larger cities, the banks are usually open a little longer one day a week (the day varies throughout the province) until 5:00 pm.

Some of the larger banks in Munster have an ATM machine either outside their main doorways, or just inside the bank. The ATMs are part of the Cirrus and Plus international networks. Note: check with your bank to see if your personal identification number (PIN) will work on international ATMs. Most international ATMs only accept four-digit PINs.

Buses, Planes, & Trains

If you're flying around Ireland, you'll want to use the following airports:
- **Cork Airport**, *Tel. (021) 313131 – ten miles south of Cork City*
- **Kerry Airport**, *Farranfore, Tel. (066) 64644*
- **Shannon Airport**, *Shannon, Tel. (061) 471444*
- **Waterford Airport**, *Killowen, Tel. (051) 75589*

For buses, use the following stations:
- **Cork City**, *Parnell Station, Parnell Place, Tel. (021) 508188*
- **Killarney**, *Killarney Bus Station, Cork Road, Tel. (064) 34777*
- **Limerick**, *Colbert Station, Parnell Street, Tel. (061) 313333*
- **Waterford**, *Plunkett Station, Plunkett Street, Tel. (051) 73401*

For trains, use the following stations:
- **Cork City**, *Kent Station, Lower Glanmire Road,Tel. (021) 506766*
- **Killarney**, *Killarney Train Station, Cork Road, Tel. (064) 31067*
- **Limerick**, *Colbert Station, Parnell Street, Tel. (061) 315555*
- **Waterford**, *Plunkett Station, Plunkett street, Tel. (051) 73401*

Emergencies

Remember this: dialing 999 in Ireland = dialing 911 in the States. Use it in the event of any emergency where you need assistance from the police, fire department, or the medical community.

Exchanging Money

You can exchange money at banks, most post offices, and at larger hotels.

Lost Credit Cards
- **American Express Card**, *Tel. (01) 288-3311*
- **American Express Traveler's Checks**, *Tel. 800-626-0000*
- **Diners Club**, *Tel. 800-709-944*
- **Visa/MasterCard**, *Tel. (01) 269-7700*

Restrooms

Public restrooms are not prevalent in Ireland; your best bet is usually a hotel or a pub. (Hint: most hotels have at least one pub, and the restrooms are usually located near the pub.)

Note: in the Gaeltacht (Irish-speaking) areas of Munster, some of the restrooms may only be marked in Irish. If you guess, you'll probably guess wrong: *Mna* is for women, and *Fir* is for men.

Tourist Offices

Tourist offices are located throughout Munster. The main offices are:
- **Cashel**, *Town Hall, County Tipperary, Tel. (062) 61333*
- **Tipperary**, *James Street, County Tipperary, Tel. (062) 51457*
- **Waterford**, *41 The Quay, County Waterford, Tel. (051) 77388*

16. CONNACHT

Connacht is the province that covers central and western Ireland. It consists of five counties, all of which are on the sea except County Roscommon. Counties Galway and Mayo are by far the largest counties in Connacht, and two of the four largest counties in the country.

Connacht is the least populated of Ireland's four provinces. Indeed, large areas of land are relatively unpopulated; driving through portions of County Mayo makes you think you've strayed off the map and are traveling in Wyoming. But in late summer when the heather has changed to purple, the scenes are splendid and you know for sure you're not in the American West.

Connemara is an area of quiet beauty. In western Galway, **Connemara** is home to the "Twelve Bens," twelve mountains that rise seemingly out of nowhere to dominate the landscape. Here and there Connemara is dotted with beautiful loughs, hillocks, and vales.

Galway is the principal city of Connacht, with a population in excess of 50,000. It's a pretty city with a small town feel. Across from the mouth of Galway harbor are the **Aran Islands**, islands that hearken back to an ancient time. A fun place to visit, the Aran Islands are wind-swept and barren. It's a hearty people that call the Aran Islands home. I think you'll enjoy meeting them.

Further up the coast is the pretty seaport town of **Westport**, primarily a fishing port, but tourism is a close second.

ARRIVALS & DEPARTURES

Connacht is easily accessible via several different modes of transportation.

BY AIR

Visitors arriving on transatlantic flights, or from Europe or Britain, fly into Shannon Airport. As soon as you clear Customs, you'll see over a dozen rental car agencies awaiting you with open arms. If it's bus service you prefer, the bus stop is right outside the arrivals hall, and for £4, it will take you into Limerick.

Buses leave every half hour throughout the day, beginning at ten minutes after the hour (e.g. 7:10 am, 7:40 am, 8:10 am, etc.). Evening bus service isn't quite as frequent, with buses leaving for Limerick at 6:00 pm. 7:00 pm, 9:00 pm, and midnight. If you want a taxi, the taxi stand is right outside the Arrivals hall, and the ride into Limerick will cost about £16.

Visitors from Britain can fly into **Horan International Airport**, *located in the small town of Knock in County Mayo, Tel. (094) 67222*, and known most frequently as Knock Airport. Horan International Airport has about a half dozen rental car desks awaiting you as you enter the small terminal. One of these would be a good choice – there are no other options as far as taxi or bus service to any of the surrounding towns.

Coming from Britain, you can also fly into **Galway Airport**, *about seven miles from Galway City, Tel. (091) 755569*. When you arrive, a number of rental car agencies will be available to you. There is only one bus into town, and that leaves at 1:30 every day.

Taxis are available right outside the main doors, and they will whisk you into downtown Galway for about £7.

BY BUS

As with the other provinces, there is frequent bus service to Connacht from Dublin. Buses leave from Dublin's **Busaras Station**, *Store Street, Tel. (01) 836-6222*, in Dublin. There are frequent routes into Connacht, and the rates are quite inexpensive. In most cases, the round-trip fare is the same as the one-way fare, and if it's different, it's only by a pound or two. Call Busaras Station at the number above for exact schedule information.

For **Galway**, the bus depot is **Ceannt Station**, *Station Road just off Eyre Square, Tel. (091) 64222*, where nine buses a day arrive from Dublin. The nearly four-hour trip will cost you about £10. The area the bus station is fine, and only a short walk to the hotels and sights to see in Galway.

There is no bus station in **Westport**, even though three buses a day arrive from Dublin. Passengers are dropped off at the Grand Central Hotel on the Octagon in town. The neighborhood is fine, and you'll be right where all the action is.

BY CAR

The main roads into Connacht are the N6 and N17 into Galway, and the N60 into Westport. The N17 runs between Galway and Sligo. The N5 makes a hearty attempt to come into Connacht, but dead-ends at Castlebar, outside of Westport. Unlike other areas in Ireland, there are not myriads of roads running everywhere within the province. When traveling in Connacht, there are usually only one or two roads to choose from to get where you're going. This is especially true in the Connemara District and in County Mayo.

BY TRAIN

Train service to Connacht is pretty abbreviated, especially when compared to how large the province is. Train lines run to Galway and Westport. Given Connacht's size, wide-open spaces, and few inhabitants, you would be well-advised to have additional transportation plans if you wish to see much of Connacht.

For **Galway**, the train depot is also the bus depot: **Ceannt Station**, *Station Road just off Eyre Square, Tel. (091) 64222*. Ten trains a day arrive from Dublin after their three-hour journey. The fare for the trip is £24. The station, just off Eyre Square, is near hotels and Galway's sights.

For **Westport**, the train depot is **Westport Station**, *Altamount Street, Tel. (098) 25253*. Three trains a day arrive from Dublin. The fare for the three and a half hour ride is £24. The station is in a very nice section of town, and a short walk to all of Westport's shops.

GREAT CONNACHT SIGHTS!

ACHILL ISLAND – *Achill Island is the largest island off the Ireland coast. It is relatively tourist-free, so you might want to venture here for a relaxing and quiet visit.*

ARAN ISLANDS – *A trip to the Aran Islands is like a journey into Ireland's past. It'll take a day, but it will be well worth the time.*

ASHFORD CASTLE – *Unfortunately, Ashford Castle is not open to the public unless you are a guest at the luxury hotel now occupying the premises. But its grounds are impressive, and it's worth the time to drive around or stroll through.*

CONNEMARA – *The Connemara District of Connacht is unlike any other area of Ireland. Lots of wide open spaces provide serenity and tranquillity.*

CREEVYKEEL COURT TOMB – *Creevykeel Court Tomb is one of the finest examples of a classic court tomb in existence. Archaeologists estimate it has been here since 3,000 BC.*

CROAGH PATRICK – *Known as Ireland's Holy Mountain, Croagh Patrick sits regally on the south side of Clew Bay and holds an important position in Irish legend, as it is the site where St. Patrick rid the Emerald Isle of all those nasty snakes.*

DRUMCLIFFE – *Poets take note: this is the site of the gravestone of W. B. Yeats, inscribed with the epitaph he wrote years before his death.*

GALWAY CITY – *Galway City is my favorite Irish city. Spend a little time here walking in and out of the shops on Quay/High Street, and take in Eyre Square, Lynch's Memorial Window, and the Salmon Weir Bridge.*

KYLEMORE ABBEY – *As you are driving through the open expansive of Connemara, you'll have an opportunity to stop and see Kylemore Abbey, an impressive abbey set on the shores of a lake. It has a fairytale quality about it.*

WHERE TO STAY

Galway City

SEA BREEZE B&B, *13 Whitestrand Avenue, Lower Salthill, Galway, Tel. (091) 61530. 4 rooms. Rates for singles: £19 to £21, doubles: £14 to £16 per person sharing. Rates include breakfast. No credit cards accepted. No service charge.*

If you want a wonderful place to stay in Galway, you can't go wrong with the Sea Breeze B&B. This clean and comfortable B&B is enhanced by the great cooking of Colette O'Donnell, and all is complemented by the warm and friendly welcome Colette and husband Joe extend to all their guests. Just a block off Galway Bay in a quiet cul-de-sac, the Sea Breeze is within walking distance of downtown Galway, or within a block of public transportation if you'd prefer. Two rooms are ensuite, and two share a bath. Baby-sitting services are available if you've brought your children and wish to have a little time to yourself.

CONNACHT'S BEST HOTELS

THE CORAL REEF B&B, *Lecanvey, Westport, Tel. (098) 64814. 5 rooms. Rates for singles: £21 en suite, £19 standard, doubles: £16 per person sharing for en suite and £14 per person sharing for standard. Beautiful views of Clew Bay or Croagh Patrick await those who stay here.*

LOUGH INAGH LODGE, *Recess, Connemara, Tel. (095) 31006, fax (095) 31085. 20 rooms. Rates for singles: £55 to £59, doubles: £40 to £52 per person sharing, suites: £47 to £60 per person sharing. This former hunting lodge has been restored and is a wonderful place to stay while in Connemara.*

BALLYNAHINCH CASTLE HOTEL, *Recess, Connemara, Tel. (095) 31006, fax (095) 31085. 28 rooms. Rates for singles: £55 to £69, doubles: £80 to £104, suites: £94 to £120. Ballynahinch Castle has been converted into a four-star hotel with beautiful views of either the mountains or the lake.*

CASHEL HOUSE HOTEL, *Cashel, Connemara, Tel. (095) 31001, fax (095) 31077, US toll free 800-223-6510. 32 rooms. Rates for singles: £49 to £66, doubles: £49 to £66 per person sharing. Pound for pound, pence for pence, this is probably the best lodging for the money in western Ireland!*

ROSLEAGUE MANOR, *Letterfrack, Connemara, Tel. (095) 41101, fax (095) 41168, US toll free 800-223-6510. 18 rooms. Rates for singles: £45 to £70, doubles: £45 to £70 per person sharing, suites: £140. Antiques, large, comfortable rooms, marvelous views, and lovely gardens.*

GLENLO ABBEY, *Bushypark, Galway, Tel. (09) 526666, fax (091) 527880, US toll free 800-525-4800. 45 rooms. Rates for singles: £110, doubles: £135 to £150, suites: £175 to £375. Originally an 18th-century manor house, now a lovely four-star hotel.*

ASHFORD CASTLE, *Cong, Tel. (092) 46003, fax (092) 46260, US toll free 800-346-7007. 83 rooms. Rates for standard rooms: £116 to £202, deluxe rooms: £180 to £245, state rooms: £180 to £292, suites: £245 to £414. I don't believe there is another Irish hotel in the same class as Ashford Castle. Elegance and regal splendor.*

RONCALLI HOUSE, *24 Whitestrand Avenue, Lower Salthill, Galway, Tel. (091) 584159. 6 rooms. Rates for singles: £21, doubles: £16 per person sharing. Rates include breakfast. No credit cards accepted. No service charge.*
This modern two-story B&B comes highly recommended by numerous other B&B owners, as well as tourists I spoke with. Right on Galway

Bay, you'll enjoy the setting almost as much as the hospitality. And if it's a little cool out, the fireplace will keep you warm. There are six bedrooms, two on the ground floor and four upstairs, and all have their own bathrooms. The rooms are pleasant, light, and airy. Tea- and coffee-making facilities are available in each of the rooms. You're within a short walk of downtown Galway.

MARLESS HOUSE, *Threadneedle Road, Salthill, Galway, Tel. (091) 23931, fax (091) 529810. 6 rooms. Rates for singles: £22, doubles: £17 per person sharing. Rates include breakfast. No credit cards accepted. No service charge.*

This pretty two-story red and white neo-Georgian home is a stone's throw from the beach (well, maybe a little farther – about 100 yards). The rooms are large and comfortably furnished. Mrs. Geraghty knows how to take care of her guests. Tea- and coffee-making facilities are available in each room.

LISCARRA HOUSE, *6 Seamount, Threadneedle Road, Salthill, Galway, Tel. (091) 21299. 4 rooms. Rates for singles: £22, doubles: £17 per person sharing. Rates include breakfast. No credit cards accepted. No service charge.*

This lovely new home overlooks Galway Bay and has great views. The rooms are light and tastefully decorated. This B&B will be a pleasant place to put your feet up after a long day.

JURY'S GALWAY INN, *Quay Street, Galway City, Tel. (091) 566444, fax (091) 568415, U.S. toll free 800-843-3311. 128 rooms. Rates for singles: £43 to £56, doubles: £43 to £56 per person sharing. Restaurant. All major credit cards accepted. No service charge.*

Jury's Galway Inn is located at the foot of the key shopping street in Galway (Quay/High/Shop/William Street). The idea behind this inn is to provide basic, no-frills accommodations at a reasonable price. The location is an excellent one to base your exploration of Galway.

The hotel lobby is open, pleasant, and modern. Many of the rooms overlook the River Corrib near the end of its journey to Galway Bay. The rooms themselves are large and plain, but comfortable. You'll find the basics here – telephone and television – but nothing extra such as tea- and coffee-making facilities, flowers, mineral water, etc.

Because of its budget focus and nifty location, Jury's Galway Inn fills up quickly during the summer months. If you'd like to stay here, be sure and call ahead.

GREAT SOUTHERN HOTEL, *Eyre Square, Galway City, Tel. (091) 564041, fax (091) 566704. 116 rooms. Rates for singles: £67 to £77, doubles: £50 to £57 per person sharing. Restaurant, indoor swimming pool, sauna, hair salon. All major credit cards accepted. 12.5% service charge.*

Located at the eastern side of Eyre Square in downtown Galway, the Great Southern Hotel has seen Galway City grow up around it. Built in

1845 as a hotel for railroad passengers, the hotel must have been an incredibly grand place for its day. Today, its age is beginning to show, but much of its former grandeur still shines through as you walk into its lobby.

The public rooms have all been renovated, and they retain their old-world feel. O'Flaherty's Pub is a delight, and its decor recalls the hotel's days as the railway hotel for Galway. Guest rooms feature mahogany and brass furnishings, and most are quite large and roomy, although there are a few that are a bit on the small side. The hotel offers a number of fitness activities for its guests, including an exercise room, sauna, and rooftop pool that offers some of the most splendid views of the city.

ARDILAUN HOUSE HOTEL, *Taylor's Hill, Galway City, Tel. (091) 21546. 89 rooms. Rates for singles: £45 to £65, doubles: £70 to £115, suites: £175 to £375; children under 4 stay free, and 50% reduction for kids under age 10 in their parents' room. Rates include breakfast. Restaurant, pub, gardens, tennis, fitness center, sauna. All major credit cards accepted. 10% service charge.*

This hotel is located amid a quiet residential neighborhood in the Taylor's Hill area of Galway City. Over the years, Ardilaun House has been one of the best places to stay in the Galway City area. Currently, however, it is in need of some attention to things like carpet and wallpaper.

The rooms are of varying sizes, decorated in soft colors, and are comfortably furnished. Each room is provided with trouser press to help you stay unwrinkled. There are a number of fitness activities available to guests at the Ardilaun House, including an exercise room, sauna, and a solarium. There's also a snooker room available.

BRENNANS YARD HOTEL, *Lower Merchants Road, Galway, Tel. (091) 568166, fax (091) 568262. 24 rooms. Rates for singles: £55, doubles: £70; children under 12 are free in parents' room. Rates include breakfast. Restaurant. All major credit cards accepted. 12.5% service charge.*

Brennan's Yard Hotel is found in Galway's "Left Bank" area, and is a delightful place. From what was once an old warehouse, Brennan's Yard has arisen as a clean and classy place. The bedrooms are each uniquely decorated in a light and airy manner. Antique pine furniture, pottery, and art from local artists grace the somewhat small rooms. Tea- and coffee-making facilities are available in each room.

CORRIB GREAT SOUTHERN, *Dublin Road, Galway City, Tel. (091) 755281, fax (091) 751390. 180 rooms. Rates for singles: £72, doubles: £104; children under 12 stay free in parents' room. Rates include breakfast. Restaurant, indoor swimming pool, spa, snooker. All major credit cards accepted. No service charge.*

This modern low-rise hotel overlooking Galway Bay has benefited greatly from a recent refurbishment. The rooms are a mix of large, comfortably furnished rooms to smaller but functional rooms. All are well-kept and clean and have a trouser press.

The hotel is noted for its animated pub called O'Malleys, and it is popular with both tourists and Galwegians. The views of Galway Bay from O'Malleys are an added bonus. The hotel has a number of amenities available for its guests, including an indoor pool, jacuzzi, and a steam room. The hotel really caters to families, allowing children under twelve years of age to stay free in their parents' rooms, and offers a discount in their restaurant for children twelve years old and younger. The hotel has a number of rooms that are wheelchair-accessible.

GLENLO ABBEY HOTEL, *Bushypark, Galway, Tel. (09) 526666, fax (091) 527880, US toll free 800-525-4800. 45 rooms. Rates for singles: £110, doubles: £135 to £150, suites: £175 to £375. Rates include breakfast. Restaurant, pub, golf. All major credit cards accepted. No service charge.*

Just four miles outside Galway City, Glenlo Abbey Hotel is a marvelous place. Connected to an 18th-century abbey via a breezeway, this five-star hotel was built in 1993.

Originally this was a manor house built in 1740 by and belonging to Lord Ffrench, one of the principal families of Galway. Lady Ffrench felt she needed her own personal chapel if she was to keep up with the Jones's (or the Blakes, Bodkins, Brownes, D'Arcys, etc.). Lord Ffrench was appalled by the hypocrisy and strongly opposed the proposition, but Lady Ffrench prevailed, sort of. The abbey was begun, but Lord Ffrench gave strict instructions that the work was to take a long time. Lady Ffrench died before its completion, and it sat unfinished until the current owners of the Glenlo Abbey Hotel finished it according to the original plans.

They have done a nice job of blending the new sections of the hotel into the existing portions of the original manor house. The rooms are huge and lavishly decorated befitting a five-star hotel. Check out the bars in the Canfield Lounge and the River Room. Both were made from the converted altars of an old Catholic church in Kilkenny.

There is an interesting 9/18 hole golf course associated with the hotel. It's actually nine fairways, and each fairway has two greens. On the "front" nine you play one green, and on the "back" nine you play the other green.

County Galway

BROOKSIDE YOUTH HOSTEL, *Hulk Street, Clifden, Connemara, Tel. (095) 21812. 36 beds. Rates are £5 to £7 per person. No credit cards accepted. No service charge.*

At the edge of Clifden, you'll find Brookside Youth Hostel. The furnishings, rooms, and about everything else here are pretty basic, but they'll meet your needs if you're looking for a hostel. Two self-catering kitchens are available for guests. Linens are included.

SUNNYBANK GUESTHOUSE, *Westport Road, Clifden, Connemara Tel. (095) 21437. 11 rooms. Rates for singles: £22 to £27, doubles: £22 to £27 per person sharing. Rates include breakfast. No credit cards accepted. No service charge.*

The Sunnybank Guesthouse sits proudly and regally atop a hill overlooking Clifden. The converted Georgian house (circa 1814) boasts large, tastefully decorated rooms with high ceilings. All rooms are a little different, and all have been well refurbished. The rooms are quite comfortable. In addition to fine sleeping accommodations, Sunnybank also offers a nice fitness package for their guests. They have an outdoor swimming pool (it's heated), sauna, solarium, and tennis courts.

Sunnybank Guesthouse is the recipient of a number of industry awards, including one for outstanding breakfasts.

THE QUAY HOUSE, *Clifden, Tel. (095) 21369, fax (095) 21608. 10 rooms. Rates for singles: £30 to £35, doubles: £30 to £35 per person sharing. Rates include breakfast. Restaurant, gardens. Diner's Club, MasterCard, Visa accepted. No service charge.*

The Quay House is most renowned for its excellent restaurant (see *Where to Eat* section), but it also has a few rooms to rent. The rooms are nice sized, and are tastefully decorated. The rooms at the front of the house overlook Clifden Harbor and cost a few pounds more. If you've an extra few minutes, see if you can eat lunch – or at least chat with – one of the owners, Paddy or Julia Foyle. They are both truly delightful, and are exceptionally pleasant to visit with.

RENVYLE HOUSE, *Renvyle, Tel. (095) 43511, fax (095) 43515. 65 rooms. Rates for singles: £60, doubles: £62 per person. Rates include breakfast. Restaurant, swimming pool, sauna, gardens, tennis, snooker, putting and bowling greens, riding, fishing. All major credit cards accepted. 10% service charge.*

Once considered one of the finest hotels in Ireland, the Renvyle Hotel is still nice but in need of modernization and upgrading. Recent refurbishment of several dozen of their rooms has gone a long way to reclaiming their past glory when, for example, world leaders like Winston Churchill stayed here. Many of the public areas are endowed with photos of past personalities enjoying their stay at Renvyle.

The bedrooms are small for the most part and unmemorably decorated. Several of the suites have balconies overlooking the pool, but the best views are on the drive to the hotel. Stunning seascapes follow you along the mountain road, but are mostly hidden from view once you reach the hotel.

The hotel has a number of amenities that their guests find enjoyable. They have a swimming pool, tennis court, snooker room, and a playground for the kids. They also offer a discount for families traveling with children, and they'll arrange baby-sitting services for you if you need them. Pets are welcome, and the hotel is wheelchair-accessible.

ABBEYGLEN CASTLE HOTEL, *Clifden, Connemara, Tel. (095) 21201, fax (095) 21797. 36 rooms. Rates for singles: £64 to £78, doubles: £49 to £65 per person sharing, suites: £69 to £85 per person sharing. Rates include breakfast. Restaurant, swimming pool, sauna, gardens, tennis, snooker, pitch and putt golf. All major credit cards accepted. 12.5% service charge.*

Clifden's own *faux-castle*, the Abbeyglen Castle Hotel, offers nice views of Clifden from some of its rooms and from its grounds. Rooms are of adequate size, but the furnishings are largely unremarkable. The hotel is set in twelve acres of well-manicured grounds, with gardens, verdant lawns, a swimming pool and tennis courts. But don't expect to stay here if you are traveling with small children; the hotel requests no children under ten years of age. Seniors, however, are treated with a discount all year except July and August.

THE ARDAGH HOTEL, *Ballyconeely Road, Clifden, Tel. (095) 21384, fax (095) 21314. 21 rooms. Rates for singles: £45 to £52, doubles: £35 to £42 per person sharing. Restaurant. All major credit cards accepted. No service charge. Open from March through October.*

About two miles outside Clifden on the road to Ballyconeely sits the Ardagh Hotel. Overlooking Ardbear Bay, the views are just enough to make you want to stay one more night (or two).

The rooms are nice sized, and the floral print wallpaper gives them a quiet, homey feeling. The best rooms overlook the Bay, although the views out over the mountains around Clifden are very nice too. Each room has tea- and coffee-making facilities.

CASHEL HOUSE HOTEL, *Cashel, Connemara, Tel. (095) 31001, (095) 31077, US toll free 800-223-6510. 32 rooms. Rates for singles: £49 to £66, doubles: £49 to £66 per person sharing. Rates include breakfast. Restaurant, gardens, riding, walking trails. All major credit cards accepted. 12.5% service charge.*

Cashel House Hotel is a warm, comfortable, and delightful hotel. It has the feel and personality of a B&B, but the facilities and amenities of a hotel. Built in the 19th century, Cashel House has been magnificently renovated. It's chock full of antiques and old (*old!*) oil paintings. Plush Connemara hand-made rugs grace the floors throughout the hotel.

If that's not enough, their restaurant is considered one of the best in Ireland (see *Where to Eat* section). The restaurant is in a semi-circular conservatory with large windows that overlook the well-manicured lawn and gardens. The food is exceptional, and features the freshest ingredients that add just the right subtle flavorings necessary to make the meals a wonderful dining experience. Whether you prefer fish, beef, or vegetarian meals, there is a tradition of excellence here.

Each hotel room is lavish and unique. Each is tastefully wallpapered and carpeted. Flowers from the extensive gardens are found daily in your room – just the right touch to make you feel that much more welcome.

Riding stables on-site are constantly in use by the guests; in keeping with their thoughtful manner, the owners have provided boots and riding helmets for their guests to ensure they have a safe and enjoyable ride. Luxurious gardens make for a quiet beginning or a romantic end to your day. Pound for pound, pence for pence, this is probably the best lodging for the money in western Ireland! The owners, Dermot and Kay McEvilly, have been in the hotel business since 1968, and the product they offer is full of grace and quiet elegance.

ROSLEAGUE MANOR, *Letterfrack, Connemara, Tel. (095) 41101, fax (095) 41168, US toll free 800-223-6510. 18 rooms. Rates for singles: £45 to £70, doubles: £45 to £70 per person sharing, suites: £140. Rates include breakfast. Restaurant, gardens, sauna, fishing, boat trips, walking trails, billiards, tennis. American Express, MasterCard, and Visa accepted. No service charge. Closed from November through Easter.*

About nine miles out of Clifden between Clifden and Westport sits pretty Rosleague Manor, an elegant Georgian manor house overlooking Ballinakill Bay. Rosleague Manor is jointly owned by the brother-sister team of Paddy and Anne Foyle. (Along with his wife, Paddy also owns The Quay House and Destry Rides Again in Clifden.) Together, the Foyles have out-serened the serene with Rosleague Manor, which has become a favorite base of those touring Connemara. There are thirty acres of lush lawns and gorgeous gardens available for guests to stroll through.

The house is as exceptional inside as it is outside. Antiques, turf fires, and old portraits set the perfect atmosphere. Spacious bedrooms furnished thoughtfully with antiques and comfortable furniture are complemented by nice bathrooms with modern fixtures. The rooms have wonderful views that make them seem even more tranquil and comfortable.

Resident in the house is an excellent restaurant presided over by Nigel Rush, a Swiss-trained chef. He works his magic with fresh ingredients, imaginative menus, and superb cuisine. A specialty of the house is fish from the nearby Atlantic and many of the inland lakes found scattered throughout Connemara. Beef, lamb, and fowl are also available.

LOUGH INAGH LODGE, *Recess, Connemara, Tel. (095) 31006, fax (095) 31085. 20 rooms. Rates for singles: £55 to £59, doubles: £40 to £52 per person sharing, suites: £47 to £60 per person sharing; children under 12 stay free in their parents' room. Rates include breakfast. Restaurant, gardens, croquet, riding, fishing, walking trails. All major credit cards accepted. 10% service charge.*

Once the hunting lodge associated with Ballynahinch Castle, Lough Inagh Lodge is now a fine hotel with a reputation for excellence all its own. Its owners, John and Moira O'Connor, have overseen its refurbishment with a zeal for perfection. The results are outstanding: turf fires, period antiques, and a wonderful, friendly atmosphere.

Like her sibling, Lough Inagh Lodge's rooms are large, tastefully decorated, and all have lovely views of either Lough Inagh or the mountains and countryside. Lough Inagh Lodge caters to families, with a discount available for children. If you've brought a pet, the hotel accepts them also.

BALLYNAHINCH CASTLE HOTEL, *Recess, Connemara, Tel. (095) 31006, fax (095) 31085. 28 rooms. Rates for singles: £55 to £69, doubles: £80 to £104, suites: £94 to £120. Rates include breakfast. Restaurant, gardens, croquet, riding, shooting, walking trails. All major credit cards accepted. 10% service charge.*

Simply put, Ballynahinch Castle is an entrancing place, from the live red fox that often greets tourists at the front door to the impeccable service. Ancestral home of the Martin Clan of Connemara, Ballynahinch Castle has been converted into a four-star hotel. The rooms – all individually decorated – are spacious and offer beautiful views of either the mountains or the lake.

During the 1930s, the eccentric (and wealthy) Maharajah Ranjitsinji purchased Ballynahinch Castle as a winter get-away to relax and entertain his friends. Pictures of the Maharajah grace some of the walls and help put a name with the face.

In recent years, Ballynahinch Castle Hotel has earned the reputation as a shooting center, where sportsmen and sportswomen come from all over the world to participate in five annual woodcock bird hunts sponsored by the hotel. In addition to the exceptional service and the warmth of Ballynahinch Castle, the restaurant is also impressive. Looking out over the Owenmore River as it quietly fills Ballynahinch Lake, the flood-lit shores add a peaceful touch to your dining experience. The food is delicious, the service efficient, and the atmosphere tranquil.

Ballynahinch Castle Hotel is rightfully proud of their designation as *Ireland's Hotel of the Year* in 1994.

County Mayo

THE CORAL REEF B&B, *Lecanvey, Westport, Tel. (098) 64814. 5 rooms. Rates for singles: £21 en suite, £19 standard, doubles: £16 per person sharing for en suite and £14 per person sharing for standard. Rates include breakfast. No credit cards accepted. No service charge.*

One of my personal favorite B&Bs in Ireland, The Coral Reef is located on the shores of Clew Bay and at the foot of Croagh Patrick. The rooms are nice-sized and comfortably furnished. Mrs. Ann Colgan is your ever-friendly and efficient hostess. She was recently awarded the coveted "Personal Touch" award by Bord Failte (the Irish Tourist Board).

Two of the rooms are en suite, and three are not. The en suite rooms carry a slight premium over the others.

CEDAR LODGE, *Kings Hill, Westport, Tel. (098) 25417. 4 rooms. Rates for singles: £21 en suite, £19 standard, doubles: £16 per person sharing for en suite and £14 per person sharing for standard. Rates include breakfast. No credit cards accepted. No service charge.*

This highly recommended inn is a delightful and pleasant B&B within minutes of downtown. Mrs. Maureen Flynn is a gracious hostess and you'll like the bright and airy rooms she has. You'll also enjoy the gardens that flank the house.

ROSBEG HOUSE, *Westport, (Tel. 098) 25879. 5 rooms. Rates for singles: £30 en suite, £25 standard, doubles: £20 per person sharing for en suite and £17.50 for standard. Rates include breakfast. No credit cards accepted. No service charge.*

What a lovely old Georgian home to have a B&B in! As is typical with these old Georgian homes, the rooms are large, with high ceilings that make them seem even more spacious. Three of those spacious rooms overlook Clew Bay and the views are a pure pleasure. Mrs. Kay O'Brien is rightfully proud of her B&B, which is located on a lane just off the R395 on the western edge of town.

THE OLDE RAILWAY HOTEL, *The Mall, Westport, Tel. (098) 25166. 24 rooms. Rates for singles: £38 to £55, doubles: £28 to £40 per person sharing; children up to 12 stay free in their parents' room. Rates include breakfast. Restaurant, gardens. All major credit cards accepted. 12.5% service charge.*

The Olde Railway Hotel has been serving guests since 1780, when it was a coaching inn. Today, it stands across from the tree-lined banks of the Carrowbeg River on the Mall in Westport. Classic-looking, it is renowned for its generous collection of antiques placed liberally throughout the hotel.

The rooms are tastefully furnished in warm colors and comfortable furniture, and each room has a fine bathroom en suite. A newly added set of self-catering apartments are an option offered by the hotel. These self-contained units include kitchenettes, and continue the comfortable feeling felt in the rest of the hotel. If you are traveling with children, you can take advantage of the hotel's discount for children. (Children under twelve stay free in their parents' rooms).

WESTPORT WOODS HOTEL, *Louisburgh Road, Westport, (098) 25811, (098) 26212 (fax), 95 rooms. Rates for singles: £31, doubles: £47. Rates include breakfast. Restaurant, tennis, miniature golf. All major credit cards accepted. No service charge.*

This low-rise hotel built in the 1970s is comfortable, but is in need of updating. A recent addition which added 38 new rooms was greatly needed. Those rooms are of adequate size, and are decorated tastefully and furnished comfortably. The older rooms are little smaller, and not as nicely furnished, but functional, and include a trouser press. The hotel focuses on families traveling with children, as they offer special discounts, baby-sitting service, both an indoor and outdoor play area, and goofy golf. Special rates are also available for seniors.

HOTEL WESTPORT, *Westport, Tel. (098) 25122, fax (098) 26739. 130 rooms. Rates for singles: £54, doubles: £44 per person sharing, suites: £175 per person sharing. Rates include breakfast. Restaurant, swimming pool, spa, fitness center, sauna. All major credit cards accepted. 12.5% service charge.*

This modern low-rise hotel on the outskirts of Westport is convenient to town (about five minutes' walk) and provides a quiet place to stay. The rooms are of average size and decor, but are clean and comfortable.

THE NEWPORT HOUSE, *Newport, Tel. (098) 41222, fax (098) 41613. 19 rooms. Rates for singles: £55, doubles: £55 to £66 per person sharing. Rates include breakfast. Restaurant, gardens, fishing, walking trails. All major credit cards accepted. 10% service charge. Open from mid-March through the end of September.*

As you pull up to Newport House, you'll see an attractive ivy-clad old Georgian manor house standing amid beautiful gardens. It oozes character, personality, and a certain mystery.

Ancient portraits, a liberal dose of antiques, and exquisite furnishings are found throughout the house. The grand staircase is nearly enough to take your breath away; the carpets are hand-made in Connemara. The bedrooms are large, even spacious, and feature some of the home's fine antiques.

Newport House has gained a well-deserved reputation as a base for fishing, and in the mornings you'll run into a number of ghillies (guides) waiting to take their clients out for a spot of fishing.

ASHFORD CASTLE, *Cong, Tel. (092) 46003, fax (092) 46260, US toll free 800-346-7007, 83 rooms. Rates for standard rooms: £116 to £202, deluxe rooms: £180 to £245, state rooms: £180 to £292, suites: £245 to £414. Restaurant, gardens, tennis, grounds, fishing, walking trails, golf. All major credit cards accepted. No service charge.*

What an exquisite hotel this is. Ashford Castle has been highlighted several times on *Lifestyles of the Rich and Famous,* and was one of the hotels Ronald Reagan stayed in during his visit to Ireland.

Resting regally amid 350 acres of lush parkland, this 13th-century Norman castle is a sight to behold. Inside, the amount, quality, and sheer presence of scores of antiques and old portraits combined with rich paneled walls and plush carpets gives you the feeling you've stumbled into the private chambers of an ancient ruler. The public rooms are elegant, filled with rich leather chairs, dark paneling, and views of the verdant grounds.

The bedrooms are unique, all well-appointed with beautiful furnishings, and are probably the largest you'll find in Ireland for each class of room. All have antiques aplenty, plush carpets, and marvelous bathrooms. Thick robes, slippers, mineral water, and a bowl of fruit greet you upon arrival.

There is no question that Ashford Castle is the *créme de la créme* of hotels in Ireland. However, as exquisite and elegant as Ashford Castle is, it has a reputation for a certain amount of stuffiness. Perhaps it's the sign at the front stairs letting you know that if you are not a guest, you are not welcome inside. Or perhaps it's their own brochure, which boasts that the hotel was "...built for the pleasure of the elite few...." Either way, it seems to be a reputation they are proud of and strive to maintain. The service is supremely efficient but lacks the customary warmth and familiarity associated with Irish hotels.

Having said this, if you choose to stay at Ashford Castle, I predict it will be one of your most memorable experiences in Ireland.

County Sligo

CROMLEACH LODGE, *Castlebaldwin, Boyle, Tel. (071) 65155, fax (071) 65455. 10 rooms. Rates for singles: £55 to £70, doubles: £40 to £65 per person sharing. Rates include breakfast. American Express, MasterCard, and Visa accepted. No service charge.*

Don't stay at Cromleach Lodge if you have your heart set on staying in one of those gorgeous Georgian homes or if you have dreamed of staying in a renovated 11th-century Norman castle. But if you're willing to depart a bit from the stereotypical Irish accommodation, you might find yourself pleasantly surprised by this lodge.

Christy and Moira Tighe have a gem atop a hill outside of Castlebaldwin. Splendid views of Lough Arrow complement the fine service Cromleach Lodge has come to be known for. In fact, every room has stunning views of the surrounding countryside. The rooms are large, even spacious by some accounts. They are lavishly furnished, and coupled with the view, are some of the best rooms in the west of Ireland. Each room offers tea- and coffee-making facilities, complimentary fruit bowls, mineral water, and even small bottles of Bailey's Irish Whiskey!

COOPERSHILL HOUSE, *Riverstown, Tel. (071) 65108, fax (071) 65466. 7 rooms. Rates for singles: £54, doubles: £44 per person sharing. Rates include breakfast. All major credit cards accepted. No service charge.*

Seven generations of O'Hara's have lived at Coopershill House, which was built in 1774. The house itself is regal – sitting in the midst of

500 verdant acres. But don't let this intimidate you. Once inside the doors, you'll feel as comfortable as if you are long-lost and well-loved family coming for a visit.

The bedrooms are large and spacious, and are generously endowed with antiques, old portraits, and four poster bed in most rooms. Complement those amenities with fresh flowers from the gardens and mineral water and you've all the trappings for a restful stay. (Bring a book – with no television to mar the tranquillity, you may need something besides the late movie to get you ready for sleep.) Lindy O'Hara will be delighted if you choose to stay for dinner, as she serves some of the finest meals in County Sligo. The dining room is grand, and features beautiful antique tables, silver candelabra, and crisp Irish linen. You'll be warmed – physically and emotionally – by a fine log fire.

Aran Islands

Note: Most of the B&Bs on the Aran Islands are only open from April through October.

RADHARC NA MARA, *Kilronan, Inishmor, Aran Islands, Tel. (099) 61115. 4 rooms. Rates for singles: £19; doubles: £14 per person sharing.*

The views are outstanding from this family-run B&B and Anna Beatty's welcome is among the warmest you'll encounter on the Aran Islands.

BEACH VIEW HOUSE, *Kilronan, Inishmor, Aran Islands, Tel. (099) 61141. 6 rooms. Rates for singles: £19; doubles: £14 per person sharing.*

Mrs. Bridie Coneely will greet you with a warmth that will thaw the chill you may feel from the winds of Inishmor. Her modern Bed and Breakfast is minutes from a picturesque sandy beach and a short walk from the ancient Celtic fortress of Dun Aengus. All of the rooms are standard, which means there is no separate bath associated with the rooms.

AN CRUGAN, *Kilronan, Inishmor, Aran Islands, Tel. (099) 61150. 6 rooms. Rates for singles: £19; doubles: £14 per person sharing.*

Bridie and Patrick McDonagh run this modern B&B, and it is as pleasant as its surroundings. None of the rooms are en suite, so you'll have an opportunity to meet other guests!

KILMURVEY HOUSE, *Kilronan, Inishmor, Aran Islands, Tel. (099) 61218, fax (099) 61397. 8 rooms. Rates for singles: £21.50; doubles: £17 per person sharing. MasterCard and Visa accepted.*

This beautiful large home at the foot of the ancient Dun Aengus fort is lovely. The large, pleasant rooms are exceptional, and the greeting you receive from Patricia and Terry Tyson make you feel right at home.

WHERE TO EAT

County Galway

MCDONAGH'S RESTAURANT, 22 *Quay Street, Galway City, Tel.* (091) 565001. £5.95 to £10.95. *Open noon to 10:00 pm Monday through Saturday, and from 7:00 pm to 10:00 pm on Sunday. Diner's Club, MasterCard, and Visa accepted. No service charge.*

At the end of High/Quay Street sits the colorful exterior of McDonagh's Restaurant, an award-winning seafood restaurant and a popular eatery with the local folk as well as tourists. Inside, part of the building is a store where you can buy fresh fish, and the other half is an interesting restaurant area. The tables and booths are themselves unremarkable, but there is interesting marine paraphernalia adorning the walls. Lunch and dinner are both inexpensive.

BRIDGE MILLS RESTAURANT, *O'Brien's Bridge, Galway City, Tel.* (091) 566231. £2.95 to £9.95. *Open daily from 9:00 am to 5:30 pm, and for dinner during the summer from 6:00 pm to 10:30 pm. MasterCard and Visa accepted. No service charge.*

Overlooking the Corrib River is the Bridge Mills Restaurant, a casual eatery that is a pleasant diversion from the normal vibrancy of Galway. The restaurant has been divided into a number of small rooms that make you feel as though you are in a much smaller place. The food is primarily snacks: scones, pastries, soups and salads, although dinner is also available in the evenings. Vegetarians in particular will like Bridge Mills Restaurant, as a number of vegetarian dishes are available.

CONNACHT'S BEST RESTAURANTS

MCDONAGH'S RESTAURANT, 22 Quay Street, Galway City, Tel. (091) 565001. £5.95 to £10.95. Diner's Club, MasterCard, and Visa accepted. No service charge. Nothing fancy, but very good seafood at reasonable prices.

NEWPORT HOUSE, Newport, Tel. (098) 41222. Set dinner menu for £20. All major credit cards accepted. 12.5% service charge. Many of the ingredients they use in their dishes are home-grown in their own organic kitchen garden.

BALLYNAHINCH CASTLE RESTAURANT, Recess, Ballynahinch, Tel. (095) 31006. Set dinner menu for £23. All major credit cards accepted. 10% service charge. The restaurant for Ballynahinch Castle Hotel is as elegant as a castle dining experience should be, and the food is delicious.

CASHEL HOUSE RESTAURANT, Cashel, Tel. (095) 31001. Set dinner menu for £29. All major credit cards accepted. 12.5% service charge. The menu is simple yet offers plenty of options. The food is splendid. What more could you ask for?

HOUSE OF JAMES, *Castle Street, Galway City, Tel. (091) 565507. £3.95 to £15. Open from 9:00 am to 5:30 pm. All major credit cards accepted. No service charge.*

Pop into the House of James for a quick sandwich, bowl of soup, or a salad during your shopping. The House of James is noted for its excellent breads and pastries, as well as a number of vegetarian dishes. Dress is very casual.

HOOKER JIMMY'S STEAK & SEAFOOD BAR, *The Fishmarket, Spanish Arch, Galway City, Tel. (091) 568351. £4.95 to £14.95. Open daily from 11:30 am to 11:00 pm. All major credit cards accepted.*

Hooker Jimmy's relies on the freshest ingredients to ensure that their traditional Irish fare is flavorful. The Glanville family is so intent on this that they own a trawler and much of the fish, mussels, and lobster served in the restaurant are caught off it. The menu is not extensive, but offers standard fare like Irish beef with potato and stir-fried vegetables, and baked oysters with an herb and garlic sauce. Dress is casual.

O'GRADY'S SEAFOOD RESTAURANT, *Market Street, Clifden, Tel. (095) 21450. £6.95 to £12.95. From June through September O'Grady's is open daily from 12:30 pm to 2:30 pm, and 6:30 pm to 10:00 pm. The rest of the year those are their hours, except that they are closed on Sunday. American Express, MasterCard, and Visa accepted. No service charge.*

O'Grady's is a nice quiet restaurant on the main shopping street in Clifden. They are also known for serving excellent seafood. Samples of their menu include fillet of cod, braised monkfish, or grilled fillet of turbot with a compote of rhubarb and champagne butter cream. There are a few non-seafood dishes, but the specialties here are from the depths of the deep blue.

DESTRY RIDES AGAIN, *Main Street, Clifden, Tel. (095) 21722. £3.50 to £11.95. Open Tuesday through Sunday from noon to 3:00 pm, and from 6:00 pm to 10:00 pm. They are closed December through the end of February. MasterCard and Visa accepted. No service charge.*

Destry's is a small sandwich shop cafe in the center of town on Main Street. A pleasant place, the furnishings are simple, the service great, and the food memorable. Destry's is owned by Paddy and Julia Foyle, and if you visit, you will assuredly meet one or the other (if not both) of them.

THE QUAY HOUSE, *Clifden, Tel. (095) 21369. Á la carte menu available from £3.50 to £14.95, set dinner menu for £19.50. Open daily for dinner from 7:00 pm to 9:30 pm, and during the high season (from the end of May through the end of August) they are open for lunch from noon to 4:00 pm. MasterCard and Visa accepted. No service charge.*

The Quay House sits quietly overlooking Ardbear Bay, an estuary of the Atlantic ocean. Paddy and Julia Foyle run the Quay House as well as the cafe Destry Rides Again (see entry above), and while they are quite different as far as atmosphere and ambiance, they have one critical thing in common: the food is of the highest quality and simply delicious. Some of the winners here include warm mussel and bacon salad with anchovy dressing, and the smoked salmon chowder. The dining room is pleasant and bordering on elegant, but not stuffy. A conservatory adjoins the dining room and is a wonderful place to have a spot of afternoon tea.

O'DOWD'S SEAFOOD BAR AND RESTAURANT, *Roundstone, Tel. (095) 35809. £4.95 to £14.95. The bar and the restaurant are open daily from 12:30 pm to 9:30 pm. (On Sunday the bar is open 12:30 pm to 2:00 pm, and 4:00 pm to 9:30 pm.) American Express, MasterCard, and Visa are accepted. No service charge.*

O'Dowd's is a popular seafood bar and traditional Irish pub. The views of the Atlantic are an added bonus. Food is served in both the bar as well as the restaurant area. Seafood is the specialty, and the menu provides a wide selection: lobster, mussels, crab salad, salmon and oysters. They also offer traditional Irish dishes if that's what you're looking for, and a pretty decent wild game menu, including venison, quail, duck, and pheasant.

CASEY'S WESTWOOD RESTAURANT, *Dangan Upper, Newcastle, Galway City, Tel. (091) 521442. Set lunch menu for £12 and set dinner menu for £19.50. Open daily from 12:30 pm to 2:15 pm for lunch and from 6:30 pm to 9:45 pm for dinner. American Express, MasterCard, Visa accepted.*

Casey's is a popular eatery, frequented by many Galwegians as well as tourists. The building houses a series of bars and lounge areas, each with its own slightly different atmosphere. The main restaurant offers a variety of modern Irish fare, including such specialties as sausage of duck and wood pigeon on a bed of colcannon with a port and orange *jus*, crab salad with autumn leaves and mango salsa, and a fabulous rack of lamb with a brioche crust and parsnip crumble. Vegetarian dishes are also available, as are excellent desserts. Dress is nice casual.

THE MALT HOUSE RESTAURANT, *High Street, Galway City, Tel. (091) 63993. £9.95 to £16.95. Open daily from noon to 3:00 pm and from 6:30 pm to 10:30 pm daily. All major credit cards accepted. 10% service charge.*

Amid the hustle and bustle of High Street you'll come across the Malt House Restaurant. This small restaurant has a nice atmosphere and is known primarily for its fine fish dishes. Other offerings include Duckling a l'orange and escalope of veal Normandy. Dress is casual.

THE FFRENCH RESTAURANT, *Bushypark, N59, Galway, Tel. (091) 526666. Set dinner menus for £19 and £27. Open to the public from 6:30 pm to 10:30 pm daily. All major credit cards accepted. No service charge.*

No, the name is not a misspelling. Glenlo Abbey offers guests more than just rooms and golf. Their dining room, called the Ffrench Room, specializes in modern Irish and international cuisine. The ambiance is quietly elegant; the room is graced with plush maroon carpets that add a regal feeling. The menu is not large, but the selections are varied. Try the roast loin of pork, or baked black pudding and spinach wrapped in filo pastry on a white onion sauce. Nice casual dress is fine, although a number of the diners will probably be in jacket and tie.

DRIMCONG HOUSE, *N59, Moycullen, Tel. (091) 85115. Set dinner menus from £15.50 to £23. Open daily from 6:30 pm to 10:30 pm from mid-March through the end of November, when they are closed on Monday and Sunday. All major credit cards accepted. No service charge.*

In many circles, Drimcong House is considered one of the best restaurants in the country. They have garnered many awards over the years. The menu is surprisingly varied and guests will have a number of selections to choose from. Entrees include such tasty offerings as ham-stuffed chicken legs with sweet peppers, honey and onion compote, roast rack of lamb with herb and honey *jus,* or skate with black butter and capers. There are vegetarian offerings as well.

County Mayo

McCORMACK'S CAFE, *Bridge Street, Westport, Tel. (098) 25619. £1.50 to £5. Open daily from noon to 2:30 pm and from 5:30 to 9:00 pm. MasterCard and Visa accepted. No service charge.*

A great little cafe for a snack or quick sandwich. Nothing fancy, just convenient to the shopping areas and good, inexpensive food.

JOHN J. O'MALLEY'S, *Bridge Street, Westport, Tel. (098) 27307. £6.95 to £9.95. Open Monday through Friday from 2:00 pm to 11:30 pm. MasterCard and Visa accepted. No service charge.*

"John J's," as the locals call John J. O'Malley's, is a hot hangout for the younger set who live in or visit the city. Kind of a cross between a cafe and a pub, John J's specializes in burgers, pasta, and some seafood.

THE QUAY COTTAGE, *Westport House Road, Westport, (098) 26412, £8.95 to £15.50. Open Monday through Saturday from 6:00 pm to 10:00 pm, and Sunday from 1:00 pm to 10:00 pm. MasterCard and Visa accepted.*

The Quay Cottage is famed for its seafood by the local clientele. The restaurant lies just outside the gates to the grounds of the Westport House. Seafood is the specialty here, and they do it well. Fillet of lemon sole, fresh scallops, crab salad cocktail, and monkfish with tagliatelle are just a few of the seafood offerings available. There are other dishes, such as lamb and good Irish beef, but seafood is clearly the main focus.

NEWPORT HOUSE RESTAURANT, *Newport, Tel. (098) 41222. Set dinner menu for £20. Open daily from 7:30 pm to 9:30 pm. All major credit cards accepted. 12.5% service charge.*

The restaurant for the Newport House relies heavily on fresh produce and herbs to give their gastronomical concoctions just the right flavor. Many of the ingredients they use in their dishes are home-grown in their own organic kitchen garden. Fruits, vegetables, and herbs come from there and add that little extra flavorful touch.

The Newport House is especially noted for seafood. Typical fare includes escalope of monkfish in a shellfish sauce, salmon cured with whiskey, and grilled turbot with creamed leeks and champagne sauce. There is a nice wine list as well. Dress is nice casual, although many of the diners will have jackets and ties.

ASGARD TAVERN AND RESTAURANT, *The Quay, Westport, Tel. (098) 25319. Set dinner menu £17. Open daily from 6:30 pm to 10:30 pm. During the off-season, they are only open Tuesday through Saturday. All major credit cards accepted. No service charge.*

Overlooking Clew Bay, Asgard Tavern and Restaurant is another of the find seafood restaurants in Westport, although they do have a fair selection of other dishes to choose from. Typical dishes include poached fillet of salmon hollandaise, lobster in brandy cream, and peppered beef fillet on a warm salad. There are also several vegetarian dishes available, although it's not a wide selection.

THE ARDMORE RESTAURANT, *Quay Street, Westport, Tel. (098) 25994. Set dinner for £18.95. Open daily from 7:00 pm to 9:30 pm. All major credit cards accepted. 10% service charge.*

The Ardmore Restaurant serenely sits on a small hill overlooking Clew Bay. This is the place for a romantic candlelight dinner. The menu is varied, and offers dishes that range from fresh wild mussels and baked clams to medallions of beef with cognac and cream sauce. Many locals will tell you that this is *the* place to eat in Westport.

BALLYNAHINCH CASTLE RESTAURANT, *Recess, Ballynahinch, Tel. (095) 31006. Set dinner menu for £23. Open from 7:00 pm until 9:30 pm. All major credit cards accepted. 10% service charge.*

The romantic setting of Ballynahinch Castle holds for the dining room as well. The atmosphere is relaxed yet elegant, with service as efficient and attentive as any restaurant in Ireland. Overlooking the Owenmore River as it serenely fills Ballynahinch Lake, it's easy to get distracted from the excellent fare prepared by the chef – until the food arrives, and your attention is diverted back to the task at hand.

Typical offerings include poached breast of guinea fowl with herbs and vegetables, and pan-fried pork fillet with sherry and mushroom sauce. Desserts are terrific; try the three-chocolate mousse with puree of fresh fruit. Jacket and tie are requested.

CASHEL HOUSE RESTAURANT, *Cashel, Tel. (095) 31001. Set dinner menu for £29. Open for dinner daily from 6:30 pm to 9:30 pm and for lunch from 1:00 pm to 2:00 pm. All major credit cards accepted. 12.5% service charge.*

Cashel House the restaurant is as impressive as Cashel House the hotel, which is why heads of state dine here on occasion. The dining room overlooks the pretty grounds. The menu is simple yet offers plenty of options. The food is splendid. What more could you ask for?

Offerings might include sautéed monkfish with a shrimp sauce, roast rack of spring lamb, filo chicken in a tarragon sauce, or and guinea fowl with grapes and Madeira. Vegetarian dishes are also available.

County Sligo

TRUFFLES, *The Mall, Sligo Town, Tel. (071) 44226. £5.95 to £14.95. Open Tuesday through Saturday from 5:00 pm to 10:30 pm. No credit cards accepted. No service charge.*

Truffles specializes in pizza, and we're not talking your basic cheese and pepperoni here. Here's a sampling of the toppings you may find when you arrive: seven different cheeses (okay so far), sausage, grilled leeks, pine nuts, salmon. And let's not forget cabbage (this is, after all, an Irish restaurant!).

The atmosphere is relaxed and casual, with an eclectic collection of statues and paintings in the dining area. They have become quite popular – maybe even trendy – of late, so during the summer months you may want to call ahead for a reservation so as not to be disappointed.

BISTRO BIANCONI, *44 O'Connell Street, Sligo Town, Tel. (071) 41744. £11.95 to £16.95. Open daily from 5:30 pm until midnight. All major credit cards accepted.*

This nice bistro is stylishly decorated with frescos, plants, and muted lighting. The menu is primarily Italian, with plenty of fresh home-made pastas. Vegetarian dishes are also offered.

Aran Islands

DUN AONGHASA RESTAURANT, *Kilronan, Inishmor, Aran Islands, Tel. (099) 61104. £7.95 to £14.95. Open from noon to 3:00 pm and 6:00 pm until 10:00 pm. They are closed from November through March. MasterCard and Visa accepted.*

If you come to an island, expect to get good seafood. And if you come to Dun Aonghasa Restaurant on Inishmore, you won't be disappointed. The exceptional seafood is as tasty as the decor is welcoming: the warmth of dark wood and stone, and an open fire will make this a memorable meal for you. Ask for a table near the window and you'll have gorgeous views of Galway Bay.

FISHERMAN'S COTTAGE, *Inishere, Aran Islands, Tel. (099) 75073, £7.95 to £13.95. Open daily from noon to 5:00 pm and from 7:00 pm to 8:30 pm. They are closed from October through mid-April. All major credit cards accepted.*

Fisherman's Cottage is located on the smallest of the Aran Islands, but the meal they serve is anything but small. Try any number of wonderful seafood dishes, including scallops, lobster, oysters, or mussels. If for some odd reason you don't feel like seafood, succulent Aran lamb is also available here.

SEEING THE SIGHTS

Galway City

Galway is one of the nicest towns in Ireland, and one I fell in love with the first time I visited it. Galway is derived from the Irish word *Gaillimh*, which means "Gailleams's Place." An ancient town, Galway is thought to be the village of Magnata identified on a map by Ptolemy in the 2nd century AD. Sitting at the head of Galway Bay, this has always been a fishing town.

In 1232, Richard de Burgh decided this would be an excellent seat of operations in western Ireland, and he made it so. It remained an Anglo-Norman stronghold for several hundred years. The main families of the settlement formed an important contingent whose descendants would fill the leading legal, political, and business positions in the city and region for several hundred years. The names of these prominent families were Blake, Bodkin, Browne, D'Arcy, Dean, Fonts, Ffrench, Kirwan, Joyce, Lynche, Morris, Martin and Skerrit.

The native Irish did not think much of their fellow County Galwegians. The feeling was mutual. In 1518, a city law was passed that stated "...neither a O' nor Mac shall strutte nor swagger through the streets of Galway." Of course, the Irish didn't take that sitting down, and Galway's history is marred with many battles between the Anglo-Norman families of Galway City and the native Irish of County Galway. The O'Flaherty Clan was a particularly irritating thorn in the side of these Anglo-Norman interlopers; at one time, the west gate of the city was inscribed with the following prayer: "From the fury of the O'Flahertys, good Lord deliver us."

Galway City sits at the head of Galway Bay on the west coast of Ireland. The **River Corrib** flows through the center of Galway City on its way to Galway Bay. Galway is reached via the N17 and N59 from the north, and the N16 from the south. The N6 enters Galway from the east and is considered the main road to Dublin.

The downtown area of Galway is compact and easy to get around in – if you park your car. You can cruise the main streets and side streets, but I'd suggest that you head directly for one of several car parks in the downtown area. The closest carpark to the downtown area is about a block northwest of Eyre Square.

Eyre Square is the ideal place to begin your exploration of Galway City. From there, you are within less than a half mile from all the main streets in Galway. The streets are a series of one-way thoroughfares that seem perpetually busy. But since you're going to park your car anyway, that's okay, right? As with most cities in Ireland, their streets change names every block or two. For example, if you are standing at the northeast corner of Eyre Square (near the fountain), the street running along the north side of the square is Eyre Street. If you walk southwest on that street for five blocks, the street will change names from Eyre Street to William Street to Shop Street to High Street, and finally to Quay Street. By the way, this is a pretty good street to stroll down, with many interesting shops and restaurants along the way.

Eyre Square, *Galway*. Eyre Square is a pretty little square that serves as Galway's center point. It's often busy with tourists and business people. It's not a large park, but it is a pleasant one. The gardens in the park are a memorial to John F. Kennedy. The late American President visited Galway on his trip to Ireland less than six months before his assassination in 1963.

One side of the square has **Browne's Doorway**, the old doorway to the Browne mansion which has been re-located here. The statue of a man sitting atop a rock is in honor of Irish-language poet Padraic O'Conaire.

Lynch's Castle, *Galway*. At the corner of Shop Street sits the relatively unimpressive square Allied Irish Bank building, formerly known as Lynch's Castle. During the 14th century, members of the Lynch family were wealthy aristocrats in the city of Galway, active in community affairs and politics.

Lynch's Memorial Window, *Galway*. From Lynch's Castle on Shop Street, turn right on Abbeygate Street, then left on Market Street. Look for the Lynch Memorial Window, a black marble skull and cross-bones memorializing the actions of one James Lynch Fitzstephen. It's by the grave yard at St. Nicholas' church. Look up – it's about eight feet off the ground. As mayor of Galway at the time, he had the unenviable task of sentencing his own son to death for murdering a Spanish visitor to the city. When no one could be found to carry out the sentence, Mayor Lynch did the unhappy job himself. From these unfortunate circumstances arose the term "lynch law." The marker reads, "This memorial of the stern and unbending justice of the chief magistrate of this City, James Lynch Fitzstephen, elected mayor AD 1493, who condemned and executed his own guilty son, Walter, on this spot."

Spanish Arch, *Galway*. Just below Claddagh Bridge, on the south end of town. In former years it served as one of the town gates.

Galway City Museum, *Galway, open Easter through September daily from 9:00 am to 5:00 pm, July through August daily from 9:00 am to 8:00 pm, and*

October through Easter on Wednesday and Friday from 10:00 am to 5:15 pm. Admission is 50p for adults and 30p for children. Tel. (091) 67641. Located at the Spanish Arch, the Galway City Museum includes several exhibits on the city's history. It's not a particularly large museum, but it is well-done.

Salmon Weir Bridge, *Galway.* An enjoyable and very popular site is the view from the Salmon Weir Bridge in Galway. Bridging the Corrib River at Newtown Smith Street, the stretch of water is often packed with salmon preparing for their journey upstream to Lough Corrib for spawning, much like planes waiting in queue at JFK Airport. They are clearly visible, and a memorable sight in Galway.

The Aran Islands

So much of what you see in Ireland is a trip into the past. Now take a day and travel even further back by visiting the Aran Islands. Off the western coast of Ireland, these islands open the door into an Irish past like no other place in Ireland. Winding rock walls, ancient ruins, prehistoric forts, and megalithic tombs greet visitors with stony silence. Contrast that silence with the warmth of the thatch-roofed cottages, the friendly island population, and the pubs you'll also find here.

There are several ways to get to the Aran Islands – by air, by sea, or a combination of both. The Tourist Information Office in Galway has many brochures of companies that provide service to the islands. Your options will be via ferry from Galway or Rossaveal, or by air from Inverin, nineteen miles from Galway. The rates among the companies are similar.

The ferry is the least expensive: £12 each way for adults, £6 for children. The ferry takes ninety minutes from Galway, and thirty minutes from Inverin. Flying with some of the local air charter companies costs £33 per adult, and £20 for children.The air companies also have several combination packages, including a mix of air and sea transportation, overnight lodging, etc.

The ferry trips to the Aran Islands take ninety minutes from Galway, and thirty minutes from Rossaveal. Following are the ferry companies that ply the waters to the Aran Islands:
- **Doolin Ferries**, *Tel. (091) 67283*
- **Aran Ferries**, *Tel. (091) 68903*
- **Island Ferries**, *Tel. (091) 61767*

Ferry service runs daily to the Aran Islands, but the frequency varies throughout the year. During the week, ferries run from Galway at 9:30 am, 10:00 am, and 11:00 am. Return trips are at 4:00 pm and 6:00 pm. These are general times; each of the ferry companies has their own times, and they vary throughout the year.

All three ferry companies have offices a half block southwest of Eyre Square (Victoria Place), either next to or across the street from the Tourist

Office that is at the corner of Victoria and Merchant's Streets. All three ferry services have shuttle service to Rossaveal. The bus costs £3 from Galway to Rossaveal. They also leave from the Galway docks, a leisurely five minute stroll from Eyre Square.

Aer Arann, *Tel. 091 93034*, flies to the Aran Islands from the small Connemara Airport in Inverin. The flight takes all of six minutes. A shuttle bus will take you from the Tourist Office in Galway to the airport one hour before their flights depart, which are at 9:30 am, 11:00 am, 4:00 pm, and 5:00 pm. Return flights from the islands are at 9:45 am, 11:15 am, 4:15 pm, and 5:15 pm.

When you get to the islands, you can explore on foot, by bicycle (rented either there or in Galway or Inverin), or hire a jaunting car. If you are of a mind to spend the evening in the many pubs that feature traditional Irish music and dance, there are also a few B&Bs on the islands that are hospitable and accommodating (see *Where to Stay*). Be sure and make certain you have lodging before you allow the last flight or ferry to depart for the mainland!

Connemara in County Galway

Connemara is an area of quiet beauty. In western Galway, Connemara is home to the **Twelve Bens**, twelve mountains that rise seemingly out of nowhere to dominate the landscape (see below for more detail). Connemara is dotted with beautiful loughs, hillocks, and vales.

Connemara lies between Lake Corrib on the east and the Atlantic Ocean on the west. The best way to see Connemara is to drive from Galway on the N59 to Oughterard, then on Maam Cross and Recess. From Recess, bear left on the N59 to Clifden, and on around the loop that the N59 makes. If you're not in any particular hurry (you shouldn't be while you're driving through Connemara), you might want to take a few detours. The Cashel Bay area is quite pretty, as are jaunts to Roundstone and Ballyconneely, and Cleggen, and Renvyle. Watch for signposts on the N59 directing you to these places.

A drive through Connemara gives you time to think and enjoy the country you are driving through. Depending on your mood, and how often you stop, you could easily spend a half day or better in Connemara.

Connemara National Park & Visitor Center, *open April through October daily from 10:00 am to 6:00 pm. Admission is free, although the car park costs £1. Tel. (095) 41054.* This is the starting point for a number of walking trails through Connemara State Park. Walking trails are short or long, depending on your pleasure.

Locals will tell you that the only true way to appreciate the beauty of Connemara is to get out and walk its hills and vales. If you're interested in a serious exploration of Connemara on foot, I'd recommend one of the following trekking companies: **Connemara Heritage Walks**, *Clifden, Tel. (095) 21379* and **Western Trekking**, *Galway, Tel. (091) 25806.* They have a number of walks available, and they'll be glad to help you plan a trip.

Oughterard. Oughterard, pronounced "Ook-ter-ard," is known as the Gateway to Connemara. Sitting pretty on the banks of the River Owenriff, about a mile from the western side of Lough Corrib, this small town is a delightful place to stop before continuing on to Connemara. It is also an important angling center in this part of the country.

Aughnanure Castle, *near Oughterard, open mid-May through September daily from 10:00 am to 6:00 pm. The rest of the year the caretaker has a key. Admission is £1 for adults and 50p for children.* Watch for the signposts in Oughterard pointing you to Aughnanure Castle, the former stronghold of the vaunted Irish warriors named O'Flaherty. Members of the O'Flaherty clan were frequent visitors to Galway City during the 15th and 16th centuries. But welcome visitors they were not. In fact, the west gate to Galway City once held the inscription: "From the fury of the O'Flahertys, good Lord deliver us." Another story of the O'Flaherty's fierceness tells of the time they paid the rent on their castle by sending the head of the rent collector to his father!

Their castle is a six-story tower house with several squat round towers. It was recently restored and is now open to the public.

Lough Corrib. This splendid lake in the west of Ireland is large – over thirty miles long – and narrow, at some points only about a half mile wide. Tradition holds that it possesses one island for every day of the year: 365. The lake is reached from several points, but you can receive a tour of parts of the lake in the small village of Oughterard. Local fishermen can be enticed to take small groups out on the lake. A favorite stopping point is Inchagoill, a small island with the ruins of a 5th-century church as well as a 12th-century church. Prices vary and are subject to negotiation, but expect to pay from £5 to £10 per person.

Ross Abbey, *near Headford.* East of Lough Corrib, about a mile north of Headford on the R334, stand the ruins of Ross Abbey. Built in the mid-14th century by Raymond de Burgo, Ross Abbey was intended for use by the Franciscans. The extensive ruins include the nave, transepts, chapel, choir, cloister, kitchen and bakery. At the end of the 15th century the splendid tower was added. The Franciscans called this home until it was abandoned in 1753.

Cashel Bay. This is a pretty secluded cove. A popular fishing spot, Cashel Bay is actually one of the inland fingers of Betraghboy Bay.

Clifden. Clifden is a pretty little village at the junction of the R341 and the N59. It has a serene setting sheltered between the mountains and the Atlantic Ocean.

The steeples of the local Catholic and Protestant churches lift skyward above the town, and beyond them are even higher *natural* steeples – the Twelve Bens – that rise majestically in the distance.

Take the time to stroll through the shops here. The two-block (side-by-side) shopping district is a pleasant one. Perhaps not as picturesque as Westport or Galway, there are still some interesting shops and pretty good prices. Take a moment and slip into **O'Hehirs Woolen Shop**, *Market Street, Tel. 095 21282*. They have a wide selection of sweaters, caps, and other Irish clothing. If you're interested in Irish craft work, you might also want to stop by the **Celtic Shop**.

Look for the signposts directing you to the **Sky Drive**. This short (ten mile) drive takes you out on the peninsula west of Clifden and offers brilliant ocean views.

The Twelve Bens, *near Clifden*. As you travel along in Connemara National Park, you'll note the Twelve Bens, twelve peaks of Connemara. The highest is Benbaun at 2,355 feet in elevation. These mountains are largely devoid of vegetation, except tundra-height small plants and low-lying heather. The Twelve Bens are often shrouded in clouds, giving off a brooding feeling as they stand guard over the rugged Connemara beauty.

Kylemore Abbey, *near Letterfrack; grounds are open from February through December 24 daily from 10:00 am to 6:00 pm. Admission is free. Tel. (095) 41113.* On the N59 between Letterfrack and Leenane, you'll find the impressive Kylemore Abbey. One of the most photographed abbeys in Ireland, it nestles on the shores of Kylemore Lake. Originally built as a residence for a wealthy Member of Parliament in the late 1800's, it now serves as a convent for the Benedictine nuns of Ypres. Unfortunately, very little of the Abbey itself is open to the public – one or two rooms in addition to the entry hall. Several hundred yards from the Abbey, around the shores of the lake, is a lovely little Gothic Chapel that's worth walking to and looking at: it reminds me of a doll house.

If you come from the direction of Letterfrack, and are headed for Leenane, be sure to look over your shoulder. The best views of Kylemore Abbey are from across the lake, and the pretty little chapel peeking through the treetops almost steals the show from its much more publicized neighbor.

County Leitrim

Parke's Castle, *near Sligo, open June through September daily from 9:30 am to 6:30 pm, and April, May and October daily from 10:00 am to 5:00 pm. Admission is £1. Tel. (071) 64149.* On the R286/R288 west of town sits Parke's Castle. This 17th-century house was partially built using stones taken from the nearby Breffni Castle. In so doing, the English owner incurred the ire of the native Irish. A short video on the history of the house is also shown.

The Old Hall, *Dromahair (not open to the public)*. On the R288 on the outskirts of Dromahair sits a fine old mansion called the Old Hall. It was built in the early 17th century for Sir William Villiers with the stones taken from an old O'Rourke stronghold that was located here.

Glencar Lough, *near Manorhamilton*. This pretty little lake lies just off the N16 between Sligo Town and Manorhamilton. Near the north end of the lake are several waterfalls, one of which free-falls about fifty feet over the edge of the mountain.

County Mayo

Cong. In 1951, Cong gained international recognition and interest when it served as the primary setting for the John Ford movie *The Quiet Man*, starring John Wayne, Maureen O'Hara and Barry Fitzgerald. It's not changed much over the ensuing years. The residents are proud of their Hollywood experience and they remember it fondly. On the edge of Cong lies Ashford Castle. Built in the 18th century, this lovely building on the banks of an estuary of Lough Corrib is now a five star luxury hotel.

Cong Abbey, *Cong*. On the edge of Cong are the ruins of Cong Abbey, an abbey of the Augustinian order dating from the early 12th century. The abbey was the benefactor of Turlough Mor O'Connor. He also commissioned the Cross of Cong, a beautiful work of religious art. It stood proudly at Cong Abbey for centuries, but has since been moved to the National Museum in Dublin, as it was considered one of Ireland's religious masterpieces.

As you walk through the abbey, look at some of the gravestones. There are some old and interesting ones there – many of which unfortunately serve as flagstones for the paths.

Ashford Castle, *Cong, not open to the public unless you are a guest staying there*. Built in the 13th century, this grand castle, now a five-star luxury hotel, is set in the midst of 350 acres of beautiful park-like lands. This is one of the hotels at which President Ronald Reagan stayed during his 1984 visit to Ireland. But you'll only be able to tour its paneled halls and gaze upon its many antiques if you are a guest of the hotel. (See the entry on Ashford Castle under the *Where To Stay* section.)

Croagh Patrick, *near Westport*. Known as Ireland's Holy Mountain, Croagh Patrick sits regally on the south side of Clew Bay and holds an important position in Irish history and legend. Just a few miles west of Westport, Croagh Patrick rises abruptly and majestically over 2,500 feet above the Atlantic waters at its base.

Croagh Patrick is the legendary peak where tradition holds that St. Patrick enticed all the snakes of Ireland to gather. When they were all assembled, St. Patrick rang his bell, and all the snakes cast themselves to their deaths over a cliff. Whether you believe the legend or not (by the way – there are no snakes in Ireland), Croagh Patrick is an impressive mountain, and the site of yearly pilgrimages by many Catholic faithful.

If you desire, there is a good hiking path up Croagh Patrick that begins in the little town of Murrisk, about five miles west of Westport. The well-worn path ascends to the top of the mountain. The last Sunday of July is the traditional time of the pilgrimage, when worshipers, many of them barefoot, make the two hour trek to the top. But you can do it anytime of the year, and the views from the top are nothing short of stunning.

Westport. Westport is at the head of Clew Bay, an island-studded estuary on this western edge of Ireland. Its Irish name bears no resemblance to its English name: *Cathair na Mart* means "The Stone Fort of the Beeves." Unlike so many other Irish cities, this one was well-planned from the beginning. It was plotted by James Wyatt, a famed architect. Of particular note is The Mall (Westport's main street), which has lines of lime trees on either side of the Carrowbeg River.

The Quay, *Westport.* Watch for the signposts in town pointing you toward the Quay, which is about a mile outside of Westport. Here you'll find an assortment of pubs and restaurants.

Westport House, *Westport, open April, May and September daily from 2:00 pm to 5:00 pm, June Monday through Friday from noon until 5:00 pm, Saturday and Sunday from 2:00 pm until 6:00 pm, July and August Monday through Saturday from 10:30 am until 6:00 pm, and Sunday from 2:00 pm until 6:00 pm. Admission is £5.50 for adults and £2.50 for children. A family ticket is available for £17.50 (2 adults and 4 children). Tel. (098) 25430.* Home of the Marquess of Sligo, Westport House is a lovely Georgian Mansion begun in 1730 and completed in 1778. Built on the site of a castle from years gone by, it features an ornate marble staircase and a wide collection of period furnishings. It sits amid nice park lands, although the quest for commercialization overshadows the serenity that would otherwise be here. A caravan (travel trailer) park, arcade games, and camp site on the grounds detract from the otherwise elegant ambiance.

Clare Island. Resting offshore at the mouth of Clew Bay is the 4,000 acre Clare Island. You can arrange for a boat ride out to Clare Island by calling the Bay View Hotel on Clare Island, *Tel. (098) 26307.*

By far its most famous occupant over the centuries was Grace O'Malley, the "Uncrowned Queen of the West." Grace was the daughter of Owen O'Malley, chieftain of western Ireland. But she was quite the power in and of herself. She was recognized as a gutsy pirate full of daring and bravado, and more than one ballad has been sung to her feats.

One of her more celebrated exploits involved her second husband. She wed one MacWilliam Oughter, another powerful figure of the day.

Since both had extensive real estate holdings, demure Grace proposed that the marriage begin on somewhat of a trial partnership. If at the end of one year either party wanted out of the relationship, all that was required was for one or the other to say, "I dismiss you." (The original pre-nuptial agreement?)

Over the course of the year, Grace used her wiles to finagle her allies into positions of power in various of Mr. Oughter's strongholds. One year after their marriage when he returned home to **Carrigahooley Castle** on Clare Island, he was dismayed to hear Grace shout from inside the castle, "I dismiss you!" Grace lived and died near the end of the 16th century. Her grave is marked with a plaque in the Clare Island abbey.

Achill Island. Achill Island is a large island off the west coast of County Mayo. To get to Achill Island, take the R319 off the N59 in Mulrany. The road takes you across a causeway and deposits you in the town of Achill Sound.

The island is about fifteen miles long and twelve miles wide. There's not much in the way of vegetation other than the heather, which is pretty in the late summer. On the north side of the island are some impressive cliffs, including some that offer a 2,000 foot drop to the ocean. The island offers shark fishing off its western coast if you're interested.

Owing to the remoteness of the island, tourism hasn't completely taken over. It's more austere than the rest of Ireland, but there are some nice sandy beaches along the coast in between the cliffs. Some of the prettiest beaches are at Keel, Keem Bay, Dugort, and Dooega. There are also lots of walking paths around the island, many of them drawn to the cliffs on the one hand and the mountains that grace the island on the other.

Newport. Just north of Westport on the N59 ten miles or so is Newport, a pretty fishing village. It is a popular haven for Salmon fishermen when the salmon are running.

Ballina. At the southern end of Killala Bay sits the little town of Ballina. It may be small (population around 6,500), but it is the largest town in County Mayo. It has been an important fishing center for generations, and continues to draw interest from the fishing public, who come there to fish for salmon and sea trout in nearby River Moy and Lough Conn.

To get to Ballina from Westport, either take the N59 north to Bangor, where it then turns due east and takes you into Ballina; or you can also take the N60 from Westport to Castlebar, then east on the N5 to Ballyvary. Watch for the signposts that direct you north to Ballina from there.

Moyne Abbey, *near Killala*. Between Ballina and Killala are some ruins you should take the time to see. Two miles from Killala is Moyne Abbey, a 15th-century abbey that still retains its tower and cloisters.

Rosserk Friary, *between Killala and Ballina*. About five miles south of Killala on the same coastal road as Moyne Abbey is the 15th century Rosserk Friary, standing pretty next to the River Moy. It is one of the best-preserved set of ruins of this vintage in Ireland. It still retains its tower and the cloisters are also in good condition.

County Roscommon

Roscommon Abbey, *admission is free*. On the south end of Roscommon Town on the N61, you come to Roscommon Abbey. The Dominican abbey was built in the 13th century. The tomb of its founder, Felin O'Connor, is found on the north wall, still guarded by the statues of eight *gallowglasses* – soldiers of fortune.

Roscommon Castle, *admission is free*. At the other end of town from Roscommon Abbey is Roscommon Castle. The old ruins are interesting. The castle was built in the 13th century, and was the stronghold of Anglo-Norman rulers who were in the area at the time.

Strokestown Park House, *Strokestown, open June through September 15, Tuesday through Sunday from noon to 5:00 pm. Admission is £3 for adults, £2 for seniors and £1 for children. Tel. (078) 33013*. The tiny town of Strokestown is about twenty miles north of Roscommon. To get there from Roscommon, take the N61 north to Four Mile, then watch for signposts directing you to the R368 and Strokestown. The R368 deadends into the N5; turn left, and you'll be in Strokestown in a matter of a few minutes.

Once there, you'll find the palatial home of the Mahon family, which they lived in from 1660 through 1979. The home itself is a not-always-congruent combination of several architectural motifs, owing to several additions over the past three hundred years. But it is interesting and is worth a visit, as are their extensive gardens.

Lough Key Forest Park, *near Boyle, Co. Roscommon. Parking in the car park costs £2*. Pretty Lough Key Forest Park lies east of the town of Boyle, and it is over 800 acres along the shores of a lake. Camping sites, walking paths, boat rentals (the ancient ruins of an abbey to explore are on the island), and bog gardens are a few of the things to do while here. The bog gardens offer you a pretty setting of heather and small plants that flourish in the moist peat of the bog.

Cisterian Abbey, *Boyle Abbey, free admission*. On the northern outskirts of Boyle you'll find the pretty and well-preserved ruins of Boyle Abbey. Dating from 1161, the nave, choir, and transepts are in good condition and there are a number of interesting carvings.

County Sligo

Sligo Town. The Irish name for Sligo is *Sligeach*, which means "The Shelly River." It's a mid-sized town bounded by mountains on three sides.

Once a strategic town on the Garavogue River, Sligo attracted the attention of just about every group of invaders who hit Ireland: the Vikings, the Anglo-Normans, and of course, Oliver Cromwell didn't want to leave this stone unturned either (twice). Not to be out-done, the native Irish tried their hand numerous times also. Today it's a quiet market town, the largest in this section of Ireland.

Some of the most interesting sights around Sligo are the ancient dolmens, cairns, and stone circles. Dolmens are megalithic tombs with three or more stones that serve as pillars or pedestals for a large stone (capstone) that is placed on top of them. Sometimes these capstones weigh up to one hundred tons. Head out on about any road into the mountains surrounding Sligo and watch for the signposts, and you're sure to find them. The greatest number are west and south of town.

Sligo County Library and Museum, *Sligo, Steven Street, open June through September Tuesday through Saturday from 10:30 am to 12:30 pm, and from 2:30 pm to 4:30 pm, April, May, and October Tuesday through Friday from 2:30 pm to 4:30 pm, and November through March on Tuesday and Friday from 2:30 pm to 4:30 pm. Admission is free. Tel. (071) 22122.* Even though it's billed as the County Library and Museum, the museum features a fine collection of W. B. Yeats memorabilia, a former resident of Sligo. The art gallery also has a number of paintings by Yeats' brother Jack and their father.

Sligo Abbey, *Abbey Street, Sligo, open year round. Admission is free.* Just a block off Kennedy Parade/Riverside Street on Abbey Street are the ruins of an abbey built by Maurice Fizgerald for the Dominicans. The ruins are open to the public. They feature a lovely set of lancet windows in the choir. On the south end of the ruins, look for the memorial to the O'Conor, a powerful chieftain among the Celts. The abbey was originally built in 1253, but suffered a fire in 1414. It was rebuilt, but a mere two and a half centuries later it gained the malevolent attention of the Cromwellian minions, who destroyed it.

Strandhill. Strandhill is located a few miles east of Sligo on the R292. It's a pretty seaport town with pretty beaches that are tailor-made for early morning or late evening walks; mid-day isn't bad, either!

Drumcliffe. Five miles north of Sligo Town on the N15 lies the ruins of the monastic settlement of Drumcliffe. Its Irish name, *Droim Chliabh,* means "Back of the Baskets." Originally the site of a monastery founded in 574 by St. Columba, the settlement lasted until the early 16th century. The only remaining artifacts are a series of gravestones, the remains of a round tower, and an elaborately carved high cross. The high cross and the round tower sit right next to the road. The high cross was placed here about the year 1000, and is deeply carved with a number of figures. Can you identify the scriptural stories depicted there?

Perhaps the most interesting aspect of your visit here is the grave of revered writer W. B. Yeats in the nearby Protestant graveyard. His simple epitaph reads:

Cast a cold eye
On life, on death.
Horseman, pass by!

Benbulben. Next to Croagh Patrick, Benbulben is perhaps the next most recognizable mountain in Ireland. Lying just east of the N15 as you travel north from Sligo Town to Bundoran is the large, flat-topped mount called by some as "Table Mountain." Deep ravines ring the edges of the steep slopes of Benbulben.

It is a mountain of legends as well as historical events. Once such event took place on the slopes of Benbulben: the "Battle of the Books" took place in 561, between the followers of St. Columba and St. Finian. St. Finian had lent a book to St. Columba, who copied it (by hand, of course). St. Finian claimed not only the original, but also the copy that had been made. The two could come to no agreeable solution, so it was presented to the king of Ireland, who judged in favor of St. Finian. He said, "To every cow its calf, and to every book its copy." (Early copyright law?). Rather than return the copy, St. Columba decided to fight (not very saintly); over three thousand men lost their lives in the ensuing battle.

Recent archaeological discoveries have been made near Benbulben's summit. They have uncovered traces of stone age settlements. Visitors can climb Benbulben, although there are no pre-defined routes. Check with locals to get an idea of how to attack its steep sides. It is dangerous if you don't know what you're doing.

Creevykeel Court Tomb, *between Cliffony and Castlegal.* Creevykeel Court Tomb is one of the finest examples of a classic court tomb in existence today in Ireland. Archaeologists estimate it has been here since 3,000 BC. Upright stones mark the circular ritual court, and lead to a burial chamber.

HELP (OR SUSTENANCE) AT CREEVYKEEL

If you are so anxious to see the Creevykeel Court Tomb that you lock your keys in your car, there's an obscure pub about one hundred meters down the road (on the N15 between Sligo and Ballyshannon) with a comforting turf fire burning, and locals – James and P.D. – willing to help a tourist in need!

PRACTICAL INFORMATION

American Express

American Express uses **John Ryan Travel**, *1 Williamsgate Street, Galway, Tel. (091) 67375*, as their representative.

Banks

Banks in Connacht are open Monday through Friday from 10:00 am to 12:30 pm, and from 1:30 pm to 3:00 pm. In the larger cities, the banks are usually open a little longer one day a week (the day varies throughout the province) until 5:00 pm.

Some of the large banks in Connacht have an ATM machine either outside their main doorways, or just inside the bank. The ATMs are part of the Cirrus and Plus international network. Check with your bank to be sure your personal identification number (PIN) will work on international ATMs. Most international ATMs only accept only accept four-digit PINs.

Buses, Planes, & Trains

If you're flying into or out of Connacht, you'll want to use the following airports:
• **Galway Airport**, *Galway, Tel. (091) 755569*
• **Horan International Airport**, *Knock, Tel. (094) 67222*

For buses, use the following stations:
• **Galway**: *Ceannt Station, Station Road, Tel. (091) 64222*
• **Westport**: *Grand Central Hotel, The Octagon, Tel. (098) 25253*

For trains, use the following stations:
• **Galway**: *Ceannt Station, Station Road, Tel. (091) 64222*
• **Westport**: *Westport Station, Altamount Street, Tel. (098) 25253*

Emergencies

Remember this: dialing 999 in Ireland = dialing 911 in the States. Use it in the event of any emergency where you need assistance from the police, fire department, or the medical community.

Exchanging Money

You can exchange money at banks, most post offices, and at larger hotels.

Lost Credit Cards
• **American Express Card**, *Tel. (01) 288-3311*
• **American Express Traveler's Checks**, *Tel. 800-626-0000*

- **Diners Club**, *Tel. (01) 1-800-709-944*
- **Visa/MasterCard**, *Tel. (01) 269-7700*

Restrooms

Public restrooms are not prevalent in Ireland; your best bet is usually a hotel or a pub. (Hint: most hotels have at least one pub, and the restrooms are usually located near the pub.)

Note: in the Gaeltacht (Irish-speaking) areas of Connacht, some of the restrooms may only be marked in Irish. If you guess, you'll probably guess wrong: *Mna* is for women, and *Fir* is for men.

Tourist Offices

- **Galway Town**, *Eyre Square, Tel. (091) 63081*
- **Sligo Town**, *Temple Street, Tel. (071) 61201*
- **Westport**, *The Mall, Tel. (098) 25711*

17. ULSTER

The province of **Ulster** covers the northern quarter of the Emerald Isle. There are nine counties in Ulster, six of which comprise **Northern Ireland**, a possession of the United Kingdom. The counties of Ulster that are not in Northern Ireland are Donegal, Cavan, and Monaghan.

The question usually asked by foreigners is: isn't travel to Northern Ireland dangerous? I asked that question of a shop owner in the US who was from Northern Ireland. He smiled, and patiently explained that not going to Northern Ireland for that reason was roughly comparable to not visiting the United States because of high crime rates in some cities or the Los Angeles riots of a few years back. He conceded there are areas you don't want to go, but there are those areas in the United States, too.

Northern Ireland is delightful and provides some of the most spectacular and awe-inspiring scenery of the island. Shop owners are

delighted to greet American tourists. I discussed my earlier concerns with one of the Northern Ireland proprietors. She quipped, "I know we get a lot of bad press in the States, but we haven't lost a tourist yet!"

There are a few areas you should definitely steer clear of – Derry (Londonderry) and Armagh. These are the primary hot-beds of dissent. Derry really is a pretty city, and it's a shame that things are still unstable there. And, on occasion, things do flare up in Belfast.

Certainly the choice is yours whether you travel into Northern Ireland or not. But don't discount Northern Ireland because of some unpleasantness in a few parts of the country.

The history of Ulster is the history of conquest, suppression, and **plantation** (repopulation or resettlement). The idea behind plantation was to replace the native (Catholic) population with those who would follow and support the Crown (Protestants). In the south, these efforts largely met with failure. For, while Protestant landlords were given Irish land, the Irish did not leave. The landlords needed their labor, and made life relatively tolerable for them.

After years of fighting with the English and their mercenaries, the Irish suffered crushing defeats in Kinsale and Ulster. The leading Irish chieftains in Ulster abandoned the fight, and in 1607, they fled from Ireland to France and Spain, never to return. This was called the "Flight of the Earls," and many historians feel this was *the* critical turning point in the history of Ulster. After their departure, hundreds of thousands of acres of land that had belonged to the Irish chieftains was confiscated by the Crown and given to Protestants: reward for former officials and soldiers who had fought against the Irish.

Because of the mass influx of these Protestants into Ulster, about two-thirds of the population of Northern Ireland today is Protestant, primarily Anglican, compared to the population in the Republic, which is 93% Catholic. Many of the Protestants who came to this part of Ireland and never left were Scottish *galloglasses* – mercenaries who fought for the English (and at times, for the native Irish). Even today, the accent in rural parts of County Antrim is much more akin to a Scottish brogue than to an Irish lilt.

As the Catholics in the south tried repeatedly to rebel against the English, the Protestants in the north became more and more English. In the late 19th century and the early part of the 20th century, when it looked like Ireland might actually have a chance at winning Home Rule – independence from England – the Ulster Protestants became militant in their opposition. They felt that "Home Rule" meant "Rome Rule," and they pledged to fight it – in Parliament and in the streets, if necessary.

In early 1914, when it appeared that Ireland might just win Home Rule, and that their triumph would assuredly result in armed conflict in

Northern Ireland, a compromise was reluctantly reached. The compromise granted Home Rule to Ireland, but allowed six counties in the north to remain a part of the United Kingdom. It was an unpopular compromise with most, but was agreed to nonetheless. In 1921, Ireland and Britain signed the **Anglo-Irish Treaty**, which gave independence to Ireland, but which also exempted the six counties – Northern Ireland – from that independence.

And there have been troubles since that time. **Republicans** felt that Ireland would never completely be a republic until all of the island was united and independent from Great Britain. **Unionists** or **Loyalists**, mostly the Protestant majority in Ulster, vowed that Northern Ireland would remain forever tied to the UK. At the same time, a generation has passed. Many of the people in the North consider themselves British citizens: they pay British taxes (which are far lower than Irish taxes, by the way), take part in Britain's national health care plan, and 17% of them draw their unemployment checks from the British government.

I see no settlement of the differences of opinion that divide Northern Ireland. Let's just hope that those differences can be aired and resolved constructively without bloodshed.

ARRIVALS & DEPARTURES

There are a number of ways to get to Ulster and Northern Ireland. Air, car, bus, rail and ferry are all viable options. There is regular bus and train service between the Republic and the North, and recently Aer Lingus expanded their service into Belfast, making it easier to get there by air. Ferry service from England via Wales and Scotland is also available.

Derry has a small regional airport, primarily used by small airlines flying in from some of England's regional airports.

BY AIR

The main airport for Ulster is also the main airport for Belfast and Northern Ireland. **Belfast International Airport**, *Tel. (01849) 422888*, formerly called Aldergrove Airport, is located twenty miles northwest of downtown Belfast out in the country. Aer Lingus has recently opened transatlantic service to Belfast from the United States. They fly to Belfast from New York City (Kennedy Airport) stopping over in Shannon en route. They also fly to Belfast from Boston, but they stop first in Shannon, then change planes (onto the flight coming from New York) and continue on to Belfast.

In addition to Aer Lingus' flights from the United States, a number of airlines fly to Belfast from a host of English airports, including Heathrow, Gatwick, Luton (London), Birmingham, Bristol, Liverpool, and Manchester. Airlines flying into Belfast International Airport include

Aer Lingus, British Airways, Britsh Midland, Manx, Jersey European, and KLM (from Amsterdam).

Renting a Car at the Airport

Once you land at Belfast International Airport, you will be directed into an Arrivals hall, where you will immediately see a bevy of rental car agency booths clamoring for your business. They include Avis, EuropCar, EuroDollar, and Hertz, plus a host of local companies.

Getting to Belfast By Bus from the Airport

Buses run from Belfast International Airport to the center of Belfast every half hour (at ten minutes after the hour and twenty minutes to the hour). The ride will take about forty minutes, and cost you UK£3.70. The bus stop is right outside the Arrivals hall.

Getting to Belfast By Taxi from the Airport

Another option for getting into Belfast from the airport is to take a taxi. The taxi stand is right outside the Arrivals hall, and the ride into town will take about twenty-five minutes and cost you around UK£20.

BY BUS

Ulsterbus, *Tel. (01232) 333000,* is the bus service that serves all of Ulster. Its main terminal in Belfast is **Europa Station**, *10 Glengall Street, just around the corner from the Europa Hotel.* The neighborhood is decent enough and should pose no problems for you, especially once you walk the short distance to Great Victoria Street.

Buses run from Europa Station throughout Ulster on a regular basis. In addition, they run between Belfast and Busaras Station in Dublin seven times a day Monday through Saturday, and three times on Sunday.

BY FERRY

Ferry service from England (Wales) and Scotland to Ulster is also available. Ferries between Larne (a port town just north of Belfast) and Stranaer, Scotland, are run by **Stena Sealink Ferries** *(toll free in the US and Canada at 800-677-8585 or (01223) 647047 in England).* The trip takes about thirteen hours. There is also a modern new ferry run by **Seacat Ferries**, *Tel. (01304) 240241 in England,* that runs between Stranaer and Belfast that takes about two hours.

Belfast Ferries, *Tel. (01519) 226234 in England,* operates ferry service between Liverpool and Belfast that takes about nine hours.

BY TRAIN

Six trains a day run between Belfast and Dublin. The trains at 8:00 am and 6:00 pm are express trains and take two hours and five minutes; the other four trains are not express and take about fifteen minutes longer. Catch the train in Dublin at **Connolly Station**, *Tel. (01) 836-6222 on Amiens Street*, and in Belfast go to **Belfast Central Train Station**, *Tel. (01232) 800411 on East Bridge Street*. On Sundays there are only four trains running between the two cities. The ride between these two capital cities will cost you about £23.

Belfast Central Train Station is in an industrial section of Belfast, not the best, but relatively safe. It will take you ten to fifteen minutes to walk to the city center, or you can catch a taxi to take you on your way. The taxi ride to the center of the city should run about UK£3.

Is it Safe to Travel to Ulster?

Before my first trip into Northern Ireland, I was a little nervous, not knowing what to expect. I had expressed my concerns to a cousin in Northern Ireland before my visit. She said, "When you get to the check-points, just be nice, and everything will be fine." I did, and it was.

When I first traveled to Northern Ireland, there was still an unde-clared war going on between the **Irish Republican Army** (IRA) and the English government. Most of the time, I was oblivious to any concerns or tension. However, as I approached and crossed check-points, I could feel the tension. (Armed guards with bullet-proof vests may have been at least partly to blame.)

Sounds pretty dreary, doesn't it? Well, as of this writing, that situation no longer exists. Several years ago, a cease-fire was called between the IRA and the English government. Since that time, although there have been a few tense moments when it looked like hostilities were going to escalate again, things have been pretty quiet. As a symbol of their commitment to the cease-fire, the English government took down all check-points at border crossings. Now you can drive from the Republic into Northern Ireland and back without even realizing you have crossed the border, unless you look at a map.

Unfortunately, this book isn't timeless. And neither is the peace process in Northern Ireland. At any point, tempers could flare and negotiations will end, and the check-points will be back. But even if that happens, unless it gets far worse than it has been in recent years, I would not hesitate to recommend that you visit Northern Ireland. But you have to make that decision. The only times I felt uneasy were at border crossings (and one time when I got lost in Armagh, but that's another story).

A BORDER CROSSING TALE

If the fighting escalates again, and check-points are once more erected, here's what you can expect if you drive into the North:

As you cross from the Republic into the North, you must go through a check-point. As you approach any check-point, there will be large speed bumps in the road. You will notice closed-circuit television cameras. Depending on your point of entry, you may even see armed military personnel.

When my wife and I traveled into Northern Ireland, we worked our way through the check-point, slowly going over the speed bumps, and advancing to a stop light. As we sat at the stop light, I could see the camera centered on us. I also noted that the stop light had two green arrows. If one was illuminated, we would be directed to go around the check-point area and on our way. If the other was illuminated, it would direct us to drive into the check-point area. After about ten seconds, the arrow indicating we were to go around the area came on, and we proceeded on our trip. (I understand from reliable sources that while we were waiting at the stop light, our car was under electronic surveillance – it was being "swept" for weapons.)

On one occasion I was crossing the border alone. This time, the arrow directed me to enter the compound. I pulled forward, and two armed guards came out to talk to me. One of them came to my side of the car, and the other to the passenger side. As the guard approached me, he asked to see identification. I gave him my passport, which he studied carefully. Then he asked me a series of rapid-fire questions: Where was I from? What state did I live in? Where was that state located geographically in the United States? Why was I coming to Northern Ireland, and how long did I intend to stay?

After the questions, he handed me my passport, stepped back, and said, "Sorry for all the questions, sir. But there are those who make these sort of things necessary. Enjoy your holiday." Then he motioned me on my way.

I'd be less than honest if I didn't say it was a bit unnerving. But the rest of the trip was pleasant, enjoyable, and without incident..

For those of us who are unaccustomed to such sights, it may all seem very intriguing. But it is a matter of life and death to those who man the check-points. When you do see the military guards, they will be heavily armed and will have bullet-proof vests on. They are also very cautious. Photography of these areas is forbidden, of course. If you hazard a snapshot, you may find yourself asked – politely but firmly – to surrender your camera so the film can be taken out of it.

The entire experience will take (probably) less than three minutes. Remember: "Just be nice, and everything will be fine."

TOP ULSTER SIGHTS

BONAMARGY FRIARY – *On the outskirts of Ballycastle sit the ruins of Bonamargy friary. Take a few minutes and prowl through the ruins.*

CARRICK-A-REDE ROPE BRIDGE – *Take a walk across a chasm above the Atlantic on a narrow rope bridge.*

DUNLUCE CASTLE – *Dunluce Castle is perhaps the most photographed ruins on the Emerald Isle. These brooding ruins are perched atop a rocky outcropping into the Atlantic Ocean.*

GIANT'S CAUSEWAY – *Forty thousand symmetric natural basalt columns will amaze you.*

GLENVEAGH NATIONAL PARK – *This an area of outstanding natural beauty.*

TORR HEAD – *Talk about a sensational seaside drive! You'll snake along the hills of Ulster as they cascade down to the Irish Sea.*

ULSTER FOLK AND TRANSPORT MUSEUM – *If you visit only one folk park in Ireland, choose this one. The extensive displays are impressive.*

ULSTER MUSEUM – *This museum in Belfast isn't particularly large, but it is well done with some interesting exhibits.*

WHERE TO STAY

"The troubles" of recent years have had a serious impact on tourism in general, and on the hotel industry in particular. To be honest, it lags behind its southern cousins in the number and quality of tourist accommodations. For example, in Belfast, the second largest city on the Emerald Isle, it's difficult to find ten hotels to recommend (literally). Several wouldn't have "made the cut" if the competition had been as stiff as it is in the Republic of Ireland.

But the last several years have been banner years for the tourism and hotel industries in the North. As a consequence, several new hotels, B&Bs, and guesthouses have been built, and numerous existing hotels have expansion and renovation plans.

A number of the B&Bs I have recommended in this chapter are brand new. With the upturn in tourism in the North, B&Bs are springing up like dandelions in spring lawns – they're everywhere. The owners of these new B&Bs are delighted to see American tourists, and quite desirous to see that all needs are met. They are outgoing and anxious to please.

One nice aspect of the hotel industry in Northern Ireland is that most of the hotels don't participate in the odious practice of foisting service charges on their guests.

ULSTER'S TOP LODGING

THE ARCHES COUNTRY HOUSE, *Lough Eske, Barnesmore, Donegal, Tel. (073) 22029. 5 rooms. Rates for singles: £21, doubles: £16 per person sharing. The Arches wins my Best Irish B&B award.*

WHITEPARK HOUSE COUNTRY HOME, *150 Whitepark Road (Coast Road), Ballintoy, Ballycastle, BT54 6NH, Tel. (012657) 31482. 6 rooms. Rates for singles: UK£25, doubles: UK£25 per person sharing. Mrs. Siobhan Isles runs one of the prettiest country homes in the north.*

BUSHMILLS INN HOTEL, *25 Main Street, Bushmills, BT57 8QA, Tel. (012657) 32339, (012657) 32048. 11 rooms. Rates for singles: UK£42, doubles: UK£85. The Bushmills Inn feels like an old stagecoach hotel. Recently inducted into "The Best Loved Hotels of the World."*

TEMPLETON HOTEL, *882 Antrim Road, Templepatrick, Ballyclare, Tel. (01849) 432984, fax (01849) 433406. 24 rooms. Rates for singles: UK£85, doubles: UK£110, suites: UK£100 to UK£125. The nicest hotel in the Belfast area.*

HARVEY'S POINT COUNTRY HOTEL, *Lough Eske, Donegal Town, Tel. (073) 22208, (073) 22352. 32 rooms. Rates for singles: £50 to £65, doubles: £40 to £80 per person sharing, suites: £50 to £60 per person sharing. Sitting on the banks of pretty Lough Eske, Harvey's Point Country Hotel provides a feel of continental Europe mixed with warm Irish hospitality.*

Belfast

The Templeton Hotel, located some miles outside Belfast on the road to the airport is the nicest. In town, the Wellington and Dukes hotels are probably your best bets.

BELFAST INTERNATIONAL YOUTH HOSTEL, *22 Donegall Road, Tel. (01232) 315435, fax (01232) 439699. 120 beds. Rates are UK£9 per person. American Express, MasterCard, and Visa accepted. No service charge.*

This is a surprisingly nice hostel just off Shaftesbury Square in central Belfast. The rooms are small but quite clean and in pretty good condition. Each bunk has a small "armoire" for hanging clothes and a deep locking drawer. The hostel is staffed 24 hours a day, so there is no curfew to worry about (some hostels have a curfew and lock the doors at certain hours). It has a nice sitting/TV room and laundry service. Linens are included.

Renshaws is located near Queens University, and is within easy walking distance to Shaftesbury Square, the Botanic Gardens, and the Ulster Museum. The hotel offers discounts for families traveling with children.

RENSHAWS HOTEL, *75 University Street, Belfast BT7 1HL, Tel. (01232) 333366, fax (01232) 333399. 22 rooms. Rates for singles: UK£55, doubles: UK£65. Restaurant, pub. Rates include breakfast. All major credit cards accepted. No service charge.*

This old Victorian schoolhouse has been converted into a homey hotel just around the corner from Queen's University. The rooms, as is typical in these old Victorians, are large and spacious. All are pleasantly furnished, including writing desks for all those postcards you'll be sending.

ALDERGROVE AIRPORT HOTEL, *Belfast International Airport, Tel. (01849) 422033, fax (01849) 423500. 108 rooms. Rates for singles: UK£56 to UK£75, doubles: UK£66 to UK£75; children under 10 stay free in their parents' room. Restaurant, pub, fitness center, sauna, bicycles. Rates include breakfast on the weekends. All major credit cards accepted. No service charge.*

I had planned to write "Except for the noise of the airport..." – but after staying here I realized the entire hotel is incredibly well sound-proofed. This is a nice, newer hotel that's just a few steps (literally) from the airport. The rooms are small, but very clean and comfortably furnished. They are decorated in light and airy colors, which give the rooms a larger feel. The rooms reminded of me of single dorm rooms at college, although they were spotlessly clean, and had their own bathroom.

The hotel was built a few years ago and was a part of the Novotel hotel chain; however, it has since left Novotel and is now under local management. They have kept the attention to cleanliness. The hotel offers a pub and an informal restaurant, exercise room, sauna, and bicycles (free of charge) for touring the surrounding countryside. There are also discounts for children, and two children under ten years old can stay free in their parents' rooms. Several rooms are wheelchair-accessible.

HOLIDAY INN GARDEN COURT, *15 Brunswick Street, BT2 7GE, Tel. (01232) 333555, fax (01232) 232999, US toll free 800-465-4329. 76 rooms. Rates for singles: UK£75, doubles: UK£85. Restaurant. All major credit cards accepted. No service charge.*

This 1970s hotel is clean and functional, but that's about it. They are located just off Great Victoria Street not far from the Europa Hotel. The rooms are small and the furnishings a little on the old side. The hotel is located in the heart of Belfast's business and shopping district, and it's within easy walking distance of city hall, the Crown Liquor Salon, Shaftesbury Square, and a number of top-notch restaurants.

DUKES HOTEL, *65 University Street, Belfast, Tel. (01232) 237177. 21 rooms. Rates for singles: UK£85, doubles: UK£100; children under age 12 stay in their parents room free. Restaurant, gym, sauna. All major credit cards accepted. No service charge.*

Dukes Hotel was a pleasant find in the university district near Queen's University. The hotel is within walking distance of the university, Ulster Museum and Botanic Gardens, and Shaftesbury Square. In addition to its convenient location, the hotel features a sauna and exercise room. This modern hotel has a Victorian facade, but the interior is anything but Victorian. The lobby features chrome and leather furnishings, and the staircase follows an intriguing waterfall in clear Lucite troughs. The bedrooms are done in pastels and floral prints. But they are nice-sized, comfortably furnished, and have double-glazing on the windows to help hold down traffic noise.

TEMPLETON HOTEL, *882 Antrim Road, Templepatrick, Ballyclare, Tel. (01849) 432984, fax (01849) 433406. 24 rooms. Rates for singles: UK£85, doubles: UK£110, suites: UK£100 to UK£125. Restaurant, pub, fitness center, sauna, bicycles. Rates include breakfast. All major credit cards accepted. No service charge.*

This is the nicest hotel in the Belfast area, and one of the nicest in all of Northern Ireland. It is a newer hotel about six miles from Belfast International Airport on the main road to the airport, and just a mile or so off the M2. The decor in the public areas is a combination of warm wood and lots of crystal and bright lights – a nice effect that is sort of a cross between modern and rustic, yet not stuffy or stand-offish at all. Furniture and furnishings range from Scandinavian to medieval, depending on which areas of the hotel you are in.

The rooms are of a nice size, and are decorated in soft colors, giving it a restful feeling. All furnishings are new and well-chosen to afford the greatest comfort to guests. There are several family rooms that are very large, furnished in new pine furniture, and exceptionally inviting for families. Combine that with the hotel's discounts for children, and you've got a nice place to stay with your children.

Several executive suites are available in a separate addition. The suites are spacious, and feature jacuzzis and mini-bars. This would be an ideal location from which to tour Belfast and the surrounding areas of County Antrim.

WELLINGTON PARK HOTEL, *21 Malone Road, Belfast BT9 6RU, Tel. (01232) 38111. 50 rooms. Rates for singles: UK£90, doubles: UK£90; children under 12 stay free in their parents' room. Restaurant, pub. Rates include breakfast. All major credit cards accepted. No service charge.*

Just up the street from Queen's University, the Wellington Park Hotel is an older low-rise hotel that has undergone, and is undergoing, renovation. The public areas suffer a little from the low ceilings and dim lighting, but the staff makes up for any darkness of decor with a brightness and lightness of spirit that is rare in hotels this size, even in Ireland.

When you are in the public areas of the hotel, take time to notice the paintings and sculptures – they are the works of a number of local artists, and are proudly displayed by the hotel. The rooms are large and comfortable, although none of them have anything approaching a good view. Each room offers tea- and coffee-making facilities. Children's discounts and baby-sitting services are available should you need them.

STORMONT HOTEL, *587 Upper Newtownards Road, Belfast BT4 3LP, Tel. (01232) 658621, fax (01232) 480240. 106 rooms. Rates for singles: UK£75, doubles: UK£135. Restaurant. All major credit cards accepted. No service charge.*

This modern new hotel is outside of Belfast on the Newtownards Road across from picturesque Stormont Castle. It is a busy hotel, serving as a business and conference center. The public rooms always seem to be abuzz with activity from the latest conference or exhibition. The pub is a popular spot, and one of the lounges has large windows that look out over the castle grounds.

The bedrooms are large and well-lit, providing the opportunity for business people – the hotel's primary clientele – to review proposals, rewrite responses, or catch up on necessary reading. They are furnished comfortably, and the new marble tile baths are spacious.

EUROPA HOTEL, *Great Victoria Street, Belfast BT2 7AP, Tel. (01232) 327000, fax (01232) 327800. 184 rooms. Rates for singles: UK£68 to UK£95, doubles: UK£98 to UK£130, suites: UK£120 to UK£175. Two restaurants, pub, beauty salon. All major credit cards accepted. No service charge.*

The Europa has a similar feel to the Gresham Hotel in Dublin: older, but not run down. Built in the 1970s, they have been busy in recent years refurbishing some of their public areas, including the entire front of the hotel. They are proud that President Clinton stayed here when he visited Northern Ireland in 1995 – in fact, they have memorialized the room with photographs of the president, and a saxophone hangs on the wall!

The pubic areas of the hotel are an eclectic collection striving to meet the needs and tastes of all their guests. There is an informal brasserie on the ground floor, as well as a pub.

Upstairs above the lobby is a not-quite-stuffy lounge that provides a bit more of an upscale feel. But at the edge of the lounge is a large open area that overlooks the front lobby entrance and keeps the atmosphere light and conversational. A pianist supplies guests in the lounge with background music most nights. And for the jet-setters (or those that need to work a few kinks out), a disco is also available five nights a week.

The rooms are of average size and with conventional furnishings. The thing that most impressed me about the Europa was their attention to customer service. They seem to go the extra mile to ensure happy and satisfied customers.

County Antrim

CASTLE HOSTEL, *62 Quay Road, Ballycastle, Tel. (012657) 69822. 42 beds. Rates for singles are UK£7.50 per person sharing in a double room, or UK£6 per person sharing in a dormitory. No credit cards accepted. No service charge.*

The Castle Hostel is located in the heart of Ballycastle just off the round-about at the eastern side of town. Drab from the outside, it's not a castle and never was, but it's a good, relatively clean hostel to hole up for the night. They offer a variety of accommodations, from two double rooms to dormitories that house 4, 6, or 8 occupants. They have two self-catering kitchens, a washing machine, and a place to pitch your tent out back if you prefer.

During the season don't expect to drop in and find a room available for the night – they turn away between 25 and 40 guests per night from June through August.

HILLVIEW B&B, *36 Belfast Road, Larne, Tel. (01574) 260584. 8 rooms. Rates for singles: UK£15, doubles: UK£15 per person sharing. Rates include breakfast. No credit cards accepted. No service charge.*

Sitting atop a hill above the main Belfast Road into Larne, Hillview B&B gives you fine views of Northern Ireland's templed hills. Mrs. Muriel Rainey runs a nice B&B, with comfortable, nice-sized rooms.

SEA VIEW B&B, *12 Shingle Cove, Carnlough, BT44 0EH, Tel. (01574) 885033. 2 rooms. Rates for singles: UK£18, doubles: UK£18 per person sharing. Rates include breakfast. No credit cards accepted. No service charge.*

This new B&B just off the main road through Carnlough is clean and comfortable. Mrs. Brenda McAuley is a gracious hostess just beginning in the B&B business, and she is anxious to provide you a pleasant B&B experience. The rooms are tastefully decorated, and are nice sized.

SHINGLE COVE B&B, *6 Shingle Cove, Tel. (01574) 885593. 3 rooms. Rates for singles: UK£18, doubles: UK£35 for the room. Rates include breakfast. No credit cards accepted. No service charge.*

At the end of a cul-de-sac off the Coast Road, the Shingle Cove B&B has lovely views of the North Channel. The new B&B is comfortable, tastefully decorated, and a warm welcome will greet you from Mrs. Jennifer McAuley. Be sure and call ahead – they fill up quickly.

ROWAN'S B&B, *7 Shingle Cove, Carnlough, BT44 0EH, Tel. (01574) 885638. 2 rooms. Rates for singles: UK£18, doubles: UK£15 per person sharing. Rates include breakfast. No credit cards accepted. No service charge.*

Another new B&B on the same cul-de-sac as the Sea View, Margaret and John Rowan are also new to the business, and just as anxious to please. Their rooms are light and airy, and comfortably furnished.

THE MEADOWS B&B, *81 Coast Road, Cushendall BT44 0QW, Tel. (012667) 72020. 5 rooms. Rates for singles: UK£18, doubles: UK£15 per person sharing. Rates include breakfast. No credit cards accepted. No service charge.*

Another of the new B&Bs on the Coast Road along the eastern coast of County Antrim, The Meadows is a lovely new facility. Mrs. Anne Carey is proud of this tastefully decorated B&B that looks out on the sea. Rooms at the front of the house have views of the North Channel, and the rooms at the back have views of the countryside. Even though the sea views out the front bedrooms are pretty, the B&B sits on a rather busy road, and the traffic noise is noticeable. Try the rooms in the back of the house for the best night's sleep.

CAIREAL MANOR, *90 Glenravel Road, Glens of Antrim, Martinstown, Ballymena, BT43 6QQ, Tel. (012667) 58465. 5 rooms. Rates for singles: UK£25, doubles: UK£25 per person sharing. Rates include breakfast. No credit cards accepted. No service charge.*

You'll find this brand new B&B on the A43 between Ballymena and Waterfoot at the edge of Martinstown. The mauve and blue interior is pleasant and warm, and the rooms are tastefully and comfortably furnished. The Caireal Manor is owned by Mr. Pat O'Neill, owner of the Manor Lodge Restaurant. The B&B features wheelchair access, one of the few in the country to do so. But Mr. O'Neill knows very well the necessity of that service, as he, too, requires it. A little pricey for a B&B, but a nice place.

WHITEPARK HOUSE COUNTRY HOME, *150 Whitepark Road (Coast Road), Ballintoy, Ballycastle, BT54 6NH, Tel. (012657) 31482. 6 rooms. Rates for singles: UK£25, doubles: UK£25 per person sharing. Rates include breakfast. Restaurant, gym, jacuzzi, solarium. Credit cards not accepted. No service charge.*

Mrs. Siobhan Isles runs one of the prettiest country home B&Bs in the country. Built in 1734, this home has been lovingly restored and is richly and tastefully decorated. Several of the rooms overlook the ocean, and the others overlook the wonderful gardens. The main drawback to this house is that none of the rooms are en suite, but if you can handle that, this would be a great central point for touring the Antrim coast.

DRUMNAGREAGH HOTEL, *Coast Road, Glenarm BT440BD, Tel. (01574) 841651. 16 rooms. Rates for singles: UK£40, doubles: UK£60; children under age 12 stay free with their parents. Rates include breakfast. Restaurant and pub. All major credit cards accepted. No service charge.*

This one hundred year old Victorian inn sits atop a hill above the Coast Road, offering stunning views across the Irish Sea to Scotland. It is far enough above the road below that noise from traffic is not an issue. The rooms are all spacious and nicely decorated. Some rooms have views of the Irish Sea, and the others look out on verdant hills and pastoral sheep.

LONDONDERRY ARMS HOTEL, *Glens of Antrim, Carnlough BT44 OEH, Tel. (01574) 885255, (01574) 885263. 35 rooms. Rates for singles:*

UK£45, doubles: UK£65. Restaurant and pub. All major credit cards accepted. No service charge.

Note that while this is called the Londonderry Arms, it is not in Londonderry, but rather in Carnlough among the Glens of Antrim.

A lovely old Victorian coaching inn once owned by Winston Churchill, this creeper-clad hotel is a popular base from which to explore the Glens of Antrim and this part of the Antrim coast. The hotel is scattered with antiques throughout, newly refurbished from top to bottom. Across the street from the hotel is their carpark, and beyond that is a series of gardens and patios for guests to enjoy. The views of Carnlough Harbor from here are beautiful.

The public areas are a bit cramped. However, on the first floor there is a delightful sitting room chock full of interesting antique oddities and a warm and aromatic turf fire burning in the fireplace. It's a nice place to relax before or after you investigate the surrounding areas. Two pubs in the hotel are well attended by locals as well as guests. Rooms are large, spacious, and comfortable. Those overlooking the harbor are a little noisy due to the traffic on the street below. The hotel offers discounts for children on room rates as well as in their restaurant. Baby-sitting service is also available.

BUSHMILLS INN HOTEL, *25 Main Street, Bushmills, BT57 8QA, Tel. (012657) 32339, (012657) 32048. 11 rooms. Rates for singles: UK£42, doubles: UK£85; children under age 12 stay free with parents. Rates include breakfast. Restaurant. American Express, MasterCard, and Visa accepted. No service charge.*

Call ahead and make reservations, because you're going to love this hotel. Located in downtown Bushmills, the Bushmills Inn feels like an old stagecoach hotel. Well-kept and clean, you get an old world feel as you walk into the hotel (the structure dates back to the 1600s). The small reception area is warmed – figuratively as well as literally – by an open turf fire, warm dark wood, gas lights, and a grand staircase leading upstairs. The rooms are light and airy and of a decent size. The rooms facing the main street are a bit noisy, so ask for a room off the street.

The Bushmills Inn is proud of their recent induction into *"The Best Loved Hotels of the World."*

DUNADRY INN, *2 Islandreagh Drive, Dunadry BT41 2HA, Tel. (01849) 432474, fax (01849) 433389. 67 rooms. Rates for singles: UK£50, doubles: UK£55 per person sharing; children up to 5 stay free in their parents' room. Rates include breakfast. Restaurant, indoor swimming pool, spa, fitness center, garden, croquet, miniature golf, bicycles, sauna, solarium. All major credit cards accepted. No service charge.*

The Dunadry Inn is a converted 18th-century paper and linen mill, and they have succeeded in providing a nice facility. The hotel is really striving for a country-club feel, and offers an indoor swimming pool, exercise room, sauna, solarium, and even goofy golf. The rooms are large and well-furnished. If you've brought your computer along to do a little work, ask for one of the executive rooms, as they offer computer ports. Special discounts for children and seniors are available.

BALLYGALLY CASTLE HOTEL, *Coast Road, Ballygally BT40 2QR, Tel. (01574) 583212, fax (01574) 583681. 60 rooms. Rates for singles: UK£49, doubles: UK£74 per person sharing, suites: UK£90 per person sharing. Rates include breakfast. Restaurant and pub. All major credit cards accepted. No service charge.*

Unlike many hotels that call themselves the "Castle Hotel," Ballygally Castle Hotel (or at least parts of it) was once a genuine castle. Built in 1625 (you can still see the date inscribed in one section of the hotel), it was converted into a hotel in the 1970s. The rooms are nice sized and comfortable. They recently expanded the hotel, adding thirty new rooms.

The hotel boasts their own friendly, albeit mischievous, ghost. Legend has it the Lady Isabel Shaw had been locked in one of the tower rooms by her cruel husband. To escape her confinement, she cast herself from the window. They say she still visits on occasion, moving softly through the halls, amusing herself by tapping on the doors of guests' rooms. Her room has not been converted to a guest room, and it is furnished much like it might have been during her confinement. You can see the room by ascending a narrow, winding staircase up one of the turrets of the original castle.

GALGORM MANOR, *136 Fenaghy Road, Ballymena BT42 1EA. 23 rooms. Rates for singles: UK£65, doubles: UK£65 to UK£90 per person sharing, suites: UK£125 per person sharing. Rates include breakfast. Restaurant, pub, gardens, riding, fishing. All major credit cards accepted. No service charge.*

This converted Georgian "gentlemen's residence" is off by itself near the River Main. The grounds impart a pleasant serenity. The public areas have been recently redecorated, with antiques to set the atmosphere. The best rooms are the Executive bedrooms, as they continue the traditional Irish motif, including a number of antiques. The rest of the rooms, although large and spacious, are more modern and don't give you quite the same feel.

Gillies Pub is a popular venue with both the locals as well as the hotel's guests, and would be a good place for you to rub (and bend!) elbows with a few real characters. The pub, along with the rest of the public areas, carries through the traditional Irish feel and atmosphere.

Galgorm Manor sits amid eighty-five acres, and they have an equestrian center on-site that enables you to see the grounds via horseback if you wish (although there is an extra charge).

County Donegal in the Irish Republic
GALLAGHER'S FARM HOSTEL, *Darney, Tel. (073) 37057. 18 beds. Rates are £7 per person, (£6 per person after the first night) for the hostel, or £3.50 per person for campsites. No credit cards accepted – only cash. No service charge.*

This farmhouse hostel is in the converted barn on this Irish farm. But the owners have done a nice job in the conversion, and the accommodations are pretty comfortable. The dormitory rooms have four, six, and eight beds. There are self-catering kitchen facilities and a washer is available (£2.50 per load). This is a pretty decent place to put up for the night. Linens are included.

THE ARCHES COUNTRY HOUSE, *Lough Eske, Barnesmore, Donegal, Tel. (073) 22029. 5 rooms. Rates for singles: £21, doubles: £16 per person sharing. Rates include breakfast. No credit cards accepted. No service charge.*

The Arches wins my Best Irish B&B award. Mrs. Noreen McGinty is the primary reason. She is a gracious and enjoyable hostess. Her house is immaculate, and rests on a hill with stunning views of Lough Eske.

The B&B itself is a newer one, and the rooms are all well-lit and decorated in a bright and cheery manner. The rooms at the front of the house have large windows that open to provide spectacular views of Lough Eske in the distance. The rooms at the back of the house are equally as nice, with lovely views of the Bluestack Mountains. A nice sitting room is available to visit with other guests or just relax after the rigors of touring.

ARDEEVIN, *Lough Eske, Barnesmore, Donegal, Tel. (073) 21790. 6 rooms. Rates for singles: £18, doubles: £16 per person sharing. Rates include breakfast. No credit cards accepted. No service charge.*

Next door to The Arches, Ardeevin is another pleasant B&B in the Lough Eske area. The views are great here too. This Mrs. McGinty is the wife of Sean McGinty, who owns the sweater shop where you probably bought your sweater today (or will tomorrow)! Together, they have been in the B&B business since 1967, and know their stuff. Recent and extensive renovations have been made, and their B&B is nicer than ever. You probably won't have to twist Sean's arm too much to get him to help you experience a "real" Irish pub – it's one of his regular routines.

SMUGGLER'S CREEK INN, *Waterville (near Rossnowlagh), Tel. (066) 74330, fax (066) 74422. 6 rooms. Rates for singles: £30, doubles: £24.50 per person sharing. One restaurant, pub. All major credit cards accepted. No service charge.*

This 100-year old house overlooking the ocean was converted recently into an award-winning restaurant with six bedrooms. Several of the rooms are of a nice size with beautiful views of the ocean and an expansive sandy beach. One of the rooms has a balcony. The remaining rooms are smallish, but their distressed pine furnishings give them a homey feeling.

The rooms are actually a side business for Smuggler's Creek Inn. Their real business appears to be a wonderful pub and restaurant (See *Where To Eat* section.) If you are looking to turn in early on Friday and Saturday evenings, this probably isn't a good place to stay – the rooms are above the pub where traditional Irish music is featured from 10:00 pm to midnight on the weekend.

CASTLE MURRAY HOTEL, *Dunkineely, Tel. (073) 37022, (073) 37330. 10 rooms. Rates for singles: £26, doubles: £26 per person sharing. Rates include breakfast. Restaurant, pub. All major credit cards accepted. No service charge.*

Not a castle at all, but a nice, new hotel, sitting atop a hill and overlooking the scant ruins of its castellated namesake and the ocean beyond. Many of Castle Murray's rooms have gorgeous views of McSweeney Bay and the rugged Donegal coastline. The rooms are nice sized and are tastefully decorated with warm pine. There is more of a B&B feel here than at most hotels. The rooms at the front of the hotel offer the best views by far: the Atlantic Ocean crashes onto the shore and the rugged Donegal shoreline is picturesque and photogenic.

The owners, Thierry and Clare Delcros, also run a wonderful seafood restaurant on the first floor (see *Where To Eat*). In addition to marvelous food, the views are stunning.

CASTLEGROVE COUNTRY HOUSE, *Letterkenny, Tel. (074) 51118, fax (074) 51384. 7 rooms. Rates for singles: £30 to £45, doubles: £30 to £45 per person sharing. Rates include breakfast. MasterCard and Visa accepted. No service charge.*

It's hard to say which you will enjoy more: the beautifully restored 17th-century house, the splendid views of Lough Swilly, or the warm welcome you'll receive by Mrs. Mary Sweeney. No matter. Every one of them is above expectations, and no matter what you're looking for here, you'll find them at Castlegrove Country House. The pleasant public areas have open fires, the rooms are tastefully decorated, and the service attentive.

KEE'S HOTEL, *Stranolar, Ballybofey, Tel. (074) 31018, fax (074) 31017. 48 rooms. Rates for singles: £33 to £40, doubles: £54 to £67, executive rooms: £60 to £73. Restaurant, indoor swimming pool, gym, jacuzzi, solarium, sauna, spa, steam room. All major credit cards accepted. 10% service charge.*

Four generations of the Kee family have hosted guests in Kee's Hotel in Ballybofey, and they are very good at their trade. The reception you receive here will be more akin to the personal attention you get at a B&B than what you often find at hotels. Kee's Hotel was built in 1842, and has been carefully renovated through the years.

The rooms are large and comfortably furnished, including the thirteen new Executive rooms that offer pretty vistas of the Bluestack

Mountains. The rooms in the front of the hotel have been thoughtfully soundproofed to afford a quiet stay to go along with the fine views. All the rooms have tea- and coffee-making facilities and trouser presses.

In recent years the hotel has added some wonderful amenities for their guests, and include an indoor swimming pool, sauna, and exercise room. A nice touch is that entrances to these areas have been added with direct access to guests' rooms – no need to walk through public areas to get to any of these facilities.

The hotel is proud of their fine restaurant, and I was impressed with it also (see *Where to Eat*). In fact, I was so impressed with it after my first visit, that I wandered the Donegal roads trying to find it on my last visit. I discovered that my memory hadn't played tricks on me: the food is still incredible.

THE CENTRAL HOTEL, *The Diamond, Donegal Town, Tel. (073) 21027, fax (073) 22295. 85 rooms. Rates for singles: £43 to £50, doubles: £66 to £85. Rates include breakfast. Restaurant, bistro, pub, gym, jacuzzi, solarium. All major credit cards accepted. 10% service charge.*

You can't get much more central in Donegal town than the Central Hotel, which sits right on the main square in the downtown area. The rooms are nice sized, although all have pretty much the same decor. The hotel is older but clean and functional. The rooms in the front overlook the busy Diamond, but they can be noisy. Opt instead for the rooms in the back that overlook the gardens and an estuary of the sea.

ARDNAMONA HOUSE, *Lough Eske, Donegal Town, Tel. (073) 22650, fax (073) 22819. 6 rooms. Rates for singles: £40, doubles: £40 per person sharing. Rates include breakfast. Gardens, forest walks, fishing, boating. No credit cards accepted. No service charge.*

This is a pleasant B&B overlooking Lough Eske. The rooms are nice sized, and the rooms in the front of the house offer splendid views of the lake and surrounding woodlands. Ardnamona House offers more than mere accommodations: beautiful gardens and acres of woods available for walks.

THE SAND HOUSE HOTEL, *near Waterville (near Rossnowlagh), Tel. (073) 51777, fax (073) 52100. 45 rooms. Rates for singles: £48 to £55, doubles: £38 to £43 per person sharing. Rates include breakfast. Restaurant, several pubs. All major credit cards accepted. 10% service charge. Open from Easter through October.*

A Manor House Hotel, the Sand Hotel sits along one of the most popular surfing beaches in the country. Several pubs are on the premises, including a 1960s-era "surfer's bar." Traditional Irish sessions are held Wednesday evenings from June through August.

All the rooms are decorated differently, and antiques are sprinkled throughout. The rooms with an ocean view are of course the most popular. There are no televisions in the rooms to distract you from the beautiful ocean views. The hotel offers a wide variety of activities to its guests, including tennis courts, snooker, a game room, a playground, and even a croquet court.

The hotel is delighted to accommodate children, and offers discounts for them. If you've brought a pet with you, it is welcome too.

THE BAY VIEW HOTEL, *Main Street, Killybegs, Tel. (073) 31950, fax (073) 31856. 38 rooms. Rates for singles: £43 to £45, doubles: £65 to £75, suites: £80 to £90. Rates include breakfast. Restaurant, gym, jacuzzi, solarium. All major credit cards accepted. 10% service charge.*

This is a nice older hotel in "downtown" Killybegs, overlooking the harbor and its plentiful fishing boats. The rooms are large and the furnishings simple. Ask for a room facing the harbor – the double-pane windows cut down on the noise considerably, and the sights are interesting. The hotel has a number of leisure activities to offer their guests, including an indoor swimming pool, exercise room, jacuzzi, and solarium. In addition, they make it nice for their guests who are traveling with children or pets, as they offer a discount for children and can accommodate pets. Seniors can also benefit from discounts most months of the year (but not in July and August).

HARVEY'S POINT COUNTRY HOTEL, *Lough Eske, Donegal Town, (073) 22208, (073) 22352, 32 rooms. Rates for singles: £50 to £65, doubles: £40 to £80 per person sharing, suites: £50 to £60 per person sharing. Rates include breakfast. Restaurant, walking and bicycle paths, boating. All major credit cards accepted. 10% service charge.*

Sitting along the banks of pretty Lough Eske, Harvey's Point Country Hotel provides a feel of continental Europe mixed with warm Irish hospitality. The setting is pretty – in the trees and beside the lake. Lots of nature is available to explore via walking or bicycling (bikes are provided free to guests).

The hotel is owned by Jody Gysling, and it fosters a Swiss-German resort feel. Lots of light wood and chalet-style buildings contribute to the feel of a country inn someplace in the Swiss or German Alps. The public areas are light and airy, with lots of windows on the side of the building that faces the lake. An informal brasserie offers delicious meals and a pleasant atmosphere. Another, more formal restaurant features Swiss and French cuisine.

The rooms are spacious and tastefully decorated. If you can afford them, the executive suites are of course the nicest, and most have views of the lake out at least one window. All the rooms feature tea- and coffee-making facilities, and the executive suites offer trouser presses. Although this may sound like a fun place to bring your children, the management requests that you not bring them if they are younger than ten years old.

ST. ERNAN'S HOUSE HOTEL, *Donegal Town, Tel. (073) 21065, fax (073) 22098. 12 rooms. Rates for singles: £75 to £90, doubles: £55 to £62 per person sharing. Rates include breakfast. Restaurant, gardens, walking paths. All major credit cards accepted. 10% service charge.*

St. Ernan's has an idyllic setting – this pretty four-star Victorian hotel sits grandly on its own timbered tidal island, joined to the mainland by a causeway. Serenity is the goal here, and serenity is what the staff helps provide. The rooms are of a nice size, decorated graciously, and each has outstanding views of the surrounding sea. Whether you just need a break from charging all over the country, or are just looking for a good night's sleep before charging about again, St. Ernan's is a very pleasant respite.

County Down

MARINE COURT HOTEL, *18 Quay Street, Bangor BT20 5ED, Tel. (01247) 451100, fax (01247) 451200. 51 rooms. Rates for singles: UK£40, doubles: UK£45 per person sharing. Rates include breakfast. Restaurant, garden, tennis, riding, beaches. Visa accepted. No service charge.*

The public areas as well as the service here are underwhelming, but the rooms are the saving grace: large, well furnished, and pleasantly decorated. But as close as they are to the harbor, it's a little disappointing that none of the rooms have views. Each room offers tea- and coffee-making facilities as well as trouser presses. The hotel offers guests an indoor swimming pool, sauna, and fitness center. In addition, discounts for children are offered.

CLANDEBOYE LODGE HOTEL, *10 Estate Road, Clandeboye, Bangor BT19 1UR, Tel. (01247) 852500, fax (01247) 852772. 43 rooms. Rates for singles: UK£50, doubles: UK£46 per person sharing; children stay free in their parents' room. Rates include breakfast. Restaurant, pub, bikes, fishing, riding, beaches. American Express, MasterCard, Visa accepted. No service charge.*

Just outside the town of Clandeboye sits the Clandeboye Lodge Hotel. This new brick hotel is already popular with the business community, as it joins an existing business and conference center. The rooms are large, and some of them are even spacious. They are well-equipped and comfortably furnished. Since the hotel caters primarily to the business community, the rooms are well-lit and offer lots of room for writing or reading. They also offer additional phone jacks for modems. Children under twelve stay free in their parents' room.

A traditional Irish pub is located outside of the main building in an old Victorian building, and you will enjoy meeting other tourists as well as some of the local populace there.

GLASSDRUMMAN LODGE, *85 Mill Road, Annalong, BT34 4RH, Tel. (01396) 768451, fax (01396) 767041. 10 rooms. Rates for singles: UK£45, doubles: UK£55 per person sharing. Rates include breakfast. Restaurant, garden,* *tennis, riding, beaches. American Express, MasterCard, Visa accepted. No service charge.*

If it's magnificent views you want, then the Glassdrumman Lodge ought to satisfy you. Along with your room you can either have seascapes or mountain scenes. The rooms of this converted farmhouse are large and comfortable, with little additions such as mineral water, fresh flowers, and warm and friendly Irish hospitality. There is an excellent restaurant associated with this guest house also.

WHERE TO EAT

Belfast City

Unlike the dearth of hotels in Belfast, there are quite a number of restaurants in and around the city. Still, on the whole, the quantity and quality of restaurants is nowhere near the level you'll find in Dublin. There are only a few that could go toe-to-toe in competition with Dublin restaurants such as Number 10, The Commons, Restaurant Patrick Guilbaud, or Alexandra's.

Many of the following restaurants are found in and around Shaftesbury Square:

BACKPACKER'S CAFE, *22 Donegall Road, Tel. (01232) 315435. UK£6.50 to UK£11.95. Open daily from 7:30 am to 8:00 pm. Breakfast is served from 7:30 am to 11:30 am. American Express, MasterCard and Visa accepted. No service charge.*

You don't need to stay at the youth hostel at the same address, but the food is decent, filling, and inexpensive. Just off the corner of Shaftesbury Square, it's a good place to grab an inexpensive sandwich, quick breakfast, or just a cup of coffee.

THE BUTLER, *39 Dublin Street, Tel. (01232) 322153. UK£3.80 to UK£5.50. Open Monday through Saturday from 9:30 am to 10:00 pm. American Express, MasterCard, and Visa accepted. No service charge.*

This quiet little cafe offers unexceptional ambiance, but the food is good and reasonably priced. Dress is very casual – grubbies are fine.

BISHOP'S FISH AND CHIPS, *Bradbury Place, Tel. (01232) 311827. UK£2.90 to UK£5.95. Open Monday through Friday from 9:00 am to 2:00 am, and 9:00 am to 3:00 am Saturday and Sunday. MasterCard and Visa accepted. No service charge.*

You'll find a little bit o' London at Bishop's Fish and Chips, located close to Shaftesbury Square. Here's where you can go to satisfy your palate for honest-to-goodness fish and chips. This establishment has a cafeteria atmosphere – noisy and chattery, booths lining the walls and down the center. They also have a variety of burgers available, but fish and chips is the main attraction.

THE REVELATIONS INTERNET CAFE, *27 Shaftesbury Square, Tel. (01232) 320337. UK£3.50 to UK£7.95. Open Monday through Friday from 10:00 am to 10:00 pm, Saturday from 10:00 am to 8:00 pm, and Sunday from noon to 10:00 pm. No service charge.*

This small nondescript cafe gives new meaning to Surf and Turf – it is a combination coffee shop/computer lab. Guests can order cappuccino and a sandwich while surfing the net on any of the half dozen computers they have set up for internet access. The sandwiches will run you around £4, and connect time is £4.50 per hour. They also offer one-on-one tutorials for £15 per hour. If you want to contact them, their internet address is http:www.revelations.co.uk.

THE CELLARS, *Belfast Castle, Antrim Road, Tel. (01232) 776925. UK£6.50 to UK£10.95. Open 12:15 pm to 2:30 pm and 6:30 pm to 9:45 pm. MasterCard and Visa accepted. No service charge.*

Located in the basement of Belfast Castle, the atmosphere is decidedly cozy and the food is good. Casual dress is fine.

AUBERGINES AND BLUE JEANS, *1 University Street, Tel. (01232) 23370. UK£3.95 to UK£10.50. Open Sunday through Wednesday from 12:30 pm to 9:00 pm and Thursday through Saturday from 12:30 pm to 11:00 pm. All major credit cards accepted. No service charge.*

A part of but also separate from Saints and Scholars Restaurant (see below). There is a separate entrance and name, but if you walk around the bar, you find yourself in the bistro section of Saints. But Aubergines is really different, and I mean *really* different! Apparently it has an irresistible appeal to the many students who frequent it. Lots of interesting things on the walls to hold your attention. Keeping with the cafe motif, it has a nice selection of burgers, sandwiches, soups, and salads. Vegetarians will also find a good selection here. Dress is casual

SAINTS AND SCHOLARS, *3 University Street, Tel. (01232) 325137. UK£5.95 to UK£11.95. Open Sunday through Wednesday from 12:30 pm to 9:00 pm and Thursday through Saturday from noon to 11:00 pm. All major credit cards accepted. No service charge.*

This restaurant in the heart of the University area seems unable to decide what it wants to be: a bistro, upscale trendy cafe, or quiet and elegant restaurant. But don't worry – it's designed that way. Owner Dirk Lakeman explained how he hoped to cater to any and every diner's taste. He indicated that patrons often don't know exactly what they feel in the mood for until after a drink or two, so he offers them a nice range from which to choose.

The menu – which is the same for all "three" restaurants – successfully bridges different tastes: from soups and salads to Thai chicken to pink roasted duck breast with red cabbage and bittersweet port jus. Overall, the food is good and reasonably priced. Casual dress is more than fine here.

ULSTER'S BEST DINING

ESPERANTO CAFE, 89 Dublin Road, Belfast, Tel. (01232) 248708. UK£7.95 to UK£13.95, American Express, MasterCard, and Visa accepted. No service charge. Esperanto Cafe is a popular restaurant just off Shaftesbury Square.

***MANOR HOUSE CANTONESE CUISINE**, 43 Donegall Pass, Belfast, Tel. (01232) 238755. UK£7.95 to UK£14.50. All major credit cards accepted. No service charge. This is probably the best Chinese food in Belfast.*

KEE'S RESTAURANT, Stranolar, Ballybofey, Tel. (074) 31018. £10.95 to £17.00. All major credit cards accepted. In my humble opinion, the restaurant at Kee's Hotel is among the top ten in all of Ireland.

***THE OLD SCHOOLHOUSE RESTAURANT**, 106 Ballyrobin Road, Muckamore. Set dinner menu for UK£19.95. All major credit cards accepted. No service charge. This old schoolhouse is a comfortable and homey country restaurant warmed by open turf fires. The food is pretty good, too!*

ANTICA ROMA, 67 Botanic Avenue, Belfast, Tel. (01232) 310787. Set dinner menus UK£17.95 to UK£21.95, American Express, MasterCard, and Visa accepted. No service charge. Antica Roma is probably my favorite Italian restaurant on the Emerald Isle.

RESTAURANT 44, 44 Belfast Road, Belfast, Tel. (01232) 244844, 238755. UK£14.95 to UK£24.95. All major credit cards accepted. No service charge. Great food, intriguing decor!

DUKES HOTEL RESTAURANT, *65 University Street, Tel. (01232) 236666. UK£5.95 to UK£10.50. Open Monday through Saturday from 7:00 pm to 9:45 pm, and Sunday from 1:00 pm to 7:45 pm. All major credit cards accepted. No service charge.*

This is a nice chatty restaurant, and the food is good and reasonably priced: try their fried cheese beignet with black currant and cranberry sauce. For more traditional fare, you might try the fillet of cod. Dress is informal.

BELFAST CASTLE RESTAURANT, *Antrim Road, Tel. (01232) 776925. UK£4.95, to UK£14.50. Open daily from 6:30 pm to 9:30 pm. All major credit cards accepted. No service charge.*

Sitting regally on the slopes of Cave Hill overlooking the city, Belfast Castle affords beautiful views of both the city and Belfast Lough. The castle was built in 1870 on the site of several castles that preceded it. The restaurant is elegant and tranquil. But it's not overly expensive. Menu selections include roast chicken with leek and smoked bacon in Dijon mustard sauce, or roast salmon and scallops with oysters and mushrooms. Jacket and tie are requested.

DRAGON PALACE, *16 Botanic Avenue, Tel. (01232) 32369. UK£6.50 to UK£11.95. MasterCard and Visa accepted. No service charge.*

This is a nice, quiet Chinese restaurant. Hanging lamps provide each of the tables with muted light, giving the impression of intimacy and privacy. The menu is pretty typical of Chinese restaurants. It's also pretty busy, so consider calling ahead for reservations. Casual dress.

PONTE VECCHIO, *73 Great Victoria Street. UK£9.85 to UK£12.95. Open Tuesday through Saturday from 5:00 pm to 11:30 pm and Sunday from 5:00 pm to 10:00 pm. MasterCard and Visa accepted. No service charge.*

This small Italian cafe gives you the impression of being in a similar cafe on the streets of Rome – except for the New Age music. But the food is good. Try their pollo marsala or tournedos rossini.

ESPERANTO CAFE, *89 Dublin Road, Tel. (01232) 248708. UK£7.95 to UK£13.95. Open Monday through Friday from 5:00 pm to 11:00 pm, Saturday from 4:00 pm to 11:00 pm, and Sunday from 4:00 pm to 10:00 pm. American Express, MasterCard, and Visa accepted. No service charge.*

Esperanto Cafe is a popular restaurant just off Shaftesbury Square. The evening I was there it was packed – waiting diners were lined up down the stairs out into the entryway. Once you make it to this upstairs restaurant, you'll find checkered table cloths, candles on the table, and a trellis with grape vines hanging down that add a nice touch to your dining experience. Try the chargrilled steak fillet or the frilled salmon fillet. Casual dress is fine here.

MANOR HOUSE CANTONESE CUISINE, *43 Donegall Pass, Tel. (01232) 238755. UK£7.95 to UK£14.50. Open daily from noon to 2:30 pm and 5:00 pm to 11:30 pm (Sunday 12:30 pm to 11:00 pm). All major credit cards accepted. No service charge.*

This is probably the best Chinese restaurant in Belfast. Owned by Joe Wong and his family since 1982, they are very good at what they do. The menu is extensive. Soft colors in the restaurant add a tranquil feeling to the dining experience, even though the place gets busy most of the time. There is a set dinner menu for UK£14.50, and a bargain of a set lunch menu for UK£5.50. Nice casual is the dress.

THE STRAND, *12 Stranmillis Road, Tel. (01232) 682266. UK£10 to UK£16.95. Open daily noon to 11:00 pm, Sunday from noon to 3:00 pm and 5:00 pm to 10:00 pm. All major credit cards accepted. No service charge.*

Located close to Queen's University, The Strand is an intimate café relying on muted lighting and candlelight to set a quiet atmosphere. The food is good but not exceptional. Numerous vegetarian menus dishes are available for those who prefer them. Their lunch menu is very reasonable at £4.50.

RENSHAWS RESTAURANT, *75 University Street, Tel. (01232) 333366. UK£12.95 to UK£16.95. All major credit cards accepted. No service charge.* This restaurant associated with Renshaws Hotel has a nice atmosphere with its dark wood and cozy ambiance. The food is decidedly European with an Eastern theme. Dress is nice casual.

CAFE SOCIETY, *3 Donegall Square East, Tel. (01232) 439525. Set dinner menus from UK£12.50 to UK£17.50. Open Monday from noon to 3:00 pm, Tuesday through Saturday noon to 3:00 pm and 6:00 pm to 10:30 pm. MasterCard and Visa accepted. No service charge.*

This new modern cafe near Belfast City Hall offers up excellent fare for sagging shoppers, tired tourists, and busy business people. The menus offer a nice selection, and presentation is an important aspect of the fare. Try their fillet of salmon in herb crust or roasted rack of pork. The dessert menu is great.

GALLERY RESTAURANT, *Great Victoria Street, Tel. (01232) 327000. Set dinner menu for UK£21.50. Open daily from 12:30 pm to 2:30 pm and 6:30 pm to 10:00 pm (or, as the manager says, "until people quit coming"). Reservations are strongly suggested, especially on the weekends. All major credit cards accepted. No service charge.*

This is a pleasant restaurant. The quiet ambiance is accented by crystal and starched linens. The menu is also impressive, with such offerings as pan-fried pheasant with juniper berries and fresh trompettes de la mort and wild mushroom melange, and noisettes of North Down spring lamb sprinkled with red currant cream.

ANTICA ROMA, *67 Botanic Avenue, Tel. (01232) 310787. Set dinner menus UK£17.95 to UK£21.95. Open Monday through Saturday for dinner from 6:00 pm to 11:30 pm, and for lunch Monday through Friday from noon to 3:00 pm. American Express, MasterCard, and Visa accepted. No service charge.*

Antica Roma could well be my favorite Italian restaurant on the Emerald Isle. Authentic decor (mosaic floors, columns, murals, etc.) combined with a fine wine list and an extensive and interesting menu add up to an enjoyable Italian meal. The menu items are Italian, but not your standard run-of-the-mill Roman eatery. Examples of the fare include roast guinea fowl with mushrooms, pasta, and rice, or Mediterranean sea bream on a bed of fennel with wild rice and pasta. Dress is nice casual, although you'd not feel out of place with a jacket and tie in the evenings.

RESTAURANT 44, *44 Belfast Road, Tel. (01232) 244844, 238755. UK£14.95 to UK£24.95. Open Monday through Friday 12:30 pm to 2:30 pm, 6:30 pm to 10:00 pm, and Saturday from 6:30 pm to 10:00 pm. All major credit cards accepted. No service charge*

This unlikely restaurant a couple of blocks down the street from City Hall is a pleasant surprise. The look and feel is that of having walked into a bar in India rather than one on the Emerald Isle. Green cane furniture, ceiling fans, and an elephant theme mural graces one wall. A nice selection of traditional Irish dishes cooked with a continental flair are offered, plus a number of vegetarian dishes. Dress is casual, but no grubbies, please.

ROSCOFF RESTAURANT, *7 Shaftesbury Square, Tel. (01232) 331532. Set lunch menu for UK£15.50, and set dinner menu for UK£24.95. Open daily from 12:15 pm to 2:15 pm for lunch, and from 6:30 pm to 10:30 pm for dinner. Reservations are recommended on the weekends in particular. All major credit cards accepted. No service charge.*

This owners of this modern restaurant are frequent guests on local cooking shows, and their restaurant is a great showcase for their talent. The set menu changes on a regular basis, and you're never left with too few decisions: often you can choose from five to eight items per course. The main courses consist of such delicacies as confit duck, glazed monkfish, venison with roast shallots, and roast cod with a lobster and tarragon vinaigrette. Combine those offers with an eclectic assemblage of fresh appetizers, vegetables, and desserts, and you've got a feast on your hands.

It may surprise you to discover this is one of the most highly regarded restaurants in the North. Chrome and cloth chairs and small two-person tables define the ambiance. Coat and tie are suggested. Dress is nice casual.

County Antrim

VALERIE'S PANTRY, *125 Main Street, Bushmills, Tel. (012657) 32660. UK£1.40 to UK£3.50. Open April through October Monday through Saturday from 9:00 am to 6:00 pm, and Sunday from 1:00 pm to 9:00 pm. During the winter, the hours are Monday through Saturday from 9:00 am to 5:00 pm. No credit cards accepted. No service charge.*

Just up the hill on Main Street from the round-about in the center of town is Valerie's Pantry, a delightful little cafe that offers snacks and sandwiches for a quick bite. From scones to roast beef sandwiches, Valerie's offers you good food at fair prices. The furnishings are simple and the food is good.

TEMPLETON HOTEL RESTAURANT, *882 Antrim Road, Templepatrick, Ballyclare, Tel. (01849) 432984. UK£7.95 to UK£12.95. Open daily from 7:00 pm to 9:45 pm. All major credit cards accepted. No service charge.*

The restaurant in the Templeton Hotel is a nice place bordering on elegant. Wedgewood china, crystal, and starched linen tablecloths add accent to the traditional Irish (with French influences) menu. The fare is well-presented, tasty, and reasonably priced. Dress is nice casual.

TERRACE RESTAURANT, *Belfast international Airport, Tel. (01849) 422033. UK£6.50 to UK£14.50. Open daily from 6:00 am to 10:00 am, noon* *to 3:00 pm, and 6:00 pm to 10:00 pm. All major credit cards accepted. No service charge*

You probably won't drive out to Belfast International Airport specifically to eat dinner at the Terrace Restaurant in the Aldergrove Hotel, but if you're staying here or find yourself in the area, it's a pretty decent and reasonably priced restaurant. Try their gammon and pineapple or their roast beef wrapped in bacon. Dress is nice casual.

LONDONDERRY ARMS HOTEL RESTAURANT, *20 Harbor Road, Glens of Antrim, Carnlough, Tel. (01574) 885255. Set lunch menu for UK£10.95, and set dinner menu for UK£14.95. Open 8:00 am to 10:00 am for breakfast, noon to 3:00 pm for lunch, and 5:00 pm to 9:00 pm for dinner. All major credit cards accepted. No service charge.*

The restaurant for the Londonderry Arms Hotel is popular with hotel guests, tourists, and the Irish themselves. The atmosphere and decor are unmemorable (although they were planning extensive renovations), but the food is considered a good buy for the money. Try the roast leg of lamb with mint or the grilled fresh cod. They offer set menus as well as á la carte. Dress is casual.

MANOR LODGE RESTAURANT, *120 Glen Road, Glenariff, Tel. (012667) 58221. Set lunch menu for UK£11.95, and set dinner menu for UK£15.95. Owner Pat O'Neill says they are open from 11:00 am to 9:00 pm "or whenever everyone has gone home." American Express, MasterCard, and Visa accepted. No service charge.*

This wonderful restaurant set at the foot of Glenariff Waterfall is a favorite among tourists as well as natives alike. Always busy, the restaurant offers excellent fare for a reasonable price. Try the fresh fillet of Red Bay plaice poached in white wine, or the tenderized Irish beef topped with prawns and sautéed in garlic butter. The dress ranges from casual to jacket. Plenty of patrons here are mid-hike on one of the numerous walking trails at Glenariff National Park.

BUSHMILLS INN RESTAURANT, *25 Main Street, Bushmills. UK£9.45 to UK£17. Open daily from noon to 9:30 pm. (They close at 9:00 pm on Sunday.). American Express, MasterCard, and Visa accepted. No service charge.*

From the moment you enter, you'll be warmed – first by the open turf fire in the reception area, and then by the service. The restaurant is proud of its membership in the "Taste of Ulster," an elite restaurant society in Northern Ireland. Their secret is in the freshness of the local produce, poultry, meat, and seafood they provide. Look for such main courses as roast rack of lamb or braised barony duckling, poached salmon, or smoked sea trout. The menu varies, but you're sure to find something you'll like. The restaurant itself is a series of booths; old white-washed stone walls and distressed pine gives kind of an old world ambiance. Casual dress is fine.

THE OLD SCHOOLHOUSE RESTAURANT, *106 Ballyrobin Road, Muckamore. Set dinner menu for UK£19.95. Open Tuesday through Sunday noon to 2:30 pm and 5:00 pm to 9:30 pm. All major credit cards accepted. No service charge.*

The Old Schoolhouse Restaurant is on the road from Belfast City to the airport, and might just be worth the drive (twenty minutes or so) out from the city. Jim Kelly is the owner of this family-run restaurant, which in former times served as the local schoolhouse (from 1850 to 1960). Today it is a comfortable and homey country restaurant warmed by open turf fires.

The menu is classical European with French influences. The menu changes monthly, but one of the choices might well be boneless lamb cutlets pan-fried and finished in the oven with herb crust and a Madeira sauce. Casual dress is fine, but you wouldn't feel out of place with a jacket and tie.

County Donegal in the Irish Republic

THE BLUEBERRY TEA ROOM, *Castle Street, Donegal Town, Tel. (073) 22933. £2.50 to £3.95. Open daily from 9:00 am to 9:00 pm during the summer, 9:00 am to 7:00 pm Monday through Saturday the rest of the year. No credit cards accepted.*

Just off the Diamond up a narrow staircase between the Olde Castle Bar and Restaurant and Melody Maker is The Blueberry Tea Room, a popular little sandwich shop. I asked several of the merchants in the area where they took their lunch, and a surprising number indicated this little shop. The decor is unmemorable, but the sandwiches are good and inexpensive. Casual dress – grubbies are acceptable.

CENTRAL HOTEL RESTAURANT, *The Diamond, Donegal Town, Tel. (073) 21027. £12.95 to £16.95. Open daily for dinner from noon to 2:30 pm and 5:30 pm to 9:30 pm. All major credit cards accepted. 10% service charge.*

The restaurant in the Central Hotel serves a pretty decent dinner. The atmosphere is unexceptional, but the food is pretty good. Try their roast duckling a l'orange or roast spring leg of lamb in rosemary. Nice casual dress is fine.

ABBEY RESTAURANT, *The Diamond, Donegal Town, Tel. (073) 21014. £12.95 to £16.95. Open daily from 8:00 am to 10:00 am, 12:30 pm to 3:00 pm, and 5:30 to 9:30 pm. All major credit cards accepted. 10% service charge.*

The restaurant at the Abbey Hotel offers a nice dining experience set with an open fire, with views looking out onto The Diamond. The food is middling, but try their oak-smoked chicken in mushroom sauce, or one of their beef dishes.

SMUGGLER'S CREEK INN, *Rossnowlagh, Tel. (072) 52366. £9.75 to £12.95. Open daily from 9:00 am to 10:00 am, 12:30 pm to 5:00 pm, and 6:30 pm to 9:15 pm. MasterCard and Visa accepted. No service charge.*

The Smuggler's Creek Inn, a seafood restaurant, has splendid views of Donegal Bay and a long wide sandy beach. They have a number of tables out on a veranda overlooking the ocean, and it is a very popular place during the summer months. You probably won't get in without a reservation from June through August. An added bonus is the traditional Irish music played in the bar on Friday and Saturday evenings from 10:00 pm until midnight.

Nice casual dress is recommended. Lunch is a little less casual.

KEE'S RESTAURANT, *Stranolar, Ballybofey, Tel. (074) 31018. £10.95 to £17. Open Monday through Friday from 6:30 pm to 9:30 pm, and Saturdays from 6:30 pm to 10:00 pm. All major credit cards accepted.*

This is a wonderful restaurant. Located on the N15 in Stranolar on the left-hand side of the road (if you're traveling to Donegal from Strabane), the food at Kee's remains as delicious as the first time I visited years ago. Chef Frederic Souty is the master behind the fare, and he didn't disappoint me this time. The menu is well represented by beef, seafood, and other wonderful concoctions. Try the roast rack of Donegal spring lamb or the grilled fillet steak with wild mushroom essence. Add one of the finest wine lists in the country, and you have a combination that's difficult to beat. The dark wood enhances the quiet, private atmosphere of the room. Framed tapestries around the walls are the work of past owners of the hotel and restaurant.

Without reservation, I would put Chef Souty's handiwork up against any in the country. Try it yourself, and see if you agree. (I guarantee you will.) Nice casual dress is nice. Coat and tie would not be out of place.

CASTLE MURRAY HOUSE RESTAURANT, *St. John's Point, Dunkineely, Tel. (073) 37022. Set menu £13 to £26 or á la carte menu. Open Monday through Saturday from 7:00 pm to 9:30 pm, and Sunday from 3:00 pm to 8:00 pm. MasterCard and Visa accepted. No service charge.*

Just outside the drab little town of Dunkineely, not far from Donegal Town and overlooking McSweeney Bay, is Castle Murray House Restaurant. This light and airy restaurant offers stunning views of the bay to complement a varied menu. The owners, Thierry and Clare Delcros, are French, and the menu is "French with an Irish flair" according to Clare. You can select a lobster and eat it within site of its home, McSweeney Bay. Or, if you prefer, try the *piece de veau du jour* (the veal of the day). Casual dress is fine.

SAND HOUSE RESTAURANT, *Rossnowlagh, Tel. (072) 51777. £12.95 to £21.50. Open daily from 7:00 pm to 8:30 pm. (Closed from October through Easter). All major credit cards accepted. 10% service charge.*

Overlooking Donegal Bay, this award-winning restaurant provides a wonderful, pleasant atmosphere with a menu to whet your appetite. Try the escalope of veal aux champignon or the roast leg of lamb with rosemary and fresh mint sauce. Nice casual dress is requested.

HARVEY'S POINT COUNTRY RESTAURANT, *Lough Eske. £12.95 to £22. Open daily from 12:30 pm to 2:30 pm and 6:30 pm to 9:30 pm. All major credit cards accepted. 10% service charge.*

Harvey's Point Country Restaurant and Hotel sits on the banks of lovely Lough Eske in County Donegal. The setting is marvelous, and parts of the dining room have views of the lake. Starched linens, crystal, and silver complement the excellent food, like the crepinette of tender farmhouse chicken or the grilled salmon fillet with leek and chive sauce. Or, if beef is your preference, you can't miss with the beef stroganoff and tagliatelle. Casual dress is requested.

ST. ERNAN'S HOUSE RESTAURANT, *St. Ernan's House Hotel, Tel. (073) 21065. Set dinner £25. Open for dinner daily from 6:30 pm until 8:30 pm. MasterCard and Visa accepted.*

Associated with St. Ernan's House Hotel, the restaurant is designed primarily for guests of the hotel, but you might luck out and be able to savor the fare here. Call ahead to see how likely it is that you'll get in. If you do, the seafood is the specialty here. Casual dress is requested.

County Down

VILLA TOSCANA, *Toscana Park West Circular Road, Bangor. UK£11.95 to UK£17.95. Open daily from 5:00 pm to 11:30 pm, and Sunday lunch from noon to 3:00 pm. American Express, MasterCard, and Visa accepted. No service charge.*

This nice Italian restaurant is located not far from Belfast City in Bangor. The decor is unmemorable, but they have a pretty recognizable Italian menu with everything you're accustomed to seeing at other Italian restaurants.

SHANKS RESTAURANT, *Blackwood Golf Center, 150 Crawfordsburn Road, Bangor. Set lunch menu for UK£14.95, and set dinner menu for UK£24.95. Open Tuesday through Friday from 12:30 pm to 2:30 pm, and from 7:00 pm to 9:00 pm. Saturday they are open for dinner only from 7:00 pm to 9:00 pm. American Express, MasterCard, Visa accepted. No service charge.*

Shanks is considered one of the best restaurants in the Belfast area. Chef Robbie Millar is gaining quite a reputation for top-notch fare, including marvelous steaks – beef as well as venison – and seafood dishes. Choices for dinner include such tasty treats as roast monkfish with penne, pancetta, and roast garlic; duck with wild mushroom risotto; and an excellent chargrilled angus steak. The ambiance is bright and airy, with contemporary art, yellow walls, and modern furnishings.

SEEING THE SIGHTS

Belfast

Grand Opera House, *Great Victoria Street, (01232) 241919. Tickets range from UK£3 to UK£20.* Across from the Europa and the Crown Liquor Saloon is the Grand Opera House of Belfast. Built in 1895, but allowed to grow seedy over the years, this beautiful Victorian Theater was restored to all its finery in 1980. The restoration was faithful to the original heavy gilding and ornamental plasterwork. Productions range from plays and operas to ballet.

Belfast City Hall, *open Monday through Friday from 9:00 am to 5:00 pm. Admission is free. Tel. (01232) 327000.* The central area of Belfast is Donegall Square, and the central attraction of the square is the City Hall of Belfast. Columned and domed, the building was erected at the turn of the century (1907). The entrance for the general public is located around back. You are free to go in and walk around the open public areas. As you'd suspect, it's marbled and grand. The statue of the woman out front of City Hall is Queen Victoria. On Wednesdays a guided tour takes you into other areas of the structure.

Garden of Remembrance, *Belfast City Hall grounds.* This is an interesting war memorial on the west side of Belfast City Hall

Crown Liquor Saloon, *44 Great Victoria Street, open daily 11:30 am to 11:30 pm, Sunday from 12:30 pm to 2:30 pm and 7:00 pm to 10:00 pm. Tel. (01232) 325368.* Don't miss the most popular pub in Belfast and Northern Ireland. This marvelous Victorian bar sits proudly across the street from the Europa Hotel. Stepping into the bar is like stepping into a movie set in Victorian times. Gaslights glisten, mosaics on the floor shine, *snugs* (small, semi-private booths with high walls) beckon patrons to share their most intimate secrets, brass blazes, and the ornate mirrors are a sight to behold. The building is so important to Belfast that it has been maintained by the National Trust. No fear, though – it is a working bar run by an independent company. If you visit only one pub in Northern Ireland, make this be the one.

Shaftesbury Square. Shaftesbury Square is a square formed by the confluence of Great Victoria Street, Dublin Street, Botanic Avenue, Bradbury Place, and Donegall Road – sort of a Times Square of Belfast, complete with a large electronic billboard! There are lots of restaurants, bookies, pubs, movie theaters, the main post office, and a fun place to watch the panorama of Belfast streetlife.

Linen Hall Library, *open Monday through Wednesday, and Friday from 9:30 am to 6:00 pm, Thursday from 9:30 am to 8:30 pm, and Saturday from 9:30 am to 4:00 pm. Membership fee runs UK£28 per year.* The Linen Hall Library sits on the north side of Donegall Square. Built in 1788, this fine old library

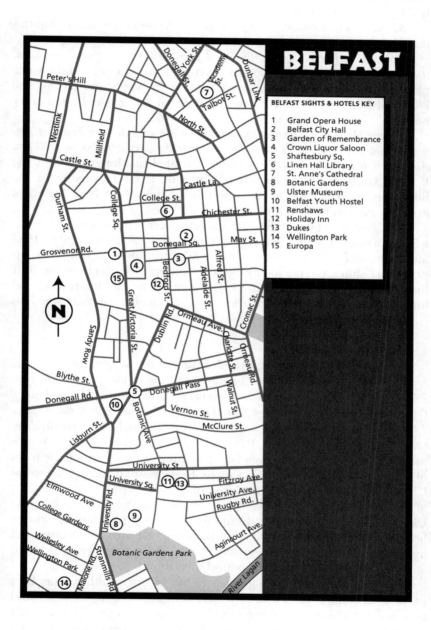

BELFAST

BELFAST SIGHTS & HOTELS KEY

1. Grand Opera House
2. Belfast City Hall
3. Garden of Remembrance
4. Crown Liquor Saloon
5. Shaftesbury Sq.
6. Linen Hall Library
7. St. Anne's Cathedral
8. Botanic Gardens
9. Ulster Museum
10. Belfast Youth Hostel
11. Renshaws
12. Holiday Inn
13. Dukes
14. Wellington Park
15. Europa

is an architecturally interesting place. They also have a display on the history of linen manufacture.

St. Anne's Cathedral, *Donegall Street*. St. Anne's is the main Anglican church in Northern Ireland. It is suitably austere and imposing.

Botanic Gardens, *Stranmillis Road, open daily from sunup to sundown. Admission is free.* This pretty spot sits next to Queens's College, and is a nice place to stroll and enjoy the beauty of the flowers, plants, and shrubs. The Ulster Museum is located on the grounds of the gardens. (see entry below.)

Ulster Museum, *Stranmillis Road, open Monday through Friday 10:00 am to 5:00 pm, Saturday 1:00 pm to 5:00 pm, Sunday 2:00 pm to 5:00 pm. Admission is free. Tel. (01232) 381251.* Located on the grounds of the Botanic Gardens, this museum is Northern Ireland's version of the Smithsonian. It is an eclectic collection of important Irish historical artifacts, natural history, and art.

My favorite exhibit is the paraphernalia recovered from the *Girona*, a Spanish ship that sunk in the cold waters off the Antrim Coast in 1588 after their ill-fated expedition against England. Jewelry, weaponry, articles of clothing, and personal effects are among the collection. The four floors are nicely done, and the exhibits are generally interesting and informative. A third floor cafe serves a reasonable lunch if you find yourself getting hungry.

Elsewhere in County Antrim

Ulster Folk and Transport Museum, *near Bangor, open May to September from Monday through Saturday 11:00 am to 6:00 pm, Sunday from 1:00 pm until 6:00 pm, (open Wednesdays until 9:00 pm during May and June). October to April Monday through Saturday from 11:00 am to 5:00 pm, Sunday 1:00 pm to 5:00 pm. Admission is UK£3 for adults and UK£2 for children. Children under five are free. Tel. (01662) 243292.* To get to the folk park, take the A2 from Belfast toward Bangor. Just after you go through the town of Hollywood (still on the A2), watch for the signpost directing you to the Ulster Folk Park and Transport Museum.

Perhaps the finest recreation of its kind on the Emerald Isle, the Ulster Folk and Transport Museum features cottages, chapels, schoolhouses, and farms all brought from their original sites and transported here from all over Ulster. They have been painstakingly reconstructed and extensively equipped with period furnishings.

The museum gives you a glimpse of the 18th and 19th century lives of the Ulster folk, from priests to peasants, farmers to fiddlers. What kind of a living could a weaver eke out? How about a tailor? The open-air museum invites you into the very homes of those who practiced these and other professions, so you can more readily visualize their living conditions. The buildings are located over a sprawling seventy acre park-like area, so you get to combine a nature walk with a field trip into Irish history.

A fascinating and informative aspect of the Ulster Folk and Transport Museum is the transportation section. You follow the history of Ulster from horse and buggy days (actually, in Ulster it's *donkey and creel* days) to the mighty ocean liners (the *Titanic* was built in Belfast) and on into the jet age.

It may well take a half day or better to tour all the exhibits. Don't be rushed, as there is plenty to see.

Carrickfergus Castle, *Carrickfergus, open April through September Monday through Saturday from 10:00 am to 6:00 pm, Sunday from 2:00 pm until 6:00 pm, and October through March Monday through Saturday from 10:00 am until 4:00 pm and Sunday from 1:00 pm to 4:00 pm. Admission is UK£2.70 for adults and UK£1.35 for children under 16. A family ticket is available for UK£7.30. Tel. (01969) 351273.* Take the A2 north out of Belfast. As you pass the end of Belfast Harbor, follow the signposts for Carrickfergus. The Castle is at the far edge of town – you won't miss it if you stay on the A2.

Sitting beside Belfast Lough on a small rocky peninsula, Carrickfergus Castle is a large example of the structural excesses the Anglo-Normans went to as they established their footholds on the Emerald Isle. This beautiful castle (particularly at night when it is lit) was built in 1180 by one of the earliest Anglo-Norman intruders, John de Courcy. But the castle proved a large and desirous target for a host of assailants, from Irish chieftains to the French and even the Scottish. Sometimes they were successful in taking the castle, but always lost it a short time later to concentrated English efforts.

It was at Carrickfergus Castle that William of Orange stopped en route to his momentous victory at the Battle of the Boyne. In fact, a large stone in the harbor marks the spot he stepped from his boat onto Irish soil. And U.S. naval history was made in the veritable shadow of Carrickfergus Castle; while aboard his ship *Ranger*, the legendary John Paul Jones defeated the English warship *HMS Drake* in America's first-ever naval victory just outside Carrickfergus.

The castle itself is magnificent and well worth a visit. Inside the castle is an impressive five-story Keep, about 60 feet wide and over 90 feet high, which originally held the well for the castle's drinking water as well as a dungeon. On the third floor is a grand Great Hall. The Keep is also home to a Cavalry Regimental Museum, with several fine examples of ancient weaponry. The views from the top of the Keep are splendid.

Glens of Antrim, *between Larne and Ballycastle*. As you drive on the A2 between Larne and Ballycastle, take in the incredible seascapes as well as the famous Glens of Antrim. Nine of them in all, they are deep, heavily forested glades, some of then with quasi-tropical greenery. The prettiest of these is Glenariff, and its Glenariff Forest Park (see below) provides numerous paved walking trails of varying lengths through the lush greenery.

Glenariff Forest Park, *near Cushendall*. At Cushendall, watch for signposts for Glenariff Forest Park (B14). Known as the "Queen of the Glens," Glenariff Forest Park is billed as an "area of outstanding natural beauty," and it truly is. You have a choice of numerous walking paths, featuring cascading waterfalls, beautiful wild flowers, and dense undergrowth. The beautiful, moist gorges support a wide variety of plant life. Several walking trails are available from a half mile stroll up to a nine mile scenic trek. The three mile waterfall trail is the most popular and, I think, the prettiest.

Bonamargy Friary, *Ballycastle*. Lying next to a golf course on the south-eastern edge of Ballycastle on the A2 is the overgrown ruins of Bonamargy Friary. Founded in the 1500s by Rory McQuillan, the friary thrived for several centuries before its destruction by the (dratted) McDonnells, arch-enemies of my kinsmen the McQuillans.

Take a few minutes and wander among the ruined walls of this Franciscan friary. See if you can find the small round stone cross of **Julia McQuillian**, the Black Nun (it's easy to find – it's marked). Legend has it that Julia still roams the now deserted friary (see sidebar on next page). By the way, watch your head – the entranceways are very low. I have painful first-hand experience.

Torr Head Road, *between Cushendun and Ballycastle*. After prowling about Bonamargy Friary, follow the signposts for Torr Head Road (about two miles southeast of Bonamargy Friary on the A2). This is not the time to be in a hurry. The ribbon-like road snakes around the northeastern tip of Northern Ireland, a scarce twelve miles from Scotland at its closest point. It is a very narrow road, but well-maintained.

On a clear day the views are stunning, and you might enjoy pulling off the road and listening to the surf crashing against the rocks below you. If you do – hold onto your hat; or better yet, leave it in the car. Otherwise, it may become part of the flotsam below. If you picked up Torr Head Road in Ballycastle, you'll end up in Cushendun. Conversely, if you picked it up in Cushendun, you'll end up in Ballycastle.

Ballycastle. Ballycastle lies on the northeast coast of Northern Ireland on the A2. Ballycastle is famous for two fun festivals each year. On the last Tuesday and Wednesday of August each year, they hold their *Oul' Lammas* Fair, a festival that has been held here every year since 1606. It is a modern celebration of the Celtic harvest festival called *Lughnasa*. During mid-June, Ballycastle hosts the *Fleadh Amhran agus Rince*, a lively three-day folk festival featuring lots of dancing and traditional music.

Rathlin Island. Lying offshore from Ballycastle is the large, stony Rathlin Island. Its main claim to fame is that it was from Rathlin Island that **Guglielmo Marconi** established the first radio link between the Rathlin Island lighthouse and Ballycastle.

THE BLACK NUN OF BALLYCASTLE

Despite the fact that he built the Bonamargy Friary – see previous page – the only member of Rory McQuillan's Clan to be buried at Bonamargy Friary is a woman named Julia McQuillian, known as the **Black Nun**. *Born in the 17th century, Julia was known as a religious recluse and noted for her humility and piety. In addition, she was considered by many in the country to be a prophetess. She prophesied of the day when carriages would travel the roads of Ballycastle without the use of horses, and that ships would sail the seas without the assistance of sails – clear prophecies of the automobile and steamship.*

As the local prophetess, she was also known for her intolerance of the improprieties of the human creature. Her demands of excessive penance for minor transgressions became legendary, even during her lifetime. But such was the respect bestowed upon her that the local townsfolk supported her enthusiastically.

Even her death is the stuff of legends. One legend is that she died violently during a battle when the McDonnell Clan took the friary from the McQuillians. She is said to have met her death from a McDonnell arrow. As she slumped on the steps of the friary, she reportedly cursed all McDonnells.

Her fame grew after her death when locals learned that Julia had requested to be buried near the steps to the chapel, so that worshipers would tread on her grave as they came to pray – another example of her abject humility.

Her grave marker is a small cross with a round hole in it. Over the centuries since her death, many have reported seeing a shadowy figure dressed in a dark nun's habit, gliding through the friary near the cross. Most claim it's the spirit of Julia McQuillian, doing her own penance for cursing the McDonnell Clan with her dying words.

Carrick-a-Rede, *near Ballintoy, open May through September daily from 9:30 am to 6:00 pm. Admission is free, although the carpark costs UK£2.* Just off the A2 on the B15 near Ballintoy, watch for the signposts directing you to Carrick-a-Rede rope bridge. The rope bridge is suspended 80 feet above the ocean across a chasm 60 feet wide. Now, neither of those may seem high, until you are in the middle of this swaying rope bridge. Access is via a pleasant half-mile walk up a slight incline. The rope bridge is installed each May and taken down each September by salmon fishermen who need access to the fishery on the small island.

As you walk across the bridge and near the middle, you'll swear there is a prankster behind you jumping up and down on the bridge, causing it to undulate wildly under your feet. A quick glance over your shoulder will prove that it is your own amplified movement on the bridge that is causing the swaying.

Hold tight, move slowly, and you're sure to leave with a pleasant memory and feeling a little bolder for the effort.

Giant's Causeway, *near Bushmills, Causeway Head, open all year. September through June the hours are variable, depending on demand, but generally 10:00 am to 5:00 pm; July and August it is open daily from 10:00 am to 7:00 pm. Admission to the audiovisual presentation is UK£2. for adults and UK£1 for children. The car park is UK£2.50, or you can park for free on the road, about 100 yards from the entrance. Tel. (012657) 31855.* The Giant's Causeway lies on the B146 road just off the A2 between Ballintoy and Bushmills. Watch for the signposts directing you here, whether you are coming from Bushmills or Ballintoy.

Giant's Causeway is one of two things: it is either an incredibly interesting work of nature, or it might be, as the legends say, the handiwork of the giant Finn MacCool who was trying to build a stepping-stone bridge to Scotland to find a wife. Either way, the sight is fascinating.

Geologists tell us that Giant's Causeway is a group of 40,000 symmetric hexagonal stone columns formed millions of years ago by rapidly-cooling molten lava. They are absolutely fascinating and probably unlike anything you have ever seen.

Stop first at the Visitors Center. It is well done, and helps you understand the scientific explanation for the geological oddity you're about to see. You'll also learn here about the fate of the *Girona*, a Spanish ship of the ill-fated Spanish Armada, that foundered on the rocks now called *Port-na-Spania*. Her cargo of gold and jewelry was recovered in the late 1960s, and much of it is on display in the Ulster Museum in Belfast.

From the Visitors Center, you have two options to reach the Causeway. The first (my preference) is a cliff-top walk of about a mile and a half to some very steep steps descending to the shore below. You actually overshoot the main attraction by several hundred yards, but the scenery is well worth it. You can come back that way, or do the more direct shot from the rocks up a fairly steep hill back to the Visitors Center. A shuttle bus runs constantly between the two points, and is available for UK£1 each way. The second way is to head straight down the hill by foot or shuttle.

What you find there nearly defies description – you'll almost believe it's not possible that what you are seeing is really the work of mother nature. All these hexagonal basalt pillars stacked next to one another, more than you can possibly count. They're fun to sit on, walk amongst, and get your picture taken on. Don't miss this sight if you're in the area.

Bushmills Distillery, *Bushmills, open June through August Monday through Saturday from 9:00 am to 5:30 pm, September through May Monday through Thursday from 9:00 am until noon, and from 1:30 to 5:00 pm, Friday from 9:00 am to 1:00 pm. Admission is UK£2.50 for adults, UK£1 for seniors and children, and a family ticket is available for UK£6.50. Tel. (012657) 31521.* Bushmills is a quiet village famous for its wild drinks. The Bushmills Distillery produces their famous brand of Irish whiskey here on the northern coast of Ulster. Guided tours are conducted to give you a "flavor" for their process, including a wee nip at the end!

Dunluce Castle, *between Portrush and Bushmills, open April 1 through September 30 Monday through Saturday from 10:00 am until 7:00 pm, Sunday from 2:00 pm until 7:00 pm; July and August daily from 10:00 am until 9:00 pm. Admission is UK£1.50 for adults and 75p for children.* Dunluce Castle stands between the A2 and the coast between Portrush and Bushmills, just outside of Portrush. Described variously in tourist brochures as brooding, romantic, somber, and inspiring, Dunluce is perched atop a natural basalt tower that rises abruptly out of the ocean. Surrounded on three sides by the ocean, and on the fourth by a gorge, Dunluce Castle was once considered an impregnable fortress. Its picture graces the cover of almost every tourist brochure for Northern Ireland.

Originally built in the 14th century, Dunluce Castle was the ancestral home of the McQuillans. What war could not accomplish, marriage and intrigue did, and the castle fell into the hands of the hostile McDonnells in the mid-1500s. (Do I sound bitter? Nah....) Many are the stories and legends that surround Dunluce Castle. Perhaps one of the most startling is the true story about the large banquet that was being hosted within the castle in 1639. The elite guests were gathering, and anticipation was running high when a horrible sound shattered the gaiety. The kitchen, along with its complement of cooks, crashed into the churning sea below.

There is a twenty minute slide and audio show that covers the history of the area, and touches briefly on Dunluce Castle's role in it. The show really could spend more time on the history of the castle, but it is still well done.

County Cavan in the Irish Republic

Cavan Folk Museum, *Cavan Town, open mid-June through October. Admission is £1.50 for adults and 50p for children. Tel. (049) 37248.* Cavan is about an hour and a half northwest of Dublin on the N3. The museum contains a collection of clothing, home, and farm implements from the 1700s to the present. It's actually quite interesting.

County Donegal in the Irish Republic

County Donegal is one of the most secluded areas of the entire Emerald Isle, and it is beautiful. It is associated with Ulster but aligned politically with the Republic. It features little in the way of civilization, but lots in the way of scenic drives, templed hills and wooded vales. Lakes seem to be around every bend and twist of the road, and the lush green of Ireland seems to shine brightest here.

Just about any road you choose is going to treat you to bounteous beauties. So have fun exploring!

Donegal Town. This pretty little town of less than 2,500 inhabitants sits quietly at the head of Donegal Bay on the western shore of Ireland, along the N15. The Irish name for Donegal, *Dun na nGall*, which means "The Fort of the Foreigners," gives you an inkling of the tenuous and rocky beginnings of Donegal. The town was founded originally in the 9th century by the Vikings to provide a base of operations for their depredations further into the countryside. The town was eventually taken by the McDonnell clan, and served as their seat of power for centuries.

Donegal Craft Village, *Donegal*. About a mile outside of town on the N15 is a bevy of craft shops where you can shop for knit-wear, pottery and china, and assorted other items.

Donegal Castle, *Donegal, Tirchonaill Street*. In the center of town near the area called the Diamond sits the regal-looking Donegal Castle. Originally the home of O'Connell Clan chieftain Hugh O'Donnell, the stronghold passed through several hands before being taken by Sir Basil Brooke. In 1610, he reworked the structure, adding the mansion and turrets that you see today. The castle's interior is not open to the public.

Killybegs. To get to Killybegs, take the N56 west out of Donegal for about thirty miles. Watch for signposts directing you to Killybegs on Road R263. The Irish name for Killybegs is *Na Cealla Beaga*, which means "The Little Churches," referring no doubt to some long forgotten churches that have long since faded from memory and history.

Today this pretty little harbor town sits abreast a pretty cove. The fishing fleet here is big business. Another big business is the hand-tufted carpets produced here. These prized works of art have found their way into the Vatican, the White House, Buckingham Palace, and a number of other important places.

Slieve League Mountains. Continue west from Killybegs on the R263 to get to the Slieve League Mountains.The cliffs of Slieve League Mountains are the highest in Ireland, dropping nearly 2,000 feet into the ocean. They are quite pretty, although for sheer dramatics, I prefer the Cliffs of Moher. Several cliff walks are available in the area. One of them, "One Man's Pass," feels not unlike a high-wire act, and is not for the faint of heart or people suffering from fear of heights.

Glencolumbkille. Further west along the R263 fom Killybegs, watch for the signpost directing you to Glencolumbkille. This pretty little fishing village, scattered as it is on the rocks just out of reach of the Atlantic Ocean, is a nice place to stop and visit. To call it a village is almost an overstatement, as it is not very large. Originally it was a monastic settlement of St. Columba and his followers (its Irish name means Columba's Church of the Glen). But the settlement of this region is even older than that, as evidenced by the presence of dozens of prehistoric cairns in the vicinity.

St. Columba's House, *Glencolumbkille*. On a crag just north of the village is a small oratory which legend says was used by the good saint himself. Every year at midnight on June 9, worshippers form a processional where they walk barefoot for two miles around a circuit called the "Stations of the Cross."

The Folk Village, *Glencolumbkille, open April, May, and October from Monday through Saturday from 10:00 am to 6:00 pm and Sunday from noon to 6:00 pm, June through September Monday through Saturday from 10:00 am to 7:00 pm and Sunday from noon to 7:00 pm, November they're open Monday through Saturday from 10:00 am to 6:00 pm and Sunday from noon to 6:00 pm. Admission is £1.50 for adults, 75p for children. Tel. (073) 30017.* This is an exhibit that depicts three centuries of life in Ireland. The cottages are realistically simple, effectively showing the spartan lifestyle of past days. Thatched roofs, dirt floors, and simple furnishings are the rule in this folk village.

Lough Swilly. From Donegal Town, take the N15 north to Stranorlar, then north to the N56 to reach Lough Swilly, a beautiful long narrow lake in the northeast corner of Donegal. It's a peaceful and pretty lake to just sit and watch, or to walk along her banks.

Rathmullan. As you are driving north on the N56 toward Letterkenny, watch for the signposts directing you to the R245 and Ramelton, then take the R247 from there to Rathmullan, a picturesque little village on the western shores of Lough Swilly. The harbor at Rathmullan witnessed the "flight of the Earls" in 1607. This was the departure of the Ulster chieftains from Ireland. Most never returned. Their departure opened the way for the large-scale settlement of Protestants on the confiscated lands of the departed nobles.

Rosguill Peninsula. Near the tiny town of Carrigart is the pretty Rossguill Peninsula, one of the northernmost points of Ireland. To get there, take the R245 from Ramelton to Carrigart. From there, follow the signs to Downings and the Rosguill Peninsula.

Downings. Downings is just northwest of Carrigart on the R245. Some of the signposts may only show the Irish name for Downings, which is *Dunaibh*. The resort town of Downings (to confuse matters even further, some maps list the town as *Downies*) provides pretty sandy beaches and plenty of good fishing for its visitors. Sitting on the southwestern edge of Rosguill Peninsula as it does, Downings affords lovely seascapes.

Atlantic Drive. Leave Downings on the only road north out of town to begin the Atlantic Drive, which is the circular route around Rosguill Peninsula. It's a pretty drive.

MacSwyne's Gun. When you're in the small town of Dunfanaghy (you come to Dunfanaghy by taking the N56 north of Letterkenny), watch for the sign directing you to an oddity of nature: McSwyne's Gun. During rough weather, the incoming tide strikes this large natural hole and it sounds as though a cannon has been fired.

Horn Head. When you're in Dunfanaghy, park your car and take a stroll out to Horn Head. County Donegal has many awe-inspiring sights, but this may be the topper of them all. Dramatic drops of six hundred feet enable you to see great distances over these cliffs. If you don't feel like walking, you can take a narrow, unnumbered road out on Horn Head to see the sights.

Tory Island. Lying nine miles northwest off the northwest coast of Ireland is Tory Island. You reach Tory Island via ferry from Meenlaragh. You can reach Meenlaragh by taking the N56 south from Dunfanaghy, and then taking the R257 west from Gortahork. But you'll only have access to the island if the weather is good, and it can be brutal off the coast here. The island itself is a rocky lump sitting amid the crashing surf. If you take the ferry out, be sure to leave early enough in the day to get back, since there are no overnight accommodations available on Tory Island.

In recent years the hearty folk who live on Tory Island have discovered a market for their paintings, to supplement their normal fishing income. There are a number of ruins on the island, mute witnesses to the extent past generations have gone to retain their seclusion.

Bloody Foreland Head, *near Meenlaragh*. As the R257 sweeps along through the back-country of Donegal, the vistas just get more and more scenic. One of the high points is Bloody Foreland Head, on the northwestern tip of Ireland. It has earned this name because the rays from the setting sun seem to linger on the granite boulders that line the Atlantic coast, causing them to seemingly "blush" as the day wanes.

Ailt an Chorrain. Also called Burtonport, this is the jumping-off point for Aranmore Island. You can reach Ailt an Chorrain by taking the R257 back east to the N56, then heading south to Dungloe. At Dungloe, watch for signposts directing you west on the R259 to Ailt an Chorrain. This small fishing village on the rocky coastline of The Rosses Headland remains frozen in time, with very little tourist development.

Aranmore Island. Aranmore lies four miles offshore from the village of Ailt an Chorrain. Aranmore is the largest island off the Donegal coast.

Prehistoric ruins on the island are witnesses that hearty men and women have made this their home for many centuries. Boat trips to the island leave roughly every hour throughout the day. Expect to pay around £2 to £3 per person for a round-trip to the island.

Glenveagh National Park, *near Letterkenny, open April 18 through October 26 daily from 10:00 am to 6:30 pm (7:30 pm June through August), closed every Friday in April and October. Admission is £2 for adults, £1.50 for senior citizens, and £1 for children. If you'd like a guided tour, you pay an additional admission charge (same rates as above). Tel. (074) 37088 or (074) 37090.* Glenveagh National Park lies just a few miles northwest of Letterkenny. To get there from Letterkenny, take the R250 west of town to the R251, andhead north. If you are coming from the coast, take the N56 to the R252, head east for a short distance until you come to the R254 in Doochary, then take that north until you intersect the R251. Turn left, and you're almost there.

In a land of incredible beauty, Glenveagh National Park can hold its own. Glenveagh Lough is simply gorgeous, as is Glenveagh Castle. It boasts a set of Castle gardens that are exquisite.

You can't drive through the 24,000 acre park. It is similar to wilderness areas in American parks – no motorized vehicles are allowed in most of the park. You may park at the front gate, and a bus will take you to the castle. Once you arrive, there are walking paths that allow you to see a bit of the park more closely.

It is interesting to note that Americans played an important part in Glenveagh National Park. During the mid-19th century, John Adair began acquiring the land that is now Glenveagh National Park. In 1861 he evicted all the tenants who had been living and working the land. He commissioned the building of Glenveagh Castle in 1870. Immediately upon its completion, he left Ireland for Texas. He never returned. His wife Cornelia left Texas and returned to Glenveagh, where she supervised the care of the land. The gardens you see around the castle are a result of her labors. In 1984, American millionaire Henry McIlhenny graciously donated the estate to Ireland.

Grianan of Aileach, *between Letterkenny and Burnfoot.* When you've had your fill of Glenveagh National Park, follow the signposts to Letterkenny. Follow the N13 southeast out of Letterkenny, and then bend northeast on the N13 until you come to the signpost indicating Grianan of Aileach. Follow it for about a mile up a winding lane to the top of an 800 foot hill and you're at Grianan of Aileach – the impressive stone fort that was once the stronghold of the O'Neills, formerly the rulers of Ulster. From atop the circular tiers of rock and grass you'll have outstanding views of the surrounding area including two large lakes: Lough Swilly to the north and Lough Foyle to the east.

Archaeologists speculate that the fort dates from the Iron Age. It is a circular structure with three terraced rings one inside the other. On the inside a series of stone walks bring you to the top of the 17 foot tall walls. Their base is a mere 13 feet.

Malin Head. Malin Head is the northernmost point of the Emerald Isle. You've got to go here if for no other reason than to be at Ireland's northernmost point! But there are definitely other reasons to come to Malin Head. The views, especially those along the southern shoreline, are fabulous, and it's hard to beat the incredible sunsets from this particular vantage point.

County Down

Mourne Mountains. The poets say that the Mourne Mountains "sweep down to the sea" and in many cases they certainly do. The highest peaks (these are really very old and rounded granite mountains – not really peaks, *per se*) are 2,800 feet tall. Wind-swept and mostly devoid of trees, the Mournes offer an ominous starkness to the rest of this lush country.

The Mourne Mountains sit serenely on the southeast portion of both County Down and Northern Ireland. They are circumscribed on the west, south and east by the A2 as it glides along the Irish coastline. The B8 between Newry and Newcastle hems them in on the North.

St. Patrick Heritage Centre, *Downpatrick, open Monday through Friday from 11:00 am to 5:00 pm, Saturday and Sunday from 2:00 pm to 5:00 pm. Admission is free. Tel. (01396) 615218).* An 18th-century jail houses St. Patrick Heritage Centre as well as the **County Down Museum**. Take a few minutes and tour both (they're not very extensive) for a secular and religious history of the area. Downpatrick is in eastern County Down at the junction of the A7 and the A25. The A7 comes southeast from Belfast directly into Downpatrick, and the A25 comes northwest from the coastal city of Newcastle.

County Fermanagh

Lough Erne. Of all the pretty lakes in Ireland, Lough Erne may well be the prettiest. Deep and blue, long and narrow, punctuated often by green islands, Lough Erne is a favorite with fishermen and families alike.

Lough Erne lies in the northwest corner of County Fermanagh. You can reach it by taking the N15 south from Donegal Town to Ballyshannon, and then east on the R230 into Beleek. From there you can take the A47 to head around the northern and eastern sides of the lake, or you can take the A46 to drive along the southern and western shores of Lough Erne.

Belleek Pottery Factory, *Belleek, open Monday through Thursday 9:30 am to 4:15 pm, and Friday from 9:30 am to 3:15 pm. Admission is free. Tel.*

(013656) 58501. The creamy china known as Belleek pottery is produced here near the northern banks of Lough Erne. Tours are available during the week. And of course you can purchase some of their goods if you wish. You can reach Beleek Pottery by driving south from Donegal Town on the N56 to Ballyshannon, and then taking the R230 east to Beleek. The little town of Beleek sits at the junction of the R230, the A46, and the A47. If you're coming from elsewhere in Northern Ireland, take the A32 south out of Omagh, and you'll drive right to the center of Lough Erne.

Castle Caldwell, *near Drennan.* Castle Caldwell is just a few miles outside of Beleek, on the A47 as it skirts the northern shores of Lough Erne. Watch for the entrance to the ruins of Castle Caldwell. The most intriguing artifact here is the tombstone of one Denis McCabe, a fiddler of some ability. While on a pleasure ride on the lake in 1770, Denis fell overboard and drowned. The epitaph chiseled into his headstone gives us a clue as to why he may have drowned: *On firm land only exercise your skill, That you may play and safely drink your fill.* Poor Denis!

Devenish Island, *near Enniskillen, accessible from April through September, daily except for Monday. The fare is UK£2.* About three miles north of Enniskillen on the A32, watch for signposts directing you to Devenish Island. A short ferry ride to the island will introduce you to the ruins of a 12th-century monastery, several Celtic carvings, and a fine high cross.

Royal Inniskilling Fusiliers Regimental Museum. Enniskillen is a pretty town that sits alongside the River Erne as it flows the short distance between Lower Lough Erne and Upper Lough Erne. Along the banks of the River Erne you'll find Enniskillen Castle, home to the Royal Inniskilling Fusiliers Regimental Museum (what a mouthful!). The museum is devoted to soldiers who fought in the Napoleonic Wars. A pretty impressive display of mementos from the war is included in the exhibit, including medals, weaponry, and bright, colorful uniforms.

County Monaghan

Inniskeen Folk Museum, *Inniskeen, open May through August on Sundays from 2:00 pm to 5:00 pm. They will make appointments for other times if you call. Admission is free, although donations are accepted and appreciated. Tel. (042) 78109.* The hamlet of Inniskeen is about nine miles west of Dundalk on the R178. A small museum here commemorates one of Ireland's great poets, Patrick Kavanaugh. Kavanaugh's body was interred at Inniskeen after his death.

Monaghan Town. Monaghan Town is located northwest of Dublin on the N2, and southwest of Belfast on the M1/A3. Monaghan is the county seat. *Muineachain*, its Irish name, means "Little Hills" and describes much of the land in this county. A monastery was built on this site in the 9th century, and weathered a series of sieges, sacks, and plunderings until

1161, when it was abandoned. The site was rededicated anew, when a Franciscan friary was built here in 1462.

There are a few interesting sights in and around Monaghan. On the south end of town is **St. Macartan's Cathedral**, a Gothic structure built in the 19th century, topped by a graceful spire. Downtown in the central square called "The Diamond" is an interesting memorial known as **Rossmore Monument**, which looks like a medieval spaceship ready for blast-off! At **St. Patrick's Cathedral** (1836), look for the **Lloyd Monument**, a poignant memorial to a son (Henry Craven Jesse Lloyd) who died while fighting in South Africa during one of the modern wars, and features exquisite sculpting depicting a variety of unique and interesting scenes (native tribesmen, horses, cavalry, an African village, etc.).

Monaghan County Museum, *Monaghan, open year around Tuesday through Saturday from 11:00 am to 1:00 pm, and from 2:00 pm until 5:00 pm. Admission is free. Tel. (047) 82928.* Housed in the old Market House, the Monaghan County Museum is a good place to stop and discover the history of the area from ancient times up through the present day.

Rossmore Forest Park, *near Monaghan.* Leave Monaghan via the R189 toward Newbliss and you'll come to Rossmore Forest Park, nearly seven hundred acres of pretty park land featuring rolling hills, lakelets, and plenty of walking trails.

County Tyrone

Ulster American Folk Park, *Camphill, open Easter through September Monday to Saturday 11:00 am to 6:30 pm, Sunday from 11:30 am to 7:00 pm; October through Easter Monday through Friday from 10:30 am to 5:00 pm. (Last entrance allowed 90 minutes before closing.) Admission is UK£3 for adults and UK£1.50 for children. Tel. (01662) 243292.* The Ulster American Folk Park is located three miles north of Omagh on the A5.

This particular folk park presents an interesting angle to tourists. They have reconstructed a typical 18th-century County Tyrone village, as well as an American settlement from the same period. Their attempt is to compare and contrast the life immigrating Irish left for the life they found in America.

The main museum in the park is a whitewashed cottage believed to be the home of the ancestors of Andrew Mellon, the famous American millionaire.

The park is interesting, although not nearly as extensive as others of its ilk, like the Ulster Folk and Transport Museum outside Belfast.

PRACTICAL INFORMATION

American Express

The American Express office in Belfast is located at *Kyrenia House, 108 Royal Avenue, Belfast, Tel. (01232) 242341.*

Banks

Banks in the part of Ulster that is in the Republic of Ireland are open Monday through Friday from 10:00 am to 12:30 pm, and from 1:30 pm to 3:00 pm. In the larger cities, the banks are usually open a little longer one day a week (the day varies throughout the province) until 5:00 pm.

In the Northern Ireland portion of Ulster, banks are open from 9:30 am to 4:30 pm and closed from 12:30 pm to 1:30 pm. Banks in Belfast and Derry don't close for lunch.

Some of the large banks in Ulster have an ATM machine either outside their main doorways, or just inside the bank. The ATMs are part of the Cirrus and Plus international networks. Check with your bank to be sure your personal identification number (PIN) will work on international ATMs. Most international ATMs only accept four-digit PINs.

Buses, Planes, and Trains

If you're flying into or out of Ulster:
- **Belfast International Airport**, *Belfast, Tel. (018494) 22888*

For buses, use the following station:
- **Europa Bus Center**, *10 Glengall Road, Belfast, Tel. (01232) 333000*

For trains, use the following station:
- **Central Station**, *East Bridge Street, Belfast, Tel. (01232) 899411*

Embassies and Consulates
- **American Consulate**, *14 Queen Street, Belfast, Tel. (01232) 328239*

Emergencies

Remember this: dialing 999 in Northern Ireland = dialing 911 in the States. Use it in the event of any emergency where you need assistance from the police, fire department, or the medical community.

Exchanging Money

You can exchange money at banks, most post offices, and at larger hotels.

Lost Credit Cards
- **American Express Card**, *Tel. (01) 288-3311*
- **Visa/MasterCard**, *Tel. (01) 269-7700*

Restrooms
    Public restrooms are not prevalent in Northern Ireland; your best bet is usually a hotel or a pub. (Hint: most hotels have at least one pub, and the restrooms are usually located near the pub.)

Tourist Offices
- **Belfast**, *St. Anne's Court, 59 North Street, Belfast, Tel. (01232) 231221*
- **Ballycastle**, *Sheskburn House, 7 Mary Street, Tel. (02657) 62024*
- **Donegal Town**, *Quay Street, Tel. (073) 21148*

18. SEARCHING FOR YOUR IRISH ROOTS

Many Americans – an estimated forty million – trace their ancestry to the Emerald Isle. Because of that, many are prompted to return to Ireland and, in many cases, search a bit for their roots. In this chapter, I have included over five hundred and fifty Irish surnames and their traditional ancestral counties. Many Irish surnames originated in Scotland or England (Italy as well!), but since many of them have been in Ireland since the 16th and 17th centuries, they are now considered Irish, so I have included them in this listing.

Indeed, my love affair with Ireland came about as a result of an intense interest in renewing my acquaintance with the country of my forefathers. But my interest didn't end there – I was also interested in seeing if I could connect with any of my long-lost cousins. Never shy, I decided on a bold plan. First of all, it required a letter written to my Irish cousins. This is what I wrote:

Dear McQuillan Family,

Greetings from your long-lost American cousin! Doubtless you were unaware that you had a long-lost American cousin, at least not this one. But you do. In 1619 my tenth-great grandfather Teague McQuillan left County Antrim to see if he could improve his fortunes in the wilds of America. Ten generations later here I am, intensely interested in visiting the part of Ireland he left so long ago.

But that's not all. I am as interested in meeting other members of the McQuillan family as I am in seeing the Emerald Isle. Hence my letter. In May of next year, my wife and I are planning to visit Ireland and would like to be able to visit some of the cousins as well as the part of Ireland Teague was from.

We will be in Northern Ireland from May 3 through May 10, and would love to stop by and meet you. Please let me know if you will be available during that time, and we'll arrange our schedule to meet with you. Please write to us at the address below.

I know this may seem rather presumptuous and just a bit bold, but I really am interested in meeting other members of the McQuillan Clan, however distant along the family tree they may be.

Thanks, and I look forward to meeting with you when we are there.

Daniel McQuillan

After I wrote the letter, I made twenty copies. Then, from a map of Northern Ireland, I selected twenty small towns in County Antrim. (I think something like this will work better with small towns rather than larger cities.) I addressed each envelope with the family name and the name of one of the towns. For example, one of the letters was addressed as follows: *McQuillan Family, Larne, Northern Ireland.*

And then, in the bottom left-hand corner of the front of the envelope I wrote: *POSTMASTER: PLEASE DELIVER THIS LETTER TO ANY McQUILLAN FAMILY IN THE VICINITY.*

I sent the letters six months prior to our trip to Ireland. I was delighted to receive seven responses to my rather unorthodox method of contacting family. But the results were marvelous! We met a number of these Irish families, were entertained in their homes, and they showed us great kindness. We left much richer for our time with them.

The vast majority of Irish-Americans are here because of the mass migration here during the potato famine years of 1845 through 1847. During that dark period, it's estimated that over one million Irish men, women, and children sailed for America. That's almost two hundred and fifty years after my ancestors sailed for America. It is entirely possible that you may find some very near cousins, especially if you know a grandfather's or great-grandfather's name.

So, if you are of Irish extraction, give it a try. If you know nothing of your Irish connection, use the following information on traditional ancestral counties and send letters there. Cousin or not, you're sure to meet some wonderful people, and you'll likely establish some long-lasting friendships.

Another way for you to meet family if you are planning to go to Ireland is to see if your clan holds an annual or semi-annual clan rally (reunion). There is an organization in Ireland called the Clans of Ireland, and they serve as a clearinghouse for information on clan reunions. They are a non-profit organization working under the auspices of the Irish Tourist Board (Bord Failte). To contact the Clans of Ireland office, write or call the following:

Anne Kavanaugh, Clans of Ireland
2 Kildare Street, Dublin 2 Ireland
Tel. (01) 661-8811, extension 410

Below is a partial list of clans who hold rallies. Ms. Kavanaugh can help put you in contact with their representatives.

Allen	Gleeson
Baker	Greene
Barry	Griffin
Bradshaw	Gormley
Brennan	Hanly
Buckley	Hennessy
Butler	Heery
Burke	Heffernan
Callan	Herlihy
Carroll	Hickey
Cassidy	Hogan
Clancy	Horkan
Cleary	Huley
Clune	Jones
Collins	Joyce
Comerford	Kavanagh
Connolly	Keating
Cormican	Kelly
Crawford	Kennedy
Cronin	Kenny
Crowe	Keohane
Crowley	Kiely
Daly	Kilkenny
Dalton	Killoran
Delaney	Kinnane
Devlin	Kissane
Duffy	Lafferty
Dunne	Larkin
Elliott	Lewis
Evans	Long
Ferris	Lynch
Fitzgerald	MacClancy
Fitzgibbon	MacDermot
Gallahue	MacGeoghegan
Geraghty	MacRaith
Gettings	McAnallen

McAteer
McAuliffe
McCabe
McCarthy
McCullagh
McDonagh
McDuffee
McEgan
McGettigan
McGillycuddy
McKenna
McLoughlin
McManus
McNally
Namara
McQuillan
McSweeney
McGennis
Maguire
Maher
Marmion
Managan
Marnane
Moloney
Mooney
Moore
Muireagain
Mulcahy
Mullaney
Nolan
Noonan
O'Brien
O'Byrne
O'Callagan
O'Carragher
O'Cathain
O'Connell
O'Connor
O'Dea
O'Dochartaigh
O'Donnell
O'Donoghue
O'Dowd

O'Driscoll
O'Dubhda
O'Dwyer
O'Farrell
O'Flaherty
O'Flynn
O'Gara
O'Grady
O'Hanlon
O'Higgins
O'Keefe
O'Leary
O'Loughlin
O'Madden
O'Mahony
O'Malley
O'Meara
O'Neill
O'Rahilly
O'Reilly
O'Rourke
O'Shaughnessy
O'Scanlan
O'Shea
O'Sullivan
O'Toole
Patterson
Pierce
Quinlan
Quinn
Rafferty
Riordan
Ronan
Ryan
Shaw
Sheehan
St. John
Sugrue
Tierney
Troy
Turley
Whitty
Wingfield

BIG MAC OR BIG MC?

Some of the books you read about Irish genealogy will claim that names beginning with "Mc" are Irish, while those beginning with "Mac" are Scottish. In *The Surnames of Ireland*, Edward MacLysaght indicates this is essentially rubbish. He contends that "Mc" is merely an abbreviation for "Mac." "Mc/Mac" means "son of", while "O'" means simply "of" (as in descended of – for example: O'Donnell signified "the descendants of Donnell," or "one who is part of the house of Donnell").

If your name isn't listed below, don't despair (certainly don't be offended!). It is simply not possible to list every Irish name; however, if your name isn't listed here, you can get a more complete listing (along with a history of the names) in several books. The first, *Irish Family Names* (W. W. Norton & Company, Inc., New York, NY 1982) by Brian de Breffny has an excellent listing of many Irish family names and their counties of origin. The other, mentioned above, is *The Surnames of Ireland* (Irish Academic Press Limited, Blackrock, Co. Dublin) by Edward MacLysaght. Both are well-researched and list hundreds of Irish names and the counties the families originated in. Those chosen for this book are the more common names found throughout Ireland and Northern Ireland.

If you can't find your surname, add (or remove) a "Mc" or "O" to (or from) your name. Irish emigrants often anglicized their names by dropping the prefix from their surnames. On the other hand, many Irish families dropped the prefixes while still in the "ould" country, only to have their descendants add the prefix back later.

In the list below, "Co." stands for County.

Acheson - Co. Fermanagh, Wicklow
Adair - Co. Antrim
Ahren - Co. Clare, Cork
Aiken - Co. Antrim
Allison - Co. Antrim, Donegal
Ambrose - Co. Cork, Limerick, Wexford
Anderson - Co. Antrim
Archbold - Co. Wicklow
Arthur - Co. Limerick
Athy - Co. Kilkenny
Aylmer - Co. Kildare

Bagott - Co. Dublin
Bannon - Co. Tipperary
Barnewall - Co. Dublin
Barnwall - Co. Cork, Meath

Barrett - Co. Cork, Mayo
Barron - Co. Waterford
Barry - Co. Cork
Bell - Co. Antrim, Derry, Down
Bellew - Co. Louth, Meath
Bergin - Co. Offaly
Bertagh - Co. Meath
Billry - Co. Limerick
Birmingham - Co. Galway, Kildare
Birn - Co. Mayo
Bissett - Co. Antrim
Blair - Co. Antrim
Blake - Co. Galway
Bodkin - Co. Galway
Bolger - Co. Carlow
Boyd - Co. Antrim, Derry
Boyle - Co. Donegal

Brady - Co. Cavan, Clare
Brehan - Co. Galway
Brehon - Co. Wexford, Tipperary
Brody - Co. Mayo
Brogan - Co. Sligo
Brosnaghan - Co. Kerry
Browne - Co. Galway, Limerick,
  Mayo, Wexford
Bryan - Co. Kilkenny
Buckley - Co. Cork
Burke - Co. Galway, Kildare, Limer-
  ick, Mayo, Sligo, Tipperary
Burnell - Co. Dublin
Butler - Co. Carlow, Kilkenny, Laois,
  Meath, Tipperary, Waterford,
  Wexford, Wicklow
Byrne - Co. Wicklow

Cahaney - Co. Mayo
Cahill - Co. Galway, Tipperary
Campbell - Co. Antrim, Tyrone
Carew - Co. Carlow
Carey - Co. Kerry, Kildare
Carrigan - Co. Cork
Carroll - Co. Kilkenny, Louth
Casey - Co. Cork, Kerry,
Cassidy - Co. Fermanagh
Cavanaugh - Co. Carlow, Wexford
Cheevers - Co. Carlow, Meath,
  Wicklow
Clancy - Co. Leitrim
Cleary - Co. Clare, Galway
Clerkin - Co. Limerick
Clifford - Co. Kerry
Clinton - Co. Louth
Cody - Co. Kilkenny
Cogan - Co. Laois
Colclough - Co. Wexford
Coleman - Co. Louth, Sligo
Coll - Co. Limerick
Comerford - Co. Kilkenny,
  Waterford
Commiskey - Co. Cork

Conaghty - Co. Sligo
Condon - Co. Cork
Connelan - Co. Tyrone
Conran - Co. Waterford
Conroy - Co. Roscommon
Considine - Co. Clare
Conway - Co. Longford
Cooke - Co. Carlow
Cody - Co. Kilkenny
Coghlan - Co. Cork, Offaly
Collins - - Co. Cork, Limerick
Concannon - Co. Galway
Connery - Co. Limerick
Coogan - Co. Galway, Kilkenny
Copeland - Co. Down
Coppinger - Co. Cork
Corcoran - Co. Fermanagh
Corrigan - Co. Fermanagh
Costello - Co. Mayo
Courtney - Co. Kerry
Creagh - Co. Clare
Cronin - Co. Kerry
Crotty - Co. Waterford
Crowley - Co. Roscommon
Cruise - Co. Dublin, Meath
Cullen - Co. Dublin, Kildare,
  Wexford
Culmore - Co. Donegal
Cunningham - Co. Tyrone
Curran - Co. Clare, Galway
Cusack - Co. Clare, Limerick, Meath

Dalton - Co. Meath, Westmeath
Daly - Co. Clare
Danaher - Co. Cork, Limerick,
  Tipperary
Darcy - Co. Galway, Meath
Dardis - Co. Meath
Dargan - Co. Meath
Davis - Co. Antrim, Dublin
Davoren - Co. Clare
Deane - Co. Donegal, Galway, Mayo
Dease - Co. Westmeath

De Bathe - Co. Meath
De Burgo - Co. Antrim, Down,
  Galway
De Clare - Co. Clare
De Cogan - Co. Cork
d'Exeter - Co. Mayo
De Geneville - Co. Meath
De Gernon - Co. Louth
DeLacy - Co. Antrim, Down
Delahoyde - Co. Dublin
Delamare - Co. Westmeath
Delgany - Co. Wicklow
De Martimer - Co. Meath
De Montmorency - Co. Kilkenny,
  Wexford
Dempsey-Co. Kildare, Laois, Offaly
Dennehy - Co. Cork, Kerry
De Prendergast - Co. Wexford
De Renzy - Co. Wexford
Dermody - Co. Clare
Desmond - Co. Cork
Devane - Co. Galway, Kerry
Devenish - Co. Fermanagh
De Verdon - Co. Westmeath
Devereux - Co. Wexford
De Vesey - Co. Kildare, Laois
Devine - Co. Fermanagh, Tyrone
Devlin - Co. Derry, Sligo, Tyrone
Dickson - Co. Donegal, Mayo
Dillon - Co. Galway, Mayo,
  Westmeath
Dineen - Co. Cork
Dobbins - Co. Antrim
Dobbs - Co. Antrim
Doherty - Co. Donegal
Dolan - Co. Cavan, Mayo
Donlevy - Co. Tyrone
Donnegan - Co. Armagh, Tyrone
Donnelly - Co. Donegal, Tyrone
Dowling - Co. Laois, Carlow
Doyle - Co. Dublin
Duffy - Co. Donegal, Monaghan
Duggan - Co. Cork, Galway

Dunluce - Co. Antrim
Dunn(e) - Co. Laois

Egan - Co. Galway, Tipperary
Ennis - Co. Dublin, Offaly
Enright - Co. Limerick, Cork
Eustace - Co. Carlow, Kildare

Fagan - Co. Dublin, Westmeath
Farrell - Co. Longford
Fay - Co. Westmeath
Feeney - Co. Galway, Mayo
Fenton - Co. Cork, Kerry
Ferguson - Co. Antrim
Finnegan - Co. Cavan, Galway
Fitzgerald - Co. Cork, Limerick
Fitzgibbon - Co. Cork, Limerick
Fitzmaurice - Co. Kerry, Mayo
Fitzpatrick - Co. Laois, Cavan
Flanagan - Co. Roscommon
Flannery - Co. Limerick, Mayo
Fleming - Co. Cork, Meath
Flynn - Co. Cork, Mayo
Fogarty - Co. Tipperary
Foley - Co. Kerry, Waterford
Ford - Co. Cork, Leitrim
Fox - Co. Meath
Furlong - Co. Wexford

Gallagher - Co. Donegal
Galligan - Co. Sligo
Garvey - Co. Armagh, Down
Garvin - Co. Mayo, Meath
Gannon - Co. Mayo
Getty - Co. Antrim
Gibbons - Co. Mayo
Gibson - Co. Antrim
Gillen - Co. Sligo, Tyrone
Gillespie - Co. Antrim, Donegal
Gilligan - Co. Derry
Gilmore - Co. Antrim
Gormly - Co. Donegal, Mayo
Gould - Co. Cork

Grace - Co. Kilkenny, Tipperary
Graham - Co. Antrim
Gray - Co. Antrim
Green(e) - Co. Clare, Fermanagh
Greer - Co. Antrim, Down
Griffin - Co. Clare, Kerry
Grimes - Co. Offaly

Hackett - Co. Carlow, Dublin
Hagerty - Co. Derry, Donegal
Hallahan - Co. Cork
Halligan - Co. Armagh
Hamill - Co. Antrim, Tyrone
Hamilton - Co. Antrim
Hanley - Co. Roscommon
Hanrahan - Co. Limerick
Hanratty - Co. Louth
Harrington - Co. Cork, Galway
Harris - Co. Dublin
Harrison - Co. Dublin
Hart - Co. Limerick, Meath
Harty - Co. Kerry, Laois
Healy - Co. Cork, Sligo
Hennessey - Co. Offaly
Henry - Co. Antrim, Donegal
Hickey - Co. Clare, Limerick
Higgins - Co. Sligo, Meath
Hogan - Co. Tipperary
Horan - Co. Galway, Mayo
Houlihan - Co. Clare, Offaly
Hughes - Co. Donegal, Meath
Hurley - Co. Clare, Cork
Hussey - Co. Meath, Kerry

Irwin - Co. Fermanagh
Ivers - Co. Louth, Clare

Jameson - Co. Antrim, Dublin
Jennings - Co. Mayo, Roscommon
Jordan - Co. Mayo
Joyce - Co. Galway, Mayo

Kane - Co. Derry

Kavanaugh - Co. Carlow, Wexford
Keane - Co. Derry, Galway
Kearney - Co. Clare, Mayo
Kearns - Co. Leitrim, Sligo
Keating - Co. Carlow, Wexford
Keegan - Co. Dublin
Keenan - Co. Antrim, Fermanagh
Kelleher - Co. Cork, Kerry
Kelly - Co. Antrim., Galway
Kenneally - Co. Limerick
Kennedy - Co. Clare, Wexford
Kenny - Co. Galway, Tyrone
Keogh - Co. Tipperary, Wicklow
Kerr - Co. Antrim
Kerrigan - Co. Mayo
Keyes - Co. Fermanagh
Kidd - Co. Dublin
Kiernan - Co. Cavan
Kilkelly - Co. Galway
Kilpatrick - Co. Antrim
Kirk - Co. Louth
Kirwin - Co. Galway
Kirkpatrick - Co. Antrim
Kitt - Co. Galway
Knox - Co. Derry, Mayo

Lacy - Co. Limerick
Laffan - Co. Wexford
Lambert - Co. Galway, Wexford
Landers - Co. Kerry
Larkin - Co. Galway, Wexford
Lavelle - Co. Galway, Mayo
Law - Co. Antrim
Lawless - Co. Galway
Lawlor - Co. Laois
Leahan - Co. Galway
Leech - Co. Mayo, Wicklow
Lennon - Co. Cork, Galway
Leonard - Co. Fermanagh
Lindsay - Co. Tyrone
Lockhart - Co. Antrim
Loftus - Co. Galway
Logan - Co. Antrim

Lonergan - Co. Tipperary
Lowry - Co. Tyrone
Lynch - Co. Galway, Tipperary
Lyons - Co. Cork, Galway

Madden - Co. Galway, Offaly
Madigan - Co. Clare, Limerick
Maguire - Co. Fermanagh
Magee - Co. Antrim
Magrath - Co. Fermanagh
Maher - Co. Tipperary
Malone - Co. Offaly, Westmeath
Mannion - Co. Galway
Martin - Co. Tyrone
Mason - Co. Fermanagh
Masterson - Co. Cavan, Wexford
Maxwell - Co. Antrim
Meagher - Co. Tipperary
Meehan - Co. Cork, Leitrim
Molloy - Co. Offaly
Monaghan - Co. Roscommon
Mooney - Co. Dublin, Offaly
Moore - Co. Kerry
Moran - Co. Galway, Kerry
Moriarty - Co. Kerry
Moroney - Co. Clare
Morris - Co. Galway
Morrison - Co. Antrim, Down
Morrissey - Co. Sligo
Moynihan - Co. Cork, Kerry
Mulcahy - Co. Cork, Limerick
Muldoon - Co. Clare, Galway
Mulholland - Co. Derry, Donegal
Mullane - Co. Derry, Tyrone, Kerry
Mulligan - Co. Donegal
Mullins - Co. Clare
Mulrooney - Co. Galway,
   Fermanagh
Mulroy - Co. Mayo
Murdoch - Co. Antrim
Murphy - Co. Cork, Donegal, Mayo
Murray - Co. Roscommon
Murtagh - Co. Meath

McAdam - Co. Cavan, Monaghan
McAllister - Co. Antrim
McAuley - Co. Fermanagh,
   Westmeath
McAuliffe - Co. Cork
McBride - Co. Donegal
McCabe - Co. Cavan, Monaghan
McCafferty - Co. Cavan, Mayo
McCaffrey - Co. Cavan, Fermanagh
McCann - Co. Armagh, Louth
McCarthy - Co. Cork, Tipperary
McCartney - Co. Antrim
McClean - Co. Antrim, Donegal
McClelland - Co. Donegal
McClintock - Co. Donegal
McClure - Co. Antrim
McConnell - Co. Derry, Tyrone
McCormick - Co. Longford,
   Tipperary
McCoy - Co. Galway
McCullough - Co. Antrim
McDermott - Co. Roscommon, Sligo
McDonnell - Co. Antrim, Clare
McDowell - Co. Roscommon
McElhinney - Co. Derry, Donegal
McEvoy - Co. Armagh, Westmeath
McFadden - Co. Donegal
McFarland - Co. Armagh
McGafney - Co. Cavan
McGarry - Co. Antrim, Leitrim
McGill - Co. Antrim, Donegal
McGeraghty - Co. Mayo, Sligo
McGibbon - Co. Mayo
McGilfoyle - Co. Tipperary
McGillicuddy - Co. Kerry
McGilligan - Co. Derry
McGilmore - Co. Monaghan
McGinty - Co. Donegal
McGonigle - Co. Derry, Donegal
McGovern - Co. Cavan
McGowan - Co. Cavan, Donegal
McGrath - Co. Donegal, Fermanagh
McGuiness - Co. Down

McGuire - Co. Fermanagh
McHale - Co. Mayo
McHugh - Co. Cavan, Donegal
McIlroy - Co. Antrim, Tyrone
McInerney - Co. Clare, Limerick
McIntyre - Co. Antrim
McKee - Co. Antrim, Derry
McKenna - Co. Kerry, Monaghan
McKeon - Co. Antrim
McKinley - Co. Antrim
McKnight - Co. Antrim, Derry
McLoughlin - Co. Derry, Donegal
McMahon - Co. Clare, Monaghan
McManus - Co. Fermanagh
McMaster - Co. Antrim
McMillan - Co. Antrim
McMurrough - Co. Carlow
McNally - Co. Antrim, Armagh
McNamara - Co. Clare
McNamee - Co. Derry
McNeill - Co. Antrim, Derry
McNulty - Co. Donegal, Mayo
McQuaid - Co. Antrim, Monaghan
McQuillan - Co. Antrim
McRory - Co. Down
McShane - Co. Antrim, Derry
McSharry - Co. Donegal, Leitrim
McSweeney - Co. Cork, Donegal

Nagle - Co. Cork
Neville - Co. Kildare
Newell - Co. Antrim, Kildare
Newman - Co. Cork
Nolan - Co. Carlow
Noonan - Co. Cork
Noone - Co. Galway, Mayo
Nugent - Co. Meath, Westmeath

O'Bannon - Co. Mayo, Offaly
O'Boyle - Co. Donegal
O'Bradley - Co. Cork
O'Breslin - Co. Donegal
O'Brien - Co. Clare, Limerick

O'Callaghan - Co. Clare, Cork
O'Carey - Co. Kildare
O'Carroll - Co. Kerry, Louth
O'Casey - Co. Limerick, Fermanagh
O'Cassidy - Co. Derry, Fermanagh
O'Coffey - Co. Galway
O'Connell - Co. Kerry
O'Connor - Co. - Kildare
O'Corcoran - Co. Tipperary
O'Cullen - Co. Cork
O'Curran - Co. Donegal
O'Curry - Co. Cavan, Cork
O'Daly - Co. Cavan, Cork
O'Dea - Co. Clare, Cork
O'Dennehy - Co. Waterford
O'Devin - Co. Fermanagh
O'Dell - Co. Limerick
O'Donnell - Co. Donegal, Galway
O'Donnelly - Co. Tipperary
O'Donohoe - Co. Tipperary
O'Donovan - Co. Cork, Limerick
O'Dooley - Co. Westmeath
O'Doolin - Co. Kerry
O'Dowd - Co. Mayo, Sligo
O'Doyle - Co. Carlow, Kilkenny
O'Driscoll - Co. Cork
O'Duffy - Co. Donegal
O'Dugan - Co. Mayo
O'Dunn - Co. Kildare, Meath
O'Dwyer - Co. Tipperary
O'Fallon - Co. Roscommon
O'Feeney - Co. Galway, Sligo
O'Finegan - Co. Roscommon
O'Flaherty - Co. Galway
O'Flanagan - Co. Fermanagh,
  Roscommon
O'Flynn - Co. Antrim, Cork, Kerry
O'Fogarty - Co. Tipperary
O'Gara - Co. Sligo
O'Garvey - Co. Armagh, Wexford
O'Grady - Co. Clare, Kerry,
  Limerick
O'Hagan - Co. Tyrone

O'Hagarty - Co. Derry, Kerry
O'Halahan - Co. Cork
O'Halligan - Co. Meath
O'Halloran - Co. Clare, Galway
O'Hanlon - Co. Armagh
O'Hanrahan - Co. Galway
O'Hara - Co. Antrim, Derry
O'Hare - Co. Armagh, Down
O'Hea - Co. Cork, Limerick
O'Healy - Co.
O'Hurley - Co. Cork
O'Kane - Co. Antrim, Derry
O'Kean - Co. Tipperary
O'Keefe - Co. Cork
O'Keenan - Co. Derry, Fermanagh
O'Kelly - Co. Down, Galway
O'Larkin - Co. Armagh
O'Leary - Co. Cork
O'Looney - Co. Cork
O'Lynch - Co. Cavan, Cork
O'Mahon - Co. Down
O'Mahony - Co. Cork, Kerry
O'Malley - Co. Mayo
O'Meara - Co. Tipperary
O'Moran - Co. Mayo, Sligo
O'Mulcahy - Co. Tipperary
O'Muldoon - Co. Fermanagh
O'Mullen - Co. Derry
O'Mulvey - Co. Leitrim
O'Murray - Co. Derry
O'Neill - Co. Antrim, Carlow
O'Neill - Co. Clare, Donegal
O'Nolan - Co. Carlow
O'Quigley - Co. Derry
O'Quinn - Co. Donegal, Limerick
O'Quinlan -Co. Kerry, Tipperary
O'Quinlevan - Co. Clare
O'Rafferty - Co. Donegal
O'Regan -Co. Cork, Laois, Meath
O'Reilly - Co. Cavan, Meath
O'Riordan - Co. Tipperary
O'Rooney - Co. Down
O'Rourke - Co. Leitrim

O'Ryan - Co. Carlow, Kilkenny
O'Scanlan - Co. Kerry
O'Scully - Co. Tipperary
O'Shanahan - Co. Tipperary
O'Shaughnessy - Co. Galway
O'Shea - Co. Kerry, Tipperary
O'Sheehan - Co. Limerick
O'Sullivan - Co. Cork, Kerry
O'Tierney - Co. Armagh
O'Toole - Co. Kildare, Wicklow
O'Tully - Co. Fermanagh
O'Toumey - Co. Cork

Patton - Co. - Antrim, Donegal
Peppard - Co. Louth
Petit - Co. Mayo, Westmeath
Phelan - Co. Kilkenny, Waterford
Phillips - Co. Kilkenny Mayo
Plunkett-Co. Cavan, Dublin, Louth
Power - Co. Waterford
Prendergrast-Co. Mayo, Waterford
Prunty - Co. Antrim, Derry
Purcell - Co. Kilkenny, Tipperary

Quigley - Co. Derry, Mayo
Quillen - Co. Antrim
Quinlan - Co. Meath, Tipperary
Quinn - Co. Antrim, Clare, Derry
Quirk - Co. Kilkenny, Tipperary

Rafferty - Co. Donegal, Sligo,
  Tyrone
Raftery - Co. Galway
Redmond - Co. Wexford, Wicklow
Reynolds - Co. Leitrim
Riddell - Co. Down
Riordan - Co. Antrim
Roche - Co. Cork, Kilkenny
Rogers - Co. Armagh, Meath
Ross - Co. Donegal, Wexford
Rooney - Co. Down
Rossiter - Co. Wexford
Ryan - Co. Limerick, Tipperary

Sarsfield - Co. Cork, Dublin, Limerick
Savage - Co. Down
Scanlan - Co. Cork, Kerry, Louth
Scott - Co. Laois
Scully - Co. Tipperary, Westmeath
Segrave - Co. Dublin
Sexton - Co. Cavan, Limerick
Shanahan - Co. Clare
Shanley - Co. Leitrim
Shannon - Co. Clare, Fermanagh
Sharkey - Co. Derry, Donegal, Tyrone
Shaw - Co. Cork, Tipperary
Sheehan - Co. Cork, Limerick
Sheehy - Co. Kerry, Limerick
Sheridan - Co. Cavan, Longford
Shields - Co. Donegal
Sherlock - Co. Kildare, Meath
Shortall - Co. Kilkenny
Slattery - Co. Clare, Limerick, Kerry
Spillane - Co. Cork, Kerry, Sligo
Stack - Co. Cork, Kerry
Sutton - Co. Wexford

Taafe - Co. Louth
Taggart - Co. Antrim
Talbot - Co. Waterford, Wicklow
Tierney - Co. Donegal, Mayo
Tobin - Co. Cork, Limerick
Toner - Co. Derry, Donegal
Tracey - Co. Cork, Galway
Troy - Co. Clare, Limerick
Tulley - Co. Cavan, Longford
Tynan - Co. Laois
Tyrell - Co. Dublin, Westmeath

Ventry - Co. Kerry

Wadding - Co. Waterford, Wexford
Wade - Co. Dublin, Longford
Waldron - Co. Cavan, Mayo
Wall - Co. Carlow, Kilkenny
Walsh -Co. Cork, Mayo, Kilkenny
Walsh - Co. Waterford, Wexford
Ward - Co. Donegal, Galway
Warren - Co. Monaghan, Wicklow
Weir - Co. Antrim, Derry
White - Co. Down, Limerick
Wilkinson - Co. Donegal
Woulfe - Co. Cork, Kildare
Wright - Co. Antrim, Derry
Wylie - Co. Antrim

INDEX

FROM THE PUBLISHER

Our goal is to provide you with a guide book second to none. Please bear in mind, however, that things change: phone numbers, admission price, addresses, etc. Should you come across any new information, we'd appreciate hearing from you. No item is too small for us, so if you have a great recommendation, find an error, see that some place has gone out of business, or just plain disagree with our recommendations, write to:

Ireland Guide
Open Road Publishing
P.O. Box 20226
Columbus Circle Station, New York, NY 10023

ORDER FORM

Name and Address: _____

_____

_____ Zip Code: _____

Quantity	Title	Price

Total Before Shipping _____

Shipping/Handling _____

TOTAL _____

Orders must include price of book <u>plus</u> shipping and handling. For shipping and handling, please add $3.00 for the first book, and $1.00 for each book thereafter.

Ask about our discounts for special order bulk purchases.

Order from:
OPEN ROAD PUBLISHING
P.O. Box 20226, Columbus Circle Station, New York, NY 10023